Readings in Russian Civilization

Readings

VOLUME III

SOVIET RUSSIA, 1917-PRESENT

in Russian Civilization

EDITED, WITH INTRODUCTORY NOTES, BY

THOMAS RIHA

SECOND EDITION, REVISED

THE UNIVERSITY OF CHICAGO PRESS

CHICAGO AND LONDON

THE UNIVERSITY OF CHICAGO PRESS, CHICAGO 60637
The University of Chicago Press, Ltd., London

First published 1964
Second edition, revised, 1969
Printed in the United States of America
89 88 87 86 85 84   8 7 6

ISBN: 0-226-71856-5 (clothbound); 0-226-71857-3 (paperbound)
Library of Congress Catalog Card Number: 69-14825

CONTENTS VOLUME III

*Items added in 2d edition.

Contents

CONTENTS VOLUME I

*Items added in 2d edition.

CONTENTS VOLUME II

*Items added in 2d edition.

PREFACE TO THE SECOND EDITION

This new and enlarged version of *Readings in Russian Civilization* is the result of fairly extensive revisions. There are now 72 instead of 64 items; 20 of the selections are new. The first volume has undergone the least change with 3 new items, of which 2 appear in English for the first time. In the second volume there are 6 new items; all of them appear in English for the first time. The third volume has undergone the greatest revision, with 11 new items, of which 6 are newly translated from the Russian. It is the editor's hope that items left out in the new edition will not be sorely missed, and that the new selections will turn out to be useful and illuminating. The aim, throughout, has been to cover areas of knowledge and periods which had been neglected in the first edition, and to include topics which are important in the study of the Russian past and present.

The bibliographical headnotes have been enlarged, with the result that there are now approximately twice as many entries as in the old edition. New citations include not only works which have appeared since 1963, but also older books and articles which have come to the editor's attention.

The editor would like to thank several persons who have contributed to the improvement of the text. Some sixty professors answered a questionnaire sent out by the University of Chicago Press and suggested changes or improvements in the *Readings*. Most of these suggestions have been heeded, and the editor is grateful for this generous cooperation by his colleagues. Professor Josef Anderle should be singled out, since he offered particularly detailed comments and had been most helpful in the preparation of the first edition as well. Professors Richard Wortman and Richard Hellie suggested new documents and, in the case of Mr. Hellie, translated them as well. Howard Goldfinger, Sylvia Fain, and Walter Gleason helped with the translations.

Once again I should like to dedicate this new version of my work to my students at the University of Chicago and at the University of Colorado. They have made this enterprise not only a duty but also a pleasure.

BOULDER, COLORADO
JUNE, 1968

THOMAS RIHA

PREFACE TO THE FIRST EDITION

In selecting the readings for these volumes, I was guided by several considerations. The selection, first of all, was to be important for the period of Russian history under consideration. Second, it was to lend itself fairly easily to class analysis—if possible, by the discussion method. This meant that polemics were preferable to descriptions, though I could not, and indeed did not wish to, manage without the latter. The selection was to stimulate curiosity to the point where the reader would wish to pursue the subject further.

All things being equal, I tended to lean toward primary sources. Thus, of the final sixty-four items, forty-six, or 70 per cent, are of this nature. Nevertheless, this remains a book of readings, not a collection of documents. I did not want snips and pieces, no matter how important; each essay is intended to be of sufficient length to develop a point of view or an argument reasonably and sensitively. I wanted my selections to be readable; there is not all that much good writing in this often turgid field, and I made a deliberate attempt to hunt for those authors who took pride in their language and exposition.

At certain crucial points I made a deliberate effort to bring a Soviet point of view into play. This I found to be not only healthy for argument's sake but sometimes quite enlightening in its own right. I carried this principle into the bibliographies as well. These were intended to provide a few guideposts to those who might wish to investigate an individual problem. Paperback editions were indicated because they might lead to the building of small private libraries. One could, these days, build quite a respectable collection of paperbacks on Russia.

I tried to give each period of Russian history its due. The order of selections will be found to be approximately chronological, though in a few places items are grouped topically for the sake of convenience. Each volume concludes with a general assessment of the period where more than one point of view is presented. It was my hope that Russian civilization would thus be given certain stages and a definable shape. If the general contours turn out to be approximately accurate, my aim will have been achieved.

ACKNOWLEDGMENTS

My thanks are due, to begin with, to the College at the University of Chicago, which conceived of the Russian civilization course and gave it elbow room to develop. Donald Meiklejohn, Warner Wick, and Alan Simpson were sympathetic initiators and tolerant supervisors. For a colleague they provided Meyer Isenberg, whose warm participation was essential to the first years of the enterprise and who always reminded me of the aims of general education. Chicago's Russian specialists —Michael Cherniavsky, Leopold Haimson, Arcadius Kahan, and Hugh McLean— gave their time to make improvements in the selections. Richard Hellie, Jean Laves, and Marianna Tax Choldin acted as able assistants. Elizabeth Ireland and Wells Chamberlin first suggested publication. Michael Petrovich inspected the volumes and made valuable suggestions. Ruth Jensen piloted the manuscript through its many stages over three years and proved to be the ideal secretary. Last, but most important, my students at the University of Chicago supplied the curiosity and enthusiasm which is their valued hallmark. To them these three volumes are dedicated.

THOMAS RIHA

CHICAGO

44

TESTIMONY ON THE FEBRUARY REVOLUTION

By General Sergei Khabalov

When disorders broke out in Petrograd in late February 1917 no one believed that this was the end of the old regime. The Emperor ordered the suppression of all disorders. But this turned out to be impossible. The street fighting developed into a large-scale rebellion which, in a few days, toppled the emperor and the monarchy itself. In the excerpt below General Khabalov, Commander of the Petrograd Military District during these days, recounts his inability to restore order in the capital. He is responding to the questions of the Extraordinary Commission appointed, after the revolution, to investigate the activities of ministers and other high officials of the deposed regime.

There are several histories of the February Revolution. Three paperback ones should be mentioned. Leon Trotsky's *The Russian Revolution* is the most famous. The others are Nikolai Sukhanov's *The Russian Revolution, 1917*, and William H. Chamberlin's *The Russian Revolution*. A recent account is George Katkov's *Russia, 1917: The February Revolution*. A large number of documents on the February Revolution is printed in Robert Browder and Alexander Kerensky, *The Russian Provisional Government*, and in Frank Golder, *Documents of Russian History, 1914–1917*. For the situation in the army see General Nikolai Golovin, *The Russian Army in the World War*, and A. Nikolaieff, "The February Revolution and the Russian Army," *Russian Review*, Vol. VI.

Khabalov: On Sunday the 26th the troops appeared and, as usual, took up positions as scheduled. . . It turned out that they had to fire into the crowd at various places. The Volhynians fired into the crowd at Znamenskii Square and on Suvorov Street. Subsequently the Pavlovsk Regiment[1] fired into the crowd on Nevskii Avenue near the Kazan cathedral. Then, about four o'clock in the afternoon. . . But I cannot report to you, gentlemen, where and how many were shooting. . . The situation here, it must be said, was ghastly! I myself was in the town governor's building where a great many people were crowded in. . . I no longer made any provisions for the distribution of bread that day. After four o'clock I was informed that the Fourth Company of the

---

[1] The Volhynians, the Pavlovsk Regiment: Russian military units usually bore geographic names.

Translated by Walter Gleason from P. Shchegolev (ed.), *Padenie Tsarskogo Rezhima*, I (Moscow, 1926), 225–31.

Pavlovsk Regiment household troops, which was quartered in the Court stables' buildings, and which, as it later turned out, consisted primarily of evacuated men, upwards of 1,500 men, ran out into the street, shooting into the air, and, shouting various slogans, mustered on Koniushennyi Square, near the foot bridge, not far from the Church of the Resurrection of Christ. When I asked for the battalion commander over the telephone, I was informed, though not by him, but by someone else, that this company demanded that the troops be withdrawn to the barracks and that there should be no shooting. And it was reported that this company had fired into a platoon of mounted police. This information appeared unreliable to me. Why should they shoot at the mounted police? Subsequently it became clear that this company had actually revolted; in fact it had not gone out into the streets: it had never been so ordered—the training detachments and other companies had been called. But this company had not been called and sat in its barracks. And so this company revolted, demanding that the other companies return to the barracks and that there be no shooting. Then I ordered the battalion commander to admonish the troops, to keep this company in the barracks, and to make sure that officers were with the company. According to my information, there were two officers there, but there should have been not two, but many more. . .

I instructed Colonel Pavlenkov[2] that he should take steps so that this would not spread, not break out any further. . . Besides the battalion commander and the officers, I also gave orders to the regimental chaplain so that he might persuade them, shame them, and induce

them to swear obedience so that the company would return to the barracks, and hand in their rifles. . . Finally, because of the exhortations of the battalion commander and the chaplain, this company returned to its barracks, and the rifles were gradually passed in. But not all the rifles; twenty-one had disappeared! Evidently, the people disappeared with them. . . The Minister of War continuously required me to inform him by telephone of what was happening in the city. I reported to him over the telephone. When, during the evening report, I told him about this company, he demanded an immediate court-martial and execution. . . I considered it impossible not only to have executions but even to punish a man without hearing his side, at least through some simplified court procedure. . . How could one even speak of executions! . . . Therefore I asked for the procurator of the military court, Mende, to inquire what should be done with this company, which initially consisted of eight hundred men. "Without doubt there should be an inquiry, and only then a court-martial," he told me. Well, in that case, I said, eight hundred men—this is a joke! an unthinkable affair: you cannot examine them even in a week. I ordered my chief of staff, General Khlebnikov, or perhaps it was Chizhevskii, to appoint a commission of inquiry: five persons under the chairmanship of a general were appointed. And in the meanwhile I gave orders that the regiment itself should surrender the culprits in order that they might be arrested. Initially it was proposed to arrest the entire battalion and imprison them here—in the Fortress of Peter and Paul,[3] and so, late in the evening, I in-

---

[2] Colonel Vladimir Pavlenkov commanded the Petrograd military police during the February days.

[3] "Here, in the Fortress of Peter and Paul": the hearings during which Khabalov testified were held in the Fortress, where the important personages of the old regime were kept under arrest.

quired whether space could be found for such a mass of people. When it turned out that there were actually not eight hundred but fifteen hundred men, this proved physically impossible, for there were no such accommodations. . . Then I ordered the arrest of at least the most prominent instigators, and ordered them interrogated; there were nineteen men, and they were conveyed to the fortress.

Chairman: Did the regiment itself surrender them?

Khabalov: The regimental command turned them over, it was undoubtedly the authorities. Forgive me, I speak of a regiment, but there were no regiments in this instance, we are talking about reserve battalions. They are so large that they exceed the peacetime numerical strength of a regiment three to four times. . . Thus, there were fifteen hundred men in this company, whereas an entire regiment during peace time has 1,770 men. This company alone represented the peacetime quota of a regiment. . . And so those who were in the fortress were by no means men who would be shot on the morrow, but men subject to trial. . . Whether they would be shot or not was still a question; prior to this I had never had anyone shot; I substituted penal servitude of various terms. This development, this revolt of the Pavlovsk Regiment, showed that all was not well. The following day the troops were to occupy the same posts. . .

Chairman: Excuse me! You are now passing to Monday! But, General, did you inform Headquarters about the results?

Khabalov: Yes I did inform Headquarters of the following: "I cannot carry out Your Majesty's command," and that the disorders are continuing. . .[4] On Monday morning, the fol-

---

[4] Khabalov had received a telegram from Nicholas II ordering him to suppress the disorders in the capital immediately.

lowing occurred. . . Let me go back a little bit: it must be stated that this unfortunate order to use rifles was issued in the meantime, and was due to the fact that the cavalry was exhausted. As soon as it scattered one crowd, another would gather. In a word, thirsty horses and unfed men jostled and exhausted themselves, and lost their energy. . . During the night we were informed that the Second Baltic Naval Depot would raise the standard of revolt during that night. . . And that some agitators were there. This was being conveyed to me during the night, but they could not reach me, and it was brought to the attention of my chief of staff. The city governor conveyed this to me early in the morning—probably about six or seven o'clock. (Remember that I arrived during the night at three o'clock: i.e., I didn't get any sleep.) During the night I was informed that the Naval Depot was astir, would revolt, and would be at the head of the insurgents. I found out that measures had already been taken during the night, a search had been made, and it turned out that there had been nothing of the kind—all this had been false information. . . During the first days, and during the disorders in general, there was a mass of erroneous information. There was a whole lot of false news!. . . That same morning, at about six or seven o'clock, I received a call from the Volhynian regiment. The battalion commander told me that the training detachment of this regiment refused to leave the barracks; at first I was told that they had apparently killed the commander of the training detachment; other reports indicated that he had shot himself in front of the ranks when they refused to obey him. . . At this point I told the battalion commander: "Be sure that this does not spread, does not flare up any further. Return the troops to the barracks, and try to

disarm them: let them stay indoors. . ."
I myself went directly to the office of the
city governor. It must be added that
Colonel Pavlenkov was suffering from
chest spasms (in general all the officers
stationed here were ill, for all the healthy
ones were at the front, all those evacuated here were sick). And that morning
Colonel Pavlenkov was in no condition
for service. . . I therefore summoned
his deputy, Colonel Mikhailichenko, of
the household troops of the Moscow
Regiment, and went there myself. When
I arrived, it turned out that a company of the Preobrazhenskii Regiment
consisting of evacuated troops had joined
the rebellious Volhynians, who remained
on the street and refused to surrender
their rifles; subsequently a unit of the
Lithuanian Regiment did likewise. Further information indicated that this
armed crowd, joined by groups of factory workers and others, was moving
along Kirochnii Street, that it had raided
the barracks of the gendarmes' division
and was looting the barracks of the Engineers' Academy. I had to think of
pacifying this crowd. I formed a detachment made up of two companies of the
Keksgol'm Regiment, two companies
of the Preobrazhenskii Regiment, companies of His Majesty's Riflemen—in a
word, those who could be withdrawn
from nearby neighborhoods, from Nevskii Avenue. . . A machine-gun company
from the Strel'na area, joined by a
squadron of dragoons of the 9th Reserve
Regiment was added by Colonel Mikhailichenko. . . And this force, composed of six companies, fifteen machine
guns, and a troop and a half of cavalry,
under the command of Colonel Kutepov,
an officer decorated by the Order of St.
George, was sent against the rebels demanding that they lay down their
weapons, and, should they refuse, to take
decisive action against them. . . And now
something unbelieveable began to happen. Namely, the detachment advanced,
under a brave, decisive officer. But it
somehow left the scene, and there were
no results. . . But something should have
happened: if he acted decisively there
should have been a collision with this
electrified crowd, the troops should have
dispersed the mob and driven it into a
corner toward the Neva, toward the Tau-
rida Gardens. . . But there were no
results! I dispatched men, I got no news
—I sent three mounted patrols of Cos-
sacks—of the Cossack troops at my disposal. Having sent this detachment, I
remained without troops, and I had to
gather another detachment so as to be
able to oppose any possible further disorders. And so I sent these three
mounted patrols, I was informed that
the Kutepov detachment had advanced
only as far as Kirochnii Street, that
it was moving along Kirochnii and Spas-
skii Streets, but was unable to advance any further—reinforcements were
needed. Then I received the news that
the Circuit Court building had been
burned. Litvinov, the fire chief, informed
me over the telephone that he and the
firemen had arrived to extinguish the
fire but that the crowd would not give
way, and that he was not able to make
them. . . Then two companies, I don't
remember which ones, were sent to the
Circuit Court to scatter the mob and
enable the firemen to put the fire out. . .
But again these companies, once they
had left, disappeared, and were missing!
After that information was received
from the Moscow Regiment. The Moscow Regiment was deployed thus: part
of it was deployed along Sampsonevskii
Avenue near the barracks—this unit was
to stop the crowd from gathering on
Sampsonevskii Avenue near the factories.
A second unit, the Fourth Company with
machine guns, was to occupy the Liteinii

Bridge and Nizhnii Novgorod Street and stop the crowd of workers from moving in and out of the Liteinii Area, so as to control, if possible, the approach to the arsenals. Information was received near midday that the Fourth Company had been dispersed by the crowd, that, of the officers who tried to resist, some had been killed, others wounded, that huge crowds were blocking Sampsonevskii Avenue, that the remaining companies were standing in the barracks yard, evidently powerless to do anything. The situation was becoming critical! It was becoming difficult to furnish any reinforcement—wherever I turned I was told that they did not have any available companies, that they could not give me any. . . Only toward the evening did it become clear how much the Semenevskii, Ismailovskii and Chasseur Regiments could offer; but of this number, in the end, only three companies of the Ismailovskii men and three companies of Chasseurs appeared. The Finnish Regiment could not offer any help. Excuse me, I do not know whether this interests you. . .

Chairman: Please, please!—it is very important.

Khabalov: Along with this came a stream of demands: furnish a company for protection here, supply one there for security—give the Chairman of the Council of Ministers a guard for his personal protection. . . I must admit that I wondered how much a few soldiers could help: what are twenty men?— They cannot provide protection; there will only be more unnecessary bloodshed. It seemed to be better where there was no guard! But in view of the demands made, I did send a company which was to occupy both ends of Mokhovaia Street, on the Simeonovskii and the Panteleimonovskii side. Then, when it became clear. . .

Chairman: Did the Minister of Interior, Protopopov, demand that a unit be sent for his personal security?

Khabalov: I don't remember. .·. No, it seems this was not the case. In fact I am sure that this was not the case. At that point there were many demands: for example, the Lithuanian Palace reported. . .

Chairman: What about the former Chairman of the Council of Ministers, Sturmer?

Khabalov: No, there was no demand from him either. Of the ministers only Prince Golitsyn[5] made demands; and there was a demand to send troops to the Mariinskii Palace, and a detachment was sent there during the evening. Subsequently a company was sent to occupy the telephone building, and it defended it. And so when it became clear that the Vyborg side had been seized by the revolting mob, and subsequently the Liteinii section, but that the remaining areas of the city were relatively calm, I intended to gather a reserve force under Colonel Prince Argutinskii-Dolgorukov of the Preobrazhenskii Regiment on Palace Square, and I directed the following: a unit was to be sent to support Kutepov, who, evidently, could not cope with the situation, and another unit was to be sent to the Petersburg side, together with the Grenadiers and a company of the Moscow Regiment. They were to try to force these mutineers back if possible to the north, toward the sea. . . The situation was all the worse because the Porokhovyi plants for explosives were in the rear. God forbid! one explosion in these plants, and nothing would remain of Petrograd. The outlook was becoming more serious. And the

[5] Prince Nikolai Golitsyn was Chairman of the Council of Ministers from December 27, 1916, to February 27, 1917; he was the last premier of the old regime.

task of forming reserves proved very hard, because the third company of the Preobrazhenskii Regiment arrived without cartridges, and to obtain them was impossible since the rebellious mob held the Vyborg side. There was no place to get them. Then it was decided to obtain these cartridges from other units (Pavlenkov was in charge, but I was present as senior commander) of the 181st Infantry Regiment. But it turned out that, although the regiment had not actually rebelled, the commander was only barely able to restrain it. And the commander of the Finnish Reserve Regiment, asked to send a company of troops, replied that his regiment had only two loyal companies, and only their presence contained the regiment. Then we tried to obtain cartridges from the military schools, from the Pavlovsk and Vladimir schools.

Chairman: Was that on Monday evening?

Khabalov: It was during the night. . . This revolt of soldiers and workers occurred on Monday. Our attempt to obtain cartridges failed because they could not be delivered; had the shells been sent, they would have fallen into the hands of the mutineers—the revolutionaries. . . Seeing that I could not collect troops here, that we had only a handful, I telephoned to the commander at Kronshtadt, asking him to send troops, and if not troops then at least cartridges. . . But the commander told me that he could send nothing, since the fortress itself was in danger. Thus, toward the evening the situation became almost hopeless—in terms of an attack. . .

45

THE RUSSIAN VILLAGE, SUMMER 1917

The February Revolution was made in the cities, not in the countryside. At first Russia's peasants sat by quietly, waiting to see what would happen. When they discovered that the Provisional Government was postponing all major decisions on the land question till the convocation of the Constituent Assembly they took matters into their own hands. They would not wait for any legislative solution, particularly since there was no effective government authority in the countryside. The documents below illustrate the nature of the elemental revolution going on in the Russian villages—a process which no one seemed able to stop and which Lenin and the Bolsheviks would utilize in their drive for power.

There are numerous documents on the agrarian situation in 1917 in Robert Browder and Alexander Kerensky, *The Russian Provisional Government.* A most interesting government survey of the situation is in C. Vulliamy (ed.), *From the Red Archives*, pp. 227–70. For major studies of the Russian land problem see Geroid Robinson, *Rural Russia under the Old Regime*; G. Pavlovsky, *Agricultural Russia on the Eve of the Revolution*; and L. Owen, *The Russian Peasant Movement, 1906–1917*, as well as his "The Russian Agricultural Revolution of 1917." *Slavonic and East European Review*, XII, 155–66, 368–86. Victor Chernov, who was Minister of Agriculture during the summer of 1917, writes on the problem in *The Great Russian Revolution.*

A. FROM A MEMORANDUM OF KIRSANOV LANDOWNERS ON THE ACTIVITIES OF THE COMMITTEES AND THE PRESENT SITUATION IN KIRSANOV COUNTY, TAMBOV PROVINCE[1]

The old men, the sick, and the women remaining in the countryside have accepted the overthrow calmly, and consider it to be the result of the Tsar's foolish management of the country. It might have been expected that the demand for a social revolution would not penetrate into the countryside soon and would at first remain only the demand of the army and the workers. But the replacement of the entire local administration, the elimination of the police and the usual authorities in the villages, and the amnesty granted criminals hastened the advent of the revolution. Approach-

Translated by Walter Gleason from "Agrarnoe dvizhenie v 1917 g. po dokumentam Glavnogo Zemel'nogo Komiteta," *Krasnyi Arkhiv*, XIV (Moscow, 1926), 191–95, 204–5, 218.

[1] The memorandum was received by the Chief Land Committee in Petrograd in June, 1917.

507

ing the village from without, the revolution found no state institutions there. This tendency was hastened even more in Tambov province, specifically in Kirsanov county, because of the abdication of the provincial and county commissars.

In Kirsanov a Committee of Public Safety was formed, chosen not on the basis of universal suffrage, which was technically impossible, but by a random selection of individuals. Through its initiative committees were formed in the districts. A section of the population protested the illegal election of these committees and the destruction and replacement of the district and village authorities, but found no support anywhere. This made the population think that under the new regime the will of the people, as embodied in the committees, was the highest law of the land and that there was no control over the decisions of the popular will. The peasants concluded this from the fact that none of the decrees of the committees, no matter how illegal, was annulled by the authorities. Not once did the authorities leave Kirsanov to settle the misunderstandings which had arisen in the villages. The villages were left entirely to themselves. Here are some examples of certain excesses of the peasants and the committees.

On Count Perovskii's estate peasants dismissed the manager, V. Ia. Khovelko, a provincial and county zemstvo deputy, with whose assistance the owner and his father sold 16,000 of the 24,000 desiatins to the peasants at a price significantly below market value. The managers on the estates of Senator Martynov and Mrs. Goriainova were also dismissed, while Count Nosov's manager was arrested.

The Kurdiukovsk District Committee seized the landowners' oats for seed and sold it to the peasants considerably below the fixed price. In many districts search and seizures on estates were made by the committees, weapons were taken away, and the removal and sale of the estates' products prohibited. All business transactions were inspected by the district committees which could alter the price and conditions of such transactions. All activity on the estates was hampered by demands and permits. It became impossible to run the estates, and many landowners gave up and left for the cities.

At the height of the sowing season the district committee permitted the rural committees to release war prisoners at their discretion.[2] The sowing suffered, and production in various branches of the village economy ceased because of the impossibility of finding replacements, all the more so since Russian workers were also laid off. It was forbidden to hire workers from nearby districts. The committees charged extremely high prices for day laborers.

The county committee decided to audit the records of financial institutions and their method of distributing money. It decided to charge the expenses for the upkeep of the committees only to the landlords and church properties. It interfered with the allocation of zemstvo funds. It reduced the fixed prices on grain announced by the government by one-third, thus halting the transport of grain to the city and obstructing government purchases.

The committees conferred upon themselves the right to levy all taxes, duties, and payments; they assumed jurisdiction over business transactions by imposing conditions, for example, prohibiting the inhabitants of other districts to attend

---

[2] During the war many German and Austro-Hungarian prisoners of war were put to work in Russian fields and factories to replace the men at the front.

sales.

The county committee destroyed the right to property, the right to the management and use of one's belongings, contractual rights, without first consulting the landowners. Thus the county committee lowered rental prices on land by 25 per cent compared to the preceding year's price. The district committee went even further and lowered prices by 60 per cent. In some localities the peasants seized the land free. The following account reveals the confiscatory nature of such rental fees. With the price of rye fixed at 2 rubles 40 kopecks, and an average harvest in Kirsanov county of 80 puds per desiatina,[3] a desiatina of rye should provide a gross income of 184 rubles in grain and 25 rubles in straw. Allowing 70 rubles to cover the cost of harvesting and processing, a net profit of 140 rubles remains. In view of this income, the rental fee of 9–20 rubles, which was the price of the rented land, was quite minimal, all the more so since the tenants put down only a very insignificant deposit, leaving the balance until next year. This rent was even more insignificant with regard to the leasing of meadows. Irrigated and sown meadows were rented for 10–25 rubles. Counting a harvest of hay in such meadows as 200 puds per desiatina, and the price of hay at 1 ruble 50 kopecks, the income turns out to be 300 rubles per desiatina, the expense of harvesting the grass being no more than 25 rubles per desiatina.

The peasants jumped at such cheap rents, and with the help of the committees forced the landowners to rent almost all their land. In some localities the peasants seized so much land that they were forced to plow hurriedly and carelessly. In many places the fallow was not plowed, and it is now too late for such plowing. The land available to

[3] A pud is 36 pounds, a desiatina 2.7 acres.

the landlords for sowing decreased on the average by 80 per cent.

The committees were eager to distribute land allotments among poorly landed peasants, according to a labor norm. This aspiration met opposition in the very advantageous rents which each tried to receive. In addition, it ran against the tendency to divide the land equally, per soul. In some localities the rich peasants seized much of the land and are now seeking storage space for the grain grown on seized land. In some places the low land rents produced a land rush and speculation.

It should be noted that in the past thirty years, and especially before the revolution of 1905, the landlords sold half their land to the peasants—150,000 desiatins. These lands fell into the hands only of the former manorial peasants, who lived near the liquidated estates. Thus this group of peasants became relatively prosperous, as opposed to the former state peasants, who lived at a distance and received nothing from the sales made by the landowners. This year when the peasants imposed their will upon the landowners, all the landowners' arable land was again turned over to peasants living nearby, since the latter did not let peasants of other villages near these lands.

The new socialists, dreaming of the socialization of the land, continued to live under the influence of serfdom and were firmly convinced that the right to ownership of the land leased by them from landowners could be obtained only by those who had formerly been serfs of these landowners. In this way the former manorial peasants are, for the second time, overloaded with land, while the former state peasants again obtained nothing. And the first attempt at the social task sought by the land reform, the just distribution of land according to a labor norm, failed because ot the anarchy of Russian life.

Under another directive of the county committee general pasturage rights were granted for all meadow lands after the harvest. As a result great masses of peasants overran and destroyed in a few days all pastures the landowners had prepared for milk cows, pedigree cattle, and horses. The manorial cattle farms will be completely ruined. The peasants worsened the situation by invading the landowners' pastures during the spring, thus ruining the seeded meadows, fodder, and clover.

A third land measure of the county committee was even more decisive: it handed all the lands which had been fully sown to the peasants. In one section of the county fully sown land is fairly widespread, since there are landowners who, for lack of equipment and money, rent out all their land. This measure deprived them of all their sown land, but it also should have penalized some peasants. Soldiers' wives and some well-to-do peasants also rent out all their lands. By a unique logic this transfer of land was applied only in the case of estates. This measure clearly represents the seizure of the landowners' sown lands. It violates the government's order guaranteeing this land. Nonetheless the transfer of land was completed, to the bewilderment of the peasants themselves.

In other decrees the committees also forbade the cutting of trees. If the landowners sought permission to cut down a tree or two for domestic needs, they had to petition the committees, who did not always grant these petitions.

In vain did the landowners beseech the county and provincial commissars with requests that the decrees ruining their livelihood be changed. The commissars acknowledged the complete illegality of these decrees but stated that they had no right to change them. They only repeated: liquidate your estates. This encouraged the arbitrary actions of the peasants. To the charge that the decrees were illegal, the peasants would respond that they were probably legal, since the government had not opposed their implementation. It would have been easy to direct the current of arbitrary actions into normal channels at the outset. Now it is of course more difficult to do as some sections of the peasantry are convinced that the people have already transferred the lands into their own hands, the people meaning the closest village. In any case the intention of the government to forbid any seizures until the meeting of the Constituent Assembly has failed. The seizures have been completed, and the government itself, timid in the face of the committees' actions, is guilty of this.

One should conclude from what has been said that organizations which were either formed arbitrarily or appointed by the government, such as the Provisioning and Land Committees, are in need of supervisory control, which would review their decrees and annul the illegal ones. This function could be transferred to the temporary judges, who are now left without any real duties. In addition the commissars should snap out of their inactivity and become active agents of the government, implementing its policies. They should not be subservient to arbitrary public organizations which must be controlled, because our democracy is not yet used to the exercise of power.

B. MEMORANDUM OF THE DIRECTOR OF THE CHISTOPOL'SK BRANCH OF THE STATE BANK OF JULY 2, 1917

. . . The destructive consequences of the authorities' laxity are already evident here. All the land, meadows, and forests have passed from the hands of the owners to the peasants. For this reason we cannot, in the coming year, expect either the usual quantity (since much of the land will have been left fallow) or quality of grain (the plowing has been quite shallow—worse than the peasants' usual plowing). Pedigreed horned cattle have been seized and in some cases slaughtered for meat, the rest sold and led away. Stables have been destroyed, trotters and racing horses put behind stolen plows, harrows, seeding machines, and rollers, most of which are already on the verge of ruination owing to the lack of experienced hands. Cultivated orchards underwent reckless ravaging, young trees were torn up at the roots, while the bark was stripped off old trees. Forests were mercilessly cut down for firewood and household needs; in some localities they were burned down. The owners are not permitted to take with them their furniture and other household fixtures, including wardrobes. They themselves, and their managers or bailiffs, are being expelled. "You have lived on our labor and drunk our blood long enough; now our time has come," they are told. In the cities small groups of men, women, and youngsters, taking a soldier with them, break into apartments and make arbitrary searches, pretending to act on the orders of the Committee of Soldiers' and Workers' Deputies or the Committee of Public Safety. Innocent people are arrested without cause and put in prison, as was the case in Chistopol' with the chairman of the zemstvo board, the mayor, the military commander, and others. Now there is talk in the countryside of renewed agitation; the peasants are urged not to take their grain into the city for the fixed price, but to demand 5 to 10 rubles or more for a pud of rye. The peasants will glad-

ly listen to this type of agitation, as they did in case of the land (the land should be yours, don't delay, seize it now and don't wait for the Constituent Assembly). Our villages are again preoccupied with idle musing and discussions about new windfalls.

C. TELEGRAM OF THE COMMISSAR OF SIMBIRSK PROVINCE, AUGUST 28, 1917

Petrograd. Central Militia Board. Copies to the Chairman of the Council of Ministers and the Ministers of Justice and Agriculture.

On August 20 in the village of Chipikovo, Sengileev county, the population beat up a member of the Chertanovskii supply board, Lobanov, while he was going about his official duties. An inquiry is being conducted. According to the information received, the citizens of the village of Kliukovka, in Korsun county, undertook arbitrary seizures of timber and cut down trees as well. The district commissar was advised to take extraordinary measures, together with the land council, to put an end to the seizures. According to information received, in the village of Atiashevo, Ardatov county, the soldiers Froklin and Rezkin are agitating against the grain monopoly and hindering the requisitioning process. They were arrested. An inquiry is being conducted. In the village of Maliachkino, Syzran county, the population refused to submit to the grain estimates and threatened the members of the supply board. The district commissar was advised to take the most decisive measures immediately. The supply board of the Timoshkin district, Sengileev county, telegraphed that the local inhabitants Abdriazikov, Baimashev, and Absaliamov agitated against the district supply board. This agitation had a harmful influence on the population, interfering with its work. Board members are resigning. The workers are starving. Measures are being taken to eliminate the agitators' activities. According to a communiqué from the Syzran county supply board, the population of that county is refusing to surrender its grain at the established prices, considering them too low. The situation in the city and in the rural areas is critical. The district commissar was advised to take the most energetic steps to enforce the grain monopoly regulations, using military force if need be. The chairman of the Simbirsk county supply board reported to the provincial executive committee that soldiers led by the garrison commander arrived in the village of Ishcheevka at the request of the committee to enforce the regulations on the grain monopoly. However, the soldiers not only did not assist in the transfer of the grain supplies from the government warehouses to the Aratskii factory but went over to the peasants' side and, brandishing their rifles, declared that the grain will not leave the warehouses. I am instructing the garrison commander to take the strictest measures and to call the offenders to account. There were no other outstanding events during the past week.

46

RUSSIA'S ONE-DAY PARLIAMENT

By Victor Chernov

The Bolsheviks had used the demand for the convocation of the Constituent Assembly as a major slogan in their rise to power. But when free elections gave them only a minority in that body, they liquidated the institution. Chernov (1873–1952) was the Assembly's freely elected chairman, representing its non-Bolshevik majority. Born a peasant, he had become the leader of rejuvenated populism. In 1901 he was one of the leaders of the Socialist Revolutionary organization (the S.R.'s), Russia's largest political party representing the peasantry. In 1917 he became minister of agriculture in the Provisional Government. Hunted by the Soviet police, he left Russia in 1920; he came to New York in 1941. He wrote the brief account below on the thirtieth anniversary of the Constituent Assembly's brutal dissolution.

Chernov's memoirs, in an abridged English translation, are entitled *The Great Russian Revolution*. For documents on the Assembly, see the relevant portions of the three-volume collection, *The Russian Provisional Government*, edited by Robert Browder and Alexander Kerensky. For a brief history of the Assembly, see Oliver Radkey's *The Elections to the Russian Constituent Assembly of 1917*. For a history of the S.R. party, see the same author's *The Agrarian Foes of Bolshevism* and *The Sickle under the Hammer*. There are chapters on the Constituent Assembly in Karl Kautsky's *The Dictatorship of the Proletariat* (paperback), and Ariadna Tyrkova-Williams, *From Liberty to Brest Litovsk*. Boris Sokoloff, in *The White Nights*, recounts the ill-fated attempt to defend the Assembly. There is a section on the Assembly in James Bunyan and Harold Fisher, *The Bolshevik Revolution, 1917–1918*. Lenin's theses on the Assembly are in Volume XXVI of his *Collected Works*. See also Truman Cross, "Chernov and 1917," *Russian Review*, October, 1967.

When we, the newly elected members of the Constituent Assembly, entered the Tauride Palace, the seat of the Assembly in Petrograd, on January 18, 1918, we found that the corridors were full of armed guards. They were masters of the building, crude and brazen. At first they did not address us directly, and only exchanged casual observations to the effect that "This guy should get a bayonet between his ribs" or "It wouldn't be bad to put some lead into this one." When we entered the large hall, it was still empty. The Bolshevik deputies had not yet appeared.

Reprinted from *The New Leader* (New York), January 31, 1948.

A tank division billeted in Petrograd remained faithful to the Assembly. It intended to demonstrate this faithfulness by participating in the march to the Palace which was to pass on its way the barracks of the Preobrazhenski and Semenovski Regiments, the two best units of the Petrograd garrison. At the meetings held by these regiments, resolutions were invariably adopted demanding the transfer of state power to the Constituent Assembly. Thus a prospect was open for the consolidation of democratic forces.

But the Bolsheviks were not caught off guard. They attacked the columns of demonstrators converging on the Tauride Palace from various parts of Petrograd. Whenever the unarmed crowd could not be dispersed immediately, the street was blocked by troops or Bolshevik units would shoot into the crowd. The demonstrators threw themselves on the pavement and waited until the rattle of machine guns quieted down; then they would jump up and continue their march, leaving behind the dead and wounded until they were stopped by a new volley. Or the crowd would be bayoneted by enraged Bolshevik outfits, which would get hold of the banners and placards carried by the demonstrators and tear them into scraps.

The Assembly hall was gradually filled by the deputies. Near the dais were placed armed guards. The public gallery was crowded to overflowing. Here and there glittered rifle muzzles. Admission tickets for the public were distributed by the notorious Uritski.[1] He did his job well.

* * *

At last all the deputies had gathered in a tense atmosphere. The left sector was evidently waiting for something. From our benches rose Deputy Lordkapanidze, who said in a calm, businesslike voice that, according to an old parliamentary custom, the first sitting should be presided over by the senior deputy. The senior was S. P. Shvetsov, an old Socialist Revolutionary (SR).

As soon as Shvetsov's imposing figure appeared on the dais, somebody gave a signal, and a deafening uproar broke out. The stamping of feet, hammering on the desks and howling made an infernal noise. The public in the gallery and the Bolshevik allies, the Left Socialist Revolutionaries, joined in the tumult. The guards clapped their rifle butts on the floor. From various sides guns were trained on Shvetsov. He took the President's bell, but the tinkling was drowned in the noise. He put it back on the table, and somebody immediately grabbed it and handed it over, like a trophy, to the representative of the Sovnarkom (Soviet of Commissars), Sverdlov. Taking advantage of a moment of comparative silence, Shvetsov managed to pronounce the sacramental phrase: "The session of the Constituent Assembly is open." These words evoked a new din of protest. Shvetsov slowly left the dais and joined us. He was replaced by Sverdlov, who opened the session for the second time, but now in the name of the Soviets, and presented its "platform." This was an ultimatum: we had just to vote Aye or No.

In the election of the Assembly's President, the Bolsheviks presented no candidate of their own. They voted for Maria Spiridonova, nominated by the Left SR's. Later they threw Spiridonova into jail and tormented her until she was on the verge of insanity. But at this moment they wanted to take full advantage of her popularity and reputation as a martyr in the struggle against Tsarism. My nomination as candidate for the Presidency received even greater support than had been expected. Some leftist peasants evidently could not bring themselves to oppose their own "muzhik

[1] Head of the Soviet secret police.

minister." I obtained 244 votes against 150.

I delivered my inauguration address, making vigorous efforts to keep self-control. Every sentence of my speech was met with outcries, some ironical, others spiteful, often buttressed by the brandishing of guns. Bolshevik deputies surged forward to the dais. Conscious that the stronger nerves would win, I was determined not to yield to provocation. I said that the nation had made its choice, that the composition of the Assembly was a living testimony to the people's yearning for Socialism, and that its convention marked the end of the hazy transition period. Land reform, I went on, was a foregone conclusion: the land would be equally accessible to all who wished to till it. The Assembly, I said, would inaugurate an era of active foreign policy directed toward peace.

* * *

I finished my speech amidst a cross-fire of interruptions and cries. It was now the turn of the Bolshevik speakers—Skvortsov and Bukharin. During their delivery, our sector was a model of restraint and self-discipline. We maintained a cold, dignified silence. The Bolshevik speeches, as usual, were shrill, clamorous, provocative and rude, but they could not break the icy silence of our majority. As President, I was bound in duty to call them to order for abusive statements. But I know that this was precisely what they expected. Since the armed guards were under their orders, they wanted clashes, incidents and perhaps a brawl. So I remained silent.

The Social Democrat Tseretelli rose to answer the Bolsheviks. They tried to "scare" him by levelling at him a rifle from the gallery and brandishing a gun in front of his face. I had to restore order—but how? Appeals to maintain the dignity of the Constituent Assembly evoked an even greater noise, at times turning into a raving fury. Dybenko and other demagogues called for more and more assaults. Lenin, in the government box, demonstrated his contempt for the Assembly by lounging in his chair and putting on the air of a man who was bored to death. I threatened to clear the gallery of the yelling public. Though this was an empty threat, since the guards were only waiting for the order to "clear" us out of the hall, it proved temporarily effective. Tseretelli's calm and dignified manner helped to restore peace.

There was a grim significance in the outburst that broke loose when a middle-of-the-road deputy, Severtsov-Odoievski, started to speak Ukrainian. In the Assembly the Bolsheviks did not want to hear any language except Russian. I was compelled to state emphatically that in the new Russia, each nationality had the right to use its own language whenever it pleased.

When it appeared that we refused to vote the Soviet "platform" without discussion, the Bolsheviks walked out of the sitting in a body. They returned to read a declaration charging us with counter-revolution and stating that our fate would be decided by organs which were in charge of such things. Soon after that the Left SR's also made up their minds. Just before the discussion of the land reform started, their representative, I. Z. Steinberg, declared that they were in disagreement with the majority, and left the Assembly.

We knew that the Bolsheviks were in conference, discussing what to do next. I felt sure that we would be arrested. But it was of utmost importance for us to have a chance to say the last word. I declared that the next point on the agenda was the land reform. At this moment somebody pulled at my sleeve.

"You have to finish now. There are orders from the People's Commissar."

Behind me stood a stocky sailor, accompanied by his armed comrades.

"What People's Commissar?"

"We have orders. Anyway, you cannot stay here any longer. The lights will be turned out in a minute. And the guards are tired."

"The members of the Assembly are also tired but cannot rest until they have fulfilled the task entrusted to them by the people—to decide on the land reform and the future form of government."

And leaving the guards no time to collect themselves, I proceeded to read the main paragraphs of the Land Bill, which our party had prepared long ago. But time was running short. Reports and debates had to be omitted. Upon my proposal, the Assembly voted six basic points of the bill. It provided that all land was to be turned into common property, with every tiller possessing equal rights to use it. Amidst incessant shouts: "That's enough! Stop it now! Clear the hall!" the other points of the bill were voted.

Fearing that the lights would be extinguished, somebody managed to procure candles. It was essential that the future form of government be voted upon immediately. Otherwise the Bolsheviks would not fail to charge the Assembly with having left the door open for the restoration of the monarchy. The motion for a republican form of government was carried unanimously.

In the dawn of a foggy and murky morning I declared a recess until noon.

At the exit a palefaced man pushed his way to me and beseeched me in a trembling voice not to use my official car. A bunch of murderers, he said, was waiting for me. He admitted that he was a Bolshevik, but his conscience revolted against this plot.

I left the building, surrounded by a few friends. We saw several men in sailor's uniforms loitering near my car. We decided to walk. We had a long distance to go, and when I arrived home I learned that rumors were in circulation that the Constituent Assembly had dispersed, and that Chernov and Tseretelli had been shot.

At noon several members of the Assembly were sent on reconnaissance. They reported that the door of the Tauride Palace was sealed and guarded by a patrol with machine guns and two pieces of field artillery. Later in the day a decree of the Sovnarkom was published by which the Constituent Assembly was "dissolved."

Thus ended Russia's first and last democratic parliament.

47

DAYS WITH LENIN

By Maxim Gorky

During the 1890's Gorky (1868–1936) became Russia's most popular writer. Much of his large literary income went to the Social Democrats, whom he joined before the turn of the century. His name and prestige became a valuable asset of the Bolsheviks. After 1917 he found himself opposed to many of the new regime's policies. His close friendship with Lenin resulted in the saving of many Russian intellectuals. In 1921 he left Russia for Capri but returned in 1928. In 1934 he became the president of the Union of Soviet Writers. The cause of his death in 1936 remains a mystery.

His warm tribute to Lenin is one of the best pieces written about the Soviet leader. The essay is reprinted here with only minor cuts. For Lenin's writings, see his *Collected Works* (38 vols.). For biographies see *Memories of Lenin* by his wife, Nadezhda Krupskaya; David Shub's *Lenin* (paperback is abridged); Louis Fischer's *The Life of Lenin* (paperback), which has a chapter on "Lenin and Gorky"; Adam Ulam's *The Bolsheviks*; and the recent compendium edited by Leonard Schapiro and Peter Reddaway, *Lenin: The Man, the Theoretician, the Leader*. For recent biographies of Gorky see Richard Hare, *Maxim Gorky*; Dan Levin, *Maxim Gorky*; and Irwin Weil, *Gorky* (paperback). For a recent Soviet biography of Lenin see Lydia Fotieva, *Pages from Lenin's Life*. Two new looks at Gorky in the years covered by this excerpt are Bertram Wolfe's *The Bridge and the Abyss: The Troubled Friendship of Maxim Gorky and Lenin*, and *Untimely Thoughts* by Maxim Gorky himself.

. . . It would be a difficult task to paint the portrait of Vladimir Ilyitch[1] Lenin. His words were as much a part of his external appearance as scales are of fish. The simplicity and straightforwardness of everything he said were an essential part of his nature. The heroic deeds which he achieved are surrounded by no glittering halo. His was that heroism which Russia knows well—the unassuming, austere life of self-sacrifice of the true Russian revolutionary intellectual who, in his unshakable belief in the possibility of social justice on the earth,

[1] Ilyitch—Lenin's patronymic by which his close friends and comrades always liked to refer to him.—*Ed.*

From Maxim Gorky, *Days with Lenin* (New York, 1932), pp. 3–7, 11–57, by permission of International Publishers Co., Inc. Footnotes in original.

renounces all the pleasures of life in order to toil for the happiness of mankind.

What I wrote about him directly after his death, when I was overwhelmed with grief, was hastily written and inadequate. There were things which I could not write then because of considerations of tact, which, I hope, are fully comprehensible. He was a man of piercing vision and great wisdom and "in much wisdom there is much grief. . . ."

THE FIRST MEETING

The unsatisfactory character of my former reminiscences was increased by the presence of many bad gaps and inconsistencies. I ought to have begun with the London Congress,[2] when the figure of Vladimir Ilyitch stood out in strong relief against a background of doubt and mistrust, of open hostility and even of hate.

I still see vividly before me the bare walls of a wooden church on the outskirts of London, unadorned to the point of absurdity, the lancet windows of a small, narrow hall which might have been a classroom in a poor school. . . .

I had never met Lenin before this, nor read as much of him as I ought to have done. But what I had managed to read, and above all the enthusiastic accounts of those who knew him personally, had attracted me strongly towards him. When we were introduced, he shook me heartily by the hand, and, scrutinizing me with his keen eyes and speaking in the tone of an old acquaintance, he said jocularly: "So glad you've come. I believe you're fond of a scrap? There's going to be a fine old scuffle here."

I did not expect Lenin to be like that.

[2] The Congress of the Russian Social-Democratic Labor Party, held in London in 1907. —*Ed.*

Something was lacking in him. He rolled his "r's" gutturally, and had a jaunty way of standing with his hands somehow poked up under his armpits. He was somehow too ordinary, did not give the impression of being a leader. As a literary man, I am obliged to take note of such little details, and this necessity has become a habit, sometimes even an irritating habit, with me. G. V. Plekhanov, at our first meeting, stood with folded arms, looking at me with the severe, slightly bored expression with which an overworked teacher regards an additional pupil. Nothing that he said has remained in my memory except the extremely trite remark: "I am an admirer of your work"; and neither of us, during the whole time of the Congress, felt any desire to have a heart-to-heart talk with the other.

Before me now stood a baldheaded, stocky, sturdy person, speaking with a guttural roll of his "r's," and holding my hand in one of his, while with the other he wiped a forehead which might have belonged to Socrates, beaming affectionately at me with his strangely bright eyes.

He began at once to speak about the defects of my book *Mother*—evidently he had read it in the manuscript which was in the possession of S. P. Ladyzhnikov. I was hurrying to finish the book, I said—but did not succeed in saying why. Lenin with a nod of assent, himself gave the explanation: Yes, I should hurry up with it, such a book is needed, for many of the workers who take part in the revolutionary movement do so unconsciously and chaotically, and it would be very useful to them to read *Mother*. "The very book for the moment." This was the single compliment he paid me, but it was a most precious one to me. . . .

I was in a festive mood. I was in the

midst of three hundred picked Party men, who, I learnt, had been sent to the Congress by one hundred and fifty thousand organized workers. Before my eyes were all the Party leaders, the old revolutionaries, Plekhanov, Axelrod, Deutsch. My festive mood was quite natural and will be understood by the reader when I add that I had become extremely low-spirited during the two years I had spent away from my native country. . . .

AT THE LONDON CONGRESS

But my festive mood lasted only until the first meeting when they began wrangling about "the order of the day." The fury of these disputes at once chilled my enthusiasm, and not so much because I felt how sharply the Party was divided into reformers and revolutionaries—I had realized that in 1903—but because of the hostile attitude of the reformers to Lenin. It oozed and spouted out of their speeches like water under high pressure out of an old hose.

It is not always what is said that is important, but how it is said. When Plekhanov, in a frock coat, closely buttoned up like a Protestant pastor, opened the Congress, he spoke like a preacher confident that his ideas are incontrovertible, every word and every pause of great value. Way above the heads of the delegates he skillfully weighed out his beautifully rounded phrases, and whenever anyone on the Bolshevik benches uttered a sound or whispered to a comrade, the venerable orator made a slight pause and sent his glance into him like a needle. One of the buttons on his frock coat was a great favorite with Plekhanov; he stroked it caressingly all the time with his finger, and when he paused, pressed it like an electric bell —it seemed to be this pressure which interrupted the flowing current of his speech. . . .

While Plekhanov was speaking at the first meeting, the person who did the most fidgeting on the Bolshevik benches was Lenin. At one time he hunched himself up as though he were cold, then he sprawled as if he felt hot. He poked his fingers in his armholes, rubbed his chin, shook his head, and whispered something to M. P. Tomsky. When Plekhanov declared that there were no "revisionists"[3] in the Party, Lenin bent down, the bald spot on his head grew red, and his shoulders shook with silent laughter. The workers sitting next to him and behind him also smiled, and from the back of the hall a voice called out loudly and morosely: "And what about the people sitting over there?"

Little Theodore Dan spoke like a man whose relationship to the authentic truth is one of father and daughter—he has begotten and fostered it, and still fosters it. He is Karl Marx incarnate, and the Bolsheviks—half-educated, ill-mannered children, a fact which is quite clear from their relations with the Mensheviks among whom are to be found, he said, "all the most eminent Marxist thinkers."

"You are not Marxists," he said disdainfully. "No, you are not Marxists" —and he thrust out his yellow fist. One of the workers asked him: "When are you going to tea again with the Liberals?"

I don't remember if it was at the first meeting that Martov spoke. This amazingly attractive man spoke with the ardor of youth and was evidently especially deeply affected by the tragic drama of the dissension and split. He trembled all over, swayed backward and forward spasmodically unfastening the collar of his starched shirt and waving his hands about. His cuff fell down from under the

---

[3] Supporters of the reformist Bernstein's attempts to "revise" Marxism.—*Ed.*

sleeve of his coat, he raised his arm high up and shook it to send the cuff back again to its proper place.

Martov did not give so much the impression of arguing as of urging and imploring: we must put an end to the split, the Party is too weak to be divided, the workers must get freedom before anything else, we mustn't let them lose heart. At times, during the first part of his speech he sounded almost hysterical; he became obscure through abundance of words, and he himself gave a painful impression. At the end of his speech, and without any apparent connection with it, he began in the same "militant" tone and with the same ardor, to shout against the militant group and against all work directed to the preparation of an armed uprising. I remember distinctly that someone from the Bolshevik benches cried out, "Well, there you are!" and Tomsky, I think it was, said: "Have we got to cut our hands off for Comrade Martov's peace of mind?"

Again, I do not remember exactly if Martov spoke at the first meeting. I only mention it in order to describe the different ways in which people spoke.

After his speech there was a gloomy discussion among the workers in the room which led into the hall of the meeting. "There's Martov for you; and he was one of the 'Iskra' group!"[4] "Our intellectual friends are changing their color!"

Rosa Luxemburg spoke eloquently, passionately and trenchantly, using irony with great effect.

LENIN SPEAKS

But now Vladimir Ilyitch hurries to the

[4] From 1900 to 1903 the *Iskra*, with Lenin at its head, was the leading organ of the Russian Social-Democracy. After Lenin's resignation in November, 1903, it continued publication until 1905 as the organ of the Mensheviks.—*Ed*.

pulpit, and cries "Comrades!" in his guttural way. He seemed to me to speak badly, but after a minute I and everybody else were absorbed in his speech. It was the first time I had heard complicated political questions treated so simply. There was no striving after eloquent phrases with him, but every word was uttered distinctly, and its meaning was marvelously plain. It is very difficult to pass on to the reader the unusual impression which he made. . . .

He gave a shorter speech than the orators who spoke before him, but he made a much greater impression. I was not alone in feeling this. Behind me was an enthusiastic whispering: "Now, he has got something to say." It really was so. His conclusions were not reached artificially, but developed by themselves, inevitably. The Mensheviks made no attempt to hide their displeasure at the speech and more than displeasure at Lenin himself. The more convincingly he showed the necessity to the Party of the utmost development of revolutionary theory so that the practice might be thoroughly surveyed in the light of it, the more exasperatedly did they interrupt him.

"A Congress isn't the place for philosophy!" "Don't act the teacher with us, we're not school-boys!"

One tall, bearded individual who looked like a shopkeeper was especially aggressive. He jumped up from his seat and stuttered: "Little p-plots—p-playing at little p-plots! Blanquists!"

Rosa Luxemburg nodded her head in approval of Lenin. She made a neat remark to the Mensheviks at one of the later meetings. "You don't stand on Marxism, you sit on it, rather lie down on it. . . ."

LENIN AND THE WORKERS

His free minutes or hours Lenin spent among the workers, asking them about the most petty details of their lives.

"What about their wives? Up to the neck in housework? But do they manage to learn anything, to read anything?"

Once in Hyde Park a group of workers who had seen Lenin for the first time at the Congress was discussing his conduct there. One of them made a striking remark:

"For all I know there may be other fellows as clever as he in Europe on the side of the workers. But I don't believe you'll find another one who could get you on the spot like that fellow!"

Another one added with a smile, "He's one of us all right."

"Plekhanov's just as much one of us," some one replied. The answer I heard just hit the mark—"You feel that Plekhanov's always teaching you, lording it over you, but Lenin's a real leader and comrade." One young fellow said jokingly: "Plekhanov's frock coat is too tight for him."

On one occasion we were on our way to a restaurant, when a worker, a Menshevik, stopped Lenin to ask him a question. Ilyitch dropped behind while the party went on. He entered the restaurant frowning, five minutes later, and said: "Curious that such a simpleton should have got into the Party Congress. He asked me, what was after all the real reason for the discussion. 'This is what it is,' I said to him. 'Your friends want to get into Parliament, while we believe that the working class has got to prepare for a struggle.' I think he understood."

Several of us always had our meals together in the same cheap little restaurant. I noticed that V. Ilyitch ate very little—two or three fried eggs, a small piece of ham, and a mug of thick, dark beer. He obviously took very little care of himself and his amazing care for the workers struck one all the more.

M. F. Andreyeva looked after the canteen, and he would ask her: "What do you think, are the workers getting enough to eat? No? H'm, h'm. Perhaps we can get more sandwiches?"

Once when he came to the inn where I was staying, I noticed him feeling the bedding with a preoccupied air.

"What are you doing?" I asked.

"I'm just looking to see if the sheets are well aired."

At first I didn't understand. Why should he want to know what the sheets were like in London? Then, noticing my perplexity, he explained, "You must take care of yourself."

In the autumn of 1918 I asked a worker from Sormovo, Dmitry Pavlov, what he thought was Lenin's most striking feature. He answered: "Simplicity. He is as simple as truth itself." He said this as though it has been thought out and decided long ago.

It is well known that one's severest critics are those who work under one. Lenin's chauffeur, Gill, a man of great experience, said: "Lenin is quite unique. There are no others like him. Once I was driving him along Myasnitskaya Street when the traffic was very heavy. I hardly moved forward. I was afraid of the car getting smashed and was sounding the horn, feeling very worried. He opened the door, reached me by standing on the footboard, meanwhile running the risk of being knocked down, and urged me to go forward. 'Don't get worried, Gill, go on like every one else.' I am an old chauffeur. I know that nobody else would do that. . . ."

Two years later in Capri, when he was discussing the Utopian novel with A. A. Bogdanov, he said, "If you would write a novel for the workers on the subject of how the sharks of capitalism robbed the earth and wasted the oil, iron, timber and coal—that would be a useful book, Signor Machist!"[5]

A MEETING IN PARIS

When he said good-bye to me in London he promised to come to Capri for a rest. But before he had made up his mind to come, I saw him in Paris in a two-roomed student's flat (it was a student's flat only in size, not in the cleanliness and order that reigned there). Nadejda Konstantinovna[6] had gone out after giving us tea and we remained alone together. . . .

With his invariably striking vividness and clarity, he began to talk about the Duma and the Cadets[7] who, he said, are "ashamed to be Octobrists"[8] and have only one way open to them, the road to the right. Then he brought forward a series of arguments for the imminence of war and "probably not of one, but of a whole series of wars"; *a prophecy which was speedily fulfilled in the Balkans.* He got up and with characteristic gesture, putting his thumbs in his waistcoat armholes, paced slowly up and down the little room, screwing up his bright eyes, saying:

"War is coming. It is inevitable. The capitalist world has reached the stage of putrescent fermentation. People are already beginning to poison themselves with the drugs of chauvinism and nationalism. I think we shall yet see a general European war.

"The proletariat? The proletariat will hardly be able to find in itself the strength to avert the carnage. How could it be done? A general strike of workers all over Europe? They are not yet sufficiently organized or class-conscious for that. Such a strike would be the signal for a civil war but we as practical politicians cannot count on that."

He paused, scraping the soles of his shoes on the floor, then said gloomily: "The proletariat of course will suffer terribly. Such must be its fate for some time yet. But its enemies will weaken each other, that also is inevitable."

Coming up to me he said forcibly but not loudly, as if in amazement: "No, but think of it. Why should people who are well-fed force hungry ones to fight against each other? Could you name a more idiotic or more revolting crime? The workers will pay a dreadfully heavy price for this, but in the end they will gain. It is the will of history."

He often spoke of history but I never felt in what he said any fetishistic worship of its will or power. . . .

LENIN IN ITALY

The next time we met after Paris was in Capri. I had a very strange impression at that time—as though V. Ilyitch were twice in Capri and in two sharply different moods. One Ilyitch, when I met him at the wharf, immediately declared to me resolutely: "I know, A. M., that you are always hoping that it will be possible to reconcile me with the Machists although I warned you of the futility of it in a letter. So don't make any attempts. . . ."

Then I told him that in my eyes A. A. Bogdanov, A. Lunacharsky and V. A. Bazarov were important people, highly and thoroughly educated, and had no equals in the Party.

"Granted. Well, what follows?"

"I consider them to be people aiming finally at the same thing, and if profoundly understood and realized, the unity of their aim should wipe out and annihilate philosophical contradictions."

[5] Machism was the name given to the tendency at that time to revise Marxism by diluting it with a new version of philosophical idealism based on the mechanist theories of the Austrian physicist Ernst Mach.—*Ed.*

[6] N. K. Krupskaya, Lenin's wife.—*Ed.*

[7] Members of the bourgeois-liberal Constitutional Democratic Party.—*Ed.*

[8] The party of big capital and landowners. —*Ed.*

"That means that the hope of reconciliation is still alive after all? It is quite useless," he said. "Put it out of your head, as completely as possible, I advise you as a friend. Plekhanov, according to you, has the same aim as well, and I, between ourselves, consider that he has quite another aim, although he is a materialist and not a metaphysician. . . ."

A. A. Bogdanov, who was an extremely attractive person, of a very mild character and very fond of Lenin, though with a rather high opinion of himself, had to listen to these biting and painful words: "Schopenhauer said that 'clear thinking means clear speaking' and I think he never said a truer word. You don't explain yourself clearly, Comrade Bogdanov. Explain to me in a few words what your 'substitution' will give to the working class, and why Machism is more revolutionary than Marxism?"

Bogdanov tried to explain but he really did speak in a confused and wordy fashion.

"Drop it," advised V. Ilyitch. "Somebody or other, Juares, I think, said, 'It is better to speak the truth than to be a minister'—or a Machist, I would add." Then he plunged into a game of chess with Bogdanov, and when he lost grew angry and even despondent like a child. It is worthy of remark that even this childish despondency, like his astonishing laugh, did not impair the completeness and unity of his character.

There was in Capri another Lenin— a splendid comrade, a light-hearted person with a lively, inexhaustible interest in everything in the world, and strikingly gentle. Late one evening when everyone had gone out for a walk, he said to me and M. F. Andreyeva sadly and with deep regret: "Such clever and talented people, who have done a great deal for the Party, and could do ten times more—and they will not go with us! They cannot do so. And scores, hundreds of such people are ruined and mutilated by this criminal regime."

Another time he said: "Lunacharsky will return to the Party. He is less of an individualist than the other two. He has a highly gifted nature such as is rarely met with. I 'have a weakness' for him. What stupid words, 'to have a weakness'! I am really very fond of him, you know, he is a splendid comrade! There is something of the French brilliancy about him. His levity is the result of his estheticism. . . ."

There was a certain magnetic quality in him which drew the hearts and sympathies of the working people to him. He did not speak Italian, but the Capri fishermen, who had seen Chaliapin and many other outstanding Russians, by a kind of instinct put Lenin in a special place at once. His laugh was enchanting —the hearty laugh of a man, who through being so well acquainted with the clumsy stupidity of human beings and the acrobatic trickery of the quick-witted, could find pleasure in the child-like artlessness of the "simple in heart." One old fisherman, Giovanni Spadaro, said of him: "Only an honest man could laugh like that. . . ."

I do not remember if it was before Lenin's visit or after that Plekhanov came to Capri. Some of the emigrants in the Capri colony, the writer Oliger, Lorentz-Mettner, who was condemned to death for organizing the rising in Sotchi, Paul Vigdorchik, and, I think, two others, wanted to speak to him. He refused. He had a right to do so. He was ill and had come for a rest. But Oliger and Lorentz told me that he had refused in a very offensive way. Oliger, who was of a highly-strung temperament, insisted that Plekhanov had said something about "being sick of the crowd of people who all want to speak but are incapable of doing anything." When he was with me, he really did not wish to see any one from the local colony. Ilyitch saw them all. Plekhanov never asked about anything. He already knew it all and told you all about it himself. Talented in the wide Russian way and with a European education, he loved to parade his wit, and for the sake apparently of a pungent jest would lay the cruelest emphasis on the weak points of foreign or Russian comrades. To me his witticisms often appeared pointless and only such have remained in my memory: "Immoderately moderate Mehring; Enrico Ferri is an imposter; there is neither gold nor iron in him." This pun was built up on the word *ferro*, meaning iron. All of them were after this pattern. As a general rule he had a condescending manner towards people, as if he were a god. I felt deep respect for him as a very talented writer and the theoretical inspirer of the Party, but no sympathy. There was too much of the "aristocrat" in him. I may be mistaken in my judgment. I am not fond of indulging in mistakes, but like everybody else cannot always avoid them.

But the fact remains that I have rarely met two people with less in common than G. V. Plekhanov and V. I. Lenin; and this was natural. The one was finishing his work of destroying the old world, the other was beginning the construction of a new. . . .

I have never met in Russia, the country where the inevitability of suffering is preached as the general road to salvation, nor do I know of, any man who hated, loathed and despised so deeply and strongly as Lenin all unhappiness, grief and suffering. In my eyes, these feelings, this hatred of the dramas and tragedies of life exalted Lenin more than anything, belonging as he did to a country where the greatest masterpieces have been gospels in praise and

sanctification of suffering, and where youth begins its life under the influence of books which are in essence descriptions of petty, trivial dramas monotonously unvarying. The literature of Russia is the most pessimistic in Europe. All our books are written on one and the same theme—how we suffer in youth and middle-age from our own foolishness, from the oppressive weight of autocracy, on account of women, from love of one's neighbor, from the unsuccessful structure of the universe; how we suffer in old age from consciousness of the mistakes we have made in our lives, from lack of teeth, from indigestion and the imminence of death. Every Russian who has passed a month in prison for some political offense, and a year in exile, considers it his sacred duty to present Russia with a book of reminiscences about his sufferings. But a happy life no one has ever thought of putting into the form of memoirs. As Russians are in the habit of thinking out what their lives shall be, but unable to make them come out that way, maybe such a book would teach them how to devise a happy life. . . .

DIFFERENCES WITH LENIN IN 1917

In the years 1917–18 my relations with Lenin were not what I would have wished them to be, but they could not be otherwise. He was a politician. He had to perfection that clear-sighted directness of vision which is so indispensable in the helmsman of so enormous and heavily burdened a ship as Russia with its dead-weight of peasants. I have an organic distaste for politics, and little faith in the reasoning powers of the masses, especially of the peasants. Reason without ordered ideas is yet far from being the force which lives in creative activity. There can be no ideas in the minds of the mass until the community of interests of all the separate individuals is realized. . . .

When in 1917 Lenin on his arrival in Russia published his theses[9] I thought that by these theses he was sacrificing to the Russian peasantry the small but heroic band of politically educated workers and all the genuine revolutionaries of the intelligentsia. The single active force in Russia, I thought, would be thrown like a handful of salt into the vapid bog of village life, and would dissolve without leaving any trace, would be sucked down without effecting any change in the mind, life or history of the Russian people. The professional intelligentsia, in general, the scientists and technicians, were, from my point of view, revolutionaries by nature, and this socialist intelligentsia, together with the workers, were for me the most precious force stored up in Russia. In 1917 I did not see any other force capable of taking power, and organizing the village. But only on condition of complete inner unity could this force, numerically insignificant and split by contradictions, fulfill its rôle. Before them stood a tremendous task—to bring order into the anarchy of the village, to discipline the mind of the peasant, teach him to work rationally, to reorganize his economy, and by such means make the country progress. All this could only be achieved by subjecting the instincts of the village to the reason of the town. . . .

In order to make myself quite clear I will add that all my life, the depressing effect of the prevalency of the illiteracy of the village on the town, the individualism of the peasants, and their almost complete lack of social emotions had weighed heavily on my spirits. The dictatorship of the politically enlightened

workers, in close connection with the scientific and technical intelligentsia, was, in my opinion, the only possible solution to a difficult situation which the war had made especially complicated by rendering the village still more anarchical. I differed from the Bolsheviks on the question of the value of the rôle of the intelligentsia in the Russian Revolution, which had been prepared by this same intelligentsia to which belonged all the Bolsheviks who had educated hundreds of workers in the spirit of social heroism and genuine intellectuality. The Russian intelligentsia, the scientific and professional intelligentsia, I thought, had always been, was still, and would long be the only beast of burden to drag along the heavy load of Russian history. In spite of all shocks and impulses and stimulation which it had experienced, the mind of the masses of the people had remained a force still in need of leadership from without.

So I thought in 1917—and was mistaken. This page of my reminiscences should be torn out. But "what has been written by the pen cannot be cut down by the ax"; and "we learn by our mistakes," as V. Ilyitch often repeated. Let the reader know my mistake. It will have done some good if it serves as a warning to those who are inclined to draw hasty conclusions. Of course, after a series of cases of the most despicable sabotaging by a number of specialists, I had no alternative but to change my attitude towards the scientific and technical professionals. Such changes cost something —especially in old age.

The duty of true-hearted leaders of the people is superhumanly difficult. A leader who is not in some degree a tyrant is impossible. More people, probably, were killed under Lenin than under Thomas Münzer; but without this, resistance to the revolution of which Lenin was the leader would have been more widely and more powerfully organ-

[9] An analysis of the nature of the February Revolution and the Bolshevik program to continue the revolution until the workers in alliance with the poor peasants have wrested power from the bourgeoisie.—*Ed.*

ized. In addition to this we must take into account the fact that with the development of civilization the value of human life manifestly depreciates, a fact which is clearly proved by the growth in contemporary Europe of the technique of annihilating people, and the taste for doing so. . . .

Much has been said and written about Lenin's cruelty. I have no intention, of course, of doing anything so ridiculously tactless as to defend him against lies and calumny. I know that lying and slandering is a legitimate method in petty bourgeois politics, a usual way of attacking an enemy. It would be impossible to find a single great man in the world to-day who has not had some mud thrown at him. This is known to everybody. Besides this, there is a tendency in all people not only to reduce an outstanding man to the level of their own comprehension, but to roll him beneath their feet in the viscid noisome mud which they have created and call "everyday life."

The following incident is for me repulsively memorable. In 1919 there was a congress in Petrograd of "the village poor." From the villages in the north of Russia came several thousands of peasants, some hundreds of whom were housed in the Winter Palace of the Romanovs. When the congress was over, and these people had gone away, it appeared that not only all the baths of the palace, but also a great number of priceless Sèvres, Saxon and oriental vases had been befouled by them for lavatory use. It was not necessary to do this since the lavatories of the palace were in good order and the water system working. No, this vandalism was an expression of the desire to sully and debase things of beauty. Two revolutions and a war have supplied me with hundreds of cases of this lurking, vindictive tendency in people, to smash, deform, ridicule and

defame the beautiful. It must not be thought that I emphasize the conduct of the village poor because of my skeptical attitude to the peasants. This is not the case.

This malicious desire to deface things of exceptional beauty is fundamentally the same as the odious tendency to vilify an exceptional man. Anything exceptional prevents people from living as they want to live. People long, if they have any longings, not for any fundamental change in their social habits, but to acquire additional habits. The gist of the wailing and complaining of the majority is, "Do not interfere with the way of living to which we are accustomed!" Vladimir Lenin was a man who knew better than anyone else how to prevent people from leading the life to which they were accustomed. The hatred of the world bourgeoisie for him is nakedly and repellently manifest; the livid plague spot of it shows unmistakably. Disgusting in itself, this hatred yet tells us how great and terrible in the eyes of the world bourgeoisie is Vladimir Lenin, the inspirer and leader of the proletarians of the whole world. . . .

THE PERFECTLY FASHIONED FIGURE OF TRUTH

. . . It was an unusual and extraordinary thing to see Lenin in the park at Gorky,[10] so much has the idea of him become associated with the picture of a man sitting at the end of a long table and expertly and skillfully guiding the comrades in their work, with the observant eyes of a pilot, smiling and beaming; or standing on a platform with head thrown back, casting clear distinct words to the hushed crowd, before the eager faces of the people thirsting for

[10] A country place near Moscow to which Lenin would retire for rest, where he spent his period of illness and where he died January 21, 1924.—*Ed.*

truth.

His words always brought to my mind the cold glitter of steel shavings, From these words, with amazing simplicity, there rose the perfectly fashioned figure of truth. . . .

He loved fun, and when he laughed it was with his whole body; he was quite overcome with laughter and would laugh sometimes until he cried. He could give to his short, characteristic exclamation, "H'm, h'm," an infinite number of modifications, from biting sarcasm to noncommittal doubt. Often in this "H'm, h'm" one caught the sound of the keen human which a sharp-sighted man experiences who sees clearly through the stupidities of life.

Stocky and thick set, with his Socratic head and quick eyes, he would often adopt a strange and rather comical posture—he would throw his head back, inclining it somehow on to his shoulder, thrust his fingers under his armpits, in his waistcoat armholes. There was something deliciously funny in this pose, something of a triumphant fighting cock; and at such a moment he beamed all over with joy, a grown-up child in this accursed world, a splendid human being, who had to sacrifice himself to hostility and hatred, so that love might be at last realized.

ABOUT INTELLECTUALS AND SPECIALISTS

I did not meet Lenin in Russia, or even see him from afar, until 1918, when the final base attempt was made on his life.[11] I came to him when he had hardly regained the use of his hand and could scarcely move his neck, which had been shot through. When I expressed my indignation, he replied, as though dismissing something of which he was tired: "A brawl. Nothing to be done. Everyone acts according to his lights."

We met on very friendly terms, but of course there was evident pity in dear Ilyitch's sharp and penetrating glance, for I was one who had gone astray.

After several minutes he said heatedly: "He who is not with us is against us. People independent of the march of events—that is a fantasy. Even if we grant that such people did exist once, at present they do not and cannot exist. They are no good to anyone. All, down to the last, are thrown into the whirl of an actuality which is more complicated than ever before. You say that I simplify life too much? That this simplification threatens culture with ruin, eh?"

Then the ironic, characteristic "H'm, h'm. . . ."

His keen glance sharpened, and he continued in a lower tone: "Well, and millions of peasants with rifles in their hands are not a threat to culture according to you, eh? You think the Constituent Assembly could have coped with that anarchy? You who make such a fuss about the anarchy of the country should be able to understand our tasks better than others. We have got to put before the Russian masses something they can grasp. The Soviets and Communism are simple.

"A union of the workers and intelligentsia, eh? Well, that isn't bad. Tell the intelligentsia. Let them come to us. According to you they are true servants of justice. What is the matter then? Certainly, let them come to us. We are just the ones who have undertaken the colossal job of putting the people on its feet, of telling the whole world the truth about life—it is we who are pointing out to the people the straight path to a human life, the path which leads out of slavery, beggary, degradation."

He laughed and said without any trace

11 Dora Kaplan, a Socialist-Revolutionary, made an attempt on Lenin's life in 1918, when he was leaving a factory where he addressed a meeting of workers.—*Ed.*

of resentment: "That is why I received a bullet from the intelligentsia."

When the temperature of the conversation was more or less normal, he said with vexation and sadness: "Do you think I quarrel with the idea that the intelligentsia is necessary to us? But you see how hostile their attitude is, how badly they understand the need of the moment? And they don't see how powerless they are without us, how incapable of reaching the masses. They will be to blame if we break too many heads. . . ."

At the Eighth Congress of the Party,[12] N. I. Bukharin said among other things: "The nation is the bourgeoisie together with the proletariat. To recognize the right of some contemptible bourgeoisie to self-determination is absolutely out of place."

"No, excuse me," retorted Lenin, "it certainly is not out of place. You appeal to the process of the differentiation of the proletariat from the bourgeoisie, but let us wait and see how it will turn out." Then pointing to the example of Germany, and to the slowness and difficulty with which the process of differentiation develops, and declaring that they would never succeed in planting Communism by means of force, he went on to discuss the question of the importance of the intelligentsia in industry, in the army, in the coöperative movement. I quote from *Izvestia*,[13] from the debates of the Congress.

"This question must be decided at the coming Conference with complete definiteness. We can only build up Communism when it has become more accessible to the masses by means of bourgeois science and technique. For this, it is necessary to take over the apparatus

from the bourgeoisie, to attract all the specialists to work in this connection. Without the bourgeois specialists it is impossible to increase the forces of production. They must be surrounded by an atmosphere of comradely coöperation, by workers' commissars, by Communists; conditions must be created which will not allow them to break away, but they must be given the possibility of working better than under capitalism, for otherwise this layer which has received its education from the bourgeoisie will not begin to work. It is impossible to make a whole layer work by main force.

"The bourgeois specialists are used to doing cultural work, they carried it on within the framework of the bourgeois régime, that is, they enriched the bourgeoisie by enormous material work and construction and gave a miserable share in this wealth to the proletariat. Nevertheless, they did carry forward the work of the culture—that is their profession. In so far as they see that the workers not only value culture but also help to spread it among the masses, they will change their attitude towards us. Then they will be morally won over and not only politically divided from the bourgeoisie. . . ."

REVOLUTIONARY TACTICS

I often used to speak with Lenin about the cruelty of revolutionary tactics and life.

"What do you want?" he would ask in astonishment and anger. "Is it possible to act humanely in a struggle of such unprecedented ferocity? Where is there any place for soft-heartedness or generosity? We are being blockaded by Europe, we are deprived of the help of the European proletariat, counter-revolution is creeping like a bear on us from every side. What do you want? Are we not right? Ought we not to struggle and

---

[12] In 1919.—*Ed.*

[13] Official organ of the Soviet Government. —*Ed.*

resist? We are not a set of fools. We know that what we want can only be achieved by ourselves. Do you think that I would be sitting here if I were convinced of the contrary? . . ."

I often overwhelmed him with requests of a different nature, and often felt that all the bother I went to for various people made Lenin pity me. He would ask, "Don't you think you are wasting your energies on a lot of rubbish?"

But I continued to do what I thought ought to be done, and was not put off when the man who knew who were the enemies of the proletariat looked at me askance, in anger. He would shake his head crushingly and say, "You are compromising yourself in the eyes of the comrades and workers."

I pointed out that comrades and workers, when their passions were roused and they were irritated, not infrequently hold too lightly the life and liberty of valuable people, and that this in my view not only compromised the honest hard work of the revolution by too great, sometimes even senseless, cruelty, but was objectively and strategically bad, as it repelled many important people from participation in the revolution.

"H'm, h'm," Lenin muttered skeptically, and pointed out to me many cases when the intelligentsia betrayed the interests of the workers. . . .

Yet I don't remember a single instance when any request of mine met with a refusal from Ilyitch. If they were not always fulfilled, it was not his fault but the fault of the mechanism in which the clumsy Russian state machine has always abounded, and, let us grant, a certain malicious reluctance to lighten the lot or save the lives of people of worth. Perhaps, too, there were cases of willful harming, which is an enemy as cynical as it is cunning. Revenge and malice are often effective through force of inertia; and of course there are petty persons with unhealthy minds, with a morbid thirst for the delight of contemplating the sufferings of their neighbors. . . .

I was often struck by Lenin's readiness to help people whom he considered to be his enemies, and not only readiness to help but even care for their future. One general, for example, a scientist, a chemist, was threatened with death. "H'm, h'm," said Lenin, after listening attentively to my story. "So you think he didn't know that his sons had hidden firearms in his laboratory? That seems rather unlikely. But we must leave it for Dzerzhinsky to unravel. He has a keen instinct for the truth."

Several days later he rang me up in Petrograd and said, "We are letting your general go—I think he has already been set free. What does he intend to do?"

"Homoemulsion."

"Yes, yes—carbolic acid. Well, let him boil his carbolic. Tell me if he is in need of anything."

Lenin spoke ironically in order to conceal the joy, which he did not wish to show, of saving a man's life. Several days later he asked again: "Well, how is the general getting on? Everything arranged? . . ."

He was silent. Then he got up and, sorting the papers on the table, said thoughtfully: "Yes, those people are in great straits. History is a cruel stepmother, and when it retaliates, it stops at nothing. What is there to say? It is bad for those people. The clever ones among them understand of course that they have been torn up by the roots and will never grow again; and transplantation in Europe won't satisfy the clever ones. You don't think they will strike root there, do you?"

"I don't think they will."

"That means that they will either go our way or attempt to make another intervention."

I asked him: "Does it only seem to me so, or do you really pity people?"

He answered: "I am sorry for the clever ones. We haven't enough clever people. We are for the most part a talented people, but mentally lazy." Recollecting several comrades who had outlived their class psychology and were working with the Bolsheviks, he spoke of them with astonishing warmth.

LENIN'S QUALITIES

. . . In the hard famine year of 1919 Lenin was ashamed to eat the food which was sent to him by comrades, soldiers and peasants from the provinces. When the parcels came to his bleak flat he would frown, grow embarrassed, and hasten to give the flour, sugar and butter to the sick comrades or to those who were weak from lack of food.

Once, when he invited me to dine with him, he said: "I shall give you some smoked fish—it was sent to me from Astrakhan." And with a frown on his Socratic forehead, turning his sharp glance away from me, he added: "They send things to me as though I were a lord! How can I prevent them doing it? If you refuse and don't accept it, they are hurt. And everyone around me is hungry."

Entirely without any personal fads, a stranger to tobacco and wine, occupied from morning to night with complicated and difficult work, he had no thought of looking after himself, but kept a vigilant eye on the health of the comrades. . . .

An old acquaintance of mine, P. A. Skorokhodov, another Sormovo worker, a tender-hearted man, complained of the painfulness of work in the Tcheka.[14] I said to him, "I think that is not the right work for you. It isn't congenial to you." He agreed sadly, "Absolutely uncongenial." But after thinking a little, he said: "But you know Ilyitch too has to stifle his emotions, and I am ashamed to be so weak."

I knew and still know many workers who had to, and have to, grit their teeth hard, and stifle their emotions, to overcome their organic "social idealism" for the sake of the triumph of the cause they are serving. Did Lenin too have to stifle his emotions? He paid too little attention to himself to talk about himself to others; he, more than anyone, could keep silent about the secret agitation of his soul.

Once, however, in Gorky, when he was caressing some children, he said: "These will have happier lives than we had. They will not experience much that we lived through. There will not be so much cruelty in their lives."

Then, looking into the distance, to the hills where the village nestled, he added pensively: "And yet I don't envy them. Our generation achieved something of amazing significance for history. The cruelty, which the conditions of our life made necessary, will be understood and vindicated. Everything will be understood, everything." He caressed the children with great care, with an especially gentle and tender touch.

Once I came to him and saw *War and Peace* lying on the table.

"Yes. Tolstoy. I wanted to read over the scene of the hunt, then remembered that I had to write to a comrade. Absolutely no time for reading. Only last night I managed to read your book on

[14] Abbreviated name for the Extraordinary Commission for Combating Counter-revolution and Sabotage; since the defeat of counter-revolution renamed State Political Administration (OGPU).—*Ed.*

Tolstoy."

Smiling and screwing up his eyes, he stretched himself deliciously in his armchair and, lowering his voice, added quickly, "What a Colossus, eh? What a marvelously developed brain! Here's an artist for you, sir. And do you know something still more amazing? You couldn't find a genuine muzhik in literature until this Count came on the scene."

Then screwing up his eyes and looking at me, he asked, "Can you put anyone in Europe beside him?" and replied himself, "No one." And he rubbed his hands, laughing contentedly. . . .

One evening in Moscow, in E. P. Pyeskovskaya's flat, Lenin was listening to a sonata by Beethoven being played by Isaiah Dobrowein, and said: "I know nothing which is greater than the Appassionata; I would like to listen to it every day. It is marvelous superhuman music. I always think with pride—perhaps it is naive of me—what marvelous things human beings can do!"

Then screwing up his eyes and smiling, he added rather sadly: "But I can't listen to music too often. It affects your nerves, makes you want to say stupid, nice things, and stroke the heads of people who could create such beauty while living in this vile hell. And now you mustn't stroke anyone's head—you might get your hand bitten off. You have to hit them on the head, without any mercy, although our ideal is not to use force against anyone. H'm, h'm, our duty is infernally hard!"

When he himself was nearly a sick man, quite worn out, he wrote me, August 9, 1921:

A. M!

I sent on your letter to L. B. Kamenev. I am so tired that I am incapable of the slightest work. And you are spitting blood and yet don't go away? That really is dis-

gracefully imprudent. In Europe, in a good sanatorium, you will get well and be able to do something else worth while. Really, really. But here you can neither get well, nor do anything. There is nothing for you here but bother, useless bother. Go away and get well. Don't be obstinate, I implore you!

Yours,
LENIN

For more than a year, he insisted with astonishing persistence that I should leave Russia. I was amazed that, entirely absorbed in work as he was, he should remember there was a sick person somewhere in need of rest. He wrote letters like this to different people —scores, probably.

ATTITUDE TOWARD COMRADES

I have already described his quite exceptional attitude to the comrades, his attention to them, which penetrated down even to the smallest details of their lives. But in this feature of his I never caught the note of that self-interested care which a clever master sometimes exhibits towards an honest and expert workman. This was not the case with Lenin. His was the heartfelt interest of a sincere comrade, the love which exists between equals. I know that it is impossible to consider as Lenin's equals even the greatest people in his Party, but he himself didn't seem to realize this, or more probably, did not want to realize it. He was sometimes sharp with people, when arguing with them, pitilessly ridiculed them, even laughed at them in a venomous fashion. All this he did. But how many times, when judging the people whom yesterday he criticized and rebuked, was there clearly evident the note of genuine wonder at their talents and moral steadfastness; at their unflagging labor under the abominable conditions of

1918–21, work amid spies of all countries and parties, amid the plots which swelled like festering sores on the body of the war-exhausted country! . . .

The only regret he ever expressed in my presence was "I am sorry, deeply sorry, that Martov is not with us. What a splendid comrade he was, what an absolutely sincere man!"

I remember how long and heartily he laughed at reading Martov's remark somewhere, "There are only two Communists in Russia, Lenin and Kollontay." He laughed and then sighed, "What a clever woman she is!"

It was with genuine respect and wonder that he remarked, after conducting one comrade, an administrator, out of his study, "Have you known him for long? He would be at the head of the cabinet in any country in Europe." Rubbing his hands and smiling, he added: "Europe is poorer than we are in talent."

Once I proposed that we should go together to the Chief Artillery Department to see an apparatus which had been invented by a Bolshevik, an old artillery man, to adjust artillery fire directed against airplanes. "What do I understand about that?" he said, but he went with me.

In a dark room around a table on which stood the apparatus were gathered seven generals with scowling faces, gray, bewildered old men, all scientists. Among them the modest civilian figure of Lenin was lost, dropped into insignificance.

The inventor began to explain the construction of the apparatus. Lenin listened to him for two or three minutes, then said approvingly, "H'm, h'm," and began to question the man with as much ease as if he were examining him on some political question.

"And how do you manage to get the machine to do two things simultane-ously, when it is laying the sight? Would it be impossible to form an automatic connection between the mounting of the barrel and the indications of the mechanism?" He asked how far the dangerous space extended, and something else. The inventor and the generals gave eager explanations, and next day the former said to me:

"I had told my generals that you were coming with a comrade, but I didn't say who the comrade was. They didn't recognize Ilyitch and probably would never have imagined that he could appear without a great deal of ceremony or a bodyguard. They asked me, 'Is he a technical engineer or a professor? What? Lenin? What a surprise! How is it possible? How does he know so much about these things we're concerned with? He asked those questions like a technologist.' What mystification!"

Apparently they didn't really believe that it was Lenin. On the way from the Chief Artillery Department, Lenin kept chuckling, and talked about the inventor. . . .

Yes, he often praised the comrades in my hearing, even those with whom he was not personally in sympathy. Lenin knew how to appreciate their energy. I was very surprised at his high appreciation of L. D. Trotsky's organizing abilities. V. Ilyitch noticed my surprise.

"Yes, I know there are lying rumors about my attitude to him. But what is, is, and what isn't, isn't—that I know also. He was able at any rate to organize the military experts."

After a pause he added in a lower tone, and rather sadly: "And yet he isn't one of us. With us, but not of us. He is ambitious. There is something of Lassalle in him, something which isn't good."

These words, "with us, but not of us," he used twice in my hearing, the second time about another prominent man, who died soon after V. Ilyitch himself. . . .

48

DOWN WITH FACTIONALISM!

By Nikolai Bukharin

Bukharin, who wrote the speeches from which we print an excerpt, and Leon Trotsky, who is the subject of his attack, were among the top leaders of the Bolsheviks after Lenin's death in 1924. In his testament Lenin said of Bukharin that he was "not only the most valuable and biggest theoretician of the party, but also may be legitimately considered the favorite of the whole party." Of Trotsky Lenin said that he was "the most able man in the present Central Committee." In the struggle for power which began during Lenin's illness and was finally resolved by Stalin, the two men, Bukharin and Trotsky, found themselves in opposing camps. The pages which follow are intended to give the reader a sample of the extraordinary public debates which raged in the party during the twenties, debates which would never be repeated. Both Bukharin and Trotsky perished at the hands of Stalin, and today are "unpersons" in the Soviet Union. Fortunately we have their writings, and a considerable literature about them.

For a listing of Bukharin's writings see Sidney Heitman, *An Annotated Bibliography of Nikolai Bukharin's Published Works.* Heitman is also the editor of *The Path to Socialism in Russia: Selected Writings of N. A. Bukharin,* and the author of an essay on Bukharin in Leopold Labedz, *Revisionism.* For speeches by both Bukharin and Trotsky see Robert Daniels, *A Documentary History of Communism* (2 vols. in paperback), and his *The Conscience of the Revolution,* which is an account of the debates of the twenties. *The Great Purge Trial* (paperback), by Robert Tucker and Stephen Cohen, is an account of Bukharin's last public appearance, in the prisoner's dock. Warren Lerner discusses Bukharin in his "The Unperson in Communist Historiography," *South Atlantic Quarterly,* Autumn, 1966. Bukharin's most famous work, *The ABC of Communism,* has been recently reissued in paperback. Trotsky's published works are too numerous to mention. For a useful paperback anthology see *The Basic Writings of Trotsky,* edited by Irwing Howe. There is a famous biography of the man by Isaac Deutscher, in three paperback volumes, entitled *The Prophet Armed; The Prophet Unarmed;* and *The Prophet Outcast.* Two works of Leonard Schapiro, both in paperback, present a history of the intraparty struggles during the twenties; they are A *History of the Communist Party of the Soviet Union,* and *The Origin of the Communist Autocracy.*

In his article "On Groups and Factions" Comrade Trotsky calls on us "to try to understand each other," for "we will have time to get excited later." Comrade Trotsky considers his article to be "of

Translated by Howard Goldfinger from N. Bukharin, *K Voprosu o Trotskizme* (Moscow, 1925), pp. 7–20.

534

explanatory nature," and he expects "a calm and thoughtful response to the subject."

These counsels are very fine and perfectly appropriate. Unfortunately, Comrade Trotsky did not apply them to himself. For if he had not published his famous letter (i.e., if he had not become excited), if he had tried to *understand* the Central Committee's position "thoughtfully and calmly," he might not have had to "clarify" his own speeches *ex post facto,* and the party might have been spared the tension of debates which shake it and weaken it. It is not the first time that Comrade Trotsky gets "excited" (despite his own advice), and it is not the first time that "through excitement" he *opposes* himself to the party's Central Committee.

In his pamphlet *Once Again on the Trade Unions* Comrade Lenin emphasized "the danger to the Party from factional statements." Comrade Lenin then wrote about a speech of Comrade Trotsky:

Just imagine: after the Central Committee had spent two plenary meetings (November 9 and December 7) in an unprecedentedly long, detailed and heated discussion of Comrade Trotsky's original draft theses and of the entire trade-union policy which he advocates for the Party, one member of the Central Committee, *one out of nineteen,* forms a group outside the Central Committee and presents its "collective work" as a "platform," inviting the Party Congress "to choose between *two trends.*"![1]

History repeats itself; but, unfortunately, tragedy is not always followed by

farce. Comrade Trotsky is once again subjecting the Party to a period of crisis.

"Just imagine": after a series of meetings, after the Politburo *unanimously* adopts a resolution, after all this *"one member of the Central Committee"* comes out with an article on "The New Course" which makes unheard-of accusations against both the Central Committee and the entire Bolshevik Old Guard! These charges are taken over by the entire opposition (including the "vulgar democrats" mentioned by Trotsky), a systematic attack is conducted against the Central Committee, and, after all this, Comrade Trotsky graciously invites us not "to get excited." Heat will not help, of course. Comrade Trotsky, more than anyone else, ought to remember this wise rule. For the publication by Comrade Trotsky of an article which provoked a burst of indignation among the ranks of seasoned Bolsheviks, a pronouncement coming *two days* after a unanimous decision, cannot be taken as anything other than a product of Comrade Trotsky's *factional heat.*

Incidentally, at the countless discussion meetings which have been held, the representatives of the opposition (Comrade Preobrazhenskii and others) have frequently alleged improper interference by the Central Committee in the discussion which supposedly prevents the consideration of important questions. Now we are presented with a new statement by Comrade Trotsky on the *old* resolution despite the fact that the Central Committee has published a new resolution on economic matters; this is only an additional illustration of who, in the final analysis the Central Committee or someone else, is "interfering" with a *businesslike* order of discussion. *The Central Committee is forced* to turn backward: Comrade Trotsky's factional ardor presents an obstacle to it.

[1] The entire pamphlet, printed in January 1921, is reproduced in the English edition of Lenin's *Collected Works,* XXXII (Moscow, 1965), 70–107. Incidentally, Bukharin conveniently overlooks the fact that in the piece Lenin attacks him as well and puts him in the same "factional grouping" with Trotsky.

1. *The essence of our disagreements. Leninism and deviations from it.* There is a striking feature about all the discussions we have been witnessing: many party members, particularly the young ones, are bewildered by the sudden outbreak of dissent. To a significant extent this is explained by the fact that many of these disagreements have never been aired in the open before. Under Comrade Lenin's leadership and later the frequent differences between Comrade Trotsky and the majority of the Central Committee were resolved within the Central Committee. Duty-bound to act this way, the Central Committee thus protected the Party from the excesses of factional disputes. On the other hand, disagreements which went beyond the closed doors of the Central Committee (Brest-Litovsk, the trade-union disputes) were not dragged out later, and the mistakes of a number of comrades, including Comrade Trotsky, were not subjected to critical analysis. Undoubtedly this situation had its weakness: now that Comrade Trotsky has introduced the dispute into the wide arena of mass party discussions, this weakness appears very clearly. Many do not understand *the essence* of the controversy. That is why a patient explanation and "a calm and thoughtful response to the subject" are called for.

Our Party has undergone three great crises since the October Revolution: Brest, the trade unions, and the present situation. Comrade Trotsky erred at each stage. It is necessary to try to comprehend the root of his mistakes "calmly and thoughtfully." Only thus can we *correct* these deviations, which are inevitable consequences of the past.

The Brest Peace. What was the error of Comrade Trotsky (and the Left Communists)? It was their love of revolutionary phrases, blueprints, beautiful *paper plans.* The opponents of the Brest peace were blind to cursed *reality* which Lenin's genius apprehended so perfectly. They failed to see that *the peasants* could not and would not fight on.

The trade unions. What was the basic mistake of Comrade Trotsky and a group of other comrades here? Again they had a splendid blueprint for industry, and spoke of the unification of the trade unions, their reorganization, and their adjustment to "industrial democracy." But the plan was *utopian,* despite the great exactitude of its formulas. Why? Because once again its political line ran directly counter to the realities.

At the time of Brest the peasants, the basic element of the population, cried: peace at any price! We must have peace whatever it may cost. But Comrade Trotsky and the Left Communists preached either a revolutionary war or the worthless formula: neither peace nor war. At the time of the trade-union discussion, the nation demanded the loosening of the fetters of War Communism which were blocking the growth of the productive forces. But Comrade Trotsky proposed to tighten the screws even more. Here, too, there was a misunderstanding of *reality,* and, above all, of the *peasant* psychology. The proletariat is in no condition to rule in our country without a proper appreciation of this psychology.

The present disagreements with Comrade Trotsky have the same foundation. These disagreements existed when our work was directed by Lenin, and they recurred later. Comrade Trotsky heaps all our troubles on shortcomings in planning. In his opinion, this shortcoming is leading to the country's "ruin." This is Comrade Trotsky's chief and systematic accusation against the Central Committee.

It goes without saying that "ruin" is to be found only in Comrade Trotsky's excited factional imagination. It goes without saying that no member of the Central Committee can object to improved order and planning in our work. But the Central Committee holds that Comrade Trotsky has exaggerated ruinously in this question. The Central Committee believes that the plan for our economic development must be developed extremely cautiously, if it is to be realistic and not insane. Despite Comrade Trotsky, the Central Committee believes that we cannot yet speak of "the dictatorship of industry" but must, as Lenin taught, continue to travel on the peasant's skinny nag in order to save our industry and lay a firm basis for the dictatorship of the proletariat.

Here is the root of the present disagreements. One can ask whether we do not have here, in a new form, the very same old error? Of course the answer is yes. Again we have before us a hyperbolic *plan* without the means of bringing it into accord with reality. And once again an underestimation of peasant reality is at the root of the trouble. This is the foundation of foundations of Comrade Trotsky's mistakes and constitutes *a deviation from Leninism*. For the new element that Lenin introduced into Marxism was his remarkably clear exposition (theoretically), and achievement (in practice) of the union of "the proletarian revolution" with "a peasant war," the interrelationship of the working class and the peasantry, their economic and political alliance.

Comrade Trotsky's deviation from Leninism can be explained by his past, by the peculiarity of his views regarding the development of the revolution. No use getting angry about recalling this past once we have begun the work of "explanation." Comrade Trotsky has often and courageously admitted that he came to Lenin "not without struggle." Evi-

dently, however, he did not quite reach Lenin.

2. *Leninism and deviations from it in the organization question.* Deviations from the correct line on basic questions of politics are usually paralleled by deviations in a number of other questions, vitally significant for the fate of the proletarian party. In the present discussion, as in Comrade Trotsky's last article, we clearly see how the faction of Comrades Trotsky, Sapronov, and Preobrazhenskii *deviate*, willy-nilly, *from Leninism* on questions of *inner party politics*.

What was the Bolshevik party's general organizational principle? Our party was always distinguished by its monolithic nature and its unity. There was always a sharp distinction between our party's organizational nature and the opportunistic parties. It was in conflict with opportunism that our party developed and grew into a party of one piece. Our party *has never been*, and, we hope, *will never be, a federation of splinters, groups and tendencies negotiating with each other*. In contrast the Mensheviks, the Socialist Revolutionaries, and other "softies" opposed themselves to the "intolerant," "hard-as-rock" Bolsheviks, and jealously guarded their "freedom of opinion," "freedom of groupings," and "freedom of tendencies." At the trial of the Socialist Revolutionaries not so long ago the accused boasted of their party's "tolerance": they had a wing which supported the Whites, they had an "Administrative Center," they had leftists, centrists, etc. In a word, the party had a pair of every beast. It was the same with the Mensheviks. But as you know, one reason why our party smashed its foes was that it turned itself into a single "iron cohort" of fighters, achieved and strengthened its unity of will, and so structured itself that all shades of opinion would run into a *single stream* and would not divide the party into factions struggling with each other.

If some comrades, headed by Comrade Trotsky, now renounce this tradition, then they renounce the organizational *tradition of Leninism*. One can, of course, ridicule traditions, including Leninist traditions, but then one should do it directly and openly. Of course, no tradition can claim absolute authority for all time. But it is necessary to point out *why* Leninism has become obsolete on this point. We do not think it has become obsolete, for our party remains at its battle post, surrounded by enemies, and must remain as united and fraternal as before.

Bolshevism has always highly valued and continues to value the *party apparatus*. It does not follow that Bolsheviks must be blind to the diseases peculiar to this system (including its bureaucratization). I will speak of this in a moment. But Bolshevism (Leninism) never opposed the party to the apparatus. From the Bolshevik point of view, this would be elementary illiteracy because there would be no party *without* the apparatus. Eliminate the apparatus, and the party becomes at atomized mass of individuals. In contrast the Mensheviks, for example, always felt "democratic" contempt for the "committee-mindedness" and "Jacobinism" of the Bolsheviks. Under the guise of defending the "independence" of the party mass against the apparatus, the Mensheviks defended the opportunistic petty-bourgeois "workers' politicans" against the proletarian discipline and organization of the Bolsheviks.

It is possible and necessary to fight with all passion against the diseases of the apparatus which reflect the illness in the party, but to oppose the party to the apparatus is another *deviation from Leninism*.

Among organizational questions, a major role was always played by the question of *party leadership*, the question of the central institutions of the party. The Bolsheviks never subscribed to a formal, empty democratism which always covers up lack of principle. Lenin taught us to value the leadership of the chief cadres who had accumulated the greatest experience in the struggle. It is true that he savagely satirized "old fools" who did not and could not apply the lessons of the past to the *new* demands of the present. He always warned, however, against "playing" at *formal* democracy which *verbally* asks for only a registering role of the center, but *in fact* becomes the plaything of demagogues of the worst sort. Here Bolshevism represents a practice which has always taken full account of reality. If some comrades now consider it permissible to make satirical accusations against the leading party center, it is because they do not understand the role and significance of the leading party organ. And here they are traveling a road which leads away from Bolshevism.

The question of "The Old Guard" is related to this matter. But here we merely wish to mark out the stages found in the positions of Comrades Trotsky, Preobrazhenskii, Sapronov, and the others. In the following pages we shall see how these deviations appear in the statements of these comrades, Comrade Trotsky first of all. But one must not get "excited" about charges of anti-Leninist deviations. It must be *proved* that they do not exist. Unhappily, they do exist. And the entire party could only be overjoyed if this "calm and careful" exchange of opinions resulted in the disappearance of the deviations, and their replacement by a solidarity based on the tried and confirmed political and organizational views of Leninism.

3. *Monopolizing democracy and the*

factional opposition. "We stand," writes Comrade Trotsky in his latest article ("On Groups") "before a new onslaught of the party apparatus which peremptorily blames *every criticism* [italics ours —Bukharin] of the old, formally condemned but not yet liquidated course on factionalism." "The lid has to be screwed down more tightly. Dozens of speeches and articles 'against factionalism' are permeated by this limited wisdom." "The most militant wing of the old apparatus is deeply convinced of the error of the Central Committee's resolution." "Furious bureaucracy. . . It was from this camp that came the voices which can only be described as those of provocateurs. It was here that they said: we do not fear a split! It is the representatives of this camp who rake up the past for anything which might further embitter the party discussions; artfully they reawaken memories of past struggles and old splits in order gradually to get the party used to the possibility of a crime as monstrous and suicidal as a new split." It is thus that Comrade Trotsky— why hide it or keep it secret—characterizes the Central Committee's official line. If the Central Committee has led the nation to ruin, if it is on the path of Kautsky and Bernstein, then why not accuse it of fomenting a *new* party split? (And what was the old one? The one with the Mensheviks? Was that so bad?)

Comrade Trotsky is clearly excited, and he obviously evaluates the facts improperly; more correctly, he skirts the facts. At the same time, he commits the same mistake which he made during the trade-union discussion. Comrade Lenin noted Comrade Trotsky's passion for freewheeling accusations, among his other factional tendencies. . . This time we are dealing not with "hints" but with direct accusations. It is asserted that the Central Committee, despite its own resolution, is convinced of the error of the new course and dreams only of "screwing down the lid more tightly," and so on. What are the facts? Where is the slightest *shadow* of proof besides dubious interpretations of other people's minds? The *facts* run directly *counter* to the positions of Comrade Trotsky and the entire opposition. Comrade Trotsky himself speaks of the outburst of discussion, about *excesses* in this area, etc. Where, when, and who was ever "forbidden" to speak? Where, when, and to whom was the bridle applied? Are we not living through an unprecedentedly wide and intense discussion? Where was it that Comrade Trotsky saw "every" criticism of the old course blamed on factionalism"?

These are truly monstrous accusations. I do not know a single member of the Central Committee who did not agree with the criticism of the "old course" at the discussion meetings—criticism which was formulated in the Central Committee's resolution to begin with. It is most unlikely that Comrade Trotsky will point out a single Central Committee member who still supports "the old course." Then what is all the noise about? The fact is that Comrade Trotsky needs "democracy" for strategic purposes, in order to weaken the old "cadres," to "correct" the Central Committee's *political line. Subjectively,* from the point of view of his aims, Comrade Trotsky is perfectly right. *Objectively,* he is cruelly mistaken: the party will permit no corrections of the basic line taught to us by Comrade Lenin.

Comrade Trotsky and the entire opposition love to insist that *they* spoke the first word about inner party democracy, for which they were condemned by the "furious bureaucracy." This completely *reverses* the facts. The Politburo voted for a new course in September, before any of the opposition's statements. The Central Committee's October plenum confirmed the Politburo's decision. These actions formed the *basis* for the unanimously accepted resolution. These *facts,* however, are deliberately avoided, hidden, and rearranged, apparently for strategic reasons. It is necessary to make it appear that the "opposition" wears the crown of martyrdom and suffers for "democracy." . . .

4. *Comrade Trotsky's valuable admission (on factions and groupings).* The opposition comrades, led by Comrade Trotsky, love to employ one argument in particular: "The Central Committee is *intimidating* the party with the threat of a split." The shouting about a split is an attempt to strangle discussion. ("Intimidation is generally the result of fear," writes Comrade Trotsky.)

Here, too, history repeats itself surprisingly. Dear comrades, whatever name you use, you may not *want* a split. It usually happens that splits are not made but occur. There is an objective logic of struggle, in which the elements tend toward a split independently of the subjective wishes of the comrades who lead the factions. This danger becomes extremely serious when the workers' party rules over a country in which the working class forms an oasis in a peasant desert.

We say history repeats itself. At the Tenth Party Congress, Comrade Lenin said: "The circumstances of the dispute [the speech concerned the trade-union discussion] have become extremely dangerous. When I told some comrades several months ago during a discussion: 'Look, this is a threat to the domination of the working class, to its dictatorship,' they replied: 'This is a method of intimidating us. You are terrorizing us.' "[2]

[2] Lenin's speeches at the Tenth Party Congress in March, 1921, are reprinted in the same volume of his *Collected Works,* XXXII, 165–270.

Now the same thing is being said of the Central Committee, which has taken a Leninist line. It is well to remember also that, in his last articles, Comrade Lenin stressed the danger of a split and called attention to this danger in every way. Did Lenin want to "terrorize the party" by this? An absurd accusation! But if the danger exists and is increasing, should the party's leading department remain *silent?* What kind of Central Committee would it be that would not *point out* the danger? And what, finally, is the worth of these old, moss-grown charges of intimidation? Do they reflect any credit on the patented defenders of the new course?

Unlike Comrade Preobrazhenskii, who asserts that there are not and cannot be any factions, that the groupings (quite harmless and not factional groupings, of course) rest on no social base, and that to imagine such a base is a departure from Marxism, unlike these "perfectly innocent" views Comrade Trotsky puts the question quite differently. He does not hide his head under his wing, and states openly: Yes, there are groupings; they have a tendency to become factions, and factions "represent the greatest evil in our circumstances."

This is a very frank statement of the question, and we must be grateful to Comrade Trotsky for his valuable admission. The question is put correctly, and without the juridical alchemy which representatives of the opposition usually employ. However, Comrade Trotsky wishes to squeeze "a little advantage" for his "unfactional" faction out of this correct exposition of the question. "It is necessary only to ponder on our party's history," writes Comrade Trotsky, "during the period of the revolution, i.e., precisely when factional struggle was particularly dangerous, and it becomes clear that a formal judgment against and prohibition of groupings does not in the least terminate the struggle with this danger." At the time of Brest, there was no mere "prohibition": "The Party adopted . . . more complex methods—discussions, clarifications, tests based on experience. It reconciled itself temporarily with such abnormal and threatening phenomena as the existence of an organized faction within the party." At the Tenth Congress, the party "dealt with" the opposition through its economic decisions, etc.

Very well, Comrade Trotsky. But please apply the same criteria to the present situation. *First,* Comrade Trotsky admits the existence of factional groupings (or groupings with factional tendencies). *Second,* the party "dealt with" factionalism in the resolutions on inner party democracy, and on the economy. *Third,* to use Comrade Trotsky's words, the party is applying "the most diverse methods: discussions [haven't there been any?]; clarifications [plenty of them]; tests based on experience, *temporary reconciliation* [italics ours] with fractional groupings."

Remarkable formulations! Yet they point, as you see, completely against Comrade Trotsky! Incidentally, they fully answer Comrade Preobrazhenskii's question: If we are a faction, why don't you strike us down immediately? Because, dear Comrade Preobrazhenskii, the Central Committee is following Comrade Trotsky's wise advice, and "temporarily reconciles itself" with the situation while continuing the job of clarification. Now we may ask: Does "clarification" include stressing what Comrade Trotsky himself notes, namely, that factions are dangerous and might ruin the revolution? We think yes. For Comrade Trotsky, however, who is not consistent, this constitutes "intimidation."

Make it out if you can! It somehow does not come out for Comrade Trotsky. And this is because he speaks from a factional perspective, which, of course, cannot be reconciled with pointing to the mortal danger of factions.

We must finally point out one more of Comrade Trotsky's inconsistencies. He claims that the Central Committee represents the *bureaucratic* "faction." One can only agree with him that the bureaucratization of the ruling party would be extremely dangerous. But if the Central Committee represents this bureaucracy, if it heads this bureaucratic faction, then why allow it to *remain?* Why not *drive it out?* The country's ruin, social treachery, degeneration into bureaucracy—surely these are sufficient causes to *drive* such a Central Committee *out?* Why is this not being proposed? Is that how to save the party? Why vote unanimously with such a Central Committee?

Here again Comrade Trotsky is not consistent. The truth is that he does not *believe* in these charges. If he believed in them, he would manfully draw all conclusions from them. But he is not drawing these conclusions. Why? Because, in the interests of his faction, he wants to *shake* up the party, and replace the Leninist Old Guard with comrades who will debolshevize our Bolshevik party.

The party did not permit this earlier. It will not permit it now. . . .

49

THE HISTORY OF A SOVIET COLLECTIVE FARM

By Fëdor Belov

The account of collective farming which appears below reflects the situation as of 1950. Let us first look at some of the factors of continuity as of 1967, taken from a summary by Basile Kerblay entitled "The Peasant," which appeared in *Survey,* July, 1967. Since 1945 one family in three on the farms has rebuilt its house, but 50 per cent of the farmhouses are of wood throughout. In 1917 22 per cent of all peasants had no cow; in 1960 this was true of 37 per cent of the kolkhoz families. Over 60 per cent of these families still bake their own bread. Only 61 per cent of the kolkhoz houses are lit electrically. In 1966 the rural population comprised 107.1 million persons; in 1897 it was 106.7 million. According to the 1959 census only 3 per cent of the kolkhoz members had completed their secondary education. In 1962 only 7 per cent of peasant families owned a television set. Of all the roads in the Russian Republic 78 per cent are simple earth tracks. Only 5 per cent of farm children under three are looked after in public nurseries. Wages paid by the kolkhoz represent only 29 per cent of the family's cash income. In 1917 the average family holding was four hectares; today the average private plot in the Russian Republic is 0.3 hectares. Family size, however, shrank from 5.9 members in 1897, to 4.9 members in 1926, and to 3.6 members in 1959.

Now for some of the impressive gains made by Soviet agriculture since 1953. The government has raised prices on most food products several times since then, producing a large rise in the kolkoznik's income. In 1958 the notorious Machine Tractor Stations were abolished; the collective farm can now do its own work, using its own machines, at much reduced cost. A very large investment has been made in agriculture for machinery, fertilizer, etc. The current Five-Year Plan (1966–70) envisages a 100 per cent increase in state capital investment in' agriculture, as well as a 200 per cent increase in the consumption of electric power in agriculture. Though the Soviet Union has recently had to import grain from Canada, total agricultural output has grown impressively since 1953. For

From Fëdor Belov, *The History of a Soviet Collective Farm* (New York: Frederick A. Praeger, Inc., 1955), pp. 3–13, 16–23, 25–27, 34–38, 40–41, 44–45, 48–51, 176–88, 191–93, 233. Reprinted with the permission of the Committee for the Promotion of Advanced Slavic Cultural Studies.

the first time in Soviet history Soviet collective farmers are now eligible for state old-age pensions. A scheme is beginning to be put into effect which will eventually guarantee a minimum wage to all collective farm workers. Modest prosperity has finally arrived to the collective farms of which there are only 37,000 now; in 1950 the figure was 250,000. Forty-four per cent of all agricultural output now originates on the collective farms, 32 per cent on the private plots, and 24 per cent on the state farms. One figure to compare Soviet and American agriculture: in 1963 the total U.S. labor force was 68.8 million, of which only 4.9 million were employed in agriculture. The figures for the USSR were 92.1 million and 30 million, respectively.

The literature on Soviet agriculture is enormous. What will be noted here are some of the more interesting studies of certain basic problems, with an emphasis on the most recent work. On collectivization see Herbert Ellison, "The Decision to Collectivize Agriculture," *American Slavic and East European Review*, Vol. XX; M. Lewin, "The Immediate Background of Soviet Collectivization," *Soviet Studies*, October, 1965; O. Narkiewicz, "Stalin, War Communism, and Collectivization," *ibid.*, July, 1966; Victor Kravchenko, *I Chose Freedom*, pp. 91–131; and three chapters of Merle Fainsod's *Smolensk Under Soviet Rule* (paperback). On the famine of 1932–34 see Dana Dalrymple, "The Soviet Famine of 1932–4," *Soviet Studies*, January, 1964 and Dmytro Solovey, "On the 30th Anniversary of the Great Man-Made Famine in the Ukraine," *Ukrainian Quarterly*, XIX (1963), 237–46, 350–63. For a Soviet view of these problems see the two paperback novels of Mikhail Sholokhov, *Harvest on the Don*, and *Virgin Soil Upturned*; Iakov Iakovlev, *Red Villages*; V. Pogudin, "Soviet Historiography on the Problem of the Elimination of the Kulaks as a Class," *Soviet Studies in History*, Winter, 1965–66; I. Volkov, "The Collective Farm Village in the First Post-War Year," *ibid.*, Summer, 1966; and "A New Look at Stalin's Role in Collectivization," *Current Digest of the Soviet Press*, October 2, 1963. For general studies of Soviet agriculture in the 1930's and 1940's see two paperbacks by John Maynard, *The Russian Peasant*, and *Russia in Flux*; Lazar Volin, *A Survey of Soviet Agriculture*; and Naum Jasny, *The Socialized Agriculture of the USSR*, as well as *The Economics of Soviet Agriculture* by L. Hubbard. For the situation in recent years see Roy Laird and E. Crowley, *Soviet Agriculture: The Permanent Crisis*; Sidney Ploss, *Conflict and Decision Making in Soviet Russia: A Case Study of Agricultural Policy, 1953–63*; Jerzy Karcz, *Soviet and East European Agriculture*; A. Avtorkhanev, "A New Agricultural Revolution," *Bulletin of the Institute for the Study of the USSR*, July, 1967; and Folke Dovring, "Soviet Farm Mechanization in Perspective," *Slavic Review*, June, 1966. There is a regular section on agriculture in the weekly *Current Digest of the Soviet Press*.

For two very recent studies see M. Lewin, *Russian Peasants and Soviet Power*, as well as Jerzy Karcz, "Thoughts on the Grain Problem," *Soviet Studies*, April, 1967.

ABOUT THE AUTHOR

Fëdor Belov was born shortly after the Revolution in the Ukrainian village which is the scene of his narrative. He attended school in the village until he was sixteen, working on the collective farm during his holidays. During the summer when he reached sixteen he worked in the collective farm office and then went to Kiev, where he attended a more advanced school for four years.

In 1941 he joined the army, serving during the war in Poland, Hungary and Germany. At the end of the war he was discharged with the rank of captain and was then sent as a civilian technician to the Carpathians. On a visit home to his village in 1947 he decided to remain there and help look after his family.

The secretary of the raion[1] Party committee offered him the chairmanship of a collective farm in the raion in accordance with a general policy after the war of putting former army officers into managerial jobs. Despite misgivings over his lack of experience, he eventually accepted, on condition that he be named chairman of one of the two collective farms in his own village. The officials were not pleased with this condition, but it was popular with the villagers, who wanted to have one of their own people in the job. In due course Mr. Belov was elected chairman, serving in that capacity for nearly three years. At the end of 1949 he was recalled to the army and sent to Germany. In the fall of 1950 he spent a month and a half on the collective farm on furlough, and then returned to his unit in Germany. Shortly thereafter, in 1951, finally disillusioned with the Soviet regime, he managed to escape to Western Germany. He now lives in the United States.

Mr. Belov's account of the life on the collective farm is based mainly on the diaries which he was able to bring with him out of the Soviet Union. The diaries included statistical reports of collective farm operations, but for some of the facts and figures the author has had to rely on his memory.

THE HISTORY OF OUR VILLAGE TO 1947

I. FROM PREREVOLUTIONARY DAYS THROUGH THE CIVIL WAR

The village which is the site of the kolkhoz I want to describe is situated in the western part of the Ukraine, in a small valley. In 1950 it numbered 772 households; their dwellings were spread out along the banks of a stream for a distance of six kilometers (a little under four miles).

Before the Revolution, part of the village lands belonged to the landlord F., whose estate lay nearby; he owned 10,000 hectares (25,000 acres) of plowland and 2,000 hectares of forest in various parts of the district. About 1,000 hectares of his property formed part of the lands of our village. On his estate he had 300 oxen, 200 horses and over 100 cows; he also owned a large brickyard, a lumber mill and several flour mills. His residence and farm buildings were located in the center of the village, dividing it into two parts which later became the sites of the two kolkhozes set up in the village. All of his farm and administrative buildings, such as dairies, granaries and workshops, were built of stone; other buildings on his estate were of brick, and some of these, among them the school, the hospital and several shops, are still standing. The bricks used in these buildings are marked A. F., the initials of F.'s wife—an unobtrusive reminder of the contrast between things past and things present, for almost all the newer structures of the village are built of clay.

The village was proud of its church, the largest and most beautiful one in the district. It had been built largely at the expense of the landlord. Religious festivals were important events in the life of the village, which in general was

---

[1] An administrative unit roughly equivalent to a county in the United States.

peaceful and predictable. The land was fertile, food was always plentiful and the peasants were able to supplement their income by selling the products of the home industries which they carried on during the winter.

The calm routine of village life was disrupted by the outbreak of war in 1914. The army took many of the men; some never returned, others came back crippled and embittered.

In the summer of 1917 the first deserters from the front appeared in the village. The soldiers brought back guns, Bolshevik leaflets and the seeds of disloyalty to the Tsar. One of them (who was subsequently shot by the Germans) secretly began to prepare an anti-government uprising in the village; the same sort of activity was going on in the surrounding villages, but before anything could be accomplished the ringleaders were arrested and sent to Siberia.

News of the revolutionary uprising of October 25, 1917,[2] reached the village the following day and was greeted with enthusiasm; to the peasants it meant free land and an end to the war. On the very day the news arrived the landowner's manor house was looted, his stock farms were "requisitioned," and his vast orchard was cut down and sold to the peasants for wood; all his farm buildings were torn down and left in ruins while the land was distributed among the peasants, who were prepared to live the new Soviet life.

But the triumphant and exciting days of the Revolution were quickly followed by evil days; the Germans came almost immediately, drove off most of the peasants' livestock and left the village devastated. Then came the Civil War, with robberies, murders and general economic ruin.

The political situation in the Ukraine at that time was so complex that the

[2] November 7, New Style.

peasants, who were poorly educated and knew little of politics, were incapable of understanding it. No one knew whom to believe, whose leadership to follow. One government followed another, and the peasants hung on grimly and waited for the end of the confusion.

It was a long time before the peasants felt safe in relinquishing their guns, for it was not till 1923 that the village was free from the raids of armed bands, whether Communists, anti-Communists or ordinary brigands.

II. From the End of the Civil War to Collectivization

Following the Civil War, with all its anxieties and confusion, the village gradually began to revive. After the famine of 1921 (I should mention that no one in the village died of hunger during this time), the village lands were repartitioned according to the new regulations. At that time the village numbered more than three thousand inhabitants, with total holdings of 4,380 hectares. This total included the homestead strips, or individual garden plots, which averaged 6 to 7 hectares per household.

Our land produced good crops. On an average, the yields obtained per hectare were 30 to 40 centners of wheat, 25 to 30 centners of rye, 20 to 25 centners of barley, and 200 centners of beets. Every household had large surpluses of grain which it could dispose of as it saw fit; for the most part, the grain went to market for sale.

Since at that time the tax burden was light, the majority of the peasants were able to increase and improve their holdings. They built houses, barns and sheds, and bought agricultural implements. By 1926 the village had more than 500 cows, 300 horses, 600 swarms of bees, 2 watermills, 13 windmills, and 6 stores. More than 100 houses were fitted out with sheet-iron roofs, a sure sign of peasant prosperity. A villager who did not kill one or two pigs a year (for Christmas and Easter) was a rarity. As a rule, lard and eggs could be found in every home. These were the golden days of the NEP,[3] which the peasants still look back upon with longing. . . .

In the spring of 1928 the first wave of the "attack on the kulaks" swept over our raion. As a rule, it was the Committees of the Poor[4] and the members of the Komsomol[5] in the villages on whom the government depended. In our village the Committee of the Poor was headed by one of the poorest peasants, Kapan.

Kapan had appeared in our village after the Civil War; he had married a widow and squandered almost all her money on drink. He went about dressed in a soldier's overcoat and a huge sheepskin cap, and was always slightly tipsy. Somehow his appearance made one think of a beast of prey about to pounce on its victim.

Eighteen of the poorest households joined the Committee of the Poor. In many of these households the young people were members of the Komsomol. Frequently, in the "attack of the kulaks," father and son marched together. Though the Komsomol of the village had only nine members, they were held in even greater awe by the villagers than members of the Communist Party are today.

The "dekulakization" took place in the following manner: in the office of the village soviet, where the Committee of the Poor had its headquarters, a victim would be selected at a board meeting, and on the next day the entire group of active members would raid the victim's household. Such raids resembled

those of the locusts which destroy everything in their path. The raiders made a clean sweep of everything—grain, agricultural implements, harness, livestock, furniture, and clothing. The entire company was armed with revolvers and long iron rods; with the latter they probed the walls, the floors, the stove, and so forth of the raided peasant's home, in search of "kulak property." The members of the kulak family would sometimes dress themselves in several layers of clothing hoping to save at least something, but the clothes would be taken off by force in spite of all pleas and tears. Articles taken from the kulak farms were sold at auction in the village club. Most of the peasants did not go to these sales, saying "one's happiness cannot be built on the tears of others." The stolen goods usually fell to the "active" peasants.

During this period twenty-one kulak households were "dekulakized" in the village. The members of nine households were sent to Siberia and Kazakhstan. (After the war some of them returned to the village.) The singing of the young girls was no longer heard in the evenings; at night the baying of the dogs on the ruined farms gave rise to a feeling of sadness and vague foreboding.

III. The First Attempts at Collectivization

It was in the same year that the first attempts at collectivization began. A commune was set up, using two former kulak farms as a base. The commune consisted of thirteen families, with a total of seventy persons, the majority of whom were poor peasants, hired farmhands and orphans. The farm tools taken from the "dekulakized" farms were turned over to the commune, since its members had almost none of their own. The members ate in a communal dining hall, and income was divided in accordance with the principles of "co-

---

[3] The New Economic Policy, approximately 1921 to 1928.

[4] Groups composed of the poorest peasants.

[5] The Young Communist League.

operative communism." The entire proceeds of the members' labor, as well as all dwellings and facilities belonging to the commune, were shared by the commune members. The orphans and the homeless of the commune lived in a separate building called the "bachelor house." The same building was used for the club, from which propaganda was carried on among the peasants. At the head of the commune was a five-man council which managed the entire administrative and economic life of the commune and drew up ambitious plans for the future. But in spite of all propaganda, more peasants did not enter the commune. It was the same in other villages. The communal form of collective farming soon lost favor and Party efforts to promote it were gradually abandoned in the late twenties.

At about the same time the members of the Evangelist sect in the village set up another commune on a religious basis. This one included six families with a total of twenty-four persons. In order not to harm any peasants by taking their land, the commune asked the village soviet to give them the poorest lands. They built a community house, a store and a dairy; they lived and worked as one family, in friendship and harmony. They taught their children at home, since disbelief in God and church was being taught at school. Many peasants who were not members of the sect attended their church and spoke well of them. They were against war and every kind of violence and falsehood.

Nevertheless, the religious commune was broken up by an order from above; the authorities found in it the dangerous germ of "counterrevolution."

After the dissolution of the religious commune, a new form of collective farm, the TOZ,[6] appeared in the village.

TOZ's were created on a voluntary basis; usually they were joined by former commune members and poor peasants. In the spring of 1929, the TOZ in our village included thirty-four households which had pooled their lands and implements. In the distribution of the profits, not only the amount of labor performed by the members on the society's farm but also the means of production which they had contributed were taken into account. The income of each society member thus depended on the acreage he provided, on his livestock and implements, and on his labor contribution. Such distribution caused intense dissatisfaction in the households of the poor peasants who, because they did not have any livestock or implements, received very small incomes. These households fought for a distribution of profits according to the number of mouths and the amount of labor contributed; the other households, however, defended the existing system of distribution. In this way the TOZ soon split into two camps.

By the autumn of 1929 the TOZ numbered fifty-seven households and received a charter from the government. Notwithstanding special advantages such as reduced taxes, however, the TOZ gained no new members after that time; by the end of 1929 eleven households had withdrawn, six of them leaving the village entirely to seek their fortunes in the Soviet Far East. Soon other households followed the example of the first group, and the TOZ was in danger of collapse.

The experience in our village with these early types of collective farms was typical of what was taking place in many other Soviet villages at this time. . . .

---

[6] Society for the Joint Cultivation of Land (*Tovarishchestvo po sovmestnoi obrabotke zem-*

li). The purpose of the TOZ was to combine manpower, draft animals and agricultural machinery of individual peasant farms for joint field work.—EDS.

In the winter of 1930, the TOZ was reorganized as an artel,[7] the form of collective farm which the government decided should be generally adopted and which evolved into the present-day kolkhoz.

General collectivization in our village was brought about in the following manner: Two representatives of the Party arrived in the village. All the inhabitants were summoned by the ringing of the church bell to a meeting at which the policy of general collectivization was announced. At the meeting, however, someone distributed leaflets entitled "This Is How It Will Be on a Collective Farm." The leaflet showed a picture of a mother and child, the mother bent under the burden of overwork. The upshot was that although the meeting lasted two days, from the viewpoint of the Party representatives nothing was accomplished.

After this setback the Party representatives divided the village into two sections and worked each one separately. Two more officials were sent to reinforce the first two. A meeting of our section of the village was held in a stable which had previously belonged to a kulak. The meeting dragged on until dark. Suddenly someone threw a brick at the lamp, and in the dark the peasants began to beat the Party representatives, who jumped out the window and escaped from the village barely alive. The following day seven people were arrested. The militia[8] was called in and stayed in the village until the peasants, realizing their helplessness, calmed down.

It was difficult, however, for the Party and government to break down the old principles and traditions. The peasants stubbornly clung to their possessions. But "there are no fortresses which Bolsheviks cannot storm."[9] Heavy taxes and fear of the future drove even the middle-peasant households into the collective farm. Those households which refused to join were loaded with burdensome taxes and allotted the poorest lands. The independent peasants feared particularly "the household plan," a special tax regulation under which monetary payments in kind were required to be made on twenty-four hours' notice; after the expiration of the time limit, the delinquent farm was subject to a raid by the Committee of the Poor and the Komsomol members.

IV. THE FIRST KOLKHOZES AND THE FAMINE OF 1932–33

By the end of 1930 there were two kolkhozes in our village. Though at first these collectives embraced at most only 70 per cent of the peasant households, in the months that followed they gradually absorbed more and more of them. . . .

Our kolkhoz was built on the site of the former commune, the acreage of which had been increased at the expense of households which had been evicted to other parts of the village. The farm and administrative buildings of the collective were constructed from sheds which had formerly belonged to kulaks, the farm buildings of collectivized peasants, and other miscellaneous sources. Tombstones and stone crosses from the cemetery were used for the foundations of the buildings; for the roofs, the sheet-iron was ripped off the former kulak dwellings on the kolkhoz land. Willow and linden wood, of which the village

[7] Members of an artel were allowed to have small plots for their vegetable gardens and to own some livestock, but most of the means of production, such as peasant land holdings, livestock and farming implements, were collectivized.—EDS.

[8] In the Soviet Union, the regular police force.

[9] A common Party slogan of the times.

The History of a Soviet Collective Farm

had an ample supply, was also used in the farm's construction. By the summer of 1931, the kolkhoz had its own stud farm with space for 120 horses, a large barn for grain and a steam-operated flour mill. It included in its membership 85 per cent of all the peasant households of our section of the village, and had 90 horses, 24 oxen, 80 sheep, 160 swarms of bees, and several cows and pigs. . . .

By late 1932 more than 80 per cent of the peasant households in the raion had been collectivized. In the twenty-four villages of the raion there were fifty-two kolkhozes and three state farms (sovkhozes).[10] That year the peasants harvested a good crop and had hopes that the calculations would work out to their advantage and would help strengthen them economically. These hopes were in vain. The kolkhoz workers received only 200 grams of flour per labor day for the first half of the year; the remaining grain, including the seed fund, was taken by the government. The peasants were told that industrialization of the country, then in full swing, demanded grain and sacrifices from them.

That autumn the "red broom"[11] passed over the kolkhozes and the individual plots, sweeping the "surplus" for the state out of the barns and corn-cribs. In the search for "surpluses," everything was collected. The farms were cleaned out even more thoroughly than the kulaks had been. As a result, famine, which was to become intense by the spring of 1933, already began to be felt in the fall of 1932.

The famine of 1932–33 was the most terrible and destructive that the

Ukrainian people have ever experienced. The peasants ate dogs, horses, rotten potatoes, the bark of trees, grass—anything they could find. Incidents of cannibalism were not uncommon. The people were like wild beasts, ready to devour one another. And no matter what they did, they went on dying, dying, dying.

They died singly and in families. They died everywhere—in the yards, on streetcars, and on trains. There was no one to bury these victims of the Stalinist famine. People traveled for thousands of kilometers in search of food—to Siberia, the Caucasus. Many perished by the wayside or fell into the hands of the militia. To protect what little grain they had from the raids of the militia, the peasants often banded together in groups of thirty or forty persons and defended their gleanings with sticks and knives.

I was thirteen years old then, and I shall never forget what I saw. One memory especially stands out: a baby lying at his mother's breast, trying to wake her.

A man is capable of forgetting a great deal, but these terrible scenes of starvation will be forgotten by no one who saw them. The worst time came during May and June 1933. In the fields of the kolkhoz a bumper crop was ripening, but the peasants were too weak to live until the new grain was ripe. Many went out to the waving fields of wheat and rye, tore off the half-ripened ears and ate them. But they were so weak that the indigestible grain was fatal and they would drop dead on the spot. In our village alone the famine claimed 479 lives. . . .

V. LIFE ON THE KOLKHOZ
BEFORE THE WAR

. . . The kolkhoz enjoyed its greatest

---

[10] Later the number of kolkhozes dropped to forty-six. Sovkhoz is the contraction for *sovetskoye khozyaistvo.*

[11] The name given to groups of Party members, often from the cities, who were sent out to search for food the peasants might have hidden.

prosperity during the years 1936–38. In these years it had a five-field system of crop rotation and planted an area of 72 hectares in sugar beets. The total vegetable plantings ran as high as 200 hectares.

Since it had excellent draft power— 160 horses and 80 oxen—the kolkhoz tried to cultivate its land with its own motive power and thus avoid the large payments in kind for the use of the tractors provided by the Machine-Tractor Stations (MTS). Since the tractor station was not large—one tractor brigade (four tractors) serviced two or three kolkhozes—the collective performed about 55 per cent of its cultivation with its own power. The total payments in kind for the work of the tractors amounted to no more than 1,200 to 1,300 centners of grain annually. It should be mentioned, too, that because of its fine stock of draft animals the kolkhoz had thousands of tons of manure for its fields, which contributed to its success.

Having a surplus of grain, the kolkhoz members decided at the general meeting to sell it to the state each year and with the credit thus obtained to buy machinery and necessary implements. The kolkhoz had such surpluses up until 1939, when a new system of deliveries of agricultural products was initiated. Thereafter the amount of obligatory deliveries of individual products was based not, as before, on the area of land sown to each crop, but on the total area of arable land. Moreover, the differences in the fertility and composition of the land on different farms were ignored in computing the amount of the deliveries under the new regulations. Under this system only those kolkhozes with fertile land could operate profitably; the others were doomed to poverty. For example, although the

value of the labor day on our kolkhoz was usually about 3 to 6 kilograms of grain and 3 to 5 rubles in cash, there were other collectives in our raion in which the labor day was equal to only 1 to 2 kilograms of grain and 70 to 90 kopecks in cash. . . .

In general, from the mid-1930's until 1941, the majority of kolkhoz members in the Ukraine lived relatively well. They were never in need of bread and other foodstuffs. If the market provided insufficient clothes and shoes, the shortage was made good by items made locally. In 1939 and 1940, however, the state demanded more grain from the kolkhozes than they had contributed before. The alliance with Germany, to which the grain was sent, stirred up dissatisfaction and disapproval among the peasants. The sharp changes in the amount delivered to the state and the fluctuating remuneration for the labor day constantly aroused a fear of tomorrow's fate among the kolkhoz members and drove them to steal grain and conceal it.

On the eve of war, our kolkhoz presented the following picture: its collective livestock consisted of 180 horses, 44 cows, 90 oxen, about 300 calves, more than 400 pigs, about 100 sheep, and more than 60 chickens. It had three automobiles, a flour mill, a sawmill, a creamery, machine and wood-working shops and other buildings. It was considered a "leading" kolkhoz in the raion and had participated in the all-Union agricultural exhibitions from 1935 to 1939; its chairman had attended several republic and oblast conferences of agricultural leaders.

VI. The Destruction of the Kolkhoz and the Occupation of the Village by the Germans

At the beginning of the war most of our

collective livestock was driven to the east and turned over to other kolkhozes. (Not one head of livestock was returned at the end of the war.) Most of the remaining animals were slaughtered and the meat was distributed among the kolkhoz members. Before the arrival of the Germans in the village, the kolkhoz was dismantled: all the farm buildings were torn down and the building materials were carried away by the peasants. The implements, agricultural machinery and harness, and even the tractors, were also divided among the kolkhoz members. The allotment of the collective property was carried out under the supervision of Fëdor B., a former deacon of the church, who created a special commission for this work. The allotment of the lands to the peasants was supervised by a temporary committee elected by a special assembly of the village. This committee, which was composed of two schoolteachers, the former secretary of the village soviet and several peasants, managed the village until the Germans came.

In 1941 each peasant harvested the crop from his own strip of land. Some former kulaks moved back into their homes without disturbance; they did not demand their former lands and submitted to the generally established rules. In the same year more than forty deserters from the front appeared in the village, hoping to settle down to a new life as free peasants. When the German troops came, the village greeted them "with bread and salt"[12] and hailed them as liberators.

At first the Germans were friendly; they accepted the food they were offered, clicked their cameras and roared, "Stalin kaput." But the "liberation" did not last long. In the winter of 1942 the Germans ordered the restoration of the kolkhozes. They commanded the peas-

12 The traditional peasant welcome.

ants to surrender the implements and machinery previously distributed and threatened to execute those who evaded the order. Regulations in the two restored kolkhozes in our villages, under the management of a certain Hungarian whom the people nicknamed "Fritz," became stricter than ever. Five o'clock in the morning was the time set for going out to the fields, and nine at night for returning; for lateness, the culprit was given three or four lashes. Subsequently the Germans took away all the cows, chickens, pigs, and beehives from the individual peasant households and put them back in the kolkhoz.

As a result of such actions, the peasants' attitude toward the Germans changed to one of hostility; there was much stealing from the kolkhozes; the local population worked together in this and protected one another from German retribution. There were exceptions when the lure of reward in the form of money or land would induce a man to denounce his neighbor, but they were few. Many peasants joined the partisans, while others awaited with impatience the return of the Russians. Following the liberation of our village by Soviet troops, the active collaborators with the Germans were tried and banished to Siberia; the "emigrants" from the front were shot.

All told, the village suffered the following losses from the war: forty-four homes were burned, two bridges and two club buildings were destroyed and over three hundred male inhabitants were killed. The Germans did not bring the peasants the expected land and freedom. They brought only suffering to the peasant masses.

VII. THE RESTORATION OF THE KOLKHOZ

In the first days after the liberation from the Germans in 1944, the kolkhoz presented the following picture: Out of the five livestock barns, only one horse-stable was still intact. All the agricultural implements had been plundered. The farm had no sheep, poultry, or bees, and only sixteen horses, thirteen oxen, and twenty-three pigs. The families of the former kulaks who had settled in their old homes were forcibly evicted. The other kolkhoz in the village was in similar straits.

Promptly after the departure of the Germans, the kolkhoz was again set up. This was not, however, simply the re-establishment of the prewar kolkhoz; it was the creation of a new organization, since the entire process had to be started over from the beginning, just as in 1930. . . .

A chairman, Vasili B., was appointed by the raion Party committee as soon as the kolkhoz was re-established in 1944, and afterwards he was approved by the general meeting. He was forty-five years of age, fat, uncouth, and illiterate. His swearing, which was incessant, he called "mathematics." He was proud of the fact that the kolkhoz members were afraid of his "mathematics" and that it served him as a useful weapon. The peasants wondered why this man remained on special orders in the rear and was not sent to the front; such people, it seems, were valued by the raion Party committee as obedient and devoted tools. . . .

The kolkhoz was forced to engage in a variety of illegal activities in order to exist and fulfill its obligations. The drought of 1946 further increased its troubles; the state grain deliveries took so much that the peasants received only 300 grams of grain and 60 kopecks in cash per labor day; the seed and forage funds, moreover, were cleaned out. The farm was told to look for seed locally, despite the fact that neighboring farms were in the same plight and were doing the same thing.

Because the peasants received so little food and money, they became almost entirely dependent for their livelihood on their homestead plots. Labor discipline went to pieces, and the peasants refused to work on the collective land. The chairman found that not even his best "mathematics" was effective in this situation, and he had to threaten the peasants with trial and expulsion from the collective. This was sometimes effective, because although many people wanted to leave the kolkhoz they did not want to be expelled, for in such a case they were given no official documents, without which it was impossible to move about the country.

When I came back to the village in January 1947 in the company of two other army officers, we were struck by the contrast between living conditions then and before the war. The whole village was seething with discontent, which was particularly directed against the administration, both of the two farms and of the village. It was a measure of the strength of this discontent that the peasants managed to force the local Party leadership to let them elect new people to the posts of chairman of the village soviet and chairmen of the two kolkhozes in the village.

Thus all the top posts in the village passed into the hands of former front-line officers, who strove to improve the economic position of the collective farmers. Bohdan K., a young, energetic and intelligent officer who immediately won the respect of the peasants, was elected chairman of the village soviet. Volodymyr T., a retired colonel, became chairman of one of the kolkhozes; the other chairmanship fell to me. During this period, I made the following entries in my diary:

January 26. Tonight I went to a party at N. S.'s. It turned out that I was invited for a special reason. Almost all the "fighting *aktiv*"[13] were there. They intended to expose and evict the kolkhoz chairman, V. B., from his job.

They asked me again and again to accept the nomination as their candidate for the position of kolkhoz chairman. I didn't want to offend my fellow villagers, but at the same time I didn't agree to become chairman. It is certainly true that they don't have a suitable candidate to replace V. B., and it is rare that a person will accept this beastly job. It seems to me that the position of kolkhoz chairman is more appointive than elective, so that my friends are needlessly concerned about my candidacy. . . .

February 2. The report and election meeting began at noon. It promised to be interesting. Almost all the kolkhoz members turned up—even that well-known intrepid trio, Yelizaveta B., Tatiana Yu. and Maria P. In order to keep these dangerous women quiet, the chairman of the meeting proposed that all three of them be elected to the presidium. The trio apparently arranged things among themselves and categorically refused this honor.

Listening to V. B.'s report, which consisted merely of a reading of figures about which he knew nothing, I was amazed— why was such a person needed by the raion Party committee? Evidently he's a good man for carrying out their wishes. The discussion about the economic "activity" of V. B. and his colleagues has been going on for ten hours already. More than forty people have spoken, but the end of the meeting is not yet in sight. I didn't know that the kolkhoz members could criticize not only B. but also the raion authorities so fearlessly and angrily as they are doing. It is obvious that democracy is not yet crushed in the kolkhozes.

To sum up: in all, forty-nine kolkhoz members spoke at the meeting. The point of all the speeches was aimed primarily at B. and at the business manager. The kolkhoz members were in full control of the meeting and did not even consider the suggestions of the representative of the raion

[13] A Soviet political term designating the more active members of an organization.

Party committee. The meeting lasted fourteen hours and twenty-four minutes. The kolkhoz members elected me chairman unanimously. To my great surprise, they allowed me personally to select the board of managers. They obviously have great confidence in me. Will I be able to justify this trust? We shall see.

VIII. THE GENERAL MEETING OF THE KOLKHOZ MEMBERS

. . . The constant interference of the raion Party and administrative personnel in the internal affairs of the kolkhozes brought about a situation in which the authority of the general meetings was sharply curtailed, particularly in the case of elections. For example, in 1949, at the annual report and election meeting of one kolkhoz in our raion, persons unacceptable to the Party organization were elected to key positions. Subsequently the decisions of the general meeting were decreed invalid and countermanded by the kolkhoz Party organization, acting under orders from the raion, and more acceptable people were "elected." By the time I left in the autumn of 1949, not merely the top managerial personnel but even quite minor kolkhoz officials were being chosen by the raion Party committee. . . .

The way elections worked was as follows: at the general meeting, the representative of the raion Party committee submitted to the members of the kolkhoz the names of persons who had been designated by the raion to fill the various offices. The Party organization and the other kolkhoz activists had to "note and carry out" these suggestions, while the rank-and-file kolkhoz members merely had to raise their hands automatically in agreement with the wishes of the higher-ups. In the event that the raion was not able to place its people in the key posts of that farm, the general meeting would be broken up and a new date would be set for the continuation of the same meeting.

In some kolkhozes a meeting might last three or four days, often in the presence of the secretary of the raion Party committee and the chairman of the raion executive committee; in the long run the raion authorities achieved their aim. With every passing year the number of collective farmers who seriously opposed the decisions of the raion authorities became smaller and smaller, and by 1949 the general meetings were perfunctory rubberstamp affairs which were held on most farms no more than two or three times a year, and in a few cases only once a year, for accounting purposes.

In 1947, however, the year I came back to the village, things were rather different. The peasants in the village had got the bit between their teeth and were determined to get rid of their old administration, whether the raion authorities liked it or not. The general meeting of our kolkhoz which was called in February of that year produced some fireworks.

Almost all the members showed up at the meeting, well fortified by the consumption of large quantities of homemade liquor and determined to oust the unpopular Vasili, who had been foisted on them as chairman by the raion Party committee in 1944. They let him deliver an account of the financial and business activities of the management of the kolkhoz, and then they began to make speeches. Every speaker tried not only to recall all the illegal activities of the chairman but to insult him personally as well. One man had spent an entire year collecting and writing down all the details of Vasili's high-handedness, and now he read them, indicating the time and place of each action. He pointed out to the meeting how eighty-seven roosters had been charged off to foxes, who had presumably eaten them, but he made it

clear that the "foxes" were really Vasili and his deputy chairman.

Yet in spite of a thousand reasons why Vasili should have been removed from his post as chairman of the kolkhoz, the raion Party committee ordered its authorized representative, Boris N., to try to have him retained in his post by all possible means. Boris defended him with all his might, and so did the Party organization of the kolkhoz, but the other kolkhoz members stood their ground and would not even listen to the idea of re-electing him.

The meeting lasted fourteen hours, and it finally became quite evident that Vasili could not be re-elected. Boris got in touch with the raion Party committee, and was told to break up the meeting and reconvene it the next day to consider the candidacy of Ivan B. This man, who was notorious throughout the district, had just failed to be re-elected to the chairmanship of the other kolkhoz in our village. When the peasants got wind of Boris's intentions, they refused to break up the meeting; if anything, they wanted Ivan as chairman even less, than Vasili, for the former was a slave-driver who made the peasants fulfill the government's demands to the last letter and afterwards exploited them for his own benefit—an order of priorities which explained his popularity with the Party authorities. One of the stories told about him was of how he caught a woman stealing grain; he threatened her with criminal proceedings and ordered her to pay a five hundred ruble fine, which he pocketed, and finally he seduced her. So unpopular was he that some members of the kolkhoz Party organization opposed his candidacy and refused to carry out the instructions of the raion Party committee. (Subsequently the secretary of the Party organization was deprived of his Party card because he had been unable to impose the Party's will on the general meeting.)

Eventually the question of my candidacy was brought up. At this time there was a widespread policy of putting former army officers in positions of authority, and I had already been offered the job of secretary of the village Komsomol, which I had refused. I was then urged by the secretary of the raion Party committee to take on the job of chairman of a kolkhoz, but I said I would accept only if they gave me such a job in my own village. This the committee was rather unwilling to do, but when it had become clear that neither Vasili nor Ivan could be elected without endless trouble, they did not oppose my candidacy. The kolkhoz members, on the other hand, welcomed me because I had been born and raised in the village and they considered me as one of them, even though I had been away for a long time. So the long and short of it was that I was elected.

Normally the general meeting should also have elected a new board of managers and a new inspection committee at the same time, but because of my inexperience I asked that the personnel then holding those jobs be kept on until I had familiarized myself with the operations of the kolkhoz. I was also given the right to select the new board when the time came.[14]

[14] The reader may be struck by the degree of freedom and independence shown by the members of the kolkhoz at this meeting, which is in contrast with what the author says elsewhere about such meetings. In this connection it is worth quoting from Barrington Moore, Jr., *Soviet Politics—the Dilemma of Power*, pp. 339–40: "In the collective farms as elsewhere in the Soviet social system, the repeating cycle of alternating authoritarian and democratic procedures may be observed." He goes on to say that too great an extension of authoritarian practices and interference by state and Party organs produces a lack of enthusiasm and even opposition. "At such a point the regime typically engages in a campaign of re-democratiza-

IX. KOLKHOZ OFFICIALS—THE BOARD OF MANAGERS AND THE CHAIRMAN

According to the Model Statutes, the officials of a kolkhoz fall into two groups: those who are elected by the general meeting and those who are appointed by the elected personnel. In practice there was less and less difference between the two groups as time went on, and by 1949 almost all the officials were being appointed by the raion authorities.

The so-called elected officials comprise the chairman, the board of managers and the members of the inspection committee, all of whom are supposed to be elected for two-year terms; in practice, however, they were often changed each year. The chairman of the kolkhoz also serves as a chairman of the board of managers. The board, in turn, appoints the accountant, the warehouseman, the manager of the flour mill, the brigadiers, and other administrative personnel. . . .

The board and the chairman are responsible to the state for the execution by the kolkhoz of its obligations for the supply of agricultural products, the payment of taxes, and payments in kind for the work of the MTS.

While I was chairman, the board of managers consisted of six persons in addition to myself: the business manager, who was also the first deputy chairman of the kolkhoz, the field supervisor and

tion, in which the democratic aspects of its ideology are given not only lip service but receive additional realization in practice. In the collective farms this stage was reached again early in 1947, when the Party ordered that general meetings of the rank-and-file membership be held in all of the kolkhozy of the Soviet Union before February 15 of that year."

It is justifiable to assume that this explains what appears to have been an unusually effective expression of preference on the part of the kolkhoz members, in defiance of Party orders.

four other members, who were in charge of the workshops and the stock farms. . . .

When I first took over the chairmanship of the farm, I discovered that the existing business manager was a dishonest man who had been defrauding the farm for years. He was an ingenious fellow, who had managed to bribe the accountant, the warehouseman and the entire inspection committee, with the result that I had to make a major overhaul of the administration. When I reported what had been going on to the other members and the general meeting, there was general insistence that these people be sent up for trial. Knowing what this would involve, I tried to prevent it, but the peasants were furious and insisted on my informing the prosecutor, with the result that the guilty individuals got prison terms of ten to fifteen years.

X. Brigades and Squads

Among the appointed personnel, the brigadiers of the fieldwork brigades are an important part of the kolkhoz. A brigadier is appointed by the board of managers from among the kolkhoz members, theoretically for a term of two years. Working directly under the field supervisor, the brigadier carries out the operational directives of the board which relate to the various crops grown by the farm. He draws up the detailed work plan for his brigade, which consists of about a hundred people, selects the squad leaders and assigns members to the various squads; it is his duty to see that the members of his brigade get out to work when they should and carry out their tasks properly. He coordinates the work of his brigade with that of the tractor brigades, and assigns draft animals and implements to the members of his brigade, for which they are held responsible. He maintains labor discipline within his brigade, reporting all violations to the board of managers. He also organizes "socialist competitions" between his squads and between individual members of the brigade.

The board pays special attention to the selection of brigadiers, for on their management depends the productive success of the brigades. In the immediate postwar period the brigadiers had almost no training in agricultural technology, and it was extremely difficult to get anyone to serve in this capacity, despite the fact that the brigadier received a higher income than other members of the brigade. The reason for this reluctance to take the job was that it was difficult and thankless since the brigadier stood between a group of unwilling workers on the one hand and the higher officials of the farm on the other, to whom he was entirely accountable for the fulfillment of the production plans of his brigade. Often the brigadier had to go to each household and beg its members to go to work so that he could carry out the work orders he had received, and during the hot weather, particularly at harvest time, the entire board of managers and the Party organization of the farm were mobilized to help the brigadier get his people to work.

Work assignments are usually given to the brigadier each evening for the next day. While I was chairman, these assignments were generally 85 per cent fulfilled, and on Sundays and holidays 55 per cent. In the raion as a whole during that period, nine brigadiers of field brigades were sentenced for non-fulfillment of the orders of the board, on charges that they were responsible for losses up to 30 per cent of the grain and technical crops.

Most of the brigadiers in our raion

were men, but the field brigades themselves consisted entirely of women, and the squad leaders were all women.

The squad leader is appointed by the brigadier and is directly subordinate to him. She gives the work orders to the members of her squad, checks on labor discipline, is responsible for the implements assigned to her squad, and participates directly in the work being done. At the end of the year the squad leader receives, in addition to her share as a squad member, up to 5 per cent of the total labor days which have accumulated to the credit of the squad for the year. On our kolkhoz, each squad consisted of sixteen to eighteen women.

XI. THE KOLKHOZ PARTY ORGANIZATION

In the postwar period, Party organizations began to multiply in every village and kolkhoz. They were customarily small, consisting of seven to ten persons, most of whom had entered the Party at the front during the war. By 1949 there was no kolkhoz in the raion without a Party organization. To an ever greater extent, the kolkhoz chairmen were being appointed (the word "elected" having lost all meaning) only from among Party members and candidates. Non-Party kolkhoz chairmen in our raion numbered thirteen in 1948 and only seven in 1949 out of forty-six kolkhozes. The raion Party committee placed great stress on the appointment of Party members and candidates to various managerial positions. This policy is explained by the fact that more can be demanded from a Party member than from a non-Party individual, since the Party member is responsible for carrying out all Party policies. . . .

Before the kolkhoz holds its report and election meeting, the Party organization discusses at its own meetings the candidacy of the future chairman and the members of the board who will be presented to the general meeting. The Party organization is obligated to use all its power to put over the Party's candidates, as the very strength of the organization resides in the realization of these plans. The Party organization has the power to reverse the decision of the kolkhoz board when it finds something contrary to regulations.

The Party organization participates in elections to the governmental organs and is fully responsible for their preparation and conduct. It assists the village soviet in the collection of taxes and plays a leading part in the loan campaigns.

In our village these loan campaigns, which usually lasted two or three days, were regarded as a scourge by the collective farmers; they were supposed to be voluntary, but there was nothing voluntary about it. A few days before the campaign was due to begin, the kolkhoz would receive from the raion executive committee the control figures for its subscription, in other words the total sum which was to be levied upon the members of the farm. The kolkhoz members were each assigned a certain sum for which they had to sign up, but they did not pay cash. Instead the farm paid for them, and they then had to work off their debt to the farm. In the spring of 1948, the control figure for loans from members of our farm was 65,000 rubles, but the commission which was sent to organize the collection of subscriptions made a mistake and distributed the obligations incorrectly so that the total came out 1,400 rubles short. The missing sum was arbitrarily divided between me and the secretary of the kolkhoz Party organization, to give us a chance to demonstrate our patriotism.

In the loan campaigns, all Party members are expected to set an example and be the first to carry out their obligations. For example, if the average subscription for a loan is 200 rubles for every able-bodied member of the farm, Party members are expected to subscribe double that amount. The majority of kolkhoz Party members, however, are ordinary peasants, and the privilege of subscribing double the normal amount is a luxury some of them cannot afford. For example, in 1949 two members were ousted from the kolkhoz Party organization because they refused to help with the loan campaign and even refused to sign up themselves. To refuse to sign, however, was dangerous: it was interpreted as opposition to the rebuilding of the war-damaged towns and villages and to strengthening the defensive power of the government, and whoever refused, therefore, became an enemy of the people. Even people who were actively opposed to the government did not want to be openly identified as such, and in the end therefore almost everybody signed.

Members of the Party organization sometimes showed a lack of enthusiasm for the supplementary grain deliveries which the government was apt to impose on the farm after it had fulfilled its normal deliveries. Like everybody else, their incomes depended partly on their earnings in labor days, and the more grain the government took, the less a labor day was worth when the final distribution was made. . . .

At one kolkhoz I knew the Party organization consisted of thirteen persons, eight Party members and five candidates. Of these thirteen, three had had seven years of schooling, six had three, and four had had only two years. All had joined the Party during the years 1941–45.

During 1949, the organization held only seven meetings instead of the required twenty-four. In the course of the year one member was expelled from the Party and twenty-six Party punishments were imposed on other members for such misdemeanors as non-fulfillment of Party obligations, immoral acts, drunkenness, hooliganism, and theft. Three of the members got married, observing all the religious rites to which of course, as Communists, they were supposed to be unshakably opposed. And one Party member set fire to a stack of hay while he was drunk; he was sentenced to two years in jail. Another one deserted his wife and family and became the father of three bastards. One of the candidates for Party membership, employed as a truckdriver, managed to steal a whole truckload of sugar beets for illicit distilling.

Some of these actions were committed deliberately, in the hope of being expelled from the Party, but it was difficult to gauge the degree of one's crime so exactly that it would be bad enough to mean Party expulsion but not bad enough to involve the risk of trial.

XII. INDIVIDUAL HOUSEHOLDS

By law the individual household consists of a house, a homestead plot, implements, and livestock. The right to this property is contingent on membership in the kolkhoz and on participation in its labor by the members of the household. The household does not have the right to transfer ownership of its plot. Persistent slacking by members of the household is punished by the loss of the homestead plot, and even by expulsion from the kolkhoz. It is the threatened loss of the homestead plot which forces individual peasants to participate in the collective work of the kolkhoz, even though such work is very unrewarding.

Households are classified according

to their productive capacity as "strong," "average" and "below average." The classification is based not only on the number of persons in the family, particularly the number of able-bodied persons, but also on the availability of implements and animals. Of the 336 households in our kolkhoz, 7 were classified as "strong," 135 as "average" and the remaining 194 as "below average." It should be remembered that ours was one of the more fortunate kolkhozes in the raion.

A typical "strong" household consists of about five members, including the head of the family, his wife and usually one other person of working age. Such a household owns a house and barn, a cow, one or two pigs, fifteen to twenty chickens, several swarms of bees, and a homestead plot of a little more than half a hectare. It can afford to butcher a pig each year and have meat and lard; it can grow extra produce for the market and thus earn enough to buy clothing and household goods, and even such luxuries as a radio, a bicycle or a gramophone. The house is usually kept in good condition, and the head of the household generally works in an administrative or managerial position.

An "average" household may have the same number of people as a "strong" one, but it is apt to have more young children. Such a household owns a house, a cow, a heifer or a pig, some chickens, and a homestead plot of about half a hectare.[15]

A "below average" household usually lacks an able-bodied man as head of the household and has perhaps only one able-bodied member; it has a house but no animals other than chickens, and a homestead plot of less than half a hectare. With the passing of time, more and more households in our kolkhoz slipped from the stronger categories to the lower one, as the men left to work in industry, or as the cow had to be sold to pay taxes.

When I took up my post as chairman, I made it my business to visit every family in the kolkhoz. Nine, I found, lived in dugouts and 57 in partially destroyed houses; 108, for lack of barns or sheds, kept their animals in the house with them. More than half of the houses needed repairs, particularly to the roofs, but because of the general shortage of building materials little could be done except to patch things up with clay or straw.

Most households had no barns; they had long since been requisitioned for the needs of the collective farm. There were no fences, because they had been burned either by the Germans during the war or by the peasants themselves for fuel. The homestead plots contained no fruit trees—they had been cut down for fuel or to avoid taxation. One man, who owned an orchard of one-fifth of a hectare, had to pay an annual tax of 1,600 rubles. Since his orchard brought him an income of only about 600 rubles, he simply chopped it down.

The houses were shabby inside and out; generally the family lived in one room, with wooden bunks for beds and straw mats or loose straw as floor covering. Straw was also used for stuffing mattresses and as fuel for the stove. Potatoes, beets and pumpkins lay scattered under the furniture, and sometimes a calf or a few pigs wandered about. In every house there was a row of ikons on the wall, and usually a faded portrait of Shevchenko.[16]

In one house a woman said to me:

[15] In our oblast the homestead plots were supposed to measure seven-tenths of a hectare, but the majority of households had less, and a newly formed household received only a quarter of a hectare.

[16] Taras Shevchenko (1814–61), the Ukraine's greatest poet.

"So you want to know how I live? Just look at me and my four children and everything will be clear to you. My husband was killed at the front. I had a son who was beginning to help me; they took him away to the factory workshop school and left me with four hungry mouths to feed, four children to clothe and send to school. Am I strong enough to do that? Yesterday a commission came to the house to collect the taxes. They wanted to list my property, but there wasn't any. I suggested that they take the children instead of the taxes, but they refused."

Two per cent of the income of the kolkhoz was set aside as an assistance fund for hardship cases, but it came nowhere near sufficing for all who needed food, clothing and fuel. After we had helped the orphans and the sick, there was little left, although we tried to do what we could, officially or unofficially.

XIII. THE ECONOMY OF AN AVERAGE HOUSEHOLD

Each household derived part of its income from the kolkhoz in the form of payment for labor days. On the average, men earned 250 to 300 labor days per year, women from 150 to 180 and youngsters between 50 and 60. An ordinary family would earn about 500 labor days in a year, and since the average distribution of grain in our raion at that period was a little less than a kilogram per labor day, such a family would receive about 500 kilograms of grain for its year's work. The grain would consist typically of 250 kilograms of wheat, 50 kilograms of rye, 150 kilograms of corn, and 50 kilograms of barley. Wheat bran was often substituted for part of the wheat, which somewhat reduced its value. The household would also receive 500 kilograms of potatoes from the kolkhoz, 15 centners of straw, and 400 to 500 rubles in

cash. Such was the basic income of an average household. Under the regulations of the kolkhoz this is regarded as the principal income, and what is earned from the homestead plots is regarded as entirely subsidiary. In fact, however, it was the plots which saved the majority of households from starvation.

The homestead plot of a typical household consisted of about half a hectare, of which perhaps 10 per cent would be occupied by the house and farm buildings and an equal amount by the orchard. The remainder would be planted with cereal grains, including corn, and with potatoes, hemp or flax, oil seeds, and vegetables. The homestead plot was intensively cultivated. If a peasant grew corn, he would also plant beans on the same area, and perhaps sunflowers and pumpkins as well, while on the potato plot he would plant beets, beans and other vegetables. If the household owned a cow or a calf, the area under grain would be plowed up immediately after the harvest and planted with millet; the millet did not have time to ripen, but it made a good hay which was used for fodder. Most kolkhoz members spent a great deal of time on their plots, weeding and watering late in the evening if they had no time during the day. As a result the yields obtained from their plots were considerably higher than those from the kolkhoz fields. Grain yields came to more than 20 centners per hectare, and potato yields to about 125 centners per hectare. Thus an average plot would yield from 250 to 300 kilograms of grain and about 1,500 kilograms of potatoes.

The income from this yield, however, was offset by the taxes and deliveries in kind which the households had to make to the state. (The deliveries in kind were paid for by the state, but at such low prices that they really constituted an additional tax.) Payments were as follows:

Agricultural tax.	600 rubles
Cultural tax....	50 rubles
Insurance tax...	30–50 rubles (depending on the number of buildings on the lot)
Subscription to state loan.....	150–200 rubles for each able-bodied person
Cereal grain.....	80–100 kilograms (depending on area sown)
Potatoes........	100–150 kilograms (depending on area sown)
Milk...........	250 liters (if there was a cow)
Meat...........	40 kilograms, or equivalent in money
Eggs...........	150, or equivalent in money

It should be pointed out that the figure on agricultural tax was an average for all the households on our farm, including those which were exempt from the agricultural tax because they contained no able-bodied persons and those which paid only 50 per cent because they contained very elderly people or disabled persons. Incidentally, households entitled to exemptions found it difficult to obtain them. For those households which were not entitled to such exemptions or reductions, the tax ranged from 700 to 1,000 rubles a year. There was also an additional tax of 150 rubles a year on every childless man or woman over eighteen, while couples with two children or less had to pay 50 rubles a year.

The so-called cultural tax was really only an additional income tax, and was supposed to be used locally for such things as schools, public baths and general welfare needs. In 1949, however, the sum of 22,000 rubles, which had been collected in cultural taxes by the village soviet to build us a club, was taken over by the raion administration to pay for the building of a public bath in the raion center.

The state purchased grain from the household at the rate of 8 to 10 rubles per 100 kilograms, depending upon the quality and kind of grain; this was the same price as that paid for the compulsory deliveries of the kolkhoz. Potatoes were paid for at the rate of 4 kopecks per kilogram. Since the deliveries of grain and potatoes were based on the area sown, the peasants generally tried to falsify the area that they reported. This was not easy to do in the case of grain, for there were inspections and the penalties were severe, but it was frequently done in the case of potatoes; because of the custom of sowing other crops among the potatoes, it was possible to pass off about a third of the potato plot as a general vegetable garden and thereby reduce the deliveries.

A household which owned a cow had to deliver milk to the state, but it was never able to deliver as much as was required and had to make up the rest in cash, at the rate of 3 rubles per liter, the market price. Yet for the milk that they did deliver, the state paid from 3 to 5 kopecks per liter, depending on the cream content.

Every household had to deliver meat and ·eggs. If it owned no livestock or lacked enough to meet the delivery quotas, it had to pay 8 to 10 rubles for each missing kilogram of meat and 50 to 60 kopecks for each missing egg, although for what was delivered the state paid 14 kopecks per kilogram of pork, 9 kopecks per kilogram of beef and 1.5 kopecks per egg.

In all, the average kolkhoz household received about 30 rubles from the state in exchange for ·the deliveries it was obliged to make. Against that, it had to pay monetary taxes (which averaged about 800 rubles per household), subscription to the state loan (which raised the total to at least 1,000 rubles), and the differences in the meat, milk and egg deliveries (which might mean several hundred rubles more). Non-payment of taxes was severely punished. According to the law, the tax collectors were forbidden to attach the only cow, calf or pig for non-payment of taxes, but this regulation was frequently ignored, and tax delinquents lost even their household possessions.

Since the average household received only 400 to 500 rubles in cash income from the kolkhoz, a good deal of the produce obtained from the plot or from the kolkhoz had to be sold in order to raise money for taxes. Most years it would have to sell from 150 to 200 kilograms of grain or flour, 200 to 300 kilograms of potatoes, almost all the sugar obtained in return for cultivating the kolkhoz sugar beets, and a good part of its livestock. If it owned a pig and several shoats, the household would have to sell either the pig or the shoats; if it owned chickens, almost all had to be sold, only two or three being kept for breeding during the winter.

Most of the produce was sold on the kolkhoz markets in the nearby towns, but often the peasants on our kolkhoz walked the 9 kilometers to the railroad station and sold such things as butter, milk, lard, chickens, vegetables, fruits, pies, and small cakes to the passengers on the trains. An average household earned about 1,000 rubles a year from the sale of its produce, which usually just about covered its monetary obligations to the state.

After meeting the delivery quotas and selling what it could on the market, the average family was left with about 600 kilograms of grain and 1,500 kilograms of potatoes. Further deductions had to be made from these amounts: some grain was needed for seed, some of the potatoes were needed for fodder and some of the grain had to go as a fee for milling at the kolkhoz mill. This fee was much resented by the peasants, partic-

ularly since they also had to provide the kerosene required by the motor, and they tried to get out of it by grinding their own grain with hand-operated grindstones, a time-consuming process. One man on our farm was ingenious enough to build a small windmill, which he used to grind his own grain and also that of several other households. But in 1949 the government forbade people to grind their own grain and confiscated the grindstones; the man who had built the windmill was fined 500 rubles and his mill was destroyed.

The residue left to the average family for its own consumption came to about 500 kilograms of grain and 1,000 kilograms of potatoes. The grain usually lasted the family from seven to eight months, and thereafter it was necessary to buy grain or live on potatoes and vegetables. Additional grain could be bought from the SPO in exchange for hemp, at the rate of one kilogram of hemp for 1.5 kilograms of grain and about 25 kopecks. Wheat or rye flour would be made to go further by the addition of potato flour, bran or even oil cake.

Except for the "strong" households, the consumption of meat and fats was small, perhaps 10 kilograms of meat a year and 15 kilograms of fats. Some of the meat would be bought on the market, for special holidays, and some would be obtained from pigs, chickens or rabbits owned by the households. Some meat was served in communal meals during the harvest campaigns: this might be the only meat the poorest households ate during the year. Much of the fat eaten was vegetable fat, obtained from the oil plants such as sunflower, rape and hemp grown by the peasants; many households produced no animal fats and had to buy what little they used on the market.

The basic foods of the peasants were bread, borshch, potatoes, vegetables (fresh or salt-cured), and fruit. It was a monotonous, sometimes inadequate, diet. Food supplies were often so low just before harvest that the workers' productivity during harvesting was affected.

Most clothing was homemade, and there was always a shortage of warm clothes. A man's entire wardrobe often consisted of a sweater, a pair of trousers and two or three shirts. Many peasants went barefoot in the summer; in winter they wore old shoes, galoshes or bast-shoes. I remember in November 1948 meeting two young boys on their way to school in bare feet, although the ground was already frozen. The cold was so sharp that they had to stop from time to time to sit down and warm their feet with the scarves they wore around their heads.

XIV. THE PRIVATE LIVESTOCK PROBLEM

The number of cattle belonging to individual households decreased steadily during 1948 and 1949. For example, in 1948 there were 96 cows and 12 calves owned by individual households in our kolkhoz, but a year later the number had fallen to 76 cows and 9 calves. Most of the animals had been sold, either on the market or to the kolkhoz. Some had died of disease, and one cow had been stolen.

The major reason for the sales of cattle, besides the pressure for contracting calves to the kolkhoz, was the difficulty of getting fodder. The introduction of the ten-field system of crop rotation drastically cut down the amount of grazing land, forcing the peasants to keep their cattle at home almost all year round and feed them with fodder, which was in short supply for the kolkhoz cattle and still more so for those of the households. . . .

The necessity of making milk deliv-

eries, amounting to 250 liters of a given butterfat content per year, was yet another reason for the decrease in the number of privately owned cattle. If the milk was below standard, the quantity demanded was increased, and this added expense made many peasants feel that keeping a cow was not worthwhile. Then too, the tax law stated that possession of a cow gave the owner an annual income of 2,000 rubles, a fact which raised his income tax. Still another deterrent was the acute shortage of barns or sheds to shelter the animals. . . .

Those households which were in arrears with their meat deliveries were branded as "vicious wreckers" and were subject to various forms of reprisals. There were two or three meat-delivery agents for each village, depending on its size, whose job it was to collect the deliveries and see to it that those who did not meet the quotas were criminally prosecuted. In 1948 in our village alone fourteen persons were prosecuted and four families had their property, including animals, confiscated and sold at auction to make up for insufficient deliveries. . . .

XV. WOMEN AND CHILDREN

The women of the households led a thankless life. I have said already that they formed the major working force of the kolkhoz, but they also had a multitude of tasks to do at home. Old people and children helped out with the care of the homestead plot and with the housekeeping, but a great deal of the work fell upon the wife and mother after she returned from the kolkhoz fields. The majority of raion leaders gave no thought to the problems of the farm women and considered them merely as a working force; a woman on a kolkhoz was valued not according to her beauty or charm, but according to the number of labor days she earned. This attitude even extended to marriage: in selecting a bride a man usually checked up on her labor-day record, her dowry and her strength. I heard one man tell another, "I'm marrying the letter 'K,'" which meant that his bride-to-be was named Katya and that along with her went a room, a cow, a hog, and a goat, all words which begin with "k" in Russian.

Just as the women received almost no consideration as wives and mothers, so they were given very few positions of responsibility or authority. In our raion there were sixty-two women who were candidates or members of the Party, but only a handful held jobs of any importance. There was one woman who was chairman of her local village soviet, one zoo-technician, one kolkhoz bookkeeper, and one agronomist. There were also seven women schoolteachers.

It is true that in elections for soviets of workers' deputies a definite proportion of candidates proposed had to be women (30 per cent in 1948), but if elected these women were hardly ever given any responsible work and merely served to bolster Soviet propaganda claims about the improved position of women.[17]

There was one way for kolkhoz women to receive some public recognition, and that was to have large numbers of children. The mother of ten or more children received the title of "Mother Heroine" and a small pension, while mothers of five to nine children received lesser honors. But nobody envied them this glory and heroism. A kolkhoz woman who bears and brings up seven or eight

[17] There is another category of women, usually non-Party members, who are not so closely connected with the life of the kolkhozes. They are the teachers, midwives, doctors, and commercial workers, who constitute about 50 per cent of all the people in the above-named professions in the villages and whose life is much better than that of the kolkhoz woman.

children under the conditions of the Soviet regime really has to be a heroine. Kolkhoz women heard much about the so-called "protection of motherhood," but they did not see it in practice. Pregnant women worked almost up to the time of delivery and were exempt from work for only three weeks. Each village had a lying-in home with four to six beds and a midwife in charge, but these were supported almost completely by the kolkhozes and were therefore badly equipped, lacking adequate bed-furnishings or instruments. There were, however, portraits of Party leaders on which expectant mothers could feast their eyes. Many women distrusted the lying-in homes and preferred to give birth at home, assisted only by some old woman. In our village two women died in childbirth at the lying-in home one year, and thereafter almost all the women refused the services of the midwife.

The kolkhozes had public nurseries which were supposed to look after the children while their mothers were at work, but they were very unsatisfactory. In the first place, there were no permanent quarters for the nurseries, which were often shifted around the village and set up wherever room could be found. Then too, there was hardly any proper equipment for them; the nursery on our kolkhoz, for example, had only six cribs, although the number of infants was never less than ten or a dozen. Children over a year old had no beds at all but were put to sleep on the floor. There were no toys or books. . . .

CONCLUSION

In 1949 we had an exceptionally good harvest and over-fulfilled the compulsory grain delivery plans by 23 per cent. We were written up in the raion newspaper, and my hopes ran high that, having kept the "First Commandment," I could now go ahead and replenish the various funds and issue the remaining grain to the kolkhoz members. But the day after we had completed the regular compulsory deliveries, I was called in for a personal interview with the secretary of the raion Party committee.

He began by congratulating me on over-fulfilling the plan and then asked whether I had been reading the newspapers. Of course I replied that I had. He then showed me the front page of a recent issue of *Pravda*, with a number of reports and letters to Stalin regarding the completion of grain deliveries and the assumption of commitments for supplementary deliveries. He asked how much additional grain I could deliver to the state. I said that as soon as I had filled up the reserve funds and had given the kolkhoz members an adequate recompense for their labor days, I would turn the rest over to the state. The secretary said that the state would not wait and that the grain must be handed over immediately. I offered to deliver an additional 300 centners, but he demanded 1,500 centners. We argued, and finally he threw me out of his office, saying that I would be forced to deliver the grain.

The next day I called a meeting of all the Party members of the kolkhoz and told them about the conference. The Party members, themselves peasants who were partly dependent for their living on what they earned for their labor days, were no more enthusiastic about giving up the grain than anyone else, and they also decided that no more than 300 centners should be given up. In the name of the Party organization a letter was written to the Central Committee of the Communist Party, enclosing the newspaper clipping telling of our 123 per cent fulfillment of the grain delivery plan and other documents confirming this fact and protesting against the action of the raion Party secretary.

Needless to say, the letter remained unanswered.

A couple of days later trucks arrived to carry off the additional grain. We let them take 300 centners but then turned them away. Now the fat was in the fire. We held a general meeting of the kolkhoz, at which a representative of the raion Party committee was present. I put my case to the general meeting, and the members backed me up. The raion Party representative took the floor but was hooted down and reduced to silence.

I was then summoned to an extraordinary session of the raion executive committee, at which I was told firmly that it was my responsibility to deliver to the state a further 1,000 centners of grain. I declared that the kolkhoz had no more grain and that I would not take the responsibility for further deliveries. The secretary of the raion Party committee told me that the state had not placed me in the official position of chairman of a kolkhoz to have me sow the collective farm lands like a kulak and refuse grain to the state. Since the state had put me in office, I should think first about the state—the peasants could get along without my worrying about them. Moreover, the longer I held out, the more grain I would have to give up in the end. Other threatening and intimidating speeches followed, but I stuck to my guns. In the end the raion executive committee passed a resolution to commit me for trial on the grounds that I had ignored the decisions of the Party and the state.

I got back to the kolkhoz in the middle of the night and immediately set about distributing the grain to the kolkhoz members. Even though the state was not pleased, the kolkhoz members fared better in 1949 than they had the two previous years. During the years 1947–49 there were only two kolkhozes in the raion whose members received more than one kilogram of grain and one ruble per labor day, and one of them was ours. Our figures for the three years were as follows:

Year	Total Labor Days Earned by the Kolkhoz as a Whole	Total Grain Yield (Centners)	Total Cash Income (Rubles)
1947	96,700	10,200	422,000
1948	107,400	11,720	501,000
1949	112,800	13,680	604,000

The payments in money and kind per labor day per person were as follows:

Year	Grain	Money
1947	970 grams	1 ruble 40 kopecks
1948	1.08 kilograms	1 ruble 62 kopecks
1949	1.53 kilograms	1 ruble 90 kopecks

As soon as the grain had been distributed among the kolkhoz members, I turned the management of the kolkhoz over to the deputy chairman and awaited results, which were not long in coming. At the beginning of September I received a notice from the oblast military commissariat informing me that I was being recalled to the armed forces. The chairman of the inspection committee and the bookkeeper took a substantial bribe to the chief of the commissariat, but he said that he could do nothing about the order. The kolkhoz members knew that I was being relieved of my post because I had been uncooperative and disobedient to the Party officials. For myself, I was happy that it was no worse and was not sorry to be relieved of the job before more serious things befell me.

50

A DAY IN MAGNITOGORSK

By John Scott; Valentin Katayev

Despite the appalling conditions of living and work which he describes here, the author, who worked in Magnitogorsk for five years, makes clear the general enthusiasm of the workers whom he observed. The goals of industrialization had captured the imagination of the Soviet population. Scott says something about himself in his Introduction; at present he is an assistant to the editor of *Time* and still pays periodic visits to the Soviet Union. The book is dedicated to his Soviet wife Masha. The Soviet novelist Valentin Katayev first went to Magnitogorsk at the same time as Scott. Out of his visit came his most famous novel, available in English as *Time Forward* (1932). He revisited the city in 1966 and wrote the piece which we reprint.

For other recollections of the fervor of the first Five-Year Plan see chapter 33 of Ilia Ehrenburg's *Memoirs: 1921–1941* (paperback); Louis Fischer, *Machines and Men in Russia*; G. F. Grinko, *The Five Year Plan;* Maurice Hindus, *The Great Offensive;* and Michael Farbman, *Russia's Five Year Plan.* For studies on bourgeois specialists and Red Directors see Jeremy Azrael, *Managerial Power and Soviet Politics;* Simon Liberman, *Building Lenin's Russia*; Lubov Krassin. *Leonid Krassin: His Life and Work;* Vladimir Ipatieff, *The Life of a Chemist;* and the Soviet work by Vasilii Prokofieff, *Industrial and Technical Intelligentsia in the USSR,* as well as the article "Captains of Soviet Industry, 1926–1940," *Soviet Studies in History,* Winter, 1966–67. See also the relevant chapters of Merle Fainsod, *Smolensk under Soviet Rule* (paperback). For descriptions of Magnitogorsk today see Franklyn Holzman, "The Soviet Ural-Kuznetsk Combine," *Quarterly Journal of Economics,* August, 1957, and M. Gardner Clark, "Magnitogorsk," *Focus on Geographic Activity,* 1964, pp. 128–34, as well as the latter's book *The Economics of Soviet Steel.* For a description of industrial construction much farther East in the 1960's see Fedor Hayenko, "Living and Working Conditions at the New Construction Sites," *Studies on the Soviet Union,* 1965, No. 1. A new monograph on Soviet economic development in the East is *Beyond the Urals* by Violet Conolly.

From John Scott, *Behind the Urals* (Cambridge, Mass.: The Riverside Press, 1942), pp. 3–51. The piece by Valentin Katayev is from *Moscow News,* June 18, 1966, p. 12.

AUTHOR'S INTRODUCTION

I left the University of Wisconsin in 1931 to find myself in an America sadly dislocated, an America offering few opportunities for young energy and enthusiasm.

I was smitten with the usual wanderlust. The United States did not seem adequate. I decided to go somewhere else. I had already been in Europe three times. Now I projected more far-flung excursions. Plans for a motorcycle trip to Alaska, thence by home-made sailboat to Siberia and China came to naught. Where would I get the money to finance the project, and what would I do in China? I looked around New York for a job instead. There were no jobs to be had.

Something seemed to be wrong with America. I began to read extensively about the Soviet Union, and gradually came to the conclusion that the Bolsheviks had found answers to at least some of the questions Americans were asking each other. I decided to go to Russia to work, study, and to lend a hand in the construction of a society which seemed to be at least one step ahead of the American.

Following wise parental counsel I learned a trade before going to Russia. I went to work as welders' apprentice in the General Electric plant in Schenectady, and several months later received a welder's certificate. Armed with this, with credentials from the Metal Workers' Union of which I was an active member, and with letters from several personal friends, I set off for Berlin, where I applied for a Soviet visa.

For some five weeks I lived with friends in Wedding, went to Communist demonstrations, and attended numerous turbulent political meetings organized by several parties. Things were bad in Germany. It was shocking to see thousands of able-bodied men living with their families in the 'Laubenkolonien,' the German Hoovervilles, while block after block of apartment houses in Berlin where they had previously lived stood empty. Such things, I felt sure, did not happen in the Soviet Union.

In due course of time Soviet consular wheels ground out my visa and I entrained for Moscow. For ten days I bounced back and forth between several Soviet organizations, trying to make arrangements for a job. The welding trust was glad to give me work. They needed welders in many places. They were not able to sign me up, however, until the visa department had given me permission to remain in the Soviet Union as a worker. The latter organization could grant such permission only to people with jobs. Neither would put anything in writing.

Finally arrangements were completed, and I started out on the four-day train trip to a place called Magnitogorsk on the eastern slopes of the Ural Mountains.

I was very happy. There was no unemployment in the Soviet Union. The Bolsheviks planned their economy and gave opportunities to young men and women. Furthermore, they had got away from the fetishization of material possessions, which, my good parents had taught me, was one of the basic ills of our American civilization. I saw that most Russians ate only black bread, wore one suit until it disintegrated, and used old newspapers for writing letters and office memoranda, rolling cigarettes, making envelopes, and for various personal functions.

I was about to participate in the construction of this society. I was going to be one of many who cared not to own a second pair of shoes, but who built blast furnaces which were their own. It was September, 1932, and I was twenty years old.

A DAY IN MAGNITOGORSK

The big whistle on the power house sounded a long, deep, hollow six o'clock. All over the scattered city-camp of Magnitogorsk, workers rolled out of their beds or bunks and dressed in preparation for their day's work.

I climbed out of bed and turned on the light. I could see my breath across the room as I woke my roommate, Kolya. Kolya never heard the whistle. Every morning I had to pound his shoulder for several seconds to arouse him.

We pushed our coarse brown army blankets over the beds and dressed as quickly as we could—I had good American long woolen underwear, fortunately; Kolya wore only cotton shorts and a jersey. We both donned army shirts, padded and quilted cotton pants, similar jackets, heavy scarves, and then ragged sheepskin coats. We thrust our feet into good Russian 'valinkis'—felt boots coming up to the knee. We did not eat anything. We had nothing on hand except tea and a few potatoes, and there was no time to light a fire in our little homemade iron stove. We locked up and set out for the mill.

It was January, 1933. The temperature was in the neighborhood of thirty-five below. A light powdery snow covered the low spots on the ground. The high spots were bare and hard as iron. A few stars crackled in the sky and some electric lights twinkled on the blast furnaces. Otherwise the world was bleak and cold and almost pitch-dark.

It was two miles to the blast furnaces, over rough ground. There was no wind, so our noses did not freeze. I was always glad when there was no wind in the morning. It was my first winter in Russia and I was not used to the cold.

Down beside the foundation of Blast Furnace No. 4 there was a wooden shanty. It was a simple clapboard structure with a corrugated-iron roof nailed on at random. Its one big room was dominated by an enormous welded iron stove placed equidistant from all the walls, on a plate of half-inch steel. It was not more than half-past six when Kolya and I walked briskly up to the door and pushed it open. The room was cold and dark. Kolya fumbled around for a moment for the switch and then turned on the light. It was a big five-hundred-watt bulb hanging from the ceiling and it illuminated every corner of the bare room. There were makeshift wooden benches around the walls, a battered table, and two three-legged stools stood in a corner. A half-open door opposite the entrance showed a tremendous closet whose walls were decorated with acetylene torches, hose, wrenches, and other equipment. The floor of the closet was littered with electrodes, carbide generators, and dirt. The walls were bare except for two cockeyed windows and a wall telephone. Kolya, the welders' foreman, was twenty-two, big-boned, and broad. There was not much meat on him, and his face had a cadaverous look which was rather common in Magnitogorsk in 1933. His unkempt, sawdust-colored hair was very long, and showed under his fur hat. The sheepskin coat which he wore was ragged from crawling through narrow pipes and worming his way into various odd corners. At every tear the wool came through on the outside and looked like a Polish customs officer's mustache. His hands were calloused and dirty; the soles of the valinkis on his feet were none too good. His face and his demeanor were extremely energetic. . . .

The door opened and two besheepskinned figures entered the room. 'All right, you guys, how about a fire?' said Kolya, without looking up. 'We can't heat this whole room by electricity.'

The two riggers pulled their scarves down from around their noses, took off their gloves, and rubbed the frost from their eyelashes. 'Cold,' said one to the the other. They approached the electric stove, produced rolls of dirty newspaper and a sack of 'Makhorka,' a very cheap grade of tobacco, and rolled themselves newspaper cigarettes as big as Havana cigars. I rolled one too and we lit them from the stove. The riggers were young-ish and had not shaved for several days. Their blue peasant eyes were clear and simple, but their foreheads and cheeks were scarred with frostbite, their hands dirty and gnarled. The door opened again admitting a bearded man of fifty-odd, so tall that he had to stoop to enter. 'Good morning, comrades,' he boomed good-naturedly. . . .

Workers came, one after the other now, and gathered around to warm their cold hands, faces, and feet. At about six-forty, Ivanov, the riggers' foreman, came in, shook hands with Kolya, and picked up the telephone receiver. He was a broad-shouldered, middle-aged man with a deeply lined face and a quizzical expression around the corners of his mouth. He was a Pole and a party member who had fought three years in the Red Army and worked on bridge construction jobs from Warsaw to Irkutsk. After an unsuccessful attempt to call the storehouse and try to get some bolts he needed, Ivanov hung up and took Kolya by the arm. 'Come on, let's look the job over,' he said. The two foremen left the shanty together, Ivanov tucking a roll of blueprints into his pocket and swearing good-naturedly at the cold, the storehouse manager, the foreigners who projected structural steel with inch-and-a-half bolts, and the tele-phone operator.

In the meantime, the iron stove was nearly red-hot, and the men gathered round in an ever-widening circle, smok-ing and talking. . . .

At this point a young, boisterous, ath-letic-looking burner burst into the room and pushed his way up to the stove. 'Boy, is it cold!' he said, addressing everybody in the room. 'I don't think we should work up on top today. One of the riveters froze to death up there last night. It seems he was off in a bleeder pipe and they didn't find him till this morning.'

'Yeah?' said everybody at once. 'Who was it?'

But nobody knew who it was. It was just one of the thousands of peasants and young workers who had come to Magnitogorsk for a bread card, or be-cause things were tough in the newly collectivized villages, or fired with en-thusiasm for Socialist construction.

II

I was more or less warmed up by this time, so I pulled my scarf up around my face and went out after the two fore-men. They had ascended a rickety wood-en ladder and were walking along the blast-furnace foundation, looking at the tons and tons of structural steel in process of erection on all sides. Over their heads was a ten-foot diameter gas pipe, one section of which was not yet in place. To their left was the enormous conical bosch of the fourth blast fur-nace. They walked past this, and down through the cast house toward No. 3. A few dim bulbs cast a gray dawn around the job. Several scurrying figures could be seen—bricklayers, laborers, mechan-ics, electricians—getting things lined up for the day's work. I caught up with them and the three of us climbed up to the top of No. 3. We found a little group of riveters standing silently around a shapeless form lying on the wooden scaffold. We discovered that it was the frozen riveter, and having ascertained that a stretcher had already been sent for to take the body down, we went on to the very top to look over the coming day's work. . . .

By the time the seven o'clock whistle blew, the shanty was jammed full of riggers, welders, cutters, and their helpers. It was a varied gang, Russians, Ukrainians, Tartars, Mongols, Jews, mostly young and almost all peasants of yesterday, though a few, like Ivanov, had long industrial experience. There was Popov, for instance. He had been a welder for ten years and had worked in half a dozen cities. On the other hand, Khaibulin, the Tartar, had never seen a staircase, a locomotive, or an electric light until he had come to Magnitogorsk a year before. His ancestors for centuries had raised stock on the flat plains of Kazakhstan. They had been dimly conscious of the Tsarist government; they had had to pay taxes. Reports of the Kirghiz insurrection in 1916 had reached them. They had heard stories of the October Revolution; they even saw the Red Army come and drive out a few rich landlords. They had attended meetings of the soviet, without understanding very clearly what it was all about, but through all this their lives had gone on more or less as before. Now Shaimat Khaibulin was building a blast furnace bigger than any in Europe. He had learned to read and was attending an evening school, learning the trade of electrician. He had learned to speak Russian, he read newspapers. His life had changed more in a year than that of his antecedents since the time of Tamerlane. . . .

The foremen gathered around the table. The telephone rang incessantly—a welder was wanted at the blowing station, two of the riggers in the gang working on the open-hearth gas line had not come to work. The gang could not hoist the next section of pipe short-handed. Ivanov swore at the absentees,

their mothers, and grandmothers. Then he went out to borrow two men from another gang. Kolya wrote out a list of the welders and what they were doing. He wrote it on newspaper. The ink was a semi-frozen slush. This list formed the basis on which the workers would get paid for the day's work. He thrust it into his pocket and went to the clean gas line to see how things were going. I took my mask and electrodes and started out for No. 3. On the way I met Shabkov, the ex-kulak; a great husky youth with a red face, a jovial voice, and two fingers missing from his left hand.

'Well, Jack, how goes it?' he said, slapping me on the back. My Russian was still pretty bad, but I could carry on a simple conversation and understood almost everything that was said.

'Badly,' I said. 'All our equipment freezes. The boys spend half their time warming their hands.'

'Nichevo, that doesn't matter,' said the disfranchised rigger's brigadier. 'If you lived where I do, in a tent, you wouldn't think it so cold here.'

'I know you guys have it tough,' said Popov, who had joined us. 'That's what you get for being kulaks.'

Shabkov smiled broadly. 'Listen, I don't want to go into a political discussion, but a lot of the people living down in the "special" section of town are no more kulaks than you.'

Popov laughed. 'I wouldn't be surprised. Tell me, though. How did they decide who was to be dekulakized?'

'Ah,' said Shabkov, 'that's a hell of a question to ask a guy that's trying to expiate his crimes in honest labor. Just between the three of us, though, the poor peasants of the village get together in a meeting and decide: "So-and-so has six horses; we couldn't very well get along without those in the collective farm; besides he hired a man last year to help on the harvest." They notify the GPU, and there you are. So-and-so gets five years. They confiscate his property and give it to the new collective farm. Sometimes they ship the whole family out. When they came to ship us out, my brother got a rifle and fired several shots at the GPU officers. They fired back. My brother was killed. All of which, naturally, didn't make it any better for us. We all got five years, and in different places. I heard my father died in December, but I'm not sure.'

Shabkov got out his canvas tobacco pouch and a roll of newspaper, and thrust both toward Popov. 'Kulak smoke?' He smiled grimly.

Popov availed himself of the opportunity and rolled a cigarette.

'Da. A lot of things happen that we don't hear much about. But then, after all, look at what we're doing. In a few years now we'll be ahead of everybody industrially. We'll all have automobiles and there won't be any differentiation between kulaks and anybody else.' Popov swept his arm dramatically in the direction of the towering blast furnace. Then he turned to Shabkov. 'Are you literate?'

'Yes,' said Shabkov, 'I studied three years. I even learned a little algebra. But now, what the hell! Even if I were really well-educated, they wouldn't let me do any other work but this. What's the use of me studying? Anyhow, they won't even let me into any but an elementary school. When I get home from work I want to raise my elbow and have a good time.' Shabkov touched his throat with his index finger, to any Russian a symbol of getting drunk. We arrived at No. 3. Shabkov swung onto a ladder and disappeared up into the steel. Popov looked after him with wrinkled forehead. Shabkov was one of the best brigadiers in the whole outfit. He spared neither himself nor those un-

der him, and he used his head. And yet he was a kulak, serving a sentence, living in a section of town under the surveillance of the GPU, a class enemy. Funny business, that. Popov didn't thoroughly understand it. . . .

III

It was just about nine-fifteen when I finished one side of the pipe and went around to start the other. The scaffold was coated with about an inch of ice, like everything else around the furnaces. The vapor rising from the large hot-water cooling basin condensed on everything and formed a layer of ice. But besides being slippery, it was very insecure, swung down on wires, without any guys to steady it. It swayed and shook as I walked on it. I always made a point of hanging on to something when I could. I was just going to start welding when I heard someone sing out, and something swished down past me. It was a rigger who had been working up on the very top.

He bounced off the bleeder pipe, which probably saved his life. Instead of falling all the way to the ground, he landed on the main platform about fifteen feet below me. By the time I got down to him, blood was coming out of his mouth in gushes. He tried to yell, but could not. There were no foremen around, and the half-dozen riggers that had run up did not know what to do. By virtue of being a foreigner I had a certain amount of authority, so I stepped in and said he might bleed to death if we waited for a stretcher, and three of us took him and carried him down to the first-aid station. About halfway there the bleeding let up and he began to yell every step we took. . . .

The rigger was gurgling and groaning. His eyes were wide open and he seemed conscious, but he did not say anything. 'We should undress him, but it is so cold in here that I'm afraid to,' said the nurse. Just then the doctor came in. I knew him. He had dressed my foot once when a piece of pig iron fell on it. He took his immense sheepskin off and washed his hands. 'Fall?' he asked, nodding at the rigger.

'Yes,' I said.

'How long ago?'

'About ten minutes.'

'What's that?' asked the doctor, looking at the nurse and indicating the corner of the room with his foot. I looked and for the first time noticed a pair of ragged valinkis sticking out from under a very dirty blanket on the floor.

'Girder fell on his head,' said the nurse.

'Well,' said the doctor, rolling up his sleeves, 'let's see what we can do for this fellow.' He moved over toward the rigger, who was lying quietly now and looking at the old bearded doctor with watery blue eyes. I turned to go, but the doctor stopped me.

'On your way out, please telephone the factory board of health and tell them I simply must have more heat in this place,' he said.

I did the best I could over the telephone in my bad Russian, but all I could get was, 'Comrade, we are sorry, but there is no coal. . . .'

IV

At about ten o'clock a group assembled in the wooden shanty, far different from that which had been there three hours before. First Syemichkin, the superintendent, arrived. Then came Mr. Harris, the American specialist consultant, with his interpreter; then Tishenko, the burly, sinister prisoner specialist.[1] They came into the shanty one by one, unbuttoned their coats, warmed their hands, then set to talking over their blueprints. Mr. Harris produced a package of fat 'Kuzbas' cigarettes from the special foreigners' store. He passed

them around with a smile. No one refused. Kolya, who had just come in, got in on it too.

'Well,' said Mr. Harris, through his taciturn interpreter, 'when do you expect to get the rest of the riveting done up on top of No. 3? They were telling me about this new time limit. The whole top is to be finished by the twenty-fifth. That's ten days.'

Tishenko, the chief engineer, convicted of sabotage in the Ramzin trial in 1929, sentenced to be shot, sentence commuted, now serving ten years in Magnitogorsk, shrugged his shoulders. He did not speak immediately. He was not a wordy man. He had been responsible engineer for a Belgian company in the Ukraine before the Revolution. He had had a house of his own, played tennis with the British consul, sent his son to Paris to study music. Now he was old. His hair was white. He had heard a great deal of talk since 1917, and had decided that most of it was worthless. He did his job, systematically, without enthusiasm. He liked to think that he was helping to build a strong Russia where life would one day be better than it was for his son in Paris or his sister in London. It certainly wasn't yet, though.

Mr. Harris looked at Tishenko. He understood the older man's position and respected his silence. Still, he was a consulting engineer being paid good American dollars, being supplied with caviar in a country where there was little bread and no sugar, to push Magnitostroi through to completion on time. He pressed the point. And Tishenko finally answered slowly: 'A riveter froze

---

[1] Prisoner specialists: a group of several thousand eminent engineers and scientists convicted of various anti-Soviet activities in the late twenties and exiled to outlying industrial and construction towns where they held responsible technical and administrative posts.

to death last night. Cold and malnutrition. This morning four of the girls we have heating rivets didn't show up. Two of them are pregnant, I think, and it's cold up there. The compressor is working badly.' He stopped, realizing it was all beside the point. If he said that the job would be finished by the twenty-fifth he was a liar and a hypocrite and Mr. Harris would be perfectly aware of it. If he said that it would take longer, he was sabotaging the decision of the Commissar of Heavy Industry. He was already under sentence for sabotage. He looked out of the dusty window. 'It'll take at least a month,' he said. . . .

Syemichkin looked on. His attitude was partly one of respect, partly disdain. These 'bourzhies' didn't understand Bolshevik tempo. They didn't understand the working class. They did understand blast furnaces, though, much better than he. They had had years of experience building steel mills in several different countries, whereas he, Syemichkin, had graduated only a year ago, after a rather superficial course in engineering. When it came to questions like the construction of the tuyer zone, or the situation of the water jackets, both of these men knew by heart how every large blast furnace in the world was put together. He, Syemichkin, knew vaguely where Berlin was, knew that Paris was somewhere beyond.

The door opened and Shevchenko came in. Shevchenko was the great activist among the technical personnel. He was called engineer by his subordinates. Actually he was a graduate of the Institute of Red Directors, had been in the party since 1923, had been trade-union organizer, party functionary, director of a large Donbas construction job. His technical knowledge was limited, and his written Russian contained many mistakes. His present job was sectional

assistant director of construction. He was responsible to the director and to the party for the fulfillment of construction plans. . . .

'Have you seen the new order?' said Shevchenko belligerently, advancing toward the table and shaking hands casually with Harris and Tishenko.

'Da,' said Mr. Harris, who had understood the Russian without the aid of his interpreter.

'Well?' Shevchenko looked from one to the other.

Syemichkin, Kolya, and I listened with great interest. We all realized that Shevchenko was a boor and a careerist. But it seemed to take people like that to push the job forward, to overcome the numerous difficulties, to get the workers to work in spite of cold, bad tools, lack of materials, and undernourishment. It took all types to make Magnitogorsk. That was clear. And Syemichkin, realizing full well his limitations, was content for the moment to draw his five hundred roubles a month, fulfill his more or less mechanical functions as superintendent, and watch how those above and below him worked. Kolya was a tough foreman, trying to become an engineer, trying to build Socialist blast furnaces quickly. I was a stray American, dropped in Magnitogorsk as an electric welder through a series of accidents.

Mr. Harris was jotting down figures on a piece of paper. He beckoned to Shevchenko and began reading a list of materials necessary for the completion of the top of No. 3, none of which were available.

'Now, Mr. Shevchenko,' said the American, 'orders are orders, but you can't rivet steel with them and you can't heat rivets with them. We must have these things or the job won't be finished by next Christmas. You're an influential man in the party and with the construction administration. It's up to you to get these materials.'

Shevchenko knew that this was sound. However, Harris's remark created a situation in which it appeared that he, Shevchenko, was the one who was not doing his job as he should. This would not do. The assistant director launched into a long tirade. He quoted Marx and Stalin, referred to the records of the Ramzin group, to foreign agents and to opportunism. 'Surrounded as we are by hostile capitalist nations, we are forced to industrialize our great country in the shortest possible time, leaving no stone unturned, sparing no one. Magnitogorsk is the most important single heavy industry center in the Soviet Union. Millions of roubles have been invested, thousands of workers have come from far and wide. The country is waiting for our iron and steel. Here we have assembled all the materials and equipment for two new blast furnaces. They must be erected and blown in at the earliest possible date, and yet if I were to believe you I would be forced to think that the whole job must be held up for lack of a few rivets. You, Tishenko, you have thirty years of industrial experience, and you sit there and do nothing. Haven't you got ingenuity enough to think up some way to keep the job going, some way to surmount these obstacles? Or perhaps you're not interested. Perhaps you remain unconvinced by the last fifteen years.'

Shevchenko's rhetoric carried him away. His face was flushed, his arm extended. Then, having asserted himself, having placed the party line before the old wrecker and the foreign specialist, thus acquitting himself of his obvious political obligation under the circumstances, he took one of Mr. Harris's cigarettes, drew a stool up to the table, and proceeded to look over the list of materials that the American had made

out. There was no question about it, of course; no amount of proletarian enthusiasm, no speeches, could take the place of the inch-and-a-half rivets. Shevchenko picked up the telephone. He called the storehouse director, the director of supplies of the whole combinat, finally he called a personal friend of his who worked in the rolling mill. He talked in a low, friendly voice. There was mention of a couple of drinks the next night. Then a casual allusion to inch-and-a-half rivets. When he hung up, Shevchenko grunted, 'I think we'll get the rivets.'

The four men, as heterogeneous a group as one could find—a Cleveland engineer, a prisoner specialist, a Red director, and a young, inexperienced Soviet engineer—sat down around the table to discuss the rest of the points on Mr. Harris's list.

V

At eleven o'clock a whistle blew and the workers descended from truss and girder, roof and pipe, to go to lunch. I looked enviously at the overhead bead Popov had been laying in the bleeder pipe..It was as nearly perfect as I ever saw. Popov was a crackerjack structural steel welder, as good as or better than any of the men I had learned from in the General Electric plant in Schenectady. . . .

Both Shabkov and Popov were comparatively well-dressed. Their leather gloves, while they had some holes burned in them, were still sound. They wore valinkis coming up to their knees, long sheepskin coats with the wool inside, leather fur-trimmed hats, and woolen scarves. The two riggers who had been working on the ground, however, were not so well off. One wore ragged leather shoes instead of felt boots, and anyone who has been in a cold climate knows of the torture of leather shoes. The other wore felt boots, the soles of which were coming off. He had tied them on with a piece of wire, but the 'portyankis' or rags which he had wrapped around his feet in place of stockings showed through in two places. Their sheepskins were ragged and burned, their gloves were almost palmless. They were young recruits from the village who had not yet learned to be real steel workers and therefore got the left-overs in clothes. Shabkov clapped one of them on the back.

'Well, Grishka, want to come up this afternoon and try working high? If you get dizzy you can go down again. Misha here needs somebody to line up the flange of that expansion joint while he's tacking it.'

Grisha's chest swelled. He had been waiting for this opportunity for some time. 'What do you mean get dizzy? Of course I'll go up. Only, listen, how about some felt boots? It's cold up there.'

'I know,' said Shabkov, 'I told the foreman about you and I'll tell him again. But if there aren't any boots in the storehouse, what can I do?'

'But we have to get them,' said the young rigger, with an oath. 'It's in the collective agreement. I read it myself.'

Nobody answered. Everyone had either read the collective agreement himself or heard others read it aloud, but, as Shabkov said, if there were no boots, what could one do? The other rigger said nothing. He was a little afraid that the brigadier would suggest that he work high. At the moment he was interested in staying on the ground. He had become accustomed to stairs and short ladders, but climbing a sixty-foot steel column to work on a pipe set up on top of it, walking on these suspended wooden scaffoldings that swayed and shook—no, no. It was much better on the ground turning the crank of the hand-hoist, even if he had only third

category and made one hundred and twenty roubles a month, while the riggers that worked high generally got fourth and made up to two hundred.

We crossed numerous railroad lines, passed in front of Blast Furnace No. 2, which was already in operation, and after climbing over piles of structural steel, unfinished foundations, and mounds of earth, approached a long low wooden building toward which workers were streaming from every direction. Over the door there was a sign: 'Dining-Room No. 30.'

'How many cards have you got?' Popov asked Shabkov in a low voice. 'Oh, that's right, you're a "special" ' (by which he meant a disfranchised kulak), 'you have only one.'

Shabkov grinned. He had two. Ivanov, the foreman, had given him an extra one for the simple reason that in his opinion an extra dinner invested in Shabkov produced a maximum of return in units of labor. . . .

The dining-room was jammed full. The long bare wooden tables were surrounded by workers, and behind almost every seated client somebody was waiting. There was much noise and confusion. Young waitresses ran around the room carrying large wooden trays with plates of soup and large chunks of bread on them. It was cold in the dining-room; one could see one's breath before one's face; but it was so much warmer than outside that everybody unbuttoned his sheepskin and rolled his hat up from around his ears. At the doorway a burly Tartar examined the cards of those who entered and gave a wooden spoon to each.

The cards themselves were simple affairs, printed on very poor quality brown paper. 'Dining-Room No. 30' was stamped on each and there were numbers from 1 to 31 around the edge of the card. These numbers were torn off by the waitresses before they served the meal. One card entitled the owner to one meal per day for the month. Shabkov and I shouldered our way to a far corner, found a table where the meal had already been served and took up our stations behind two bricklayers who were eating.

'Doesn't look bad,' said Popov, sniffing, 'if they'd only give us more bread. Two hundred grams[2] isn't enough.'

'I understand they get three hundred grams in the engineers' dining-room next door,' said Shabkov, wiping his spoon on the inside of his sheepskin. 'Were you ever in there?'

'Yeah, once,' answered Popov. 'Kolya lent me his card. The meals aren't much different from ours, only you don't have to wait so long and there isn't so much of a crowd. The soup is just the same, I think.'

We were joined by other workers waiting for a free space, and before we sat down there were others waiting behind us for our places when we should have finished.

'I understand a bricklayer fell down on the inside of the swirlers yesterday,' said a rigger to Popov.

'Yes, so they say,' he answered. 'It's time the safety-first trust got to work and enforced some of these fancy regulations.'

There was talk like this every day, but the safety-first organization was not in a position to take effective steps in the direction of cutting down accidents. There were three main factors: in the first place, the inexperience of the workers and their childish lack of understanding of danger; in the second place, lack of sufficient lumber to make the necessary scaffoldings, ladders with railings, etc.; and in the third place, a shortage of electric light bulbs, which meant that workers working high on the inside of pipes or stacks, and on the

outside in the early morning and late afternoon, had to work in the dark. In all of these three cases the safety-first organization was powerless. There was not enough lumber and when some did arrive it went to more essential things than to scaffolding, or else disappeared into the stoves of workers' rooms. As for the electric light bulbs, in December something had happened at the big substation and three hundred and eighty volts had gone into all the lighting lines instead of two hundred and twenty. Every bulb turned on at the time was burned out, and there was no reserve supply.

About half an hour after entering the building, we seated ourselves on newly vacated stools, put our cards on the table, and waited for the waitress to come. She was halfway down the room serving another table, swearing good-naturedly at the workers for trying to get two meals on one card and occasionally getting her behind pinched. It was ten minutes before she arrived at the end table and began tearing off our cards. Shabkov and Popov, each having two cards, were hard put to it distracting her attention so that she would not realize there were more cards than people at the table. It did not work, however. After having torn off twelve numbers she counted and saw that there were only ten at the table. Popov saved the situation. 'Oh, yeah,' he said, 'that's Petya and Grisha left their cards and went down to wash their hands.' Popov grinned. The waitress grinned too. No one ever washed his hands in the winter in Dining-Room No. 30. However, she had witnesses, so that if the director checked up, which was highly improbable, she had an excuse. She dashed off smiling and returned shortly with twelve large lumps of black bread. On the next trip she brought twelve plates

[2] Half pound.

of hot soup. It wasn't bad soup. There was some cabbage in it, traces of potatoes and buckwheat, and an occasional bone. It was hot, that was the main thing. The workers ate with relish, some of them having put mustard in it for flavor. Most of them had eaten all their bread before the soup was gone. Shabkov and Popov, however, had two pieces each (two pieces of two hundred grams each make just one pound of black bread), so that theirs lasted through till the end of their soup and they even had some left to eat with their second course. The latter consisted of a soup-plate filled with potatoes covered with thin gravy and a small piece of meat on top. Having brought these, the waitress went on to the next table. . . .

When we got back to the job, it was twelve-thirty according to the wooden clock in the compressor house. We had spent only fifteen or twenty minutes in actual eating, but had lost an hour and a half of working time. Bad organization again. The director knew it, the trade union and party functionaries knew it. But it was another story to remedy the situation. Thousands of workers had to be fed. There were not enough dining-rooms, or tables, or stools, or spoons, or food itself. Three years later increasing food supply made possible the liquidation of the card system, much better meals, and less lost time; but in 1932 and 1933 the situation was bad and no one seemed able to do anything to improve it.

VI

The trade-union organizer pasted a piece of newspaper on the shanty door. An announcement was painted on it in misspelled Russian: 'Meeting—election of new shop committee chairman—five o'clock in the Red Corner. Attendance obligatory.' Most of the gang had seen this, but there was little interest. The shop committee had little significance to most of the workers. It organized poorly attended meetings, addressed by trade-union functionaries who talked on the building program of Magnitogorsk, the second Five Year Plan, the international situation. Also when the workers had been sick or hurt they took their clinic slips to the chairman to be O.K.'d. That was all. The administration meant a good deal to the workers. It hired and fired, gave them their orders, paid their wages. The party meant a good deal too. You could get a room through the party, get a new job, lodge complaints, or make suggestions with some assurance that they would get attention. The shop committee, however, did none of these things, and the election of a new chairman aroused no interest for most of the riggers, cutters, and welders who saw the announcement. Thus it was that at five o'clock in the Red Corner the old chairman, who was being transferred to different work, and two members of the shop committee stood around smoking and watching the door. One worker came, two, five—but no more.

'This is a hell of a note,' said the old chairman, a nervous, slick-looking, middle-aged fellow, with an expensive black sealskin hat. 'I put up the announcements all over the place. I don't know why more people didn't come.' A tall, youngish fellow with a scar on his mouth, standing near by, shrugged his shoulders. He was the one who had been sent by the district trade-union committee to be the new chairman of the blast furnace construction workers' shop committee. It did not look promising, this; when only five workers came to the elections. He made a remark to this effect to the colleague whom he was replacing. 'You seem to have done a hell of a lot of social work here. What are we going to do? I can't be elected by a meeting of five in an organization of eighteen hundred workers. And you have to leave tomorrow for your new job.' The new chairman was distressed by this formal dilemma. The others were not, however.

'Nuts,' said one of the members of the shop committee. 'Don't get upset. It's just a formality, after all, this election. We'll put you through at the next meeting, and in the meantime you can begin functioning normally. It is not so good that we couldn't get more out to the meeting than this, though.'

The reasons why the workers did not come to the meeting were pretty obvious to anyone who was looking for them. In the first place, the shop committee was almost dead. It did nothing to help defend workers against bureaucratic and over-enthusiastic administrators, and to assure the enforcement of the labor laws. For instance, most of the skilled welders on the job were working two shifts a day regularly, because there were not enough of them, and the work had to be done. This was distinctly against the law, but the shop committee did nothing at all. How could they buck Shevchenko and hinder the work by taking the welders off the job? Everywhere it was the same. Then in the matter of the elections themselves, things were bad too. The chairman of the shop committee theoretically was supposed to be one of the workers in the shop, elected by his shopmates as the one in the outfit most able and competent to represent the interests of the workers. Actually it had become the custom for the district committee to send a man, a professional trade-union functionary, trained in the representation of the interests of the workers, whose arrival was registered by an 'election.' Actually the election meant nothing, as there was only one candidate, and he was sent from a higher body. Any open criticism made by a worker of this state of

affairs would have been fruitless.

The authority of the trade unions was at a low ebb. Later, in 1934 and 1935, the trade unions reorganized their work and began to carry on activities which won back the respect and support of some of the workers. They did this by building rest homes, insisting on the observance of labor laws, even if it meant that the jobs suffered for the time being, giving out theater tickets, organizing schools and courses of all kinds, and sending workers and their wives and children to sanitariums.

VII

I left the meeting and joined Popov and several other welders who were turning their steps toward home. . . .

As we left the construction site, each of us gathered a little bundle of firewood. When possible we took scraps that were no good to the job anyway; when we could not find these, however, we split up planks and ties, anything that came to hand. We had to be warm in the barracks and the supply organization had no coal.

Before leaving the territory of the plant, we had to go around the guard, whose job it was to prevent wood from being stolen. He was an old partisan, with a rifle which might shoot, so we had to make a wide detour. According to a new law stealing Socialist property was a capital crime, and while everyone took wood home, it might just be someone's ill luck to be made an example of. We saw the old guard with his enormous sheepskin and long rifle silhouetted against the sky, but he didn't see us. . . .

Two of the welders took the wood from the whole group and started off toward the barracks while the rest of us went to the store to get bread and anything else which might be obtainable.

The blast-furnace construction workers' cooperative was a large one-story affair, almost unheated and very dirty. As we came near we saw that it was jammed full of workers and that there was a line outside the door.

'Funny,' said Popov, 'they must be giving out something special.'

We approached and asked the well-worn Russian question: 'Chto daioot?' ('What are they giving?')

'Only bread,' answered a worker who was standing in line. 'There wasn't any this morning. It just came in half an hour ago.'

We got in line. The line moved forward slowly. It was ten minutes before we got inside the door and twenty more by the time we arrived at the counter. The shelves behind the counter were absolutely bare save for four boxes of artificial coffee and a display of perfume. The only thing being sold was black bread. A salesgirl was cutting steaming fresh loaves with a cleaver. She seldom had to put a piece on the scales twice. A store clerk with a dirty white apron over his sheepskin was tearing off the numbers on the workers' bread cards as they handed them to him. A second girl took in the money, thirty-five kopeks per kilogram (about fifteen kopeks a pound). Just when Popov reached the counter, a tall fellow with Mongolian features shouldered up and tried to get his bread out of line. There was a storm of protest.

'If you're a foreman, go to the foremen's store! If you are attached to this store, then get in line!' said forty people at once. The big Mongolian protested and expostulated phrases in broken Russian about the rights of national minorities. He did not get his bread out of line, however. Too many workers of the minor nationalities had been trying to get things for nothing, or out of line, or to obtain other privileges on the basis of the Leninist national policy. It no longer worked.

Popov took out a ragged pocketbook and hunted for change to pay for the bread. The pocketbook was full of money. He had over two hundred roubles.[3] He had received his last month's pay the week before, only ten days late, and there was nothing to buy. He got bread for himself and for Grisha, who had gone to the milk station and Grisha's wife, and then shouldered his way out of the store. He had five kilograms (twelve pounds) of bread under his arm. This was two days' rations for two workers and one dependent. I got my bread and we walked across the road to a drygoods store to try to buy a pair of woolen inner-gloves Popov needed badly. The store was empty, however, and we saw through the window the little pile of silk handkerchiefs and summer shirts which, for several days, had been the only things on sale.

'Lousy business,' he said; 'in summer they have sheepskins, in winter nothing but silk handkerchiefs. I guess I'll have to go to the bazaar tomorrow for gloves and a pair of pants.'

VIII

We walked on up the hill for ten minutes between two rows of whitewashed one-story barracks. The last on the right was home. It was a low wooden structure whose double walls were lined with straw. The tarpaper roof leaked in spring. There were thirty rooms in the barrack. The inhabitants of each had made a little brick or iron stove so that as long as there was wood or coal the rooms could be kept warm. The low corridor was illuminated by one small electric light bulb. Popov stumbled along in his felt boots till he reached room 17, pushed the door open and went in. His roommate, Grisha, who worked on the

---

[3] Nominally nearly one hundred dollars; equivalent in buying power, about ten dollars.

iron mine, was just making a fire.

'Hello,' he said, without looking up.

'Cold,' answered Popov, putting his bread on the table and unbuttoning his coat. The room was about six feet by ten and had one small window, which was pasted around with newspaper to keep the cold out. There was a small table, a little brick stove, and one three-legged stool. The two iron bedsteads were rickety and narrow. There were no springs, just thin planks put across the iron frame. Popov hung up his coat and came up to the stove to warm his hands.

Our room was considerably larger than Popov's, because Kolya was a foreman and I was a foreigner. We had a table, two stools as well as two beds, and a small closet. I lit a fire and peeled some potatoes.

There were eighty men, women, and children living in our barrack. The oldest man was thirty-four. Everybody worked for the construction trust, which owned the barrack. Until 1934 we paid no rent. After that it cost us about ten roubles a month each.

There had been a kitchen, but now a family was living in it so that everybody did his cooking on his own stove. One of the rooms was the Red Corner. Here hung the barrack wall newspaper, two udarnik banners, pictures of Lenin, Stalin, and Voroshilov. Here, also, was a two-hundred-book library. Twice a week classes for the illiterates were held in the Red Corner. A few months before there had been seventeen illiterate adults in the barracks, now there were ten. To be sure, one was considered literate if one could sign one's name and read a simple sentence in any language.

IX

At about six o'clock a dozen or so young workers, men and women, gathered in the Red Corner with a couple of balalaikas and a guitar. Work was finished for the day, supper was on the stove, it was time for a song. And they sang! Workers' revolutionary songs, folk tunes. and the old Russian romantic lyrics. A Tartar worker sang a couple of his native songs. A young Ukrainian danced. The balalaikas were played very skillfully. I never ceased wondering at the high percentage of Russian workers who could play the balalaika. They learned during the long winter evenings in their village mud huts.

Then a discussion sprang up. 'Why don't we get more sugar? We've received only two hundred grams' (half pound) 'per person this month. Tea without sugar doesn't get you anywhere.' Almost everybody had something to say. One young fellow explained that the sugar crop was bad this year. The sugar industry fulfilled its plan only fifty-some per cent. Somebody else pointed out that the Soviet Union exported a great deal of candy, which meant sugar.

'We still have to export a lot to get the money to buy rolling mills and other such things that we can't make ourselves yet.'

Some of the women remained unconvinced. There had always been sugar except during the war. There was no war now. There ought to be sugar. The older women particularly had not yet become accustomed to having money which could not buy what they wanted. Previously money had always been a measure of their material situation. A good payroll meant the best of everything. This had been true all through the late twenties, particularly in the industrial districts of the Ukraine where workers with jobs usually ate well. Now, however, the meaning of money had changed. The size of the pay envelope, the number of bank notes under the mattress, no longer determined living standards. Everybody had money, but what one ate or wore depended almost exclusively on what there was to buy in the particular store to which one was attached. If one were a foreign specialist or a party or GPU top flight functionary attached to the exclusive foreigners' store, one had caviar, Caucasian wine, imported materials, and a fair selection of shoes, suits, etc. Engineers, foremen, people like Syemichkin and Kolya, had cards for a technicians' store where they could buy bread and occasionally meat, butter, fish, and some dry-goods. The majority of the people, however, like Popov, were attached to workers' stores where bread was the only thing one was reasonably sure of getting with any regularity. Occasionally there was no bread for several days; but most of the workers, schooled in famine, had a small supply of hoarded crusts which tided them over temporary shortages. . . .

Food conditions were the subject of constant discussion at spontaneous little meetings in the Red Corner at the barracks before or after dinner. There was nearly always someone to explain the official position and the majority was usually satisfied.

'Just wait five or ten years and we won't need one single thing from the capitalist world,' said Anya, a young woman welder. 'Then we won't have to export food. We'll eat it all ourselves.'

'In five or ten years there won't be any capitalist world,' said a young rigger, waving his hand. 'What do you think the workers in the capitalist world are doing? Do you think they are going to starve through another ten years of crisis, even supposing there is no war during that time? They won't stand it.'

'Of course they won't. They'll revolt,' said another. 'And we'll help them when the time comes. . . .'

X

It was nearly seven o'clock when Kolya got home and stuck his nose into the Red Corner. 'Jack, we must go if we're going to be on time.' We went into our room to get our books. Kolya had already eaten supper at the technicians' dining-room down at the mill for which he had three cards. . . .

We took our books, wrapped in newspaper, and started off for school.

Many people were leaving the barracks; some were going to the cinema, some to the club, but the packages of books wrapped in newspaper under the arms of most of them told of their destinations. They were going to school. Twenty-four men and women in the barracks were students in some organized school.

I attended the Komvuz. The course took three years and included Russian, arithmetic, political economy, Leninism, history of the Communist Party of the Soviet Union, history of the revolutionary movement of the West, party structure, and dialectic materialism. Most of the graduates of this school became professional propagandists or functionaries in the local political or administrative organizations. Most of the students entered the Communist University as semi-literates. The entrance requirements were those of the fifth grade in elementary school, but actually only reading and writing were rigorously demanded. The academic level of the Komvuz was consequently low. Textbooks caused a great deal of trouble, particularly for subjects like dialectic materialism, where the only book in print was that of Bukharin, which had been declared 'opportunist' and banned for use in schools. To give students with a very limited general education 'Anti-Duehring,' 'The Dialectics of Nature,' or 'Materialism and Empiro-Criticism' to read was only to invite blatant superficiality. The teachers were, therefore, in a difficult position. The dialectic materialism teacher in the Communist University was changed four times in the academic year 1933–34. In each case 'deviations' caused removal, and in two cases, arrest. 'Deviation hunting' was one of the main tasks of the director of the school. And if his efforts in this direction produced no results, he was liable to get into trouble himself for 'complacency' or 'harboring enemies.'

I entered the Komvuz when I had been in Magnitogorsk only three months in order to get some help in Russian. Then I became interested in the material of the courses. The history particularly was fascinating. Every experience in history was black or white, trends and tendencies were simplified. Every question had a perfectly definite answer. Not only that, the formulation of the answer must be thus and so. When you followed all the rules, everything made sense. It was a system built up like arithmetic. The only trouble with it was that often it did not always correspond to objective realities.

I remember one altercation about the Marxian law of the impoverishment of the toilers in capitalist countries. According to this law as interpreted to the students of the Magnitogorsk Komvuz, the working classes of Germany, Britain, and the United States, as well as those of all other capitalist countries, had become steadily and inexorably poorer since the beginning of the Industrial Revolution in the eighteenth century. I went up to the teacher after class, and told him that I happened to have been in Britain, for example, and that it seemed to me that conditions among workers there were unquestionably better than they had been during the time of Charles Dickens, or at the time when Engels wrote his treatise on the 'Conditions of the Working Classes in England.'

The teacher would have none of me. 'Look at the book, Comrade,' he said. 'It is written in the book.' It mattered nothing to this man that 'the book' would be declared counter-revolutionary next month. When it happened he would be given another book. The party made no mistakes. He was given a book by the party. That was enough.

Kolya attended the Technicum, a school with slightly higher academic standards than those of the Communist University. The entrance requirements were seven years of schooling and the applicants were weeded out by competitive examination. The curriculum included algebra, physics, chemistry, mechanics, strength of materials, mechanical drawing and designing of structural steel, reinforced concrete and wooden structures, with emphasis on those types of construction needed for Magnitogorsk. Most of the teachers were engineers working in the designing office or on the job. They came to do their teaching after a day's work and were often tired and unprepared. The strain on the students was even greater, inasmuch as they studied four nights a week, whereas the teachers usually taught less. The student body was picked without regard to party affiliation. A komsomol, a non-party worker, were admitted on the same basis as a party member. 'Class enemies' and members of their families, however, were rigorously excluded. Shabkov, whose father had been a kulak, could not enter the Technicum. This deprivation of rights of higher education to 'lishentsi' (disfranchised citizens) was enforced till 1936, when a decree from Moscow granted equal educational rights to all.

Half a dozen other schools were attended by workers from Barracks No. 17 every evening: the chauffeur's school; an 'Osoaviakhim' course, including various military subjects; special courses to train economists, planners, midwives, postoffice workers, and telegraph operators. These schools were run by various trusts and organizations.

School expenses, lighting, heating, teachers' salaries, and sometimes even books and paper for the students, were met from the large fund for training technicians and skilled workers. The students paid nothing. They even got special privileges, longer vacations, time off from work during examinations.

At this time Magnitogorsk boasted very few full-time adult schools. Most of the workers, like Kolya and myself, studied in the evenings. There was too much work to be done, the pressure was too great, to release several million young workers from Soviet industry and send them to school. Within five years, however, the evening professional schools practically disappeared and were replaced by bona fide full-time institutions, whose academic standards were much higher. Students of these institutions received allowances from the State, ranging from forty to five hundred roubles a month. This was true until 1940, when the government, faced with the necessity of raising billions for armaments, instituted tuition for all schooling over the seventh grade. . . .

The necessity of training a Soviet intelligentsia had even more sweeping effects than the outlay of millions of roubles for education. The graduation of wages, the increased differential between the wages paid to skilled and unskilled, educated and uneducated, was largely an attempt to stimulate the desire to study. In doing this, the lethargy and traditional sluggishness of the Russian peasantry had to be overcome. The population, and in particular the peasants, had to be made to want to study. To some extent this desire was already present as a reaction to centuries of deprivation of educational opportunities and as a result of the natural curiosity of man. But additional stimulus was necessary. If pay were the same for shepherd boy and engineer, most peasants would graze their flocks and never trouble Newton and Descartes.

In 1933 wage differentials were approximately as follows: The average monthly wage of an unskilled worker in Magnitogorsk was something in the neighborhood of 100 roubles; a skilled worker's apprentice, 200; a skilled worker, 300; an engineer without experience, 400 to 500; with experience, 600 to 800; administrators, directors, etc., anywhere from 800 to 3000. This heavy differentiation, plus the absence of unemployment and the consequent assurance of being able without difficulty to get a job in any profession learned, supplemented and stimulated the intellectual curiosity of the people. The two together were so potent that they created a student body in the Magnitogorsk night schools of 1933 willing to work eight, ten, even twelve hours on the job under severest conditions, and then come to school at night, sometimes on an empty stomach and, sitting on a backless wooden bench, in a room so cold that you could see your breath a yard ahead of you, study mathematics for four hours straight. Of course, the material was not always well learned. Preparation was insufficient, conditions were too bad. Nevertheless, Kolya, after having studied two years in the Technicum, could design a truss, calculate volumes, areas, and do many other things. Moreover, he knew from personal experience the concrete practical application of everything he had learned.

Kolya and I walked down the hill toward school. It was cold, the wind bit our cheeks, and within five minutes the moisture from our breath began to freeze on our eyebrows and eyelashes. We walked fast, as it was nearly seven o'clock. . . .

We went on in silence. The Komvuz school building was a barrack very similar to the one in which we lived, except that it was cleaner and the rooms were larger. As we approached the door, we heard Natasha, the janitress, come out of her room with her cowbell in her hand, ringing it vigorously. Just in time. Kolya went on to the Technicum. I went into my classroom. There were twenty-four students in the group. The age range was from fourteen to forty-five. The teacher was a sharp-looking little man with glasses who worked as a designer during the day. . . .

XI

It was a little after eleven when I got back to Barracks No. 17. Kolya had come in ten minutes earlier, and had started a fire. 'Hungry, Jack?' I was. We boiled a half-dozen small potatoes, and ate them with salt. They tasted very good indeed, but before Kolya had finished his last one he fell asleep squatting on his haunches in front of the little home-made iron stove.

Outside of the barrack the wind howled dismally, but in our little room it was warm. Strips of newspaper pasted around the window-panes and frames, as well as over cracks in the plaster walls, kept out the cold. The dying wood fire cast a red glow around the room.

I began to doze off when a particularly obstreperous louse bit me in the small of the back. I found the little fellow, and snapped him between my thumbnails in good Russian style. Then I woke Kolya, and we both went to bed.

IT STARTED AS A DREAM
By Valentin Katayev

I was in Magnitogorsk last in 1931. But I have never forgotten the visit. To people of my generation this city is as unforgettable as one's first love.

I shall always remember that feeling of inimitability that I experienced at the time—35 years ago—on the first day of my arrival at the foot of Mount Atach, which towered over the vast Ural steppes. I had previously seen the hydroelectric plant on the Dnieper being built. The scaffolding there reminded me of the siege of Troy. I had also witnessed the cornerstone laying ceremonies and construction of the Rostov Farm Machinery Plant and the Stalingrad Tractor Plant, I had seen the first collective farms on the Volga and Don rivers. Consequently, I was in a receptive mood for what I would see at Magnitogorsk. But what I saw literally astounded me. It was not because this was the most majestic project I had ever seen. What impressed me was the plan, bold to the point of daring, to build a giant metallurgical complex deep in the wild and barren Ural steppelands.

That was the period of construction records. The concrete pourers won world renown with their fantastic speed. I saw people marching ahead of time. They worked with inspiration to turn their backward agrarian country into an industrial power.

In the course of the construction job thousands of heroes were born—these were the real shock workers of socialist labor—the cream of the working class. Before our very eyes the old world was being uprooted and a new, unprecedented world of the socialist future was taking shape. It was a world no one had ever seen or described. I saw the Komsomols working with fiery enthusiasm on the construction jobs of our first five-year plans.

The city and the giant metallurgical complex did not even exist in embryo at the time—all that did exist was the dream to see colossal blast furnaces blown in, to see coke and open hearth furnaces and blooming mills operating, and to see in place of what was a tiny factory pond at the time—a vast man-made sea, and on its shores—a new multistory city with broad avenues ablaze with light, with luxuriant parks and boulevards.

Thirty-five years after the dream first gripped the minds of the builders, I drove through the blocks of multi-story houses, through beautifully ornamented squares: this was the dream come true, the cherished dream of the first builders of this steel center of our country.

Huge housing projects with their thousands of windows looked down at me over the low iron fences. The deep blue sky looked down at the houses in their surrounding of gardens and green alleys. This was indeed a city worthy of our epoch.

I crisscrossed this city that now has a population of about half a million. I visited the mills where I saw iron and steel in all shapes and forms: there were steel staircases, bridge girders, colossal pipes to bring in gas from Bukhara, rails stretching in all directions, locomotives hauling molten metal, the blast furnaces with their torches of flaming gas. Forgetting my age, I climbed to the top of those famous blast furnaces. I paused at the steel gangways and landings to admire the glow of the molten iron as it flowed through the zigzagging trenches into the huge buckets.

The components of this metallurgical giant are spread over 40 square kilometers. Yet it is still growing and expanding.

The original number of eight blast furnaces has been increased to ten. In the past seven years the Magnitogorsk complex built a large agglomeration mill, coke furnaces, a blast furnace, jumbo size open hearth furnaces, a hot-rolling mill and many other basic and auxiliary installations. I was present at the inauguration of a new coke furnace that will supply the recently built tenth blast furnace.

A large, beautiful city grew up together with the mills. It has the bright eye-catching showcases a modern city should have and also clubs, Palaces of Culture, theaters, sport installations, schools, and medical institutions.

I met one of the veterans of the Magnitogorsk project—Yakov Frolov. I recall how in 1931, when he was young and bubbling over with energy, enthusiastic in all undertakings, he headed the building team that laid the foundation for the first houses in the city. Frolov lived with his wife and child in a barrack hostel. There were forty narrow iron cots divided by half a meter of space. In the center stood an unpolished wooden table, a bench and several stools, and in the corner a wooden water barrel.

At that time all the builders of Magnitogorsk lived in such barracks and dugouts.

Now Yakov Frolov is on pension. He shares with his son, daughter-in-law, and their two children a three-room flat. In the kitchen there is a gas range and a refrigerator. They have hot and cold running water.

Yakov sat bouncing his grandson on his knee as he told me:

"We live well, as you see. Still, I

miss those first years when we had only started construction. It's a grand feeling to be building a city with your own hands. . . ."

I dropped in to see the fine glass-roofed studios of the local artists. I saw the spacious, well-appointed flats in which the furnace and rolling-mill men live, the flats of the welders, technologists, and building workers. They are the cream of the working class, the true masters of life, men blazing new trails in production. They are real working-class intellectuals—well read and educated, cheerful and high-spirited. They are all in love with their city, with its brilliant, enviable future. This is true of the younger generation who have just taken their place at the lathe or control panel and of the veterans who have tasted the full cup of bitter hardships and privation in the battle against the Ural steppes.

The Magnitogorsk complex supplies iron and steel to hundreds of industrial enterprises all over the country. Its output is also in considerable demand abroad. From year to year new capacities are put into operation. This is a process resembling rejuvenation and even rebirth.

In recent years a genuine technical revolution has taken place in all branches of production. Automation and cybernetic machines have been introduced together with instruments using radioactive isotopes. Output has increased 63 per cent over the last seven years. Quality has improved. New items have been put into production. The complex netted a profit of 1,500 million rubles for the country. This is the result of technical re-equipment, the result of the creative initiative of the engineers and workers who have attained genuine technical maturity. The entire staff is engaged in a collective search for ways of modernization.

It is noteworthy that every year more and more workers are acquiring a secondary and higher technical education while on the job. After graduation they all remain at the complex adding their know-how to the common effort of the engineers and technicians.

Prominent among the steelmen are Yuri Kartashov, Mikhail Manjula, Nikolai Sorokin and Ivan Verezov. They head furnace teams at the thirteenth open hearth furnace. They are given much publicity. They serve as examples to the other men—their experience is studied. What merited them this popularity and attention?

The men servicing the thirteenth open hearth furnace decided to smelt 310,000 tons of steel this year without the use of oxygen. No furnace of that type in Magnitogorsk has ever managed to produce even 300,000 tons. This explains the significance of the commitment undertaken by these men. It meant boosting production by 30,000 tons over the figure for 1965. This is not a simple thing. But the commitment was founded on a precise scientific and practical estimate. Recently a technical innovation was introduced at this furnace. The fuel feeds were placed at the top and not the base as in all other furnaces. Operation experience shows that this cuts down smelting time. Another reserve of mounting production is the increase in the weight of the smelt. The men undertook to increase it to 420 tons in 1966. The initial preparatory work has already been completed.

The workers at Magnitogorsk are constantly improving blast furnace operation and are increasing productivity. They are introducing automation and mechanization, and are furthering the traditions of the veterans who have many achievements to their credit.

I met a group of enthusiastic young men working under Igor Morev, a young engineer-innovator. Morev and his team are tackling the problem of smelting steel in an entirely new way—by taking advantage of the latest achievements of science—of quantum mechanics and physics, magnetic hydrodynamics, electronics, and cybernetics. It is too early to speak of results as yet but the experiments have already advanced to the preproduction stage. There is every reason to expect something really big. They have also invented a plasma burner that can cut any metal quickly, leaving no rough edges.

. . . These young men keep alive the tradition and enthusiasm of the Komsomols of the thirties, when such scenes were typical:

. . . Ivan Zapyantsev walked up to the desk of the personnel chief of the Magnitogorsk complex.

"What job do you hold?"

"I'm an apprentice."

"Can you work as a smelter?"

"They haven't given me that job yet."

"But if they do?"

"I'll manage!"

"But you've got to be a good technician to hold that job."

"I'll be a good technician!"

And that was not an empty promise. It was the tradition of the thirties.

FIERY SOUL

Before leaving Magnitogorsk, I visited Vladimir Zudin, who comes from a dynasty of metallurgical workers. He was a steelman for many years. Then he went to college and later became director of the complex, engineer, and professor. Now he is on pension but he continues to act as professor at the Mining and Metallurgical Institute, training young innovators and preparing a new generation of engineers and technicians, a new generation of highly educated and qualified metallurgists.

As we sat over our tea, I asked him:

"How would you explain the source of the enthusiasm that flared up here more than thirty-five years ago and which still keeps burning? How would you explain the constant creative quest of the Soviet people?

The scientist, a former worker with a long career behind him, pondered my question. Then, weighing every word, he said:

"As I see it, there are people of two sorts. One tries to give as little as possible while taking as much as he can himself. This is the grabbing kind. Luckily for all of us, there are fewer and fewer of this kind. The other kind experience satisfaction and joy only when doing something for other people, and in the long run, for all of mankind. It's this feeling of joy of constantly devoting all one's energy to the common cause of building communism that is the spiritual *fire* that is passed down from generation to generation. Since the October Socialist Revolution this has been the main tradition of the working class of our country and the glorious Leninist Komsomol."

51

SOCIALIST GOLD

By John Littlepage

In 1927 the head of the Soviet Gold Trust, Alexander F. Serebrovsky (liquidated in the 1937 purges), came to Alaska to study gold mines. There he hired his American guide, John D. Littlepage, to help him increase Soviet gold production. Littlepage spent the years 1928–37 in the Soviet Union and helped bring Soviet gold output to second place in the world. Commissar of Heavy Industry Sergei Ordjonikidze (pushed into suicide by Stalin, according to Khrushchev) gave him a Ford car, an extremely valuable possession in Russia at that time. Soviet President Mikhail Kalinin awarded him the Order of the Red Banner of Labor in 1935. Despite these rewards, Littlepage remained an impartial judge of the Soviet industrial scene. Of particular interest is his account of industrial sabotage by both Party members and ordinary workers, since it is generally believed outside Russia that Soviet charges to that effect were fabricated.

For other accounts of American engineering in Russia see Andrew Steiger, *American Engineers in the Soviet Union;* Walter Rukeyser, *An American Engineer in Russia;* Wladimir Naleszkiewicz, "Technical Assistance of American Enterprises to the Growth of the Soviet Union," *Russian Review,* January, 1966; and three articles by Dana Dalrymple: "The American Tractor Comes to Soviet Russia," *Technology and Culture,* Spring, 1964; "American Technology and Soviet Agricultural Output, 1924–33," *Agricultural History,* July, 1966; and "The Stalingrad Tractor Plant in Early Soviet Planning," *Soviet Studies,* October, 1966. For an account by an American worker see Andrew Smith, *I Was a Soviet Worker.* For an uncompromising view of Russian technical backwardness see Werner Keller, *East Minus West=Zero: Russia's Debt to the Western World, 862–1962.* On the training of engineers see Stephen Timoshenko, *Engineering Education in the USSR.* A Soviet account of a sabotage trial is *The Case of N. P. Vitvitsky Et Al.;* a Western comment on this trial is A. J. Cummings, *The Moscow Trial.* Georgii Piatakoff was a defendant in *Report of Court Proceedings in the Case of the Anti-Soviet Trotskyite Center* (the transcript was published in English in Moscow, 1937). See also Andrew Rothstein, *Wreckers on Trial.* On the subject of women in industry see the recent scholarly survey, *Women in the Soviet Economy,* by Norton Dodge. See also Tatiana Cherna-

From *In Search of Soviet Gold,* copyright, 1937, 1938, by John D. Littlepage and Demaree Bess, pp. 39–45, 86–93, 96–100, 198–200, 225–34. Reprinted by permission of Harcourt, Brace & World, Inc., and Brandt & Brandt.

vin, *We Soviet Women*, and Fannina Halle, *Woman in Soviet Russia*. Since 1945 the Soviets have published an English-language monthly, *Soviet Woman*. The place of gold in Soviet output is assessed in Demitri Shimkin, *Minerals: A Key to Soviet Power*. See also A. Zauberman, "Gold in Soviet Economic Theory and Policies," *American Economic Review*, Vol. LXI. There is interesting information on Soviet gold holdings today in John Jessup, "How Golden Is the Dollar," *Life*, August 25, 1967. A recent Soviet report is "The Country's Gold," *Current Digest of the Soviet Press*, March 27, 1968.

. . . In our first year in Russia, the tempo was much slower than it became later, and is now. The mines at Kochkar were closed on Sundays, and everybody took the day off; the idea of continuous production hadn't caught on anywhere. The nearby steppes provided plenty of good duck hunting, which had been my favorite recreation in Alaska. I found some Russian acquaintances who liked hunting as well as I did, and we usually made up a party. And when the weather was especially fine, we had family picnics in the woods and along the river.

The country and the people and the life suited us fine. We paid no rent, and food was abundant and cheap. Eggs cost a ruble a hundred, or half a cent apiece. Other prices were comparable. The peasants brought in their produce to a great bazaar, and sat in their carts or spread out their vegetables, fruits, meat, eggs, and cheese on the ground, and spent a sociable day while they disposed of their produce.

And my work absorbed every bit of energy I could generate. Serebrovsky had sent me to Kochkar because these were the first Soviet gold mines to receive modern equipment. He wanted me to rehabilitate these mines and use them as a model and training ground for the industry. When I arrived, they were just being brought into production. Some of these mines had been worked for a hundred and fifty years, and in one place there were still traces of a ring in which gold ore had been crushed by driving horses over it. The mines had formerly been worked in three groups, divided among Russian, English, and French companies. Now they were all being brought under the central Gold Trust and equipped with up-to-date imported machinery. . . .

It didn't take me very long to discover that I had a huge job on my hands. None of the workmen had had any experience with mechanized mining, and even the older engineers had never seen any of the new milling equipment except as pictures in catalogues. I saw that it would be necessary to teach each individual workman drilling, timbering, blasting, operation of the milling machinery, and especially, care of equipment. I put on some digging clothes and went to work with the men, and I followed that practice during all my years in Russia. . . .

The people in Berlin had told me the truth, however, when they said that Russian engineering traditions tended to keep engineers and officials in good clothes and in their offices, well out of the dirty mine shafts. One day soon after I arrived at Kochkar, a group of two hundred engineering students came along to our mines for some practical experience; most of them were just beginning university work. The Gold Trust had hurriedly set up special schools in order to train additional mine managers, and the few existing mining academies were being expanded as rapidly as possible to supply the growing need for technical personnel.

When I went through the mill, this

group of Young Communists was standing around with notebooks and pencils, drawing pictures of machinery. I called some of them around me, and suggested that they go to work at once as operators in the mill. I told them that, by actually performing the different operations, they would learn better than in any other way, and could later train workmen more easily.

They were outraged, and curtly informed me that they were future engineers, not workmen. I decided to make an issue, and posted orders that they would not be permitted to enter the plant unless they followed my instructions. Some of them tried to stir up trouble for me; they demanded to know how a foreigner could forbid Soviet citizens to enter their own property, and even appealed to their institutes for help.

Fortunately for my prestige, the authorities backed me up and ordered the students to do as I had suggested. If these young people yielded with bad grace in the first place, they came around to my point of view later. In a few weeks a committee waited upon me and thanked me, in the name of the group, for showing them how to get the best out of their limited time in the mines.

This incident threw some light on Serebrovsky's astonishment in Alaska, when he discovered the general superintendent of our largest gold mine coming out of the tunnel in his digging clothes and sitting down just as he was, to eat with his own miners. I saw that Russians, even under their Soviet system, were a long way from our American forms of industrial democracy. And they still are so; although I must say that the authorities are trying to break down the caste lines between ordinary labor and so-called specialists. . . .

As soon as I had looked over the mines in Kochkar, I began to dig into the figures for output per man and similar information, and after some difficulty discovered that the output per man per day was less than one-tenth that of American workmen in Alaskan mines. Even after accounting for the ignorance and lack of training of the Russian miners, this discrepancy was altogether too great, and showed that something serious was wrong with the methods of operation.

I put my mind to the matter, and reached my own conclusions. Then I asked the Communist manager of the mines to call a conference of the Russian managing staff, including the engineers, and laid my figures before them.

"As I see it, the trouble is that your men are all working for wages by the day," I said. "For that reason, they don't do any more work than they have to in order to get by. They must have more incentive if they are to be induced to work harder. I suggest that we install a system of piece-work or bonus and arrange for some kind of contract labor."

My suggestion was received in a kind of horrified silence, and the manager abruptly changed the subject. A friendly engineer later advised me not to mention this proposal again, as it was contrary to Communist ideas, and might get me into trouble.

That's the sort of things engineers were up against in the Soviet Russia of 1928. The Communists were in complete control, as they still are, but the Communists in those days were even more hampered than they are today by several such fantastic formulas as the one I have mentioned. They surrendered these fetishes of theirs reluctantly, one by one, as the years went by, and it became more and more obvious that they didn't make sense.

It is hard to believe now, looking back over the changes which have occurred in Soviet industrial practice since I began to work in Russia in 1928, that the Communists ever possessed this attitude toward piece-work, contract labor, and cost-accounting, all of which have become the most striking features of their industrial system in recent years. . . .

During the latter part of 1930, our Gold Trust was combined with the Copper and Lead Trust in one gigantic Nonferrous Metals Trust. Although I didn't know it at the time, this move meant plenty of grief for me. The copper and lead mines were giving a lot of worry to the authorities, and for this reason they assigned Serebrovsky to take them over in addition to gold, and see what he could do with them. . . .

Our Gold Trust, while theoretically under the Commissariat of Heavy Industry, had actually maintained an autonomous position, on account of Serebrovsky's personal influence in the Kremlin, and his close relationship with Ordjonikidze. But the copper and lead mines had been directed by the leading Communist authorities in the Urals, and in particular by Yuri Piatakoff, the Vice-Commissar of Heavy Industry, who was an Old Bolshevik like Serebrovsky.

I had become well enough acquainted with some Russians by this time to hear part of the gossip going around, and I had known for some time that there was bad feeling between Serebrovsky and Piatakoff. My chief was very blunt in his speech, and spared nobody's feelings when he felt he should say something, although he was usually very mild-mannered. In fact, there was a saying in the Gold Trust that Serebrovsky would yell and curse only when he liked a man; if he was always polite, it was a sign he didn't like you. . . .

Conditions were reported to be especially bad in the copper mines of the Ural Mountain region, at that time Russia's most promising mineral-producing area, which had been selected for a lion's share of the funds available for production. American mining engineers had been engaged by dozens for use in this area, and hundreds of American foremen had likewise been brought over for instruction purposes in mines and mills. Four or five American mining engineers had been assigned to each of the large copper mines in the Urals. and American metallurgists as well.

These men all had been selected carefully; they had excellent records in the United States. But with very few exceptions they had proved disappointing in the results they were obtaining in Russia. When Serebrovsky was given control of copper and lead mines, as well as gold, he wanted to find out why these imported experts weren't producing as they should, and in January, 1931, sent me off, together with an American metallurgist and a Russian Communist manager, to investigate conditions in the Ural mines, and try to figure out what was wrong and how to correct it. . . .

We discovered, in the first place, that the American engineers and metallurgists were not getting any cooperation at all; no attempt had been made to provide them with competent interpreters, and in some places there was no means of communication possible between them and the Russian engineers and managers. Most of them had tried hard to earn their money and make themselves useful; they had carefully surveyed the properties to which they were assigned, and drawn up recommendations for exploitation which would have been immediately useful if applied. But these recommendations had either never been translated into Russian or had been stuck into pigeonholes and never brought out again. . . .

Our Gold Trust was better run in every way than the copper-lead industry and, above everything else, the personnel had a different spirit. Our workmen sometimes didn't have enough to eat, and there was plenty of grumbling, but it was more or less good-natured. Everybody connected with the Gold Trust felt that we were getting ahead, and the sense of succeeding made up for discomforts.

But it was different in the copper and lead mines. They were enveloped in an atmosphere of failure. The shortage of food and other consumer goods was worse here, because distribution was badly organized. There was also a serious lack of equipment, largely because the materials purchased abroad and manufactured in Soviet factories was clumsily apportioned to get the best results. The mining methods used were so obviously wrong that a freshman engineering student could have pointed most of them out. Areas were being opened up too large for control, and ore was being removed without the proper timbering and filling. In an effort to speed up production before suitable preparations had been completed, several of the best mines had been badly damaged, and some ore bodies were on the verge of being lost beyond recovery. There had been serious cave-ins in several mines, and many others had caught fire, with much loss of valuable ore.

I shall never forget the situation we found at Kalata. Here, in the northern Urals, was one of the most important copper properties in Russia, consisting of six mines, a flotation concentrator, and a smelter, with blast and reverberatory furnaces. Seven American mining engineers of the first rank, drawing very large salaries, had been assigned to this place some time before. Any one of them, if he had been given the opportunity, could have put this property in good running order in a few weeks.

But at the time our commission arrived they were bogged down in red tape. Their recommendations were ignored; they were assigned no particular work; they were unable to convey their ideas to Russian engineers through ignorance of the language and lack of competent interpreters. They had become so disgusted with the situation that they were occupied almost entirely with operating an "American boarding house" which they had set up for themselves. These expensive engineers, so badly needed in Russia at that time, were taking turns as bookkeepers and house-managers and buyers for their little eating and rooming house, and that is just about all they were doing. I must say that their talents were being exerted to good effect within this limited field; I didn't find a better boarding house in Russia. . . .

In July, 1931, after Serebrovsky had examined the report of conditions made by our commission, he decided to send me back to Kalata as chief engineer, to see if we couldn't do something with this big property. He sent along with me a Russian Communist manager, who had no special knowledge and had sense enough not to interfere with men who did have special training.

The seven American engineers brightened up considerably when they discovered we really had sufficient authority to cut through the red tape and give them a chance to work. They neglected their boarding house, I am afraid, for the next few months, and went down into the mines alongside their workmen, in the American mining tradition. Before long, things were picking up fast, and within five months, production rose by 90 per cent. . . .

At the end of five months, I decided I could safely leave this property. The seven American engineers were still on the job, and although still handicapped by lack of knowledge of the Russian language, had been enabled to get their ideas across and had been assigned regular work, for which they were all anxious enough. Mines and plant had been thoroughly reorganized; there seemed to be no good reason why production could not be maintained at the highly satisfactory rate we had established.

I drew up detailed instructions for future operations, which the seven American engineers had helped to work out. I explained these thoroughly to the Russian engineers and to the Communist manager, who was beginning to get some notion of mining. The latter assured me that my ideas would be followed to the letter, and I went off pretty well pleased with myself, with a sense of a sound job of work completed. Not only were the production figures at these mines vastly improved, but I flattered myself sound foundations had been laid for future steady progress. I was never more hopeful anywhere about the future of a Soviet project than I was when I left Kalata. I suppose it was fortunate that I couldn't foresee what would happen to these mines; it might have discouraged me too much to continue my work. . . .

Soon after my return to Moscow, I was informed that the copper mines at Kalata were in very bad condition; production had fallen even lower than it was before I had reorganized the mines in the previous year. This report dumbfounded me; I couldn't understand how matters could have become so bad in this short time, when they had seemed to be going so well before I left.

Serebrovsky asked me to go back to Kalata to see what could be done. When I reached there, I found a depressing scene. The Americans had all finished their two-year contracts, which had not been renewed, so they had gone home. A few months before I arrived, the Communist manager, who had learned something of mining under my direc-tion, had been removed by a commission which had been sent in from Sverdlovsk, Communist headquarters in the Urals. The commission had reported that he was ignorant and inefficient, although there was nothing in his record to show it, and had appointed the chairman of the investigating commission to succeed him—a funny sort of procedure.

During my previous stay at the mines we had speeded up capacity of the blast furnaces to seventy-eight metric tons per square meter per day; they had now been permitted to drop back to their old output of forty to forty-five tons. Worst of all, thousands of tons of high-grade ore had been irretrievably lost by the introduction into two mines of methods which I had specifically warned against during my previous visit. . . .

Much discouraged, I set to work to try to recover some of the lost ground. The atmosphere around the place impressed me as unpleasant and unwholesome. The new manager and his engineers were sullen, and made it plain that they wanted little to do with me. The food shortage was at its height in the Urals at this time, and the workmen were in a more ugly mood than I had ever seen them. Living conditions had been permitted to decline along with production.

I worked as well as I could to get things moving again; but I didn't have seven American engineers and a friendly Communist manager to help me out, as I had before. Then one day I discovered that the new manager was secretly countermanding almost every order I gave. I saw there was no need to stay any longer, and caught the first train I could get back to Moscow. I was so disheartened at that time that I was prepared to resign and leave Russia for good.

When I reached Moscow, I reported exactly what I had discovered at Kalata to Serebrovsky. He brushed aside my resignation and told me I was needed more than ever now, and shouldn't think of leaving. I told him it was no use for me to try to work in Russia, when I could get no cooperation from the men in the mines. "You needn't worry about those men," he said. "They will be attended to."

He started an investigation right away, and in a short time the mine manager and some of the engineers were put on trial for sabotage. The manager got ten years, the maximum prison sentence in Russia, and the engineers lesser terms. The evidence indicated that they had deliberately removed the former manager in order to wreck the mines.

I was satisfied at the time that there was something bigger in all this than the little group of men at Kalata; but I naturally couldn't warn Serebrovsky against prominent members of his own Communist party. It has never been my policy to get mixed up in politics. But I was so sure that something was wrong high up in the political administration of the Ural Mountains that I agreed to stay on in Russia only after Serebrovsky had promised me that I would not be sent back to work in the copper mines of the Urals. . . .

I studied all the information I could get hold of about the trial of the manager and engineers at Kalata. It seemed clear to me at the time that the selection of this commission and their conduct at Kalata traced straight back to the Communist high command in Sverdlovsk, whose members must be charged either with criminal negligence or actual participation in the events which had occurred in these mines.

However, the chief secretary of the Communist Party in the Urals, a man named Kabakoff, had occupied this post since 1922, all through the period of great activity in developing the mines and industries of the Urals. For some reason which was never clear to me he

had always commanded the complete confidence of the Kremlin, and was considered so powerful that he was privately described as the "Bolshevik Viceroy of the Urals."

If this man's record was examined, there was nothing to justify the reputation he appeared to have. Under his long rule, the Ural area, which is one of the richest mineral regions in Russia and which was given almost unlimited capital for exploitation, never did produce anything like what it should have done.

This commission at Kalata, whose members later admitted they had come there with wrecking intentions, had been sent directly from this man's headquarters, and yet when this evidence came out at the trial, there was no reflection against Kabakoff. I told some of my Russian acquaintances at the time that it seemed to me there was a lot more going on in the Urals than had yet been revealed, and that it came from somewhere high up.

All these incidents became clearer, so far as I was concerned, after the conspiracy trial in January, 1937, when Piatakoff, together with several of his associates, confessed in open court that they had engaged in organized sabotage of mines, railways, and other industrial enterprises since the beginning of 1931. A few weeks after this trial had ended and Piatakoff had been sentenced to be shot, the chief Party Secretary in the Urals, Kabakoff, who had been a close associate of Piatakoff's, was arrested on charges of complicity in this same conspiracy. . . .

I can testify that the only "employer" in Russia, the state, hires more labor spies than American industry could ever afford to do. It is always assumed, in every Soviet mine or factory or office, that a certain number of workers are police agents, and no one is ever quite sure which workers are agents and which are not. The police are known to have amateur agents almost everywhere, with instructions to report suspicious actions or conversation of any kind. There is so much vigilance of this kind in every Soviet enterprise that Soviet citizens seldom speak their real minds, even in a small group, for fear one of the group is a police agent. All reports of agents, whether professional or amateur, are apparently cleared through the Secret Department. It is known that these agents even report workers who grumble regularly.

Of course, there is plenty of need for close police supervision in Soviet industry. In the gold industry the police guard shipments of gold, which don't take up much space, and might easily be diverted. But they are kept even busier looking out for sabotage.

Sabotage was something strange to my experience before I went to Russia. In all my fourteen years' experience in Alaskan gold mines, I had never run across a case of sabotage. I knew there were people who sometimes tried to wreck plant or machinery in the United States, but I didn't know just how or why they operated. However, I hadn't worked many weeks in Russia before I encountered unquestionable instances of deliberate and malicious wrecking.

One day in 1928, I went into a power station at the Kochkar gold mines. I just happened to drop my hand on one of the main bearings of a large Diesel engine as I walked by, and felt something gritty in the oil. I had the engine stopped immediately, and we removed from the oil reservoir about a quart of quartz sand, which could have been placed there only by design. On several other occasions, in the new milling plants at Kochkar, we found sand inside such equipment as speed reducers, which are entirely enclosed, and can be reached only by removing the hand-hold covers. . . .

Why, I have been asked, is sabotage of this description so common in Soviet Russia, and so rare in most other countries? Do Russians have a peculiar bent for industrial wrecking?

People who ask such questions apparently haven't realized that the authorities in Russia have been, and still are, fighting a whole series of open or disguised civil wars. In the beginning, they fought and dispossessed the old aristocracy, the bankers and landowners and merchants of the Tsarist régime. I have described how they later fought and dispossessed the little independent farmers and the little retail merchants and the nomad herders in Asia.

Of course, it's all for their own good, say the Communists. But many of these people can't see things that way, and remain bitter enemies of the Communists and their ideas, even after they have been put back to work in state industries. From these groups have come a considerable number of disgruntled workers who dislike Communists so much that they would gladly damage any of their enterprises if they could.

For this reason, the police have records of every industrial worker, and have traced back their careers to the time of the Revolution, so far as possible. Those who belonged to any group which has been dispossessed are given a black mark, and kept under constant watch. When anything serious happens, such as a fire or a cave-in in a mine, the police round up such people before they do anything else. And in the case of any big political crime, such as the Kirov assassination, the roundup becomes nation-wide.

However, the police assigned to Soviet industrial enterprises do not confine themselves to watching potential wreckers. I know from my own observation that they also organize a network of labor spies. It is a fact that any troublemaker among the workmen, who grumbles excessively or shows any tendency to criticize the Government, is likely to disappear quietly. The police handle such cases with great skill, and seldom raise a rumpus. I don't mean to suggest that such workers are treated violently; they are probably shipped off to out-of-the-way enterprises, perhaps to some of those operated by the police themselves. . . .

When I first went to Russia, no women were actually working in the mines. A few girls and young women had started their training as engineers and geologists, and were scandalizing oldtime miners by puttering around in drifts and tunnels and mills. But some two years after I arrived in Russia, late in 1929, when the first Five Year Plan got under way, women began to take over some of the light jobs, such as running compressors and hoists, distributing drill steel around the mines, assisting surveyors, and sometimes acting as trammers, pushing ore cars.

When the first women appeared in the mines, there was considerable opposition from male miners, who clung for some time to the old superstition that accidents invariably occur when women visit mines. Inasmuch as accidents had occurred just as often in Soviet mines before there were any women to be blamed for them, this superstition didn't get much consideration. It wasn't long before the presence of women was taken for granted, although some of the older miners never did entirely get over their resentment, and sometimes still show it.

Women took jobs in mills and smelters in much larger numbers than in the mines. They labored alongside men as operators, doing work which is dirty but not particularly heavy. From the beginning, they were shown no favors. They were expected to do an equivalent amount of work for a day's pay, under the same working conditions, with the same responsibilities.

From the engineer's point of view, the question of woman's labor is whether or not she can pull her weight. Judging from my experience in Soviet mines and mills, I should say that women average better than men in production. As a general rule, women proved to be more conscientious in their work and better disposed to maintain discipline. These qualities compensated for their physical inferiority except on such jobs as require an exceptionally strong physique.

Even on such jobs, women sometimes found places. I came across a big husky Russian peasant woman working as a drill-runner in a mine in the Urals. Her job consisted in taking a rock-drill weighing about fifty pounds, and drilling holes with this bulky machine in the solid rock. The hammer of a rock-drill strikes about eighteen hundred blows a minute, and it takes a hefty man to handle the machine for long. After watching this woman operate her drill for a while, I suggested that the job was hardly suited to a woman. She thought I was joking, and I never was able to convince her that I was serious. She was intensely proud of the fact that she was the only woman drill-runner in that group of mines.

This woman was an exception. Most women workers in Soviet industry do not undertake such heavy work; they are usually confined to mechanized shops or mills or mines, where manual skill is more important than brawn. But Soviet women do tackle all sorts of jobs which the girls and women of western industrial countries are never expected to do. They clean streets and sewers, they help to build subways and railroads and canals, they work in steel mills throwing around heavy bars of red hot metal. They do a large share of the manual work of the country. In 1936, according to official figures, 28 per cent of the workers in the Soviet mining industry were women.

In considering differences between the kinds of work done by Soviet and other women, I think it is necessary to bear in mind that women of most of the races in Russia have been accustomed to physical labor for generations. About 85 per cent of the adults were engaged in agriculture in Russia as late as 1928. Russian farm women worked out in the fields with their men. They still do to-day.

When the Moscow authorities began to apply their ambitious industrializing program, beginning in 1929, they were smart enough to realize that they could not accomplish what they wanted unless they could attract husky peasant girls into the new factories, mills, and mines. These farm girls were more adaptable than farm men, and found it easier to pick up the knack of operating machinery. Without their help, it might have proved impossible to keep Russia's new industries going during the critical years following 1929. . . .

On the one hand, the elaborate propaganda machine was set to work inducing women to go into every kind of industrial occupation. The Communists had made a great point of the equality of women after 1917, and now they said in effect: "Women, here's your chance to show whether you take equality seriously. We've opened all our schools to you, we've opened all our jobs to you on a basis of equal pay for equal work in every line. Now we need your help in our new industries. We need your assistance in our mines and subways and steel mills as well as in our offices and on our farms. Will you help us build our industries, even if the work is dirty or unpleasant, or will you leave that to men?"

That was the general tone of the appeal made to Soviet women, and it proved effective. At a time when working conditions were bad, when housing and the supply of food was inadequate, when male workers were roaming around in droves looking for a "better 'ole," women stuck to their jobs more faithfully than the men, and played a considerable part in putting across the industrial program.

But the authorities accompanied these emotional appeals to their women by another method of persuasion which was indirect and more or less hidden but probably even more effective. This was the solid method of economic necessity. Controlling the entire national economy, the authorities at Moscow could fix both wages and prices to an extent which would not be possible in most countries. During the years following 1929, they fixed wages and prices so as to make it extremely difficult for a workingman to support his wife and family in the least degree of comfort. If the wife didn't work, the family was likely to find itself on short rations. . . .

But I believe that the wholesale use of women in such work as mining, steel fabrication, and the like, is a temporary phase of Soviet development and is already passing. During my last two years in Russia, from 1935 to 1937, I noticed that there was less tendency for women to work, and less agitation to entice women into heavier industrial jobs. The word was beginning to get around that such work was better left to men.

Why was this? It was largely due to the increased wages earned by many skilled male workers through the wider application of the piecework system. These workers, finding they could support a wife and family again, wanted their women back in the home, and the women were not averse to going back. The authorities also made no objection; in fact, they seemed to be encouraging the return to the home.

The economic motive was chiefly responsible for bringing so many Soviet women into heavy jobs in industry, and the same motive is now operating to send many of them back into the home. The wider application of piecework in the last three or four years has made it possible for more skilled workers and managers to support their wives and families in comfort, and a large number of women are proving themselves quite willing to allow their husbands to support them. . . .

I don't want to give the idea that women are being pushed back into the home and out of heavy industries. In theory, at least, they are still as welcome as ever in the mines and mills. The law provides penalties for industrial managers who refuse to employ women on an equal basis with men, and to give them the same pay. But in practice, Soviet industrial managers are naturally not anxious to have their payrolls overloaded with women. These managers are between the devil and the deep blue sea in this respect, as in many others. They are under obligation to show substantial profits in their enterprises, to cut down labor costs and increase production. This is almost impossible to do if they have too many women workers who take time off on full pay to have babies. So industrial managers, if they are smart, contrive in one way and another to avoid hiring too many women.

In some ways, the Soviet attitude toward women's equality seems to be more logical than our own. They say that women must pay for equal privileges by assuming equal responsibilities. So long as this principle is enforced, there doesn't seem to be much danger of a matriarchy growing up in Russia. So far, women have reached very few of the highest posts in any line of activity. But in the mines an increasing number of women are becoming executives and foremen, and male workers are learning to take orders from them without grumbling.

I have been interested to note that Soviet women in the mines and mills, even when performing the dirtiest and most severe manual labor, manage to retain their feminine appearance. At work, the women often wear trouser outfits resembling ski suits, and these clothes are quite becoming to them. But as soon as they get away from work, they take off their work clothes and get back into skirts. The Soviet women don't show any tendency to become like men just because they perform more of what is called man's work in most other countries.

Just as Soviet men and women are treated equally in free labor, so they are also impartially assigned to forced labor under police supervision if they offend the authorities. The prison workcamps contain women workers performing the same manual tasks as men. Women prisoners have helped to build railways in the Far East in temperatures 80° to 90° below zero, and they have also helped to dig canals and construct power stations.

The wives and daughters of kulaks usually accompanied them at forced labor in some of the mines I supervised, and they sometimes also worked in the mines. These women had worked hard in the fields, and thought nothing of performing manual labor. They were not compelled to work in the mines, but were permitted to do so, and preferred to eke out their husbands' modest earnings. In this way, thousands of Soviet peasant women got their first training for industry, and many of them later went into mills and factories as operators. . . .

52

THE SOVIET CONSTITUTION

The first Soviet Constitution of 1918 applied only to the Russian Republic (R.S.F.S.R.). It disfranchised the former "exploiting classes," legislated other inequalities, and made no mention of the Communist party. In 1924 the first Constitution of the U.S.S.R. came into effect. It maintained the principle of unequal representation for city and countryside and this time affected not only the Russian but also the Ukrainian, White Russian, and Transcaucasian Republics. Turkmenistan and Uzbekistan came into the Union in 1925, while Tadzhikistan joined in 1929. Since 1936 the Soviet Union has had a third constitution, the full text of which appears below. At the 22d Party Congress in 1961 Khrushchev announced plans for a new constitution, which will thus be the fourth since the revolution.

On Soviet elections, see George Carson, *Electoral Practices in the USSR*. On Soviet federalism, see V. Aspaturian, *The Union Republics in Soviet Diplomacy*. On the treatment of non-Russians in the Union, see Rudolf Schlesinger, *The Nationalities Problem in Soviet Administration: Selected Readings*. For a recent Soviet view of the same subject, see I. Tsamerian and S. Ronin, *Equality of Rights between Races and Nationalities in the USSR*, published by Unesco in 1962. The text of the 1918 Constitution can be found in *Intervention, Civil War and Communism in Russia*, ed. James Bunyan, pp. 507–24. See also Nicholas Timasheff, "The Soviet Constitution," *Thought*, XVI, 626–44; N. Alexeiev, "The Evolution of Soviet Constitutional Law," *Review of Politics*, II, 463–76; and Alex Nove, "Some Aspects of Soviet Constitutional Theory," *Modern Law Review*, XII, 12–36. On Bukharin and the Constitution of 1936 see Boris Nicolaevsky, *Power and the Soviet Elite*, pp. 3–25. For recent contributions see Robert LeFevre, *Constitutional Government Today in Soviet Russia*; Casimir Gecys, *Two Worlds: An Analytical Study of the Soviet Constitution*; Max Mote, *Soviet Local and Republic Elections*; J. A. Newth, "Some Constitutional Conventions in the USSR?" *Soviet Studies*, July, 1964; and "The Composition of the USSR Supreme Soviet, 1958–1966," *ibid.*, July, 1967. For a Soviet view see V. Kotok, *The Soviet Representative System*.

CONSTITUTION OF THE UNION OF SOVIET SOCIALIST REPUBLICS

As Amended and Added to at the Ninth Session of the Supreme Soviet of the U.S.S.R., Fourth Convocation (December 1957)

Reproduced from *Constitution of the Union of Soviet Socialist Republic* (Moscow, 1960).

CHAPTER I. THE SOCIAL STRUCTURE

Article 1.—The Union of Soviet Socialist Republics is a socialist state of workers and peasants.

Article 2.—The political foundation of the U.S.S.R. is the Soviets of Working People's Deputies, which grew and became strong as a result of the overthrow of the power of the landlords and capitalists and the conquest of the dictatorship of the proletariat.

Article 3.—All power in the U.S.S.R. belongs to the working people of town and country as represented by the Soviets of Working People's Deputies.

Article 4.—The economic foundation of the U.S.S.R. is the socialist system of economy and the socialist ownership of the instruments and means of production, firmly established as a result of the liquidation of the capitalist system of economy, the abolition of private ownership of the instruments and means of production, and the elimination of the exploitation of man by man.

Article 5.—Socialist property in the U.S.S.R. exists either in the form of state property (belonging to the whole people) or in the form of co-operative and collective-farm property (property of collective farms, property of co-operative societies).

Article 6.—The land, its mineral wealth, waters, forests, mills, factories, mines, rail, water and air transport, banks, communications, large state-organized agricultural enterprises (state farms, machine and tractor stations and the like), as well as municipal enterprises and the bulk of the dwelling-houses in the cities and industrial localities, are state property, that is, belong to the whole people.

Article 7.—The common enterprises of collective farms and co-operative organizations, with their livestock and implements, the products of the collective farms and co-operative organizations, as well as their common buildings, constitute the common, socialist property of the collective farms and co-operative organizations.

Every household in a collective farm, in addition to its basic income from the common collective-farm enterprise, has for its personal use a small plot of household land and, as its personal property, a subsidiary husbandry on the plot, a dwelling-house, livestock, poultry and minor agricultural implements —in accordance with the rules of the agricultural artel.

Article 8.—The land occupied by collective farms is secured to them for their use free of charge and for an unlimited time, that is, in perpetuity.

Article 9.—Alongside the socialist system of economy, which is the predominant form of economy in the U.S.S.R., the law permits the small private economy of individual peasants and handicraftsmen based on their own labour and precluding the exploitation of the labour of others.

Article 10.—The personal property right of citizens in their incomes and savings from work, in their dwelling-houses and subsidiary husbandries, in articles of domestic economy and use and articles of personal use and convenience, as well as the right of citizens to inherit personal property, is protected by law.

Article 11.—The economic life of the U.S.S.R. is determined and directed by the state national-economic plan, with the aim of increasing the public wealth, of steadily raising the material and cultural standards of the working people, of consolidating the independence of the U.S.S.R. and strengthening its defensive capacity.

Article 12.—Work in the U.S.S.R. is a duty and a matter of honour for every able-bodied citizen, in accordance with the principle: "He who does not work, neither shall he eat."

The principle applied in the U.S.S.R. is that of socialism: "From each according to his ability, to each according to his work."

CHAPTER II. THE STATE STRUCTURE

Article 13.—The Union of Soviet Socialist Republics is a federal state, formed on the basis of a voluntary union of equal Soviet Socialist Republics, namely: The Russian Soviet Federative Socialist Republic, The Ukrainian Soviet Socialist Republic, The Byelorussian Soviet Socialist Republic, The Uzbek Soviet Socialist Republic, The Kazakh Soviet Socialist Republic, The Georgian Soviet Socialist Republic, The Azerbaidzhan Soviet Socialist Republic, The Lithuanian Soviet Socialist Republic, The Moldavian Soviet Socialist Republic, The Latvian Soviet Socialist Republic, The Kirghiz Soviet Socialist Republic, The Tajik Soviet Socialist Republic, The Armenian Soviet Socialist Republic, The Turkmen Soviet Socialist Republic, The Estonian Soviet Socialist Republic.

Article 14.—The jurisdiction of the Union of Soviet Socialist Republics, as represented by its higher organs of state power and organs of state administration, embraces:

a) Representation of the U.S.S.R. in international relations, conclusion, ratification and denunciation of treaties of the U.S.S.R. with other states, establishment of general procedure governing the relations of Union Republics with foreign states;

b) Questions of war and peace;

c) Admission of new republics into the U.S.S.R.;

d) Control over the observance of the Constitution of the U.S.S.R., and ensuring conformity of the Constitutions of the Union Republics with the Constitution of the U.S.S.R.;

e) Confirmation of alterations of boundaries between Union Republics;

f) Confirmation of the formation of new Autonomous Republics and Autonomous Regions within Union Republics;

g) Organization of the defence of the U.S.S.R., direction of all the Armed Forces of the U.S.S.R., determination of directing principles governing the organization of the military formations of the Union Republics;

h) Foreign trade on the basis of state monopoly;

i) Safeguarding the security of the state;

j) Determination of the national-economic plans of the U.S.S.R.;

k) Approval of the consolidated state budget of the U.S.S.R. and of the report on its fulfilment; determination of the taxes and revenues which go to the Union, the Republican and the local budgets;

l) Administration of the banks, industrial and agricultural institutions and enterprises and trading enterprises of all-Union importance; over-all direction of industry and construction under Union Republic jurisdiction;

m) Administration of transport and communications of all-Union importance;

n) Direction of the monetary and credit system;

o) Organization of state insurance;

p) Contracting and granting of loans;

q) Determination of the basic principles of land tenure and of the use of mineral wealth, forests and waters;

r) Determination of the basic principles in the spheres of education and public health;

s) Organization of a uniform system of national-economic statistics;

t) Determination of the principles of labour legislation;

u) Establishment of the principles of legislation concerning the judicial system and judicial procedure, and of the principles of the criminal and civil codes;

v) Legislation concerning Union citizenship; legislation concerning rights of foreigners;

w) Determination of the principles of legislation concerning marriage and the family;

x) Issuing of all-Union acts of amnesty.

Article 15.—The sovereignty of the Union Republics is limited only in the spheres defined in article 14 of the Constitution of the U.S.S.R. Outside of these spheres each Union Republic exercises state authority independently. The U.S.S.R. protects the sovereign rights of the Union Republics.

Article 16.—Each Union Republic has its own Constitution, which takes account of the specific feature of the Republic and is drawn up in full conformity with the Constitution of the U.S.S.R.

Article 17.—The right freely to secede from the U.S.S.R. is reserved to every Union Republic.

Article 18.—The territory of a Union Republic may not be altered without its consent.

Article 18-a—Each Union Republic has the right to enter into direct relations with foreign states and to conclude agreements and exchange diplomatic and consular representatives with them.

Article 18-b—Each Union Republic has its own Republican military formations.

Article 19.—The laws of the U.S.S.R. have the same force within the territory of every Union Republic.

Article 20.—In the event of divergence between a law of a Union Republic and a law of the Union, the Union law prevails.

Article 21.—Uniform Union citizenship is established for citizens of the U.S.S.R.

Every citizen of a Union Republic is a citizen of the U.S.S.R.

Article 22.—The Russian Soviet Federative Socialist Republic includes the Autonomous Soviet Socialist Republics: Bashkirian, Buryat-Mongolian, Daghestan, Karbardino-Balkarian, Karelian, Komi, Mari, Mordovian, North Ossetian, Tartar, Udmurt, Chechen-Ingush, Chuvash, Yakut; Autonomous Regions: Adygei, Gorno-Altai, Jewish Kalmyk, Karachai-Cherkess, Tuva and Khakass.

Article 24.—The Azerbaidzhan Soviet Socialist Republic includes the Nakhichevan Autonomous Soviet Socialist Republic and the Nagorno-Karabakh Autonomous Region.

Article 25.—The Georgian Soviet Socialist Republic includes the Abkhazian Autonomous Soviet Socialist Republic, the Ajarian Autonomous Soviet Socialist Republic and the South Ossetian Autonomous Region.

Article 26.—The Uzbek Soviet Socialist Republic includes the Kara-Kalpak Autonomous Soviet Socialist Republic.

Article 27.—The Tajik Soviet Socialist Republic includes the Gorno-Badakhshan Autonomous Region.

Article 28.—The decision of questions relating to the Regional and Territorial Administrative Structure of Union Republics is left to the jurisdiction of Union Republics.

CHAPTER III. THE HIGHER ORGANS OF STATE POWER IN THE UNION OF SOVIET SOCIALIST REPUBLICS

Article 30.—The highest organ of state power in the U.S.S.R. is the Supreme Soviet of the U.S.S.R.

Article 31.—The Supreme Soviet of the U.S.S.R. exercises all rights vested in the Union of Soviet Socialist Republics in accordance with article 14 of the Constitution, in so far as they do not, by virtue of the Constitution, come within the jurisdiction of organs of the U.S.S.R. that are accountable to the Supreme Soviet of the U.S.S.R., that is, the Presidium of the Supreme Soviet of the US.S.R., the Council of Ministers of the U.S.S.R., and the Ministries of the U.S.S.R.

Article 32.—The legislative power of the U.S.S.R. is exercised exclusively by the Supreme Soviet of the U.S.S.R.

Article 33.—The Supreme Soviet of the U.S.S.R. consists of two Chambers: the Soviet of the Union and the Soviet of Nationalities.

Article 34.—The Soviet of the Union is elected by the citizens of the U.S.S.R. voting by election districts on the basis of one deputy for every 300,000 of the population.

Article 35.—The Soviet of Nationalities is elected by the citizens of the U.S.S.R. voting by Union Republics, Autonomous Republics, Autonomous Regions, and National Areas on the basis of 25 deputies from each Union Republic, 11 deputies from each Autonomous Republic, 5 deputies from each Autonomous Region and one deputy from each National Area.

Article 36.—The Supreme Soviet of the U.S.S.R. is elected for a term of four years.

Article 37.—The two Chambers of the Supreme Soviet of the U.S.S.R., the Soviet of the Union and the Soviet of Nationalities, have equal rights.

Article 38.—The Soviet of the Union and the Soviet of Nationalities have equal powers to initiate legislation.

Article 39.—A law is considered adopted if passed by both Chambers of the Supreme Soviet of the U.S.S.R. by a simple majority vote in each.

Article 40.—Laws passed by the Supreme Soviet of the U.S.S.R. are published in the languages of the Union Republics over the signatures of the President and Secretary of the Presidium of the Supreme Soviet of the U.S.S.R.

Article 41.—Sessions of the Soviet of the Union and of the Soviet of Nationalities begin and terminate simultaneously.

Article 42.—The Soviet of the Union elects a Chairman of the Soviet of the Union and four Vice-Chairmen.

Article 43.—The Soviet of Nationalities elects a Chairman of the Soviet of Nationalities and four Vice-Chairmen.

Article 44.—The Chairmen of the Soviet of the Union and the Soviet of Nationalities preside at the sittings of the respective Chambers and have charge of the conduct of their business and proceedings.

Article 45.—Joint sittings of the two Chambers of the Supreme Soviet of the U.S.S.R. are presided over alternately by the Chairman of the Soviet of the Union and the Chairman of the Soviet of Nationalities.

Article 46.—Sessions of the Supreme Soviet of the U.S.S.R. are convened by the Presidium of the Supreme Soviet of the U.S.S.R. twice a year.

Extraordinary sessions are convened by the Presidium of the Supreme Soviet of the U.S.S.R. at its discretion or on the demand of one of the Union Republics.

Article 47.—In the event of disagreement between the Soviet of the Union and the Soviet of Nationalities, the question is referred for settlement to a conciliation commission formed by the Chambers on a parity basis. If the conciliation commission fails to arrive at an agreement or if its decision fails to satisfy one of the Chambers, the question is considered for a second time by the Chambers. Failing agreement between the two Chambers, the Presidium of the Supreme Soviet of the U.S.S.R. dissolves the Supreme Soviet of the U.S.S.R. and orders new elections.

Article 48.—The Supreme Soviet of the U.S.S.R. at a joint sitting of the two Chambers elects the Presidium of the Supreme Soviet of the U.S.S.R., consisting of a President of the Presidium of the Supreme Soviet of the U.S.S.R., sixteen Vice-Presidents, a Secretary of the Presidium and fifteen members of the Presidium of the Supreme Soviet of the U.S.S.R.

The Presidium of the Supreme Soviet of the U.S.S.R. is accountable to the Supreme Soviet of the US.S.R. for all its activities.

Article 49.—The Presidium of the Supreme Soviet of the U.S.S.R.:

a) Convenes the sessions of the Supreme Soviet of the U.S.S.R.;

b) Issues decrees;

c) Gives interpretations of the laws of the U.S.S.R. in operation;

d) Dissolves the Supreme Soviet of the U.S.S.R. in conformity with Article 47 of the Constitution of the U.S.S.R. and orders new elections;

e) Conducts nation-wide polls (referendums) on its own initiative or on the demand of one of the Union Republics;

f) Annuls decisions and orders of the Council of Ministers of the U.S.S.R. and of the Councils of Ministers of the Union Republics if they do not conform to law;

g) In the intervals between sessions of the Supreme Soviet of the U.S.S.R., releases and appoints Ministers of the U.S.S.R. on the recommendation of the Chairman of the Council of Ministers of the U.S.S.R., subject to subsequent confirmation by the Supreme Soviet of the U.S.S.R.;

h) Institutes decorations (Orders and Medals) and titles of honour of the U.S.S.R.;

i) Awards Orders and Medals and confers titles of honour of the U.S.S.R.;

j) Exercises the right of pardon;

k) Institutes military titles, diplomatic ranks and other special titles;

l) Appoints and removes the high command of the Armed Forces of the U.S.S.R.;

m) In the intervals between sessions of the Supreme Soviet of the U.S.S.R., proclaims a state of war in the event of military attack on the U.S.S.R., or when necessary to fulfil international treaty obligations concerning mutual defence against aggression;

n) Orders general or partial mobilization;

o) Ratifies and denounces international treaties of the U.S.S.R.;

p) Appoints and recalls plenipotentiary representatives of the U.S.S.R. to foreign states;

q) Receives the letters of credence and recall of diplomatic representatives accredited to it by foreign states;

r) Proclaims martial law in separate localities or throughout the U.S.S.R. in the interests of the defence of the U.S.S.R. or of the maintenance of public order and the security of the state.

Article 50.—The Soviet of the Union and the Soviet of Nationalities elect Credentials Committees to verify the credentials of the members of the respective Chambers.

On the report of the Credentials Committees, the Chambers decide whether to recognize the credentials of deputies or to annul their election.

Article 51.—The Supreme Soviet of the U.S.S.R., when it deems necessary, appoints commissions of investigation and audit on any matter.

It is the duty of all institutions and

officials to comply with the demands of such commissions and to submit to them all necessary materials and documents.

Article 52.—A member of the Supreme Soviet of the U.S.S.R. may not be prosecuted or arrested without the consent of the Supreme Soviet of the U.S.S.R., or, when the Supreme Soviet of the U.S.S.R. is not in session, without the consent of the Presidium of the Supreme Soviet of the U.S.S.R.

Article 53.—On the expiration of the term of office of the Supreme Soviet of the U.S.S.R., or on its dissolution prior to the expiration of its term of office, the Presidium of the Supreme Soviet of the U.S.S.R. retains its powers until the newly elected Supreme Soviet of the U.S.S.R. shall have formed a new Presidium of the Supreme Soviet of the U.S.S.R.

Article 54.—On the expiration of the term of office of the Supreme Soviet of the U.S.S.R., or in the event of its dissolution prior to the expiration of its term of office, the Presidium of the Supreme Soviet of the U.S.S.R. orders new elections to be held within a period not exceeding two months from the date of expiration of the term of office or dissolution of the Supreme Soviet of the U.S.S.R.

Article 55.—The newly elected Supreme Soviet of the U.S.S.R. is convened by the outgoing Presidium of the Supreme Soviet of the U.S.S.R. not later than three months after the elections.

Article 56.—The Supreme Soviet of the U.S.S.R., at a joint sitting of the two Chambers, appoints the Government of the U.S.S.R., namely, the Council of Ministers of the U.S.S.R.

CHAPTER IV. THE HIGHER ORGANS OF STATE POWER IN THE UNION REPUBLICS

Article 57.—The highest organ of state power in a Union Republic is the Supreme Soviet of the Union Republic.

Article 58.—The Supreme Soviet of a Union Republic is elected by the citizens of the Republic for a term of four years.

The basis of representation is established by the Constitution of the Union Republic.

Article 59.—The Supreme Soviet of a Union Republic is the sole legislative organ of the Republic.

Article 60.—The Supreme Soviet of a Union Republic:

a) Adopts the Constitution of the Republic and amends it in conformity with article 16 of the Constitution of the U.S.S.R.;

b) Confirms the Constitutions of the Autonomous Republics forming part of it and defines the boundaries of their territories;

c) Approves the national-economic plan and the budget of the Republic and forms the economic administrative Regions;

d) Exercises the right of amnesty and pardon of citizens sentenced by the judicial organs of the Union Republic;

e) Decides questions of representation of the Union Republic in its international relations;

f) Determines the manner of organizing the Republic's military formations.

Article 61.—The Supreme Soviet of a Union Republic elects the Presidium of the Supreme Soviet of the Union Republic, consisting of a President of the Presidium of the Supreme Soviet of Union Republic, Vice-Presidents, a Secretary of the Presidium and members of the Presidium of the Supreme Soviet of the Union Republic.

The powers of the Presidium of the Supreme Soviet of a Union Republic are defined by the Constitution of the Union Republic.

Article 62.—The Supreme Soviet of a

Union Republic elects a Chairman and Vice-Chairmen to conduct its sittings.

Article 63.—The Supreme Soviet of a Union Republic appoints the Government of the Union Republic, namely, the Council of Ministers of the Union Republic.

CHAPTER V. THE ORGANS OF STATE ADMINISTRATION OF THE UNION OF SOVIET SOCIALIST REPUBLICS

Article 64.—The highest executive and administrative organ of the state power of the Union of Soviet Socialist Republics is the Council of Ministers of the U.S.S.R.

Article 65.—The Council of Ministers of the U.S.S.R. is responsible and accountable to the Supreme Soviet of the U.S.S.R., or, in the intervals between sessions of the Supreme Soviet, to the Presidium of the Supreme Soviet of the U.S.S.R.

Article 66.—The Council of Ministers of the U.S.S.R. issues decisions and orders on the basis and in pursuance of the laws in operation and verifies their execution.

Article 67.—Decisions and orders of the Council of Ministers of the U.S.S.R. are binding throughout the territory of the U.S.S.R.

Article 68.—The Council of Ministers of the U.S.S.R.:

a) Co-ordinates and directs the work of the all-Union and Union-Republican Ministries of the U.S.S.R. and of other institutions under its jurisdiction and exercises direction over the Economic Councils of the economic administrative Regions through the Union Republic Councils of Ministers;

b) Adopts measures to carry out the national-economic plan and the state budget, and to strengthen the credit and monetary system;

c) Adopts measures for the mainte-

nance of public order, for the protection of the interests of the state, and for the safeguarding of the rights of citizens;

d) Exercises general guidance in the sphere of relations with foreign states;

e) Fixes the annual contingent of citizens to be called up for military service and directs the general organization of the Armed Forces of the country;

f) Sets up, whenever necessary, special Committees and Central Administrations under the Council of Ministers of the U.S.S.R. for economic and cultural affairs and defence.

Article 69.—The Council of Ministers of the U.S.S.R. has the right, in respect of those branches of administration and economy which come within the jurisdiction of the U.S.S.R., to suspend decisions and orders of the Councils of Ministers of the Union Republics and the Economic Councils of the economic administrative Regions and to annul orders and instructions of Ministers of the U.S.S.R.

Article 70.—The Council of Ministers of the U.S.S.R. is appointed by the Supreme Soviet of the U.S.S.R. and consists of: the chairman of the U.S.S.R. Council of Ministers; the first vice-chairman of the U.S.S.R. Council of Ministers; the vice-chairmen of the U.S.S.R. Council of Ministers; Ministers of the U.S.S.R.; the chairman of the U.S.S.R. Council of Ministers' State Planning Committee; the chairman of the U.S.S.R. Council of Ministers' Soviet Control Commission; the chairman of the U.S.S.R. Council of Ministers' State Committee on Labour and Wages; the chairman of the U.S.S.R. Council of Ministers' State Scientific and Technical Committee; the chairman of the U.S.S.R. Council of Ministers' State Committee on Aviation Technology; the chairman of the U.S.S.R. Council of Ministers' State Committee on Defense

Technology; the chairman of the U.S.S.R. Council of Ministers' State Committee on Radio Electronics; the chairman of the U.S.S.R. Council of Ministers' State Committee on Shipbuilding; the chairman of the U.S.S.R. Council of Ministers' State Committee on Construction; the chairman of the U.S.S.R. Council of Ministers' State Committee on Foreign Economic Relations; the chairman of the U.S.S.R. Council of Ministers' State Committee on State Security; the chairman of the Board of the U.S.S.R. State Bank; the director of the U.S.S.R. Council of Ministers' Central Statistical Administration.

The U.S.S.R. Council of Ministers includes the chairmen of the Union Republic Councils of Ministers ex officio.

Article 71.—The Government of the U.S.S.R. or a Minister of the U.S.S.R. to whom a question of a member of the Supreme Soviet of the U.S.S.R. is addressed must give a verbal or written reply in the respective Chamber within a period not exceeding three days.

Article 72.—The Ministers of the U.S.S.R. direct the branches of state administration which come within the jurisdiction of the U.S.S.R.

Article 73.—The Ministers of the U.S.S.R., within the limits of the jurisdiction of their respective Ministries, issue orders and instructions on the basis and in pursuance of the laws in operation, and also of decisions and orders of the Council of Ministers of the U.S.S.R., and verify their execution.

Article 74.—The Ministries of the U.S.S.R are either all-Union or Union-Republican Ministries.

Article 75.—Each all-Union Ministry directs the branch of state administration entrusted to it throughout the territory of the U.S.S.R. either directly or through bodies appointed by it.

Article 76.—The Union-Republican Ministries, as a rule, direct the branches of state administration entrusted to them through corresponding Ministries of the Union Republics; they administer directly only a definite and limited number of enterprises according to a list confirmed by the Presidium of the Supreme Soviet of the U.S.S.R.

Article 77.—The following Ministries are all-Union Ministries: Foreign Trade; Merchant Marine; Transportation; Medium Machine Building; Transport Construction; Chemical Industry; Power Plants.

Article 78.—The following Ministries are Union Republic Ministries: Internal Affairs; Higher Education; Geology and Conservation of Mineral Resources; Public Health; Foreign Affairs; Culture; Defense; Communications; Agriculture; Trade; Finance; Grain Products.

CHAPTER VI. THE ORGANS OF STATE ADMINISTRATION OF THE UNION REPUBLICS

Article 79.—The highest executive and administrative organ of the state power of a Union Republic is the Council of Ministers of the Union Republic.

Article 80.—The Council of Ministers of a Union Republic is responsible and accountable to the Supreme Soviet of the Union Republic, or, in the intervals between sessions of the Supreme Soviet of the Union Republic, to the Presidium of the Supreme Soviet of the Union Republic.

Article 81.—The Council of Ministers of a Union Republic issues decisions and orders on the basis and in pursuance of the law in operation of the U.S.S.R. and of the Union Republic, and of the decisions and orders of the Council of Ministers of the U.S.S.R., and verifies their execution.

Article 82.—The Council of Ministers of a Union Republic has the right to suspend decisions and orders of the Councils of Ministers of its Autonomous Republics and to annul decisions and orders of the Executive Committee of the Soviets of Working People's Deputies of its Territories, Regions and Autonomous Regions and of the Economic Councils of the economic administrative Regions.

Article 83.—The Council of Ministers of a Union Republic is appointed by the Supreme Soviet of the Union Republic and consists of:

The Chairman of the Council of Ministers of the Union Republic;

The First Vice-Chairmen of the Council of Ministers;

The Vice-Chairmen of the Council of Ministers;

The Ministers;

The Chairman of the State Planning Commission;

The Chairman of the State Committee of the Council of Ministers of the Union Republic on Construction and Architecture;

The Chairman of the State Security Committee under the Council of Ministers of the Union Republic.

Article 84.—The Ministers of a Union Republic direct the branches of state administration which come within the jurisdiction of the Union Republic.

Article 85.—The Ministers of a Union Republic, within the limits of the jurisdiction of their respective Ministries, issue orders and instructions on the basis and in pursuance of the laws of the U.S.S.R. and of the Union Republic, of the decisions and orders of the Council of Ministers of the U.S.S.R. and the Council of Ministers of the Union Republic, and of the orders and instructions of the Union-Republican Ministries of the U.S.S.R.

Article 86.—The Ministries of a Union Republic are either Union-Republican or Republican Ministries.

Article 87.—Each Union-Republican Ministry directs the branch of state administration entrusted to it, and is subordinate both to the Council of Ministers of the Union Republic and to the coresponding Union-Republican Ministry of the U.S.S.R.

Article 88.—Each Republican Ministry directs the branch of state administration entrusted to it and is directly subordinate to the Council of Ministers of the Union Republic.

Article 88-a.—The Economic Councils of the economic administrative Regions direct the branches of economic activity entrusted to them and are directly subordinate to the Union Republic Council of Ministers.

The Economic Councils of the economic administrative Regions, within the bounds of their competence, make decisions and issue directives on the basis and in execution of the laws of the U.S.S.R. and the Union Republic and of the decrees and directives of the U.S.S.R. Council of Ministers and the Union Republic Council of Ministers.

CHAPTER VII. THE HIGHER ORGANS OF STATE POWER IN THE AUTONOMOUS SOVIET SOCIALIST REPUBLICS

Article 89.—The highest organ of state power in an Autonomous Republic is the Supreme Soviet of the Autonomous Republic.

Article 90.—The Supreme Soviet of an Autonomous Republic is elected by the citizens of the Republic for a term of four years on a basis of representation established by the Constitution of the Autonomous Republic.

Article 91.—The Supreme Soviet of an Autonomous Republic is the sole legislative organ of the Autonomous Republic.

Article 92.—Each Autonomous Republic has its own Constitution, which takes account of the specific features of the Autonomous Republic and is drawn up in full conformity with the Constitution of the Union Republic.

Article 93.—The Supreme Soviet of an Autonomous Republic elects the Presidium of the Supreme Soviet of the Autonomous Republic and appoints the Council of Ministers of the Autonomous Republic, in accordance with its Constitution.

CHAPTER VIII. THE LOCAL ORGANS OF STATE POWER

Article 94.—The organs of state power in Territories, Regions, Autonomous Regions, Areas, Districts, cities and rural localities (stanitzas, villages, hamlets, kishlaks, auls) are the Soviets of Working People's Deputies.

Article 95.—The Soviets of Working People's Deputies of Territories, Regions, Autonomous Regions, Areas, Districts, cities and rural localities (stanitzas, villages, hamlets, kishlaks, auls) are elected by the working people of the respective Territories, Regions, Autonomous Regions, Areas, Districts, cities or rural localities for a term of two years.

Article 96.—The basis of representation for Soviets of Working People's Deputies is determined by the Constitutions of the Union Republics.

Article 97.—The Soviets of Working People's Deputies direct the work of the organs of administration subordinate to them, ensure the maintenance of public order, the observance of the laws and the protection of the rights of citizens, direct local economic and cultural affairs and draw up the local budgets.

Article 98.—The Soviets of Working People's Deputies adopt decisions and issue orders within the limits of the powers vested in them by the laws of the U.S.S.R. and of the Union Republic.

Article 99.—The executive and administrative organ of the Soviet of Working People's Deputies of a Territory, Region, Autonomous Region, Area, District, city or rural locality is the Executive Committee elected by it, consisting of a Chairman, Vice-Chairmen, a Secretary and members.

Article 100.—The executive and administrative organ of the Soviet of Working People's Deputies in a small locality, in accordance with the Constitution of the Union Republic, is the Chairman, the Vice-Chairman and the Secretary elected by the Soviet of Working People's Deputies.

Article 101.—The executive organs of the Soviets of Working People's Deputies are directly accountable both to the Soviets of Working People's Deputies which elected them and to the executive organ of the superior Soviet of Working People's Deputies.

CHAPTER IX. THE COURTS AND THE PROCURATOR'S OFFICE

Article 102.—In the U.S.S.R. justice is administered by the Supreme Court of the U.S.S.R., the Supreme Courts of the Union Republics, the Courts of the Territories, Regions, Autonomous Republics, Autonomous Regions and Areas, the Special Courts of the U.S.S.R. established by decision of the Supreme Soviet of the U.S.S.R., and the People's Courts.

Article 103.—In all Courts cases are tried with the participation of people's assessors except in cases specially provided for by law.

Article 104.—The Supreme Court of the U.S.S.R. is the highest judicial organ. The Supreme Court of the U.S.S.R. is charged with the supervision of the judicial activities of all the judicial organs of the U.S.S.R. and of the Union Republics within the limits established by law.

Article 105.—The Supreme Court of the U.S.S.R. is elected by the Supreme Soviet of the U.S.S.R. for a term of five years. The Supreme Court of the U.S.S.R. includes the Chief Justices of the Supreme Courts of the Union Republics, ex officio.

Article 106.—The Supreme Courts of the Union Republics are elected by the Supreme Soviets of the Union Republics for a term of five years.

Article 107.—The Supreme Courts of the Autonomous Republics are elected by the Supreme Soviets of the Autonomous Republics for a term of five years.

Article 108.—The Courts of Territories, Regions, Autonomous Regions and Areas are elected by the Soviets of Working People's Deputies of the respective Territories, Regions, Autonomous Regions or Areas for a term of five years.

Article 109.—People's Courts are elected by the citizens of the districts on the basis of universal, direct and equal suffrage by secret ballot for a term of three years.

Article 110.—Judicial proceedings are conducted in the language of the Union Republic, Autonomous Republic or Autonomous Region, persons not knowing this language being guaranteed the opportunity of fully acquainting themselves with the material of the case through an interpreter and likewise the right to use their own language in court.

Article 111.—In all Courts of the U.S.S.R. cases are heard in public, unless otherwise provided for by law, and the accused is guaranteed the right to defence.

Article 112.—Judges are independent and subject only to the law.

Article 113.—Supreme supervisory power to ensure the strict observance of the law by all Ministries and institutions subordinated to them, as well as by officials and citizens of the U.S.S.R. generally, is vested in the Procurator-General of the U.S.S.R.

Article 114.—The Procurator-General of the U.S.S.R. is appointed by the Supreme Soviet of the U.S.S.R. for a term of seven years.

Article 115.—Procurators of Republics, Territories, Regions, Autonomous Republics and Autonomous Regions are appointed by the Procurator-General of the U.S.S.R. for a term of five years.

Article 116.—Area, district and city procurators are appointed by the Procurators of the Union Republics, subject to the approval of the Procurator-General of the U.S.S.R., for a term of five years.

Article 117.—The organs of the Procurator's Office perform their functions independently of any local organs whatsoever, being subordinate solely to the Procurator-General of the U.S.S.R.

CHAPTER X. FUNDAMENTAL RIGHTS AND DUTIES OF CITIZENS

Article 118.—Citizens of the U.S.S.R. have the right to work, that is, the right to guaranteed employment and payment for their work in accordance with its quantity and quality.

The right to work is ensured by the socialist organization of the national economy, the steady growth of the productive forces of Soviet society, the elimination of the possibility of economic crises, and the abolition of unemployment.

Article 119.—Citizens of the U.S.S.R. have the right to rest and leisure.

The right to rest and leisure is ensured by the establishment of an eight-hour day for industrial, office, and professional workers, the reduction of the working day to seven or six hours for arduous trades and to four hours in shops where conditions of work are particularly arduous; by the institution of annual vacations with full pay for industrial, office, and professional workers, and by the provision of a wide network of sanatoria, holiday homes and clubs for the accommodation of the working people.

Article 120.—Citizens of the U.S.S.R. have the right to maintenance in old age and also in case of sickness or disability.

This right is ensured by the extensive development of social insurance of industrial, office, and professional workers at state expense, free medical service for the working people, and the provision of a wide network of health resorts for the use of the working people.

Article 121.—Citizens of the U.S.S.R. have the right to education.

This right is ensured by universal compulsory seven-year education; by extensive development of ten-year education, by free education in all schools, higher as well as secondary, by a system of state grants for students of higher schools who excel in their studies; by instruction in schools being conducted in the native language, and by the organization in the factories, state farms, machine and tractor stations, and collective farms of free vocational, technical and agronomic training for the working people.

Article 122.—Women in the U.S.S.R. are accorded equal rights with men in all spheres of economic, government, cultural, political and other public activity.

The possibility of exercising these rights is ensured by women being accorded an equal right with men to work, payment for work, rest and leisure, social insurance and education, and by state protection of the interest of mother and child, state aid to mothers of large families and unmarried mothers, maternity leave with full pay, and the provision of a wide network of maternity homes, nurseries and kindergarten.

Article 123.—Equality of rights of citizens of the U.S.S.R., irrespective of their nationality or race, in all spheres of economic, government, cultural, political and other public activity, is an indefeasible law.

Any direct or indirect restriction of the rights of, or conversely, the establishment of any direct or indirect privileges for, citizens on account of their race or nationality, as well as any advocacy of racial or national exclusiveness or hatred and contempt, are punishable by law.

Article 124.—In order to ensure to citizens freedom of conscience, the church in the U.S.S.R. is separated from the state, and the school from the church. Freedom of religious worship and freedom of anti-religious propaganda is recognized for all citizens.

Article 125.—In conformity with the interests of the working people, and in order to strengthen the socialist system, the citizens of the U.S.S.R. are guaranteed by law:

a) freedom of speech;

b) freedom of the press;

c) freedom of assembly, including the holding of mass meetings;

d) freedom of street processions and demonstrations.

These civil rights are ensured by placing at the disposal of the working people and their organizations printing presses, stocks of paper, public buildings, the streets, communications facilities, and other material requisites for the exercise of these rights.

Article 126.—In conformity with the interests of the working people, and in order to develop the organizational initiative and political activity of the masses of the people, citizens of the U.S.S.R. are guaranteed the right to unite in public organizations: trade unions, co-operative societies, youth organizations, sport and defence organizations, cultural, technical and scientific societies; and the most active and politically conscious citizens in the ranks of the working class, working peasants and working intelligentsia voluntarily unite in the Communist Party of the Soviet Union, which is the vanguard of the working people in their struggle to build communist society and is the leading core of all organizations of the working people, both public and state.

Article 127.—Citizens of the U.S.S.R. are guaranteed inviolability of the person. No person may be placed under arrest except by decision of a court or with the sanction of a procurator.

Article 128.—The inviolability of the homes of citizens and privacy of correspondence are protected by law.

Article 129.—The U.S.S.R. affords the right of asylum to foreign citizens persecuted for defending the interests of the working people, or for scientific activities, or for struggling for national liberation.

Article 130.—It is the duty of every citizen of the U.S.S.R. to abide by the Constitution of the Union of Soviet Socialist Republics, to observe the laws, to maintain labour discipline, honestly to perform public duties, and to respect the rules of socialist intercourse.

Article 131.—It is the duty of every citizen of the U.S.S.R. to safeguard and fortify public, socialist property as the sacred and inviolable foundation of the Soviet system, as the source of the wealth and might of the country, as the source of the prosperity and culture of all the working people.

Persons committing offences against public, socialist property are enemies of the people.

Article 132.—Universal military service is law.

Military service in the Armed Forces of the U.S.S.R. is an honourable duty of the citizens of the U.S.S.R.

Article 133.—To defend the country is the sacred duty of every citizen of the U.S.S.R. Treason to the Motherland—violation of the oath of allegiance, desertion to the enemy, impairing the military power of the state, espionage—is punishable with all the severity of the law as the most heinous of crimes.

CHAPTER XI. THE ELECTORAL SYSTEM

Article 134.—Members of all Soviets of Working People's Deputies—of the Supreme Soviet of the U.S.S.R., the Supreme Soviets of the Union Republics, the Soviets of Working People's Deputies of the Territories and Regions, the Supreme Soviets of the Autonomous Republics, the Soviets of Working People's Deputies of the Autonomous Regions, and the area, district, city and rural (stanitza, village, hamlet, kishlak, aul) Soviets of Working People's Deputies—are chosen by the electors on the basis of universal, equal and direct suffrage by secret ballot.

Article 135.—Elections of deputies are universal: all citizens of the U.S.S.R. who have reached the age of eighteen, irrespective of race or nationality, sex, religion, education, domition of insane persons and persons who have been convicted by a court of law past activities, have the right to vote in the election of deputies, with the excepcile, social origin, property status or and whose sentences include deprivation of electoral rights.

Every citizen of the U.S.S.R. who has reached the age of twenty-three is eligible for election to the Supreme Soviet of the U.S.S.R., irrespective of race or nationality, sex, religion, education, domicile, social origin, property status or past activities.

Article 136.—Elections of deputies are equal: each citizen has one vote; all citizens participate in elections on an equal footing.

Article 137.—Women have the right

to elect and be elected on equal terms with men.

Article 138.—Citizens serving in the Armed Forces of the U.S.S.R. have the right to elect and be elected on equal terms with all other citizens.

Article 139.—Elections of deputies are direct: all Soviets of working People's Deputies, from rural and city Soviets of Working People's Deputies to the Supreme Soviet of the U.S.S.R., are elected by the citizens by direct vote.

Article 140.—Voting at elections of deputies is secret.

Article 141.—Candidates are nominated by election districts.

The right to nominate candidates is secured to public organizations and societies of the working people: Communist Party organizations, trade unions, co-operatives, youth organizations and cultural societies.

Article 142.—It is the duty of every deputy to report to his electors on his work and on the work of his Soviet of Working People's Deputies, and he may be recalled at any time upon decision of a majority of the electors in the manner established by law.

CHAPTER XII. ARMS, FLAG, CAPITAL

Article 143.—The arms of the Union of Soviet Socialist Republics are a sickle and hammer against a globe depicted in the rays of the sun and surrounded by ears of grain, with the inscription "Workers of All Countries, Unite!" in the languages of the Union Republics. At the top of the arms is a five-pointed star.

Article 144.—The state flag of the Union of Soviet Socialist Republics is of red cloth with the sickle and hammer depicted in gold in the upper corner near the staff and above them a five-pointed red star bordered in gold. The ratio of the width to the length is 1: 2.

Article 145.—The Capital of the Union of Soviet Socialist Republics is the City of Moscow.

CHAPTER XIII. PROCEDURE FOR AMENDING THE CONSTI- TUTION

Article 146.—The Constitution of the U.S.S.R. may be amended only by decision of the Supreme Soviet of the U.S.S.R. adopted by a majority of not less than two-thirds of the votes in each of its Chambers.

53

ON THE CONSTITUTION

By Joseph Stalin

In 1935 the Seventh Congress of Soviets elected a commission, headed by Stalin, to draft a new Soviet Constitution. Among the commission members were three who would soon be liquidated in the purges—Bukharin, Radek, and Sokolnikov. When adopted, the document became known as the Stalin Constitution, though Bukharin and Radek were its chief authors. Addressing the Eighth Congress of Soviets on November 25, 1936, Stalin delivered a report on the constitution which is reprinted below in abbreviated form.

For a listing of Stalin's writings see Robert McNeal, *Stalin's Works: An Annotated Bibliography*. Those translated into English are available in Joseph Stalin, *Works* (13 vols.) which, however, goes only to 1934. The best biography is Isaac Deutscher, *Stalin* (paperback). A portrait by his chief rival is Leon Trotsky, *Stalin* (paperback). A recent anthology is T. Rigby, *Stalin* (paperback). The literature on Stalin is discussed by Francis Randall, "Books on Stalin," *Problems of Communism*, Vol. XII, No. 2. On Soviet constitutionalism see Nicholas Timasheff, "The Soviet Concept of Democracy," *Review of Politics*, Vol. XII; Marc Vishniak, "Sovereignty in Soviet Law," *Russian Review*, Vol. VIII; and V. Aspaturian, "The Theory and Practice of Soviet Federalism," *Journal of Politics*, Vol. XII. A famous Soviet text, now condemned by Soviet scholars, is Andrei Vyshinsky, *The Law of the Soviet State*, the bible of Stalinist constitutionalism.

CHANGES IN THE LIFE OF THE U.S.S.R. IN THE PERIOD FROM 1924 TO 1936

What are the changes in the life of the U.S.S.R. that have been brought about in the period from 1924 to 1936 and which the Constitution Commission was to reflect in its Draft Constitution?

What is the essence of these changes?

What was the situation in 1924? . . .

At that time we were in the first period of the New Economic Policy, the begining of NEP, the period of a certain revival of capitalism; now, however, we are in the last period of NEP, the end of NEP, the period of the complete liquidation of capitalism in all spheres of the national economy. . . .

And what does this mean?

It means that the exploitation of man has been abolished, eliminated, while the Socialist ownership of the implements and means of production has been established as the unshakable foundation of our Soviet society. [Prolonged applause.]

As a result of all these changes in the sphere of the national economy of the

Condensed from Joseph Stalin, *Problems of Leninism* (Moscow, 1940), pp. 561–89.

615

U.S.S.R., we now have a new, Socialist economy, which knows neither crises nor unemployment, which knows neither poverty nor ruin, and which provides our citizens with every opportunity to lead a prosperous and cultured life. . . .

In conformity with these changes in the economic life of the U.S.S.R., the class structure of our society has also changed.

The landlord class, as you know, had already been eliminated as a result of the victorious conclusion of the civil war. As for the other exploiting classes, they have shared the fate of the landlord class. The capitalist class in the sphere of industry has ceased to exist. The kulak class in the sphere of agriculture has ceased to exist. And the merchants and profiteers in the sphere of trade have ceased to exist. Thus all the exploiting classes have now been eliminated.

There remains the working class.

There remains the peasant class.

There remains the intelligentsia.

But it would be a mistake to think that these social groups have undergone no change during this period, that they have remained the same as they were, say, in the period of capitalism.

Take, for example, the working class of the U.S.S.R. By force of habit, it is often called the proletariat. But what is the proletariat? The proletariat is a class bereft of the instruments and means of production, under an economic system in which the instruments and means of production have been taken from the capitalists and transferred to the state, of which the leading force is the working class. Consequently, there is no longer a capitalist class which would exploit the working class. . . . This being the case, can our working class be called the proletariat? Clearly, it cannot. . . . And what does this

mean? This means that the proletariat of the U.S.S.R. has been transformed into an entirely new class, into the working class of the U.S.S.R., which has abolished the capitalist economic system, which has established the Socialist ownership of the instruments and means of production and is directing Soviet society along the road to Communism. . . .

Let us pass on to the question of the peasantry. . . . In our country there are no longer any landlords and kulaks, merchants and usurers who could exploit the peasants. Consequently, our peasantry is a peasantry emancipated from exploitation. Further. Our Soviet peasantry, its overwhelming majority is a collective farm peasantry, i.e., it bases its work and wealth not on individual labour and on backward technical equipment, but on collective labour and up-to-date technical equipment. Finally, the economy of our peasantry is based, not on private property, but on collective property, which has grown up on the basis of collective labour. . . .

Lastly, let us pass on to the question of the intelligentsia, to the question of engineers and technicians, of workers on the cultural front, of employees in general, and so on. The intelligentsia, too, has undergone great changes during this period. It is no longer the old hidebound intelligentsia which tried to place itself above classes, but which actually, for the most part, served the landlords and the capitalists. Our Soviet intelligentsia is an entirely new intelligentsia, bound up by its very roots with the working class and the peasantry. In the first place, the composition of the intelligentsia has changed. People who come from the aristocracy and the bourgeoisie constitute but a small percentage of our Soviet intelligentsia; 80 to 90 per cent of the Soviet intelligentsia are people who have come from the working class, from the peasantry, or from other strata of the working population. Finally, the very nature of the activities of the intelligentsia has changed. Formerly it had to serve the wealthy classes, for it had no alternative. Today it must serve the people, for there are no longer any exploiting classes. And that is precisely why it is now an equal member of Soviet society, in which, side by side with the workers and peasants, pulling together with them, it is engaged in building the new, classless, Socialist society. . . .

What do these changes signify?

Firstly, they signify that the dividing lines between the working class and the peasantry, and between these classes and the intelligentsia, are being obliterated, and that the old class exclusiveness is disappearing. This means that the distance between these social groups is steadily diminishing.

Secondly, they signify that the economic contradictions between these social groups are declining, are becoming obliterated.

And lastly, they signify that the political contradictions between them are also declining and becoming obliterated.

Such is the position in regard to the changes in the class structure of the U.S.S.R. . . .

II

THE PRINCIPAL SPECIFIC FEATURES OF THE DRAFT CONSTITUTION

How are all these changes in the life of the U.S.S.R. reflected in the draft of the new Constitution? . . .

In drafting the new Constitution, the Constitution Commission proceeded from the proposition that a constitution must not be confused with a program.

. . . Whereas a program speaks of that which does not yet exist, of that which has yet to be achieved and won in the future, a constitution, on the contrary, must speak of that which already exists, of that which has already been achieved and won now, at the present time. A program deals mainly with the future, a constitution with the present.

Two examples by way of illustration.

Our Soviet society has already, in the main, succeeded in achieving Socialism; it has created a Socialist system, i.e., it has brought about what Marxists in other words call the first, or lower, phase of Communism. Hence, in the main, we have already achieved the first phase of Communism, Socialism. The fundamental principle of this phase of Communism is, as you know, the formula: "From each according to his abilities, to each according to his work." Should our Constitution reflect this fact, the fact that Socialism has been achieved? Should it be based on this achievement? Unquestionably, it should. It should, because for the U.S.S.R. Socialism is something already achieved and won.

But Soviet society has not reached the higher phase of Communism, in which the ruling principle will be the formula: "From each according to his abilities, to each according to his needs," although it sets itself the aim of achieving the higher phase of Communism in the future. Can our Constitution be based on the higher phase of Communism, which does not yet exist and which has still to be achieved? No, it cannot, because for the U.S.S.R. the higher phase of Communism is something that has not yet been realized, and which has to be realized in the future. It cannot, if it is not to be converted into a program or a declaration of future achievements.

Such are the limits of our Constitution at the present historical moment. . . .

Further. The constitutions of bourgeois countries usually proceed from the conviction that the capitalist system is immutable.

Unlike these, the draft of the new Constitution of the U.S.S.R. proceeds from the fact that the capitalist system has been liquidated, and that the Socialist system has triumphed in the U.S.S.R. The main foundation of the draft of the new Constitution of the U.S.S.R. is the principle of Socialism, whose main pillars are things that have already been achieved and realized: the Socialist ownership of the land, forests, factories, works and other instruments and means of production; the abolition of exploitation and of exploiting classes; the abolition of poverty for the majority and of luxury for the minority; the abolition of unemployment; work as an obligation and an honorable duty for every able-bodied citizen, in accordance with the formula; "He who does not work, neither shall he eat"; the right to work, i.e., the right of every citizen to receive guaranteed employment; the right to rest and leisure; the right to education, etc. The draft of the new Constitution rests on these and similar pillars of Socialism. It reflects them, it embodies them in law.

Such is the second specific feature of the draft of the new Constitution.

Further. Bourgeois constitutions tacitly proceed from the premise that society consists of antagonistic classes, of classes which own wealth and classes which do not own wealth; that no matter what party comes into power, the guidance of society by the state (the dictatorship) must be in the hands of the bourgeoisie; that a constitution is needed for the purpose of consolidating a social order desired by and beneficial to the propertied classes.

Unlike bourgeois constitutions, the draft of the new Constitution of the U.S.S.R. proceeds from the fact that there are no longer any antagonistic classes in society; that society consists of two friendly classes, of workers and peasants; that it is these classes, the labouring classes, that are in power; that the guidance of society by the state (the dictatorship) is in the hands of the working class, the most advanced class in society; that a constitution is needed for the purpose of consolidating a social order desired by and beneficial to the working people.

Such is the third specific feature of the draft of the new Constitution.

Further. Bourgeois constitutions tacitly proceed from the premise that nations and races cannot have equal rights, that there are nations with full rights and nations without full rights, and that in addition, there is a third category of nations or races, for example, the colonies, which have even fewer rights than the nations without full rights. This means that, at bottom, all these constitutions are nationalistic, i.e., constitutions of ruling nations.

Unlike these constitutions, the draft of the new Constitution of the U.S.S.R. is, on the contrary, profoundly internationalistic. It proceeds from the proposition that all nations and races have equal rights. It proceeds from the fact that neither difference in colour or language, cultural level, or level of political development, nor any other difference between nations and races, can serve as grounds for justifying national inequality of rights. It proceeds from the proposition that all nations and races, irrespective of their past and present position, irrespective of their strength or weakness, should enjoy equal rights in all spheres of the economic, social, political and cultural life of society.

Such is the fourth specific feature of the draft of the new Constitution.

The fifth specific feature of the draft of the new Constitution is its consistent and thoroughgoing democratism. From the standpoint of democratism bourgeois constitutions may be divided into two groups: One group of constitutions openly denies, or actually nullifies, the equality of rights of citizens and democratic liberties. The other group of constitutions readily accepts, and even advertises, democratic principles, but at the same time it makes reservations and provides for restrictions which utterly mutilate these democratic rights and liberties. They speak of equal suffrage for all citizens, but at the same time limit it by residential, educational, and even property qualifications. They speak of equal rights for citizens, but at the same time they make the reservation that this does not apply to women, or applies to them only in part. And so on and so forth.

What distinguishes the draft of the new Constitution of the U.S.S.R. is the fact that it is free from such reservations and restrictions. For it, there exists no division of citizens into active and passive ones; for it, all citizens are active. It does not recognize any difference in rights as between men and women, "residents" and "non-residents," propertied and propertyless, educated and uneducated. For it, all citizens have equal rights. It is not property status, not national origin, not sex, nor office, but personal ability and personal labour, that determines the position of every citizen in society.

Lastly, there is still one more specific feature of the draft of the new Constitution. Bourgeois constitutions usually confine themselves to stating the formal rights of citizens, without bothering about the conditions for the exercise of these rights, about the opportunity of exercising them, about the means by which they can be exercised. . . .

What distinguishes the draft of the new Constitution is the fact that it does not confine itself to stating the formal rights of citizens, but stresses the guarantees of these rights, the means by which these rights can be exercised. It does not merely proclaim equality of rights for citizens, but ensures it by giving legislative embodiment to the fact that the citizens have been emancipated from all exploitation. It does not merely proclaim the right to work, but ensures it by giving legislative embodiment to the fact that there are no crises in Soviet society, and that unemployment has been abolished. It does not merely proclaim democratic liberties, but legislatively ensures them by providing definite material resources. . . .

III

BOURGEOIS CRITICISM OF THE DRAFT CONSTITUTION

I must admit that the draft of the new Constitution does preserve the regime of the dictatorship of the working class, just as it also preserves unchanged the present leading position of the Communist Party of the U.S.S.R. [Loud applause.] If the esteemed critics regard this as a flaw in the Draft Constitution, that is only to be regretted. We Bolsheviks regard it as a merit of the Draft Constitution. [Loud applause.]

As to freedom for various political parties, we adhere to somewhat different views. A party is a part of a class, its most advanced part. Several parties, and, consequently, freedom for parties, can exist only in a society in which there are antagonistic classes whose interests are mutually hostile and irreconcilable—in which there are, say, capitalists and workers, landlords and peasants, kulaks and poor peasants, etc. But in the U.S.S.R. there are no longer such classes as the capitalists, the landlords, the kulaks, etc. In the U.S.S.R. there are only two classes, workers and peasants, whose interests—far from being mutually hostile—are, on the contrary, friendly. Hence, there is no ground in the U.S.S.R. for the existence of several parties, and, consequently, for freedom for these parties. In the U.S.S.R. there is ground only for one party, the Communist Party. In the U.S.S.R. only one party can exist, the Communist Party, which courageously defends the interests of the workers and peasants to the very end. . . .

They talk of democracy. But what is democracy? Democracy in capitalist countries, where there are antagonistic classes, is, in the last analysis, democracy for the strong, democracy for the propertied minority. In the U.S.S.R., on the contrary, democracy is democracy for the working people, i.e., democracy for all. But from this it follows that the principles of democratism are violated, not by the draft of the new Constitution of the U.S.S.R., but by the bourgeois constitutions. That is why I think that the Constitution of the U.S.S.R. is the only thoroughly democratic Constitution in the world. . . .

IV

AMENDMENTS AND ADDENDA TO THE DRAFT CONSTITUTION

1. First of all about the amendments to Article 1 of the Draft Constitution. There are four amendments. Some propose that we substitute for the words "state of workers and peasants" the words "state of working people." Others propose that we add the words "and working intelligentsia" to the words "state of workers and peasants." A third group proposes that we substitute for the words "state of workers and peasants" the words "state of all the races and nationalities inhabiting the territory of the U.S.S.R." A fourth group proposes that we substitute for the word "peasants" the words "collective farmers" or "toilers of Socialist agriculture."

Should these amendments be adopted? I think they should not.

What does Article 1 of the Draft Constitution speak of? It speaks of the class composition of Soviet society. Can we Marxists ignore the question of the class composition of our society in the Constitution? No, we cannot. As we know, Soviet society consists of two classes, workers and peasants. And it is of this that Article 1 of the Draft Constitution speaks. Consequently, Article 1 of the Draft Constitution properly reflects the class composition of our society. It may be asked: What about the working intelligentsia? The intelligentsia has never been a class, and never can be a class— it was and remains a stratum, which recruits its members from among all classes of society. In the old days the intelligentsia recruited its members from the ranks of the nobility, of the bourgeoisie, partly from the ranks of the peasantry, and only to a very inconsiderable extent from the ranks of the workers. In our day, under the Soviets, the intelligentsia recruits its members mainly from the ranks of the workers and peasants. But no matter where it may recruit its members, and what character it may bear, the intelligentsia is nevertheless a stratum and not a class. . . .

The same must be said of the nations and races comprising the U.S.S.R. In Chapter I of the Draft Constitution it is stated that the U.S.S.R. is a free union of nations possessing equal rights. Is it worthwhile repeating this formula in Article 1 of the Draft Constitution, which deals not with the national composition of Soviet society, but with its class composition? Clearly, it is not worthwhile. As to the rights of the nations and races comprising the U.S.S.R., these are dealt with in Chapters I, X, and XI of the Draft Constitution. From these chapters it is evident that the nations and races of the U.S.S.R. enjoy equal rights in all spheres of the economic, political, social and cultural life of the country. Consequently, there can be no question of an infringement upon national rights. . . .

2. Then follows an amendment to Article 17 of the Draft Constitution. The amendment proposes that we completely delete from the Constitution Article 17, which reserves to the Union Republics the right of free secession from the U.S.S.R. I think that this proposal is a wrong one and therefore should not be adopted by the Congress. The U.S.S.R. is a voluntary union of Union Republics with equal rights. To delete from the Constitution the article providing for the right of free secession from the U.S.S.R. would be to violate the voluntary character of this union. Can we agree to this step? I think that we cannot and should not agree to it. It is said that there is not a single republic in the U.S.S.R. that would want to secede from the U.S.S.R., and that therefore Article 17 is of no practical importance. It is, of course, true that there is not a single republic that would want to secede from the U.S.S.R. But this does not in the least mean that we should not fix in the Constitution the right of Union Republics freely to secede from the U.S.S.R. In the U.S.S.R. there is not a single Union Republic that would want to subjugate another Union Republic. But this does not in the least mean that we ought to delete from the Constitution of the U.S.S.R. the article dealing with the equality of rights of the Union Republics.

3. Then there is a proposal that we add a new article to Chapter I of the Draft Constitution, to the following effect; that on reaching the proper level of economic and cultural development Autonomous Soviet Socialist Republics may be raised to the status of Union Soviet Socialist Republics. Can this proposal be adopted? I think that it should not be adopted. It is a wrong proposal not only because of its content, but also because of the condition it lays down. Economic and cultural maturity can no more be urged as grounds for transferring Autonomous Republics to the category of Union Republics than economic or cultural backwardness can be urged as grounds for leaving any particular republic in the list of Autonomous Republics. This would not be a Marxist, nor a Leninist approach. The Tatar Republic, for example, remains an Autonomous Republic, while the Kazakh Republic is to become a Union Republic; but this does not mean that from the standpoint of cultural and economic development the Kazakh Republic is on a higher level than the Tatar Republic. The very opposite is the case. The same can be said, for example, of the Volga German Autonomous Republic and the Kirghiz Union Republic, of which the former is on a higher cultural and economic level than the latter, although it remains an Autonomous Republic.

What are the grounds for transferring Autonomous Republics to the category of Union Republics?

There are three such grounds.

First, the republic concerned must be a border republic, not surrounded on all sides by U.S.S.R. territory. Why? Because since the Union Republics have the right to secede from the U.S.S.R., a republic, on becoming a Union Republic, must be in a position logically and actually to raise the question of secession from the U.S.S.R. And this question can be raised only by a republic which, say, borders on some foreign state, and, consequently, is not surrounded on all sides by U.S.S.R. territory. Of course, none of our republics would actually raise the question of seceding from the U.S.S.R. But since the right to secede from the U.S.S.R. is reserved to the Union Republics, it must be so arranged that this right does not become a meaningless scrap of paper. Take, for example, the Bashkir Republic or the Tatar Republic. Let us assume that these Autonomous Republics are transferred to the category of Union Republics. Could they logically and actually raise the question of seceding from the U.S.S.R.? No, they could not. Why? Because they are surrounded on all sides by Soviet republics and regions, and, strictly speaking, they have nowhere to go if they secede from the U.S.S.R. [Laughter and applause.] Therefore, it would be wrong to transfer such republics to the category of the Union Republics.

Secondly, the nationality which gives its name to a given Soviet republic must constitute a more or less compact majority within the republic. Take the Crimean Autonomous Republic, for example. It is a border republic, but the Crimean Tatars do not constitute the majority in that republic; on the contrary, they are a minority. Consequently, it would be wrong and illogical to transfer the Crimean Republic to the category of Union Republics.

Thirdly, the republic must not have too small a population; it should have a population of, say, not less but more than a million, at least. Why? Because it would be wrong to assume that a small Soviet Republic with a very small population and a small army could hope to maintain its existence as an independent state. There can hardly be any doubt that the imperialist beasts of prey would soon lay hands on it.

I think that unless these three objective grounds exist, it would be wrong at the present historical moment to raise the question of transferring any particular Autonomous Republic to the category of Union Republics. . . .

8. Then follows an addendum to Article 40, proposing that the Presidium of the Supreme Soviet be granted the right to pass provisional acts of legislation. I think that this addendum is wrong and should not be adopted by the Congress. It is time we put an end to a situation in which not one but a number of bodies legislate. Such a situation runs counter to the principle that laws should be stable. And we need stability of laws now more than ever. Legislative power in the U.S.S.R. must be exercised only by one body, the Supreme Soviet of the U.S.S.R.

9. Further, an addendum is proposed to Article 48 of the Draft Constitution, demanding that the President of the Presidium of the Supreme Soviet of the U.S.S.R. be elected not by the Supreme Soviet of the U.S.S.R. but by the whole population of the country. I think this addendum is wrong, because it runs counter to the spirit of our Constitution. According to the system of our Constitution there must not be an individual president in the U.S.S.R., elected by the whole population on a par with the Supreme Soviet, and able to put himself in opposition to the Supreme Soviet. The president in the U.S.S.R. is a collegium, it is the Presidium of the Supreme Soviet, elected, not by the whole population, but by the Supreme Soviet, and accountable to the Supreme Soviet. Historical experience shows that such a structure of the supreme bodies is the most democratic, and safeguards the country against undesirable contingencies. . . .

12. Next follows an amendment to Article 124 of the Draft Constitution, demanding that the article be changed to provide for the prohibition of the performance of religious rites. I think that this amendment should be rejected as running counter to the spirit of our

Constitution.

13. Finally, there is one other amendment of a more or less material character. I am referring to an amendment to Article 135 of the Draft Constitution. It proposes that ministers of religion, former White Guards, all the former rich, and persons not engaged in socially useful occupations be disfranchised, or, at all events, that the franchise of people in this category be restricted to the right to elect, but not to be elected. I think that this amendment should likewise be rejected. The Soviet government disfranchised the non-working and exploiting elements not for all time, but temporarily, up to a certain period. There was a time when these elements waged open war against the people and actively resisted the Soviet laws. The Soviet law depriving them of the franchise was the Soviet government's reply to this resistance. Quite some time has elapsed since then. During this period we have succeeded in abolishing the exploiting classes, and the Soviet government has become an invincible force. Has not the time arrived for us to revise this law? I think the time has arrived. . . .

Such is the position with regard to the amendments and addenda to the Draft Constitution of the U.S.S.R.

54

THE SOVIET SYSTEM OF GOVERNMENT

By John Hazard

It would require an entire volume to provide an adequate commentary on the Soviet Constitution. What is attempted in this selection is far more modest; it is to throw light on some aspects of Soviet politics which the constitution proclaims but does not describe. It is Hazard's thesis that the U.S.S.R. can afford to utilize "democratic forms" since it is free to deal with them effectively by a system of "totalitarian counterweights." Mr. Hazard studied in the Soviet Union for two years in the 1930's. He has been for many years professor of government at Columbia University, where he is a member of the Russian Institute.

The best-known text on Soviet politics is Merle Fainsod, *How Russia Is Ruled.* See also his *Smolensk under Soviet Rule* (paperback), based on captured Soviet documents never before published. A British work is Robert Conquest, *Power and Policy in the USSR.* An older but still useful textbook is Julian Towster, *Political Power in the USSR.* A Soviet view may be obtained in A. Denisov, *Soviet State Law;* V. Karpinsky, *The Social and State Structure of the USSR;* and P. Romashkin, *Fundamentals of Soviet Law.* On the Communist Party see Leonard Schapiro, *The Communist Party of the Soviet Union* (paperback). Two recent works are Frederick Barghoorn, *Politics in the USSR,* and Alfred Meyer, *The Soviet Political System.* On law in the USSR see Harold Berman, *Justice in the USSR* (paperback), and his *Soviet Criminal Law and Procedure.* See also "Law and Legality in the Soviet Union," a special issue of *Problems of Communism,* March–April, 1965.

STRUCTURE OF THE STATE APPARATUS

Under the second Constitution of the U.S.S.R., adopted in 1936 and presently in effect, the soviets have both policy-making and administrative functions. At levels above the local one, they are structured in the same way as is the Communist party. There is, therefore, a Supreme Soviet of the U.S.S.R. which corresponds to The All-Union Congress of the Communist Party. The Supreme Soviet is authorized to choose a presidium as its alter ego to make policy decisions in the form of legislation during intervals between its meetings, these intervals being usually six to eight

From John Hazard, *The Soviet System of Government* (4th ed., rev.; University of Chicago Press, 1968), pp. 43–59, 92–97, 175–81. Copyright 1957, 1960, 1964, 1968 by The University of Chicago.

months. Each sitting of the Supreme Soviet lasts only from four to six days under normal circumstances. The Supreme Soviet also chooses formally a council of ministers to be the executive branch of government.

Below the level of the Supreme Soviet of the U.S.S.R., there are supreme soviets in each of the fifteen republics which are federated in the U.S.S.R. Each such supreme soviet has its own presidium and its own council of ministers. Below the republic level there is a soviet in each province. At the level below the province there are soviets in cities and in rural counties. Each has its executive committee. The various soviets in the republics are elected, formally and directly by the people, every four years, while deputies to the lesser soviets are named in direct election for two-year terms. In these elections, all adult citizens of the geographical area defined as under the jurisdiction of the soviet may vote and be represented, regardless of their place of work. There is no system of indirect elections, such as in the Communist party conferences functioning at the level of the county, the big city, the province, the republic, and the union, according to which delegates to higher levels of the party system come from the party conference immediately below.

At the local level there is a marked difference between the soviet apparatus and the party apparatus. While the party apparatus comprises all party members of the local employment group at a given level of the organizational hierarchy, the soviet apparatus is composed of only a selected group of persons, nominally elected every two years, and thus bears some formal structural resemblance to the town or city council, or board of selectmen, of many an American village or city. In

substance, however, it is very different, as will be indicated below.

The soviet at each level of the hierarchy is not in permanent session but is called together by its executive committee at intervals specified in the Constitution. In practice, the intervals are often longer than those specified, as indicated by complaints in the Moscow press that executive committee chairmen are not doing their duty in calling the required meetings of local soviets. Since meetings of the soviet are called only infrequently, the opportunity is afforded the local party bosses to prepare its business in small, easily controlled committees. Thus in each soviet there is created a group of "permanent committees" to which are assigned those of the deputies who have special knowledge of the subject matter to be discussed. Schoolteachers and parents are assigned to the permanent committee on education; doctors, nurses, and sanitary workers are assigned to the permanent committee on public health; engineers and bench workmen are assigned to the permanent committee on local industry; and so on.

Skilled individuals who are not deputies to the soviet are assigned to the "permanent committees" to initiate large numbers of citizens into the problems with which they deal. Some Soviet commentators have declared that through these assignments many citizens will be trained to assume the responsibilities of government. This has been interpreted variously either as a preparation for the eventual withering away of the state and the substitution of unpaid staff serving in rotation for the regular civil service, or as the development of a new kind of democracy symbolic of the "state of the whole people," which in Soviet eyes has replaced the "dictatorship of the proletariat" and the "state of the working people" to which allegiance was required in turn during the two earlier periods of Soviet history.

A meeting of a soviet, when it is called, brings together a rather large number of people. While the usual number of deputies in a rural community is not more than 35, this number increases in the provinces to 208 and in the large cities such that after elections in 1967 there were 1,120 in Moscow. The total number of people elected to sit as deputies in all of the soviets of the U.S.S.R. is correspondingly large. Statistics indicate that in the elections of 1967 some 2,045,277 persons were named to sit in the soviets below the republic level. The elections of 1966 seated 1,517 deputies in the two chambers of the Supreme Soviet of the U.S.S.R.

PARTY INFLUENCE ON THE SOVIETS

By no means all of the deputies in the various soviets are members of the Communist party. In 1966 the percentage of Communist party members and candidates among the deputies elected to the Supreme Soviet of the U.S.S.R. was 75.7 in one chamber and 74.6 in the other. The Republics' Supreme Soviets reported party representation of 68 per cent following the 1967 elections.

At lower levels the number is much smaller. The statistics reveal for 1965 a range from 49.9 per cent Communist party members in the provincial and lower soviets of the Azerbaidjan Republic to 38.9 per cent in the same-level soviets of the Lithuanian Republic. The other republics fall between, the correlation seemingly being established on a basis of number of years during which a republic's territory has been part of the U.S.S.R.

These statistics suggest that the Communist party is able, through the soviets, to spread the influence of its limited membership among a large number of people. More important, it is thus able to bring many of the most active non-party people into an apparatus which makes some policy decisions, even though these decisions are limited in character, and, in so doing, develop in them a sense of participation and, presumably, a corollary sense of loyalty to the regime.

Reports from the soviets indicate the subjects of their policy debates. A school milk program is one such subject. The manner of distribution of schoolbooks, whether to be through kiosks in the schools or through regular bookstores throughout the city, is another. The distribution of natural gas to consumers for their cooking stoves is studied and a policy established. Those few party members who are deputies can, through their caucus, prevent an undesirable conclusion to the debate, and meanwhile they may learn from an irate mother or from an angry housewife what needs to be done to improve the distribution of schoolbooks or milk or cooking gas. The end result is that the party need not spend the time of all its members on such details.

In the Supreme Soviet of the U.S.S.R., to which matters of greater national concern are presented, the pattern of Communist party membership is, as we have seen, different. Every election prior to that of 1954 named to the office of deputy to the Supreme Soviet of the U.S.S.R. a higher percentage of party members than to the preceding Supreme Soviet. One can conclude either that the matters presented were of such great concern that the party felt increasingly that its members had to be present in mass or that almost all politically active citizens had already been made members of the party.

Such crowding of the Supreme Soviet of the U.S.S.R. with party members may have defeated the purpose for which it was established as the peak of the state apparatus, for it brought very few people in touch with policy matters who would not ordinarily be close to them anyway by virtue of their Communist party membership. Such an approach may have been that of the Communist party leadership for two years after Stalin's death. A suggestion that party thinking was along these lines is to be found in the manner in which important changes in the national economic plan were made. A decision to introduce a greater quantity of consumers' goods into production was made by the Central Committee of the party and issued over the signatures of the Central Committee, together with the signatures of the officers of the Presidium of the Supreme Soviet and the Council of Ministers. The same was done with a program of agricultural expansion into virgin lands that was adopted in 1953. Both these very important matters would in earlier years have been brought before the Supreme Soviet or discussed at a meeting of the Supreme Soviet following adoption by the Supreme Soviet's Presidium. Yet neither program was brought before the Supreme Soviet for discussion in any form, except in so far as the programs were reflected in the annual budget approved by the Supreme Soviet at its annual sessions of 1954 and 1955. Perhaps the Supreme Soviet was being permitted to lose even the limited importance it had had in the past in bringing a group of the most active of the non-party citizens into close relationship with the economic policies of the government.

If the tendency of Communist party leaders was to ignore the Supreme Soviet on important economic issues immediately after Stalin's death, that policy began to change in 1955. Sessions of the soviets were held on schedule, and the work of each was enlivened by activity of the standing committees, which during Stalin's time had met in secret if at all.

It is these committees which have provided the measure of change in attitude toward the work of the Soviets. Under arrangements made for organization of the Supreme Soviet after the 1937 elections these committees functioned to discuss the budget, new legislation, foreign affairs, and credentials of the deputies, and they were established in both chambers. The first of these to become active publicly after 1955 was the committee on the budget of each chamber. Hearings were held prior to the plenary sessions of the Supreme Soviet, and ministers were questioned on the justification for requested appropriations. With the major reforms in the codes of law initiated after Stalin's death, the legislative committees also came to life, and reviewed over long periods drafts submitted by the Council of Ministers. Witnesses were heard, issues debated, and some drafts returned to the Council of Ministers for revision. Still, the committees did not participate in all cases, for from 1961 to 1965 its preliminary consideration was limited to 53 of the 241 laws enacted.

Foreign policy was not debated in the same way, even when the Supreme Soviet was asked to ratify treaties signed by the government. Khrushchev and his ministers merely stated the positions they had taken and asked for confirmation. The committee made a report supporting what had been done, and the report was then adopted by a show of hands in the assembly without debate or dissent.

The work of the Soviets was a major item of concern of the twenty-third congress of the party, held in 1966. The party's General Secretary stated that in the soviets was to be found the place to manifest a new emphasis upon democracy. Practice since that time has pointed the finger at the committees of the soviets as the focus of the attempt at democratization of what used to be moribund bodies. The committees have proliferated. Thus, for example, the Supreme Soviet at its 1966 organizational meeting added six new committees in each chamber to those already existing, these being to consider matters of transportation and communication, construction and the building materials industry, agriculture, public health and social security, public education, science and culture, trade and services. The budget committees' duties were expanded to include review of the national economic plans, which had formerly issued from the party alone. Since the budget concerned economic matters, the Economic Committee, formerly existing only in the Council of Nationalities, was discontinued as no longer necessary.

The movement reached into the Republic Supreme Soviets in 1967, when they were organized after new elections. The Russian Republic followed the federal soviet's pattern to create seven new committees to add to the traditional ones. These corresponded in the main to those in the federal soviet, but concerned some matters reserved by the Constitution to the republics alone, such as sports, which were added to the new committee on public education and culture, and public catering, which was added to the committee on trade. Committees for which nothing comparable existed at the federal level were created in the republic for activities conducted by the local soviets in providing communal services, as well as for civic improvements and nature conservatiu... The committees were small, numbering from 30 to 40 persons, while that for foreign affairs had but 13.

From these events, it is evident that the role of the soviets is being reassessed. From bodies which served Stalin to ratify his proposals and publicize them among the people of the deputies' homelands, they are becoming forums for discussion and perfection of plans and performance in economic and cultural fields, and for discussion of legislative proposals affecting the personal life of large numbers of citizens. They are not, however, places for voting contests, as the decisions are based on consensus and are always unanimous.

The conclusion seems justified that the state apparatus, which Lenin created out of necessity when his party had to share with others in the formulation of policy and which was continued by Stalin to serve the useful purpose of radiation of party influence throughout the whole population, has been reformed. Its functions are now dual: radiation of influence as before, but also the gathering of experts in administration and with specialized knowledge to consult on detail necessary to the formulation of policy. The Communist party members among these relatively popular bodies are always present to provide guidance, but the new vitality of the soviets permits party members to hear witnesses from outside the ruling circles in meetings which could not easily be organized inside the party where the tradition has been one of secrecy of meetings.

CONTROLLED MASS PARTICIPATION

A strengthened socialist democracy was the theme of the fiftieth anniversary year, but it presented problems to the Communist party leaders. Even with a tradition of firm leadership by the party of the political life of the country, Soviet citizens have become restless. Increasing numbers travel abroad to represent the state or to study or to tour. Ideas from abroad in a form sympathetic to Western democracies are still withheld from the masses by limitation of foreign newspapers except those published by foreign Communist parties, but foreign radio broadcasts can be heard. Soviet citizens know that modernized mankind now measures democracy in terms of opportunity to choose leaders and to influence policy formulation. The Communist party leaders cannot escape consideration of the reflection of these world-wide aspirations upon their own people. They are trying to meet the demand, but without sacrificing what they believe essential to progress at the U.S.S.R.'s current stage of economic and social development, namely strong leadership by the party.

The Soviet state apparatus provides the means through which democratic aspirations are balanced with the desire to retain strong leadership. Fortunately for the Communist party leadership, the state apparatus was never merged by Stalin with the party, so that there is ready for use in execution of the new policy a form preserved by Stalin. Still, that form is not to be developed as Western Jeffersonian democrats would expect. Communists cannot bring themselves to open wide the gates to unrestricted selection of leaders and determination of policy. They insist on creation of a pattern of action designed to balance freedom of choice with control over what they believe to be its irresponsible use. The theme is to be controlled mass participation, differing from Stalin's concept in that emphasis is to be on participation rather than on control.

ELECTIONS AND THE ONE-PARTY SYSTEM

The key to mass participation in the eyes of the world is the electoral process, and since 1936 the Communist party has opened elections to all when deputies are to be chosen for the bodies comprising the representative agencies of the Soviet state apparatus. The restrictions existing until 1936 denying the vote to those who hired labor, served as priests or monks, or had been former members of the Imperial Police or the royal family were revoked at that time. Elections were simultaneously opened to every person of eighteen years of age and over, regardless of social origin, occupation, race, or creed.

Elections were also made direct for all levels of soviets. Since 1936 the indirect system of election, still maintained within the Communist party, under which delegates to all higher levels within the party are chosen not by the rank and file of party members but by the next lower party body, has been abandoned. Further, since 1936 all elections to the various soviets have been secret. Printed ballots are used, and curtained booths are provided for the voter to scrutinize and mark the ballot. Herewith, the U.S.S.R. is able to offer to its citizens and to the world a picture of general, direct, and secret elections, and to claim that it has established institutions that are the cornerstones of democracy.

To understand how little risk is really being taken by the Communist party in reforming the electoral procedure, the Westerner must note the counterweights that have been set up to prevent popular selection of state functionaries who might be unwilling to accept the guidance of the party. The most important of these counterweights is the constitutional provision establishing the Communist party as the sole political party within the U.S.S.R. No other political party may be organized in competition for votes.

While Western peoples do not consider one-party systems compatible with the processes of democracy, it must be admitted that there are parts of the world that are accepted as democratically governed and in which there is only one effective party because the competing party is traditionally too weak to make the slightest challenge to its rule. It is possible, therefore, for a system to merit attribution of the democratic label if there be only one effective party, but, in such cases, there must be a choice of candidates within that party. In many places this choice is provided through a party primary, in which the citizen can select the candidate he prefers. If he belongs to the traditional minority party, he may even declare membership in the perpetual majority party, so as to have an opportunity to vote in its primary and thus share in the selection of candidates.

Opportunity for such choice of candidates is denied in the U.S.S.R. The Communist party holds no primaries, nor does it permit the placing of more than one name per office on a ballot. Nothing in the law prevents a multiple-candidate election. On the contrary, the new constitutional provisions applied in elections for the Supreme Soviet in 1937 provided for a ballot on which was printed the instruction to the voter to cross out all but one name. This same form of ballot is still in use. There is nothing in the regulations to show that there is no choice.

The nominating procedure provided by law appears to make possible the naming of more than one candidate for each office of deputy. Under this procedure, public organizations, such as sports clubs, trade unions, and cooperative associations; may propose candidates in addition to those named by the Communist party. However, none of these organizations may be a political party or conceal the mechanism of a political party under a mask, so it is clear that its basic program must conform to that of the party. It can be imagined that one organization would propose a candidate who would emphasize local school improvement, another might enter a candidate who favored building branch libraries or sports fields. All would have to favor basic party policies such as progression toward communism. None could seek to retrace steps from state-owned enterprise to private enterprise, but candidates could differ in emphasis and, easily, in ability.

In spite of the legal possibility of a choice of candidates in the elections of 1937, the first held under the new rules, there was no choice. On the day the ballots were printed, there appeared on each ballot only one name for each position. The individuals who had been nominated by different organizations within each district had been reduced to one, presumably after the executive committee of the party conference at the county or big-city level had made its selection from among the nominees. To this day, there has appeared on the ballot only one name for each place.

Since the Second World War, the variety of nominations has been reduced so that only one real candidate is nominated within each district by all the nominating groups in factories, in universities, in sports organizations, and in trade unions. The other nominees are nationally known members of the government who are nominated in all but their customary constituency for honorary reasons alone. This very fact —that the established leaders of the party are nominated in many precincts but ultimately have their names withdrawn from all but their customary constituency, leaving only one real candidate for election in each district—indicates that the nominating agencies have been advised whom they are to nominate. If they were not advised, withdrawal of the names of national figures might leave two, or no, candidates. Such pat results can be achieved only when there has been some planning at party headquarters.

Soviet defenders of the claim that the soviet system of government is democratic often point to the fact that citizens may cross out the name of the sole candidate appearing upon the ballot. The voter may even write in a name, so the defenders say. Soon after each election the electoral commission in each voting district publishes statistics on the number of scratches, and on each occasion a considerable number are reported. For example, in the 1966 elections for the Supreme Soviet, the scratches were said to have totaled 345,643 for deputies to one chamber of the Supreme Soviet and 289,298 for deputies of the other chamber. In spite of these scratches all candidates were elected, for in no instance did the scratches exceed the number of affirmative ballots for a candidate.

In the local elections of 1967 there were reported 129 cases in which the single candidate for the position of deputy to a village, city, or county soviet failed of election because the total number of scratches constituted a majority of the votes cast. These failures were not many, however, for over two million deputies were successful in the elections at these local levels. Clearly, the public opposition was to individuals and not to basic party positions.

The desire to express opposition to individuals led to proposals in the press in 1965 to give the voters a choice of candidates. No one needed to explain that the choice would not concern party programs, but only personalities and their concern for local issues. No change in electoral procedures has resulted, nor has there even been public discussion of the matter by high party officials. Still, the fact that they were published at all in a controlled press indicates some desire to extend the concept of socialist democracy to include a choice of candidates in an election, even when all have to adhere to the fundamental strategy of the party.

CONTROLS OVER VOTING PROCEDURE

Foreign correspondents who have visited U.S.S.R. polling booths since World War II report that there has developed another practice which yet further reduces the possibility of dissent. Although curtained booths are always provided for the marking of ballots, voters are not required on pain of punishment to enter the booths whether or not they wish to mark the ballot, and zealous citizens are permitted to stand ostentatiously in the open room, fold their ballot without marking it, and then move to the urn and deposit it. Such a practice illustrates the possibilities open to leaders who want to control the vote: folding the ballot unmarked, in plain view of the poll watchers, can and probably has become a sign of loyalty to the regime, which timorous persons dare not fail to give.

It is clear that even though the elections for soviets at all levels are now open to all and are also secret and direct, they are subject to various strict controls so that they cannot result in a serious surprise to the Communist party leaders who guide them. The laws provide the formal framework of democratic institutions, but the counterweights prevent their operation toward an unhindered expression of opinion.

Notwithstanding this, Soviet leaders make much of full participation in elections. It is impossible for foreigners to verify the attendance, but it is currently reported to be in the neighborhood of 99.9 per cent of the eligible voters. It may be that the attendance indeed approaches this percentage, for by all accounts nearly everyone votes, if need be in the ballot boxes that are carried into the hospitals and the homes of the sick, onto Soviet ships at sea, or to Soviet troops abroad. Communist party pressure to vote is so great that it results in an even higher percentage of participation than is found in those democratic countries where the law itself requires a citizen to vote and provides a penalty if he does not.

Voting by deputies within the soviets is controlled by the simple procedural expedient of voting by show of hands. It may be that a deputy would always choose to vote for the party's program out of gratitude for the prestige brought him by election to the soviets, for prestige obviously accrues to being a deputy. Yet, even if he wished to vote against some measure, he would probably think twice lest he lose the confidence of the party and the seat he holds. He might even fall under the observation of the repressive agencies, of which more will be said later. That there are no such public dissenters—at least in the Supreme Soviet, to which foreign diplomats and correspondents are invited as observers—is proved by the fact that there has never yet been a vote, on any subject, which has not been unanimous. This was so even on the dramatic occasion when in 1955 Malenkov was replaced as Prime Minister by Bulganin. Although the move came as an obvious surprise to some of those in the room, not a voice was raised against it. Everyone must have assumed that the change had been arranged by the Presidium of the Central Committee of the Communist party, and, with such sponsorship, there was no likelihood of opposition from the floor.

Given the system that evolved during Stalin's time for the election of deputies to soviets and their participation in meetings, the representative function was that of a rubber stamp on a program prepared by the Communist party. Still the drama of deputy participation in budget-making was presented in realistic form. After the Minister of Finance had read the budget proposals, the two chambers of the Supreme Soviet met separately to hear the reports of their respective budget committees. These reports made detailed suggestions for changes in the government's proposals, recommending items to be added to the revenue and expense sides of the budget. When the draft was resubmitted for action by the deputies, the committees' proposals were always incorporated.

The drama was too well acted in Stalin's time to have substance, particularly for those with knowledge of the planning of the Communist party for each Supreme Soviet meeting. For the Communist party there could be no surprises, and it seemed obvious that the drama had been planned in advance.

Since 1955 the emergence of committee hearings well before the Supreme

Soviet sessions to which reference has been made in the preceding chapter may be preparing the way for a change. The Communist party, notably since 1966, gives evidence of having decided that it is to its advantage to utilize the committee structure to seek to improve efficiency through consultation with the republic and provincial experts who sit on committees. Such consultation would, of course, be possible within party circles alone, but it is being sought through Supreme Soviet committees as well.

Explanation of the increasing importance of budget committees suggests that the drama of committee consideration without the substance of real participation may have seemed undignified to those who participated in it, especially in light of the exposure of its lack of substance by critics abroad. The value the drama may have had in winning friends for the U.S.S.R. among peoples who really did not know that it was being staged may have been reduced as explanations of competent observers of the Soviet scene reached their ears through advanced media of mass information.

Whatever the explanation, a report on activity within the Supreme Soviet cannot omit consideration of increasing committee activity. Yet, the conclusion is still justified that the forum provided by the Supreme Soviet is still a highly controlled forum. It provides nothing like the place provided by parliaments in Western lands for the introduction of ideas unexpected by a party in power and for the possible rejection in totality of a scheme introduced by that party.

LIMITATIONS ON FREEDOM OF EXPRESSION

Democracy is measured in the public mind by more than parliamentary representation. Before the Russian Revolu-

tion, Communist party leaders claimed for their adherents the right to speak their minds, and the first Soviet Constitution included this as a right to a free press and to free speech, but a qualification was added. In this qualification the policy-makers of the new state showed their concern with a counterweight to complete freedom of expression. They provided that the constitutional freedoms be extended to the general public for a limited purpose. They might be exercised solely in the interest of the socialist revolution, and, if exercised contrary to that interest, the responsible person might be deprived of them.

Limitations upon freedom of the press and of speech have been stated less clearly in subsequent Soviet constitutions but they seem still to exist. The 1936 Constitution retains the limitation mentioned above, in the form of a declaration that the right of free speech is granted "in accordance with the interests of the toilers and for the purpose of strengthening the socialist structure" of the U.S.S.R. The Criminal Code states that it is for the courts to determine whether speech is contrary to the interests of the toilers and whether it is exercised with the intention of harming the Soviet state.

Probably few among those who supported the Soviet regime in the early years thought that the limitations on the right to free speech and press would prevent a significant part of the citizens from expressing their views. None of the revolutionaries felt sorry about constitutional limitations on their enemies. The opponents of the regime were thought to be relatively few and all to be members of classes that had supported Tsarism or the provisional government that followed it. These classes were accused of having failed to provide the masses with economic benefits, and Marxist supporters of the new regime felt them to be outright traitors to the Russian people in opposing a development that was an outgrowth of a scientific analysis of the course of history. As political failures or even as traitors who would prey with their ideas upon the uninformed millions who had not yet come to understand the program of the revolutionaries, these opposition elements had to be silenced, at least until the new regime had established its own power. Writers of the time indicated that the restraints which they espoused were to be operative solely upon the enemies of the regime. They did not anticipate that any but the obviously capitalist elements would be denied the exercise of democratic rights, and they cared nothing for these elements. They trusted the new state apparatus to preserve the rights inviolate for their own purpose.

History has proved the peril of thinking that democracy can be preserved if any group is deprived of the right to a free press and to freedom of speech unless it is established beyond reasonable doubt that a clear and present danger to the state is threatened by persons attempting to exercise the constitutional freedom of speech and press. The Soviet authorities began with a limitation which seemed to them to be beyond question a reasonable measure for preserving power over their enemies. They have since turned it, again and again, against citizens who have no desire to upset the regime but who have wanted to grumble against some detail immensely important to them.

Early judicial decisions interpreting the constitutional guarantees in the course of application of the criminal code's ban on speech designed to overthrow the regime exemplify the type of extreme action that was taken by local officials to silence the opposition. A man was convicted for opposing the plan for spring sowing in his village by speaking up in the meeting of the village soviet in which he was a deputy. His opposition was in no sense an effort to overthrow the regime; he simply wanted to discuss a very concrete problem, since it affected his personal life, and was doing no more than many an American farmer who opposes his government's plan for agricultural subsidies. Yet the local soviet judge, on motion of the local prosecutor, found the soviet peasant guilty of violating the criminal law. Only on appeal to the Supreme Court of the Russian Republic was the peasant successful in having his conviction quashed, and then it was not because his words were not deemed seditious. It was concluded that he could not have intended to overthrow the regime since he "was a workman, he had been at the front in the civil war, he was an invalid, and he was not a class enemy." In short, the Supreme Court felt that the speaker had been one of those who were presumed to support the regime, and his criticism of the sowing plan must therefore have been intended by him to be a proper, rather than an improper, exercise of the constitutional guarantee of free speech.

A class enemy in the form of a well-to-do peasant also was convicted of counterrevolutionary speech, in opposing a plan of self-taxation introduced for approval of the village soviet. His conviction was appealed, and the Supreme Court of the Republic freed him because it found that no harm had come from his opposition to the plan since it had been adopted by an overwhelming majority. The peasant was, however, convicted of criminal defamation because he had cursed the officials of the Soviet in "unprintable words" while registering his opposition to the proposal.

The Supreme Court of the Russian Republic reveals in these two decisions of the early 1930's that it was trying to establish some yardstick which would remove from the ban against seditious speech grumbling against proposals introduced into soviets, even when those proposals were deemed necessary by local party bosses to the success of a program. The court, in establishing its yardstick, examined the class origin of the speaker to see if he could be presumed to be a class enemy and also looked to the result of the speech. The court seems to have felt that the local authorities needed correction for reading revolutionary intent into speech of a limited critical character.

Examination of class origin to determine the real intent of a critic continued into the 1940's. For example, a Soviet army sergeant training recruits on the drill field during World War II was heard to make derogatory remarks about the rights granted by the Soviet Constitution. In a trial for counter-revolutionary speech in violation of the criminal code, he was acquitted because the court could not believe that he meant to harm the regime. He was found to have served most of his life in exemplary fashion in the army, had been a member of the Communist party for twenty-three years, and had always conducted himself in a manner which suggested that he was devoted to the motherland.

By these court decisions top Soviet authorities are obviously trying to make a good impression upon the public. They are hoping to put a popular meaning into their constitution's guarantee of free speech. They have built an official record designed to show that while the guarantee is not unlimited, it will be held to be meaningful in circumstances when no real harm is caused, or when the speaker can be presumed loyal because of his record of loyalty or class origin. Testimony of *émigrés* indicates that lower Soviet officials are not so careful and that here the guarantee provides very little restraint on repressive action against the vocal dissenter, even when his dissent is expressed on a subject of local concern having no connection with the stability of the regime.

PRACTICAL RESTRICTIONS ON PRINTING AND MEETINGS

Limitation upon the constitutional guarantee of freedom of the press is even more clearly defined by Soviet law and regulation. Because of a constitutional ban on the employment of labor by a private individual for any commercial purpose, no private individual may own a printing establishment in which labor is employed. In consequence, operation of a mass-circulation daily paper or even of a less frequent periodical is impossible, unless it were to be by a co-operative association of printers. But even this is forbidden, because the licensing instructions under which private enterprise without employed labor may be conducted, within limits, excludes specifically the operation of any reproductive apparatus. A citizen may not, therefore, so much as operate a mimeograph or duplicating machine for the publication of handbills. He may not use the printed word to spread his ideas, except through channels provided by the state.

Even state-operated printshops have been censored under a law requiring submission to a central censorship office prior to publication of all matter prepared for reproduction. During

Stalin's time this office on occasion licensed a book or drama only to have the license revoked when Stalin saw the play or read the book and demanded that the play end and the books be destroyed. Private citizens at that time even hesitated to keep a questionable book in an apartment lest it be taken as indication of lack of support for Stalin and subject the owner to suspicion and surveillance. Khrushchev claimed to have abolished centralized censorship, and to have left the decision to publish to the editorial committee of each state publishing house, but there have been indications that a central office still exists for the difficult decisions. Soviet authors even protested publicly against central censorship in 1967.

The right of assembly as a popular democratic right is also guaranteed by the Soviet constitution, but a statute requires that all public meetings be licensed, whether to be held indoors or out of doors. No meeting to which representatives from all parts of the country are to be invited may be licensed without the consent of the Council of Ministers of the U.S.S.R. If the meeting is to bring together only people from within a single republic, the consent of the council of ministers of that republic is required. If the gathering is to include only members of a single ministry, the minister must consent. When the people to be invited are only from within a single province or smaller unit, the Provincial Soviet's Executive Committee has discretion to determine what shall be permitted.

The right of association is also guaranteed by the Constitution, but, again, is subject to limitation. Any association must be licensed, regardless of the purpose for which it is to be formed, and each republic is authorized to establish a procedure under which such associations may receive a charter.

By virtue of these licensing provisions, public opinion can be effectively expressed only through a licensed agency. This is not to say that the Communist party wants to hear no public opinion. The contrary is true. The party has always been attentive to restlessness among the masses, for such restlessness can spell difficulties for the leadership. If there were no way short of violent revolution for dissent to find expression, the Communist party would not only have little chance of convincing anyone at home, much less abroad, that a democratic system existed within the U.S.S.R., but would find out about the unrest so late that it would have to apply expensive measures of repression, causing perhaps even greater unrest.

The state-owned and -licensed press is therefore thrown open to letters to the editor. Analysis of great numbers of these letters has indicated that their subject matter is far different from that which might be found in any American newspaper. For one thing it is limited to complaints about public administration, and never refers to a basic matter of policy. Further, criticism of administrators is limited to those only slightly higher in the administrative hierarchy than the writer. Thus no bench operator would write in criticism of the minister under whose supervision his factory might be but rather of his foreman or, at most, of his factory manager. No one has ever had published a criticism of the Presidium of the Central Committee of the Communist party, or even of the Presidium of the Supreme Soviet. The highest position to be criticized seems to be that of minister, and such criticism is usually made by a deputy to the Supreme Soviet either in a letter to the editor of the local newspaper or in a speech from the floor of the Supreme Soviet.

All letters to the editor are obviously

subject to clearance in the editorial office of the party-controlled newspaper, just as any proposed speeches in the Supreme Soviet must clear the office of those who plan the agenda. It can be presumed that censorship, or anticipation of censorship, causes the exclusion of those letters and speeches which touch upon matters too sensitive to air. Still, many criticisms are aired, and a letter to the editor is usually followed some days later by an article in which the editor reports on action taken to set right the administrative shortcoming in question. It is quite possible that many Soviet citizens interpret such action as proof that the public can influence administration and that the Soviet system is democratic.

Soviet citizens with little knowledge of the extent of public criticism in Western countries and of the influence brought to bear upon major policies by associations of irate citizens cannot measure their success against anything but the experience of their own limited past. Although Soviet youths sometimes think out for themselves the political shortcomings of the Soviet system, it has been more usual to find the defectors from the Soviet system among those who are sufficiently old to remember accounts of the freedoms of Western democracies read in their childhood or who have been brought into touch with Western practices through capture during the war, visits outside the U.S.S.R., or Western broadcasts.

LIMITATIONS ON THE RIGHTS OF REPUBLICS

Both in his 1912 manual and in subsequent statements, Stalin had made it clear that he felt that the Communist party should oppose any movement for secession if it meant that a people would return to the capitalist form of economy, for, in Marxist terms, a return to capitalism was a retrogressive step and, by definition, should be opposed by Communists. With Communist opposition assured against any effort to secede, it seemed to foreigners inconceivable that any republic could exercise the right successfully.

Stalin's argument for categorizing peoples in "union" or "autonomous" republics seems especially empty in the light of his writings on secession. The argument can have been thought to have value only for propagandizing the peoples who live on the frontiers of the U.S.S.R., such as the Iranians, the Afghans, the Latvians, the Poles, and others. At the time of his utterance, Stalin probably had not anticipated that some of these territories could be brought within the Soviet orbit so soon by military action rather than by the subversion to which his argument might be said to have appealed.

The limited nature of the powers reserved to the republics in the Soviet federal system is most clearly demonstrated in the law governing the budget of the U.S.S.R. Annually, the Supreme Soviet of the U.S.S.R. adopts a budget for the entire Union that is broken down republic by republic in its totals. No republic has its own source of revenue subject to its own control, and no republic can spend on its institutions any funds except those allocated by the federal budget. Only after the Supreme Soviet has adopted the budget for the entire country do the supreme soviets of each of the union republics meet in annual session to adopt their budgets. The total for a republic has to be the total established by the federal budget for that republic, but the republic may divide that total among its various provinces as it thinks fit. Obviously, the federal planners have drafted the federal budget with knowledge of the needs and possibilities of each province in each republic, but a republic's government can provide some variation. It can, through the budget debate, give to the deputies from the various provinces and from the various "autonomous republics," "autonomous regions," and "national districts" within the republic some sense of participation in the process of government. As has been seen, this sense of participation is probably one of the primary reasons why the Communist party has maintained the system of soviets alongside its own institutions.

To the outsider who knows the jealousy with which the states in the United States have guarded their budgets from federal encroachment, it is evident that one of the bases on which the autonomy that is still maintained by the American states rests is the power of the purse. In relinquishing this power to their federal government, the republics of the U.S.S.R. have given away the key to much of the independence possible within a federal system.

Of recent years, Soviet leaders have sought to enhance the appearance of independence in their republics by amending the clause in their federal Constitution that relates to the division of powers between federal and republic governments. In 1944 the Supreme Soviet of the U.S.S.R. extended to each of the then existing sixteen union republics the power to conduct its foreign relations, within the limits of policy established by the federal government, and to establish military formations of its own, within limits established by the federal government. The republics were permitted to organize ministries of foreign affairs and of defense to administer their affairs in these areas, but federal ministries of the same names were retained to co-ordinate policy. Further,

the federal government was charged with "the representation of the Union in international relations, conclusion and ratification of treaties with other states, and the establishment of the general procedure in the mutual relations between the Union Republics."

Various reasons have been suggested for the changes of 1944. The most cogent is that Stalin was preparing to ask for sixteen seats in the United Nations, which was then being planned. He made such a request of the planning group at Dumbarton Oaks and, again, at the Yalta Conference. The world now knows the compromise that was accepted by Franklin D. Roosevelt and by Winston Churchill, under which the Byelorussian and Ukrainian republics received membership in the United Nations along with the U.S.S.R. while the other fourteen republics received no international recognition. The voting and debating records of these two Soviet republics in the United Nations since that time indicate that the federal government of the U.S.S.R. sets policy on all matters, as its Constitution requires it to do.

An additional reason for the 1944 amendments may lie in their possible appeal to the U.S.S.R.'s neighbors in Asia. For example, the Afghan government could deal directly with the governments of the Central Asian republics on border matters, though, when any cession of territory is made, as was the case in 1955 when territory was ceded to Iran, the treaty is made with the U.S.S.R. The republics concerned indicated their formal consent to the Presidium of the Supreme Soviet of the U.S.S.R. There was no negotiation between Iran and the two republics whose territory was affected.

Since Stalin's death in 1953 changes have appeared in his pattern of federation. Instead of an ever increasing number of union republics, there has been a decrease, and there are further signs of merger. The Karelo-Finnish Republic was demoted in 1956 from union status to autonomous status, losing in consequence its union republic quota of delegates in the second chamber of the Supreme Soviet and subordinating its administrative departments to the Russian Republic into which it was merged.

While no other republic has been demoted since that time, there was evidence under Khrushchev's leadership of his desire to establish the conditions for merger, at least of economic and political controls, if not of territory, probably as a means of co-ordination of the numerous economic regions in which he placed his hope for revivification of managerial efficiency at the local level. Thus, he created a Central Asian Regional Economic Council with authorization to co-ordinate the economies of the republics in the region. After his ouster and the complete abandonment of his regional economic system of administration, the Council had no further reason to exist and was abolished. Plans which seemed afoot in 1963 for similar regionalization of economic activity in the three republics south of the Caucasus and in the three on the shores of the Baltic also ceased to be discussed, since they were no longer needed.

The post-Khrushchev return to centralized economic command through ministries located in Moscow suggests that there is a return to the concept of federation as it emerged in 1923. Ethnic boundaries take precedence over economic boundaries in structuring the federation, even when economic boundaries would be economically more rational. This had been the rule established in 1928 by the party for the State Planning Commission when the economists suggested that it was economically

rational to attach all of Byelorussia and part of the Ukraine to the Russian Republic for purposes of economic integration. Only the Finnish case now remains to represent the triumph of economics over ethnic considerations, but the example is not a strong one, for the Finnish ethnic unit was never large; it was very much intermingled with Great Russians, and its importance sprang in some degree from the desire of Soviet policy makers of the time to attract all of Finland to the U.S.S.R. by offering them a show piece in the Finno-Karelian Union Republic, a hope long since abandoned.

The system of representation of union republics within the Supreme Soviet of the U.S.S.R. was questioned during Khrushchev's tenure by some Soviet political scientists. Suggestions were made during the early period of drafting a new constitution; since ethnic rivalries and suspicions had faded over the years, it had become unnecessary to continue the institution of a bicameral legislature to give ethnic minorities a sense of equality with the Russians and the Ukrainians. It was noted that both chambers had met since their inception in 1938 in joint session to hear presentation of the economic plan and the annual budget as well as foreign policy statements, and that their budget committees had proposed identical changes in the budget. Chamber deliberations had produced no differences in discussions. No case is on record of a conflict of views between the chambers, although Soviet professors have said in conversation that on one occasion the Soviet of Nationalities refused in the early 1950's to accept the proposal that the names of ministries be removed from the Constitution. They were said to have feared that the authority of the smaller union republics could be reduced without their consent if ministries could be altered in status without the necessity of constitutional amendment. But ministries were changed radically in status by Khrushchev with no audible objection from the small union republics.

The trend toward a unicameral legislature and reduction in the dignity of the union republics ceased after Khrushchev's ouster. On the contrary, there began an effort to enhance their dignity by formal measures. The membership of the Soviet of Nationalities was increased by constitutional amendment in 1966 so that this chamber might regain its parity in numbers with the Soviet of the Union, which had been enlarged for each successive four-year term to keep pace with the growing population. In so doing the number of seats for each union republic was increased from twenty-five to thirty-two, which resulted in even more one-sided importance being given to a seat in the Soviet of Nationalities than had previously existed. After the change Estonia as the smallest union republic had thirty-two deputies in the Soviet of Nationalities and only four in the population-based Soviet of the Union.

Even before the restoration of dignity to the union republics after Khrushchev's ouster, there had been a trend toward strengthening their position in the field of legislation. In 1957, the authority to enact codes of law that had been taken from the union republics in the Constitution of 1936 was restored to them by amendment. To be sure, fundamental principles for each branch of law were established by the federal legislature to guide the draftsmen in the republics, but the ethnic groups for whose satisfaction the republics were originally created were given the right to reflect in their codes such cultural

peculiarities as they wished. Under the amendment the codes have been enacted at intervals in each republic since 1960, and some diversity of administrative structure in cultural matters has also been evident, as in the means of directing the republic colleges of advocates, the state notaries, and the prison administrations.

Considering all of the events since 1922 when the federation was brought into being, the hypothesis can be supported that federation was chosen primarily as a means of quieting the potential opposition of ethnic groups which would otherwise have resisted Russification had it emerged in the Tsarist pattern. Its secondary purpose was to attract border peoples in other lands to join their blood brothers in the U.S.S.R. who were Finns, Ukrainians, Azerbaidjanis, Mongols, or Uigurs. When the Finns demonstrated in the Russo-Finnish War of 1940 that they would not join the union voluntarily, the second reason lost its validity, and it was given its death blow in 1956 when it became evident that the Communist-led states which had come into existence after the war on the U.S.S.R.'s frontiers were to be permitted to develop their own "paths to socialism," without thought of eventual adherence to a greater U.S.S.R.

Why then, does the federation continue to exist? The Russian language is now an international tongue, no longer used because of any command but because the smaller peoples know that their place in the sun, not only within the U.S.S.R. but in the world as a whole, depends on their using the language of their preponderantly large ethnic neighbor. Still, there is an urge to preserve cultural distinctions, notable especially among the Ukrainians. This has sometimes led to the emergence of national protest groups, especially in the Ukraine, which are nipped in the bud whenever they appear but which nevertheless make headlines in the press of their fellow Ukrainians outside the U.S.S.R. From what is known about these movements, they are not now significantly powerful, but they could become so if there were any evidence of complete loss of ethnic identity to the Great Russians, as the schemes proposed during Khrushchev's time might have suggested. It is simply easier to govern within a federation than to suppress ethnic minorities. The economy, which is the major factor of importance requiring in Soviet minds strong centralization for efficiency, can be centralized through the administrative structure without arousing ethnic hostilities, and so long as that is possible, it is expedient to let well enough alone.

POPULARIZATION OF THE BENCH

The Soviet court system has borrowed from Germany a substitute for the jury of the Anglo-American common-law court. Together with the single professional judge, chosen in the manner just indicated, there sit for each civil or criminal case two lay judges. This is the rule not only in the peoples' courts at the bottom of the judicial ladder but also for each of the higher courts, including the supreme court of the republic, when these higher courts sit as a court of original jurisdiction, i.e., when they try a case that has not been heard in any lower court. This is the rule also for the federal courts, including the Supreme Court of the U.S.S.R., when it tries a case as a court of original jurisdiction.

The lay judges are chosen differently for each court. At the bottom level, they are elected, under a 1958 reform, for two years at general meetings of col-

leagues at their place of work or residence. At the upper levels, they are appointed by the same soviet that appoints the professional judge. While they are, therefore, chosen to serve over a period of years, they sit for not more than ten days each year. They are not lawyers but laymen, who are supposed to add a democratic flavor to the bench. They are selected to bring to a case, whether criminal or civil, the common-sense approach of the members of the community, just as the jury contributes this element in the common-law court of the United States.

The lay judges of the Soviet courts have greater authority in a sense than the American jury, because they are permitted by law to share with the professional judge the decision of all questions, whether relating to the determination of the credibility of a witness or to the meaning of a statute. In the United States the jury is not permitted to determine the meaning of a statute. The American jury is ordered only to determine facts. Its task is usually to decide whether to believe a witness.

While he has greater formal authority than the American juror, the Soviet lay judge is subjected to more guidance than the American juror, for the Soviet professional judge sits with the lay judges to determine the court's decision. In the United States the judge may not go to the jury room with the jurors. He can tell them what law is applicable and sometimes what he thinks of the evidence, but he cannot sit with them. They are free to do as they please when they are alone, and they occasionally make a finding which is quite contrary to what the judge has suggested.

Although Soviet lay judges can under their law outvote a professional judge, the outside world has been informed of only a very few cases in which this has happened. These cases have been recounted by former Soviet lawyers who have fled to the West, and one is reported in the Soviet official reports. Generally the lay judges are believed to be quite docile in accepting the proposals of the professional judge. They rarely ask questions at the trial or show any independence of view. Nevertheless, they provide an opportunity to the general public to share in the decision, and as such they may help the Soviet leaders to maintain popular support for the regime.

It is not entirely accurate to say that the Soviet lay judges represent the general public. While very few of them are members of the Communist party, they are selected by institutions in each district, such as factories, farms, universities, retail stores, and army units. The Communist party shares in the selection by these institutions, and the nominations are unopposed. In consequence, the panels from which lay judges are called for service are not cross-sections of the entire population as are the panels from which jurors are selected in the United States. For trials in the Supreme Court of the U.S.S.R., the panel of lay judges is even less representative, for it is small and is comoposed of the cream of Communist party leadership to be found in the various major institutions of the country, the army, and soviets, the administrative apparatus, the trade unions, the educational institutions, and the collective farms.

PROCEDURAL GUARANTEES AND THE EXCEPTIONS

Procedure within the courts has been made to correspond in general with what the world accepts as necessary for a fair trial. The code of criminal procedure established the basic principles of orality, publicity, confrontation of witnesses, the right to introduce evidence, the right to counsel, the right to be informed of the charge, and the right to appeal. The code of civil procedure offers the same opportunities to present one's case and to rebut the position of the other party in open court with counsel.

Some of the procedural guarantees are incorporated in the U.S.S.R. Constitution, such as the right to counsel, the right to public trial, and the right to an interpreter. In spite of this fact, these guarantees are made subject to such exceptions as may be established by law, and the law has, in fact, created exceptions. One of the exceptions established by law is that public trial not be granted when the offense involves a sex crime or when relevant military or diplomatic interests of the U.S.S.R. cannot be disclosed. Another exception which was kept until 1956 was that right to counsel did not extend to trials involving terroristic acts against Soviet officials or attempts to unseat the regime defined in that part of the criminal code devoted to "counterrevolutionary" crime. Further, there was in the law in effect until 1956 denial of the right to appeal in such cases, and in trials for terroristic acts or assassination of Soviet officials, the accused did not have to be present at the trial.

In the political exceptions to the usual rules of procedure, the Soviet policy-makers again demonstrated their readiness to withdraw from the general pattern of protection espoused by all democratic peoples those cases which in their opinion threatened the very continuation of the regime. Their decision to maintain such exceptional methods until 1956 was the more remarkable because of the opportunities they have had to control the final outcome of any case. Through the appellate courts, they always have had the opportunity to bring an undesirable decision of a lower court before judges chosen for the appellate courts because of their extensive political training. There would seem to have been no danger in permitting a defendant to appeal through the usual procedure to the court next higher above the one in which his trial occurred. The appellate bench for the peoples' court is the provincial court, and appeals from the provincial court when it sits as a court of original jurisdiction go to the supreme court of the republic concerned. Perhaps in recognition of the protection provided by the appellate procedure, Stalin's heirs made their decision in 1956 to eliminate the political exceptions to ordinary procedural rights. In doing so, they have probably won praise from those who do not appreciate the controls remaining.

When a court hears an appeal, it has no lay judges on the bench. All three judges are selected from the panel of professional judges available at that level. Under such circumstances, the policy-makers' decision under Stalin to allow no appeals seems to have been a vote of no confidence in the political wisdom of the professional judges in the higher courts. This conclusion is fortified by the fact that, even if the appellate court should have taken a position contrary to the desires of the policy-makers at the highest level, the procedural code provided before 1956 and still provides another chance for the government to require a review. Under the code, either the Prosecutor-General of the U.S.S.R. or the President of the Supreme Court of the U.S.S.R. may ask for a review of the record by the appellate college of the Supreme Court of the U.S.S.R. Should the appellate college of the Supreme

Court of the U.S.S.R. again decide against the interests of the state, as interpreted by the highest policy-makers of the Communist party, another review may be had by the Plenum of the Supreme Court of the U.S.S.R., on which sit all judges of the various colleges of the Supreme Court.

With so many possibilities to change the decision of the trial court on appeal to the next higher court and on subsequent review by courts right up to the level of the full bench of the Supreme Court of the U.S.S.R., the denial prior to 1956 of the right of appeal in political cases could have had only one object, to deter potential assassins and those seeking to bring about a new revolution by striking terror into their hearts. They were being advised that they could be assured of no escape from execution. In this is another example of the value the Communist party has found in terrorizing as an instrument of government to prevent the unseating of the regime. The good will of the people at home and abroad that was gained from the adoption of procedural due process for the routine cases was sacrificed when the vital cord of the regime was in danger.

THE STATUS OF THE PRESUMPTION OF INNOCENCE

Another element of what the American court considers vital to the concept of due process of law is missing from Soviet codes. This is the presumption of innocence, which operates to require the state, through the prosecutor, to prove that the crime has actually been committed. Under the system in use in most Western countries, the prosecutor may not lay his charge before the judge and ask the defendant to disprove it. The prosecutor must prove his charge, even when the defendant refuses to take the stand and respond to questions. While this procedural protection of the defendant is often exasperating to a prosecutor who feels that he has a good case, so good in fact that he can presume the defendant guilty and especially if the defendant will not take the stand in his own defense, mankind throughout the centuries has reached the conclusion that the only fair trial is the one in which the defendant must be presumed innocent at the outset.

Soviet law contains no such written statement of presumption of innocence, but Soviet text writers have said that the presumption exists. They argue that it exists because the law guarantees the right of counsel and they say that such a guarantee is meaningless unless the attorney retained by the defendant can have an opportunity to present his client's defense. These authors seem to feel that if a citizen were presumed guilty, there would be no reason to give him any chance to defend himself, so that any right to defense naturally carries with it the presumption of innocence.

This view was restated in 1958 when new fundamental principles for criminal procedure were adopted. Although jurists on the drafting committee urged specific declaration of the existence in Soviet law of a presumption of innocence, non-jurists argued that common people would not understand what it meant, for they could not but suppose that when an accused was brought to trial, the prosecutor and the preliminary investigator must have had good reason to conclude him guilty. The presumption was not incorporated, although the President of the Supreme Court of the U.S.S.R. restated in his speech to the Supreme Soviet as a deputy, perhaps in an effort to make his point in the stenographic minutes, that the procedural guarantee of the new codes rested on the assumption of the existence of a presumption of innocence, even though it was not stated explicitly.

Westerners have been rather doubtful of the effectiveness of such an argument in times of stress. They would prefer having the presumption of innocence spelled out, and this is usually done in the West. It is particularly important in procedural systems structured upon the customary pattern of Continental European countries, as is the U.S.S.R., for in those countries there is always a lengthy preliminary investigation before trial, which is unknown to Anglo-American procedure. The Soviet preliminary investigation is a hearing before an investigator who is a civil servant subject to the administrative control of the prosecutor's office. Under the Soviet procedural code, he is supposed to conduct an impartial hearing like that of a judge, in spite of his administrative link to the prosecutor. He is required by law to hear not only those witnesses brought by the police and by the prosecutor but also all witnesses and evidence that the defendant wishes to introduce. On the basis of careful weighing of all of this evidence, the investigator prepares a conclusion supported by the record of his investigation, from which the prosecutor can prepare the indictment. The indictment and the record are then sent to the court for use in the trial, which means that at a Soviet trial the judges have before them a record, often in several volumes of typewritten and handwritten notes, of what every witness said on the occasion of the preliminary investigation. The judge has only to work through the material, calling the witnesses and seeing whether they adhere to their prior testimony.

It is a rare Soviet judge, on the admission of Soviet text writers themselves, who can resist the conclusion that the investigator's work must have proved guilt. While the judge is supposed to consider the accused innocent, he has a hard time approaching the case as if the accused were innocent. He is likely to try to prove the record before him rather than to verify it. Under Soviet rules of procedure, a judge may ask any question he wants and cross-examine witnesses himself. He is not limited to listening to the direct and cross-examination by prosecutor and defense attorney, as is the case in some American states. In consequence, the judge can, and often does, appear to be a second prosecutor acting on the basis of the record before him.

The great threat to the presumption of innocence presented by the preliminary investigation has caused even Soviet authors to argue that the accused should be permitted to have counsel at the preliminary investigation as well as at the trial. Their arguments were partially successful in obtaining reform in 1958, but only for juvenile delinquents. For them counsel is now to be permitted, but for adults the preliminary investigator may exclude counsel from the preliminary investigation until the indictment has been prepared. Exclusion has been countenanced lest he obtain suggestions that would permit the concealing of evidence from the prosecution or learn secrets that might be harmful to the state.

55

I SPEAK FOR THE SILENT

By Vladimir Tchernavin

Writing in *Pravda* on December 25, 1918, Latsis, the head of the Soviet political police, said: "Do not ask for incriminating evidence to prove that the prisoner opposed the Soviet government either by arms or word. Your first duty is to ask him what class he belongs to, what were his origins, education and occupation. These questions should decide the prisoner's fate."

Such were the guiding principles of the Soviet secret police whether it was called Cheka, NKVD, GPU, or MVD. Today the initials, less dreaded than in the past, are KGB.

Tchernavin's fate was mild. He was sentenced to "only" five years of forced labor and managed to escape to Finland. Few others were equally fortunate. Tchernavin was a scientist of humble but non-proletarian origin. A specialist in fisheries, he became in 1925 director of production and research of the Northern State Fishing Trust in Murmansk, beyond the Arctic Circle. Before his arrest in 1930 he had become professor of ichthyology at the Leningrad Agronomic Institute. He was one of the many victims used as scapegoats to explain the shortages which developed after the launching of collectivization. When food became scarce in 1930, the government blamed "wreckers" who had "penetrated" into food industries and had "disrupted" production. On September 22, 1930, the press announced that forty-eight leading scientists, one each from the food industries, had been arrested. Four days later the forty-eight men were shot, without trial. Thousands of lesser men were now arrested, including Tchernavin.

Tchernavin's wife tells her side of the story in *Escape from the Soviets*. Another account of the purge among scientists is Alexander Weissberg's *The Accused* (also published as *Conspiracy of Silence*). The most famous of the Soviet accounts of prison life is Alexander Solzhenitsyn's *One Day in the Life of Ivan Denisovich*. Other Soviet accounts are A. Gorbatov's *Years Off My Life*, Eugenia Ginzburg's *Journey into the Whirlwind*, and the novelistic treatments of Iurii Bondarev in *Silence*, and Viktor Nekrasov in *Kira Georgievna*.

The relevant articles of the Soviet Criminal Code are printed and commented upon in Harold Berman, *Soviet Criminal Law and Procedure*, and Wladimir Kulski, *The Soviet Regime*.

From V. Tchernavin, *I Speak for the Silent* (Newton Center, Mass.: Charles T. Branford, 1935), pp. 100–106, 116–20, 131–33, 199–208, 227–29, 277–84. Used by permission of the publisher.

For studies of the secret police see S. Wolin, *The Soviet Secret Police*, as well as F. Beck and W. Godin, *Soviet Purge and the Extraction of Confession*.

The economic role of the labor camps is examined in the following: James Bunyan (ed.), *The Origin of Forced Labor in the Soviet State, 1917–1921*; Boris Nicolaevsky and David Dallin, *Forced Labor in Soviet Russia*; David Dallin, *The Economics of Slave Labor*; S. Swianiewicz, *Forced Labor and Economic Development*; Naum Jasny, "Labor and Output in Soviet Concentration Camps," *Journal of Political Economy*, October, 1951, and July, 1952. A Marxist view is provided in Alexander Baykov, "A Note on the Economic Significance of Compulsory Labor in the USSR," *Bulletins on Soviet Economic Development*, Vol. VII. A Soviet account of a forced labor project of the thirties is *Belomor: An Account of the Construction of the New Canal between the White Sea and the Baltic Sea*.

"YOU WILL BE THE 49TH"

"Tchernavin!"

My name was called loudly from the other side of the grill. A passage-way was made for me and as I walked through the cell the eyes of my companions followed me with curiosity—a newcomer. At the door stood a prison guard, a Red Army soldier. He repeated my name.

"Tchernavin?"

"Yes."

"First name and father's name?"

"Vladimir Vyacheslavovich," I replied.

"Get going!—to the examining officer!"

One of the prisoners stopped me and whispered hurriedly, "You are being taken to examination. Take some food with you, and remember one thing— never believe the examining officer."

I went back and put an apple in my pocket.

"Well, get going!" hurried the guard.

. . .

"Good morning," the examining officer greeted me, calling me by name. "Sit down." He was a young man of about thirty, fair, pink-cheeked, well-groomed and well-fed.

"Well, let's talk," he began. "Why do you think you were arrested?"

"I don't know."

"How is it you don't know? Don't you even have an idea?"

"I have no idea."

"Think well, is it possible that you never even thought you would be arrested? No? Try to remember.

"No."

I was looking straight and firmly into his eyes. I was thinking—no, my friend, you will not catch me on this, it's too simple.

"No," I repeated again. "I haven't the slightest idea. I had hoped that you would give me some explanation."

"In good time. Meanwhile, remember that we are in no hurry; we have no reason for hurrying. An investigation rarely lasts less than six months, usually nine months, very often a year. You'll have plenty of time to think things over. —And so, you will not tell me that you were expecting your arrest?"

"No, I didn't expect it."

In this fashion we argued for a long time, still with the same result.

"Well, maybe later you will become more compliant. Let's get on to the questionnaire."

He went over all the questions that I had answered the night before and I replied firmly without contradicting what I had written—he would not trap me here.

"Well! well! a hereditary nobleman —and I, the man questioning you, am a hereditary proletarian," he drawled, accentuating these words with a ridiculous emphasis as he lolled in his chair.

I was looking at him and thinking: "probably the son of a merchant; the face—smooth, hands—well kept, not those of a working man; you have never seen work in your life, and I have had to work with both my head and hands since I was sixteen."

"Your attitude towards the Soviet Government?"

"Sympathetic."

He laughed.

"Why not tell the truth? You might better say 'loyal,'—this is false."

"I say—sympathetic."

"No, I won't enter it on the questionnaire, it's too absurd. Listen, this is a little thing, has no importance. I am asking this question only in order to verify your sincerity. Tell me the truth and I will deal with you in the future with full frankness. Believe me, I sympathize with you sincerely. We value and take care of specialists, but you do harm to yourself from the very beginning . . ." he was speaking in the light tone of a man of society.

I have heard all this already at the cross-examinations in Murmansk—I thought—and repeated with insistence; "Sympathetic. On what grounds don't you believe me?"

"I could refuse to answer your question, but to prove my sincere good will towards you, I will answer. You are a nobleman, the Soviet Government has deprived you of all privileges; this alone is sufficient to make you a class enemy, even disregarding your convictions, which are well known to us in every detail."

"You are wrong. I have never had a chance to make use of any privileges of the nobility. I lived on what I earned myself; my scientific career was not interrupted by the Revolution. I want to remind you that this same nobility, his

rank of a General and a high position, did not prevent my own uncle from becoming a loyal servant of the Revolution and a member of the Revolutionary War Council. You must have heard of him."

The examining officer kept silent, not knowing how to parry this unexpected move. He waited a few minutes, then filled in the questionnaire, "Is in sympathy."

Here at least was one small victory for me.

I understood why he was insisting. If it could be established that I belonged to the nobility and was not in sympathy with the Soviet Government, "wrecking activity" would be a logical deduction.

He made another attempt.

"But you *have* criticized the actions of the Soviet Government!"

"No."

"Again you don't want to be frank, even in a small matter like this. I will not conceal from you that your situation is very serious, the evidence against you is very strong, you are in danger of being shot, but I am sorry for you. Be frank and I will endeavor to come to terms with you. Is it possible that you can assert that you never criticized the actions of the Soviet Government?"

"Yes, I can."

"What are you doing this for? We Communists, we the GPU workers, don't we criticize the actions of the Soviet Government?"

"I don't know. But I never did."

"Let's take an example: didn't the bread lines ever arouse your indignation?"

"I believed the bread lines were not 'actions of the Soviet Government.'"

"All right. Let it be as you please." He picked up his pen. "No, we will not put this down."

"As you see fit."

And here again his way of procedure

was quite clear to me. If I had admitted that I had "criticized" he would have forced me to say that it had happened more than once, would have questioned me regarding when and with whom I had carried on such conversations, and this would give material for a "frank confession" which would have been classed according to Article 58, Paragraph 10 as "counter-revolutionary agitation" punishable by three to ten years in a concentration camp. The persons I might have mentioned would become the "counter-revolutionary organization," to which would be added the names of those at whose homes we could have been meeting, and this in its turn would be interpreted, according to Article 58, Paragraph 11 as "counter-revolutionary propaganda"; the two points combined would call for the death penalty.

He thought for a while and decided to make one last attack in the same direction.

"Is it also possible that you never told any anti-Soviet jokes?"

"No, I don't like jokes."

"And you never heard any?"

"No, I never listened to them."

The face of the examining officer was becoming cruel and cold. He was looking straight into my eyes, watching every movement I made.

"And do you know that one should not lie at a cross-examination?"

"I know. I didn't tell and didn't listen to anti-Soviet jokes."

We looked at each other suspiciously. This time my lie was quite apparent: there is not a single man in Sovietland, high or low, who does not tell such jokes. It is the only bit of freedom of speech left in the U.S.S.R., something that cannot be throttled by any censorship or any terror, in spite of the fact that the spreading of such anecdotes is punishable as counter-revolutionary agitation by sentences of ten years in a concentration camp.

"Very well. Your character and your 'sincerity' are clear to me. We will take it into account during the further conduct of the investigation. But—" he suddenly again changed his threatening tone to an expression of friendly and frank advice—"I advise you to give good thought to the way you behaved at this cross-examination. You are bringing about your own destruction. You belong to the nobility. We are not persecuting for social origin, but it is clear to us that you are our class enemy if only on account of your parentage. We need proofs of your sincere desire to go with us and not against us," recited the examining officer repeating words he had probably said hundreds of times before.

I replied coldly and with reserve that I was guilty of no crime, that I was quite certain that it was all a misunderstanding which would soon be cleared up and that I would be released.

"The GPU," he said, "never makes an arrest without sufficient grounds, especially in the case of an important specialist working on production. It was only after the evidence had been thoroughly checked and all the facts against you well appraised that I received authority from the Council for the search and your arrest."

It was true. My arrest was at least a month late.

"I am not going to submit these facts to you now, because I want to give you the opportunity to sincerely repent and yourself give us all the information in detail. Only under this condition will your life be spared, but in any case you get ten years in a concentration camp—this has already been decided. You see, I conceal nothing from you, I give you time to think it over. It's hard to act more humanely."

I kept silent.

He also stopped talking; then, looking me straight in the eye, he said harshly:

"You will be the 49th."

. . . .

SECOND INQUISITION

It was my second day in prison—my second cross-examination. I was called before the tea ration was given out and had only time to eat an apple.

"How do you do?" the examining officer asked, scanning me attentively to see if I showed signs of a sleepless night.

"All right."

"It isn't so good in your cell. You are in 22?"

"A cell like any other."

"Well, did you do any thinking? Are you going to tell the truth *today?*"

"Yesterday I told only the truth."

He laughed. "What will it be today—not the truth?"

Then he returned to the subject of the cell.

"I tried to choose a better cell for you, but we are so crowded. I hope we will come to an understanding and that I will not be forced to change the regime I have ordered for you. The third category is the mildest: exercise in the yard, permission to receive food parcels from outside, a newspaper and books. The first two categories are much stricter. Remember, however, that it depends entirely on me; any minute you may be deprived of everything and transferred to solitary confinement. Or rather, this depends not on me but on your own behavior, your sincerity. The more frank your testimony, the better will be the conditions of your imprisonment. . . ."

He spoke slowly, looking me straight in the eye, emphasizing his words with evident pleasure and relish, watching for their effect.

"Did you know Scherbakoff? He was a strong man, but I broke him and forced him to confess."

With great difficulty I controlled myself before replying.

"I don't doubt for a minute that you use torture, and if you believe that this assists in discovering the truth and speeding up the investigation, and since Soviet laws permit its use, I would suggest that you don't give up mediaeval methods: a little fire is a wonderful measure. Try it! I am not afraid of you. Even with that you can't get anything out of me."

"Well, we will see about that later. Now let's get down to business. Let's talk about your acquaintances. Did you know V. K. Tolstoy, the wrecker, executed in connection with the case of the '48'?"

"Yes, I knew him. How could I not know him when he was the director of the fishing industry in the north?" I replied in frank astonishment. "We both worked in it for more than twenty years."

"And did you know him well?"

"Very well."

"How long did you know him?"

"From childhood."

His manner changed completely; he hurriedly picked up a statement sheet and placed it in front of me.

"Write down your confession."

"What confession?"

"That you knew Tolstoy, that you were in friendly relation with him from such and such a time. I see that we will come to an understanding with you, your frankness will be appreciated. Write."

He evidently was in a hurry, did not quite know what he was saying, afraid that I might reverse my statements.

I took the sheet and wrote down what I had said.

"Excellent. Let's continue."

Then followed a barrage of questions

about Tolstoy, about Scherbakoff and other people that I had known. He did not find me quite so tractable and we launched into a battle of wits that kept up hour after hour. He questioned me with insistence and in great detail, trying without success to make me give dates.

"You'll not succeed in outwitting me," he snapped sharply. "I advise you not to try. I am going home to dinner now and you will stay here till evening. This examination will continue—not for a day or two, but for months and, if necessary, for years. Your strength is not equal to mine. I will force you to tell us what we need."

After threatening me still further he handed me some sheets of paper.

"You are going to state in writing your opinion regarding the building of a utilization factory in Murmansk, its equipment and work in the future. I'll soon be back; when I return, your comments on these questions must be completed."

He put on his overcoat and left. His assistant took his place, and I busied myself with my writing. It was three or four hours before he returned, already evening.

Although I had eaten almost nothing for three days, I was still in good fighting form. He questioned me about the buying of a ship from abroad, trying to make me say that here was "wrecking," because the price had been exorbitant and the ship itself had proved unsatisfactory. It was most confusing and his questions far-fetched. We talked and we argued, but I would not give the answers he wanted.

He began on another tack. . . .

"All right," he said. "And what is your attitude regarding the subject of the fish supply in the Sea of Barents in connection with the construction of trawlers as provided for by the Five-Year Plan?"

Now he had broached a subject with which I *could* have a direct connection. The evening was already changing into night, but I was still sitting in the same chair. I was becoming unconscious of time; was it my second day in prison or my tenth? In spite of the depressing weariness, mental and physical, which was taking hold of me, I told him that I thought the fresh fish supply should be minutely and thoroughly investigated. I tried to make him see the hazards of the fishing industry in Murmansk and the enormous equipment that would be necessary to meet the proposals of the Five-Year Plan.

"And thus you confess that you doubted the practicability of the Five-Year Plan?" he said with a smile of smug satisfaction.

What could one say? I believed, as did everybody, that the plan was absurd, that it could not be fulfilled. For exactly such statements—no, for only a suspicion of having such thoughts—forty-eight men had been shot. . . .

OLD MEN AND BOYS

Soon I became acquainted with everyone in the cell, knew all of them by sight, learned the names of many, what they were accused of, how long they had been in prison, what kind of "pressure" the examiners used, and so on. I collected a lot of new information which I only vaguely suspected when free. I also learned quite a few lessons: how the investigation is conducted, what methods are used to obtain a confession. I saw the results of submitting to the will of the prosecutor and becoming a "novelist," that is to say, writing fantastic confessions according to directions given by the GPU.

To understand the life of those imprisoned in the U.S.S.R. while their cases are under investigation it is necessary to realize fully that the prison regime is intended, first of all, to weaken the prisoner morally and physically and break down his resistance, thus making easier the task of obtaining from him "voluntary confessions" of crimes he had never committed. The examining officer not only determines the prisoner's regime—allowing or forbidding exercise, remittance of food parcels, visits with relatives, reading of books—but he also has the right to transfer the prisoner to the dark cell or to punishment cells—ordinary, hot, cold, wet and so on.

The punitive cell in the prison of preliminary detention in the U.S.S.R. has lost its initial function as a punishment for breaking prison regulations and serves only as a means of coercion during the conduct of the investigation. The prison administration has no power over the prisoners and only fulfills the orders of examining officers.

The purpose of solitary confinement is to force a man, who is depressed by threats of violent death and torture, to remain alone with his fears, without any possibility of distraction or moral support and encouragement from others. Those confined in solitary cells often lose their minds and after six months of this regime the majority suffer from hallucinations.

The "double cell" (single cell into which two men are placed) is perhaps the easiest form of imprisonment, but in this case the welfare of the prisoner is entirely dependent upon the companion assigned to him by the examining officer. Sometimes his companion is a man violently insane who attempts to do him harm and beats him, or else one afflicted by melancholia, who is continually attempting to commit suicide. In other instances he may be a criminal who causes annoyance by his rough behavior and profanity or a man suffering from venereal disease, or even a spy who in the cell keeps up a conversation bearing on the subjects covered at cross-examinations and who persistently advises compliance with the wishes of the examining officer and the signing of the "confession."

The common cell depresses by its filth and vermin, but more than anything else by its crowded condition, which forbids eating or sleeping in peace, and does not allow a minute of real rest. The prison diet serves the same purpose—the weakening of the prisoners. Although sufficient in quantity it is intentionally lacking in vitamins and contains almost no fats—hence scurvy and boils. Sufferers from scurvy are more compliant, more amenable to the "exhortations" of examining officers than healthy ones and can be made to sign anything. . . .

What was striking at first was the extreme pallor of the prisoners, the result of a long sojourn in prison—their colorless faces, overgrown beards and hair, dusty and shabby clothes. In the filth of the cell they could not look otherwise. And yet, the majority in this cell were not only intellectuals, but foremost specialists in their lines, men with well-known names and reputations. For instance, there were two professors of the Petrograd University, several professors and instructors of technical and engineering schools, many engineers in different lines, technicians, railroad men, aviators, artillery officers, naval officers and, finally, clergymen. We had representatives of most of the largest factories, such as Putilov, Obouhov, Prohorov, and also many men of purely scientific careers, who had spent all their lives in laboratories, or in university chairs. Unfortunately I cannot speak of them here, for men of important individual ability cannot be described as a group. To tell of their work and its significance for Russian science and culture and to unfold the grippingly tragic picture of the transfer of the Russian intelligentsia into prison and penal servitude remains for another. Only he who gains admission to the secret archives of the GPU will some day reveal the unbelievable history of the destruction of a whole generation of men of science. . . .

TORTURE IN THE LICE CELL

The night following my rowdy encounter with the examining officer the old jeweler was summoned to his first cross-examination. He was gone for four days. After having sat in prison for four months he was so upset at being called out that he left behind his set of false teeth. He was unrecognizable when he returned on the night of the fourth day. As soon as he entered the cell he began to talk excitedly. He ravenously attacked the food we had saved for him, choked over the soup and bread, shook with laughter, stumbled over words, but still kept on trying to eat and talk at the same time.

"What fun, what fun! I'll tell you all about it, but you won't believe it. You will never believe what I've been through.—Fun.—How smart they are—they certainly know how to do it. They took me to the Gorokhovaya and put me in the 'lice' cell. Yes, the 'lice' cell. You know, you've heard of it—the 'lice' cell. What fun! . . ."

"There are between two and three hundred people in the 'lice' cell, men, women and some children all thrown in together. How hot it is! And how crowded, without room to sit or lie down. They shoved me in and there was only standing room. The crowd sways back and forth incessantly—red faces and bulging eyes. It's fearful! But I found a friend in there who urged me to squeeze forward towards the grill.

May God reward him—my friend—for telling me this, for showing me what to do; otherwise I would not be living now. Towards the end of the first night I lost consciousness. What happened and how—I don't know. When I came to I was lying down. I had been hauled out into the corridor. If I hadn't been near the grill I would certainly have died. My head was resting on a woman —a fat woman with large breasts who was also unconscious, and beyond her there was another woman. What fun! Oh, what fun! . . ."

According to him the "lice" cell at the Gorokhovaya is only about *half* the size of those crowded common cells of the Shpalernaya, but two to three hundred persons are jammed into it. There the people must stand pressed closely together. To add to the torture a high temperature is maintained in the cell. Everybody is covered with lice and fighting them is quite impossible. There is no toilet in the cell. The prisoners are taken out, three at a time, heavily guarded; men and women are taken together to the same toilet. This goes on continuously throughout the day and night. And every time even one person squeezes his way to the grill a general motion is started, resulting in a continuous swaying or rocking throughout the entire cell.

No one may sit or lie down. From time to time a GPU official enters the cell and stands up on a stool in the middle of this exhausted mass of people. If he finds that any one of the prisoners is sitting he makes the entire cell do a squatting exercise—lowering themselves slowly with bended knees and then slowly raising themselves up again time after time. This is such torture when everybody's legs are swollen from long standing that the prisoners themselves watch over each other so that no one may slide down to the floor.

The underwear of those who have been in the cell for several days becomes completely rotten and worn out and their entire bodies covered with lice bites and often a rash from nervous eczema.

"Do they have anything to eat there?" we asked, horrified at this picture of torture.

"Yes, yes! Each person gets 200 grams of bread and a mug of water a day. All drink water, but no one eats the bread—it would stick in one's throat. What a farce! The whole cell can be seen from the corridor. People are taken to see it before examinations and later, on the threat of being thrown in there, give up all their money, jewels,—anything to save themselves from it. They are cunning, very cunning, those devils of the GPU."

"But you, Ivan Ivanovitch, why didn't you immediately say that you'd give up everything?"

"They didn't ask me to. That's just it —they didn't ask for anything. They kept me here four months without saying a single word to me, you know that. For almost four days they kept me in the 'lice' cell and I couldn't even speak to them about it. That's just one of their ways of terrifying people. Some are put in the cell and others are shown it from the corridor. The GPU knows how to frighten people, they're cunning!

"It was not until the fourth day," he continued, "that forty of us were picked out and taken to another cell where we waited for one hour and then another. At last a young fellow came in; he was young and alert and explained everything so clearly that we understood what it was all about.

"'You are parasites,' he said, 'and enemies of the Soviet Government. You all ought to be executed without mercy, but the Soviet Government will be lenient towards you for a time. It will let you cut your own roots. The Government needs money for the *Piatiletka*,[1] real money! Foreign currency and gold coins will do, and those who haven't any can give gold articles and precious stones. The richer the Government is, the sooner will it be able to fulfill the *Piatiletka* and establish a classless society where there will be no room for parasites like you. In a word, you must give voluntarily to the *Piatiletka* that amount which will be assigned to each one of you. And those who refuse will be returned to the "lice" cell or sent to the "conveyor." And don't forget about the concentration camps.' Then after considerable swearing at us he sent us one by one to the examining officer.

"This officer was, I'll have to admit, a clever guy—very clever, and an expert in precious stones. When he told me that my contribution must be made with a certain value in precious stones, I agreed to it all. It meant I must give away all the jewels that I had collected in my fifty-five years of work. My only worry was that these might not be enough to cover the amount required from me. He told me to sign the agreement and I did. 'I will send you today to your apartment and you, yourself, can show us where these precious stones are hidden. If there aren't enough to meet the amount you must contribute, we shall put you back into the "lice" cell.'

"And everything happened as he had said. A man was appointed to go with me and we went in a street-car straight to my home."

"You rode in a street-car and you've been home?" we asked in amazement.

"Yes, we simply took a street-car— and how strange it felt. I couldn't believe it was true, that I actually was outside, riding on a car, that the people all around me were free. And I myself

[1] The Five-Year Plan.

seemed free, but I knew that actually I was a prisoner. Oh Lord! Oh Lord! When my old woman answered the door-bell she almost fainted. But she immediately understood that something was wrong because I was with a stranger; she didn't know what to do. But my companion took me straight to the place where the stones were hidden. I took them out, counted them and entered them all on a slip of paper. Then he ordered me to get going back to the prison. But my old woman begged that she be allowed to give me some tea. And he was a good fellow and gave his consent. Well, you know, at home there is nothing to eat, but I had a glass of tea and changed to clean underwear. I cheered up the old woman as best I could, saying that everything was all right and I would soon be back home. She was crying. We are both old. And he, the Gepeist, was hurrying me, saying, 'Let's go, old man, stop moping!'

"When we got back to the Gorokhovaya the same examining officer looked over my stones and made an expert valuation. 'Good,' he said, 'everything is all right. This will be enough from you for now, old man. The day after tomorrow you will be free, and for some time we'll let you alone.' And here I am."

"But Ivan Ivanovitch, how did it happen that they·let you go so soon?" we asked. "We've always heard that people were kept in the 'lice' cell for weeks."

"Many of them are," he replied. "There was a jeweler friend of mine who'd been in there for thirty days, and twice he'd been taken to the 'conveyor.' You see, some people would rather lose their lives than give up their money. Either they won't give it up or they try to bargain about the amount. And there are still others who are asked to give up something they've never even had. That's what's really so horrible, for they're tor-

tured, really tortured, until they wish they were dead; then they're deported to the concentration camp for insubordination.

"And there are all kinds of people there: merchants, dentists, doctors, engineers—all sorts. Anyone who might have some money is being taken. No matter how carefully money or gold is concealed, the GPU scents it and demands that it be turned over to them."

Ivan Ivanovitch finished his story and we went to sleep, and the next morning he woke up the same as he had always been—silent and reticent. We tried to find out more but he would not talk. Evidently the memory of his talkativeness of the night before, occurring because of nervous strain for perhaps the first time in his naturally quiet life, was very unpleasant to him. He told us nothing more.

The following day he was sent home "with things." Ivan Ivanovitch had bought himself out of prison.

THE "CONVEYOR"

There were many men whom I came across later who had not only undergone the tortures of the "lice" cell but also those of the "conveyor." One of these was a former bank employee, a Jew, about forty-five years old, but in appearance much older. His hair was quite gray, he was bent and walked with difficulty.

"I had no gray hair when I was arrested," he said. "Half a year at the Shpalernaya and thirty days at the Gorokhovaya and look at me now; I'm an old man—gray hair, sore legs—"

"From the 'lice' cell?" I interrupted.

"The 'lice' cell is comparatively nothing," he continued. "It's fearful, it's terrible, but it's not the 'conveyor.'"

"Just what is the 'conveyor'?" I asked.

"The 'conveyor?' Well imagine if you can a torture so terrible that if they ask you to cut off your arm you cut it off. That's what the 'conveyor' is like.

"Picture for yourself a group of about forty prisoners, men and women, all worn out, hungry, eaten by lice, suffering with swollen legs from long standing—people who have not slept for many nights. Single file we were led into a big room with three or four desks, and at each desk was an examining officer. Then comes another room and more examining officers, a corridor, stairs and more rooms with examining officers. At the command 'at a run' we had to run from one desk to another. And as we approached each desk the examining officer would start shouting at us in the vilest language imaginable. They used their foulest swearing on us Jews. They would hurl their most obscene oaths at us and shriek, 'Kike, scum—Give up your money! I'll run you to death! Give it up!—You won't? Get along, you son of a bitch. Do you want to feel my stick?' And he would swing his stick across the table.

"In front of me ran a woman, a dentist, a most respectable person. She was not so young, about forty, heavy and in ill health. She gasped for breath and could hardly keep on running. They shouted at her in the foulest language, enumerating every sexual perversion imaginable. The poor woman kept on running, would fall down, be picked up and roughly pushed from one desk to another. She was screaming: 'I swear that I have no gold, I swear! I would gladly have given it all to you, but I haven't got it. What can I do if I haven't got it?' And still they shouted their oaths at her. Some examining officers shout so strenuously that they finally lose their voices and can only shake their fists and threaten with their sticks and revolvers."

"Well, and then?"

"Then, they keep on running. Running round and round again."

"But there must be an end to it?"

"The end? The end is when the person falls down and can't get up any more. He is shaken, lifted up by the shoulders, beaten on the legs with a stick, and if he can he runs again, if not —he is taken back to the 'lice' cell and the next day it's the 'conveyor' again for him.

"This sort of torture lasts for from ten to twelve hours. Examining officers go away to rest; they get tired sitting and shouting obscenities and so are relieved by others, but the prisoners have to keep on running. And yet there are some people who won't give up their money at once. They know all about the 'conveyor' but still won't give it up. It is not until they have run for several days, have lost consciousness, have come to and been forced to run some more that they surrender. At first I was angry to think that it was because of such stubborn people that the use of the 'conveyor' continued, but I soon learned that they were the clever ones, at least very often."

"But I don't understand," said one of us.

"You don't understand," he smiled sadly. "Well, at first I didn't. You see, one has to know *how* to give up money to the GPU so as not to suffer more. Let's assume that they are demanding 10,000 roubles of you and that you have exactly this sum. What should you do? If you agree to give up this 10,000, then the examining officer thinks that you probably have more—maybe 15,000 or 20,000. So he takes your 10,000, puts you in the 'lice' cell, then sends you to the 'conveyor' and demands 5,000 roubles more. And how can you convince him that you haven't got it? You might die on the 'conveyor,' but you can't give away what you haven't got. And so, in order to convince the examining officer that you are depriving yourself of your all, of something which is as vital as life itself, you must endure torture, risk your health and perhaps finally win freedom. You have to understand the psychology of the examining officer.

"But we who have nothing," he continued, "what can we do? I swear to you now, as I did to the examining officer, that I had and have no money. Before the Revolution I worked in a banking firm and therefore they thought that I must have some foreign currency. They wanted 5,000 roubles and I didn't have it. I had to bear the worst of treatment, have lost ten years of life and was sentenced to five years in concentration camp—one year for every thousand roubles that I didn't have."

"But hasn't some accusation been brought against you?" I asked.

"Accusation? What accusation? Just give up the money! If you do you'll be free, if not—it's concentration camp. They can always find some suitable article in the Code. If I had never speculated or possessed foreign currency, I would be accused just the same—according to Article 59, Paragraph 12—of speculation in foreign currency. If I had actually speculated and had the money, I would pay up and go home. This is proletarian justice!"

"And how do they pick out the people to be arrested?"

"It's all very simple. They arrest anyone who before the Revolution or at the time of the NEP was in business, since there is a possibility that such a man may still have some money. Jewelers are arrested for the precious stones and metals which they might have, dentists for the gold which they must use in their work and doctors and engineers because they formerly earned high salaries. If such people spend much money, they are accused of misappropriating funds or for receiving money for 'wrecking';

if they spend little they are suspected of having money invested in foreign currency and this currency is demanded of them. . . ."

MY SON TAKES A MESSAGE

We were to be deported the following day. Early in the morning prisoners began to be called out to meet their relatives. There was great excitement among us, each one wondering whether he would be given a last chance of seeing those he loved. During the period of investigation scarcely anyone was allowed to see members of his family, but before deportation permits for visits were granted quite freely. The only question was whether the relatives would get the news in time to go through the detailed and complicated formalities of procuring permits for such visits. The day was advancing, but still many of us had not been called out. We had lost everything—would we also be denied the right of seeing for the last time those who were dear to us?

Preparations for our departure were going on hurriedly: prison equipment such as mugs and bowls were taken away from us; a party was being made ready for the bathhouse. I tried not to think of the visit; the thought that I might be sent away without once more seeing my son was unbearable. At least one hundred of us were lined up and counted before being led out to bathe ourselves. And just as we were about to start, a warden arrived with a list of names. He called out twenty, mine among them. One minute later and we would have gone to the bathhouse and I would have missed my boy's visit.

Trembling with emotion we were led into a large room—a grilled partition in front of us. About a meter beyond was another grill behind which stood our visitors. There was a terrible crush —a hundred prisoners on our side and more than a hundred visitors on the other—all desperately trying to find their loved ones. People were jammed closely together, some holding fast to the bars and pressing their entire bodies against the grill, their faces distorted by emotion; others hopelessly trying to find an opening in the human mass through which they might squeeze. All knew that they were seeing their relatives for the last time, that in ten minutes they would be separated perhaps forever. The excitement and noise made conversations almost impossible—the strained and breaking voices of women, the ringing shouts of children—it was like one terrifying scream of torture and farewell.

In the midst of this chaos I saw my son. He was standing close to the grill, holding on to it with all his might, waving to me and shouting with his brave, little voice. I rushed towards him but could not reach the grill. "Let me pass! Let me pass, for God's sake!" I cried, but no one heard me. Each one had before him only that face which was dear to him and heeded only their words. Frantically I tried to push one prisoner aside and for a second he turned to me, his face wet with tears, his hands clutching the grill convulsively. With one great effort I shouldered my way forward and grasped the fence with one hand. There was a sharp cracking and the grill started to fall. Guards rushed out to support it and while they were propping it up I succeeded in getting close to it that I might hear the words that my son was shouting.

"Mother is in prison," he yelled through the din and moanings of other human cries. "I take remittances to her. They won't let me see her. She once sent me a letter."

"And how is N.?" I shouted.

"She is in prison."

"And N.N.?"

"She is also in prison. Misha is left alone, too. He takes remittances to her."

"And N.N.N.?"

"She died."

I was afraid of questioning him further. There was no one left on whose help I could count. Through the crowd I could vaguely distinguish a woman totally unknown to me who stood behind my boy. Evidently she had brought him to the visit.

"If Mother is deported, try to go with her," I shouted.

"All right," he replied, and his childish mouth twitched and large tears dropped fast from his eyes and ran down his cheeks. But he was not noticing them and was not wiping them off.

"Have you got any money? What are you living on?" I asked.

"I've sold your camera."

"Good, sell whatever you can. Take remittances to Mother. Send nothing to me. Now listen carefully; I am going to Kem. Kem, do you understand? For five years. And remember this: I have not written any confessions. I am being deported innocent. Remember well: I have not surrendered."

I was shouting loudly and to my surprise felt that my voice was breaking, that tears were running down my face.

The visit was ended. We were being driven out of the room.

"Good-bye, dear, good-bye!" I called out in haste amidst the terrible moaning and screaming that filled the room.

"Remember Mother! Take care of her! Good-bye...."

SLAVE LABOR AND BIG BUSINESS—A STATE WITHIN A STATE

From my own investigations of the Fisheries Section and, as time went on, from conversations with prisoners in other sections and in the central administration of the camp, its complicated structure and its operations as a productive commercial enterprise were becoming clear to me. Let me describe them.

In 1931 the Solovetzki camp reached the height of its development. It contained fourteen sections. The river Swir and Lake Ladoga formed its southern boundary; its northern limit was the Arctic Ocean. The enterprises of this so-called camp extended approximately 1500 kilometers along the Murmansk railroad, taking in also the whole of Karelia. It was still growing and tending to expand beyond these limits. To the east this was checked by another enormous enterprise owned by the GPU —the Northern Camps of Special Designation—and to the west by the closeness of the Finnish frontier. Therefore the camp was reaching out to the islands of the Arctic Ocean, Kolgoueff and Vaigash, and to the southern shore of the Kola Peninsula (Kandalaksha and Terek shores of the White Sea). The number of prisoners was increasing daily. Enormous projects were being carried out and plans for even wider activities were under way.

Operating independently on the territory of the so-called Autonomous Republic of Karelia the Solovetzki camp established there, on a large scale, its own commercial enterprises, duplicating all the enterprises of that state. The camp had its own fisheries and lumber camps, its own brickyards, road construction, agricultural and cattle farms —all of which were completely stifling Karelian industry. Besides these activities of a permanent nature the camp also undertook work of temporary character on a still larger scale. Some of this work had a definitely strategic purpose; for example, the construction of the White Sea–Baltic Canal (actually the joining of the Onega Bay of the White Sea with Lake Onega), the building of highways to the Finnish frontier,

the reclaiming and levelling of large expanses of swamps and woods for military airports, the erection in the most important strategic points (Kem, Kandalaksha, Loukhi and others) of whole towns for quartering troops, with barracks to accommodate thousands of men, hospitals, warehouses, bathhouses, bakeries and so on. Besides this, in 1930–31 the camp also engaged in activities of an economic nature: the clearing of marsh land to be used for camp farms, preliminary work for the construction of a Soroka-Kotlas railroad which was to join the Siberian trunk line with the Murmansk railroad (this work was abandoned in 1931), the preparation of firewood for Moscow and Leningrad, and other activities.

In 1932 the GPU evidently decided that the Solovetzki camp had grown too big and it was, therefore, reorganized. After many changes, two new independent camps—the White Sea–Baltic camp (for preparation of firewood for Moscow and Leningrad)—were finally formed and were no longer a part of Solovetzki.

Each camp had many sections. Every section was a complete commercial entity, similar to those which in the U.S.S.R. are called "trusts," designed to make profits by productive commercial operations. Each section had its own budget, its invested and working capitals. The administration of the section, as in all Soviet "trusts," included the following departments: planning, production, technical, commercial, bookkeeping and executive. The higher officers were usually three in number: the section chief and his two assistants. The section was composed of production and commercial units the nature of which depended on the section's activity: factories, trades, agricultural farms, lumber camps and so on. Each section worked in a definite production field and had its own distinct territory. The marketing of its product was effected either independently in the Soviet market or through intermediaries. Goods produced by sections using forced labor and sold in the home market were often stamped with their trademark. As I have said, the trademark of the Solovetzki camp was an elephant. Dealings with foreign markets were, of course, handled through the *Gostorg* (State Trade Commissariat) and sometimes even through a second intermediary, in order better to conceal the origin of the goods. The Section of Fisheries, the *Ribprom,* in which I worked, had a canning factory, a fish-smoking factory, a shop for construction and repair of ships, a net factory and over twenty fisheries scattered along the shores of Onega and Kandalaksha bays of the White Sea, on the Solovetzki Islands and on the Murman coast of the Arctic Ocean. . . .

Like all other Soviet enterprises the camp sections formulated yearly and five-year plans, which were combined, along one line, into the general plan of the particular camp, and along another line, into the general plan for the given branch of industry by the GPU. There is no doubt that these plans were finally included in the *Piatiletka*. The industrial enterprises of the GPU, based on slave labor of prisoners, are growing from year to year and becoming a factor of decisive importance in the general economic activity of the U.S.S.R.

The concentration camps, therefore, are actually enormous enterprises operating in the same field with similar "free" Soviet State institutions. The management of the former is concentrated in the GPU, of the latter, in various commissariats. In many cases the scale of the work carried on by the GPU is larger than that of the corresponding Soviet institutions; it is quite probable, for instance, that the GPU

lumber operations exceed those of free lumber "trusts." Communication construction has almost entirely passed into the hands of the GPU, and entire camps with hundreds of thousands of slaves are engaged in these works—the White Sea–Baltic Canal, the Moscow–Volga Rivers Canal, the Sizran and Koungour railroads and the gigantic Bamlag, Baikal-Amour railroad development. It would seem that the planned economy, proclaimed by the Soviets, would have precluded the existence on such a grand scale, of an industrial organization paralleling the state industry, but the point is that *the GPU in the U.S.S.R. is not simply a state institution, it is actually a state within a state.* The GPU has its own troops, its own navy, millions of its own subjects (the prisoners in camps), its own territory where Soviet authority and laws do not function. The GPU issues its own currency, forbids its subjects to use Soviet currency and does not accept it in its stores. The GPU proclaims its own laws for its subjects, has its own jurisdiction and prisons. It is not surprising, therefore, that it maintains its own industry, parallel to Soviet industry.

There can be no exact comparison between GPU and State enterprises because the former have peculiar features differentiating them from all other business ventures, whether Soviet or not. They deserve the attention of economists.

As I continued my studies of the Fisheries Section I was struck by several of these unique features which it revealed. The invested capital was negligible, the cost of production unusually low, and the profits enormous. With a catch of 700 tons, and the purchase of a similar quantity from fishermen—a total of 1400 tons—the *Ribprom* had earned in 1930 a net profit of one million roubles. Compare this with the record of the North State Fishing Trust, which in

1928, with a catch of 48,000 tons, earned a profit of less than one million roubles.

All the production buildings of this enterprise—considered as part of the invested capital—were nothing but barracks of a temporary type. The largest establishments—the canning, fish-smoking and net factories—were housed in large barns on the verge of collapse. The equipment was primitive; at the canning factory, for instance, there was neither running water nor fresh water; sea water was used. At most of the fisheries the salting was carried on in the open as no buildings were available. There was no refrigeration of any kind —not even ice-cellars. Mechanization of work was entirely absent—everything was done by hand.

In consequence, depreciation of invested capital plays almost no part in the computation of costs. In this respect all enterprises of camps, even those engaged in such complicated works as the construction of the White Sea–Baltic Canal, present an extraordinary similarity. All work is carried on by hand, not a single building of real capital type is erected, all service buildings are constructed as cheaply as possible. This is a feature unknown in Soviet enterprises, where enormous sums are being spent for capital construction and mechanization, often without any rhyme or reason except that of "overtaking and outstripping."

Why this difference? First, the camp enterprises are not intended for "show," and second—this is the chief reason— the camps have *slave labor*. This personnel is actually the invested capital of the GPU enterprises; it takes the place of expensive equipment and machinery. Machines require buildings, care, and fuel of a certain quality and in fixed quantity. Not so with these prisoner-slaves. They need no care, they can exist in unheated barracks which they build

themselves. Their fuel ration—food— can be regulated according to circumstances: one kilogram of bread can be reduced to 400 grams, sugar can be omitted entirely; they work equally well on rotten salted horse or camel meat. Finally, the slave is a universal machine; today he digs a canal, tomorrow he fells trees, and the next day he catches fish. The only requisite is an efficient organization for compelling him to work—that is the "specialty" of the GPU.

But that is not all. This invested capital costs nothing to obtain as slaves did in capitalistic countries when slavery existed; the supply is limitless and there is neither interest to pay on funded debts nor any depreciation reserve to be set up when the balance sheet is made out.

And then there is the matter of wages, salaries, social insurance, union dues, and so on, all of which may be grouped as "labor costs," of vital importance to Soviet business. The GPU does not have to worry about these. Among the thousands of workmen in a camp section not more than a few free hired employees get salaries; the remainder work without pay. It is true that the GPU pays out premiums to those prisoners who work irreproachably, but this represents not more than 3 or 4 per cent of what the GPU would have to pay a free worker. And even this miserly pay is not in Soviet money, but in GPU scrip. The prisoner can buy for it (only in GPU stores) an insignificant quantity of food which is the waste that otherwise could not be sold. Here again the GPU makes money.

Thus, labor costs cannot be said to influence seriously the cost of production in the GPU. The absence of these two items of expense—depreciation and wages—gives the GPU a saving of not less than 35 per cent in such a venture as the fisheries, and a considerably greater saving in works like the construction of the White Sea Canal.

Moreover, the GPU trademark guarantees an assured home market for its goods—a Soviet purchaser never refuses goods offered him by this "firm," which are sold in open violation of trade regulations of the Soviet Government. A mark-up of 100 to 150 per cent over cost is the usual GPU figure according to its own "plans," and this mark-up is practically synonymous with "profit"— whereas the Soviet State enterprises are not allowed a profit of more than 8 per cent. Actually the GPU is not content with the limit approved in their plans and often sells its goods with a mark-up of 200–300 per cent and sometimes even more.

Here is an example. The Section of Fisheries dealt in fish which it caught or bought from free fishermen, who sold their catch both to the GPU and to other State enterprises (Corporations and Trusts) at fixed prices established by the local executive committee. The Section of Fisheries bought frozen herring from the fishermen at the fixed price of 10 kopeks the kilogram, delivered to the warehouse of the Section, where it would be resold, on the spot, to another GPU organization—called "Dynamo"—for 1 rouble (100 kopeks) the kilogram. The new purchaser would cart it to the State Kem Inn, two blocks away, and sell it there for 3 roubles (300 kopeks) the kilogram. That ended the transaction for the GPU. I might add that the State innkeeper, who had nothing to fear from the authorities, would salt it slightly and retail it in his restaurant at one rouble a fish. The White Sea herring is small— there are fifty to sixty in a kilogram— so that the consumer was buying them at the rate of fifty to sixty roubles the kilogram, which was 500 to 600 times the fixed price of 10 kopeks established by Soviet authorities. . . .

56

THE PURGE TRIALS

The purges of the 1930's form one of the bloodiest chapters of Soviet history. The total number of their victims is unknown. In his "secret" speech of 1956 Khrushchev admitted that 7,679 persons had been rehabilitated, "many of them posthumously." The vast majority of the condemned had never had a public trial. But beginning in the late thirties a series of show trials was held. The accused were some of the Party's most prominent leaders. Our excerpts are drawn from the so-called Trial of the Seventeen.

The prosecutor was Andrei Vyshinsky, the author of the leading Soviet legal text (translated into English as *The Law of the Soviet State*) and later Soviet foreign minister. One of the defendants was Karl Radek, with Trotsky the most cosmopolitan intellectual in the Party. Born in 1885 in Lvov, Poland, he had worked with the German Social Democrats before World War I. In 1914 he joined Lenin in Switzerland. In 1918 he accompanied Trotsky to Brest Litovsk and became assistant commissar for foreign affairs. He was one of the Party's most popular members. In a 1921 vote for the Central Committee, Lenin received 479 votes, Radek came second with 475 votes, while Stalin was sixth with 458 votes and Trotsky tenth with 452 votes. But in 1923 Radek joined Trotsky's opposition and was expelled from the Party in 1927. After a year of exile in the Far North he was readmitted to the Party and began a new career as the foreign affairs spokesman for the Kremlin, writing in the official organ *Izvestia*. We have already mentioned his work on the 1936 constitution. Such was the background of this "enemy of the people." While fourteen of the seventeen defendants were sentenced to death, Radek escaped with a ten-year sentence. He was never heard from again.

In addition to the volume used here, the People's Commissariat of Justice in Moscow published two other volumes of testimony on the purge trials. One of these has been reprinted in paperback under the title *The Great Purge Trial* with a long introduction by Robert Tucker. There is a famous rejoinder exonerating Trotsky edited by John Dewey, *Not Guilty*. For a Soviet apology see Emelian Iaroslavsky, *The Meaning of the Soviet Trials*. Joseph Davies' *Mission to Moscow* was written by the American ambassador to Moscow, who believed in the guilt

From People's Commissariat of Justice of the USSR, *Report of Court Proceedings in the Case of the Anti-Soviet Trotskyite Center* (Moscow, 1937), pp. 462–64, 472–73, 512–14, 541–46, 549–51. Some of the information about Radek is drawn from the unpublished thesis of Professor Donald Fanger, now of Stanford University.

of the accused. See also the section on the purges in Peter Filene (ed.), *American Views of Soviet Russia* (paperback).

For the most famous Soviet admission of the miscarriage of justice see Khrushchev's "secret" speech printed in paperback both in Boris Nicolaevsky's *The Crimes of the Stalin Era* and in Basil Dmytryshyn's *USSR: A Concise History*. An analysis by a Soviet lawyer is in N. Zhogin, "Vyshinsky's Distortions in Soviet Legal Theory and Practice," *Soviet Review*, Winter, 1965–66.

On Radek see a biography by Warren Lerner, *The Last Internationalist*; "The Piatakov-Radek Trial," in David Dallin, *From Purge to Coexistence*; Dudley Collard, *Soviet Justice and the Trial of Radek*, and H. Schurer, "Radek and the German Revolution," *Survey*, October, 1964.

On the purges as a whole see Zbygniew Brzezinski, *The Permanent Purge*; Nathan Leites, *Ritual of Liquidation*; Merle Fainsod, *Smolensk under Soviet Rule* (paperback); Alexander Orlov, *The Secret History of Stalin's Crimes*; two chapters in John Armstrong, *The Politics of Totalitarianism*; and Boris Nicolaevsky, *Power and the Soviet Elite*.

For recent articles see Hugo Dewar, "Murder Revisited: The Case of Sergei Kirov," *Problems of Communism*, September–October, 1965; Leopold Labedz, "Rehabilitation—and Perdition," *ibid.*, March–April, 1963; and Jane Shapiro, "Soviet Historiography and the Moscow Trials: After Thirty Years," *Russian Review*, January, 1968.

ANDREI VYSHINSKY'S SPEECH FOR THE PROSECUTION

Evening Session, January 28, 1937, 4:00 P.M.

Commandant: The Court is coming. Please rise.

The President: The session is resumed. Comrade Vyshinsky, Procurator of the U.S.S.R., will speak for the Prosecution.

Vyshinsky: Comrade Judges and members of the Supreme Court of the Union of Soviet Socialist Republics. In proceeding to perform my last duty in the present case I cannot but deal with several highly important specific features of the present trial.

In my opinion these specific features are, first of all, that the present trial, in a certain sense, sums up the criminal activities of the Trotskyite conspirators who for many years have systematically, and with the assistance of the most repulsive and despicable weapons, fought against the Soviet system, against the Soviet state, against the Soviet power and against our Party. This trial sums up the struggle waged against the Soviet state and the Party by these people, who started it long before the present time, started it during the life of our great teacher and organizer of the Soviet state, Lenin. While Lenin was alive these people fought against Lenin; and after his death they fought against his great disciple, that loyal guardian of Lenin's behests and the continuator of his cause—Stalin.

Another specific feature of this trial is that it, like a searchlight, illuminates the most remote recesses, the secret byways, the disgusting hidden corners of the Trotskyite underground.

This trial has revealed and proved the stupid obstinacy, the reptile cold-bloodedness, the cool calculation of professional criminals with which the Trotskyite bandits have been waging their struggle against the U.S.S.R. They stuck at nothing—neither wrecking, nor diversions, nor espionage, nor terrorism, nor treason to their country.

When several months ago, in this very hall, in this very dock, the members of the so-called united Trotskyite-Zinovievite terrorist centre were sitting; when the Supreme Court, represented by the Military Collegium, was trying those criminals, all of us listened to the story of their crimes that unfolded itself like a nightmare scene before us, with horror and revulsion.

Every honest man in our country, every honest man in every country in the world could not then but say:

This is the abyss of degradation!

This is the limit, the last boundary of moral and political decay!

This is the diabolical infinitude of crime!

Every honest son of our country thought to himself: such hideous crimes cannot be repeated. There cannot be in our country any more people who have fallen so low and who have so despicably betrayed us.

But now we are again overcome with the sentiments that we felt not long ago! Once again across our anxious and wrathful vision pass frightful scenes of monstrous crime, of monstrous treachery, of monstrous treason.

This trial, at which the accused themselves have confessed their guilt; this trial, at which side by side with the leaders of the so-called parallel Trotskyite centre—the accused Pyatakov, Sokolnikov, Radek and Serebryakov, sit in the same dock prominent Trotskyites like Muralov, Drobnis, Boguslavsky and Livshitz; where side by side with these Trotskyites sit mere spies and secret service agents like Rataichak, Shestov, Stroilov and Hrasche—this trial has shown to what depths these people have sunk, in what an abyss counter-revolutionary Trotskyism, which long ago became transformed into the advanced and most vicious unit of international fascism, has become completely submerged.

This trial has revealed all the secret springs of the underground criminal activities of the Trotskyites, the whole mechanism of their bloody, treacherous tactics. It has once again revealed the face of real, genuine Trotskyism—this old enemy of the workers and peasants, this old enemy of socialism, loyal servant of capitalism.

This trial has shown once again whom Trotsky and his henchmen are serving, what Trotskyism really represents in practice.

Here, in this hall, before this Court, before the whole country, before the whole world, has passed a whole string of crimes committed by these people.

Whom did their crimes benefit? For what purpose, for the sake of what ideas, and finally, for the sake of what political platform or program, did these people commit their deeds? For the sake of what? And finally, why did they become traitors to their country, betrayers of the cause of socialism and of the international proletariat?

I think this trial has exhaustively answered all these questions, has clearly and precisely revealed what brought them to this.

Like a reversed cinema reel, this trial has reminded and shown us all the main stages of the historical path traversed by the Trotskyites and Trotskyism, which spent the more than thirty years of its existence on preparing for its final conversion into a storm detachment of fascism, into one of the departments of the fascist police.

The accused themselves have told us whom they served. But this was told us still more eloquently by their deeds, by their sordid, sanguinary criminal deeds.

Many years ago our Party, the working class, our whole people, rejected the

Trotskyite-Zinovievite platform as an anti-Soviet, anti-socialist platform. Our people banished Trotsky from our country; his accomplices were expelled from the ranks of the Party as traitors to the cause of the working class and socialism. Trotsky and Zinoviev were routed, but they did not subside; they did not lay down their arms.

The Trotskyites went underground, they donned the mask of repentance and pretended that they had disarmed. Obeying the instructions of Trotsky, Pyatakov and the other leaders of this gang of criminals, pursuing a policy of duplicity, camouflaging themselves, they again penetrated into the Party, again penetrated into Soviet offices, here and there they even managed to creep into responsible positions of state, concealing for a time, as has now been established beyond a shadow of doubt, their old Trotskyite, anti-Soviet wares in their secret apartments, together with arms, codes, passwords, connections and cadres.

Beginning with the formation of an anti-Party faction, passing to sharper and sharper methods of struggle against the Party, becoming, after their expulsion from the Party, the principal mouthpiece of all anti-Soviet groups and trends, they became transformed into the vanguard of the fascists operating on the direct instructions of foreign intelligence services.

The connections the Trotskyites had established with the Gestapo and the fascists were exposed by the trial of the Trotskyite-Zinovievite centre last year. The present trial has gone even further in this respect. It has provided exceptionally convincing material which has once again confirmed the existence of these connections and has brought it out more definitely; it has fully confirmed and definitely brought out, by due process

of law and in its fullest scope, the treacherous role of Trotskyism, which has utterly and unreservedly passed into the camp of the enemy, which has become transformed into one of the departments of the "SS" and the Gestapo. . . .

Comrade Judges, when today we hear in Court, in the testimony of the ringleaders of this gang, of the ringleaders of the Trotskyite underground organization, when we hear confessions that they really did receive from Trotsky directives for the restoration of capitalism in the U.S.S.R., that they accepted this line, and that, in carrying it out, they conducted wrecking, diversive and espionage work, a question may arise which, indeed, some people have actually raised, namely: How can these people who fought for socialism for so many years, people who blasphemously called themselves Bolshevik Leninists, be accused of these monstrous crimes? Does it not prove that the accusation is unfounded, that these people are being accused of crimes they cannot possibly be accused of because of the very nature of their past socialist, revolutionary, Bolshevik activities?

I will reply to this question. The accused in the present case are charged with having attempted by the most repulsive and dishonest methods to reimpose upon our country the yoke of capitalism. We accuse these gentlemen of having betrayed socialism. And we support this charge not only with evidence of what they committed today— that is the subject of the indictment— but we say that the history of their fall began long before they organized the so-called "parallel" centre, this offshoot of the criminal Trotskyite-Zinovievite united bloc. Organic connection is proved. Historical connection is proved. And what I have said would be sufficient to remove all doubt that the principal charge made by the State Procurator against the accused sitting in the dock of attempting to restore in our country the capitalist system which was overthrown 19 years ago is fully proved, proved documentarily. This accusation condemns the criminals in this dock to eternal disgrace and to the eternal execration of all honest toilers, of all the honest people in our country, and throughout the world.

From the platform of 1926, from anti-Soviet street demonstrations, from illegal printing plants, from alliance with White Guard officers to which they too resorted at that time, to diversion, espionage, terrorism and treason in 1932–36, there is only one step. And this step they took!

We have already seen this in the case of the Trotskyite-Zinovievite united bloc, in the case of the political fate of Zinoviev, Kamenev, Smirnov, Mrachkovsky, Ter-Vaganyan and the others who ended their lives in disgrace, branded as mercenaries of foreign intelligence services.

And now we see it in the fate of the accused in the present case, the majority of whom for many years before and after the October Revolution fought against Lenin and Leninism, against the Party of Lenin and Stalin, against the building of socialism in our country.

Pyatakov, K. Radek, Sokolnikov, Serebryakov, Drobnis, Muralov, Livshitz, Boguslavsky, Shestov—have all, for a number of years, fought against the cause of socialism, againt the cause of Lenin and Stalin.

Already at that time these gentlemen directed their efforts towards, as Stalin put it, "breaking the Party's back," and at the same time breaking the back of the Soviet government, the inevitable doom of which all the counter-revolutionary ravens used to croak about.

In this fight against the Soviet power these gentlemen sank lower, I think, than anyone has sunk before.

Lenin foresaw the inevitability of the shameful end which the accused have reached, and which everyone who takes the path they trod must reach. The resolution adopted on Lenin's proposal by the Tenth Congress of our Party (which then still called itself the Russian Communist Party) uttered the stern warning that those who persist in factionalism and in errors under the Soviet system must inevitably slip into the camp of the enemies of the working class, into the camp of the White Guards and imperialists. These gentlemen, by all their activities, have proved the justness of this historical forecast. . . .

It must be said that the nature of the present case is such that it predetermines the peculiar nature of the proof possible in the case. We have a conspiracy, we have before us a group of people who conspired to bring about a *coup d'état,* who organized themselves and for a number of years carried on, or secured the carrying on, of activities directed towards ensuring the success of this conspiracy, a conspiracy with fairly wide ramifications, a conspiracy which connected the conspirators with foreign fascist forces. How can the question of proof be presented under these circumstances? The question can be put this way: a conspiracy, you say, but where are the documents? You say there is a program, but where is the program? Have these people a written program anywhere? They only talk about it.

You say there is an organization, that there is some sort of a gang (they call themselves a party), but where are their decisions, where is the material evidence of their conspiratorial activities—rules, minutes, a seal, and so on and so forth?

I am bold enough to assert, in keeping with the fundamental requirements of the science of criminal procedure,

that in cases of conspiracy such demands cannot be put. You cannot demand that cases of conspiracy, of *coup
d'état* be approached from the standpoint: give us minutes, decisions, membership cards, the numbers of your
membership cards; you cannot demand
that conspirators have their conspiratorial activities certified by a notary. No
sensible man can put the question in
this way in cases of state conspiracy. In
fact we have a number of documents to
prove our case. But even if these documents were not available, we would still
consider it right to submit our indictment on the basis of the testimony and
evidence of the accused and witnesses
and, if you will, circumstantial evidence.
In the present case I can quote a brilliant authority on the law of evidence
such as the old, well-known English jurist, William Wills, who in his book on
circumstantial evidence shows how
strong circumstantial evidence can be,
and how, not infrequently, circumstantial evidence can be much more convincing than direct evidence.

I think that my esteemed opponents
will agree with me from the point of
view of the position they, as Counsel for
Defence, are taking on this question.
But we also have objective proof. I
spoke about a program and submitted
to your attention, Comrade Judges,
Trotsky's *Bulletin*, in which this very
program is printed. And identification
will be much easier here than was the
case when you were establishing the
identity of certain persons belonging to
the German intelligence service from
photographs.

We rely on a number of proofs which
in our hands may serve as a test of the
assertions of the indictment, of the theses
of the indictment. First, there is the historical connection which confirms the
theses of the indictment on the basis of
the Trotskyites' past activity. We also
have in mind the testimony of the accused, which in itself represents enormous importance as proof. In the course
of the trial when one of the proofs was
the evidence of the accused themselves,
we did not confine ourselves merely to
the Court hearing the statements of the
accused; we did all we possibly could to
verify these statements. And I must say
that we did this here with all impartial
conscientiousness, and with all possible
care.

In order to distinguish truth from
falsehood in court, judicial experience
is, of course, sufficient; and every judge,
every procurator, and every counsel for
defence who has taken part in scores of
trials knows when an accused is speaking the truth and when he departs from
the truth for some purpose or other. But
let us assume that the testimony of the
accused cannot serve as convincing
proof. In that case, it is necessary to
reply to certain questions as the science
of criminal procedure demands. If the
statements do not conform with the
truth, it is what is called in science a denunciation. And if it is a denunciation,
the reasons for it must be explained.
There may be different reasons for it. The
existence of these reasons must be
proved. It might be the pursuit of personal advantage, personal interest, a desire to take revenge on someone, and
so forth. If the case now being heard is
approached from this point of view you
will, in your conference chamber, have
to analyse all the testimony and decide
for yourselves to what extent the confessions of the accused are convincing:
you will have to put to yourselves the
question as to the motives which
prompted this or that accused or witness. The circumstances of the present
case, which have been examined here
with all possible care, convincingly con-

firm what the accused have said. There is no reason to assume that Pyatakov is not a member of the centre, that Radek was not present at the diplomatic receptions and did not speak with Mr. K——, or with Mr. H—— or with any other gentleman—whatever his name may be; that he and Bukharin did not treat certain persons who came to visit him unofficially to "fried eggs and sausage," that Sokolnikov did not speak to some representative or other, thus "putting a visa on Trotsky's mandate." All that they said about their activities has been verified by the evidence of the experts, by the preliminary interrogation, by confessions and testimony, and none of this can be subject to any doubt whatever.

I think that all these circumstances enable me to say that if there is any shortcoming in the present trial, it is not that the accused have said what they have done, but that, after all, the accused have not really told us all they have done, all the crimes they have committed against the Soviet state.

But, Comrade Judges, we had an example of this in previous trials and I ask you to bear this in mind when we hear the last pleas that will be made here in a few hours' time. I would like to remind you of how, in the case of the united Trotskyite-Zinovievite centre, say, certain of the accused vowed, right here, in this very dock, during their last pleas, some begging, others not begging for clemency, that they had spoken the whole truth, that they had said everything, that in their hearts no opposition whatever remained against the working class, against our people, against our country. And later, when the revolting skein of monstrous crimes committed by these people became more and more unravelled, we found that at every step these people had lied and deceived when they already had one foot in the grave.

If we are to speak of shortcomings of the present trial, I see only one defect: I am convinced that the accused have not said half the truth which constitutes the horrible tale of the awful crimes they committed against our country, against our great motherland! . . .

KARL RADEK'S LAST PLEA

The President: Accused Radek.

Radek: Citizen Judges, after I have confessed to the crime of treason to the country there can be no question of a speech in defence. There are no arguments by which a grown man in full possession of his senses could defend treason to his country. Neither can I plead extenuating circumstances. A man who has spent 35 years in the labour movement cannot extenuate his crime by any circumstances when he confesses to a crime of treason to the country. I cannot even plead that I was led to err from the true path by Trotsky. I was already a grown man with fully formed views when I met Trotsky. And while in general Trotsky's part in the development of these counter-revolutionary organizations is tremendous, at the time I entered this path of struggle against the Party, Trotsky's authority for me was minimal.

I joined the Trotskyite organization not for the sake of Trotsky's petty theories, the rottenness of which I realized at the time of my first exile, and not because I recognized his authority as a leader, but because there was no other group upon which I could rely in those political aims which I had set myself. I had been connected with this group in the past, and therefore I went with this group. I did not go because I was drawn into the struggle, but as a result of my own appraisal of the situation, as the result of a path I had voluntarily chosen. And for this I bear complete and sole responsibility—a responsibility which you will measure according to the letter of the law and according to your conscience as judges of the Soviet Socialist Republic.

And with this I might conclude my last plea, if I did not consider it necessary to object to the view of the trial—as regards a partial, not the main, point—which was given here and which I must reject, not from my own personal standpoint, but from a political standpoint. I have admitted my guilt and I have given full testimony concerning it, not from the simple necessity of repentance—repentance may be an internal state of mind which one need not necessarily share with or reveal to anybody—not from love of the truth in general—the truth is a very bitter one, and I have already said that I would prefer to have been shot thrice rather than to have had to admit it—but I must admit my guilt from motives of the general benefit that this truth must bring. And when I heard that the people in this dock are mere bandits and spies, I object to it. I do not object to it with the purpose of defending myself; because since I have confessed to treason to the country, it makes little difference from my point of view, from a human point of view that I committed treason in conspiracy with generals, I have not that professional pride which permits one to commit treachery in conjunction with generals but not to commit treachery in conjunction with agents.

But the matter is this. This trial has revealed two important facts. The intertwining of the counter-revolutionary organizations with all the counter-revolutionary forces in the country—that is one fact. But this fact is tremendous objective proof. Wrecking work can be established by technical experts; the terrorist activities were connected with so many people that the testimony of these people, apart from material evi-dence, presents an absolute picture. But the trial is bicentric, and it has another important significance. It has revealed the smithy of war, and has shown that the Trotskyite organization became an agency of the forces which are fomenting a new world war.

What proofs are there in support of this fact? In support of this fact there is the evidence of two people—the testimony of myself, who received the directives and the letters from Trotsky (which, unfortunately, I burned), and the testimony of Pyatakov, who spoke to Trotsky. All the testimony of the other accused rests on our testimony. If you are dealing with mere criminals and spies, on what can you base your conviction that what we have said is the truth, the firm truth? . . .

And that is why I contest the assertion that those who sit here in this dock are criminals who have lost all human shape. I am fighting not for my honour, which I have lost; I am fighting for the recognition of the truth of the testimony I have given, the truth in the eyes not of this Court, not of the Public Prosecutor and the judges, who know us stripped to the soul, but of the far wider circle of people who have known me for thirty years and who cannot understand how I have sunk so low. I want them to see clearly from beginning to end why it was I gave this testimony, and therefore, in spite of the fact that I have already in part spoken of this, I feel obliged to present a picture of the events and experiences of this latest period, especially from the time of receipt of the last instructions from Trotsky.

I must explain why the decision taken in January to reveal everything was not carried out, and I must explain why I could not do that during the interrogation, why even when I arrived at the People's Commissariat of Internal Affairs I did not at once carry this decision into effect. The doubts of the State Prosecutor are entirely legitimate. The external facts speak against the existence of such a decision. And, moreover, the State Prosecutor, who is aware of the fact that Kamenev preferred to die like a bandit without a political program, asks himself why it should be assumed that here we have complete sincerity, that the whole truth has been told to the end.

Without the slightest egocentrism— my personality plays the least part here —I must first of all mention the personal factors which made it easier for me to regard Trotsky's December directive as the finale, as the end, as a signal of the necessity to break before the others did and with greater internal conviction. These were personal factors. Some of my fellow-accused returned to the path of struggle as convinced Trotskyites who permanently denied the possibility of building up socialism in one country. I returned having ceased to believe this conception of Trotsky's. I returned because I shrank from the difficulties that confronted socialism in 1931–33. This only shows that to admit the building of socialism is easier theoretically than to possess the strength and firmness which was fostered only in those who followed the Party from profound internal conviction and did not combat it. Without confidence in the leaders, or with insufficient confidence, without sufficient contact with the cadres —the theory itself was a dead letter, it was a theoretical view and not a practical one. Here I stumbled and I returned to this underground work. And here I immediately became an object of deceit. I say this not in order to extenuate my guilt, but because I increased this deceit tenfold in relation to our rank and file, and in order that you may understand the personal elements which helped me to realize the necessity of a change of front.

When I joined the organization, Trotsky did not say a word about the seizure of power in his letter. He felt that such an idea would seem to me too reckless. He only seized upon my profound perturbation and that in this state of mind I might decide to join forces with him; and then everything would turn out as he wanted. And when during my conversation with Pyatakov in December 1932, he said, "What are you thinking about, this is of course a state conspiracy," this was the first rift from the very beginning.

In September 1933 Romm brought me a letter from Trotsky in which wrecking work was spoken of as something taken for granted. And once again —and Romm spoke of this in his evidence—I was dumbfounded. Why? Because when I held these conversations not a word was said about wrecking activity, and this was done deliberately. They knew that after the period of the fight against wrecking, after its exposure in all its hideousness, I might come to grief. And so it was concealed from me. And when Pyatakov revealed these things to me, I of course realized that the door had banged to. It was absurd to start to quarrel over this. But it was the second rift.

And, finally, after receiving Trotsky's directives in 1934, I sent him the reply of the centre, and added in my own name that I agreed that the ground should be sounded, but that he should not bind himself, because the situation might change. I suggested that the negotiations should be conducted by Putna, who had connections with leading Japanese and German military circles. And Trotsky replied: "We shall not bind ourselves without your knowledge, we shall make no decisions." For a whole year he was silent. And at the end of that year he confronted us with the accomplished fact of his agreement. You will understand that it was not any virtue on my part that I rebelled against this. But it is a fact for you to understand.

And what picture did I see? The first stage. Kirov had been killed. The years of terrorist preparation, the scores of wandering terrorist groups waiting for a chance to assassinate some leader of the Party, and the consequences of the terrorism seemed to me personally to be the sacrifice of human life without any political advantage to ourselves. We could not bring to Moscow the leaders and organizations we required for group terrorism—that showed the state of forces of the terrorist organizations. And on the other hand, I stood near enough to the government and to the leading Party circles to know that not only the precautionary measures of the organs of public security, but the masses of the people themselves had become so vigilant that the idea that the Soviet power could be cast to the ground by terrorism—even with the help of the most devoted and desperate terrorist groups—was utopian, that we might sacrifice human life, but that this would not overthrow the Soviet power.

A second aspect of the matter. I perceived that Trotsky himself had lost faith. The first variant was a concealed way of saying: "Well, boys, try to overthrow the Soviet power by yourselves, without Hitler. What, you cannot? Try to seize power yourselves. What, you cannot?" Trotsky himself already felt his complete internal impotence and staked on Hitler. The stake was now on Hitler. The old Trotskyites had held that it was impossible to build up socialism in one country, and that it was therefore necessary to force the revolution in the West. Now they were told that a revolution in the West was impossible, and so destroy socialism in one country, destroy socialism in the U.S.S.R. Yet nobody could help but see that socialism in our country had been built. . . .

When I found myself in the People's Commissariat of Internal Affairs, the chief examining official realized at once why I would not talk. He said to me: "You are not a baby. Here you have fifteen people testifying against you. You cannot get out of it, and as a sensible man you cannot think of doing so. If you do not want to testify it can only be because you want to gain time and look it over more closely. Very well, study it." For two and a half months I tormented the examining official. The question has been raised here whether we were tormented while under investigation. I must say that it was not I who was tormented, but I who tormented the examining officials and compelled them to perform a lot of useless work. For two and a half months I compelled the examining official, by interrogating me and by confronting me with the testimony of other accused, to open up all the cards to me, so that I could see who had confessed, who had not confessed, and what each had confessed.

This lasted for two and a half months. And one day the chief examining official came to me and said: "You are now the last. Why are you wasting time and temporizing? Why don't you say what you have to say?" And I answered: "Yes, tomorrow I shall begin my testimony." And the testimony I gave contains not a single correction from first to last. I unfolded the whole picture as I knew it, and the investigation may have corrected one or another personal mistake about the connections of some person with another, but I affirm that not a single thing I told the examining officials has been refuted and that nothing has been added.

I have to admit one other guilt. Having already confessed my guilt and having disclosed the organization, I stubbornly refused to testify with regard to Bukharin. I knew that Bukharin's position was just as hopeless as my own, because our guilt was the same, if not juridically, then in essence. But we are close friends, and intellectual friendship is stronger than any other kind of friendship. I knew that Bukharin was in just such a state of profound disturbance as I was, and I was convinced that he would give honest testimony to the Soviet authorities. I therefore did not want to have him brought bound to the People's Commissariat of Internal Affairs. I wanted to enable him too, like the rest of our people, to lay down his arms. This explains why it was that only towards the very end, when I saw that the trial was drawing close, did I realize that I could not appear for trial having concealed the existence of another terrorist organization.

And so, Citizen Judges, I will conclude my last plea with this. We shall answer in accordance with the full severity of the Soviet law, considering that whatever your verdict may be it will be a just one. But we want to meet it like conscious people. We know that we have no right to address the masses —it is not for us to teach them. But to those elements who were connected with us we would like to say three things.

The first thing: the Trotskyite organization became a centre for all counter-revolutionary forces; the Right organization which was connected with it and which was about to merge with it is just such another centre for all the counter-revolutionary forces in the country. The government authorities will be able to cope with these terrorist organizations. On the basis of our own experience we have not the slightest doubt of this.

But there are in the country semi-Trotskyites, quarter-Trotskyites, one-eighth-Trotskyites, people who helped us, not knowing of the terrorist organization but sympathizing with us, people who from liberalism, from a Fronde against the Party, gave us this help. To these people we say, when a sea-shell gets under a steel hammer, that is not so dangerous; but when a sea-shell gets into a screw, a propeller, there may be a catastrophe. We are living in times of great strain, we are on the verge of war. Before this Court and in this hour of retribution, we say to these elements: whoever has the slightest rift with the Party, let him realize that tomorrow he may be a diversionist, tomorrow he may be a traitor if he does not thoroughly heal that rift by complete and utter frankness to the Party.

Secondly, we must say to the Trotskyite elements in France, Spain and other countries—and there are such— that the experience of the Russian revolution has shown that Trotskyism is a wrecker of the labour movement. We must warn them that if they do not learn from our experience, they will pay for it with their heads.

And finally, we must say to the whole world, to all who are struggling for peace: Trotskyism is the instrument of the warmongers. We must say that with a firm voice, because we have learned it by our own bitter experience. It has been extremely hard for us to admit this, but it is a historical fact, for the truth of which we shall pay with our heads. . . .

57

THE BLOCKADE OF LENINGRAD

By Dmitri Pavlov

The 900-day siege of Leningrad is one of the most heroic chapters of World War II. Never in history had a huge city been besieged for so long. And yet Leningrad, the former St. Petersburg, capital of the Russian Empire from Peter the Great until 1918, endured, survived, and triumphed over its implacable enemy. The losses were staggering, but so was the courage of the inhabitants, and their resourcefulness. The Soviet regime obviously mismanaged the fate of the heroic city at first; much suffering and many deaths could have been avoided. The full story has never been told, but, in the book from which we print some excerpts, more facts are given than ever before. We have here a surprisingly frank Soviet account, which does not attempt to hide the gruesome details, though it cannot always put the blame where it belongs, which is in the highest quarters.

For an account of the siege by a participant who defected to the West see Constantine Krypton, "The Siege of Leningrad," *Russian Review*, Vol. XIII. A study by a Western social scientist is Leon Goure's *The Siege of Leningrad* (paperback). A sympathetic account by a wartime correspondent is Alexander Werth's *Russia at War* (paperback). A German account is Paul Carell's *Hitler Moves East, 1941–1943* (paperback). For a book of magnificent photographs of the city see Nigel Gosling's *Leningrad*.

HUNGER, NOVEMBER–DECEMBER, 1941

November arrived. Cold, cloudy days and heavy snowfalls replaced the clear, dry days of October. The ground was covered by a thick layer of white that rose in drifts along the streets and boulevards. An icy wind drove powdered snow through the slits of dugouts and shelters, through the broken windows of apartments, hospitals, and stores. Winter came early, snowy, and cold.

The functioning of the city's transportation system deteriorated with each day. Fuel supplies were almost gone, and industry was dying out. Workers and employees, quartered in distant parts of the city, had now to walk several kilometers to work, struggling from one end of the city to the other through deep snow. Exhausted at the close of

From Dmitri Pavlov, *Leningrad 1941: The Blockade* (Chicago: University of Chicago Press, 1965), pp. 110–12, 121–28, 132–35, 163–66.

the working day, they could barely make their way home. There they could throw off their clothes and lie down for a short while to stretch their work-heavy legs. Sleep would come instantly, in spite of the cold, but would constantly be interrupted by cramps of the legs or hands. Rising was hard in the morning. Night did not restore the strength or drive away weariness. The fatigue of great temporary exertion will pass off in a single night's rest; but this was weariness that came from the daily exhausting of physical strength. Soon, however, it would be time for work again. Arm, leg, neck, and heart muscles would have to take up their burdens. The brain worked tensely.

The demands on peoples' strength increased as their nourishment deteriorated. The constant shortage of food, the cold weather and nervous tension wore the workers down. Jokes and laughter ceased; faces grew preoccupied and stern. People were weaker. They moved slowly, stopping often. Rosy cheeks were like a miracle. People looked at the person with surprise and some suspicion. Few people in November paid any attention to the whistle and burst of shells that had shocked them into alertness only a few days before. The thunder of gunfire was like a distant, aimless, hoarse barking. People were deeply absorbed in their joyless thoughts.

The blockade was now fifty-three days old. The most severe economies in food consumption and the delivery of a small quantity of grain across the lake had only resulted in the following meager amounts being on hand on the first of November: flour for fifteen days; cereals for sixteen days; sugar for thirty days; fats for twenty-two days. There was only a very small quantity of meat. The supply of meat products depended almost wholly on the deliveries by air. Out of the whole city, however—although everyone knew that food was scarce, since the rations were being reduced—the actual situation was known to only seven men. Two specially chosen workers recorded the deliveries of food over the lake and air routes (and later over the Ice Road), and these figures and those for food on hand were restricted to a small inner circle, which made it possible to keep the secret of the beleaguered fortress.

The eve of the twenty-fourth anniversary of the October Revolution arrived.[1] There usually was such a happy fuss and bustle on that evening! Streets and houses would have been ablaze with lights; store windows would delight the eye with their decorations and lavish displays of goods. Fat turkeys, apples, prunes, pastries, thin slices of ham, and a world of other delicacies would lure shoppers. Everywhere, marketing would be going on in lively fashion, as families prepared to spend the holidays with friends. There would have been the noise of happy children excited by the gaiety in the air and the prospect of presents and shows.

In the memorable year of 1941, Leningraders were deprived of pleasure. They had cold, darkness, and the sensation of hunger constantly with them. The sight of the empty shelves in the stores woke a feeling of melancholy in them that was actually painful. The holiday was observed by issuing each child two hundred grams of sour cream and one hundred grams of potato flour. Adults received five salted tomatoes. Nothing more was to be found.

The enemy presented his gift to the city of the revolution on the night of

---

[1] The anniversary of the October Revolution is November 7 on the revised calendar.

November 6. Heavy bombers broke through at great height and dropped explosives at random. The bombs weighed at least one ton each. Falling with a terrifying whistle, some of them destroyed buildings, but many burst at the bottom of the Neva, jarring the majestic structures along the embankments; still others went deep into the ground without exploding. . . .

To fill their empty stomachs and deaden the pains of a hunger which can be compared to nothing else, the inhabitants resorted to all sorts of ways to procure food. They trapped crows and hunted down the surviving dogs and cats. They took anything that could be used for food from their medicine chests: castor oil, Vaseline, glycerin.

Soup and jelly were prepared from carpenter's glue. But by no means all the people of the vast city had these supplementary sources of nourishment available to them.

Life was especially hard for children who had just turned twelve. At twelve a "dependent's" ration card replaced the "child's" card which had been good until then. His food ration was cut just as the child was growing adult enough to take part in the work of disarming incendiary bombs and to bear on his weak shoulders some of the heavy work and responsibility of his home. Parents sometimes denied themselves bread to support the enfeebled bodies of their children but in the process did severe harm to their own bodies.

TABLE 1

Factory workers and engineer-technical workers

Bread	250 grams
Fats	20 grams
Meat	50 grams
Cereals	50 grams
Sugar and Confectionery	50 grams
Total	420 grams (1,087 calories)

Office workers

Bread	125.0 grams
Fats	8.3 grams
Meat	26.6 grams
Sugar and Confectionery	33.3 grams
Cereals	33.3 grams
Total	226.5 grams (581 calories)

Dependents

Bread	125.0 grams
Fats	6.6 grams
Meat	13.2 grams
Sugar and Confectionery	26.6 grams
Cereals	20.0 grams
Total	191.4 grams (466 calories)

Children under 12

Bread	125.0 grams
Fats	16.6 grams
Meat	13.2 grams
Sugar and Confectionery	40.0 grams
Cereals	40.0 grams
Total	234.8 grams (684 calories)

Cold had settled down to stay in the unheated apartments of the city. Remorselessly it froze the exhausted people. Dystrophy and cold sent 11,085 people to their graves during November, the first to fall under death's scythe being the old men. Their bodies, in contrast to those of women of the same age or young men, offered no resistance at all to acute hunger.

The health services set up a widespread network of medical stations to help people survive. Various treatments were tried: injections of cardiovascular preparations, intravenous glucose injections, a little hot wine. These measures saved many lives, but the "forgotten" minimum human food requirement continued to make itself felt. More and more adults and children died every day. First a person's arms and legs grew weak, then his body became numb, the numbness gradually approached the heart, gripped it as in a vise, and then the end came.

Death overtook people anywhere. As he walked along the street, a man might fall and not get up. People would go to bed at home and not rise again. Often death would come suddenly as men worked at their machines.

Since public transportation was not operating, burial was a special problem. The dead were usually carried on sleds without coffins. Two or three relatives or close friends would haul the sled along the seemingly endless streets, often losing strength and abandoning the deceased halfway to the cemetery, leaving to the authorities the task of disposing of the body. Employees of the municipal public services and health service cruised the streets and alleys to pick up the bodies, loading them on trucks. Frozen bodies, drifted over with snow, lined the cemeteries and their approaches. There was not strength enough to dig into the deeply frozen earth. Civil defense crews would blast the ground to make mass graves, into which they would lay tens and sometimes hundreds of bodies without even knowing the names of those they buried.

—May the dead forgive the living who could not, under those desperate conditions, perform the last ceremonies due honest, laborious lives.

Exceeding the previous month's mortality by almost five times, 52,881 people died of dystrophy in December and still more people of various ages reached the threshold of death. In January and February the death rate reached its peak. During these sixty days 199,187 persons died. At every step furious death tore from the besieged their battle comrades, friends, and relatives. Although the pain of loss was sharp and piercing, the great wave of death did not spread despair among the survivors. The Leningraders died like heroes, striking at the enemy till their last breath. Their deaths summoned the living to an even more dedicated struggle, which went on with unprecedented stubbornness.

It is of scientific interest that Leningrad was free of epidemics during this period, and that the incidence of acute and infectious disease was less in December, 1941, than in the same month in 1940. Details of the comparison are given in Table 2.

TABLE 2

NUMBER OF CASES OF DISEASE*

	December 1940	December 1941
Typhoid fever	143	114
Dysentery	2,086	1,778
Typhus	118	42
Scarlet fever	1,056	93
Diphtheria	728	211
Whooping cough	1,844	818

*From a report of the Leningrad Health Service, January 5, 1942.

How is the absence of epidemics to be explained, given conditions of acute hunger, shortage of hot water, lack of protection from cold weather, and physical weakness? Leningrad's experience proves that hunger need not be accompanied by the inseparable fellow travelers, infectious disease and epidemics. A good system of sanitation breaks up their comradeship, for not only during the winter months of 1941 but in the spring of 1942, when conditions were most favorable for outbreaks of disease, no epidemics occurred in Leningrad. The government set the people to cleaning streets, yards, staircases, garrets, cellars, sewer wells—in brief, all the breeding grounds where infectious disease might start. From the end of March to the middle of April, 300,000 persons worked daily at cleaning up the city. Inspections of living quarters and compulsory observance of rules for cleanliness prevented the spread of communicable disease. The inhabitants were starving. Nonetheless, they fulfillled to their last days the social obligations necessary in a crowded community.

Hunger left a heavy mark on the people: the body was wasted, slow, and dull. But microbes apparently did not grow in such bodies. Parchment-thin skin and bones evidently failed to provide the necessary environment for infectious germs. Perhaps this is not the explanation of the relative absence of disease; some other force, not understood by science as yet, may have been operating, for there are still so many secrets in nature. It is also possible that some unfavorable factors may have canceled others. Whatever the reason, however, it is a fact that there were no epidemics and, in fact, the number of cases of infectious disease decreased just at the time that alimentary dystro-phy was at its height. There was one outbreak of scurvy in the spring of 1942 as a result of the prolonged malnutrition, but scurvy was soon banished from Leningrad with very few fatalities.

The great death rate of December and the early months of 1942 was the result of the prolonged and acute shortage of food brought on by the blockade.

During the period of the blockade, 632,000 people died of starvation. Their deaths are mourned by all Soviet citizens. The painful figure is given here to suggest the depth of suffering endured in Leningrad.

Cities had been blockaded before in human history, and men had fought and suffered and perished. But in general the laws of war had somehow been observed. In the Second World War, Hitler tossed all international agreements onto the trash pile, trampled on moral standards of behavior in wartime, and unleashed the animal instincts of the German soldiers. On June 14, 1941, just before his attack on the USSR, he declared at a meeting of his commanders that it would be necessary to employ more brutal methods against the Soviet Union than against the Western countries. Keitel testified to this at the Nuremberg trials: "Hitler mainly stressed that this was a decisive battle between two ideologies and that this fact excluded the possibility of employing in the war [with Russia] the methods familiar to us soldiers and which according to international law were the only ones considered proper."[2]

Despite their monstrousness, Hitler's instructions were carried out to the letter by his commanders. They approved the dictator's policy of annihilating our people. The Fascist troops laid waste our spacious countryside and our cities with violence and wrath, and they killed

[2] Nuremberg Trial Stenographic Account.

without regarding age or sex. They threw themselves on Leningrad with frenzy and malignant joy. Leningrad, one of the most important political and economic centers of the country, was especially hated. The Fascists wanted to destroy the population of the city physically, before the eyes of the whole world. "From our point of view, in this war that is a life-and-death struggle, there is no profit in preserving even a part of the population of this large city," are the words of a directive from the chief of the German Naval Operations Staff attached to Army Group North.[3] Only through the Leningraders' inflexible will to victory, their burning hatred of the invaders, and the firm leadership of Front, party, and Soviet agencies did the spirit of the population remain adamant in the face of this terror. The energetic action of the Soviet government in delivering food, war matériel, and other necessary supplies, as well as by diversionary military strokes, frustrated the base designs of the Fascists.

German doctors informed the world in 1947 that the population of the western zone of Germany was starving to death. The population was then receiving a ration of eight hundred calories per person per day. The doctors accused the victorious countries of deliberately destroying the German people by starvation. They wrote in their memorandum:

We consider it our duty as German doctors to declare to the entire world that what is taking place here is the direct opposite of the "education in the spirit of democracy" which we were promised; it is, on the contrary, the destruction of the biological basis of democracy. The spiritual and physical destruction of a great nation is taking place before our eyes, and no one can escape resposibility for this unless he does everything in his power to rescue and help.[4]

In reality, as De Castro correctly points out, the allies had no intention of starving the population of Germany: "the low ration levels in the postwar period in Germany were the natural consequence of the destructive war and the disintegration of the world's economy which it produced."[5] It was the fault of the Germans, in other words, that hunger gripped a number of countries including Germany itself.

German doctors found powerful words and means to appeal to the consciences of the peoples of the world against "the destruction of a great nation" when hunger reached Germany and the German people began to feel privation, although this was nothing compared to the tortures the Leningraders endured. The same doctors had uttered not a word of protest against the undisguised efforts of their compatriots, the officials of Fascist Germany, to destroy the peaceful population of Leningrad by starvation.

Order was maintained strictly in Leningrad. It was supported by the authorities and by the people themselves under conditions when the incessant gnawing of hunger might have been expected to drive them to break the law. For example, a truck driver was hurrying to deliver fresh bread in time for the opening of the stores. At the corner of Rastannaya and Ligovka streets a shell burst near the truck. The front part of the body was sheared off as by a scythe, and loaves of bread spilled out over the pavement. The driver had been killed

[3] Berlin, September 29, 1941, No. 1-1a 1601/41 ("Future of the City of Petersburg"). Translation from German.

[4] Josué de Castro, *Geography of Hunger*, p. 328.

[5] *Ibid.*, p. 329.

by a shell splinter; all around it was still dark. The situation could hardly have been better for theft. Yet, having seen the unguarded bread, passersby turned in the alarm, surrounded the spot, and did not leave until a second truck arrived with the delivery manager of the bread plant. The loaves were collected and delivered to the stores. The hungry people guarding the wrecked truck had, of course, felt the urge to eat; the aroma of the still warm bread had inflamed their desire for food. The temptation was truly great, but their sense of duty overcame it.

. . . One evening a thickset man entered a bread store on one of the quiet streets in Volodarsky *raion*. After carefully and distrustfully inspecting the customers and the two saleswomen in the store, he suddenly jumped over the counter to the bread and began to throw loaves from the shelves to the customers. He shouted: "Take the loaves! They want to starve us, stand your ground, demand bread!" When the stranger noticed that no one was taking the bread or giving him any support, he struck a saleswoman and made for the door, but all the customers threw themselves on the provocateur and held him for the authorities.

Tens of thousands of letters from citizens were sent to the City Party Committee and the Leningrad City Executive Committee during the blockade. They came from workers, office workers, scholars, housewives—from people in every category of life. Not one expressed despair or spite. Not one revealed an opinion that differed markedly from the general mood of the city. The letters expressed concern for strengthening the defenses of Leningrad. They contained proposals for more rational utilization of materials in production of war supplies and for

the preservation of unique equipment, buildings, and monuments. Simple people shared their thoughts, advising how to bear adversity and preserve the city.

There are hundreds of other examples of the remarkable behavior and high-mindedness of the citizens of this large city. Although firewood was not obtainable and people suffered unspeakably from the cold, the trees in the parks and gardens were jealously protected. Leningrad's example under siege and starvation refutes the arguments of the foreign writers who assert that man loses his morals and becomes a predatory beast when hunger affects him powerfully. If this were true, anarchy should have reigned in Leningrad, where two and one-half millions went hungry for a very long time. . . .

The lack of fuel resulted in the freezing of the water pipes—and of people. Firewood is necessary to heat water and since there was none, furniture, books, fences, and houses were burned instead. A great many houses were dismantled and burned to warm the living quarters and the dormitories in the suburb of Okhta. It all burned too fast, like fireworks.

When life is normal and there is fuel, it would appear that only a bit of wood is needed to heat water and prepare a meal, two or three sticks perhaps. The city dweller never realizes what a quantity of fuel a city like Leningrad takes as a whole. To run the city's economy more or less normally, one hundred and twenty trainloads of wood a day are required. They were now throwing in only three or four trainloads of wood in a day; both the supply of wood and peat and the carrying capacity of the railroads were inadequate. No amount of houses and barns, fences and furniture, would make up for the missing firewood. Houses were without light, water, or heat. Like pieces of sculpture, they watched the human drama: the suffering of the people and their desire to live. If people did manage to fetch water home with great difficulty and to carry it safely up the ice-covered steps of the steep staircases, heating it was a problem that could not be solved. In December the City Executive Committee opened public centers at dining rooms, large apartment houses, and on the streets to supply boiling water. The measure brought great joy and relief to the population.

Time went on. Everyone, children and adults alike, strove to master hunger. They lived and worked in the firm hope that right would triumph. They did not murmur against fate; each one felt a modest pride that he, along with the rest, was fighting in this difficult time for his beloved city and the honor of the motherland. Despite the hardships and no matter how long the road might be, the engineer, the smith, the scientist, and the woodcutter were roused to heroism by the holy feeling of a just cause. This feeling inspired the artists, too, when they sang and played to divert other hungry, tired people, although their own legs were giving way and they could hardly speak for hoarseness. Only real patriots and people strong in heart could have endured such hardships.

Almost all the theatrical companies were evacuated to the interior in good time. The operetta company, however, remained, and the population loved them. As they listened to the jokes, the witty remarks, and the music, the audience escaped for a few hours from the constant burden of their thoughts.

A fantastic picture rises before the eyes. December. Twenty-five degrees of frost outside. It would be a little warmer in the unheated theater, but the room would be full of people in street clothing with many of the older people wearing their felt boots. At three o'clock in the afternoon the operetta *Rose Marie* began. The artists wore only light costumes; their faces were pinched and pale, but smiling. The ballerinas were so thin it seemed they must break in two if they moved. Between acts many performers would faint, but human willpower conquered tired flesh. They would get up, fall, rise again, and continue to perform though they could hardly see.

It was a rare performance that went off without a hitch. In the midst of the play the sound of sirens would pierce the air to warn of danger. When this happened, an intermission would be announced and the audience was led from the theater to an air-raid shelter. At the same time the performers would clamber up to the icy roof to stand guard in the tower in their grease paint and costumes. They were armed with tongs for dislodging incendiary bombs. After the all clear, the hall would fill with the spectators again and the actors, down from the roof, would continue the play. At the end of each performance the public rose. Too weak to applaud, they signified their gratitude by standing silently and reverently for several minutes. The Leningraders appreciated the performers. They understood at what a price and by what a maximum effort of will they gave pleasure to an audience and made it laugh after it had forgotten how.

The hardships of the war and blockade were felt by everyone, but the very greatest difficulties fell to the women. Taking the places of men called up for duty, they worked in production and did housework too. In the care of home and children, no one could take their places. They followed the most stringent economies day by day (and in the course of each day, hour by hour) in apportioning the scanty food. They fetched wood with great trouble and used every scrap of it sparingly so that their children would not freeze. They would bring water in buckets from the nearest river. They did the laundry and mended clothes for the children and themselves by the dim light of oil lamps. Under the burden of the deprivation caused by the blockade and the dual responsibilities of jobs in industry and at home, the health of many women was seriously affected. Their will to live, their moral strength, resolution, efficiency, and discipline will always be the example and inspiration for millions of people.

Hunger revealed character. It laid bare hitherto undiscovered feelings and traits. The vast majority bore the hardships of hunger, physical pain, and mental distress bravely and stubbornly. They continued to work honestly, but there were others for whom the material well-being of ordinary times had concealed vices and weaknesses. Hunger's bony hand ripped off the protective covering and openly displayed the essence of each individual to his own surprise and that of the people close to him. Like oil stains on clean water, there appeared the egotists who would snatch bread from their own children, the thieves who would steal their neighbor's rations or take a sick woman's overcoat for a hundred grams of horse meat—and all the other parasites eager to build their own well-being on other people's grief. They stopped at nothing. The manager of a bread store of the Smolninsky *raion*, Akkonen, and her assistant, Sredneva, sold their customers bread at false weight. They would steal four or five grams of bread from each hunger ration and barter these for

furs, antiques, and objects of gold. In the pursuit of profit, they had forgotten that they were still in a Soviet city. Although the city was er ircled by fierce enemies, the laws of the revolution were preserved and respected. The crimes of Akkonen and Sredneva were discovered, and by sentence of the court, both were shot. The air had been cleared of something foul.

Hunger tormented people. All lived in the hope that soon, very soon, the Winter Road would be ready and food would start to arrive. Only a little while longer and there would be bread. As if in spite, the lake remained unfrozen and the days of waiting dragged wearily on.

THE WINTER ROAD

. . . On January 22 the State Defense Committee by special decree ordered the evacuation of 500,000 people from Leningrad. To carry out this decision, Deputy Chairman of the Council of Ministers of the USSR A. N. Kosygin arrived in the besieged city. The massive evacuation of the population began as soon as the winter road over the lake could handle it. First priority in evacuation was given to children, women, the aged, and the sick. What could not be done in July and August, 1941, was successfully undertaken during the winter and spring of 1942. There was no need to explain matters to the people: life had taught them much.

In January they evacuated 11,296 people; in February, 117,434 people; in March, 221,947 people; and in April, 163,392 people. In all, during less than a full four months, 514,069 people were evacuated over the Winter Road.

The spring thaw interrupted traffic over the lake. In the second half of May evacuation of citizens recommenced by water. From May through November,

1942, 448,010 persons were evacuated, and, with this, evacuation ceased.

The evacuation was carefully thought out and well organized. A series of field messes was set up on the road for the evacuees. As soon as the Leningraders crossed over the lake and reached land, they were served hot cabbage soup, soup with potatoes and meat, and other nourishment such as these exhausted people had dreamed of night after night. The fragrance of bread made from pure rye flour intoxicated the famished people. From their first step on land they were surrounded by loving care. Everyone felt in his heart the desire to help them in any way he could.

Kosygin also devoted much attention to evacuating valuable and rare machinery not being used in Leningrad at the time. From January through April, 1942, several thousand different machine tools and other types of machinery were evacuated over the road to the east of the country where they were sorely needed. These machines brought life to many a reassembled factory. Industrial plants picked up speed in producing the equipment necessary for routing the Fascist armies.

The needs of the Front and the city demanded thousands of tons of kerosene, gasoline, and oil, for which there were not enough oil tankers. Tanks were filled with fuel and floated across, but even this effective method of water transportation did not solve the problem of supplying a huge city with fuel. The Front Military Council, after thoroughly analyzing the proposals of a group of specialists, decided to lay an oil pipeline under the lake. When the project had been worked out in detail, it was submitted to the government of the USSR for examination and confirmation. The State Defense Committee approved it on April 25, 1942.

Soon specialists and trainloads of pipes, materials, and machines began to arrive at the eastern shore of Lake Ladoga. Laying the pipeline started under most difficult conditions. Through the efforts of an experienced crew from the Special Underwater Work Organization, military units, and workers, the construction of a pipeline about thirty kilometers long was completed on June 16, 1942.

With the pipeline operating, there was one more serious breach in the enemy blockade. Leningrad began to receive fuel in the necessary amounts the year round. The wheels of industrial life turned with increasing speed, and the mighty productive potential of the city revived. Leningrad, which had been written off by many people abroad under the influence of Goebbels' propaganda, stood proudly and gained strength. Time began to work again in favor of the besieged; the city became an even stronger fortress with dependable supplies of food, fuel, and ammunition. The pulse of productive activity beat stronger every day.

How could the Germans permit a branch line to be built to Kabona, a pipeline to be laid across the lake, and a massive evacuation of the population and heavy ship traffic, when these measures wrecked their plans to strangle the city by the blockade? The answer is that the Germans did not remain passive observers of the tireless activity of the Soviet people hurrying to the help of the besieged. The Fascists were furious; they dropped mines in large numbers, including magnetic mines, on the shipping routes, attempted landing operations from barges and launches transferred from the North Sea, and bombed Kabona, Osinovets, and the transports themselves. In 1942 during the spring and summer alone, the enemy flew about 5,000 sorties against the Ladoga route. The Germans fired at the frail barges with countless guns and dropped depth bombs to destroy the pipeline. Their attempts often attained their objectives, and the defenders suffered heavy losses, but the enemy did not succeed in frustrating the boldly conceived plans that were carried to completion by the persistent labor of Soviet people at Lake Ladoga and that played an exceptionally important part in the eventual rout of the Fascist troops at Leningrad.

Years will pass, and from every corner of the world people will be drawn to the shore of faraway Lake Ladoga to do homage to the great city and see with their own eyes the legendary "Life Road," to understand better the conditions under which the besieged waged their struggle. The road from Leningrad to Lake Ladoga, where death was overhead every minute and the prowess of thousands of people was so clearly displayed, will surely be a living page of the history of the Leningraders' struggle. The time will come when every kilometer of the way, through its memorial monuments, will tell all who travel the road of the hard days of the blockade, about the privations of the besieged and their terrible sufferings from hunger, about those who perished in the cause of a full and equal life for man, and about the triumph of victory over the ferocious enemy of humanity: fascism.

It is impossible to pass over in silence the regrettable fact that the Leningrad Defense Museum, opened soon after the war, was unjustifiably closed in 1949. Extremely rich materials were concentrated in the Museum to depict the heroic struggle of the besieged, the living conditions in Leningrad during the fearful days of blockade, and the defense measures against war raids and artillery bombardments. The great efficiency displayed by the workers in turning out weapons and building fortifications around and inside the city was shown, the battle against fires, the disarming of delayed-action bombs, and there were many other features to bring out the inventiveness, determination, and high courage of simple people. But the Museum was founded in the years when the cult of personality flourished, when many of the heroic deeds of the Leningraders were ascribed undeservedly to single individuals. Even in 1949, however, it was not hard to correct the mistakes engendered by the cult of personality and preserve the Museum, but, unfortunately, that was not what happened. . . .

58

THE SECOND WORLD WAR

By Grigori Deborin

The cardinal assumption of Soviet writing on World War II has been that the defeat of Germany was accomplished almost entirely by the USSR. At first it seemed sufficient to deny the Western Allies any major role in bringing Hitler to heel. Later it was found necessary to assert that, far from giving the Soviet Union any effective aid, Britain and the United States actually tried to hinder the Soviet war effort, and deliberately sabotaged the common Allied aims whenever they could, in the hope of weakening the postwar might of the USSR. Below the reader will find a sample of this writing from the pen of a senior Soviet specialist on World War II. Deborin is director of the Department on World War II in the Institute of Marxism-Leninism of the Central Committee of the Communist Party of the Soviet Union, the most authoritative research body in the Soviet Union. He is the author of numerous studies, of which the one excerpted below is available in English.

For a study of Soviet historiography on our topic see Matthew Gallagher, *The Soviet History of World War II* (paperback). For bibliographies on the topic see John Erickson, "The Soviet Union at War (1941–5): An Essay on Sources," *Soviet Studies*, Vol. XIV, and John Armstrong, "Recent Soviet Publications on the Second World War," *Slavic Review*, Vol. XXI. See also Maurice Matloff, "The Soviet Union and the War in the West," in Sidney Harcave, *Readings in Russian History*, Vol. II. For a study of the relations between the Allies see William H. McNeill, *America, Britain, and Russia, 1941–1946*, as well as John Deane, *The Strange Alliance*. On the Allied conferences see U.S. Department of State, *Conferences at Cairo and Tehran, 1943*, and *The Conferences at Malta and Yalta, 1945*. See also the memoirs of former U.S. Secretary of State James Byrnes, *Speaking Frankly*. For essays on Soviet relations with the West over Germany see Philip Mosely, *The Kremlin and World Politics* (paperback). For the intense collaboration between Nazi Germany and the Soviet Union before World War II see the documents edited by Raymond Sontag, *Nazi-Soviet Relations, 1939–1941*. See also the chapter on World War II in George Kennan's *Russia and the West Under Lenin and Stalin* (paperback). For a Yugoslav view of the conflict between East and West during the war see Milovan Djilas, *Conversations with Stalin* (paperback). See also *Memoirs of a Soviet Ambassador* by Ivan Maisky.

From Grigori Deborin, *The Second World War* (Moscow, n.d.), pp. 251–62.

. . . While the U.S.S.R. was locked in single combat with Hitler Germany and its satellites, the governments of the U.S.A. and Britain kept the bulk of their fighting force on the sidelines of the war.

Some U.S. and British military and political leaders spoke quite candidly about the real reasons behind the dilatory tactics of their governments with regard to the second front. In 1941 Liddell Hart, the British war historian, said in a book[1] that Britain's past history prompted it to spare its enemy, for he was its potential ally, and to weaken its ally, for he was its most likely future enemy. Constructions of this sort were aimed, in effect, at preparing British public opinion for a future anti-Soviet compact between the British rulers and surviving German militarists.

Arnold, Assistant Attorney General of the U.S. Department of Justice, said on June 3, 1942, that American monopolists were planning a military alliance with Germany. "The small group of American businessmen who are parties to these international rings," he said, "still think of the war as a temporary recess from business as usual—with a strong Germany. They expect to begin the game all over again after the war. It is significant that all these cartel leaders still talk and think as if the war would end in a stalemate, and that, therefore, they must be in a position to continue their arrangements with a strong Germany after the war."[2]

To mislead public opinion, Western spokesmen employed "arguments" to explain the delay of the second front. They made much of the nazi legend about an Atlantic Wall, which allegedly barred the road to continental Europe. The military and political leaders of the U.S.A. and Britain pretended to believe that the Atlantic Wall existed. Eisenhower, then Supreme Allied Commander in Africa and Europe, said that "the fortified coast of Western Europe could not be successfully attacked."

"Many held," he continued, "that attack against this type of defense was madness, nothing but military suicide."[3]

Eisenhower added that "definite signs of cracking German morale would have to appear" before it would be practicable to open a second front.[4] This coincided with Churchill's opinion that a second front was more desirable at a time when "the Anglo-American forces could perform a triumphal march from the Channel to Berlin with no more than a few snipers' bullets to annoy them."[5]

The governments of the U.S.A. and Britain wanted the Soviet Union to fight it out with Germany, and then to come to the victors' table. They admitted quite frankly that they had built up enormous, but idle, armies. Speaking in the House of Commons, Churchill said, "very large numbers of troops remained on fronts which were not engaged. . . ."[6] The public was told that the menace of a German invasion of the British Isles had not yet ended. Churchill said so in April and again in July, 1942.[7]

He laid stress on the idea that "no one could be sure that Germany would

[1] Liddell Hart, *The Way to Win Wars: The Strategy of Indirect Approach* (London: Faber and Faber Ltd.).

[2] *New Times*, No. 9 (Moscow, 1948), p. 9.

[3] Dwight D. Eisenhower, *Crusade in Europe* (New York, 1948), pp. 45–46.

[4] *Ibid.*

[5] Robert Sherwood, *Roosevelt and Hopkins*, p. 767.

[6] W. Churchill, *The End of the Beginning* (Boston, 1943), p. 172.

[7] W. Churchill, *The Second World War*, IV, 447.

not break Russia, or drive her beyond the Urals."[8] One would think that in the circumstances the United States and Britain should give their ally a helping hand. Nothing of the kind. Churchill was sooner gloating over the plight of his ally than expressing concern. The myopic U.S. and British politicians overlooked the fact that the threat to the Soviet Union was also a threat to their own countries. After the war, Edward R. Stettinius, the U.S. wartime lend-lease administrator, wrote:

"The American people should remember that they were on the brink of disaster in 1942. If the Soviet Union had failed to hold on its front, the Germans would have been in a position to conquer Great Britain. They would have been able to overrun Africa, too, and in this event they could have established a foothold in Latin America."[9]

British Labour Party leaders saw eye to eye with Churchill's Cabinet in the matter of a second front. Responding to public demands in Britain for an early second front, Attlee and Bevin said that the demands of irresponsible people should not influence military decisions and that the government knew what it was doing.

The Communist Party was the only British political party to work for the early opening of a second front. The Communists issued many official statements condemning sabotage of the second front and urging the British Government to live up to its commitments.

Churchill kept deliberately delaying the solution of the second front problem and devoted himself more to the Pacific Theatre. The U.S. leaders were inclined to do the same. Every time the war against Japan cropped up in the discussions, the U.S. General Staff insisted on the Soviet Union entering it. What it wanted was to see the Soviet Union weaken Japan, and Japan weaken the Soviet Union. More than that, it wanted to gain a foothold in Eastern Siberia and the Soviet Far East. A memorandum of the Operations Division of the U.S. General Staff, of March 25, 1942, said, "Russia is most anxious to avoid belligerency in Western Siberia; but it is this area which interests us."[10]

The U.S. Government and the top U.S. generals wanted air bases in Soviet Siberia in order to gain a foothold in that area and to provoke an armed conflict between Japan and the Soviet Union.

The U.S. President insisted that large U.S. Air Force units should be stationed in the Soviet Far East and Siberia, and sought Soviet consent for an American military mission under General Omar C. Bradley to inspect Soviet military installations in the Far East and for General George C. Marshall to visit Moscow for a comprehensive discussion of matters pertaining to Siberia.

On January 13, 1943, the Chairman of the Council of Ministers of the U.S.S.R. informed the U.S. President that the Soviet Union was not in need of air force units, but of planes without pilots, for it had enough pilots of its own. He stressed that help in the way of aircraft was required "not in the Far East where the U.S.S.R. is not in a state of war, but on the Soviet-German front, where the need for aircraft aid is particularly great." The message expressed surprise over the U.S. proposal that

---

[8] *Ibid.*, p. 241.

[9] Edward R. Stettinius, *Roosevelt and the Russians* (New York, 1949), p. 7.

[10] Maurice Matloff and Edwin Snell, *United States Army in World War II* (Washington, 1953), p. 156.

"General Bradley should inspect Russian military objectives in the Far East and elsewhere in the U.S.S.R. It should be perfectly obvious that only Russians can inspect Russian military objectives, just as U.S. military objectives can be inspected by none but Americans. There should be no unclarity in this matter."[11]

The U.S. demands, veiled though they were by the professed wish to "aid" the Soviet Union, were turned down.

Instead of opening the second front in the summer of 1942 the U.S.A. and Britain undertook a series of so-called commando raids along the French shore. These raids conveyed to the Germans that no landing of large forces was to be expected in Western Europe. Furthermore, failure of the raids, which were made by insignificant forces, was meant to "prove" that it was impossible to open a second front without incurring the risk of almost certain defeat. This was why, prior to the landing of the Allied troops in Dieppe, London radio broadcast on August 19, 1942, that the operation had limited objectives. Formally, the broadcast was meant for the French patriots, to discourage premature action on their part. But in point of fact it was meant for the Germans, to give them a chance to ward off the landing of a task force made up of Canadian divisions. The men and officers involved in the raid fought bravely, but were doomed in advance.

Small wonder that many people in Britain and the United States doubted the second front would ever be opened. "Many officers employed in planning

the invasion confessed haunting, persistent fears that the planning was merely a gigantic bluff, and that we would never attempt to invade Western Europe. So, the general public may be forgiven their doubts."[12]

Official British and U.S. historians claim that the absence of the second front in summer 1942 was amply compensated by lavish supplies to the Soviet Union. J. F. C. Fuller writes, for example, that "in the autumn of 1942 the economic position of Russia was a desperate one, and had it not been for the steady stream of Anglo-American supplies then pouring into Archangel, it is doubtful whether the Russians would have been able to turn to their advantage the fantastic situation in which Hitler had placed his armies."[13] This is entirely false. There was nothing even remotely resembling a "stream of Anglo-American supplies."

Take the evidence of historian D. F. Fleming. "At first," he writes, "the stream of lend-lease supplies was only a trickle. During 1941 its value was mainly moral. During 1942 . . . the aid sent to Russia . . . could not be tremendous."[14] And Edward R. Stettinius, the U.S. lend-lease administrator, admits that "in the over-all picture, the volume of fighting equipment we sent could not have bulked large.[15] McInnis also estimates that Western aid at the time of Stalingrad was small. Furthermore, he adds that "its quality was often below

[11] *Correspondence between the Chairman of the Council of Ministers of the USSR, the President of the U.S.A., and the Prime Minister of Great Britain during the Great Patriotic War of 1941–1945* (Moscow, 1957), II, 50. Hereafter cited as *Correspondence.*

[12] John Dalgleish, *We Planned the Second Front* (London, 1945), p. 10.

[13] J. F. C. Fuller, *The Second World War*, p. 186.

[14] D. F. Fleming, *The Cold War and Its Origins* (New York: Doubleday, 1961), I, 140.

[15] Edward R. Stettinius, Jr., *Lend Lease, Weapon for Victory* (New York: Macmillan, 1944), p. 210.

that of Russian first-line equipment."[16]

Moreover, the governments of the United States and Britain tried to use supplies and temporary stoppages of deliveries at crucial periods in the war to exert pressure on the U.S.S.R. At first they said they lacked transport facilities due to the coming invasion of North Africa. Then, with a view to disrupting deliveries to the U.S.S.R., a convoy of supplies headed for Archangel was deliberately exposed to a German attack.

The reference is to convoy PQ-17, of 34 supply ships, which sailed from Iceland on June 27, 1942. The convoy was escorted by six destroyers, two anti-aircraft ships, two submarines and eleven smaller vessels. The support force consisted of two British and two U.S. cruisers, and three destroyers. Nine British and two Soviet submarines were near the north coast of Norway. Then there was a cover force of two battleships, one aircraft carrier, three cruisers and a squadron of destroyers. There were enough warships to see the convoy through seas where the Soviet fleet was keeping the Germans at bay.

On July 4, when the supply ships were in mid-sea, the escort, support and cover forces were recalled west by orders from London. The convoy was advised "to disperse and make for Soviet harbours singly." The British Admiralty issued the order, although it knew the German Command was informed of the convoy's route. The vessels were thus deliberately exposed to attack by German aircraft and U-boats. Churchill makes a very significant entry in his memoirs on this score. "I let the matter drop as far as I was concerned,"[17] he

[16] Edgar McInnis, *The War, Fourth Year* (Oxford, 1944), p. 90.

[17] Churchill, *The Second World War*, IV, 238.

writes. The British seamen had no inkling of the scheming done behind their backs. They showed supreme courage in their endeavor to help the Soviet people in their hour of need.

Convoy PQ-17 was attacked. Twenty-three of its 34 ships were sunk. This gave the U.S. and British authorities a plausible excuse to reduce shipments of supplies to the Soviet Union. On June 17 the British Government officially notified the U.S.S.R. that deliveries would be discontinued. Churchill admits in his memoirs that the Soviet Union was denied deliveries of war supplies at a time when it needed them most.

The Soviet Government informed Churchill of its opinion on the stoppage of supplies to the northern harbors. The British excuses were described as untenable.

"Given good will and readiness to honour obligations," the Soviet message said, "steady deliveries could be effected, with heavy loss to the Germans. The British Admiralty's order to the PQ-17 convoy to abandon the supply ships and return to Britain, and to the supply ships to disperse and make for Soviet harbours singly, without escort is, in view of our experts, puzzling and inexplicable."[18]

The message pointed out that the Soviet Government could not reconcile itself to the second front in Europe being postponed till 1943.

The Polish émigré government's army formed on Soviet territory was due to set out for the forward lines under the Soviet-Polish agreement. Most of its men were spoiling for a fight with the nazis. But General Anders, who was in command, had other plans.

A Polish émigré paper published in

[18] *Correspondence*, I, 56.

London said in May 1942:

"By August or September of this year both the German and Soviet armies must be rendered harmless. They will destroy each other, and the time will come for the Anglo-Saxons to strike."[19] At the height of the Volga Battle, Anders' army was evacuated to the Middle East.

The émigré government of Czechoslovakia was also eager to withdraw its units, formed in Soviet territory, to the Middle East. But its attempts to do so failed. The men of the Czechoslovakian units asked the Soviet Government to send them into action against the Hitlerites. Their request was granted. In March, 1943, they were engaged on the Soviet-German front near the village of Sokolovo, south of Kharkov.

2

Hitler Germany was not the only country that coveted Soviet oil. The U.S. and British imperialists had their eyes on it as well, and tried to make the most of the difficulties experienced by the Soviet Union. The governments of the U.S.A. and Britain worked out a program (known as the Velvet Plan) for deploying their troops from the Middle East to the Caucasus, and each wanted to be ahead of the other. This kind of race, too, was an indication of imperialist contradictions.

In August, 1942, Churchill flew to Moscow to bring belated news that the U.S.A. and Britain refused to fulfill their obligation to open the second front in 1942. In the plane Churchill made the following entry in his diary:

"I pondered on my mission to this . . . Bolshevik State I had once tried so hard to strangle at its birth. . . . What was it my duty to say to them now? General Wavell, who had literary in-

clinations, summed it all up in a poem. . . . There were several verses, and the last line of each was, 'No second front in nineteen forty-two.' "[20] Judging by this passage, Churchill considered his policy of sabotaging the second front a projection of his old anti-Soviet policy.

The conference in Moscow involved Soviet statesmen, the British Prime Minister and the U.S. Ambassador. Negotiations also proceeded between the general staffs of the U.S.S.R., the U.S.A. and Britain.

The British Prime Minister, supported by the U.S. spokesman, officially notified the Soviet Government that the second front would not be opened in 1942, and that it was timed for 1943. A Soviet Memorandum was handed to Churchill, which said:

"The British Government's refusal to open a second front in Europe in 1942 delivers a moral blow to Soviet public opinion, which had hoped that the second front would be opened, complicates the position of the Red Army at the front and injures the plans of the Soviet High Command. The difficulties in which the Red Army is involved through the refusal to open a second front in 1942 are bound to impair the military position of Britain and the other Allies."[21]

The Soviet Memorandum doubted that the second front would be opened in 1943. On January 30, 1943, the Soviet Government asked the U.S. and British governments what preparations were being made for the second front, and whether it would be opened in 1943. There was no reply, although the Soviet Government issued assurances that "the Soviet Armed Forces will do all in their power to continue the of-

[19] *Trybuna Wolnosci*, September 1, 1946.

[20] Churchill, *The Second World War*, IV, 475.

[21] *Correspondence*, I, 61.

fensive against Germany and her allies on the Soviet-German front,"[22] a pledge which, the whole world knows, it observed faithfully.

Churchill thought he could capitalize on the tremendous strain experienced by the Soviet Union at the time of the Battle on the Volga. He clamored for Soviet consent to British troops occupying Soviet Transcaucasia. But he soon saw that he would never get it. It was clear to him, moreover, that he and his U.S. colleagues were due for a disappointment. They had hoped the war would exhaust the Soviet Union. But there was no sign of this. The reverse was much more likely. This spurred Churchill, on his return to Britain in October, 1942, to issue a secret memorandum in which he called for a broad military alliance against the U.S.S.R.[23]

With the Volga Battle at its height, British Ambassador Samuel Hoare and Japanese Ambassador Suma held secret talks in Madrid. Hoare proposed that Britain and Japan conclude peace. He said Britain was prepared to recognize Japan's acquisitions in North China, but wanted Japan to return Singapore and all of Malaya. The British peace overtures, like the U.S. proposals, made on different terms, pursued the same purpose of speeding a Soviet-Japanese war.

The United States, too, attempted to profit by the tense situation on the Soviet-German front. When Washington got wind of Churchill's proposal to send British troops to the Caucasus, the United States hastened to back it and insisted that a U.S. force participate in the undertaking. This was not all. The U.S. Government offered to set up American military bases at important Soviet economic and strategic centers in the Transcaucasus, the Pacific seaboard and Kamchatka. It made a fresh demand that U.S. air bases be set up in Siberia. "We cannot let the matter rest here," wrote General Henry H. Arnold, Commander of the U.S. Army Air Forces, to Eisenhower. "We must develop the facilities as quickly as possible. Furthermore, we must move into them so that when world conditions make it necessary there can be no argument about the matter."[24]

The Soviet Union demurred, and the U.S. ruling circles retaliated by sabotaging deliveries of supplies to the Soviet Union at the height of the Volga Battle.

Despite the firm Soviet stand, the U.S. and British governments insisted on their plans of occupying the Soviet Transcaucasus. On September 28, 1942, Churchill sent the Joint Anglo-American Command an aide-memoire in which he admonished them not to miss the bus in the Caucasus. But he was troubled by the possibility of the German offensive foundering in 1942.[25] The aide-memoire also said that PQ-19, a convoy of supply ships for the U.S.S.R., was canceled, of which, he felt "most strongly," the Soviet Union should not be told. On October 5, 1942, Roosevelt sent Churchill a message in which he approved his plans of invading the Caucasus and agreed that the Soviet Union should not be told that the convoy would not sail.[26]

Meanwhile fierce fighting proceeded on the Soviet-German front. On June 28, 1942, the Germans took the offen-

---

[22] *Ibid.*, p. 89.

[23] Churchill, *The Second World War*, IV, 475.

[24] Matloff and Snell, *op. cit.*, p. 341.

[25] See Churchill, *The Second World War*, IV, 514.

[26] *Ibid.*, p. 516.

sive. The German attempt to crush the Soviet left flank south of Orel failed. But the Soviet Army was forced to retreat across the Don, fighting effective delaying actions against superior nazi forces. On July 6 the Hitlerites were stopped short near Voronezh by counterattacks from the north against the flank of the advancing enemy force. The initial German plan was frustrated. The pivot of the fighting shifted south, to the Volga sector. On July 12 the Soviet Supreme Command established the Volga Front under Colonel-General A. Jeremenko, with N. S. Khrushchov as Member of the Military Council.

The opening action of the Volga Battle was fought on the River Chir on July 17. For four harrowing months, until November 18, 1942, the Soviet Army stood its ground, putting up a stiff defense. . . .

59

THE PARTY AND THE ARTS

By Andrei Zhdanov; Nikita Khrushchev

Andrei Zhdanov (1896–1948) was one of the best educated of the Soviet leaders. If, as Stalin put it, writers were to be "engineers of the soul" then Zhdanov was the chief engineer of that corps. In 1934 he had been responsible for the new line in the writing of Russian history. In the same year he was the Party's spokesman in literary matters at the Congress of Soviet writers. In 1935 he supervised the purge of Leningrad following the murder of Kirov; he remained Party secretary of that city until his death. In 1938 he created the Party's Central Administration for Propaganda and Agitation. After 1939 he was a member of the Politburo, the Party's governing body.

Following the Second World War, Zhdanov was put in charge of tightening ideological control in the Soviet Union following the wartime relaxations. His ruthless attacks against writers, musicians, and scientists gave a name to that era: the "Zhdanovshchina" became a synonym for an ideological strait jacket.

Since Zhdanov's death his mantle passed to much inferior personalities. During the Khrushchev era the leader himself made pronouncements on culture, and a sample is reprinted here. Under the Brezhnev-Kosygin regime there have been several pronouncements, but none as open and far-reaching as those presented here.

For the Leninist text on literature which is always referred to but consistently misinterpreted see Lenin's *Collected Works*, Vol. X, the essay entitled "Party Organizations and Party Literature." The early thirties are discussed in Max Eastman, *Artists in Uniform*. For the views of an enlightened early Bolshevik who was a Commissar of the Arts see Anatole Lunacharsky, *On Literature and Art*. For the worst excesses of the Stalin period see George Counts, *The Country of the Blind*. For literary politics see Harold Swayze, *Political Controls of Literature in the USSR, 1946–1959*. For a brilliant critique of socialist realism by a Soviet writer now in a forced-labor camp see Abram Tertz, *On Socialist Realism*. On music see Alexander Werth, *Musical Uproar in Moscow;* Alexander Groth, *On Soviet Music: Documents and Discussion;* and Andrei Olkhovsky, *Music Under the Soviets.* For the plastic arts see Camilla Gray, "The Genesis of Socialist

From A. Zhdanov, *On Literature, Music and Philosophy* (London: Lawrence & Wishart, 1950), pp. 12–16, 19–20, 22–23, 35–49, 56–59, 62–63, 72–73. Used by permission of the publisher and of the International Publishers Co., Inc. The Khrushchev speech is reprinted from Vol. XV, No. 11, of the *Current Digest of the Soviet Press*, pp. 6–9. Published at Columbia University by the Joint Committee on Slavic Studies, appointed by the American Council of Learned Societies and the Social Science Research Council. Copyright, 1963, the Joint Committee on Slavic Studies.

Realism in Painting," *Soviet Survey*, October–December, 1958. For the ferment since Stalin's death see Hugh McLean and Walter Vickery, *1956: The Year of Protest*; Evgenii Evtushenko, *A Precocious Autobiography* (paperback); Priscilla Johnson, *Khrushchev and the Arts*; and "Soviet Politics and Culture," *Problems of Communism*, March–April, 1967. For an interpretation of the situation in the arts see Ralph Blum, "Freeze and Thaw: The Artists in Russia," *New Yorker*, 1965, August 28, September 4, and September 11. The 1948 decree on music was superseded by the decree of May 28, 1958; see Alexander Werth, *Russia Under Khrushchev*, pp. 262–71. For an impression by a Yugoslav writer now in jail see Mihajlo Mihajlov, *Moscow Summer*. On Zhdanov in retrospect see "Zhdanovism," in Max Hayward and Leopold Labedz, *Literature and Revolution in Soviet Russia*, and a chapter in John Armstrong, *The Politics of Totalitarianism*. On literature see Walter Vickery, *The Cult of Optimism*. See also Paul Sjeklocha and Igor Mead, *Unofficial Art in the Soviet Union*.

SPEECH AT THE FIRST ALL UNION CONGRESS OF SOVIET WRITERS, 1934

. . . There is not and never has been a literature making its basic subject-matter the life of the working class and the peasantry and their struggle for socialism. There does not exist in any country in the world a literature to defend and protect the equality of rights of the working people of all nations and the equality of rights of women. There is not, nor can there be in any bourgeois country, a literature to wage consistent war on all obscurantism, mysticism, hierarchic religious attitudes and threats of hell-fire, as our literature does.

Only Soviet literature could become and has in fact become such an advanced, thought-imbued literature. It is one flesh and blood with our socialist construction. . . .

What can the bourgeois writer write or think of, where can he find passion, if the worker in the capitalist countries is not sure of his tomorrow, does not know whether he will have work, if the peasant does not know whether he will be working on his bit of land or thrown on the scrap heap by a capitalist crisis, if the working intellectual is out of work today and does not know whether he will have work tomorrow?

What can the bourgeois author write about, what source of inspiration can there be for him, when the world, from one day to the next, may be plunged once more into the abyss of a new imperialist war?

The present position of bourgeois literature is such that it is already incapable of producing great works. *The decline and decay of bourgeois literature derive from the decline and decay of the capitalist system and are a feature and aspect characteristic of the present condition of bourgeois culture and literature.* The days when bourgeois literature, reflecting the victories of the bourgeois system over feudalism, was in the hey-day of capitalism capable of creating great works, have gone, never to return. Today a degeneration in subject matter, in talents, in authors and in heroes, is in progress. . . .

A riot of mysticism, religious mania and pornography is characteristic of the decline and decay of bourgeois culture. The "celebrities" of that bourgeois literature which has sold its pen to capital are today thieves, detectives, prostitutes, pimps and gangsters. . . .

The proletariat of the capitalist countries is already forging its army of writers and artists—revolutionary writers, the representatives of whom we are glad to be able to welcome here today at the first Soviet Writers' Congress. The number of revolutionary writers in the capitalist countries is still small but it is growing and will grow with every day's sharpening of the class struggle, with the growing strength of the world proletarian revolution.

We are firmly convinced that the few dozen foreign comrades we have welcomed here constitute the kernel, the embryo, of a mighty army of proletarian writers to be created by the world proletarian revolution in foreign countries. . . .

Comrade Stalin has called our writers "engineers of the human soul." What does this mean? What obligations does such an appellation put upon you?

It means, in the first place, that you must know life to be able to depict it truthfully in artistic creations, to depict it neither "scholastically" nor lifelessly, nor simply as "objective reality," but rather as reality in its revolutionary development. The truthfulness and historical exactitude of the artistic image must be linked with the task of ideological transformation, of the education of the working people in the spirit of socialism. This method in fiction and literary criticism is what we call the method of socialist realism.

Our Soviet literature is not afraid of being called tendentious, for in the epoch of class struggle there is not and cannot be any classless, non-tendentious and "apolitical" literature.

And it seems to me that any and every Soviet writer may say to any dull-witted bourgeois, to any philistine or to any bourgeois writers who speak of the tendentiousness of our literature: "Yes, our Soviet literature is tendentious and we are proud of it, for our tendentiousness is to free the working people—and the whole of mankind—from the yoke of capitalist slavery."

To be an engineer of the human soul is to stand four-square on real life. And this in turn means a break with old-style romanticism, with the romanticism which depicted a non-existent life and non-existent heroes, drawing the reader away from the contradictions and shackles of life into an unrealisable and utopian world. Romanticism is not alien to our literature, a literature standing firmly on a materialist basis, but ours is a romanticism of a new type, revolutionary romanticism.

We say that socialist realism is the fundamental method of Soviet fiction and literary criticism, and this implies that revolutionary romanticism will appear as an integral part of any literary creation, since the whole life of our Party, of the working class and its struggle, is a fusion of the hardest, most matter-of-fact practical work, with the greatest heroism and the vastest perspectives. The strength of our Party has always lain in the fact that it has united and unites efficiency and practicality with broad vision, with an incessant forward striving and the struggle to build a communist society.

Soviet literature must be able to portray our heroes and to see our tomorrow. This will not be utopian since our tomorrow is being prepared by planned and conscious work today. . . .

REPORT ON THE JOURNALS *ZVEZDA* AND *LENINGRAD*, 1947

MISTAKES OF TWO LENINGRAD JOURNALS

It is clear from the Central Committee's decision that *Zvezda*'s worst mistake has been that of allowing the writings of Zoshchenko and Akhmatova to appear in its pages. It is, I think, hardly necessary for me to instance Zoshchenko's "work" *The Adventures of a Monkey*. You have certainly all read it and know it better than I do. The point of this "work" of Zoshchenko's is that in it he portrays Soviet people as lazy, unattractive, stupid and crude. He is in no way concerned with their labour, their efforts, their heroism, their high social and moral qualities. He never so much as mentions these. He chooses, like the cheap philistine he is, to scratch about in life's basenesses and pettinesses. This is no accident. It is intrinsic in all cheap philistine writers, of whom Zoshchenko is one. Gorki often used to speak of this; you will remember how, at the 1934 Congress of Soviet Writers, he stigmatised the so-called *literati* who can see no further than the soot on the kitchen range and in the boiler room.

The Adventures of a Monkey is not a thing apart from the general run of Zoshchenko's stories. It is merely as the most vivid expression of all the negative qualities in his "literary work" that it has attracted the critics' attention. Since he returned to Leningrad after the evacuation, he has, we know, written several things demonstrating his inability to find anything positive whatever in the life of Soviet people or any positive character among them. He is in the habit of jeering at Soviet life, ways and people, as he does in *The Adventures of a Monkey,* and of concealing his jeers behind a mask of empty-headed entertainment and pointless humour.

If you take the trouble to read his *Adventures of a Monkey* more closely you will find that he makes the monkey act as a supreme judge of our social customs, a dictator of morality to Soviet people. The monkey is depicted as an intelligent creature capable of assessing human behaviour. The writer deliberately caricatures the life of Soviet people as unattractive and cheap, so as to have the monkey pass the judgment, filthy, poisonous and anti-Soviet as it is, that living in the zoo is better than being at liberty, that you can draw your breath more freely in a cage than among Soviet people.

Is it possible to fall morally and politically lower than this? How can the people of Leningrad tolerate such rubbish and vulgarity in the pages of their journals?

The Leningraders in charge of *Zvezda* must indeed be lacking in vigilance if a "work" of this sort is offered to the journal's Soviet readers, if it is found possible to publish works steeped in the venom of bestial enmity towards the Soviet order. Only the scum of the literary world could write such "works," and only the blind, the apolitical could allow them to appear. . . .

Zoshchenko's thoroughly rotten and corrupt social, political and literary attitude does not result from any recent transformation. There is nothing accidental about his latest "works." They are simply the continuation of his literary "legacy" dating from the twenties.

Who was he in the past? He was one of the organisers of the literary group known as the Serapion Brothers. And when the Serapion Brothers group was formed, what was he like socially and politically? Let me turn to *Literaturniye Zapiski* (3, 1922) where the founders of this group expounded their creed. This journal contains, among other things, Zoshchenko's *credo,* in an article entitled "About Myself and a Few Other Things." Quite unashamed, he publicly exposes himself and states his political and literary "views" with the utmost frankness. Listen to what he says:

. . . It is very difficult to be a writer, on the whole. Take this business of ideology. . . . Writers are expected to have an ideology nowadays. . . . What a bore! How can I have any "definite ideology," tell me, when no Party really attracts me? From the Party members' point of view I am not a man of principle. What of it? For my part,

I may say: I am not a Communist, nor a Socialist-Revolutionary, nor a Monarchist, but merely a Russian, and a politically amoral one, at that. . . . Honest to God, I don't know to this day what Party, well, Guchkov . . . say, belongs to. Heaven knows what party he's in; I know he isn't a Bolshevik, but whether he's a Socialist-Revolutionary or a Cadet I neither know nor care.

And so on and so forth. What do you make of that sort of "ideology"? Twenty-five years have passed since Zoshchenko published this "confession" of his. Has he changed since? Not so that you would notice it. Not only has he neither learned anything nor changed in any way in the last two and a half decades, but with cynical frankness he continues, on the contrary, to remain the apostle of empty-headedness and cheapness, a literary slum-rat, unprincipled and conscienceless. That is to say, now as then he cares nothing for Soviet ways, now as then he has no place in Soviet literature and opposes it.

If he has nevertheless become something approaching a literary star in Leningrad, if his praises are sung on Leningrad's Parnassus, we can but marvel at the lack of principle, of strictness, of discrimination, in the people who paved the way for him and applauded him. . . .

LENINISM AND LITERATURE

What is the cause of these errors and failings?

It is that the editors of the said journals, our Soviet men of letters, and the leaders of our ideological front in Leningrad, have forgotten some of the principal tenets of Leninism as regards literature. Many writers, and many of those working as responsible editors, or holding important posts in the Writers' Union, consider politics to be the business of the Government or of the Central Committee. When it comes to men of letters, engaging in politics is no business of theirs. If a man has done a good, artistic, fine piece of writing, his work should be published even though it contains vicious elements liable to confuse and poison the minds of our young people.

We demand that our comrades, both practising writers and those in positions of literary leadership, should be guided by that without which the Soviet order cannot live, that is to say, by politics, so that our young people may be brought up not in the spirit of do-nothing and don't-care, but in an optimistic revolutionary spirit.

We know that Leninism embodies all the finest traditions of the Russian nineteenth-century revolutionary democrats and that our Soviet culture derives from and is nourished by the critically assimilated cultural heritage of the past.

Through the lips of Lenin and Stalin our Party has repeatedly recognised the tremendous significance in the field of literature of the great Russian revolutionary democratic writers and critics Belinsky, Dobrolyubov, Chernyshevsky, Saltykov-Shchedrin and Plekhanov. From Belinsky onward, all the best representatives of the revolutionary democratic Russian intellectuals have denounced "pure art" and "art for art's sake," and have been the spokesmen of art for the people, demanding that art should have a worthy educational and social significance.

Art cannot cut itself off from the fate of the people. Remember Belinsky's famous *Letter to Gogol*, in which the great critic, with all his native passion, castigated Gogol for his attempt to betray the cause of the people and go over to the side of the Tsar. Lenin called this letter one of the finest works of the uncensored democratic press, one that has preserved its tremendous literary significance to this day.

Remember Dobrolyubov's articles, in which the social significance of literature is so powerfully shown. The whole of our Russian revolutionary democratic journalism is imbued with a deadly hatred of the Tsarist order and with the noble aspiration to fight for the people's fundamental interests, their enlightenment, their culture, their liberation from the fetters of the Tsarist regime. A militant art fighting for the people's finest ideals, that is how the great representatives of Russian literature envisaged art and literature.

Chernyshevsky, who comes nearest of all the utopian socialists to scientific socialism and whose works were, as Lenin pointed out, "indicative of the spirit of the class struggle," taught us that the task of art was, besides affording a knowledge of life, to teach people how to assess correctly varying social phenomena. Dobrolyubov, his companion-in-arms and closest friend, remarked that "it is not life that follows literary standards, but literature that adapts itself to the trends of life," and strongly supported the principles of realism, and the national element, in literature, on the grounds that the basis of art is life, that life is the source of creative achievement and that art plays an active part in social life and in shaping social consciousness. Literature, according to Dobrolyubov, should serve society, should give the people answers to the most urgent problems of the day, should keep abreast of the ideas of its epoch. . . .

Lenin was the first to state clearly what attitude towards art and literature advanced social thought should take. Let me remind you of the well-known article, *Party Organisation and Party Literature,* which he wrote at the end of 1905, and in which he demonstrated with characteristic forcefulness that literature cannot but have a partisan adherence and that it must form an im-portant part of the general proletarian cause. All the principles on which the development of our Soviet literature is based are to be found in this article.

"Literature must become partisan literature," wrote Lenin. "To offset bourgeois customs, to offset the commercial bourgeois press, to offset bourgeois literary careerism and self-seeking, to offset 'gentlemanly anarchism' and profit-seeking, the socialist proletariat must put forward the principle of *partisan* literature, must develop this principle and carry it out in the completest and most integral form.

"What is this principle of partisan literature? It is not merely that literature cannot, to the socialist proletariat, be a means of profit to individuals or groups; all in all, literature cannot be an individual matter divorced from the general proletarian cause. Down with the writers who think themselves supermen! Down with non-partisan writers! Literature must become *part and parcel* of the general proletarian cause. . . ."

And further, from the same article: "It is not possible to live in society and remain free of it. The freedom of the bourgeois writer, artist or actor is merely a masked dependence (hypocritically masked perhaps) on the money-bags, on bribes, on allowances. . . ."

There are people who find it strange that the Central Committee should have taken such stringent measures as regards literature. It is not what we are accustomed to. If mistakes have been allowed to occur in industrial production, or if the production programme for consumer goods has not been carried out, or if the supply of timber falls behind schedule, then it is considered natural for the people responsible to be publicly reprimanded. But if mistakes have been allowed to occur as regards the proper influencing of human souls, as regards the upbringing of the young, then such mistakes may be tolerated. And yet, is not this a bitterer pill to swallow than the non-fulfilment of a production programme or the failure to carry out a production task? The purpose of the Central Committee's resolution is to bring the ideological front into line with all the other sectors of our work.

On the ideological front, serious gaps and failings have recently become apparent. Suffice it to remind you of the backwardness of our cinematic art, and of the way our theatre repertoires have got cluttered up with poor dramatic works, not to mention what has been going on in *Zvezda* and *Leningrad*. The Central Committee has been compelled to interfere and firmly to set matters right. It has no right to deal gently with those who forget their duties with regard to the people, to the upbringing of our young people. If we wish to draw our members' attention to questions relating to ideological work and to set matters right in this field, to establish a clear line in this work, then we must criticise the mistakes and failings in ideological work severely, as befits Soviet people, as befits Bolsheviks. Only then shall we be able to set matters right. . . .

The lack of ideological principles shown by leading workers on *Zvezda* and *Leningrad* has led to a second serious mistake. Certain of our leading workers have, in their relations with various authors, set personal interests, the interests of friendship, above those of the political education of the Soviet people or these authors' political tendencies. It is said that many ideologically harmful and from a literary point of view weak productions are allowed to be published because the editor does not like to hurt the author's feelings. In the eyes of such workers it is better to sacrifice the interests of the people and of the state than to hurt some author's feelings. This is an entirely wrong and politically dangerous principle. It is like swapping a million roubles for a kopeck.

The Central Committee of the Party points out in its resolution the grave danger in substituting for relations based on principle those based on personal friendship. The relations of personal friendship regardless of principle prevailing among certain of our men of letters have played a profoundly negative part, led to a falling off in the ideological level of many literary works and made it easier for this field to be entered by persons foreign to the spirit of Soviet literature. The absence of any criticism on the part of the leaders of the Leningrad ideological front or of the editors of the Leningrad journals has done a great deal of harm; the substitution of relations of friendship for those based on principle has been made at the expense of the people's interests. . . .

An uncritical attitude, and the substitution of relations of personal friendship for those based on principle, are very prevalent on the Board of the Union of Soviet Writers. The Board, and its chairman Comrade Tikhonov in particular, are to blame for the bad state of affairs revealed in *Zvezda* and *Leningrad*, in that they not only made no attempt to prevent the harmful influence of Zoshchenko, Akhmatova and other un-Soviet writers penetrating into Soviet literature, but even readily permitted styles and tendencies alien to the spirit of Soviet literature to find a place in our journals.

Another factor contributing to the failings of the Leningrad journals was the state of irresponsibility that developed among the editors of these journals, the situation being such that no one knew who had the overall responsibility for the journal or for its various departments, so that any sort of order, even the most rudimentary, was impossible. The Central Committee has, therefore, in its resolution, appointed to *Zvezda* an editor-in-chief, who is to be held responsible for the journal's policy and for the ideological level and literary quality of its contents. . . .

By now it should be clear to you what a serious oversight the Leningrad City Committee of the Party, and particularly its propaganda department and propaganda secretary Comrade Shirokov (who was put in charge of ideological work and bears the main responsibility for the failure of these journals), have been guilty of.

The Leningrad Committee of the Party committed a grave political error when it passed its resolution at the end of June on *Zvezda*'s new editorial board, in which Zoshchenko was included. Political blindness is the only possible explanation of the fact that Comrades Kapustin (Secretary of the City Committee of the Party) and Shirokov (the City Committee's propaganda secretary) should have agreed to such an erroneous decision. All these mistakes must, I repeat, be set right as quickly and firmly as possible, to enable Leningrad to resume its participation in the ideological life of our Party. . . .

How could the Leningrad City Committee of the Party have permitted such a situation to arise on the ideological front? It had evidently become so engrossed in day-to-day practical work on the rehabilitation of the city and the development of its industry that it forgot the importance of ideological and educational work.

This forgetfulness has cost the Leningrad organisation dear. Ideological work must not be forgotten. Our people's spiritual wealth is no less important than their material wealth. We cannot live blindly, taking no thought for the mor-row, either in the field of material production or in the ideological field. To such an extent have our Soviet people developed that they are not going to swallow whatsoever spiritual food may be dumped on them. Such workers in art and culture as do not change and cannot satisfy the people's growing needs may forfeit the people's confidence before long.

Our Soviet literature lives and must live in the interests of our country and of our people alone. Literature is a concern near and dear to the people. So the people consider our every success, every important work of literature, as a victory of their own. Every successful work may therefore be compared with a battle won, or with a great victory on the economic front. And conversely, every failure of Soviet literature hurts and wounds the people, the Party and the state profoundly. This is what the Central Committee was thinking of in passing its resolution, for the Central Committee watches over the interests of the people and of their literature, and is very greatly concerned about the present state of affairs among Leningrad writers. . . .

However fine may be the external appearance of the work of the fashionable modern bourgeois writers in America and Western Europe, and of their film directors and theatrical producers, they can neither save nor better their bourgeois culture, for its moral basis is rotten and decaying. It has been placed at the service of capitalist private ownership, of the selfish and egocentric interests of the top layer of bourgeois society. A swarm of bourgeois writers, film directors and theatrical producers are trying to draw the attention of the progressive strata of society away from the acute problems of social and political struggle and to divert it into a groove of cheap meaningless art and literature, treating of gangsters and show-girls and glorifying the adulterer and the adventures of crooks and gamblers.

Is it fitting for us Soviet patriots, the representatives of advanced Soviet culture, to play the part of admirers or disciples of bourgeois culture? Our literature, reflecting an order on a higher level than any bourgeois-democratic order and a culture manifoldly superior to bourgeois culture, has, it goes without saying, the right to teach the new universal morals to others.

Where is another such people or country as ours to be found? Where are such splendid human qualities to be found as our Soviet people displayed in the Great Patriotic War and are displaying every day in the labour of converting our economy to peaceful development and material and cultural rehabilitation? Our people are climbing higher and higher every day. No longer are we the Russians we were before 1917; no longer is our Russia the same, no longer is our character the same. We have changed and grown along with the great changes that have transfigured our country from its very foundations.

Showing these great new qualities of the Soviet people, not only showing our people as they are today, but glancing into their future and helping to light up the way ahead, is the task of every conscientious Soviet writer. A writer cannot tag along in the wake of events; it is for him to march in the foremost ranks of the people and point out to them the path of their development. He must educate the people and arm them ideologically, guiding himself by the method of socialist realism, studying our life attentively and conscientiously and trying to gain a deeper understanding of the processes of our development. . . .

CONCLUDING SPEECH AT A CONFERENCE OF SOVIET MUSIC WORKERS, 1948

TWO TRENDS IN MUSIC

. . . All the speakers have shown that the leading part in the creative activities of the Union of Composers is being played at present by a definite group. The names of the following comrades have been mentioned: Shostakovich, Prokofiev, Myaskovsky, Khachaturyan, Popov, Kabalevsky and Shebalin. Is there any other name you would like to add?

VOICE: Shaporin.

ZHDANOV: When mention is made of any leading group holding the reins, those are the names most frequently cited. Let us consider these comrades, who are also the leading figures of the formalist trend in music, a trend which is fundamentally wrong.

The comrades in question have contributed to the discussion and have stated that they, too, are dissatisfied with the lack of criticism in the Union of Composers, with the fact that they are being overpraised, that they feel a certain loss of contact with the main body of composers and with concert audiences. It was hardly necessary, however, to wait for the production of a not very successful—or not at all successful —opera, before stating such truths. These admissions could have been made much earlier, but the crux of the matter is that the regime of the formalist sect in the musical organisations has not been entirely unpleasant, to put it mildly, for the leading group of our composers. It has required a discussion in the Central Committee of the Party for the comrades to discover the fact that this regime has its negative side. However that may be, before the conference not one of them thought of changing the state of affairs in the Union of Composers.

It has been said here that the time has come for radical changes. One cannot but agree. Inasmuch as the dominating positions in Soviet music are held by the comrades I have named, and inasmuch as any attempts to criticise them would have brought about an explosion and an immediate rallying against such criticism, in Comrade Zakharov's words, the conclusion must be drawn that the "cosy" atmosphere of stagnation and personal relations which they now wish to condemn as undesirable was in fact created by them.

Some leading comrades of the Union of Composers have asserted here that there is no oligarchy in the Union. But then the question arises: Why do they cling to the leading positions in the Union? Do they like power for its own sake? Have they developed a sort of administrative itch, so that they merely want to rule a little, like Vladimir Galitsky in *Prince Igor?* Or has this domination been established in the interests of a definite trend? I think that the first conjecture can be discarded and that the last is nearer the truth. We have no reason to say that the management of the Union has no connections with a trend. We cannot bring such a charge against Shostakovich, for instance.

It follows, then, that domination was maintained in the interests of a trend.

There is in fact, then, a sharp though hidden struggle between two trends taking place in Soviet music. One trend represents the healthy, progressive principles in Soviet music, based on the acceptance of the immense role to be played by the classical heritage, and in particular, by the Russian school, in the creation of a music which is realist and of truthful content and is closely and organically linked with the people and their folk music and folk song—all this combined with a high degree of professional mastery. The other trend represents a formalism alien to Soviet art, a rejection of the classical heritage under the banner of innovation, a rejection of the idea of the popular origin of music, and of service to the people, in order to gratify the individualistic emotions of a small group of select aesthetes.

The formalist trend brings about the substitution of a music which is false, vulgar and often purely pathological, for natural, beautiful, human music. Furthermore, it is characteristic of this trend to avoid a frontal attack and to screen its revisionist activities by formally agreeing with the basic principles of socialist realism. This sort of underhand method is, of course, nothing new. History can show many instances of revisionism behind the label of sham agreement with a given teaching. This makes it all the more necessary to reveal the real essence of the formalist trend and the damage it has done to the development of Soviet music.

As an example, there is the attitude towards the classical heritage. There is no indication whatever that the supporters of the formalist school are carrying on and developing the traditions of classical music, however much they may protest to the contrary. Any listener will tell you that the works of Soviet composers of the formalist type differ fundamentally from classical music. Classical music is marked by its truthfulness and realism, its ability to blend brilliant artistic form with profound content, and to combine the highest technical achievement with simplicity and intelligibility. Formalism and crude naturalism are alien to classical music in general and to Russian classical music in particular. The high level of the idea content in classical music springs from the recognition of the fact that classical music has its sources in the musical creative powers of the people, in a deep respect and love for the people, their music and song.

What a step backward it is along the highroad of musical development when our formalists, undermining the foundations of true music, compose music which is ugly and false, permeated with idealist sentiment, alien to the broad masses of the people, and created not for the millions of Soviet people, but for chosen individuals and small groups, for an elite. How unlike Glinka, Tchaikovsky, Rimsky-Korsakov, Dargomyzhsky, Mussorgsky, who considered the basis for development of their creative power to be the ability to express in their works the spirit and character of the people. By ignoring the wants of the people and its spirit and creative genius, the formalist trend in music has clearly demonstrated its anti-popular character.

If a certain section of Soviet composers favour the theory that they will be appreciated in fifty or a hundred years' time, and that their descendants, if not their contemporaries, will understand them, then the situation is really terrifying. To become accustomed to such an attitude is extremely dangerous. Such a theory indicates an estrangement from the people. If I, a writer, an artist, a critic, or a Party worker, do not count on being understood by my contemporaries, for whom then do I live and work? Would this not lead to spiritual sterility and a dead end? We hear that the theory is offered as consolation to our composers by certain toadying music critics. How can composers remain indifferent to counsel of that sort and not at least haul its advocates before a court of honour? . . .

NATIONAL MUSIC

Let me now deal with the relationship between national and foreign music. Some comrades here have quite correctly stated that there is a passion for, and even a certain orientation towards, contemporary Western bourgeois music, the music of decadence; and that this represents one of the basic features of the formalist trend in Soviet music.

Only a people that has a highly developed musical culture of its own can appreciate the musical riches of other nations. It is impossible to be an internationalist in music or in anything else unless one loves and respects one's own people. All the experience of the U.S.S.R. testifies to that. Our internationalism in music and respect for the creative genius of other nations is therefore based on the enrichment and development of our national musical culture which we can then share with other nations, and is not based on an impoverishment of national art, blind imitation of foreign styles, and the eradication of all national characteristics in music. All this should be borne in mind when dealing with the relationship between Soviet and foreign music.

When we speak of the formalist trend having broken with the principles of the classical heritage we must also mention the minimising of the role of programme music. This has already been mentioned here, but the principal point of the problem has not been properly clarified.

It is quite obvious that programme music has become so rare that it is almost non-existent. Matters have reached a point where the content of a composition is elucidated only after its publication. A whole new profession has come into being among the critics—that of the interpreters of new compositions, who try to decipher *post factum* and on the basis of personal intuition the content of newly published compositions, the obscure meaning of which is said to be not always clear to the composers themselves. The neglect of programme music is also a departure from progressive traditions. It is well known that Russian classical music was as a rule programme music. . . .

TASKS OF SOVIET MUSIC

What conclusions can be drawn? The significance of the classical heritage must be fully restored. The danger of destruction threatening music from the formalist trend must be stressed and this trend must be condemned as an assault upon the edifice of the art created by the great masters of musical culture. Our composers must reorientate themselves and turn towards their people. All of them must realise that our Party, expressing the interests of our state and our people, will support only a healthy and progressive trend in music, the trend of Soviet socialist realism.

Comrades, if you value the lofty calling of Soviet composer, you must prove yourselves capable of serving your people better than you have done up to the present. You are facing a serious test. The formalist trend in music was condemned by the Party twelve years ago. Since then the Government has awarded Stalin prizes to many of you, among them those guilty of formalism. The rewards you received were in the nature of a substantial advance payment. We did not consider that your compositions were free of defects, but we were patient, expecting our composers to find within themselves the strength to choose the right road. But it is now clear to everybody that the intervention of the Party was necessary. The Central Committee tells you bluntly that our music will never win glory along the road you have chosen.

Soviet composers have two highly responsible tasks. The chief one is to develop and perfect Soviet music. The other is to protect Soviet music against penetration by elements of bourgeois decay. We must not forget that the

U.S.S.R. is now the true custodian of the musical culture of mankind just as she is in all other fields, too, a bulwark of human civilisation and culture against bourgeois corruption and decay. . . .

SPEECH BY COMRADE N. S. KHRUSHCHEV ON MARCH 8, 1963, AT MEETING OF PARTY AND GOVERNMENT LEADERS WITH WORKERS IN LITERATURE AND THE ARTS[1]

We adhere to class positions in art and are resolutely opposed to the peaceful coexistence of socialist and bourgeois ideologies. Art belongs to the sphere of ideology. Those who think that in Soviet art there can be peaceful cohabitation of both socialist realism and formalist, abstractionist tendencies will inevitably slip into the position of peaceful coexistence in the sphere of ideology, a position that is alien to us. We have recently encountered such ideas. Unfortunately, this bait has been taken by some Communist writers and artists, and even some officials of creative organisations. At the same time it should be noted that some non-Party people, such as Comrade Sobolev, for instance, staunchly defend the Party line in literature and art.

At the last meeting Comrade I. Ehrenburg said that the idea of coexistence had been stated in a letter as a joke. Let us say that this was the case. But if so, it was a vicious joke. One should not joke thus in the field of ideology. Let us consider what would happen in Soviet art if the partisans of the peaceful coexistence of various ideological tendencies in literature and art were to win out. As the first step, a blow would be struck against our revolutionary conquests in the field of socialist art. According to the logic of struggle, things

[1] *Pravda* and *Izvestia*, March 10, 1963, pp. 1–4.

would certainly not end there. It is not impossible that if these people gained strength, they would undertake attempts to act against the conquests of the revolution.

I have already had occasion to say that peaceful coexistence in the field of ideology is treason against Marxism-Leninism and betrayal of the cause of the workers and peasants. Soviet society is now at a stage in which there has been achieved full and monolithic unity of all the socialist nations of the country and all strata of the people—workers, collective farmers and the intelligentsia—who are successfully building Communism under the guidance of the Leninist Party.

Our people and party will not tolerate any encroachments on this monolithic unity. One of the evidences of this phenomenon is the attempt to force us to accept peaceful coexistence of ideologies. This is why we are directing our fire both against these pernicious ideas and against those who hold them. It is my hope that we are all together on this point. (*Prolonged applause.*)

We call upon those who are still straying to consider their errors, to understand the nature and sources of these errors and to overcome them, and together with the Party in united ranks, under the red banner of Marxism-Leninism, to participate actively in the building of Communism and to multiply the successes of socialist culture, literature and art.

Abstractionism, formalism, which some of its advocates are suggesting should be given the right to exist in socialist art, is one of the forms of bourgeois ideology. One must regret that some people, including creative workers made wise by life experience, do not understand this.

There is a passage in Comrade Ehrenburg's memoirs that goes as follows, and I quote: "There was a host of literary schools: communist futurists, imagists, the Proletcult, expressionists, fuists, nonobjectivists, presentists, accidentists and even nothingists. To be sure, some of the theorists talked a great deal of nonsense. . . . But I would defend that remote period."

It is clear that the author of these memoirs has great sympathy for the representatives of so-called "left" art and has undertaken the task of defending this art. One might ask against whom he is defending it. Apparently he is defending it against our Marxist-Leninist criticism. Why is he doing this? Obviously, to defend the possibility of the existence of these or similar phenomena in our contemporary art. This would mean the recognition of the coexistence of socialist realism and formalism. Comrade Ehrenburg is making a gross ideological error, and we are under obligation to help him to see this.

At our last meeting Comrade Yevtushenko spoke in defense of abstractionism. He attempted to justify his position by saying that there are good people among both the realists and the formalists, and he cited the example of two Cuban artists who had sharply different views on art but who died in the same dugout fighting for the revolution. This might happen in life as an isolated instance. . . .

Comrade Yevtushenko's stand on abstractionism is essentially coincident with the views defended by Comrade Ehrenburg. The poet is still a young man; there is apparently a great deal he does not yet understand about our Party's policy, and he has wavering, weak views on questions of art. His speech at the session of the Ideological Commission inspired us with confidence that he will be able to overcome his waverings. I would like to advise Comrade Yevtushenko and other young writers to hold dear the trust of the masses and not to seek cheap sensation, not to bow to the ideas and tastes of the philistines. (*Prolonged applause.*) Comrade Yevtushenko, do not be afraid to admit your mistakes. Do not be afraid of what hostile people will say about you. You must be clearly aware that if we criticize you for departure from positions of principle, our enemies begin to praise you. If the enemies of our cause begin to praise you to the skies for works that are to their liking, the people will level just criticisms at you. So choose what suits you best. (*Applause.*)

The Communist Party is fighting and will continue to fight against abstractionism and against any other formalist distortions in art. We cannot be neutral toward formalism. When I was in America some artists—I don't know if they are well-known ones or not—gave me some pictures. Yesterday I showed you these daubs. Apparently these people are not my enemies, since if they were they would not have offered me the fruits of their labor. But even so, I cannot admit that these gifts to me are the highest masterpieces or any sort of masterpieces of fine art.

Tell me, what is depicted here? They say this shows the view of a city from a bridge. No matter how you look at it, there's nothing there but a band of various colors. And this daub is called a picture!

Here is another of these "masterpieces." You can see four eyes, or maybe more. They say that this is a picture of horror, fear. How ugly the abstractionists have made art! These are examples of American painting. . . .

On New Year's Eve I was returning to Moscow from outside the city. On December 31 I spent the whole day from morning to night in the woods. It was a poetic day, a beautiful day of the Russian winter, and only the Russian winter, for not everywhere do they have winters like ours in Russia. This of course is not a national phenomenon but a phenomenon of climate and nature, and so I hope you understand me correctly. (*Laughter in the hall. Applause.*)

The woods were very beautiful that day. They were beautiful because the trees were covered with downy hoarfrost. I recall reading in my youth a story in *Ogonyok* magazine. I don't remember who wrote it, but it contained the words "soft, silvery shadows." The author was describing a garden in its winter dress. The story was well written, I believe, or perhaps at that time I didn't make very high demands on literature. But I liked the story, and I still have a clear memory of it. I liked especially the description of the trees in their winter dress.

The winter forest I saw on New Year's Eve was so beautiful that it produced a strong impression on me. Perhaps the shadows weren't silvery; I don't have the words to describe the strong impression that that forest made on me. I looked at the sunrise and the forest covered with hoarfrost. Only people who have been in the forest and seen such living pictures for themselves can understand this beauty. The advantage that the artist enjoys is that he can re-create exciting pictures himself, although not all of them have this gift.

I said to the people who were with me: "Look at those fir trees and the way they are dressed, and look at the snowflakes playing and flashing in the sun's rays. How extraordinarily beautiful it all is!" But the modernists and the abstractionists want to paint these firs with their roots in the air, and they say that this is the new and progressive in art.

It is impossible that normal people would ever accept this art, that people would be deprived of the opportunity to look at pictures of nature re-created in the works by artists that decorate the halls of our clubs, our Houses of Culture, our homes.

Perhaps some will say that Khrushchev is calling for photographic portrayal, for naturalism in art. No, comrades! We call for vivid works of art that truthfully portray the real world in all its diversity of colors. Only such art will give people joy and pleasure. Man will never lose the capacity for artistic talent and will not allow dirty daubs that any donkey could paint with his tail to be foisted on him in the guise of works of art. (*Applause.*) ...

Music holds a great and important place in the spiritual life of our people, in ideological work. In this connection it appears necessary to express some considerations about the trend in composition. We do not want to be judges or to stand on the conductor's platform and lead the composers.

In music, as in other arts, there are many different genres, styles and forms. No one places any ban on a single one of these styles and genres. But we wish nevertheless to set forth our attitude to music, to its tasks and to the trend in composition.

To put it briefly, we stand for melodious, meaningful music that stirs people's souls and inspires strong emotions, and we oppose any cacophony.

Who does not know the song about Budenny's army! The composing team of the Pokrass brothers has written many good songs. I very much like their song about Moscow, written, I confess, at our order when I was Secretary of the Moscow Party Committee. I remember, we gathered in the Moscow committee and one of them played this song for the first time for us. He was not a very good singer, but the Pokrass brothers had written good music.

And how stirring are the old revolutionary songs such as "Whirlwinds of Danger" and the "Varsovienne"! Who does not know the "International"? How many years have we sung this song! It has become the international anthem of the working class. What revolutionary thoughts and feelings it inspires, how it lifts man and mobilizes him against the enemies of the working people!

When I listen to Glinka's music tears of joy always come to my eyes.

Perhaps this is unfashionable, *ancien régime;* I am no longer a young person, but I like it when David Oistrakh plays the violin; I also like very much to hear the violin group of the Bolshoi Theater—I don't know what this group is called professionally. I have heard it many times and have always experienced great pleasure.

Of course I do not pretend that my appreciation of music should be some kind of norm for everybody. But after all, we cannot encourage the claim of cacophony to be genuine music while the music loved by the people is slighted by some as outmoded.

Each people has its own traditions in music and loves its own national folk melodies and songs. I was born in a Russian village and was brought up on Russian and Ukrainian folk music, its melodies and folk songs. It gives me great pleaure to hear the songs of Solovyev-Sedoi, the song by the composer Kolmanovsky to the poet Yevtushenko's words, "Do the Russians Want War?" I also like Ukrainian songs very much; I love the song "Rushnichok" by the composer P. Maiboroda to the words of Andrei Malyshko. One listens to it and wants to hear it over again. We have many good composers and they have written many good songs, but, as you realize, I cannot enumerate them all in my talk.

There are also serious shortcomings in composition. The apparent preoccupation with jazz music and jazz bands cannot be considered normal. Do not think that we oppose all music for jazz bands, there are various kinds of jazz bands and various kinds of music for them. Dunayevsky was able to write good music for jazz bands as well as for others. I like some songs as played by the jazz band conducted by Leonid Utyosov. But there is some music that turns your stomach and gives you a pain.

After the plenary session of the Russian Republic Composers' Union, Comrade Shostakovich invited us to a concert at the Kremlin Theater. Although we were very busy, we went to hear the music; we were told the concert would be interesting. And indeed we found that it included interesting numbers. But then for some reason one jazz band performed, then another and a third, and finally all three together. Even good food makes you sick if you eat too much, and it was impossible to stand such a helping of jazz. We would have hid, but there was nowhere to hide.

Music that does not have melody evokes nothing but irritation. They say this comes from failure to understand. And indeed there is jazz music of a kind that defies understanding and is repulsive to hear.

Some so-called modern dances, brought into our country from the West, call for objections. I have had occasion to travel widely about the country. I have seen Russian, Ukrainian, Kazakh, Uzbek, Armenian, Georgian and other dances. They are beautiful dances and it is pleasant to watch them. But what is called modern fashionable dancing is simply some kind of indecency, frenzy, devil knows what! They say that one can see such indecency only among the Shaker sects. I cannot confirm this, for I have myself never attended Shaker re-

vivals. (*Laughter in the hall.*)

It seems that among workers in the arts one finds young people who strive to prove that melody in music has lost its right to existence and in its place is coming "new" music—"dodecaphony," a music of noise. It is hard for a normal person to understand what the word "dodecaphony" means, but in all likelihood it is the same thing as is meant by cacophony. Well, we are completely sweeping out this here cacophony music. Our people cannot take this garbage into their ideological arsenal.

Cries: Right! (*Applause.*)

We are for music that inspires, that summons to deeds of valor and to work. When the soldier goes into battle he takes with him what he needs, and he never leaves the band behind. On the march the band inspires him. Music for such bands can be written and is being written by composers who adhere to socialist realism, who do not alienate themselves from life, from the people's struggle, and whom the people support.

Our policy in art, the policy of firm rejection of abstract art, formalism and any other bourgeois distortions, is a Leninist policy that we unswervingly have applied, are applying and will apply. (*Applause.*) . . .

The press and radio, literature, painting, music, the cinema and the theater are a sharp ideological weapon of our party. And the Party is concerned that its weapon be always in battle readiness and that it hit the enemy accurately. The Party will allow no one to blunt its edge, to weaken its effect.

Soviet literature and art are developing under the direct guidance of the Communist Party and its Central Committee. The Party has reared remarkable, talented cadres of writers, artists, composers and cinema and theater workers who have inseparably linked their lives and their creative work with the Leninist Party and the people.

60

THE ADVENTURES OF AN APE

By Mikhail Zoshchenko

We reproduce below the story attacked so vehemently by Zhdanov in our previous selection; let the reader judge for himself. The author (1895–1958) had been perhaps the most widely read Soviet writer of the 1920's. His satires on everyday Soviet life became distinctly unfashionable in the more rigid days which followed. It is likely that Zoshchenko was condemned because the Party required a scapegoat to dramatize its new line. Zoshchenko may have been chosen because of his long career of nonconformity. He was expelled from the Union of Soviet writers and his work no longer appeared in print. After 1950 he was permitted to publish again, but he had learned to tone down his satire and to choose his themes.

For more Zoshchenko stories, see his *Nervous People and Other Satires*. There is an article devoted to his disgrace in Ernest Simmons (ed.), *Through the Glass of Soviet Literature* (paperback). For an assessment of Zoshchenko as a writer, see V. Zavalishin, *Early Soviet Writers*, and Gleb Struve, *Soviet Russian Literature*, as well as William Harkins, *Dictionary of Russian Literature* (paperback). The Party's literary policy from the end of World War II to the death of Stalin is analyzed in Avrahm Yarmolinsky, *Literature under Communism*, and Vera Alexandrova, *A History of Soviet Literature* (paperback). See the following recent contributions on Zoshchenko: a chapter in Marc Slonim, *Soviet Russian Literature: Writers and Problems*; Vera Von Wiren, "Zoshchenko in Retrospect," *Russian Review*, Vol. XXI; and her "Zoshchenko's Psychological Interests," *Slavic and East European Journal*, Spring, 1967. For a Soviet view see Mikhail Slonimsky, "Recollections of Mikhail Zoshchenko," *Soviet Studies in Literature*, Spring, 1967.

In a certain city in the south, there was a zoo. It was a small zoo, in which there were one tiger, two crocodiles, three snakes, a zebra, an ostrich, and one ape, or in other words, a monkey. And, naturally, various minor items—birds, fish, frogs, and similar insignificant nonsense from the animal world.

At the beginning of the war, when the Fascists bombed the city, one bomb fell directly on the zoo. And it exploded there with a great shattering roar. To the surprise of all the beasts.

The three snakes were killed, all at the same time, not in itself a very sad

From Mikhail Zoshchenko, *Scenes from the Bathhouse* (Ann Arbor: University of Michigan Press, 1962), pp. 177–83. Copyright © by the University of Michigan, 1961. Used by permission of the publisher.

709

fact perhaps. Unfortunately, the ostrich, too.

The other beasts did not suffer. As the saying goes, they only shook with fear.

Of all the beasts, the most frightened was the ape, the monkey. An explosion overturned his cage. The cage fell from its stand. One side was broken. And our ape fell out of the cage onto the path.

He fell out onto the path, but did not remain lying there immobile in the manner of people who are used to military activities. On the contrary. He immediately climbed up a tree. From there, he leaped on the wall. From the wall to the street. And, as though he were on fire, he ran.

He's running, and probably he's thinking: "Eh, if there are bombs falling around here, then I don't agree." And that means he's running like mad along the city streets.

He ran all the way through the city. He ran out on the highway. He runs along this highway till he leaves the city behind. Well, an ape. It's not a man. He doesn't understand the whys and wherefores. He doesn't see any sense in remaining in this city.

He ran and ran and tired himself out. He was all tired out. He climbed a tree. He ate a fly to recoup his strength. And then a couple of worms. And he fell asleep there on the branch where he was sitting.

At this time, a military vehicle came along the road. The driver saw the ape in the tree. He was surprised. Quietly he crept up to it. He flung his coat over it. And put it in his vehicle. He thought: "It's better I give him to some friend of mine rather than have him die of hunger, cold, and other hardships." So that means, on he went along with the ape.

He arrived in the city of Borisov. He went about his official business. But the monkey remained in the vehicle. He said to it: "Wait for me here, cutie. I'll be back soon."

But our monkey wouldn't wait. He climbed out of the vehicle through a broken window and went strolling along the streets.

And, so, he proceeds, the dear little thing, along the street, strolling, ambling along, tail up. The people, naturally, are surprised and want to catch him. But catching him isn't all that easy. He's lively and nimble, and runs quickly on all fours. So they didn't catch him, but only succeeded in tormenting the fugitive in vain.

Tormented, he wearied and, naturally, wanted to eat.

But in the city, where could he eat? There wasn't anything edible in the streets. With his tail, he could hardly get into a restaurant. Or a co-operative. All the more since he had no money. No discount. Ration coupons he does not have. It's awful.

Nevertheless, he got into a certain co-operative. Had a feeling that something was doing there. And they were distributing vegetables to the population: carrots, rutabagas, and cucumbers.

He scampered into this store. He sees: There's a long line. No, he did not take a place in this line. Nor did he start pushing people aside in order to shove his way through. He just leaped along the heads of the customers to where the goods were. He leaped on the counter. He didn't ask how much a kilo of carrots costs. And, as the saying goes, that's the kind he was. He ran out of the store, satisfied with his purchase. Well, an ape. Doesn't understand the whys and wherefores. Doesn't see the sense of remaining without rations.

Naturally there was commotion in the store, hubbub, confusion. The public began to yell. The salesgirl who was weighing rutabagas almost fainted from surprise. And, really, one could well be frightened, if instead of the usual, nor-mal-type customer, a hairy creature with a tail hops up. And what's more, doesn't even pay.

The public pursued the ape into the street. And he runs and on the way he chews on a carrot. He's eating. He doesn't understand the whys and where-fores.

The little boys are running at the head of the crowd. Behind them, the grown-ups. And, bringing up the rear, the policeman is running and blowing on his whistle.

And from somewhere, Lord knows where, a dog leaped out into the melee. And also sets out after our little mon-key. Not only is he yelping and yowling, but he's even trying to sink his teeth into the ape.

Our monkey picked up speed. He runs, and probably he's thinking to himself: "Och," he's thinking, "should never have left the zoo. Breathing was easier in the cage. First opportunity, I'm going to head right back there."

And, so, he runs as hard as he can, but the dog isn't giving up and still wants to grab him.

Then our ape hopped up onto some kind of fence. And when the dog leaped up to grab the monkey by the feet, as it were, the latter blipped him full force with a carrot on the nose. And he hit him so hard that the dog yelped and ran home, wounded nose and all. Probably he was thinking: "No, citizens, better I should lie quietly at home than go catch-ing monkeys and experiencing such ex-treme unpleasantness."

Briefly speaking, the dog fled and our ape leaped into the yard.

In the yard at this time a teen-age boy was chopping wood, a certain Alesha Popov.

There he is, chopping wood, and sud-denly he sees an ape. All his life he's dreamed of having an ape like that.

And suddenly—there you are!

Alesha slipped off his jacket and with this jacket he caught the monkey who had run up the ladder in the corner.

The boy brought him home. Fed him. Gave him tea to drink. And the ape was quite content. But not entirely. Because Alesha's grandma took an instant dis-like to him. She shouted at the monkey and even wanted to strike him across the paw. All this because, while they were drinking tea, grandma had put a piece of candy she had been chewing on a plate, and the ape had grabbed grandma's candy and tossed it into his own mouth. Well, an ape. It's not a man. A man, if he takes something, wouldn't do it right under grandma's nose. But this monkey—right in grandma's pres-ence. And, naturally, it brought her al-most to tears.

Grandma said: "All in all, it's ex-tremely unpleasant having some kind of macaco with a tail living in the apart-ment. It will frighten me with its inhu-man face. It will jump on me in the dark. It will eat my candy. No, I abso-lutely refuse to live in the same apart-ment with an ape. One of us is going to wind up in the zoo. Can it be that I should move straight over to the zoo? No, better let the monkey go there. And I will continue to live in my apartment."

Alesha said to his grandma: "No, grandma, you don't need to move over to the zoo. I guarantee that the monkey won't eat anything more of yours. I will train it like a person. I will teach it to eat with a teaspoon. And to drink tea out of a glass. As far as jumping is con-cerned, I cannot forbid it to swing from the lamp that hangs from the ceiling. From there, naturally, it could leap on your head. But the main thing is that you shouldn't be frightened if this hap-pens. Because this is only an ape that means no harm, and in Africa it was used to leaping and swinging."

The next day Alesha left for school. And begged his grandma to look after the ape. But grandma did not begin to look after it. She thought: "What am I going to do yet, stand here looking after every monstrosity?" And with these thoughts, grandma went and fell asleep on purpose in her armchair.

And then our ape leaped out into the street through the open casement window. And walked along on the sunny side. It isn't known whether he maybe just wanted to go for a little stroll, or whether he wanted to go have another look at the store to see if there was anything he wanted to buy for himself. Not for money, but just so.

And along the street at this time a certain old man was making his way. The invalid Gavrilych. He was going to the bathhouse. And in his hands he carried a small basket in which there were some soap and a change of linen.

He saw the ape and at first he didn't even believe his eyes that it was an ape. He thought it only seemed that way to him because he had just drunk up a jug of beer.

So he looks with amazement at the ape. And it looks at him. Maybe it's thinking: "What kind of a scarecrow is this, with a basket in his hands?"

Finally, it dawned on Gavrilych that this was a real ape and not an imaginary one. And then he thought: "With luck, I'll catch it. Tomorrow I'll take it to the market and I'll sell it there for a hundred rubles. And with that kind of money I can drink ten jugs of beer in a row." And with these thoughts in mind Gavrilych set about catching the ape, murmuring: "P'st, p'st, p'st . . . here now."

No, he knew it wasn't a cat, but he wasn't sure what language to speak to it in. But then it struck him that this was, after all, the most highly developed creature of the animal world. And then

he took a piece of sugar out of his pocket, showed it to the ape, and said, taking a bow: "Monkey, old friend, old beauty, wouldn't you like to eat a little piece of sugar?"

The latter replied: "Please, yes I would. . . ." That is, actually, he didn't say anything because he didn't know how to talk. But he simply walked right up, grabbed this little lump of sugar, and started to eat it.

Gavrilych picked him up in his hands and put him in his basket. It was warm and snug in the basket. And our monkey didn't try to get out. Maybe he thought: "Let this old sot carry me in his basket. It's even rather pleasant."

At first Gavrilych thought of taking it home. But then he really didn't want to go home again. And he went to the bathhouse with the ape. He thought: "Better I should go to the bathhouse with it. There I can wash it up. It will be clean, pleasant to look at. I'll tie a ribbon around its neck. That way I'll get more for it at the market."

And so he arrived at the bathhouse with his monkey. And began to wash himself, and to wash it too.

And it was very warm in the bathhouse, boiling—just like Africa. And our monkey was quite pleased with this warm atmosphere. But not entirely. Because Gavrilych was washing him with soap and the soap got into his mouth. Naturally, it didn't taste good, but that was no reason to scream and kick around and refuse to be washed. Our monkey began to splash furiously, but at this point soap got into his eyes. And from this, the monkey really went out of his mind. He bit Gavrilych on the finger, tore himself loose, and leaped out of the bath as though he were on fire.

He leaped out into the room where people were getting dressed. And there, he frightened them all out of their wits.

No one knew it was an ape. They see: something round, white, and foamy has leaped out. At first it leaped onto the couch. Then on the stove. From the stove onto the trunk. From the trunk onto somebody's head. And again up on the stove.

Several nervous-type customers cried out and started to run out of the bathhouse. And our ape ran out too. And went scampering down the stairs.

And there below was the ticket office, with a little window. The ape leaped through this little window, thinking it would be more peaceful there, and, most important, there wouldn't be such a fuss and commotion. But in the ticket office sat the fat woman who sold the tickets, and she sobbed and squealed. And ran out of the ticket office shouting: "Help! Emergency! Seems a bomb fell in my office. Quick, some iodine!"

Our monkey hated all this yelling. He leaped out of the office and ran along the street.

And there he is running along the street all wet and foamy with soap, and behind him, once again, people are running. The boys at the head. Behind them, the grown-ups. Behind the grown-ups, the policeman. And behind the policeman, our ancient Gavrilych, dressed harum-scarum, with his boots in his hands.

But at this point *that dog* leaped out again from some place or other, the very same one who'd been after the monkey the day before.

Having seen this, our monkey thought: "Well, now, citizens, I'm done for once and for all."

But this time the dog didn't go after him. The dog only looked at the fleeing ape, felt a sharp pain in its nose, and stopped running; even turned around. Probably thought: "They don't supply you with noses—running after apes." And although it turned around, it barked angrily: as much as to say, run where you will, I'm staying put.

At this very time our boy, Alesha Popov, returned home from school. He did not find his dear little ape at home. He was terribly roused up about it. And tears even came to his eyes. He thought that now he'd never see his glorious, divine little monkey again.

And so, from boredom and sorrow, he went out on the street. He walks along the street in a melancholy funk. And suddenly he sees—people are running. No, at first he didn't grasp that they were running after his ape. He thought they were running because of an air raid. But at this point he saw his ape—all soapy and wet. He flew toward it. He picked it up in his arms. He hugged it to himself, so as not to give it up.

Then all the people who had been running came and surrounded the boy.

At this point our ancient Gavrilych emerged from the crowd. And exhibiting his bitten finger for all to see, he said: "Citizens, don't let this fellow take my ape in his arms. I want to sell it on the market tomorrow. This is my very own ape, which bit me on the finger. Just look at this gored finger of mine. And that testifies that I'm telling the truth."

The boy, Alesha Popov, said: "No, this ape isn't his, it's my ape. Look how happily it came to my arms. And this testifies that I'm telling the truth."

But at this point yet another man emerges from the crowd—that very driver who had transported the ape in his vehicle. He says: "No, it's not your ape and it's not yours either. It's my monkey because I transported it. But I'm returning to my unit, so I'm going to give the ape to the one who keeps him kindly in his arms, and not to the one who'd sell him pitilessly on the market for the sake of a few driblets. The ape belongs to the boy."

And at this point the whole audience applauded. And Alesha Popov, beaming with happiness, hugged the ape still more tightly to himself. And triumphantly carried him home.

Gavrilych, with his bitten finger, went to the bathhouse to wash up.

And, so, from that time on, the ape came to live with the boy, Alesha Popov.

He's still living with him. Not long ago I took a trip to the city of Borisov. And I purposely went to Alesha's place to see how the ape was getting on. Oh, it was getting along very well indeed!

It didn't run away anywhere. It had become very obedient. Wiped its nose with a handkerchief. Doesn't take candy from strangers. So that even grandma is satisfied now and doesn't get mad at it, and no longer wants to move to the zoo.

When I entered Alesha's room, the ape was sitting on the table. Sitting there with a sense of importance, like a ticket taker at the movies. And was eating some rice cereal with a teaspoon.

Alesha said to me: "I've educated him like a man, and now all children and even some grown-ups can take him as an example."

61

MY WORTHLESS AND VICIOUS FILM

By Sergei Eisenstein

The Soviet system makes frequent use of public self-criticism to keep ideological nonconformity at a minimum. Eisenstein's statement below is one of these humiliations by command. It was first published in the Soviet journal *Kultura i Zhizn* ("Culture and Life"). The famous film director (1898–1948) had been in disgrace once before, in the 1930's, after he had made two films unacceptable to the regime. He redeemed himself with *Alexander Nevsky* (1937) and *Ivan the Terrible*, Part I (1945), which won the Stalin Prize, First Class. Part II of the film, however, was publicly condemned by the Party's Central Committee in September, 1946, and was not released for showing till 1958. Even today not all seems to be well in the Soviet film industry. Wrote *Pravda* on March 24, 1963: "In order to improve the guidance over the development of cinematography the Presidium of the Supreme Soviet has established a State Cinematographic Committee. Its chairman A. V. Romanov is first assistant director of the Ideological Department of the Party's Central Committee."

As noted elsewhere the three Eisenstein films mentioned here can be rented from Brandon Films (offices in New York, Chicago, and San Francisco). The leading actor of the three films, Nikolai Cherkasov, has written *Notes of a Soviet Actor*. Marie Seton, *Eisenstein* (paperback) is the best biography. See Eisenstein's own writings, *Film Form and the Film Sense* (paperback). A history of Russian movie making is Jay Leyda, *Kino*. See also *The Soviet Film Industry* by Paul Babitsky and John Rimberg. The scenario of all three parts of Eisenstein's film (Part 3 was never released), together with stills from the first two parts, is available in Sergei Eisenstein, *Ivan the Terrible*. For a discussion of Soviet films since World War II see Joseph Anderson, "Soviet Films since 1945," *Films in Review*, February, 1953, and Dwight Macdonald, "Soviet Cinema: A History and an Elegy," *Problems of Communism*, November–December, 1954, and January–February, 1955. For an English monthly devoted to films and published in Moscow see *Soviet Film*.

It is difficult to imagine a sentry who gets so lost in contemplation of the stars that he forgets his post. It is difficult to imagine a tankist eagerly reading an adventure novel while going into battle. It is difficult to believe there could be a foundryman who, instead of giving all his attention to the mass of molten metal flowing into prepared forms, turns aside from his work to contemplate a pattern of his own fantasy. They would be a bad sentry, a bad tankist and a bad foundryman. Each would be a bad soldier.

From *The New Leader* (New York), December 7, 1946.

715

In our Soviet Army and in our Socialist production there are no bad soldiers.

It is even more difficult to realize that during the stern accounting caused by demands of our Soviet reality such bad and unworthy soldiers were discovered in the front lines of literature and art.

Reading again and again the resolution of the Party Central Committee about the film *Great Life*, I always linger on the question which it put forth: "What can explain the numerous cases of production of false and mistaken films? Why did such known Soviet directors as Comrades Loukov, Eisenstein, Pudovkin, Kozentsev and Trauberg create failures while in the past they have created films of high art value?"

I cannot let the question go unanswered. First of all we failed because at a critical moment in our work we artists forgot for a time those great ideas our art is summoned to serve. Some of us forgot the incessant struggle against our Soviet ideals and ideology which goes on in the whole world. We lost for a time comprehension of the honorable, militant, educational task which lies on our art during the years of hard work to construct the Communist society in which all our people are involved.

The Central Committee justly pointed out to us that the Soviet artist cannot treat his duties in a light-minded and irresponsible way. Workers of the cinema should study deeply whatever they undertake. Our chief mistake is that we did not fulfill these demands in our creative work.

Like a bad sentry we gaped at the unessential and secondary things, forgetting the main things, and so abandoning our post. We forgot that the main thing in art is its ideological content and historical truth. Like a bad foundryman, we lightmindedly allowed the precious stream of creation to be poured out over sand and become dispersed in private, unessential sidelines. This brought us to vices and mistakes in our creations.

A stern and timely warning of the Central Committee stopped us Soviet artists from further movement along this dangerous and fatal way which leads towards creative degradation.

The resolution of the Central Committee reminds us with new force that Soviet art has been given one of the most honorable places in the decisive struggle of ideology of our country against the seductive ideology of the bourgeois world. Everything we do must be subordinated to tasks of this struggle.

In the second part of *Ivan the Terrible* we committed a misrepresentation of historical facts which made the film worthless and vicious in an ideological sense.

We know Ivan the Terrible as a man with a strong will and firm character. Does that exclude from the characterization of this Tsar the possibility of the existence of certain doubts? It is difficult to think that a man who did such unheard-of and unprecedented things in his time never thought over the choice of means or never had doubts about how to act at one time or another. But could it be that these possible doubts overshadowed the historical role of historical Ivan as it was shown in the film? Could it be that the essence of this powerful 16th-century figure lies in these doubts and not in his uncompromising fight against them or unending success of his state activity? Is it not so that the center of our attention is and must be *Ivan the builder, Ivan the creator of a new, powerful, united Russian power,* Ivan the inexorable destroyer of everything that resisted his progressive undertakings?

The sense of historical truth betrayed me in the second part of *Ivan the Terrible*. The private, unimportant and non-characteristic shut out the principal. The play of doubts crept out to the front line and the wilful character of the Tsar and his historically progressive role slipped out of the field of attention. The result was that a false and mistaken impression was created about the image of Ivan. The resolution of the Central Committee accusing me of a wrong presentation which disfigures historical truth says that in the film Ivan is presented as "weak-charactered and lacking in will, a kind of Hamlet." This is solidly grounded and just.

Some historically wrong impressions of the epoch and reign of Ivan the Terrible which were reflected in my film were widely current in pre-Revolutionary literature. This was especially true of the film's presentation of the Tsar's bodyguards [*oprichniki*]. Works of the classics of Marxism on questions of history have illustrated and made available to us the historically correct and positive evaluation of Ivan's *progressive lifeguards*. In the light of these works it should not have been difficult to overcome the false presentation of the lifeguards in the writing of Traitor-Prince Andrei Kurbsky. It should have been easy to unveil tendentious descriptions of Ivan's activity which were left us by historian spies of the Western Powers, Taube and Kruse or the adventurer Henry Staden. But it was much more difficult to overcome in one's own self the remnants of former purely imaginary presentations left over from childhood reading of such books as Alexei Konstantinovich Tolstoy's novel *Silver Prince*, or the old novel *Koudeyar*. [This Tolstoy, related neither to playwright Alexei or novelist Leo, died in 1875.]

As a result, in the film the progressive *oprichniki* were presented as a gang of degenerates something like the Ku Klux Klan. The Central Committee justly condemned this rough misrepresentation of historical fact.

On the basis of the Central Committee's resolution, all workers in art should make a most important conclusion as to the necessity of putting an end to light-minded and irresponsible attitudes toward their work. We must fully subordinate our creations to the interest of education of the Soviet people, especially youth, and not step aside one jot from this aim.

We must master the Lenin-Stalin method of perception of real life and history to such a full and deep extent as to be able to overcome all remnants or survivals of former notions which, although they have been banished from our consciousness a long time, are obstinately and maliciously attempting to infiltrate into our works as soon as our creative vigilance is weakened even for only a single moment.

This is a guarantee that our cinematography will be able to eliminate all ideological and artistic failures and mistakes which lie like a heavy load on our art in this first postwar year. This is a guarantee that in the nearest future our cinematography will again create highly ideological artistic films worthy of the Stalin epoch.

All of us workers of art must interpret the hard and just criticism of our work contained in the decision of the Central Committee as an appeal to the widest and most ardent and purposeful activity, an appeal to us masters of art to fulfill our duty before the Soviet people, state and party by creation of highly ideological artistic films.

62

THE DESTRUCTION OF SOVIET GENETICS

By Herman J. Muller

Although the Soviet regime interferes in the sciences with its own political demands, this is both more difficult and more self-defeating than is the case in
literature and the arts. Some fields of scientific endeavor appear to be almost
totally free of political control. In others the situation is less desirable. The best-
documented case of government interference in the sciences was, until recently, the
reduction of genetics under the dictatorship of Trofim Lysenko. Until the death
of Stalin, Lysenko ruled undisturbed. Under Khrushchev he lost some of his power
but remained formidable. He now seems to be decisively relegated to the background, and genetics has once again become legitimate and relatively free. A new
Genetics Institute was established by the Academy of Sciences. It sponsored an
official investigation of the allegedly model farm run by Lysenko. An entire issue
of the Academy's journal (*Vestnik Akademii Nauk SSSR*, November, 1965) was
devoted to the publication of the results of this investigation together with Lysenko's
unimpressive replies to the sharp questions posed. One of Lysenko's chief victims,
Academician Nikolai Vavilov, has been posthumously rehabilitated, and his works
have been printed again.

   The author of the article below, written in 1948, is an American Nobel Prize
winner in genetics. He was senior geneticist at the Moscow Institute of Genetics in
1933–37, and was elected Corresponding Member of the Soviet Academy of
Sciences in 1933. He resigned from the Academy in protest against the persecution
of Soviet geneticists which he describes. For a Soviet view of his action see "The
Exclusion of Prof. H. J. Muller and Prof. Henry Dale from the Academy of
Sciences of the USSR," *New Times* (Moscow), January 5, 1949.

   For a background study of the problem see David Joravsky's *Soviet Marxism
and Natural Science: The First Phase, 1917–1932*. For the excesses of Lysenkoism
see Trofim Lysenko's *Heredity and Variability* and *The Situation in Biological
Science*. For Western views see Conway Zirkle, *Death of a Science in Russia: The
Fate of Genetics*; P. Hudson and R. Richens, *The New Genetics in the Soviet
Union*; and Julian Huxley, *Heredity East and West: Lysenko and World Science*.
On the slow revival of free genetics in the Soviet Union see the following Soviet
sources: "Philosophy and the Natural Sciences in the USSR," *Daedalus*, Summer,
1960 (also available in Richard Pipes [ed.], *The Russian Intelligentsia*); frequent

articles on biology and Lysenko in the *Current Digest of the Soviet Press*; and "Hands Off Science," *Atlas*, November, 1965. For Western comments see several articles by David Joravsky: "The Lysenko Affair," *Scientific American*, November, 1962; "Lysenko's Maize," *Survey*, July, 1964; and "The Debacle of Lysenkoism," *Problems of Communism*, November–December, 1965. See also Leopold Labedz, "How Free Is Soviet Science?" *Commentary*, June, 1958.

I. THE CRUSHING OF GENETICS

The willful destruction of science in the U.S.S.R. by politicians is a tragedy of the greatest significance. Until the recently announced decision of the Central Executive Committee of the Communist Party of the Soviet Union, which made official and public their repudiation of the entire science of genetics, and their setting up in its stead of the ancient superstitions of teleologically directed germinal change and of the inheritance of acquired characters, there seemed to some outsiders room for doubt as to the genuineness of the assault on human knowledge by the Soviet governing body. But now he who runs may read.

We must confess that we no longer see any chance of saving the core of biological science, and all that goes with it, in that section of the world in our generation, short of an unexpected political overturn. Nor could it be completely restored in just one more generation. Our present task can only be that of autopsy, in the hope of finding ways of checking the already dangerous spread of the present infection to countries outside the Soviet hemisphere, and of making clear to the people of those countries the important lessons for culture and for civilization in general which are involved. . . .

It is quite evident that the Soviet politicians, being uneducated in modern science, and having proved themselves unwilling or unable to grasp the exacting technicalities involved in genetic reasoning, have through motives of their own taken a dislike to its conclusions, and have accordingly maneuvered to have it cast into the limbo. This aim they have accomplished by the use of the same combination of flagrant misrepresentation and calculated brutality which has marked their dealings with their political opponents. Yet, ironically enough, the great majority of the geneticists who have been purged were thoroughly loyal politically, and many were even ardent crusaders for the Soviet system and leadership, as the writer well knows through long personal contact with them.

What has happened to genetics and related fields during the past few months in the U.S.S.R. is only the dramatic culmination of a long drawn out campaign which for more than twelve years has been ruthlessly waged against this section of science and the workers engaged in it. Genetics in the U.S.S.R. had reached a very high state of advancement, and many eminent scientists were engaged in it. No actual scientists could be found to take up the contest against it. Hence resort was had in 1935 and the years that followed to the making of a special "build-up" for an ignorant but demagogic and fanatical peas-

An abridged version of this article was published in the *Saturday Review of Literature*, XXXI (December 4, 1948), 13–15, 65–66, and (December 11, 1948), 8–10, the latter part under the editor's title, "Back to Barbarism—Scientifically." Section I was republished in somewhat abridged form in the *Bulletin of the Atomic Scientists*, December, 1948, pp. 369–71. Used by permission of the author, the *Saturday Review*, and the *Bulletin of the Atomic Scientists*.

ant, Lysenko, who had turned plant breeder. True, Lysenko had the advantage of having achieved some doubtful success in applying (by trial and error procedures) an early American discovery concerning the influencing of the time of maturation of certain crops by pre-treatments of seeds. But this gives him no more claim to being a geneticist than does doctoring dogs for worms, and it does not, by itself, constitute Lysenko a scientist at all. His writings along theoretical lines are, to a scientist, the merest drivel, and he obviously fails to comprehend either what a controlled experiment is or those known principles of genetics that are taught in any elementary course in the subject.

The role of second in command was taken by a suave, satanic and unscrupulous juggler of words, the dialectical materialist "philosopher" Present. His authoritarian sophistries have been calculated to lend an aura of profundity and orthodoxy that confuses and impresses the earnest lay disciple of the Party Line. However, equally with Lysenko's imprecations, his argumentation is thoroughly unscientific in its method, and fails to stand up either under theoretical analysis or by the test of objective results. . . .

That Lysenko and Present are not, as they are made to appear, self-constituted leaders of the rebellion against science, but are themselves merely the tools of the highest political power, is shown by a number of telling facts. For one thing, not a few geneticists of high standing were separately martyrized on assorted pretexts in the period prior to 1937, i.e., before Lysenko and Present had risen to such high estate as to render their own allegations a sufficient excuse for the meting out of such treatment. Only a deep-seated antagonism to genetics on the part of the higher authorities can explain why, in 1933, or thereabouts,

the geneticists Chetverifkoff, Ferry, and Ephroimson had all on separate occasions been banished to Siberia and Levitsky to a labor camp in the European Arctic, or why, in 1936, the Communist geneticist Agol was quietly imprisoned and done away with in the Ukraine, after rumors that he had been convicted of "Menshevik Idealism" in genetics.

Again, it may be asked why, in 1936, the Medicogenetical Institute, founded and directed by the loyal Party member Solomon Levit, which with its numerous staff of biologists, psychologists and over 200 physicians constituted a shining example, unmatched anywhere in the world, of the possibilities of research in human genetics, was scurrilously vilified and misrepresented in *Pravda,* and then dissolved. The accusations alleged that the Institute had been attempting to exalt heredity as against environment, whereas everyone conversant with it knows that it had been entirely objective in its gathering of data but that, in its interpretations, it had been leaning as far as possible, if not even too far, in the environmentalist direction. Levit himself made, under pressure, a "confession" of scientific guilt, which he admitted to the writer was entirely false and given only out of loyalty to the Party which demanded it. Immediately afterward he was abstracted from the scene, and has not been heard from since.

Both Agol and Levit spent a year working on Rockefeller Foundation Fellowships under the writer's direction in Texas in 1931–32. They were able then to express themselves freely in private conversation without fear of reprisals. Yet the writer can vouch that both of them went out of their way on every occasion to defend the Soviet regime, the policies and person of Stalin, and the orthodox philosophy of dialectical materialism, and that they made rather a nuisance of themselves in magnifying the importance of environmental influences even where the pertinent evidence was weak or absent. In short, they were convinced Stalinists but, being scientists with dangerous knowledge and data, they had to be sacrificed, without waiting for the Punch and Judy show in which Lysenko and Present were to appear as the favorite puppets.

Other convincing evidence of the power behind the scenes is to be seen in the meteoric rise of Lysenko, Present and their hangers-on, once the stage had been set for them in 1936. In December of that year there was a carefully prearranged and widely publicized "genetics controversy," held before a packed auditorium of invited spectators and in this Lysenko appeared as the main speaker for what may be called the prosecution. It was obvious that the Party administrators, sitting as chairmen, paid no attention to the painstaking scientific arguments of the geneticist defendants, and did not use that opportunity to gain knowledge of the subject, but that they brightened up at every crude slander dropped by the attacking clique. And despite the enthusiastic siding of the entire scientifically educated portion of the audience with the geneticists, the final verdict of the administrators and of the organs of publicity, while not yet daring to damn them completely, took the geneticists heavily to task and let them out with warnings. The book of published addresses of this Congress, although already heavily expurgated when printed, was within a few months on the banned list.

In the autumn of 1936, the Seventh International Congress of Genetics, which was to have been held in Moscow in the summer of 1937, was called off without explanation and even without notification to the scientists in other countries until word of it had been smuggled out many months later, although it was then untruly claimed to have been merely "postponed." This step was taken only after the Party had first toyed with the idea of allowing it to be held with the omission of all papers on evolution and on human genetics, in spite of the fact that many foreign geneticists had intended in such papers to attack the Nazi racist doctrines! In 1939, when Edinburgh, in substitution for Moscow, finally acted as host to this Congress, all forty Soviet geneticists who had sent papers to it were at the last moment forbidden to come. At the same time the world-renowned and widely beloved Congress president, Nicolai Ivanovitch Vavilov, who was the Soviet's leading *bona fide* geneticist, sent to Edinburgh a discourteous letter of resignation which, according to information in my possession, had been written for him. During the same year, another public "genetics controversy" was staged in Moscow, and this time the now greatly exalted Lysenkoists, entirely uninjured in the administrative mind by the complete scientific refutation which they had been subjected to in 1936, were made to appear as clear-cut victors, while Vavilov and the geneticists in general, appearing as culprits, were put to shame. At about that time, Vavilov's important posts as president of the Lenin Academy of Agricultural Sciences, head of the Institute of Plant Production, and head of the Institute of Genetics were turned over to Lysenko, who was also given various high honors and decorations.

In 1941, during the time of the Soviet-Nazi liaison, Vavilov was arrested and put in prison, and it has later been learned that he was sentenced to death on the trumped-up charge of being a British spy. This was however commuted when, after the attack by the

Nazis, the U.S.S.R. allied herself with Britain. Soon afterwards an eye witness observed Vavilov in a concentration camp at Saratov in a state of physical collapse, although he had originally been a man capable of enduring the utmost rigors. He was thereupon sent to Magadan in far northwestern Siberia, near the Sea of Okhotsk, where he died in 1942. Thus ended a man of the greatest vigor, buoyancy and charm, one who was devoid of jealousy and widely loved, and who, although not a party member, had for years been one of the 400 members of the Central Executive Committee of the Soviet Government. This fabulously productive man had undoubtedly done more for the genetic development of Soviet agriculture than has ever been done by anyone else for any country in the world. It is said that after his death his matchless collection of thousands of varieties of economically important agricultural plants, with its invaluable reservoir of genes, painstakingly gathered by him and his coworkers on expeditions sent all over the world, was largely allowed to lapse, as were many of the specially constructed "pure lines" of crop plants.

During the same years, and since that time, the attack on other geneticists, and on the science of genetics in general, continued. But, owing to the imposed internal secrecy, the censorship on news leaving the country, and the existence of war conditions, it is not possible to know the real causes of death of such distinguished scientists in this field as Karpechenko, Koltzoff, Serebrovsky, and Levitsky. Certain it is however that, from 1936 onwards, geneticists of all ranks throughout the country were terrorized. Most of those who were not imprisoned, banished or executed were forced into other lines of work. And perusal of the published papers shows that, in the mildest cases, those in which

they were allowed to remain in their own laboratories, the great majority were driven to redirect their researches in such a way as to give the appearance of trying to prove the correctness of the anti-scientific views. During the disorganization attending the windup of the war, some escaped to the West. A few however were retained through it all, as showpieces who proved that the U.S.S.R. did still have its working geneticists.

In September, 1947, these remaining geneticists, and those biologists in related fields who still had the temerity to support the genetic viewpoint, were led into a trap. The columns of the *Moscow Literary Gazette* were opened to them to express their views. Three of them made use of this apparent return to freedom of scientific discussion by restating the case for genetics. Lysenko and Present thereupon replied in their characteristic style. This paved the way for a new Soviet "conference" on genetics, in July, 1948, with a considerable number of participants. This presumably was the Russian substitute for the Eighth International Congress of Genetics in Stockholm, which, according to a priceless official statement sent to that Congress by the Academy of Sciences of the U.S.S.R., the Russian geneticists were "too busy to attend." Once more the real and the spurious scientists argued. Finally, Lysenko made his historic announcement that the Communist Central Committee had in fact prejudged the case, and had already decided in his own favor. This decision by a non-scientific political body of course decided the argument.

Party members among the geneticist participants in the conference at once made public recantations of their heresies, pretending to change their convictions overnight. The presidium of the Academy of Sciences, headed by the obedient physicist Sergei Ivanovitch

Vavilov, brother of the great geneticist who had been done to death, toed the line by removing from their posts with dishonor the greatest Soviet physiologist, Orbeli, the greatest Soviet student of morphogenesis, Schmalhausen, and the best remaining Soviet geneticist, Dubinin. The entire laboratory of the latter, long known for the admirable work which had been carried out there by numerous careful investigators, was closed down. It is not to be expected that we will hear of these men again, nor of the scores of less renowned scientists who were working with them or in other institutions along similar lines.

It is noteworthy that Orbeli and Schmalhausen were biologists in other fields than genetics, who however recognized the fundamental and indispensable place occupied by genetic principles in the biological sciences in general. With most of the geneticists themselves gone, those in kindred subjects had now become more open to attack. The operation has already gone further, as more recent accounts in *Pravda* state that, at the last meeting of the Academy of Medical Sciences, September ninth and tenth, a whole group of leaders in physiology, microbiology, epidemiology, psychiatry, etc., were severely attacked for "supporting Mendelian views."

Although it has been a long time since genetics as such has been allowed to be taught in the U.S.S.R., the Academy of Agricultural Sciences has called for the rewriting of biological textbooks and the revision of courses in biology and related subjects so as to remove all traces of genetic doctrines. The minister of higher education, Kaftanov, on September ninth confessed that his own ministry had been too lax in the past and promised the eradication of all university teachers and research workers infected with the reactionary "theory" (quotations are his) of "Mendelism-

Morganism." He cited a considerable number of distinguished names as being in the list of the proscribed and gave the names of "Michurinists" who were replacing them. He also announced that the "cleansing" of the entire curriculum as well as of the personnel of the publishing houses and journals was proceeding. . . .

II. THE SIGNIFICANCE OF THE SCIENTIFIC ISSUES AT STAKE

Nowhere in the world today do either politicians or laymen in general have the kind of education which would fit them to judge the merits of a theory in natural science. In appealing to them the anti-scientist has the advantage of being able to make whatever assertions he likes and to play upon emotion and prejudice. On the other hand, the scientist's meticulous statements of the details of his evidence and of his often intricate steps of reasoning are likely to fall upon deaf ears. But if he simply resorts to truthfully calling his opponent an ignoramus or fakir he is himself suspected of prejudice. For this reason we must attempt in what follows a brief account of the nature of the scientific principles that are at stake in the attack on genetics. . . .

Among the findings of genetics we should mention first the demonstration that there is a specific genetic material, or material of heredity, which is separate from the other materials of the body. This genetic material is composed of ultramicroscopic particles, called genes, of which each cell has a whole outfit, consisting of thousands of different kinds. Most of the genes are contained in microscopically visible bodies, called chromosomes, and are inherited according to the definite rules discovered by Mendel. The other materials, making up the body as we see it, have been developed as a result of the coordinated activity of the genes, and in this process of development, both in embryo and in adult, environmental influences play a very considerable role in helping to determine just what kind of product, i.e., what bodily traits, shall be formed. Moreover, the developmental reactions started and guided by the genes are so adjusted that, in many cases, a given kind of modification in the environment results in an especially suited, or "adaptive," modification of these other materials of the body, so as to cause it to function better under the given conditions.

The genes themselves, however, are not changed in any directed or adaptive way by influences outside of themselves. Although they are relatively stable, they do sometimes undergo sudden inner changes in their chemical composition, called mutations. These mutations occur as a result of ultramicroscopic accidents, and although these can be increased in their frequency by application of X-rays, heat or special chemicals, they are essentially of a random nature, undirected, and (as is to be expected of accidents) they are usually detrimental in their effects. But order does emerge from these accidents. For the relatively frequent individual who inherits a mutated gene that is detrimental to life tends to die out, whereas the rare one who inherits a gene that chanced to change in a beneficial way tends to live and multiply. Thus, under natural conditions, a population may, in the course of ages, become ever better adapted in its characteristics, i.e., it may evolve. In this way has modern genetics implemented Darwin's theory of natural selection and given it a firm basis. The marvelous and complicated adaptations of the bodies of the living things of today (including their very capabilities of undergoing adaptive bodily responses

to changes in their environment) are thus explained as resulting from the natural selection of accidental changes in their genes, without ascribing any mysterious foresight, or power of adaptive response, to the basic elements, the genes, themselves.

This gene theory, then, gives us a unit on a lower level than the cell, and in a sense more fundamental than the cell, and even more necessary for a comprehension of all biological sciences, including agriculture and medicine. It is indispensable for a rational interpretation of the origin of life, of the relation between inanimate and animate, of the way in which organisms have undergone change in the past, and of how they may become changed, either in the course of natural breeding or in response to artificial manipulations, in the future. Moreover, through analysis of the genes of an organism, and of how they operate, we may hope to unravel ever more of the tangled web of biochemical processes which constitute its development, its physiology, and its pathology —studies which are already under way. Finally, this knowledge must affect our whole philosophical outlook, and many phases of the anthropological, psychological and social sciences.

Lightly waving away the amassed evidence for this coherent modern conception of living things, Lysenko and Present deny the very existence of genes or of a separate genetic material, ignore the all-important distinction between heredity and individual development, and offer—in the name of Darwin!—a return to pre-Darwinian days that had been all but forgotten by modern biologists. They would have the heredity itself respond in a directly adaptive way to outside influences, and would also have it able to incorporate the directly adaptive changes which the body may have undergone in its development. Thus, instead of explaining in a rational way the origin of the body's adaptive structures and reactions, they force upon the germ cells themselves (1) the ability to give that type of response which is to be the advantage of the future body, and (2) the ability somehow to mirror changes already incurred by the body that contains them. This leaves entirely unexplained the origin and the *modus operandi* of the germ cell's own supposed ability to respond adaptively, and hence it also fails to explain the origin of the body's adaptive abilities. The Lysenko-Present doctrine therefore implies a mystical, Aristotelian "perfecting principle," a kind of foresight, in the basic make-up of living things, despite the fact that it claims in the same breath not to be "idealistic" at all. And, though verbally accepting natural selection as playing some role, it fails to make use of it for the solution of the main problem, that of why organisms do have adaptability.

In support of these claims, so fantastic in this generation, the Lysenko doctrine offers no properly documented, controlled or repeatable factual evidence. Mainly it attempts to convince by citation of authority, and quotes three main authorities. First, it makes the most of Darwin's failing in having accepted (though under pressure of the universal opinion of his day) some part of Lamarck's doctrine of inheritance of acquired characters, and in even having proposed a mechanism for it—since disproved—as a supplement to his own distinctive contribution of natural selection. Second, Lysenkoism relies heavily on the theoretical weakness of the old practical plant breeders, especially the Russian Michurin and the American Burbank, producers of new varieties by trial-and-error crossing and rule-of-thumb selection. The importance of Michurin as a scientist has in fact been

insisted on by Stalin himself, so that this doctrine is now referred to by the Lysenkoists as the "Michurin doctrine." Third, it calls to witness in its favor the premature judgments concerning Mendelism of the long deceased Russian biologist Timiriazev, who lived in the days of biological confusion.

Here then we see that reaction has triumphed in the name of revolution. As this militant mysticism spreads, it is bound to have dire repercussions throughout all of natural and social science, and, indeed, throughout the whole domain of human thought, both in the U.S.S.R. and in the countries within its growing sphere of influence. As the dialecticians themselves maintain, all things are interconnected. Thus this one important falsehood, persisted in, must poison more and more of the structure of knowledge. And of course the effects are not confined to theory but extend to practice as well. Already the Lysenkoists have introduced important errors into the practices of plant breeding. One of these is the abandoning of the carefully selected pure lines of self-fertilizing crops. Another is the raising of crops for seed under the best conditions of cultivation, in the delusion that the seed will thereby be improved, instead of under those rigorous conditions which impose a more active elimination of unfavorable mutants and, conversely, relatively better chances for the multiplication of the few favorable mutants. These errors, however, will not quickly be recognized, since the effects are slow, and the methods of appraisal and comparison have at the same time become so unscientific.

One curious bearing of the new-old doctrine of Lysenko is that on the nature of man, and of human racial and class differences. It is evident that, on the official Communist view, for men as for plants, those individuals or populations which have lived under worse conditions and have thereby been stunted in their development—physical or mental—would tend, through the inheritance of these acquired characters, to pass on to successive generations an ever poorer hereditary endowment, while, in contrast, those in flourishing circumstances would produce progressively more prosperous germ cells, and so become *innately* superior. To put it bluntly, we should have inborn master and subject races and classes, as the Nazis so vociferously insisted. The writer was in fact told directly by a very high Party authority in 1936, during the genetics controversy, that this was, even then, the "official" doctrine,[1] i.e., held by those even higher in the Party peerage. . . .

Modern geneticists, on the other hand, recognizing the separateness of genes and body, of heredity and individual development, do not fall into this error of confusing the outwardly developed characters with the inner genetic endowment. Since they realize the tremendous role played by the social and physical environment in the development of human mental traits, those dealing with this field of investigation would not naively assume that the culturally or economically less developed peoples are *ipso facto* inherently less capable. So overweening, in fact, are the noninherited effects of cultural differences on mental *development* (as contrasted with innate *endowment*) that no valid conclusions concerning hereditary differences in mentality between existing human populations may be drawn at all. It was for this reason that, when the International Genetics Congress was to have been held in Moscow, groups of

Western geneticists were formed to come to the Congress and attack the Nazi racist fallacies.

The Communist authorities, however, were embarrassed by this offer of aid, and reluctant to allow any discussions concerning man, or even concerning evolution, in general, to be held at that Congress. It is easy to see the reason for this reluctance, once we realize how close their position regarding human differences is to that of the Nazis. And the explanation also becomes apparent of why they expunged all mention of man from the book of proceedings of their 1936 controversy, and why they decided to abandon work on another volume, that had been specifically designed to refute the Nazist perversion of genetics. For their own official doctrine was too close to that of the Nazis (as well as, at that time, still too confused) for them to be willing to risk having their own followers know their views. . . .

III. THE NATURE OF THE SOCIAL FORCES AT WORK

. . . Inasmuch as Lysenkoism is not founded on scientific fact, the question must be asked, what has led the Communist officials to push it so strongly? The answer is obvious: the type of thinking which sees only blacks and whites, yesses and noes, and which therefore cannot admit to itself the importance of *both* heredity and environment. Believing that it has, in its particular type of manipulation of the environment, found the complete answer to all the world's ills, it regards as a menace any concept that concedes a role in the affairs of men to something outside its own preconceived scheme. The genes happen to be outside that scheme, as it exists in the minds of the present narrow-minded leaders, hence the existence of the genes must be denied. And their

[1] The authority—Yakovlev, the head of agriculture in the Party—was later purged, but this is hardly to be held against his veracity as a mouthpiece.

reasoning does not go far enough to enable them to realize that, in this very denying of genes, they have led themselves into a still worse ideological difficulty, by setting up a doctrine according to which the peoples of the world would be saddled, biologically, with the accumulated incubus of their respective past misfortunes, and would therefore be very unequal in inherent capacities.

Lenin and most of the other older leaders of the Bolsheviks, to be sure, being better educated and more far-sighted, personally arranged important positions and the command of ample resources for scientific work to the geneticists Vavilov, Koltzoff and others, though these geneticists were even then known to hold views substantially like those of the geneticists of today. Most of these older leaders (with the exception of Lunarcharsky) saw no contradiction in ascribing an importance to the genes as well as to the outer influences that mold living things. But much water has flowed under the political bridge since those times and the official doctrine has grown much narrower and more fanatical as the reins of power have been more tightly gathered together and as freedom of discussion and criticism has disappeared.

The inner control of all scientific institutions, just as of all factories, by the Party units, which contain on the whole those weakest in science itself, and the absolute command exerted by the higher Party units over the lower, pyramidally, until the top is reached, just as in an army, create conditions maximally adapted for stamping out free thought processes. They put a premium on attitudes of subservience towards those above, combined with arbitrary domineering over those below. They create a fertile soil for rise by intrigue and by denunciation of others rather than by merit. Their fruits are seen in the amazing campaigns of defamation constantly being conducted against the conscientious workers in scientific institutions by their jealous but less capable Party "comrades." These circumstances are in themselves highly conducive to the rise of Lysenkos. But when such a Lysenko happens to provide that kind of "science" for which the uppermost circles, with their wishful thinking, are craving, is it any wonder that such a "scientist" should after a time be made Vice Chairman of the Supreme Soviet of the U.S.S.R.? In this connection, moreover, it may be recalled that Stalin himself, as far back as 1929, informed the geneticist Agol that he believed in the doctrine of inheritance of acquired characters.

One very important weapon in the attack on science lies in the permanent existence in the U.S.S.R. of an emotional condition resembling war hysteria, whereby any idea or activity can be damned or glorified, by painting it as respectively subversive or patriotic. A second major weapon lies in the existence of a mystical and unscientific but pretentious state philosophy, which might better be called a religion, known as "dialectic materialism." This is taught in credo form to young and old and it can, in any situation, be conveniently applied for purposes of blackening or whitening, as desired. It is according to the precepts of this dogma, as interpreted by its high priests, that all scientific work is supposed to be carried out and all scientific conclusions reached.

Naturally, both these weapons have been liberally employed in the attack on genetics, but it would take us too far afield to go into the details here. Suffice it to point out, as an illustration of the first method of attack, that Vavilov was charged with sabotage on a national scale for maintaining that it might take five or more years for geneticists to construct, through the only methods known to them, certain improved and needed varieties of wheat, while Lysenko on the contrary was promising that, through direct modification of the development of the plants by special treatments, followed by the immediate stable inheritance of these developmental changes, he could get as good results in a year and a half. As illustrations of the impact of the state religious dogma, we may point out that the theory of the gene and of Mendelian, chromosomal inheritance has at one and the same time been accused of the heresies of both "idealism" and "mechanism." These are supposed to stand at opposite poles, but both of them equally are anathema to the agile Party creed, which somehow manages to escape from them into another, conveniently provided dimension.

Considering all the above circumstances, it would have been very strange if genetics had been the only science to suffer. In fact, however, there have been others cases almost or quite as flagrant. Psychology likewise was set upon during the thirties and largely destroyed, although by quieter procedures. In particular, that branch of psychology dealing with tests of aptitudes and abilities, which had attained considerable advancement in the U.S.S.R. and was proving highly useful, was wiped out of existence. In medicine certain very weakly based theories—notably Speransky's, which attributes much of disease to the nutritional condition of nerves—have been politically favored to the detriment of the more scientific approaches. Physics had a narrow escape from a strong political move to condemn the relativity theory on dialectic materialist grounds, although clever maneuvering finally won the day for it. Nevertheless Joffe, the most eminent physicist in the

U.S.S.R. at the time of the writer's stay there, was under heavy Party attack at that time on various charges of having misapplied his efforts, and various other physicists were in difficulties. Even in astronomy some distinguished scientists have disappeared. And from top to bottom no scientist can feel safe, but must attempt to produce wares that will satisfy the lesser and greater Party bosses.

This situation is the more tragic because of the great spread of education, science, and culture in general in the U.S.S.R., after the revolution. In science, especially, public interest was greatly aroused. Scientific pursuits soon attained a higher prestige, far more persons were drawn into them, and they were accorded much greater material support. For the first fifteen years there was considerable freedom of discussion concerning scientific matters, and the spirit of authoritarianism in these fields was at a comparatively low ebb. Such freedom is of course the most essential requirement for scientific development. With its decline in the last fifteen years, and with the tightening and centralization of the grip of the politicans in all departments of life simultaneously, including their intrusion even into scientific thought, this delicate product of creative imagination, untrammelled communication and criticism, and scrupulous objectivity, was bound to become devitalized. A similar enfeeblement was of course to be expected in the arts, and it is well known that it has been taking place.

IV. THE VULNERABILITY OF SCIENCE TODAY

. . . For the growth of science it therefore is essential that it be left to find its own ways, unhampered by interference on the part of those who do not understand it. At the same time it must be rendered that material support without which it is left without either personnel or facilities for work. Yet the artificial pumping into it of funds and recruits will not help it, if its soul of spontaneous and independent inquiry has been put in shackles.

The conditions for relatively free inquiry on any considerable scale have existed only in modern times, in those civilized countries in which there had been generations of progress in human rights, in the toleration of minority and dissident opinions, in democratic management, in education, and in the general standard of living. Every one of these conditions is a prerequisite for the sound and continuing development of the fundamentals of our knowledge of man and the universe. And a retrogression in any of them must eventually entail a loss in science and in culture generally. This has not been understood by the present leaders of the U.S.S.R., who insist that science as well as every human activity must have its political direction, that it can never be unbiased (by implication, moreover, differences in degree of bias do not count), and that they must build a "class-conscious" science and culture. Few persons indeed would have believed that political interference could kill a thriving science as easily and quickly as it has done in the case of genetics, but this tragic example now makes the vulnerability of modern science abundantly clear.

Let us not, however, while criticizing the Soviet attack on science, neglect the motes in our own eyes or the lesson of all this in regard to our own practices. Well within the memory of many of us is the assault on the public teaching of evolution which was conducted by the Fundamentalists, led by the politician William Jennings Bryan. The trial of Scopes in Tennessee was only the most publicized of the scandals that

resulted. The writer well recalls the attentive and frequently applauding session of the Texas legislature at which the notorious preacher Norris gave, by special invitation, a fanatical two-hour harangue on the doctrine of biological evolution and its dangers (bolshevism, "nigger-loving," and the anti-Christ) as conceived by him, while no qualified person was called upon to state the case for science itself. This was followed by the lower house passing a bill against such teaching in elementary and high schools (although adjournment came before the senate acted), and by the state textbook commission's ordering the eradication of all teaching of the subject from the school and high-school textbooks. This order was rigorously carried out. While no direct action was taken against teaching in the colleges, the indirect effect was illustrated by the fact that enrollment in the writer's course on evolution, at the state university, at once dropped to a fraction of its former size. In Texas, however, the proceedings were much milder than in a number of other states. And, over wide areas, the pressure on teachers in general was sufficient to block all instruction in regard to this cornerstone of modern knowledge.

Fortunately this movement as such has died down, yet its benighting influence is still pervasive and it is doubtful whether, in many regions, there has been any real recovery yet in the teaching of biology. Moreover, practically throughout our own country the forces of superstition are strong enough to prevent the presentation in the schools of that integrated concept of biology and of man's place in nature which can only be attained through a grounding in the modern genetic interpretation of evolution. Thus a basis is laid for a popular misunderstanding which has prevented research in biological fundamentals from receiving adequate support, which has hindered the comprehension and acceptance of important genetic principles even in medical circles, and which may at any time facilitate the rise of Lysenkoism and other dangerous antiscientific movements.

A different kind of danger to science is that inherent in the support of scientific research by private foundations having ends of their own other than science in general, and by public funds administered by groups chosen by politicians or military men. Research has become increasingly expensive, and much of it is now dependent on such funds. Yet, in the case of most of the private foundations (with a few notable exceptions), the aims are dangerously narrow and some of the most important scientific problems cannot, under their aegis, be pursued freely in their own right, but only by virtue of their connection—actual or supposed—with the more specific object of the foundation. Moreover, as in the Soviet Union, instead of the scientist, once he has proved his merit, being left freely to follow the clues as they present themselves in his material and in his own brain, pretentious plans must be drawn up, usually year by year, and periodical reports must be given to show how well the objectives laid out in these particular plans have been achieved. This may be good policy in the improvement of some techniques, and in some applications of science, but it places heavy fetters on the investigation of fundamental truth and, in general, on the exploration of the unknown. For, in the battles with nature, the outcomes cannot be predicted, and the strategy must have the utmost pliability, and must sometimes change rapidly as ever new terrain comes into view. For much of the best work, moreover, it must be possible to count

on support extended over several or many years, even though the campaign cannot be mapped out far in advance. Such support is seldom given.

The funds of the government, when available, are usually distributed with the same kind of restrictions and drawbacks. True, more support will become available for fundamental work when the National Science Foundation at last gets under way, and much is now being made available by the Navy, in what at present happens to be a rather liberal spirit. But it is all too easy in this way to corrupt science, and a benign dictation may easily be followed by a malignant one. In fact, even if the administrators of such funds were first-rate scientists, chosen by the scientists themselves, they could hardly be depended upon to have the imagination in other lines than their own, the lack of personal bias in their own lines, and the broad, accurate understanding of problems and of people throughout widely scattered but technical fields, to avoid many errors in the apportionment of support. However, through their firsthand knowledge of the general conditions and prerequisites of scientific work, they could at least make a far better job of it than could any body of non-scientists, or of the "safe," unimaginative stuffed-shirt type of scientists likely to be chosen by the best-intentioned politicians. The better scientists would at least attempt to leave the utmost freedom possible to the recipient scientists themselves. It is true that much "waste" would ensue, but that is the waste inherent in all scientific work, with its constant probing into the dark, and it is far less than that incurred when the probings are misdirected in a systematic way by administrators less conversant than the working scientists with the given fields. And it is after all the possibility of having such inspired "waste," on a considerable scale, that gives rise to its very opposite: the making of those rare advances which immeasurably enrich civilization, and in the light of which all previous expenditure becomes negligible. . . .

This does not mean that really hostile or irresponsible persons should be allowed to jeopardize our applications of science to military affairs. We must recognize that it is in fact impossible, so long as the world is divided, to attain that complete freedom for science and scientists which must be our ideal. But surely, when we criticize the shocking processes against scientists which took place in Nazi Germany and which are now taking place in the U.S.S.R., we must at the same time exert ourselves to quell the shameful besmirching of scientists which is being carried on by politicians and others in our own midst. Otherwise we shall not have learned the lesson brought to us so clearly from abroad, and shall be gravitating back towards that state of stultifying intolerance which from time immemorial has been accepted as normal by barbaric societies.

63

STALIN'S COFFIN

The long line of waiting citizens in front of the Lenin Mausoleum on Red Square is a familiar Moscow sight. For almost a decade Stalin shared this supreme place of honor with Lenin. Then in late 1961 his mummified body was removed to a less prominent location. It was one of the more spectacular steps of the ongoing de-Stalinization campaign. Our excerpt is taken from the transcript of the 22d Party Congress meeting in October, 1961. It illustrates, among other things, the mystique surrounding Lenin's memory and also the recurring attempts to shake off the frightening Stalin legacy without at the same time damaging the Party's strength.

For an account of the Stalinist legacy of the present regime, see Bertram Wolfe, *Khrushchev and Stalin's Ghost.* For the extremes of adulation surrounding Stalin in his lifetime, see George Counts, *I Want To Be Like Stalin.* For a brief essay, see Alec Nove, "Was Stalin Really Necessary?" *Encounter,* April, 1962. For a picture of the circumstances surrounding Stalin's death, see *Moscow Journal: The End of Stalin,* by Harrison E. Salisbury. The March, 1963, issue of *Problems of Communism* is devoted to "Ten Years After Stalin." See also Evgenii Yevtushenko, *A Precocious Autobiography* (paperback) which has a dramatic description of Stalin's funeral, as well as Yevtushenko's poem, "The Heirs of Stalin," printed in Patricia Blake and Max Hayward (eds.), *Halfway to the Moon* (paperback). Columbia University's Russian Institute published *The Anti-Stalin Campaign and International Communism.* For recent essays on Stalin see Thomas Larson, "What Happened to Stalin?" *Problems of Communism,* March–April, 1967; Robert Conquest, "The Three Funerals of Joseph Stalin," *ibid.,* January–February, 1962; Charles P. Snow, *Variety of Men*; and the memoirs of Stalin's daughter, Svetlana Allilueva, *Twenty Letters to a Friend* (paperback).

SPEECH BY COMRADE D. A. LA-
ZURKINA, PARTY MEMBER
SINCE 1902, LENINGRAD
PARTY ORGANIZATION

Comrade delegates! I wholly and fully support the proposals of Comrade Spiridonov and other comrades who have spoken here on removing Stalin's body from the Lenin Mausoleum. (*Stormy applause.*)

In the days of my youth I began my work under the leadership of Vladimir Ilyich Lenin, learned from him and carried out his instructions. (*Ap-*

From *Current Soviet Policies,* IV (Columbia University Press, 1962), 215–16. Used by permission of the publisher. The translation comes from the *Current Digest of the Soviet Press,* copyright by the Joint Committee on Slavic Studies.

plause.) ...

And then, comrades, in 1937 I was to share the lot of many. I had an executive post in the Leningrad Province Party Committee and, of course, was also arrested. When they arrested me and when the prison doors closed behind me (this was not the first time they had closed; I was imprisoned and exiled many times in tsarist days), I felt such a horror, not for myself but for the Party. I could not understand why old Bolsheviks were being arrested. Why? This "why?" was so agonizing, so incomprehensible. I explained to myself that something horrible, obviously sabotage, had taken place in the Party. And this gave me no rest.

Not for a minute—either when I sat in prison for two and a half years or when I was sent to a camp, and later exiled (I spent 17 years in exile)—not once did I blame Stalin. I always fought for Stalin, who was assailed by the prisoners, the exiles and the camp inmates. I would say: "No, it is not possible that Stalin would have permitted what is happening in the Party. This cannot be!" They would argue with me, some would become angry with me, but I stood firm. I had high esteem for Stalin, I knew that he had done great service before 1934, and I defended him.

Comrades! And then I returned completely rehabilitated. I arrived just at the time when the 20th Party Congress was in session. This was the first time I learned the hard truth about Stalin. And now at the 22nd Congress, as I hear about the disclosed evil deeds and crimes that were committed in the Party with Stalin's knowledge, I wholly and fully endorse the proposal for the removal of Stalin's remains from the Mausoleum.

The great evil caused by Stalin consists not only in the fact that many of our best people perished, not only in the

fact that arbitrary actions were committed and innocent people were shot and imprisoned without trial. This was not all. The entire atmosphere that was created in the Party at that time was totally at variance with the spirit of Lenin. It was out of harmony with the spirit of Lenin.

I should recall only one example that characterizes that atmosphere. In May, 1937, Comrade Zhdanov was Secretary of the Leningrad Province Party Committee. He assembled us executive workers in the province committee and said: "Two enemies—Chudov and Kadatsky—have been exposed in our ranks, in the Leningrad organization. They have been arrested in Moscow." We could not say a word. It was as if our tongues had frozen. But when this meeting was over and Zhdanov was leaving the room, I said to him: "Comrade Zhdanov, I don't know Chudov. He hasn't been in our Leningrad organization long. But I vouch for Kadatsky. He has been a Party member since 1913. I have known him for many years. He is an honest member of the Party. He fought all the oppositionists. This is incredible! It must be verified." Zhdanov looked at me with his cruel eyes and said: "Lazurkina, stop this talk, otherwise it will end badly for you." But I never stopped to think whether it would end well or badly for me when I stood up for the truth. I only thought about whether it was good for the Party or not. (*Stormy, prolonged applause.*)

Under Lenin an atmosphere of friendship, comradeship and mutual faith, support and assistance prevailed in the Party. I recall the years in the underground. When we were arrested, we accepted the accusations without thought in order to protect the organization, to divert the blow from the comrades who had not yet been arrested, to save the underground literature and printshops.

And what was the atmosphere in 1937? Fear, which was uncharacteristic of us Leninists, prevailed. People slandered one another, they lost their faith, they even slandered themselves. Lists of innocent people who were to be arrested were drawn up. We were beaten so that we would slander others. We were given these lists and forced to sign them. They promised to release us and threatened: "If you don't sign, we'll torture you!" But many stood fast; they kept their Bolshevik hearts and never signed anything! (*Prolonged applause.*)

We fought to the end. We did not believe there could be such arbitrariness in our Leninist party. We wrote, wrote endlessly. If one were to look through the files of my letters, he could count volumes. I wrote endlessly to Stalin. I wrote to others also, and I wrote to the Party control body. But unfortunately, even our Party control was not at the proper level at the time; it yielded to the common fear and also refused to consider our cases.

Such was the atmosphere created by the cult of the individual. And we must root out the remnants of it! It is good that the 20th Party Congress raised this question. It is good that the 22nd Party Congress is uprooting these remnants.

I think that our wonderful Vladimir Ilyich, the most human of humans, should not lie beside someone who, although he did service in the past, before 1934, cannot be next to Lenin.

N. S. Khrushchev.—Right! (*Stormy, prolonged applause.*)

D. A. Lazurkina.—Comrades! . . . The only reason I survived is that Ilyich was in my heart, and I sought his advice, as it were. (*Applause.*) Yesterday I asked Ilyich for advice, and it was as if he stood before me alive and said: "I do not like being next to Stalin, who inflicted so much harm on the Party." (*Stormy, prolonged applause.*)

SPEECH BY COMRADE N. V. PODGORNY, UKRAINE COMMUNIST PARTY

Comrades! The delegation of the Ukraine Communist Party wholly and fully supports the proposals submitted by the delegates of the Leningrad and Moscow Party organizations and the Georgian Communist Party. (*Stormy applause.*) This is the unanimous opinion of all the Communists of the Ukraine and of all the Ukrainian people. (*Stormy, prolonged applause.*) . . .

Back in 1956 the Communists and working people of the Soviet Ukraine, like those of the other republics, after familiarizing themselves with the materials of the 20th Party Congress, voiced the opinion that Stalin's remains cannot lie in the V. I. Lenin Mausoleum, a place sacred to the Soviet people and all working people of the world. (*Shouts in the hall: "Right!" Stormy applause.*) But far from everything was yet known at that time. . . .

Discussing the materials of the 22nd Party Congress at numerous meetings and gatherings, the Communists and working people of our country vigorously demand that the organizers of the monstrous crimes—Molotov, Kaganovich and Malenkov—be severely punished. The participants in the meetings consider it inadmissible that the body of Stalin, with whose name is linked so much evil caused to our party, the country and the Soviet people, should lie beside our leader and teacher, the great Lenin, the banner of all the victories of communism. (*Applause.*)

We cannot but heed these entirely correct demands of the Communists and the working people of our entire country. The time has come to restore historical justice! (*Applause.*)

Comrades! Permit me on behalf of the Leningrad and Moscow delegations and the delegations of the Ukraine and

Georgian Communist Parties to submit for your consideration the following draft resolution of the 22nd Party Congress:

"The 22nd Congress of the Communist Party of the Soviet Union resolves:

"1. Henceforth to call the Mausoleum in Red Square at the Kremlin Wall, established to perpetuate the memory of Vladimir Ilyich Lenin, the immortal founder of the Communist Party and Soviet state, the leader and teacher of the working people of the whole world: THE VLADIMIR ILYICH LENIN MAUSOLEUM. (*Stormy, prolonged applause.*)

"2. To recognize as unsuitable the continued retention in the Mausoleum of the sarcophagus with J. V. Stalin's coffin, since the serious violations by Stalin of Lenin's behests, the abuses of power, the mass repression against honest Soviet people and other actions in the period of the cult of the individual make it impossible to leave the coffin with his body in the V. I. Lenin Mausoleum." (*Stormy, prolonged applause.*)

64

"PILFERING THE PEOPLE'S WEALTH"

In May, 1962, the Soviets raised meat and dairy product prices by about 30 per cent to stimulate increased production of these commodities. Our excerpt indicates how some enterprising Soviet citizens took advantage of this new market situation.

It is interesting to note that Soviet trade unions relied on the profit incentive in their proposal to deal with the bread-fed livestock situation. "The Presidium of the Central Council of Trade Unions," wrote *Trud* on September 29, 1962, "has authorized the Central Committee of the Trade Union of State Trade and Consumers' Cooperative Workers to work out a proposal by October 15, 1962, for changing the procedure for awarding bonuses to workers in trade organizations in the sale of grain products so that the wages system will stimulate the economic expenditure of state resources of bread and other foodstuffs and the observance of the established norms per customer for distributing food products."

It is clear that the tendency to self-enrichment on the part of the peasants is nothing new. Said Khrushchev in 1948: "We must bear in mind that the 'little worm' of individual property still sits in the mind of the kolkhoznik. Now as in the past the most important vestigial residue of capitalism in the consciousness of the collective farm peasantry is the tendency to private property." But the Soviets decided to deal with this new form of "parasitism" rather drastically. Article 154-1 of the new Russian Republic Criminal Code provides the following: "The buying up of bread or other grain products for feeding cattle or poultry committed systematically or on a large scale shall be punished by correctional tasks for a term not exceeding one year, or by deprivation of freedom for a term of one to three years with or without confiscation of the cattle."

The full text of the Criminal Code of the Russian Republic which deals with so-called economic crimes is available in Harold Berman, *Soviet Criminal Law and Procedure*. See also R. Beerman, "The Grain Problem and Anti-Speculation Laws," *Soviet Studies*, July, 1967, as well as his "The Parasites Law," *ibid.*, Vol. XIII. On the same subject see Marianne Armstrong, "The Campaign against Parasites," in Peter Juviler and Henry Morton (eds.), *Soviet Policy Making*.

From *Current Digest of the Soviet Press*, XIV, No. 38, 8–9. Published at Columbia University by the Joint Committee on Slavic Studies, appointed by the American Council of Learned Societies and the Social Science Research Council. Copyright, 1962, the Joint Committee on Slavic Studies. Reprinted by permission.

Recent Soviet fiction on farm life includes Fyodor Abramov, *One Day in the "New Life"* (paperback), and Alexander Solzhenitsyn, "Matryona's Home," in Patricia Blake and Max Hayward (eds.), *Halfway to the Moon* (paperback).

For the state of Russian agriculture in recent years see Roy Laird, *Soviet Agriculture and Peasant Affairs*; and two articles by him and Solomon Schwartz in *Problems of Communism*, March–April, 1966. See also Jerzy Karcz, "Khrushchev's Impact on Soviet Agriculture," *Agricultural History*, January, 1966.

For an analysis of the Party program on agriculture see Jerzy Karcz, "The New Soviet Agricultural Program," *Soviet Studies*, October, 1965; and Simon Kabysh, "Soviet Agriculture and the Program," in *The USSR and the Future*, edited by Leonard Schapiro.

For information about the price of meat and other foods see Harry Shaffer (ed.), *The Soviet Economy* (paperback). For a recent Soviet press account see "A Farm's Lucrative Sideline Brings Prosecution," *Current Digest of the Soviet Press*, June 28, 1967.

See also W. Klatt, "Soviet Farm Output and Food Supply in 1970," *St. Antony's Papers*, No. 19 (1966).

YOUR DAILY BREAD

(By Special Correspondent A. Michurin. *Ekonomicheskaya Gazeta*, Sept. 29, 1962, p. 37. Complete text:) The editors received a letter. In the tradition of soldiers, the envelope was folded in a triangle. This would indicate that the writer was a serviceman; however, it did not bear the postmark of a military installation but rather that of the small district center of Teikovo, in Ivanovo Province. Here is what the correspondent, a stranger to us, wrote:

Dear editors: I want to tell you about some facts that deserve attention and the strongest possible condemnation. Many residents of my town and of neighboring villages buy bread to feed to their livestock. Everyone knows what a heroic struggle our people are waging for an upsurge in agriculture, for an abundance of food products. But there are those who do not protect the people's wealth but, on the contrary, pilfer it. My neighbor Suchkova, for instance, though she has a state pension, is engaged in pilfering the state's bread and feeding it to a pig, six sheep and many chickens and ducks. The livestock and poultry that she fattens on this bread she sells at the market for triple prices. I, as a citizen of the Soviet Union, consider that such parasites and grabbers should be severely punished.— V. Golubev, worker in a cotton combine.

*   *   *

Ponder carefully every word of this brief letter. It expresses the inner distress of a man who is sincerely concerned for the homeland's welfare. It also expresses the irate protest of a citizen against the impunity with which some individuals pilfer the people's wealth.

I could not help being stirred by the letter. I left at once to make an on-the-spot check. There are two houses on Zarachenskaya Street in the small city. The first is not large, but it is very light and clean. Not a particle of dust is to be seen on the path that leads from the fence to the porch. The floors of the hallways are covered with clean white mats. One gets the feeling that the inhabitants of this house are people who like order in everything.

Vasily Vasilyevich Golubev is a veteran worker at his plant and a former front-line soldier. He can recall how in the years of the Civil War every ounce of chaff-adulterated grain was precious, how our country struggled for each pood[1] of wheat. Even in the years of the Great Patriotic War there were times in the trenches when a stale crust had to make do for almost an entire unit. For this man, bread is something sacred, a public treasure that no one should dare squander.

"I have appealed to my neighbor's conscience more than once," Vasily Vasilyevich said. "But it has done no good. She won't even listen to me but goes on feeding bread to her livestock."

The house next door is large and sturdy but poorly kept. There is dirt everywhere. From a shed could be heard the grunting of ten poods or so of hog. There were sheep there too. No, this isn't a house for human habitation but a livestock yard of some sort, and a very neglected one at that.

Nadezhda Pavlovna Suchkova has a good pension. She lives with her daughter-in-law, who earns more than 100 rubles a month. Suchkova has extra space, which she regularly rents out. However, this woman's passion for enrichment has gotten the upper hand over all her decent feelings and over her duties as a citizen. Suchkova spends the whole of each day either behind a counter at the market or worrying where to get feed for her many animals. It isn't easy to feed such a herd, but Suchkova has her methods.

Suchkova has a fine television set. She gladly invites her neighbors' children in to watch the programs.

"Enjoy it, children; I'm not selfish," she says sweetly. "But to show your thanks, you can run down to the store and buy me some bread. I'm old, and it isn't easy for me to get around."

So the children go to the store, and each brings back two loaves of rye

bread. And the pig eats the bread.

We aren't against workers' and collective farmers' having their own livestock. But it is intolerable that some livestock owners, in order to take advantage of the high market prices for meat, buy bread, groats and other food products in the stores at low prices and then feed them to their pigs, cows and sheep.

We visited the market in Teikovo. You won't find collective farmers selling meat here; it is local residents who stand behind the counters asking three or three and a half rubles for a kilogram of pork and two rubles or so for ten eggs. There's money in meat. One ruble's worth of bread will feed a pig for a day, and for this it "recompenses" its owner with a kilogram of meat. Figure out the profit for yourself!

In Suchkova's storeroom we saw a sack full of golden wheat and another full of oats.

"I bought it all on the market," she said. "You haven't anything against me."

"But why do you need so much grain?"

"What do you mean, why? For the pig, for the sheep, for the chickens."

Suchkova is far from alone in her "innocent" crime. In the same Teikovo live the sisters A. P. Krutova and A. P. Derbeneva. They have two cows and a heifer, and they feed them on bread. Ye. P. Neburchilova, a resident of the town of Rodniki, has no regular work. She owns a cow, a heifer, 13 chickens and nine ducks. She, too, buys bread to feed them. M. A. Dmitriyev, a stableman for the Furmanov District Young Communist League Committee, maintains a cow, a heifer and two pigs. Twenty loaves of bread were found in his apartment, along with some fodder he had already prepared from bread.

The sale of bread to the population

---

[1] One pood = thirty-six pounds.

in Ivanovo Province has risen greatly in the past few months. For instance, almost 2,000 tons more were sold this July than in July, 1961. In the town of Puchezh the sale of bread rose from 13 tons in the first ten days of July to 23 tons in the first ten days of August. There has also been a sharp increase in the demand for bread in Zavolzhye, Kineshma, Yuryevets and other cities. Even in Ivanovo itself, the sale of bread rose by several hundred tons in a single month.

Needless to say, the population has not suddenly begun consuming more bread and other baked goods. What has happened is that tons, tens of tons and hundreds of tons of bread are being fed to livestock.

The number of people tending their own vegetable gardens and hayfields has declined considerably. After all, this requires time and physical labor. Therefore those who fatten livestock for purposes of enriching themselves prefer to go to the stores and buy cheap bread there.

What measures are being taken against these malicious violators of the state's interests? Unfortunately, any such measures are very passive. According to the Aug. 27, 1956, resolution of the U.S.S.R. Council of Ministers "On Measures for Combating the Expenditure from State Stocks of Bread and Other Food Products To Feed Livestock,"[2] the guilty persons are fined.

But not more than ten persons have been fined in all of Ivanovo Province. No one has been fined for a second time, although the swindlers who have been caught and fined once continue to buy bread. The trade personnel, who are charged with strictly observing the norms for the sale of food products to a single individual, very often violate

2 *Current Digest of the Soviet Press*, VIII, No. 35, 9–11.

these mandatory rules. The sale of five, ten and even more loaves of bread to one person is a very frequent phenomenon.

The province Party committee and the province executive committee know perfectly well that more bread is bought in the province than the citizens could possibly eat. They also know that a great deal of this bread goes for feeding livestock. So far, however, they have done nothing more than talk about this. Only the militia agencies have been charged with the struggle against the pilferers of bread. But where are the Party and Y.C.L. [Young Communist League] *aktivs*, where are the Deputies to the district soviets, the trade union organizations and the other forces of the public? So far, they have held themselves aloof from this important state matter.

Is Ivanovo Province the only place where bread is fed to livestock?

Similar instances, and sometimes even more outrageous ones, occur in Tula, Bryansk and a number of other provinces. It is impossible to read without heartsickness a letter from Valentina Pavlovna Banchenko, a resident of the settlement of Mine No. 13 in Tula Province. She writes:

It is painful to see what happens to the grain grown with so much exertion by the collective farmers. I have been standing in line for the second day to get bread, but I cannot buy any because the same people purchase several times their quotas, making even small children and old people hardly able to walk stand in the queue for them. This bread is fed to livestock. Is it really impossible to stop this? We have been to the mine committee, but it has done nothing.

Comrades, the activities of the people who feed bread to livestock must somehow be stopped. My husband works in the mine, and I have two children; I cannot stand in line from six o'clock in the morning— it would be cruel to drag the children along, as I would have to do. I beg that you will enlist the local militia agencies and people's volunteer detachments in the struggle against pilferers of bread and will fine certain people who have been caught on several occasions buying up bread, and I think matters will straighten out. Please forgive me for troubling you, but this is a vital matter for us.

"A vital matter for us—." How can it be that the mine's trade union committee and Party organization paid no attention to the warning signal from a simple woman? How can it be that they reconciled themselves to the pilfering of the people's wealth, that they could look calmly upon the queues at the bread stores? Aren't these queues the result of the inaction of the local agencies of authority, do they not constitute tacit support of the speculators on the part of the public? How could the district Party committee remain indifferent to these facts?

The bureau of the Tula Province Party Committee recently considered the question of violations of state discipline in the expenditure of market flour stocks for baking bread and instances of the use of bread for feeding livestock. At the request of the militia administration, the province executive committee adopted a decision. However, so far there has been no improvement in the situation. The sale of bread to the population continued to rise in September. Apparently, a poor job is done in Tula Province to expose people who larcenously destroy bread products. But there are many such people in the province. For instance, N. T. Lantsov, a sawyer at the Kosogorsk Metallurgical Plant, earns 100 rubles a month. His family consists of only two people. But he has two brood sows weighing 11 to 12 poods each and three piglets of two to three poods each. Recently Lantsov slaughtered a pig and sold it. In his house

were discovered eleven loaves of rye bread, 80 kg. of flour, 30 kg. of wheat and ten kg. of barley. Sirkin, a resident of the city of Klimovo, has a brood sow, 12 piglets and one pedigreed boar. He too feeds them on bread.

Not once have the trade personnel informed the local militia agencies about people who buy more bread than they are entitled to.

Some Bryansk Province trade workers violate the Ministry of Trade's norms for the sale of grain products without a twinge of conscience. For instance, Sadovnikov, a salesclerk at Store No. 12 of the Delicatessen Office, sold 1,216 kg. of flour to eleven customers for feeding to livestock. Yeliseyeva, manager of a mobile store operated by the workers' supply department of the Shchekino Gas Construction Trust, sold as much as three sacks of flour per person in the Karachev District village of Babinko. Lysenko, manager of another of the workers' supply department's mobile stores, sold two truckloads of flour in the village of Trykovka for feeding to animals, and she too would sell several sacks of flour to a single person. Tolkacheva, manager of a store of the same workers' supply department, sold more than 10,000 kg. of flour for livestock food.

So much for illustrations. The list could be continued, but it is not the point of this article to name all the already known grabbers and speculators. It is much more important to ponder how to cut out at the roots this evil that causes our society such colossal material and moral damage. Should we raise grain and bread prices, and thus deprive the speculators of the economic basis for their crimes? No, such a path would not be to the public benefit. Speculators would still be speculators, but millions of honest working people would suffer.

The state can not take such a step. Therefore other ways must be found.

Unfortunately, the measures our legislation provides for influencing people who feed bread to livestock for their personal gain are too liberal. People infected with the disease of money grubbing aren't likely to be "re-educated" through fines. Honest working people—grain farmers, factory workers, engineers, people in all occupations—are insistently demanding that the greedy hands of the speculators be struck a hard blow. It would appear that stronger sanctions are needed. We already have a law confiscating the dishonestly earned property of bribers and money-grubbers. People who engage in transforming bread into livestock fodder for purposes of personal enrichment and speculation must also be deprived of their property.

The Ministries of Trade must also take decisive measures. No one who squanders bread should be permitted to work in a store!

The ground must be knocked from under the speculators' feet. Manifestations of indifference and liberalism in this question must become a subject for special consideration in Party and soviet agencies. This is a vital cause for every soviet person.[3]

[3] [A year went by, and the situation did not improve. It was time for more drastic action which came in the form of decrees of the Presidium of the Supreme Soviet of the RSFSR, dated May 6, 1963. These established norms for the ownership of livestock by families not belonging to the collective farm system. Such families could own a maximum of one cow and one calf as well as one pig or three sheep. For ownership of animals in excess of these norms the tax would be 150 rubles per year per cow, 55 rubles per year per pig, and 15 rubles per year per sheep. First violations would be subject to fines of 10–50 rubles; second violations would be punished by corrective labor or deprivation of freedom for a period of up to three years. The text of the decrees is reprinted in the *Current Digest of the Soviet Press*, XV, No. 22, 25–26.—ED.]

65

FROM NEW YORK TO LOS ANGELES

By G. Burkov and V. Shchetinin

Every October and November delegations of student leaders are exchanged between the Soviet Union and the United States. The groups usually number about
thirty and remain in the host country for one month. On this side the exchange is
sponsored by the Department of State in co-operation with several American youth
organizations which serve as hosts.

The article reprinted below in its entirety is a description of the Soviet visit
which took place in the fall of 1960 by two of its participants. It is an interesting
sample of Soviet writing about America. The piece appeared in the Soviet monthly
Molodoi Kommunist (Young Communist), the official organ of the Komsomol, the
most important Soviet youth organization. Some 90 per cent of Soviet youth belong
to the Komsomol.

For a study of Soviet views of the United States during the Stalin era, see
Frederick Barghoorn, *The Soviet Image of the United States.* For the same writer's
analysis of the present cultural exchange between the two countries, see his *The
Soviet Cultural Offensive.* An annotated translation of the section on American
history in the *Great Soviet Encyclopedia* is available under the title *A Soviet View
of the American Past* (Madison, Wis., 1961). A similar insight can be found in the
article "A Soviet View of Six Great Americans," *American Heritage,* October, 1960,
pp. 64–74. See also Oliver Jensen, *America and Russia.* For a recent estimate of
the role of tourism see M. Moody, "Travel and Tourism," *Problems of Communism,* November–December, 1964. A refreshingly different Soviet description
of a visit to the United States is Victor Nekrasov, *Both Sides of the Ocean* (available in abridged form in Patricia Blake and Max Hayward (eds.), *Halfway to
the Moon* (paperback). Standard Soviet reporting on America is available in
every issue of the weekly *Current Digest of the Soviet Press.* The screening of
tourists leaving the USSR is described in Yury Krotkov, *I Am From Moscow.*

At the end of the last year, at the invitation of the Council on Student Travel, a
group of Soviet youths visited the U.S.A.
The group was made up of young men
and women from various cities of the
Soviet Union: Moscow, Kiev, Tiflis,
Baku, Sverdlovsk, Kharkov, Dneprope-
trovsk. The professional composition of
the group was varied: there were young

engineers, scientific workers, journal-
ists, leaders of youth organizations, and
others. Upon arriving in the United
States, we were divided into two sub-
groups: the first travelled in the northeast, and visited Durham, Burlington,

From *Molodoi Kommunist* (Moscow), March,
1961, pp. 92–104. Trans. Jean Laves Hellie.

Boston, and Cleveland, while the second visited the middle west—Dearborn, Detroit, Chicago, and also the small university town of Beloit, Wisconsin. Subsequently meeting in Los Angeles, both groups ended their journey with a train trip to Washington, D.C., and New York, after which they returned home.

The program of our visit in the U.S.A. provided for a stay in American families, getting acquainted with student life, visiting industrial enterprises, meeting business leaders and government and party representatives, acquaintance with the activities of the UN, and also a visit to the most interesting places along the itinerary.

However, most memorable were the unplanned and unforeseen meetings with Americans representing various strata of society and different positions, with people of all sorts of religious denominations and beliefs. Now that we are home again we think of them with great gratitude since they enabled us to get to know America as well as possible, to see and hear more, to understand the way Americans live, and their aspirations and hopes. We did not agree with all with whom we spoke, some things seemed strange to us, and much seemed alien and unacceptable, but along with this there was much that was useful. The main thing was that, having covered many thousands of kilometers over a period of one month, having visited, in essence, the farthest eastern and western points of that large country, we were glad to have personal experience of the hospitality, cordiality, and peaceful character of its people.

Even several months after our return from the United States, we remember the meetings with many Americans and are more and more convinced of the benefit of such mutual visits. We tried as much as possible to answer those questions which trouble the American people, to tell them about the life and affairs of the Soviet people, about our working days and happy holidays. But such meetings were also useful for us: they allowed us to better value the advantages of the socialist system, the grandeur of those huge achievements which our people have reached and to which we have simply become accustomed, feeling that it cannot be otherwise.

"WE WANT TO KNOW THE TRUTH ABOUT YOU"

"Please, come and visit me"—a rather short, well-built student pulls us by the sleeve. We are in a hurry, but how can one really refuse when asked so sincerely? We enter a small room of the dormitory. There we see the student disorder to which we are accustomed, the scattered books and outlines. Exams are close at hand. We naturally do not confine ourselves to the allotted time, the conversation lasts a long time, and when we finally must take leave of our host— his name is U. Wagner—he gives us as a goodbye present a book of Goya's, "The Horrors of War," with eighty-five reproductions of the anti-war work of this great Spanish artist. "We are against this," says Wagner, showing us the title. "Let us prevent this together," we answer.

We had conversations—and there were many of them—about all sorts of subjects, but the center of attention invariably focused upon questions about politics and international relations and questions about war and peace. Nothing is more important for all people on any continent than guaranteeing peace on earth and safeguarding peoples from the horrible dangers of atomic war. The anxiety of Americans over the fate of peace during these conversations is particularly understandable if one takes into account that we came to the U.S.A. at a time when that power found itself compromised by policies of military ventures and the provocations of the Republican government of Eisenhower and Nixon. In particular, not long before we came to the U.S.A., supplementary military orders were made by the government in the amount of two billion dollars.

Meanwhile, the majority of the American people demanded that a different policy be carried out. The people were tired of a policy of "balancing on the brink of war" and "atomic blackmail" which guaranteed profits for the monopolists but did not defend the toilers from the oppressive consequences of the fourth postwar recession on record. The people of the U.S.A. needed the kind of program that would have guaranteed it employment and furthered the rise in minimum wages and pensions. Around the time of our arrival in America the unemployed numbered 4.5 million. Right before the change in the administration there were 5.5 million, but Eisenhower continued to maintain that 1960 was a "year of prosperity." And he said this when 15 million families were badly housed or completely without housing.

We must recognize that one would have to spend many billions of dollars in order to solve vital problems. Such sums—and ordinary Americans understand this well—may be obtained by only one means—that is: by decreasing the burden of military expenditures. From conversations with many Americans we were left with the firm conviction that the overwhelming majority of them would gladly uphold such a decision.

Under circumstances of war hysteria which prevailed in the United States during the Republican administration, it was government policy to teach people to fear the Soviet Union. At Wayne State University in Detroit, for example, on the stairs, by the entrance to the elevator, and in other places instructions were hanging telling what one must do and where to run in case of atomic alarm. "Ten short signals—everyone to the basement shelter, two long ones—danger is past." Even in elementary schools where carefree children study, at the child's eye level, hangs the following sinister announcement: "In the event of air attack, form a line and go out of the classroom, keeping to the left side." When we told the American teachers what kind of harm such instructions do to the upbringing of the younger generation, they made a helpless gesture, as if to say, "What can you do—do you think we thought this up?"

Significantly, the ordinary people of America talked and argued with us as a rule only about methods of guaranteeing peace, feeling that the preservation of peace is the main problem of governments and peoples. From conversations with them we were left with the firm conviction that the overwhelming majority of Americans, despite reactionary propaganda, consider the suggestions of the Soviet government on disarmament reasonable, and hope and sincerely wish that our peoples might live in peace and friendship. We heard quite a few good words about the address of the Chairman of the Council of Ministers of the U.S.S.R., N. S. Khrushchev. America well remembers the meeting with the head of the Soviet government at the time of his trip to the U.S.A. in 1959. In the course of conversations and meetings many spoke of the visit of N. S. Khrushchev to the U.S.A. for the General Assembly of the UN in 1960, spoke in different ways, often argued, but the main thing was that no one remained indifferent. The problems to which the head of the Soviet delegation gave clear and convincing answers troubled everyone. The ordinary Americans noted that the vivid appearance of N. S. Khrushchev at the

General Assembly in defense of the interests of the people demonstrated to the whole world and particularly to the new members of the UN how necessary it is to uphold the interests of peace and carry on a sharp political struggle. Many Americans asked us to bring greetings to Nikita Sergeevich Khrushchev, wishing him good health.

Another matter concerns the officials of government institutions who resigned from the Eisenhower administration. Our differences with them were fundamental. Since they were bound by their official positions and therefore reflected the official policies of the Eisenhower-Nixon government, none of them would admit that war should be excluded from the life of a society as a means of solving international questions. Particularly frank was Adler, former president Eisenhower's adviser on currency and finance questions, who plainly stated to us the strategy of "balancing on the brink of war." In Adler's words, according to the Eisenhower method, international questions were solved by the American government as follows: two positions were reported to the president of which one was chosen—either more advantageous or less dangerous. Thus it was, for example, according to Adler's assertions, in the solution of the question of rearming West Germany. "We thought a long time about whether or not to let Germany rearm," said Adler. "We understood that arming Germany is evil, but less so than having the powerful Soviet Union dominate(?) Europe. Therefore, out of fear of the U.S.S.R.(!) we decided to rearm Germany."

In Adler's words, it is impossible to prevent calls to a new war and military propaganda in the U.S.A. because that would supposedly violate "free speech." In essence, this means that if you raise a false fire alarm in the theatre, you'll

be arrested, while people thirsting for blood and brandishing atomic bombs can live peacefully, not fearing prosecution by the law. Therefore, to tell the truth, it was pleasant to read in the newspapers that one of the first steps of the new Kennedy administration was to lay down controls on statements by zealous generals who very often make the international situation worse with their rash speeches.

On the whole Americans are not badly informed about our scientific and technological achievements. We were often asked questions indicative of the great interest which leads many scientific and practical workers to the various investigations carried out in our country. "We were overconfident for a long time," one of them told us. "And here is the result—in a series of fields we have come out behind. We should teach each other more." But at the same time we often met sheer misunderstanding about the principles of our foreign and internal policies, and ignorance of the elementary things in our life.

"We thought that in your country only Communists could elect and be elected to governmental posts" (J. Wagner, a woman student at the University of Chicago).

"I thought that the Soviet government forbade jazz" (J. Hammen from Dearborn).

"Is there really no racial discrimination in the U.S.S.R.?" (J. Watts, union worker at the "River Rouge" Ford plant).

And what numberless questions there were beginning with the words: "But do you have . . . ?" and then there would no longer be conversation but instead continuous mutual bewilderment. But it is impossible to judge the whole American people by these questions. We repeat, in America there are many people who try more or less carefully to follow the developments in our country. In conversations with us many Americans tried to find out the truth about the life of the Soviet people, about the position and rights of young people, about the progress of the U.S.S.R. in all areas of economic and cultural life, about our system of higher education, and so on. Americans asked particularly many questions about communism, about how we imagine life in a new society, and whether the Soviets intend to "spread the communist system in other countries by force of arms."

As counter-measures to the growing interest of the common people of America in the Soviet Union imperialist circles have worked out and put into practice a complex system of misinforming Americans: of creating in them a false conception of our country; of the measures of the Communist Party and the Soviet government making possible the great rise in the standard of living of the people; of the position advanced by N. S. Khrushchev on the question of the fight for peace and universal disarmament, for the liquidation of colonialism, and so on and so forth. One could distinguish three directions in which imperialist propaganda carries out "preventive" work among the American people.

First is hushing up. There is no proposal for disarmament and there is no peaceful initiative on the part of the U.S.S.R. There is nothing—period! The method is simple, but, in the opinion of those circles who are not interested in relaxing international tension it is the correct one, leading to the misinformation of the ordinary American who is inexperienced in politics.

Away from the urban centers a person can read his newspaper regularly and in the course of a week not meet one single piece of information about the Soviet Union and about its foreign

and internal policy. And not only is this true in the rural areas. Several days before our departure from the U.S.A., N. S. Khrushchev's answers to the *Pravda* correspondent on the questions of disarmament were published in the Soviet press. At that time Khrushchev clearly told the governments of the western powers: accept our plan for disarmament and we will accept your plan for control. The American newspapers hushed up this fact. And indeed, dozens of times Americans told us that the matter of disarmament supposedly depends now on the Soviet Union and on her refusal to accept an "effective plan" of controls.

Second is the deliberate distortion of facts, presenting them in such a spirit as to leave the reader with a false impression of our country and her foreign policy.

Here is an example. On November 7, the day of the 43rd anniversary of the Great October Socialist Revolution, we were visiting the editorial office of the Chicago newspaper *The Sun-Times*. The next day's edition was prepared. Material from Moscow about the parade in Red Square was being published in it. The headline was remarkable: "The shortest war parade." Such a headline, even if only to a small degree, nevertheless reflected the ceaseless efforts of our country to relax international tensions. What was our surprise the next morning when we saw a completely different headline! Evidently, the editors of the newspaper, supporting Nixon and with him the course of preserving and aggravating tensions, reset the type and gave the article a new title: "The most powerful rockets in recent years in Red Square."[1] Of course, such a headline

[1] A thorough check of microfilms of the *Chicago Sun-Times* for Tuesday, November 8, 1960, reveals no such headline. On page 8 of the "Final Home Edition" for that date is the fol-

was calculated for an entirely different effect.

Or another example. During five days the spy Mark Kaminsky, caught red-handed in the border area of the U.S.S.R. in the summer of 1960 and not sent to jail thanks only to the charity of Soviet organs, set forth his ideas in his "memoirs" on the pages of Detroit newspapers. People like Kaminsky without a twinge of conscience lie, pour dirt on the foreign policy of the Soviet government, substitute their "personal impressions" for the true state of affairs in the U.S.S.R., and draw an unpleasant picture of our people. At this time we were living with American families—one with the family of the engineer Swanzig, another with the family of the radio-technician Hills; and we were happy to see that these people, our hospitable hosts, felt awkward before us for this gross lie which came out in print.

Third: taking into account the huge and constantly growing interest of the ordinary Americans, particularly the youth, in Marxism-Leninism, pamphlets of all sorts of renegades or "popularizer"-falsifiers of the type of Schumann, Fischer, and others are palmed off on them. The extent of this ideological diversion is all the more significant because quite a number of students from the young Asian and African countries are studying in the U.S.A., and the people of these countries regard the advice of western powers to build their social and economic life on capitalist principles more sceptically.

Conversing with many Americans, we understood well that the imperialists fear not some kind of "special propaganda" about our country, about us, the Soviet people, but precisely the truth about Soviet life. And our group tried as far as possible to bring this truth to the American people.

THE AMERICAN PEOPLE WANT CHANGES

On the first Tuesday after the first Monday in November each leap year the presidential election takes place in the United States. In 1960 the election was on November 8, which coincided with our stay in the U.S.A. We could observe the pre-election struggle, the course of the elections, and also the reaction of the Americans to the results of the voting.

Even the first minutes of our stay on American soil engage us in the heated atmosphere of the pre-election stir. Our bus forces its way with difficulty through the crowds of people, going to the pre-election meeting of Kennedy, who is appearing this evening in New York. Near the Henry Hudson Hotel where we were staying, posters pasted on huge panels announce "Nixon-Lodge. The main thing is experience" (an allusion to the experience of both candidates, in contrast to Kennedy, in solving international questions). It is clear that the Republicans also do not sit with hands folded.

The Democratic and Republican parties literally flooded the country with pre-election literature, which, as we were told, basically repeats itself from election to election. If one were to judge by the leaflets distributed, then each candidate for the presidency promised his electorate "prosperity," "freedom," "democracy," and "peace." The respective parties praised Kennedy and Nixon

---

lowing headline: "Russia Cuts Short Military Parade." On page 6 of the "Final Edition" for the same date the headline for a similar article reads: "Russia Displays 2 New Missiles in 43rd Anniversary Parade." Nor can any such headline be found in the *Sun-Times* for either Monday, November 7, 1960, or Wednesday, November 9, 1960. Furthermore, the position of the article in both November 8 editions can hardly be called inflammatory, nor can the size of the typeface used. In both cases the foreign news was eclipsed by the domestic presidential election. [Translator's note.]

as the most suitable candidates for the leadership of America in the 1960's. "Your vote should belong to the Democrats," asserted one brochure. Another named ten reasons why the nation "needs" Nixon. Many voters wore badges with pictures of the candidate and their families. But there was also the following badge: "We don't want either Nixon or Kennedy." We saw a slogan pasted on an automobile: "The nation needs Nixon like a hole in the head." Among the students there were those who would have preferred to see as president of the U.S.A. the bear-cub Pooh, who is popular among American children.

Even American children became instruments of the pre-election fight—they distributed badges and leaflets with appeals to vote for one or another candidate. In the newspaper *The Daily Defender* of November 7 we saw a photo of a little Negro girl. With pleading eyes she looked at the readers. "Vote for Kennedy!" read the caption. The families of the candidates, their wives and relatives were not left out either—they took an active part in the pre-election fight.

Some voters said that they would give their vote to the candidate whose appearance they liked better. Thus, one woman student from the University of Vermont told us that she was voting for Kennedy only because he is "more handsome than Nixon." The newspaper *Detroit News* of October 31 put a photograph on the first page with the caption: "There is no harmony at home." The smiling husband, it appears, is for Kennedy, while the beaming wife is an admirer of Nixon's.

But it would be, apparently, false to judge American elections solely by these external signs. The majority of the people voted in 1960 against the hated "cold war," against the Eisenhower-Nixon policies which brought on the

aggravation of international conditions and the worsening of the position of the wide mass of toilers. In the statement of Congressman Powell which came out in the press, it was said, for example, that Nixon "voted six times against building houses for people with low incomes, countless times against the liquidation of slums and building houses for people of middle income, four times against rent control, nine times against price control; he voted against a system of social security and the payment of unemployment compensation, and against raising the minimum wage from 50 to 75 cents an hour, even when Senator Taft voted in support of this law."

Giving their votes to Kennedy, many millions of Americans clearly expressed their desire to seek ways toward relaxing international tensions and a decrease in the burden of defense expenditures.

A not unimportant factor in securing Kennedy's victory was his promise to put an end to the situation under which there exist in the U.S.A. "second-class citizens"—Negroes, Mexicans, Puerto Ricans, and so on. "The chances of a Negro to finish high school," said Kennedy at a meeting in Harlem, "constitute at most only 60 per cent of the chances of a white person, to enter college—one third, to own his own house—one third, to educate his children—even less. As a rule he has no chance to be elected to the federal circuit court."

Very many Americans expressed the hope that as a result of Kennedy's victory new people would come to leadership of the country who could more flexibly and intelligently build the foreign policy of the U.S.A. and that this in turn would lead to the improvement of American-Soviet relations, to the lessening of international tension, and to the solution of many acute problems in the internal life of the country. During a meeting with us the the Democratic Senator E. Kefauver declared that in his opinion the relations between the U.S.S.R. and the U.S.A. can be improved and that we should meet to discuss concrete means.

THE STANDARD OF LIVING OF THE "AVERAGE AMERICAN"

The highpoint of our tour was, of course, life in an American family. "The family is the basis of society"— that is the motto of the organization "Experiment in International Living" which set up our program and the representative of which accompanied us during our trip. It is true, the families with whom we lived had means above "average," but this on the whole did not change the problems which they faced, along with Americans of average income.

At the outset we would like to note the great cordiality and hospitality which was shown to us in these families which acted as our hosts. These acquaintanceships were characteristically easy and unconstrained so that we were permitted to carry on frank conversations and useful discussions.

Acquaintanceship with the standard of living somehow always begins with showing goods and material objects, although from time immemorial it is well known that man is not satisfied by bread alone. The Americans especially liked to show what they had achieved in the area of the application to home life of all kinds of technical devices and instruments. Among them were constructions which had been solved with great technical cleverness. We gave due credit to American engineering ideas. We also liked the application in the home of plastics and cardboards of the most varied appearances. This is very economical and convenient.

Examining the American apartment houses we noticed the use made of basement and semi-basements. With the aid of all possible decorations, these tradi-

tional storage facilities are adapted for recreation. In some homes there is billiard or table tennis equipment; in others stands a television set, which one can watch while drinking tea and talking.

American food is somewhat unusual, if only because of the small consumption of bread, but there is something that one should note here. For example, on an American table one can often see tastily and appetizingly prepared dishes of corn. One would think that our cooks would have something to learn here. The housewives' labor is considerably lightened by the use of precooked foods. Once—this was in Detroit—our hostess, the hospitable Irene Hills, prepared before our very eyes a three-course dinner in literally a quarter of an hour. We welcomed such economical use of one's time.

While we estimate such phenomena at their own worth and recognize that they will undoubtedly come into our life in the next few years, we nevertheless fully realized their relationship to the system under which things are valued above all, and not man. And indeed even Americans themselves told us that most of them could reach a certain well-being only at the cost of enormous overexertion of effort during the course of a large part of their lives. We saw excellent illustrations for the chapter of Karl Marx's *Kapital* devoted to the fetishism of goods. A thing serves not so much aesthetic or utilitarian purposes but rather as a guarantee, a security, or an indispensable condition for future existence, as a means of guaranteeing life in old age. "Up to the age of thirty we create the bases of our living conditions, up to the age of fifty we work in the name of these very conditions, but after fifty—we live," sadly punned one American, who invited us once to dinner.

In fact, up to the age of thirty or thirty-five many Americans subordinate their entire lives to the creation of "conditions" under which they can buy a house, a television set, a refrigerator, etc., on installment. Not by chance are late marriages quite common, since quite a number of people cannot afford the luxury of having a family until a certain amount of money has been accumulated or until some other form of the basis of "material well-being" has been created.

When we asked Stanley Ranishevsky, the chairman of the labor dispute committee at the Ford plant in Detroit what is, in his opinion, the chief problem which faces the ordinary American, he, without even thinking, answered, "Uncertainty about tomorrow."

Here are several examples of the so-called "average" budget of American families. Actually, this budget for 1500 to 2000 dollars is better than "average," if one is to believe official statistics, but in the present case this is not important.

The family of a radio-technician lives in its "own" house, for which it still must pay for thirteen years. They bought the house not long ago and before that lived in a trailer. Now the basic goal in life is to "hold out" for these 13 years, to acquire, in the full sense of this word, their own house. And then. . . . But what "then"? He is 41, she is 38, there are no children. Their whole life has gone by in order to make their existence secure, to "buy happiness." Isn't the price high, after all? Under a comparatively high wage the "owner" of the house is forced to constantly look for additional sources of income: to repair television sets, or buy worthless cars and then, after repairing them, resell them.

Here is another example—the family of a government employee. Both the husband and wife work, both are young, they haven't any children. The house in which the couple lives was bought by the husband's mother on installment. She gave it to her son without having paid the whole amount. The couple must pay her 1000 dollars yearly until the whole debt of twenty-seven thousand is paid off. Besides going to work or staying at home they hardly ever do anything. They rarely go to the movies or to the theatre. They spend the evenings either watching television or listening to records. Even though they have no children they spend money very economically, limiting themselves mainly to food. They speak very guardedly about politics, being very careful, trying to avoid sharp questions.

The family of an engineer. In contrast to the first two families, here there are five children—almost a whole volleyball team. The husband is past forty; the wife is not forty yet, but she looks as though she weren't more than twenty-eight or twenty-nine. American women assiduously take care of their faces and figures. But their hands are working ones —with broken nails, cracked, with coarse skin. Of course—the "average budget" is fine on paper, but to live under it is considerably harder. With a yearly wage of seven thousand dollars in the course of twenty years they must pay thirty thousand for the house. After making the payment on the house and the real estate tax (still for the same house!), which goes for the upkeep of schools and for municipal needs, the family has about five thousand dollars left. Out of this money about a thousand dollars is spent for transportation and maintaining the car, 800 dollars for clothes, and 280 dollars for lighting, heating, and other municipal services. That leaves 2500 dollars, i.e., seven dollars a day for food for a family of 7 people. In practice, less is spent on food because one must always put away some money for a "rainy day." These figures differ somewhat from official calculations to a greater or lesser extent, but then official statistics deal with so-called average data.

A heavy burden for the American family is payment for medical services. A stay in the hospital comes to twenty dollars a day for the patient, not counting medicines, various analyses and other services. Blood analysis costs five dollars, an electrocardiogram eight to ten dollars, an X-ray ten dollars. An appendectomy is 250 to 300 dollars. The high cost of having a delivery obliges many women to deliver on the street, even in taxis, receiving for this the services of policemen who go through special training.

The preceding examples concern American families who receive roughly six or seven thousand dollars a year. But indeed many, very many, Americans do not receive such income. For confirmation we refer to a man whose adherence to the "American way of life" cannot be doubted. We refer to the executive secretary of the AFL–CIO, George Meany. Appearing before the Senate Labor and Welfare Committee, Meany said that at least twenty million American workers "find themselves in a state of continual poverty or worse than poverty. . . . They cannot afford good housing, enough clothes and in many cases enough food." Meany recognized that the calculations of bourgeois statistics, declaring that in the U.S.A. there supposedly exists "the highest standard of living in their world," conceal the real position of the toilers.

As acknowledged by Meany, "at least 20 million American workers are left to their own resources. Many of them earn even less than one dollar an hour." Consequently, notes G. Meany, "we have created in our society a continually growing group which can be called the 'working poor'—millions of men and women who carry out useful work but who are doomed to live in poverty all their lives."

The "colored population" is in a particularly difficult position. Even in the northeast and middle west, in states where Negroes are not subject to such discrimination as in the southern states, inequality of rights of the colored population with the white is sharply felt. Discrimination is evident even in the capital of the U.S.A., Washington. Negroes are employed in the dirtiest, hardest work. They live in the less well-built parts of towns. In recent years payment for Negro labor has gone up somewhat, but the system of social injustice and discrimination against the "colored population" is preserved as before.

Racial discrimination is one of the most characteristic features of contemporary America. In recent years in the U.S.A. all sorts of enlightened organizations have begun to be created, proclaiming as their goal the liquidation, as they say, of "national hostility" and the creation of "a single society." We visited one of these—The Chicago Urban League. It is founded on a so-called "interracial basis"—that is, both white and black are represented in it. What is the goal of this organization? According to its bylaws it is "the achievement of equal opportunities for all under equal division of responsibility by all." The bylaws explain that by equality is implied not equalization of people, not just allocation to them of opportunity, not bringing them to the same level, but helping each one to achieve his own level.

"Excuse me, but what is discrimination? How do you intend to fight it?" we ask the leaders of the organization.

"You see," they answer us, "racial discrimination has basically cultural and psychological motives. Many whites and blacks do not believe in racial equality. We have the goal of convincing them that they are equal and of helping the Negroes to get education and fair work."

"Well, but how do you work—that is, excuse me, convince people?"

Apparently there are four ways of working.

First, research. The League provides the population with "facts" which must help toward "thoughtful understanding" of interracial problems.

Second, employment. The League tries to secure the "development" and full utilization of the potential working force. Now the matter is becoming clearer. Big business needs more qualified but cheap working hands.

Third, health and welfare. The League considers it its goal to further the improvement of living conditions, safeguarding health and a system of education for all.

Fourth, citizen responsibility. The League stands for the education of citizens in civic duty.

"Whom do you try to convince of being equal?"

"Both the whites and the Negroes, but more the Negroes."

"But wouldn't it be better to fight for the adoption of a law which would prohibit racial discrimination?"

"But that would infringe upon freedom of conscience. It is necessary to prepare the ground, persuade everybody, and then secure this legally."

Leaving the meeting, we understood that the League does definite positive work, spreading facts about the difficult position of the Negroes in Chicago. But this is so little, and the main thing is that it does not lead to a solution of the Negro problem in the U.S.A.

The millions of Puerto Ricans who live in special neighborhoods are in an even more grievous position. They speak Spanish. Ignorance of English not only prevents them from taking part in the political and social life of the country, but also creates insuperable difficulties in their preparation for work, and in entering various educational institutions, beginning with elementary school.

Naturally, we were interested in how American toilers can defend their rights and what role labor unions play in this regard. In conversations with union workers, particularly at the "River Rouge" Ford plant in Detroit, we saw how restricted union rights are in the United States of America. Practically, unions do not have the right to interfere with the solution of the most important questions which concern workers, and above all questions of hiring and firing. The union can only carry on negotiations about pay and protection of workers' labor. According to the collective agreement signed with the Ford Administration, the final analysis of labor conflicts is left not to the union but to special mediators paid by the employer. Recreational organizations for workers, social security, and other questions are outside the sphere of the union. Nor can women expecting a baby count on help.

Paul Boatin, a member of the executive committee of the union at the "River Rouge" plant, told us that at Ford plants, as at many enterprises in the U.S.A., the workers are slaves of seniority, companies and unions. Seniority determines whether or not the worker will remain at the plant in case of reduced production and the decrease in staff connected with it. To receive a pension one must have a long period of service of work at a given company and belong to the union of that company.

The assurance of American propaganda that the unemployed in the U.S.A. are those who change jobs in search of better ones is laughable after hearing this. When we said this to Paul Boatin he burst out laughing. "You don't say! The main thing is to keep a job, to hang on to it. To hold out there until you get a pension. All one's efforts are directed toward this." And as though summing up our observations, it happened that we talked with a worker whose parents still live in Yugoslavia. He came up to us on one of the streets in Los Angeles which, in imitation of the well-known New York Street, is named Broadway. Stringing together in one sentence Serbian, Polish, Czech, Russian and English words, the worker quickly said with emotion, "You can't imagine how terrible it is to live here. Here they could kill you and no one would move a finger to save you. You'll die of hunger, but they won't give you a piece of bread. Here it's everyone for himself. . . . They squeeze the juice out and then throw you out the gates. Live as you can, if you survive. That's the kind of life we have." It was hard to add anything to his words.

During our stay we also became acquainted with the cultural life of the American people. After all, this is an important, integral aspect which also characterizes the living standard of the people. Although living conditions do not promote the diffusion of culture, we were glad to see that many Americans try to enrich themselves with real cultural values. In New York we heard a concert by the Philadelphia Symphony Orchestra under the direction of E. Ormandy, who is known to the Soviet public. The concert was dedicated to the 25th anniversary of his conductorship. In the huge Carnegie Hall there was nowhere to drop so much as an apple, as the saying goes. In Chicago we were also once in a concert hall filled to overflowing. The listeners came to acquaint themselves with the works of medieval composers.

Many Americans are interested in art. We saw people eager to visit art galleries. For example, during our stay in Chicago the Corot exhibition opened. In the National Gallery in Washington magnificent examples of world art are housed.

In the case of movies the situation is worse: movie theatres, as far as we could tell, are attended less well—evidently because of the quality of the products they show.

Acquaintance with the standard of living of the "average American" showed that the product of capitalism—uncertainty about tomorrow—is a heavy scourge for millions of toilers who more and more realize the injustice of the exploitation system.

MEETING AMERICAN STUDENTS

We had many interesting and instructive meetings with American students. As a rule, these meetings took place under unofficial circumstances, and this helped both sides to have frank and unconstrained conversation. Students of the University of Chicago noted that as far as the State Department (first headed by J. F. Dulles and later by C. Herter) was concerned, their age is the most dangerous. Up to the age of twenty-five people are particularly keenly concerned with the world around them. It was therefore not by chance, the students told us, that the Eisenhower administration did not like to send to the U.S.S.R. young people between the ages of twenty and twenty-five, giving preference either to "green youths" or to people older than twenty-five, who have established views and who have "settled down."

The students of America, like students of any other country, are inquisitive, and it must be added, great debaters. At times their arguments are naive, in many cases called forth either by ignorance of the subject or by false information, but the majority of them really wanted to find out the truth about the U.S.S.R. It often happened, when we came home late at night to the dormitory, that we found groups of students who came to talk with us at the door of our room. The conversations continued till long after midnight.

Receiving a higher education in the U.S.A. is an especially difficult problem for many Americans, above all because of the high cost of tuition, particularly in the nation's private colleges and universities. In many cases this predetermines the social composition of the student body and closes the doors of universities to a large part of the youth. Many students are forced to work during vacations as well as during the year, even if only in order to pay expenses partially. In the university town of Durham, for example, one can see advertisements such as: "I can work as a nursemaid, tell stories to little children, read books." Then follows the student's name and his address. In Chicago we lived in the room of the student Mike Stoken. Every summer he gets behind the steering wheel of an automobile, earning his living. One could continue a list of such examples without end.

The high cost of tuition is also one of the reasons for the big number of student dropouts. We were told that several universities graduate not more than forty-five per cent of those entering the first year. Besides that, not all students are in a position to stand a big load consisting of study and simultaneous work of 7–8 hours a day.

Individual universities have up to a hundred different student organizations —clubs, societies, associations, fraternities, etc. The different organizations carry on interesting work among the students, appear in defense of Negro rights, against racial discrimination, and acquaint their members with the progressive figures of American culture. However, not one of these organizations can exert any influence at all on the solution of questions which are connected with securing student stipends, dormitories, or rendering help to the needy. Propagating a large number of student organizations reflects a definite policy: to divide student efforts and not to give them the opportunity to act on the basic questions of student life. Americans expressed sincere surprise when they found out about the influence and strength of youth and student organizations in our country.

American students told us that in a student movement, in particular at the University of Chicago, there are two tendencies. The so-called "liberal wing" asserts that "the student is above all a citizen." Because of this the program of the liberal wing includes such questions as the fight for the defense and widening of civil rights, for disarmament, and the increase of state expenditures for education. In contrast to this, the "conservative wing" holds the point of view that "the student is only a student" and that he should not meddle in politics.

And life itself, particularly the recent events connected with the foul murder of Patrice Lumumba, confirms the rightness of those young people who feel that "the student is above all a citizen." Thousands of Americans, among them youth, angrily condemned the villainous murder of the Congolese Prime Minister Patrice Lumumba, and the infamous role which Dag Hammarskjöld played in this. The progressive forces of the American people and youth warmly upheld the demands of the Soviet government that the Judas Hammarskjöld, that detestable servant of the colonialists, should be removed from his post as Secretary-General of the UN as an accomplice and organizer of violence against the leading governmental figures of the Republic of the Congo.

Wide circles of the American people

are beginning to stand up more and more actively for the strengthening of peace, for the successful solution of the question of disarmament, and for the improvement of Soviet-American relations. The brilliant scientific and technical achievements of the Soviet Union have called forth great interest in Soviet culture, science, and technology.

In recent years, intensive study of the Russian language has been going on in many American universities. The students noted that what stimulated this were the scientific and technical achievements of our country, above all in the sphere of mastering the cosmos. To help students in universities and colleges various circles and Russian clubs are being created, the members of which are becoming acquainted with Russian literature, art, etc.

It was pleasant to hear that among the American people, as among our people, warm memories are connected with Franklin D. Roosevelt. During his presidency friendly relations were maintained between the U.S.S.R. and America which were subsequently broken off, but not through the fault of the Soviet Union. On leaving the U.S.A. we understood that many Americans sincerely wish for the restoration of such relations.

66

IS THE SOVIET UNION A WELFARE STATE?

By Alec Nove

While the Soviet standard of living is clearly lower than that of the most prosperous Western countries, certain features of Soviet family income compare most favorably with those abroad. The article below gives a wealth of concrete detail about most items of the Soviet family budget which must be considered if a realistic estimate of the Soviet way of life is to be made. Several changes that have occurred since the appearance of the article, the author of which is professor of economics at the University of Glasgow, must be noted. A 1961 currency reform devalued the ruble; therefore all ruble figures cited below must be divided by ten. Since 1965, Soviet collective farmers have been eligible for state old age pensions. Although these are lower than pensions for industrial workers, this is a significant advance in the total social welfare scheme. The implementation of the minimum wage schedule cited below has run into delays, but as of 1968 the minimum monthly wage is 60 rubles. A clear improvement is the fact that, as of 1968, Soviet industry has gone over to the five-day week.

For Soviet literature on the subject of Social welfare see V. Aralov and A. Levshin, *Social Security in the USSR*; see also two anonymous Soviet publications: *In Addition to Wages: USSR, 1965–1970*, and *Social Security USSR: 1958, 1965, 1970*. For comments on the Nove article see Samuel Hendel (ed.), *The Soviet Crucible*. On Soviet medicine see L. Fridland, *The Achievement of Soviet Medicine*; Marc Field, *Doctor and Patient in Soviet Russia* and *Soviet Socialized Medicine*. On housing see John Hazard, *Soviet Housing Law*, and Timothy Sosnovy, *The Housing Problem in the Soviet Union* and "The Soviet Housing Situation Today," *Soviet Studies*, July, 1959. For a sample of Soviet housing law as currently applied see the housing statute of the city of Erevan in Armenia, printed in the *Current Digest of the Soviet Press*, 1964, No. 15. On education see George Bereday, *The Changing Soviet School*. On wages see Janet Chapman, *Real Wages in Soviet Russia since 1928*. On social services see the following: Gaston Rimlinger, "Social Security, Incentives, and Controls in the U.S. and USSR," *Comparative Studies in Society and History*, Vol. IV, and his "The Trade Union in Soviet Social Insurance," *Industrial and Labor Relations Review*, April, 1961; Leif Bjork, *Wages*,

From *Problems of Communism*, IX (1960), 1–10. Used by permission of the United States Information Agency. Footnotes have been omitted.

Prices, and Social Legislation in the USSR; "Social Security in the USSR," *Bulletin of the International Social Security Association,* Vol. XVII, Nos. 8–9; and Wladimir Naleszkiewicz, "Social Insurance in Soviet Russia," *Industrial Labor Relations Review,* Vol. XVII (1964), No. 2.

As some critics see it, the Soviet state is exclusively an organ of oppression. The motivations of its leaders, they believe, are to be found solely in the pursuit of world revolution, of national aggrandizement, of personal power—or of all these at once. The attitude of the Soviet leaders toward their own people is often represented as if it were mainly inspired by the objective of keeping the mass of Soviet citizens on the lowest possible living standard consistent with the necessity of providing minimum work incentives.

Hence such critics are inclined to view all Soviet measures which seem to increase public welfare as "concessions" wrung from a reluctant regime by irresistible force of circumstance or popular pressure. It is but a short step from this view to the conclusion that such measures are, in themselves, proof of

the regime's weakness or instability. If more was done to improve welfare in the first years after Stalin's death, these critics might argue, it was only because the struggle for power among Stalin's successors was undecided, and because the police apparatus had lost much of its capacity to intimidate. Inversely, now that Khrushchev has become unquestioned boss, they should logically expect a return to the old ways.

The purpose of the present article is to inquire into the validity of such interpretations of the "welfare" aspect of Soviet rule. But it is necessary first of all to define the area of discussion. To take a negative approach, the author does not propose to discuss such matters as wage rates and consumer goods production. It is an acknowledged fact that real wages in the Soviet Union have been rising slowly but steadily, that peasant

TABLE 1

U.S.S.R. SOCIAL-CULTURAL BUDGET: 1950–59

(In Billions of Rubles)

Welfare Item	1950	1953	1957	1959
Total health	21.4	24.2	38.3	44.0
Hospitals and clinics, urban	10.3	12.3	18.6	....
Hospitals and clinics, rural	2.6	3.1	4.6	....
Total education	56.9	61.1	80.7	94.3
General schooling[a]	30.4	32.2	37.6	....
Higher and technical	18.3	19.3	24.2	....
Science and research[b]	5.4	6.2	13.6	23.1[c]
Total social security	22.0	22.8	52.8	88.2
Total social insurance	12.7	16.2	23.5	....
Total maternity assistance	1.2	4.5	5.2	5.5
Total, social-cultural	116.7	128.8	200.5	232.0

[a] Includes kindergarten and adult education.

[b] As most all-union expenditures for science and research are kept secret, no complete breakdown of this item is given in the budget, but nuclear research is doubtless a major element. The item as a whole has practically no relevance for "welfare" in any sense.

[c] Part of the big increase in 1959 is accounted for by a change in definition hinted at in Zverev's budget speech.

incomes and retail trade turnover have gone up, and that the present Soviet leadership has declared its intention to continue this process through the period of the Seven-Year Plan (1958–65). It is also true that the upward trend in these areas is highly relevant to welfare in the general sense and should be duly noted. In the present paper, however, attention will be concentrated rather on activities of a more direct "public welfare" nature, i.e., on the various social services (health, education, etc.), on housing, and such other state measures as affect the everyday life of Soviet citizens.

A LOOK AT THE RECORD

Before inquiring into the question of motivation, it is also necessary to set forth a few facts showing what actually *has* been done, or is being done, by the Soviet Union in the area of welfare. Such a survey of the record may best begin with a look at budget allocations for social and cultural expenditures during the 1950–59 period, presented in Table 1. Keeping the general trend toward increased outlays in mind, the individual categories of welfare listed are reviewed below with particular attention as to whether or not there has been any recent change of policy.

Health. There is no evidence that Soviet policy in this field has undergone any basic change in recent years. Vigorous efforts to expand medical and health services were already a feature of Stalin's reign, and the progress that was achieved is clearly indicated by the fact that the Soviet Union, as the following figures attest, has since 1951 boasted a larger number of doctors per thousand inhabitants than most Western countries:

U.S.S.R. (1951) 13.9
U.S.S.R. (1957) 16.9
United States (1954) 12.7

United Kingdom (1951) . . . 8.8
West Germany (1955) . . . 13.5

Thus, while the 1957 and 1959 budget figures show relatively sharp increases in health expenditures, it is clear that these are not a new departure in Soviet policy, but rather a continuation of past trends.

It is true that the equipment of many Soviet hospitals is antiquated, that drugs are often scarce, and that the general level of health facilities is not up to the best Western standards. Nevertheless, a great deal has certainly been done to spread hygiene, combat epidemics, and reduce infant mortality. The services of state doctors and hospitals are free, although most medicines have to be bought by the patient.

Education. Here again, recent Soviet policy has not basically altered Stalin's approach insofar as the latter aimed at a large-scale expansion of the educational system, but there have been important changes in emphasis and direction. Thus, the decision of the 20th CPSU Congress (February 1956) to extend full-time secondary education to all has since been modified in favor of part-time education after the age of 15, and Khrushchev's reform of higher education also seems likely to result in a reduction of the number of *full-time* university students. It is not, of course, within the scope of the present article to discuss the detailed causes and consequences of Khrushchev's reforms of Soviet education. Regardless of the effect they may have on academic standards, however, it can be stated that these reforms are unlikely to result in any modification of the upward trend in Soviet educational expenditures (except for a possible large saving in student stipends).

One notable reason for this assumption is the evident rise in the school building program, partly as a result of an overdue effort to remedy the overcrowding which at present necessitates a two-shift, and sometimes even three-shift, system of attendance, and partly to set up the new-type boarding schools in which Khrushchev plans to train the "new Soviet man." It is only fair to add that, in contrast to the continuing shortage of physical facilities, the situation of Soviet schools with regard to the ratio of teachers to pupils compares very favorably with that in many other countries including the United States, as evidenced by the following figures:

	PUPILS	TEACHERS	PUPILS PER
	(In Thousands)		TEACHER
U.S.S.R.			
(1956–57)........	30,127	1,811	16.6
United States			
(1955)...........	30,531	1,135	26.9
United Kingdom			
(1956)...........	7,981	309	25.8

Mention should also be made of the Khrushchev leadership's action in 1956 to abolish all fees in schools and universities, which reversed one of Stalin's counter-reforms. It will be recalled that free education had been a feature of the Soviet regime from the beginning and was explicitly guaranteed by the 1936 Stalin constitution. Despite the constitutional guarantee, however, educational charges were imposed in the top three grades of secondary schools and in universities by a simple decree of the Council of Ministers in 1940. Although the action did not have such a serious effect on university students because of the fact that the large majority were receiving stipends from which the fees simply were deducted, its impact on children of poor families enrolled in secondary schools, where stipends were not payable, was much more severe. Without doubt the restoration of free education was a highly popular act.

Social insurance, social security, and pensions. Sick-pay benefits in the Soviet Union have long been on a relatively generous scale, and there have been no significant changes in rates of payment in recent years, although over-all expenditures for this purpose have increased as a result of the upward trend in total numbers of employed and in the average wage. As part of the campaign launched in the 1930's to reduce the high rate of labor turnover, full rates of sick pay were made conditional upon a minimum period of work in the same enterprise or office, except in cases where workers had transferred under official orders. These rules remain in force, although with some modifications in favor of the worker.

Provided he is a trade-union member, a worker who falls ill is paid the following proportions of his actual earnings (non-members receive one-half these rates, subject to the minima referred to below):

Years of Service	Per Cent of Earnings
Less than 3	50
3–5	60
5–8	70
8–12	80
More than 12	90

Present regulations provide for minimum monthly payments of 300 rubles in towns and 270 rubles in rural areas, and a maximum payment of 100 rubles per day.[1] Those who are injured at work or suffer from diseases caused by their

[1] To give the reader an idea of the purchasing power of the ruble, here are the Soviet prices (in rubles) of a few commodities (per

work are entitled to sickness benefits at the rate of 100 per cent of their earnings regardless of length of service. Where a worker leaves his job of his own volition, he is not entitled to sickness pay for ordinary illness until a period of six months has elapsed, but this limitation does not apply (since February 1957) to cases of accident or disease caused by a person's work. Of course, the social insurance rates described here apply only to disability for a limited period of time, permanent disablement being dealt with under pension regulations.

The maternity benefit rate itself also has not been changed in recent years, but in 1956 the period of paid maternity leave was lengthened to 112 days. This was, in effect, a return to the regulation which had been in force up until 1938, when the period of maternity leave was reduced from 112 to 70 days.

The biggest improvements in this general area recently have been in the field of old-age and permanent disability pensions. Their effect, according to Finance Minister Zverev, was to raise the average rate of all pensions by 81 per cent, but certain groups of workers who had fared relatively worse under the pre-1956 pension regulations secured much bigger gains than this, for the following reasons: The previous regu-

kilogram, unless otherwise stated) : chicken, 16.5; beef (stewing), 12; pork, 19.5; average fish, 11; butter, 28; milk, 2.2 per liter; eggs (10), 7.5; rye bread, 1.24; potatoes, 1; cabbage, 1.5–2; coffee, 40; cotton print dress, 200; wool dress, 475; man's overcoat, 720; man's all-wool suit, 2,000; shoes (adequate), 200; bicycle, 450–600; motorcycle, 4,200; radio, 400; washing machine, 2,250; family divan, 1,300; toilet soap (bar), 2.2. Source: Lynn Turgeon, "Levels of Living, Wages and Prices in the Soviet and United States Economies," *Comparisons of the United States and Soviet Economies*, Joint Economic Committee of the U.S. Congress, U.S. Government Printing Office, Washington, D.C., 1959, pp. 335–36.—Ed.

lations nominally entitled a worker qualifying for an old-age pension by length of service to receive payments at the rate of two-thirds of his final wage. This looked extremely generous until one noticed the proviso, often omitted from propaganda statements, that the two-thirds was to be calculated on the basis of a *maximum* "reckonable" wage of 300 rubles per month, meaning an effective maximum pension of 200 rubles per month. This figure, when originally fixed some 25 years earlier, was quite legitimate, but wages and prices subsequently multiplied without any upward revision of the allowable maximum. The result was considerable hardship for ordinary workers, while on the other hand exceptional treatment was granted to certain categories including not only the professional and official classes but also workers in some priority occupations. For example, coal miners, steel workers, and those engaged in electricity generation were allotted a much higher reckonable maximum. Similar discriminatory rules applied also to pension benefits for surviving dependents and victims of industrial accidents and the like.

The reform of 1956, while reducing certain very high pensions, established an all-round minimum old-age pension of 300 rubles per month for those qualified by length of service, an advance of great importance. In addition, it put into effect a new scale of payments benefiting lower-paid workers, so that those earning up to 350 rubles per month now receive pensions amounting to 100 per cent of earnings, with progressively smaller percentages for those with higher earnings, and with a maximum overall ceiling of 1,200 rubles per month. An average worker earning, say, 750 rubles per month qualifies for a pension of 487 rubles under the new rules, as against probably only 200 under the old. One offsetting feature of the reform is that working pensioners are no longer permitted to receive full pensions on top of their wages. (This provision, together with the better pension rates, has very probably encouraged many old people to retire.) On balance, however, the net gain to Soviet pensioners can readily be measured by the increase in pension expenditures shown in the following table (in billions of rubles):

	1950	1956	1957 (Prelim.)	1958 (Plan)
Total pensions	30.1	36.5	59.9	66.0
Non-working pensioners	8.7	12.6	27.6	34.2
Working pensioners	4.7	5.1	5.3	5.8
Ex-military and families	15.6	17.5	23.5	23.4

The improvement in old-age pension benefits was accompanied by substantial increases in pensions for those suffering permanent disability of varying degrees and for dependents, the increases reported amounting to 50–65 per cent. Further sizable increases in minimum pension rates have also been promised under the Seven-Year Plan, along with a raising of minimum wages. No doubt exists regarding the general popularity of these measures.

There has also been a good deal of talk about extending social insurance and pension rights to collective farmers, who have thus far never enjoyed them. Some farms are reported to have adopted a system of paying fixed amounts of money and produce to their sick and aged members, which represents a step forward from the normal collective farm practice of extending relief to such members out of a small fund set aside for this purpose. Cases where fixed payments have been instituted are still the exception since the vast majority of collective farms do not yet have sufficient revenues for this purpose, but it is a fact that the number of such exceptions

is steadily growing, and the extensive publicity given to them in the Soviet press indicates that the new system is officially regarded as a desirable development. It must be noted that, at present, all such payments are made out of the resources of each farm, and that the state has no responsibility, financial or otherwise. However, as the regime's policy toward the peasants is, in principle, to reward regular collective work with regular pay, and to bring the status of

the peasant gradually closer to that of the industrial worker, it seems to follow that the state eventually will have to accept some responsibility for at least ensuring that the collective farms have now absorbed the workers of the disbanded Machine Tractor Stations, who were promised the continuation of the benefits they formerly enjoyed as state employed workers. It is too soon, however, to say how the problem will be tackled.

OTHER WELFARE BENEFITS

Holidays. Turning to other kinds of social welfare benefits for state-employed persons, there appears to have been no appreciable change in the rules governing paid holidays, which already were on a fairly generous scale under Stalin. These regulations compare favorably with those of West European countries, especially for workers in what are deemed to be arduous or unhealthy occupations. For example, miners, steel workers, and bus drivers are allowed up to four weeks of paid vacation per year. Over-all statistics showing the distribution of the total working force according to numbers of paid (working-day) holidays per years are as follows:

Days of Vacation	Per Cent of Total Workers
12	43
15	12
18	11
21	3
24	19
Over 24	12
	100

A less desirable feature of the Soviet holiday system is the practice of spreading vacations over the whole year, so that many are on vacation when the weather is unfavorable. There is also a grave shortage of holiday accommodations: despite the existence of much-publicized trade-union rest homes charging low prices, these can accommodate only a small fraction of the workers.

Working time. There has been significant improvement in respect to hours of labor, although here again the reform effected by the present leadership so far represents, in large part, a return to the more liberal regulations which prevailed prior to Stalin's oppressive labor legislation of 1938–40. A 1940 decree lengthened the standard workday from seven to eight hours, increasing total hours for the six-day work week to 48. This remained unchanged until 1956 when the Khrushchev leadership, implementing its promise at the 20th Party Congress to reduce working hours, took an initial step to cut down Saturday work to six hours, leaving most of the afternoon free and thus creating the beginnings of a Soviet "weekend."

During 1957–58 further reductions of working hours were made effective in certain industries, notably mining and metallurgy. These were followed by still greater promises at the 21st Party Congress in January 1959, when the leadership explicitly pledged a standard 40-hour week (and a 35-hour week in unhealthy occupations) by no later than 1962, with further reductions to follow later in the decade. There was even talk of achieving "the shortest working week in the world" by 1967. The promises have been so definite and attended by such great publicity that it will be hard indeed for the leadership to go back on its word, except in the event of dire emergency. Reduced hours are in fact already being put into effect in several key industries. A statement jointly issued by the CPSU Central Committee, the Council of Ministers, and the central trade union organization, and published in the Soviet press on September 20, 1959, announced a detailed time schedule for the gradual extension of the seven-hour day to "all workers and employees in the national economy." (With six-hour Saturdays, this will reduce the standard working week to 41 hours.) The process began October 1, 1959, and is to be completed in the fourth quarter of 1960.

Some Western critics, pointing to the fact that planned productivity increases are greater than would be necessary to compensate for the reduction of working hours, conclude from this that the reform is in some way not genuine since there will have to be greater intensity of effort in the shortened work period. Such a view hardly seems justifiable. It is obvious, in the first place, that a shorter working week requires greater work intensity and higher productivity not only in Russia but in the United States or any other country. If output per hour remained the same while hours were reduced by 15 per cent, the—other things being equal—total output would go down by 15 per cent and everyone would be correspondingly poorer, a situation which no one could possibly want. Nor is it true that the Soviet Union intends to increase productivity solely, or even mainly, by imposing heavier physical burdens on labor. This is quite evident from the great attention being paid to the mechanization of labor-intensive processes, especially in auxiliary occupations (loading, moving of materials, etc.).

The charge that weekly wages are being cut as part of the reduction in working hours is equally untenable. The fact that a major reform of the Soviet wage system has coincided with the reduction of the working week makes it difficult to determine the precise effect of either change, but average wages appear in any event to be displaying their usual tendency to rise slowly. Thus, the cut in the working week is as genuine as these things can be in an imperfect world. Those who assert the contrary are guilty of using against the Soviet Union the very same—quite unfounded—arguments by which Soviet propagandists seek to explain away the reduction of the working week in the United States.

Other employment reforms. Brief mention should also be made of recent steps extending the special privileges of juvenile workers. Since May 1956 workers between the ages of 16 and 18 have enjoyed a working day shortened to six hours, with extra piecework pay to make up any loss in earnings. In addition they are allowed a full month's vacation each year and special facilities for study. These privileges have, indeed, caused many managers to try to avoid employing juveniles—a tendency which has aroused official criticism and contributed to the difficulties experienced by high school graduates in seeking employment. The compulsory drafting of young people into labor reserve schools, introduced in October 1940, had already been terminated by a decree of March 18, 1955, and has been replaced by voluntary recruitment.

For another thing, the worker's right to change his occupation, while not explicitly recognized, has been made more real by the present regime's abolition, in 1957, of criminal penalties for leaving one's job without permission. These penalties, as well as others for worker absenteeism and unpunctuality, had been instituted by decree in 1940. Although the decree gradually became a dead letter under Stalin's successors and was no longer mentioned in Soviet legal textbooks from 1954 on, it apparently survived on the statute books until 1957.

In still another reversal of Stalinist policy, the 1936 decree which required the rural population to give six days' unpaid labor per year for working on roads was repealed by the present leadership in November 1958. Instead, responsibility for building and repairing local roads has been placed on the "collective farms, state farms, industrial, transport, building and other enterprises and organizations." Of course, the job still has to be done, but presumably the individual is now entitled to be paid for doing it.

Wage questions. Although wages as such are outside the province of this discussion, it may be useful to refer briefly to changes in this field insofar as they are indicative of political attitudes. The practice of the Stalin period was to maximize wage differentials, which indeed reached record dimensions; on the contrary, the trend in recent years has been in the opposite direction. In 1956, a minimum wage law was adopted, fixing a floor of 300–350 rubles per month in urban areas and 270 rubles in the country. The measure particularly benefited the appallingly underpaid groups of auxiliary personnel (janitors, cleaners, messengers, etc.) and the lowest grades of shop assistants, railroad workers, and others. This process of raising the level of the lowest-paid workers is to continue. The decree on the Seven-Year Plan provides for increasing the minimum wage to 400–450 rubles monthly during 1959–62, and to 500–600 rubles during 1963–65, as well as for a consequential (but smaller) upward revision of the pay of middle-grade workers. Since the average increase in all money wages is to be only 26 per cent, it is evident that the spread between top and bottom will be sharply reduced.

This policy is reflected in other aspects of wage reform now in progress. Apart from introducing smaller differentials in basic rates, the reforms are tending to eliminate the more exaggerated forms of progressive piecework bonuses, which will cut down disparities in actual earnings. The gap between skilled and unskilled workers' pay on collective farms is also being significantly reduced. There have apparently been cuts in very high salaries, such as those of government ministers and university professors. (Though no statement to this effect seems to have appeared in print, the cuts are apparently a matter of general knowledge in the Soviet Union and have been confirmed to the writer several times.) The relative position of the lowest-paid has also been improved as a result of a decree of March 23, 1957, reducing direct taxation on incomes below 450 rubles per month. All this certainly does not indicate that the Soviets are embracing hitherto-condemned "petty-bourgeois egalitarianism," but it does show that the *excessive* inequalities of the Stalin era are being corrected.

Housing. Something must also be said about housing, since the fact that rents in the Soviet Union are far too low to bear any relation to housing costs jus-

tifies treating it as a social service rather than as a species of commercial transaction. At 1.32 rubles per square meter per month (somewhat higher for new apartments in some cities), rents are generally insufficient even to cover bare maintenance, which may explain why this is so often neglected. At the same time, the miseries caused by the shortage of housing and consequent overcrowding are too well known to require comment here. Khrushchev has declared that his aim is eventually to provide a separate apartment for every Soviet family instead of the single room which is the usual situation today. It is evident from the housing provisions of the Seven-Year Plan, however, that the separate apartments will be very small by Western standards: the plan calls for the construction of 15 million apartment units with a total floor space (including corridors, bathroom, and kitchen) of 650–60 million square meters—or, at most, 44 square meters (430 square feet) per apartment. A British working-class family would be shocked at having to live in so little space. Still, no one can doubt that Soviet citizens will be much happier if and when each family can have its own front door and no longer have to share the kitchen with several neighbors.

There is no question about the sharp acceleration of housing construction under the post-Stalin leadership. This is fully evident from the following figures showing housing space (excluding private rural housing) completed in four different years from 1950 to 1958, and the Seven-Year Plan goals:

Despite the sharply-increased effort

	Total	State	Urban Private
	(In Million Square Meters of Total Space)		
1950	24.2	17.8	6.4
1953	30.8	23.2	7.6
1957	52.0	38.5	13.5
1958	70.1	45.6	24.5
1959 (plan)	80.0	...	...

1960 (plan)	101.0	....	....
1959–65			
Plan, total	650–60.0	....	....
Plan, annual average	93.0	....	....

since Stalin's death, it is clear that there is still a very long way to go before tolerable housing conditions will be achieved, since a large part of new construction is necessary merely to keep pace with urban population growth. It has been pointed out that the Soviet *per capita* rate of house-building, even allowing generously for peasant construction, remains below that of the (West) German Federal Republic. Nonetheless, the facts reveal considerable progress in the U.S.S.R. The ambitious plans for rebuilding villages in connection with Khrushchev's contemplated revival of the *agrogorod*[2] necessarily call for a still greater expansion of housing construction in rural areas, although the financial burden involved is to be shouldered

[2] An agricultural city.

by the collective farms.

Services. Finally, brief mention must be made of improvements in badly needed consumer services—restaurants, cafes, shops, repair facilities, and the like. This is a very backward sector of Soviet life. To cite just one example, an article in *Pravda* (March 14, 1959) estimated the total capacity of shoe-repair establishments in the Russian republic (R.S.F.S.R.) at 15 million pairs annually, although 100 million pairs of new shoes are sold each year, and may be presumed to require repair at least once annually. A recent decree embodied plans for increasing the turnover of service and repair shops of all kinds to 10.3 billion rubles in 1961, as against 6.2 million rubles in 1958. There have also been measures to increase the number of shops and restaurants. . . .

67

STANDARD BEARERS OF COMMUNIST LABOR

The Yugoslav writer Mihajlo Mihajlov, who visited Moscow in 1964 and wrote *Moscow Summer*, reports in his book: "In restaurants, shops, buses, museums, railway stations and airports—everywhere, everywhere there are red bill-boards with two kinds of signs. One, "Here Works a Brigade of Communist Labor," the other, "Here Works a Brigade Fighting for the Title of a Brigade of Communist Labor." What is this phenomenon called Communist Labor? The pages below will illustrate it. They are taken from a Soviet work describing Communist Labor Brigades and intended as a kind of textbook of the movement which began about 1960. It is the latest in a long line of Soviet experiments in building labor enthusiasm and fostering a collective spirit. Earlier names for the same phenomenon were "socialist competition," and "Stakhanovism," after the miner Stakhanov, still alive, who in the 1930's dug up, in one day, an enormous amount of coal, thus setting precedents for his fellow workers.

For a description of Soviet goals for labor see the 1961 Communist Party Program printed in Jan Triska, *Soviet Communism* (paperback). Additional Soviet views are in G. Osipov, *Industry and Labor in the USSR*; the Soviet journal *Problems of Economics*; and I Dvornikov and V. Nikitinsky, *How Labor Disputes Are Settled in the Soviet Union*. See also the section on workers in Harry Shaffer, *The Soviet Economy* (paperback). For a comparison with the United States see Walter Galenson, *Labor Productivity in Soviet and American Industry*. The fullest recent work on Soviet labor is Emily Brown, *Soviet Trade Unions and Labor Relations*. For a general study of the Soviet economy in the 1960's see Harry Schwartz, *The Soviet Economy since Stalin* (paperback). See also the article by Jerzy Glicksman, "Recent Trends in Soviet Labor Policy," *Problems of Communism*, July–August, 1956, and the chapter on workers in Abraham Brumberg, *Russia under Khrushchev* (paperback). There are occasional articles on Soviet labor in the *Industrial and Labor Relations Review*, and in the *International Labour Review*.

A. "LABOR IS LIFE'S PRIMARY NEED"

By N. Minaev, Chief of a Communist Labor Brigade and Foreman of the Red Proletariat Plant

Can you find a man who has not pondered over the question of what is the

Translated by Walter Gleason from *Znamenonostsy Komunisticheskogo Truda* (Moscow, 1961), pp. 190–92, 234–37, 252–58.

meaning of his life, or what is the significance of his work? I recently read the views of a French worker, George Novel. He writes: "Thousands of modern-day workers are slaves of serial production and the conveyor system. The work you do in the factory is of no interest, sapping your energy, fresh strength, and imagination. Sadness and a sense of despondency are daily companions of modern labor. The main defect of contemporary labor is this lack of interest." Undoubtedly Novel is sincere, but his feelings and sentiments are alien to us. Of course work is not all fun and games for a Soviet worker either; it demands a great deal of strength and persistence. But if you talked with any of our men at the "Red Proletariat" plant, you would not find a single one who would be indifferent to his labor, regardless of what it might be.

"I've worked at the 'Red Proletariat' for thirty years," says our metal-fitter, Victor Vasil'evich Ermilov. "Our plant took me into the working class and taught me about life and my trade. Here I have found my calling and have realized the incomparable romance and joy of creative work." Why do our workers view their work differently from the French workers, or the workers of any other capitalist country? The Soviet worker is interested in his labor primarily because he performs for himself and for a society of laborers like himself. It is this feeling which links his labor with the labor of the entire people who have made up their mind to build the brightest, most just society on earth —communism. Communism! How long have the working people dreamt of it, and now it is becoming a reality. We shall build it over the next twenty years. Today we already see its concrete features. "Communism is a highly organized society of free and conscious toilers, in which community self-government will establish itself. Labor for the good of society will become the primary requirement of everyone's life, a recognized necessity; the abilities of each will be employed for the greatest good of the people."

I will use my brigade to illustrate. Comprising seven men, it operated an automatic line for machining gears. At first glance what we produce is not complicated, gears for screw-cutting lathes. But if you speculate over where it goes, you unwittingly experience pride at the results of your labor. The factory's insignia, "Red Proletariat," is quite famous in our country. General purpose screw-cutting lathes, produced by the factory, can be found in practically every enterprise producing metal objects. And everywhere—in the Donbass or the Urals, in Siberia or Central Asia —they benefit workers like ourselves. Truly we work for one another, for society, and, in the last analysis, for ourselves.

The labor of the members of our brigade and the other workers in the factory flows like little streams into the common labor of our people. The same hands which grow grain, create space capsules and wondrous machines, footwear and clothes, also build villages and cities, factories and plants. Our labor is useful to those laboring in the fraternal socialist countries. We not only send them machines but we also share our experiences. A trainer in our factory, V. Shumilin, worked in factories in Czechoslovakia; an assistant to the foreman of the thermal department, A. Kurnakov, in China. I was fortunate enough to visit the German Democratic Republic. And everywhere our people were greeted joyously, as brothers in labor, as unselfish friends.

When you ponder these facts, you become convinced that your labor is needed by people. And is it not a joy to be needed by a laboring collective? I think that a worker in a capitalist country cannot derive pleasure from his work, above all because a lion's share of his labor goes toward the enrichment of the capitalists, because his heart and mind are always prey to the worm of doubts and anxieties about the future. . . .

B. "ALL FOR ONE AND ONE FOR ALL"

By T. Ivanova, Chief of a Communist Labor Brigade in the "Bolshevik" Textile Plant

. . . How do we in our brigade live up to the principle of "all for one and one for all?" Before speaking of this, I will briefly discuss the organization of production and labor in our plant. Our "Bolshevik" is a highly mechanized enterprise. For example there are eighteen machines for the twenty-two people who make up our brigade. Only one operation, sorting of sewn cutouts from pieces of cloth, is done by hand. I perform this task. The sorter must be well acquainted with the entire process of preparing this or that operation. She cannot be mistaken, since even a hardly noticeable error on her part leads to a stoppage in the production line. There is mass conveyor-line production at the factory in the basic sewing departments, including our own. This is unimaginable without a clear-cut division of labor. The success of this type of production depends on the cooperation and coordination of the workers' activities, and on their ability to fill in for one another.

Of course this does not come by itself, but is the result of a great deal of educational work with the people. For example we had the following experience. Zinaida Podkopova, a reserve worker, was sent to us in exchange for an ailing mechanic. Owing to inexperience she sewed the pattern on the flap of the back pocket incorrectly. Liusia Natalina and Tamara Tikhanova, veteran members of our brigade, noticed the mistake while doing later operations, but permitted the item to continue along the conveyor. The foreman, Alexandra Ivanova Luk'yanova, noticed the defective quality of the stitching. And so an entire lot of trousers was taken from production.

A meeting was called. Not only the brigade, but the entire department was upset over Natalina's and Tikhanova's conduct. In a collective competing for Communist Labor this was a glaring fault which might have been prevented. Everyone was interested in why Natalina and Tikhanova had acted in this way. It turned out that they had simply decided that it was none of their business. They did not consider the honor of the collective at all. Then a discussion among us turned to consciousness, the labor honor of each person. We all knew one little-noticed, yet far from unimportant, peculiarity in the character of these workers—they both lived detached from the collective, withdrawn into their own little, philistine world, thinking only about their own wellbeing. It was of no concern to them that a comrade was making mistakes and needed their help. They had less labor consciousness than anyone in the brigade, or the department.

But why did the collective, knowing all the failings of these workers, remain silent until they committed this error? Because we were occupied solely with striving to overfill the quota. Undoubtedly, this must be striven for. However, our every step should be a reflection of our high, ideological consciousness. One can learn a great deal, be thoroughly familiar with the whole process of sewing clothes, handle the quota perfectly, and yet have no comprehension of the goals which face our society. But one must live and work for the sake of its interests.

The feeling of collectivism can be developed in various ways. We in our brigade, for example, began by acquainting ourselves with the lives of each worker. Each of us sees and knows what a worker does in the production line and how she acts in the department. But what becomes of the worker beyond the factory's gates? This is not a matter of indifference for a brigade competing for Communist Labor, led by the principle of "one for all and all for one." We commissioned Liuba Borisova and Zhenia Usacheva to visit all the workers' homes and discover how they lived. Familiarity with their mode of life facilitates the education of people in the production line, it affords opportunities to help one's comrades. Thus Roza Sitdekova's husband became ill at a time when there was no one with whom to leave the child. The brigade came to her aid. Its members went to Roza's home several times. They helped out around the house, sat with the child, went shopping, and so forth. Such help ennobles a person, inspires faith in the collective, strengthens comprehension of one's public duties, and alters a person's relationship to the collective.

This principle of "all for one and one for all" forces us to think about improving our professional mastery, and our educational and cultural standards. Sometimes one of us, for a valid reason, does not show up for work. This necessitates quick modifications, since each person in the brigade accomplishes a predetermined operation. And our brigade decided that each worker should know no less than ten operations. Then it is possible easily to replace the absent comrade. If need be any of us can accomplish, instead of one operation, one and a half or two. That is how we work it. And when Roza Sitdekova did not come to work one day, Usacheva took her place. She even accomplished her own operation at the same time.

People who have just joined the brigade must be helped. Of course we do not leave them unattended. Recently Olia Kuznetskaia began to work with us. She was entrusted with operating a special machine which demands craftsmanship and skill. Tanya Esavkina is thoroughly acquainted with this machine. She helped Olia to master the assigned work quickly. We are fully aware that labor consciousness and standards of training are intimately connected with each other. Consciousness depends on the individual's education, his frame of mind, and ideological conviction. This means that everyone should study. We in the brigade also came to that conclusion. I enrolled in a technical school. Valia Vasil'eva, Zhenia Usacheva, and Liuba Borisova are busy in a school for working youth. Lena Motileva is studying to prepare herself for admission to an institute. The remaining workers attend circles, the university of culture. They are trying to do more reading on their own.

Exchanges of views on questions of public life, literature, art, arguments on what the modern young person should be like, and what constitutes beauty and the worth of the individual, all are increasingly replacing pointless conversations. The striving to find answers to troublesome questions, to enrich one's inner life, attracts our interest in visiting theaters, movies, and museums. Our group often goes in a body. Then, as a rule, we discuss what we saw. Our brigade is actively engaged in all social events. Some of the girls work as volunteer militia aids. We perform voluntary labor on Saturdays and Sundays and stay together in one-day holiday homes and tourist centers. . . .

C. "OUR EXPERIENCE IN COMPETING FOR COMMUNIST LABOR IN CONSTRUCTION"

By G. Lamochkin, Chief of a Communist Labor Brigade at the "Mosstroi" Plant No. 1

Our brigade was organized in February, 1960. At that time we were building large-scale paneled buildings in the Volkhonka region. And it must be said that things went badly at the beginning. The workers were drawn from various sectors, did not know each other, and did not coordinate their tasks, but, more importantly, the majority had no experience in construction on this scale. Among the twenty-seven men only Iurii Shikalov and I were fitters, the others specialized in bricklaying, rigging or carpentry, or were simply auxiliary workers. Thus we needed to do much and overcome a great deal if we were to unify the collective, master the art of fitting, and gain the necessary knowledge and experience. And the first step in this direction was our brigade's entry into the competition for the title of a collective of Communist Labor. We fully understood the responsibility we were assuming and did not want to fall behind the other brigades. Being "laggards," this was quite a bold step, but it was just this which somehow brought us together, gave us strength, forced us to ponder over things which earlier would have seemed too daring to us, about new methods of labor, new tech-

nological innovations in large-scale paneled buildings.

Life itself suggested an idea to us. Working under the existing techniques, we were literally overwhelmed by building parts. Our floor reminded one then of a storehouse for prefabricated constructions. This made work very difficult. In addition, analyzing the fitting process, we came to the conclusion that it was far from perfect. Parts were installed without a predetermined plan, without strict sequence. It was clear that, if we worked by the tried methods, we would not be able to obtain success and catch up with the other brigades. The technique had somehow to be changed and improved. I shared my thoughts on this matter with a section chief, Dikman. He supported my opinions, and together we worked out the details of a new technique for fitting large-scale panel homes. Our idea consisted in the following: first, work not on one section but on the fitting from both ends of two sections, using the crane according to the pendulum principle; that is, while one brigade of fitters installs one section with the help of the crane, the other brigade prepares the work space, and then they exchange roles. Second, during one of the shifts, work on the fittings of only one type of part and only in a definite sequence. For example, install only wall blocks at the beginning, and in another shift install the main internal partitions, and so forth.

This procedure permitted more effective use of the crane and made it convenient for the fitters, who did not have to shift their positions continually. In addition the new method enabled (and this is very important) an hourly labor schedule to be worked out for not only the fitters but also those supplying the parts, who would know exactly when and what kind of parts should be put on the platform. In this way we could work directly "from the supply base." The crane delivers the parts to the exact spot where they are to be installed, without overloading the building platform with material.

Estimates indicated that this procedure reduced the assembly time for one floor from seven to five days. Initially there were those who did not believe in the realization of our idea. Several comrades in other brigades who found out about our plans frankly said that nothing would come of it. But this only egged us on. No matter what, we wanted to prove to the doubting Thomases that it was not they, but we, who were right. But we understood that we had not undertaken an easy task. In order to introduce the new technique, many different agreements and permissions were required; it was necessary to coordinate with the factory suppliers. And all this was not easy because they had to disrupt fixed schedules and rearrange their own work. For this reason we decided from the outset to work not only through our management and the trust, which at once supported us and were ready to render any kind of assistance, but also through the community, especially the press.

Our brigade addressed an open letter in the newspaper *Moskovskaia Pravda* to all organizations on whom the introduction of the new technique depended with a plea that they help us. After the letter was published, our offer was discussed and approved at a meeting of the praesidium of the city's union of construction workers. Those attending the meeting for the management admitted that the new method of erecting large-scale paneled buildings was progressive and committed themselves to hastening its introduction. It was de-

cided to place at our disposal for the final elaboration of technological charts and hourly schedules the service of the Scientific Research Institute of the Chief Moscow Construction Trust.

This was the first victory. But if it was to become final, a great deal of work was necessary. The main obstacle to the introduction of the new building method was the suppliers. They did not want to rearrange their work at all, and this is understandable. An hourly schedule for delivering parts to the building platform involved a great deal of trouble. The most efficient coordination of all departments had to be arranged, a strict sequence between sections observed, and many others. But we relentlessly persisted, reminding, seeking, demanding, sending our delegations to the suppliers' offices, and turning to the Party's city committee for aid. And finally things began to roll. We began to receive parts according to our schedule.

Work done by the new method at once showed results. Our estimates were fully justified—we could assemble a story not in seven days, as the plan projected, but in five. The new method justified itself and began to spread not only in our offices but in other Moscow buildings. The elaboration of the new technique and the struggle for its introduction was a good experience for us. After a few months our brigade had turned into a friendly and cohesive collective, where each member was fully acquainted with his duties and at any moment was ready to come to the aid of a comrade.

While elaborating the schedules and holding conversations with the suppliers, we did not waste any time. It was decided that each brigade member should master no less than two to three construction skills, with fitting required of everyone. This was necessary if complete coordination were to be achieved. With this goal in mind all the comrades attended special courses for fitters in our department. In addition Iurii Shikalov and I, as the most experienced fitters, tried to transmit to them our experience. Special consideration was naturally given by the department to Victor Rybakov, Sergei Karpukhin, and Pavel Iudovskii, who, under the new organization, would be in charge of small four-man groups of fitters. When they had mastered the art of fitting they began to transfer the accumulated experience to other comrades.

Thus, over a very short period, thanks to the cooperation and the hardy encouragement of all to study, all of us in the brigade, except the plasterers, became fitters. Incidentally many did not stop at this point and began to master other specialties. At the present time the majority of the brigade members are proficient in three skills, and some have acquired four. For example fitter Bezuchko can now do competent work as a bricklayer, steel reinforcer, and carpenter. But even this is not enough for him. Recently Bezuchko enrolled in a course for electric welders.

We support this desire to gain new skills. It is not just that additional knowledge and experience never hurt, but the broad specialization of the brigade members helps a great deal at work, allowing us to shift their skills around. In addition to fitting walls, ceilings, and so forth, we ourselves make door and window frames, and rough plaster. For this reason not only fitters and bricklayers join the brigade, but also carpenters and plasterers. Under these conditions the flexibility of the brigade members is one of the most decisive sources of successful work. But the advantage in broad specialization is not confined to this alone. A knowl-edge of varied specialties broadens a man's opportunities, his professional outlook, and makes work more interesting. And you know that this is also important. When an individual likes his work and derives moral satisfaction from it, he works differently, putting a part of himself into it. In addition to his knowledge and experience, he wants to bring to his work something of his own, something new. Such was the case in our brigade.

Having acquired the art of fitting, the people began to think of ways to speed up the process, to offer rational suggestions. For example, Ivan Parshin, an electric welder, suggested that reinforcing the wall blocks would hasten their installation and make the tower crane more quickly available. A pattern for installing internal partitions was suggested by Iurii Shikalov, freeing the fitters from being occupied each time with the room partitions, which always absorbed so much time. A great deal can be drawn from such examples. There now is not one person in the brigade who has not made some improvement, however small, in our work. The following rule has been established among us: all innovations in construction methods that any of us discovers from the technical literature, the experience of other brigades, or has worked out for himself at once become the general property of the collective. And if the novelty deserves attention, we try to get the ball rolling immediately. It has become a habit for us to think continually about the perfection of construction methods.

When our management switched to constructing large-scale block homes, we also began to introduce our method here. And again the workers of the Moscow Construction Trust, with whom we were in constant contact, came to our assistance. With their help we worked out a new technique and schedules. The efficiency gained in this case was not minor. The time for assembling one floor was successfully cut from nine to seven days.

Our persistent work to perfect our professional skills through learning related skills did not go in vain. After several months we were able to advance into the vanguard and in August, 1960, six months after entering our collective in the competition for the rank of a Communist Labor brigade, we were victorious. It was not only our production success that allowed us to win the right to bear this high rank. From the outset we tried not only in words, but in deeds as well, to live up to the precept of Communist brigades—to learn to live and work the Communist way. Above all we declared war on everything superficial and negative in ourselves: on foul language and rudeness to one another, on habits of celebrating payday at a bar, on violation of the discipline at work.

Of course, since it is difficult to overcome personal habits, we try to help one another. If anyone swears or offends a comrade, we immediately stop him and remind him that he has lapsed. Swearing has now become rare. It was more difficult to overcome other habits, so closely tied to "the green serpent." Ivan Lebedev, a rigger, especially sinned in this way. After Sunday he often appeared at work with a headache, or he failed to come altogether. This showed in the work of the brigade. We talked about this with him many times. We warned him. He gave his word, but after a while he again broke loose. After one meeting, at which the comrades gave him such a scolding that the lad did not know where to turn, Lebedev did not again break a promise given to the collective. We had failures too. Maria Merkulova, a young but spoiled girl, worked as an auxiliary laborer in the brigade. She often loafed, took her time, acted arrogantly with her comrades. We talked to her many times. She repeatedly promised the collective to reform, but could not find the strength to do it. She finally left the brigade.

In order better to acquaint ourselves with the members of the brigade, to find out how they spend their free time, how they live after work, we began to visit one another, to arrange collective trips to the theaters and movies. Once almost the whole brigade went to Leningrad. There we became acquainted not only with the museums and the other sights of the hero city, but also with the advanced labor methods of the Leningrad builders. We visited the brigade of the well-known builder, Shapovalov. A warm friendship ties us to this brigade. . . .

68

SOVIET NATIONALITY POLICY

By Bobodzhan Gafurov; Richard Pipes

We saw in chapter 38 that the national problem had never been solved in the Russian Empire, and contributed to its downfall. The Soviet regime claims to have solved the problem and to have set an example to other nations on how to live together on the basis of equality and respect for each other. Our first author, Mr. Gafurov, is a prominent Soviet historian and Orientalist, a Corresponding Member of the Soviet Academy of Sciences. He is a Tadzhik by birth, and from 1946 to 1956 was the First Secretary of the Central Committee of the Communist Party of Tadzhikistan. Richard Pipes is Professor of Russian History at Harvard. His essay is part of a symposium the rest of which appears in the same issue of *Problems of Communist*. The same journal devoted a special issue in September–October, 1967, to the nationality problem.

For Soviet views on the subject see Joseph Stalin, *Marxism and the National Question*; the relevant sections of the Soviet Constitution reprinted above as chapter 52; E. Bagramov, "Lenin's Teachings on the National Question and the Situation Today," *Reprints from the Soviet Press*, December 15, 1966; I. Groshev, *A Fraternal Family of Nations* (published in Moscow); and "One Family Undivided," *Soviet Life*, September, 1967. See also Alfred Low, *Lenin on the Question of Nationality*.

For Western books on the subject see Eric Goldhagen (ed.), *Ethnic Minorities in the Soviet Union*; Allen Kassof (ed.), *Prospects for Soviet Society*; Abdurakhman Avtorkhanov, *The Communist Party Apparatus* (paperback); Robert Conquest, *Soviet Nationalities Policy in Practice* and *The Soviet Deportation of Nationalities*; Frederick Barghoorn, *Soviet Russian Nationalism*; Walter Kolarz, *Russia and Her Colonies*; Rudolpf Schlesinger, *The Nationalities Problem and Soviet Administration*; and Roman Smal-Stocki, *The Captive Nations*. A quarterly journal devoted to Soviet nationalities and printed in Munich since 1958 is *Problems of the Peoples of the USSR*.

There are a number of studies dealing with individual areas and peoples. On

The first essay is translated by the editor from B. Gafurov, "Uspekhi natsional'noi politiki KPSS i nekotorye voprosy internatsional'nogo vospitaniia," *Kommunist* (Moscow), August, 1958, pp. 10–24. The second essay is from R. Pipes, "The Forces of Nationalism," *Problems of Communism*, January–February, 1964, pp. 1–6. Published with permission of the United States Information Agency.

the Ukraine see John Armstrong, *Ukrainian Nationalism,* as well as the *Ukrainian Quarterly* and the *Digest of the Ukrainian Soviet Press* (monthly since 1956). On Central Asia see Lawrence Krader, *Peoples of Soviet Central Asia;* Michael Rywkin, *Russia in Central Asia* (paperback) ; George Wheeler, *The Modern History of Soviet Central Asia;* Edward Allworth, *Central Asia: A Century of Russian Rule, 1865-1965;* Alexander Bennigsen, *Islam in the Soviet Union;* Alec Nove, *The Soviet Middle East;* and the *Central Asian Review* (quarterly since 1953). On other nationalities see David Lang, *The Modern History of Soviet Georgia;* E. Vardys, *Lithuania under the Soviets;* Nicholas Vakar, *Belorussia;* and Salo Baron, *The Russian Jews under Tsars and Soviets.* On the last subject see also Solomon Rabinovich, *Jews in the Soviet Union* (published in Moscow).

See also "Brezhnev in Tbilisi," *Current Digest of the Soviet Press,* November 23, 1966, and "Delimitation of Competence between USSR Agencies and Republic Agencies," *Soviet Law and Government,* Winter, 1966-67.

GAFUROV: ACHIEVEMENTS OF THE NATIONAL POLICY OF THE COMMUNIST PARTY OF THE SOVIET UNION

. . . The greatest accomplishment in the solution of the national question is the establishment of brotherly friendship and collaboration of all the nationalities of the USSR in place of the former national prejudices and hatred. History knows other examples of the peaceful coexistence of nations, of the establishment among them of various kinds of unions; but the unity of Soviet socialist nations is in principle different from such precedents. The objective basis of the union of Soviet peoples is the existence and dominance in our country of socialist ownership of the means of production which results in the collaboration and mutual help of men free from exploitation. It was also historically significant that the largest, and economically and culturally most developed, Russian nation, having played the role of the dominant nation in pre-revolutionary conditions, decisively and selflessly renounced its former privileged position. Moreover, this nation expended much energy and made many sacrifices in order to help the formerly oppressed nationalities consolidate themselves into independent nations; it

helped them to develop their statehood, economy, and culture.

This example of the Russian nation, whose revolutionary vigor and readiness to fight for the victory of Communism received universal acclaim, had a favorable influence on all the other socialist nations of the Soviet Union. . . . The great accomplishments of the USSR in the solution of the national question serve as the source of hope and inspiration for all peoples struggling against imperialism and for independent development. This is why imperialist propaganda is forced to resort to shameless lies and monstrous inventions in order to represent the relations between nationalities in the Soviet Union in a perverted way. . . . All these dirty concoctions do not deserve refutation, since they are invented from beginning to end, based on false testimony of traitors to the Motherland, and all the "statistics" are simply manufactured. Really, who in our country could believe that we "persecute" national languages, that we "do not advance but oppress" cadres, that we "destroy" Islamic culture, etc.? We cite these examples to show that the imperialists, helpless in their fury against the USSR, resort to the lowest forms of slander, prevert facts, manufacture false "testimonials," in order to lie about the USSR and deceive the American reader. But as an Eastern proverb has it: "The dog barks, but the caravan moves on." The American apologists for imperialism wish to promote distrust and strife among the peoples of our great country, and to hide their own nationality policy. But their efforts are in vain. The brotherly solidarity of the peoples of the USSR is firm and unshakable. The imperialists will not succeed in hiding their low aims. . . .

The successful solution of the national question in the USSR is based on the fact that the Party has always conducted a determined struggle both with great-power chauvinism and with local nationalism, whatever forms these might take. As a result of the victory of socialism and the Party's vast educational work, the ideology of proletarian internationalism and the friendship of peoples have come to prevail in our country. In the USSR, where the social basis of national strife has been liquidated, there are no nationalist aims or groups. But we still find some nationalist prejudices and examples of nationalist narrow-mindedness. Nationalist prejudices are sometimes observed in the fields of economy and ideology, in the matter of selecting cadres. Correcting the mistakes connected with the cult of personality our Party has, in recent years, promoted a fuller and more correct realization of the principle of democratic centralism. The rights of Union Republics in the fields of planning, the distribution of revenues, and the management of the economy and of cultural affairs have been widened. These measures have already played an enormous positive role.

Nevertheless some comrades interpret these decisions of the Party and the government incorrectly. In some localities a tendency has appeared to juxta-pose cadres of the local nationality to the cadres of other nationalities. Such an approach to the problem is exceptionally harmful. True, these are only individual instances, and no generalizations can be made on their basis. But if a decisive struggle is not waged with even the most insignificant violations of the Party's national policy, they may grow stronger, and this may do harm to the interests of Communist construction. There is no doubt that in the future the growth of national cadres will move in an ever faster tempo; this does not mean, however, that we may permit any limitations on the rights of other nationalities. The selection and placement of cadres cannot be conducted merely in conformity with their national origin. This contradicts the principles of our internationalist world view and the firm traditions of the Communist Party. The selection and placement of cadres must be governed above all by the Leninist principle of judging people by their political and businesslike qualities. A closer union of the peoples of our country will be realized not only as a result of strengthening economic and cultural ties between them, but also in the course of a brotherly exchange of cadres of workers, scholars, representatives of culture, in the process of an exchange of cultural achievements, of all the best which each republic and each nationality possesses.

At the present time, when the system of managing the economy has been reorganized, and regional economic councils have been created, national narrow-mindedness in some districts takes the form of localist tendencies, which express themselves in the non-fulfilment of cooperative plans; there are attempts by individual leaders to "seize" more for their locality at the expense of the country as a whole. Recently the Party's Central Committee condemned the actions of certain leaders who had incorrectly utilized the revenues reserved for the development of undertakings of all-Union significance; these leaders had used the revenues for local needs, which are secondary in importance. Sometimes localism is accompanied by invented exaggerations of the national peculiarities of one or another republic, which gives rise to unreasonable demands for particular advantages and large investments from the all-Union budget into the republican economies.

Tendencies which cannot be called other than nationalist also appear in the efforts of some leaders to juxtapose the interests of their republic to the interests of Communist construction in our country as a whole. At one time the Kazakh Party organization condemned the incorrect behavior of certain leaders who took a negative attitude toward the question of the virgin lands. Now, when tens of millions of hectares of virgin soil have been plowed, and Kazakhstan gives the country a million puds of grain, this promotes our country's might and makes possible the further flowering of the economy and culture of the Kazakh SSR; it has become clear how wise were the decisions of the Central Committee of the CPSU on the plowing of the virgin lands, and how wrong and blind were those persons who did not understand the significance of this question. The Party cannot be indifferent even to the slightest attempts to juxtapose the incorrectly understood interests of a given republic to the interests of the entire Soviet Union.

In the field of ideology nationalist survivals find their expression in an idealization of the historical past, in an uncritical attitude toward various national movements, in forgetting the party principle in the discussion of questions of culture, literature, and art.

Some scholars are attempting to justify the activities of reactionary bourgeois-nationalist organizations in Central Asia and the Transcaucasus, motivating this by the allegation that the Twentieth Party Congress corrected the dogmatic errors in the assessment of the role of the national bourgeoisie in the countries of Asia and Africa. . . . It is necessary to dwell on another important question. The Soviet government has corrected the violations of socialist legality which took place in the past and rehabilitated those unjustly sentenced. In this lies the great merit of the Party and the government. This does not mean, however, that we must make concessions to ideological errors which were made in the past by some of the now rehabilitated persons. The Communist Party has fought and will always fight against expressions of bourgeois nationalism in our socialist society. Communists see their prime obligation in this.

In recent years the Western reactionary press has published a number of articles devoted to the republics of the Soviet East. These articles allege that national traditions are being destroyed in the Soviet Union. This, of course, is lie and slander. We Soviet people are the heirs of the best traditions of our ancestors. We shall promote all that is best in the national treasure house, we shall cultivate love for our rich past, for our classical literature and art, for the best traditions of the peoples of the USSR. But we shall fight against survivals of the exploiting society such as the cases, still found in the Soviet Union, of limiting the rights of women and harmful clan and other customs; we shall fight against backwardness and lack of culture.

Not for a moment must we forget that imperialist circles, the U.S.A. above all, are fighting against an internationalist ideology, banking on the as yet unconquered nationalist survivals in the people's consciousness. Speaking of the attempt of American imperialists to utilize the survivals of bourgeois ideology in the struggle against the socialist camp, one cannot but dwell on one of the methods which clearly illustrate the principles of American policy. The ruling circles of the U.S.A., when addressing themselves to their allies in the capitalist camp and to the nonsocialist countries in general, stress *cosmopolitan* slogans. Under the aegis of a fight against the danger of "international communism" they urge these countries to give up their national sovereignty to a "union" into aggressive blocs under the leadership of the U.S.A. On the other hand, they attempt to arouse *nationalist* tendencies in the countries of the socialist camp. These apparently contradictory goals are in fact aimed at one result—the ideological disarmament of countries which will facilitate American rule over them and enforce the domination of this imperialist power.

The imperialists' faithful ally in the spreading of bourgeois nationalism is contemporary revisionism which opposes Marxism-Leninism, the genuine internationalist teaching of the toilers. One of the theses of contemporary revisionists, which they took over bodily from the bourgeois politicians of the Dulles type, is the proposition about so-called national communism. Reactionary imperialist propaganda supports this thesis willingly and generously. The enemies of the toilers hope, with the help of this slogan, to break up the socialist camp, and to turn its countries against each other. And yet it is clear to every genuine Marxist that there is not and cannot be any specific "national" communism. Comrade N. S. Krush-

chev said at the jubilee session of the Supreme Soviet in 1957: "The opponents of socialism are hoping that the Communists will start to elaborate some sort of entirely "new" artificial roads to socialism for each country in particular, and will abandon the great experience of socialist construction available in the Soviet Union, China, and other countries."

What is the basic teaching of contemporary revisionism on the national question? The revisionists reduce their conception of internationalism to mere coexistence, on the basis of which countries with differing social systems can operate. But relations in the spirit of proletarian internationalism inevitably presuppose mutual collaboration, a rational division of labor, and joint resistance to the attempts of the imperialists.

Proletarian internationalism represents the solidarity and mutual help of the toilers of all lands in their common struggle for the victory of socialism against imperialism; it signifies above all the support of the world socialist system—the USSR, the Chinese People's Republic, and the other countries of socialism, the unity of the international communist movement, solidarity with the national liberation movement. It is firmly connected with patriotism, because the genuine patriotism of a proletarian of any country represents the strengthening of the forces of progress and democracy in their fight against the exploitation of the ruling classes, against national oppression, etc. In expressing love for their Motherland and attempting to turn it into an advanced socialist country, the workers and toilers become genuine patriots. By this very act they also fulfil their international obligation. To counterpose the national tasks of the proletariat to its international duties means to condemn the fulfilment of national tasks to failure, to bring harm to the cause of social progress, to the cause of socialism.

The revisionists deny the meaning for other countries of the experience of the Soviet Union in the building of socialism. Rejecting such views Comrade Mao Tse-tung remarked at the jubilee session of the Supreme Soviet of the USSR in November, 1957: "The people of all countries see their future more clearly every day in the successes of the Soviet people. The path of the Soviet Union, the path of the October Revolution is, in its fundamentals, the chief road for the development of all mankind."

We cannot underestimate the dangers of revisionism for the socialist camp and the entire international labor movement, because it attempts to break the unity of the peoples of the socialist camp, to weaken the struggle of the Communist and workers' parties for peace and socialism. It is therefore the first international duty of the Communists of all lands to struggle relentlessly against all the manifestations of revisionism.

With characteristic foresight Lenin showed that the struggle with nationalism, with deeply rooted petty bourgeois nationalist prejudices, will grow ever more important as the dictatorship of the proletariat becomes established in a number of countries, outgrowing the boundaries of one state and exercising a decisive influence on world politics. "The struggle with this evil," wrote Lenin, "with the most deeply rooted petty bourgeois national prejudices, will come to the forefront as the goal becomes to turn the dictatorship of the proletariat from a national to an international one (that is, a dictatorship of the proletariat in one country unable to influence world policy will change

into a dictatorship of the proletariat of several advanced countries capable of having a decisive influence on world affairs)." . . .

Despite the libelous assertions of our enemies, a thorough study of the Russian language and a mastery of the richest accomplishments of Russian culture have an enormous significance for the peoples of our country because this will, to a considerable extent, facilitate the exchange of cultural riches between the peoples of the USSR. The Russian language is a mighty means of communication between the peoples of the USSR; thanks to it, the accomplishments in the field of science, technology, and culture of the Russian people, as well as those of every national republic, become the property of all the peoples of our country. This is why the Russian language is justly regarded as the second native language of all the nationalities inhabiting the country of socialism. This does not mean, however, that the enormous role of the languages and cultures of the fraternal peoples of our Motherland should be underestimated in the slightest. The practice of our cadres in learning the language of the people among whom they live and work has justified itself and deserves all support. The most thorough study of the languages, literatures, and of the remarkable cultural heritage of all nations and nationalities remains an important task of Soviet scholars.

The publication of books criticizing the theory and practice of imperialism on the national question has the greatest significance in the task of educating the peoples in the spirit of socialist internationalism and patriotism. The racist and neo-fascist theories, fabricated in the U.S.A. and other capitalist countries, must be ruthlessly combatted. This will aid the progressive forces of all mankind in sharpening the struggle against imperialist reaction and racist dogmatism. Our scholarly and popular literature must propagandize the great accomplishments of the countries of the socialist camp more widely and deeply; we must describe the mutual help of the peoples of these countries. At the same time we must continue exposing contemporary revisionism which opposes the Leninist principles of proletarian internationalism and the unity and collaboration of the countries in the camp of socialism.

There is no question that we have as yet a too weakly developed fraternization between the youth of a number of Union and autonomous republics and the youth of the RSFSR, the Ukrainian SSR, etc. We must develop this fraternization. In particular, we must stress the further and broader development of economic, cultural, sport, and tourist ties of the youth of all nationalities in our country.

The task of constructing Communism, of educating the toilers, also demands a decisive struggle against all survivals of medieval and patriarchal practices, against religious prejudices, against improper attitudes toward women which occur in some localities. Only the best national traditions and customs must be supported. . . .

PIPES: THE FORCES OF NATIONALISM

There was a time—and not so long ago—when merely to assert the existence in Russia of a "national problem" evoked skepticism. This was a reaction common to both émigrés of pre–World War II vintage and Americans knowledgeable in Russian affairs. The majority of Russian émigrés consisted either of nobles, officials, and officers, who denied the existence of this problem on principle, from a misguided

sense of patriotism, or of urban intellectuals, who simply had no experience of it: they knew of an agrarian problem, of a labor problem, of a constitutional problem, even of a Jewish problem, but not of, say, a Ukrainian or a Moslem national problem. The latter they were inclined to regard as phantoms raised by German and Austrian propagandists during the First World War in an effort to weaken and dismember the Russian Empire.

The American attitude was, and continues to be, inspired by other considerations. First, there is the unsophisticated approach which takes at face value Soviet assertions that the abolition of private property in means of production and the constitutional guarantee of equality have in fact done away with national discrimination and animosities. Behind this kind of reasoning lie many uncritical and largely false assumptions about the nature of nationalism. Is nationalism really a "function" of economics? Do constitutional guarantees of equality assure actual equality—in Russia any more than in the United States? And would equality, even if realized, neutralize nationalism? Such questions are rarely asked by those who believe in what may be called a manipulative solution of the national question.

The more sophisticated and at the same time more prevalent attitude rests on a more or less conscious equation of the American and Russian experiences with national minorities. It assumes that in Russia, as in the United States, gradual assimilation of the minorities is both progressive and inevitable: progressive because it tends toward the establishment of true equality, inevitable because it is backed by superior culture and economic power. How persuasive such considerations can be is best illustrated by the example of an eminent American jurist who was shocked to find upon visiting Soviet Central Asia that native children were attending separate schools instead of Russian ones! Still fresh in memory are comparisons equating the Ukraine with Pennsylvania, and Georgians with the Welsh or Scots.

It is safe to say that such attitudes no longer prevail today, or at least are encountered less frequently than a decade ago. The national problem in the Soviet Union is widely recognized as a true and valid problem: it exists. But if one probes behind this admission, one still finds a very pronounced reluctance to concede that the problem is really something important and enduring. Men of good will are against nationalism, because nationalism has been responsible for so much bloodshed, hatred, and various other forms of irrational behavior. And because men of good will, like men of bad will, so often allow wishes (or fears) to interfere with their judgment of facts, they sometimes think that to recognize the reality of something one does not approve is tantamount to approving it; hence they are inclined to deny reality to that which they disapprove. Thus, though they may concede that the national problem exists, they like to think it will disappear.

NATIONALISM AND MODERNIZATION

It is quite striking that in this respect the attitudes of very many Russians and Americans fully coincide. When the issue is raised, one can hear quite similar responses from intellectuals in Moscow or Leningrad and New York or Washington. Why should this be so? It may well be that behind it lies a very fundamental factor linking American and Russian cultures: an impatience with, and underestimation of, historical

roots. For all their differences—and they are very profound—the American and Russian cultures are young cultures having been essentially molded in the past 250 years, that is, in an era when the prevailing intellectual tendencies have been antitraditionalist and scientific. They are forward-looking, more concerned with the life to be built than with the life that has been inherited. Both are imbued by a strong millennial spirit. Having given up many of their own traditions for the sake of modernization, Americans and Russians are not inclined to show undue respect for the traditionalism of other nations, especially when this traditionalism runs contrary to the requirements of modern life. So they tend to deprecate nationalism and advocate assimilation—and sometimes, to assume that the desirable is also the inevitable.[1]

Now, if we try to take a more dispassionate look at the problems of nationalism and nationality in the modern world, we must acknowledge that they show no sign whatever of becoming less urgent, let alone of disappearing. This is in some respects puzzling, because nationalism runs contrary to the needs of economic development which exert such a powerful influence on contemporary life. Certainly, the maximal use of economic resources requires a degree of rationalization that cannot brook interference from traditionalism. National barriers must be broken, and the

---

[1] It is curious that in spite of all the propaganda value which the Soviet Union has derived from discrimination against Negroes in the United States, one often encounters scorn for the whole "Negro question" among Soviet citizens. Many Russian have not much sympathy either for the economic plight of the American Negro, which is less acute than their own, or for the Negro's national aspirations. In this respect Russian tolerance of American intolerance matches the indifference of some Americans toward the Russians' maltreatment of their national minorities.

ground must be cleared of the old vegetation—sometimes luxuriant, sometimes merely disorderly and lifeless—which centuries of spontaneous cultural growth have produced. The discipline of the clock, the techniques of a money economy, and all the other complex features of modern industrial life are not compatible with national traditions that are usually rooted in agricultural or commercial mores. An ideal economic arrangement would be one in which all states would merge into one world union, and all mankind dissolve into one nation.

If, in fact, such an amalgamation is not taking place, it is because the process of modernization has a reverse side which preserves and even intensifies national allegiances and distinctions. This is the social aspect of modernization, which finds expression in the leveling of class differences and the involvement of the entire population in the national life. The rational organization of life requires that the whole citizenry be treated as one vast reservoir of manpower; consequently, it calls for democratization (in the social, if not necessarily the political, sense). Now, by pulling into national life the mass of previously isolated and passive population groups, the process of modernization inadvertently promotes nationalism and national differences, because national identity is most deeply rooted among these very groups. To cite but one example, in the days of mercenary armies nationalism was no factor in the maintenance of military morale, but it has become one with the introduction of the modern nonprofessional mass army. Mass education and mass literacy also promote national distinctions by institutionalizing local languages, histories, literatures, etc. So does the intelligentsia, whose emergence everywhere accompanies the breakdown of

the old class-stratified social structure.

This push and pull exerted on nationalism by the process of modernization has been the essence of the "national problem" of our time. On the one hand, modernization demands cultural leveling; on the other, it releases social forces that are least prone to such leveling. Since the latter tendency is often stronger than the former, because it represents real pressures as against ideal considerations, nationalism has made remarkable headway and is likely to continue to do so.

AMERICAN VS. SOVIET EXPERIENCE

The relentless assimilation of the ethnic groups residing in the United States is certainly a unique instance which neither vitiates these general considerations nor has any bearing on the situation in the Soviet Union.

(I leave aside the question of whether the American population is really as much assimilated and culturally integrated as it is often assumed to be.) Some nine-tenths of American citizens are descendants of immigrants who voluntarily severed their native roots and migrated to the United States to start a completely new life. Moreover, because many of them belonged to underprivileged groups of the population in their countries of origin, their ties to their national cultures were quite tenuous in any event. What occurred in American history was a mass-scale renunciation of one nationality in favor of a new one.

Nothing of the sort happened in Russia. The national minorities of that country consist largely of historic peoples who came or were brought under Russian sovereignty between the sixteenth and nineteenth centuries. While some of these nationalities passed under Russian rule more or less voluntarily, they did so in order to secure Russian protection against hostile neighbors, and not with any idea of surrendering their right to self-rule. Today, each has an intelligentsia and an officialdom of its own; they receive much of their education in native languages; they reside on their historic territories, surrounded by places and monuments with strong national associations. The differences between Soviet and American national minority groups could be further elaborated upon, but this is scarcely necessary. It seems obvious that the two situations are fundamentally different: in one case, we are dealing with a new nation created, as it were, through a voluntary multinational effort; in the other, with an ordinary empire of many nations dominated by one. It is meaningful to speak of an American nation, because the inhabitants of the United States refer to themselves as "Americans." Has anyone ever heard an inhabitant of the Soviet Union refer to his nationality as "Soviet"?

One of the reasons why the national problem in the Soviet Union is difficult to grasp is the confusion that surrounds the number of nationalities involved. The figures of 175, 188, or over 200 "nationalities" which are sometimes cited are quite misleading, because they confuse the term "nationality" as understood by the ethnographer and anthropologist with the term as it is used by the historian or political scientist. To the former, any group displaying certain common ethnic characteristics may well be a nationality—the six hundred Tofalars as much as the six million Uzbeks. To the historian and political scientist, on the other hand, a "nationality" all of whose members reside in one medium-sized Caucasian *aul* or Siberian settlement is of no interest whatever. Actually, there are in the Soviet Union only a dozen or so national groups of significance to the student of

the national question. The fate of the national minorities and of the "national problem" depends in large measure on them, or, more specifically, on their ability or inability to resist Russification and to evolve viable national cultures.

THE ASSIMILATION PROCESS

This Russification has been carried out by a great variety of methods, some crude, some subtle. The most effective have been connected with the semi-official policy of elevating the Great Russians to the position of the leading ethnic group in the Soviet Union. This policy, formulated by Stalin, has not been repudiated by his successors. In a country where personal relations play so important a function, serving as something of a substitute for the weakly developed legal system, such an attitude on the part of the rulers has a direct bearing on the life of all the citizens. It means, above all, that the road to prestige, power, and material benefits entails adaptation to Russian culture: in the party, in the army, in the higher educational establishment.

The message of Russian primacy is conveyed to the minorities in a variety of ways, among which one may mention the linguistic (imposition of the Cyrillic alphabet on the Muslim minority), the historiographic (emphasis on the progressive role of conquest by Tsarist Russia), and the religious (more acute persecution of religious bodies other than the Orthodox church). That the ultimate intent of all these measures is the Russification of all the various ethnic groups is made quite clear by the statement in the new party program that "full-scale communist construction constitutes a new stage in the development of national relations in which the nations will draw still closer together until complete unity is achieved." It is fair to assume that the language and culture of the eventual "completely unified" nation will not be Komi-Zyrian, Chukchi, or even Uzbek.

There are many ways in which the reaction of the national minorities can be studied, some quantitative, others not. Useful indexes can be obtained from population censuses, which furnish data on such vital matters as population movement, fertility, intermarriage, and linguistic habits. Information of a different kind, less measurable but equally important, can be derived from literary sources, from ethnographic data, and from political intelligence. Only when both these types of data—the quantitative and nonquantitative—are juxtaposed and placed against the historic background of the national groups concerned is it possible to draw meaningful and more or less scientific conclusions about the situation of Soviet minorities.[2]

The publication by the Soviet Central Statistical Administration of the abstract of the 1959 population census, imperfect as this volume is, permits for the first time in a quarter-century a study of the vital statistics bearing on the Soviet national minorities. The data it supplies, when compared with those given in the 1926 census, give a better picture than we have ever had of the various nationalities' actual tendencies of development.[3] And none of this information is more significant than the figures which tell, black on white, what has happened to the linguistic habits of the minorities. In considering these figures, one must bear in mind that the inter-census period (1926–59) coincided with the most intense Russification effort in modern Russian history. What we now have is, as it were, the fruits of that gigantic and ruthless effort. What do we find?

LINGUISTIC TRENDS

In 1926 Russians constituted 54 per cent of the total population of the USSR by nationality, but 58.5 per cent by language. In other words, in 1926, 4.5 per cent of the total population may be said to have been linguistically Russified. In 1959, the corresponding figures are 54.3 and 59.3 per cent, giving 4.8 per cent as the proportion of those linguistically Russified. The net gain of 0.7 per cent represents approximately 600,000 citizens. But even this minute gain disappears if we recall that in the intervening period the Nazis had slaughtered some two million Yiddish-speaking Jews on Soviet soil, reducing the number of Jewish Soviet citizens who consider Yiddish their native language from 1.8 million (1926) to less than one-half million (1959). Thus, the proportion of linguistically Russified non-Russians has actually decreased somewhat. In absolute terms, of course, the number of citizens who speak their national languages has grown far more than the number of those who have become linguistically assimilated. While the number of Soviet citizens who have

[2] The author tried to apply both these methods to Central Asia and Transcaucasia in the following articles: "Muslims of Soviet Central Asia: Trends and Prospects," *Middle East Journal*, Nos. 2 and 3, 1955, and "Demographic and Ethnographic Changes in Transcaucasia, 1897–1956," *ibid.*, Winter, 1959.

[3] Tsentralnoe statisticheskoe upravlenie pri Sovete Ministrov SSSR, *Itogi vsesoiuznoi perepisi naseleniia 1959 goda: SSSR (Svodnyi tom)* (Moscow, 1962), pp. 184–243. The data

from the 1926 census are drawn largely from F. Lorimer, *The Population of the Soviet Union: History and Prospects* (Geneva, 1946), supplemented by R. Pipes, *Formation of the Soviet Union* (Cambridge: Harvard University Press, 1954), pp. 289–99.

abandoned their native language in favor of Russian has grown from 6.4 million (1926) to 10 million (1959), the number of those who adhere to their native language has increased in the same period from 60 to 85 million.

Such, in its broadest aspect, is the impact of thirty years of Russification carried out with all the instruments at the disposal of the totalitarian state. But if we delve deeper into the statistical material and break down the figures for over-all linguistic assimilation into figures for each of the various national groups, and, within these, for different age-groups, we discover even more surprising facts.

Linguistic assimilation has always been and continues to be most rapid among ethnic groups that enjoy a high level of culture, but whose historic roots, and often ethnic centers, are located outside the Soviet Union. In this category belong, first of all, the groups of Europeans, such as Poles, Germans, or Greeks, between one-quarter and one-half of whom have become linguistically denationalized.[4] It also includes the groups representing ancient Oriental cultures, such as Koreans, Chinese, or Persians. In all these groups linguistic Russification is proceeding apace. The reason for it is not far to seek. Members of these nationalities in the Soviet Union regard themselves as isolated fragments of their nations and

[4] It must not be assumed, however, that all linguistic denationalization benefits Russification. Among Soviet Poles, for example, more than half (756,000) had given up Polish, but of these, two-thirds had opted for Ukranian and Belorussian, only one-third for Russian. (Undoubtedly, many of these Poles preferred to deny their mother tongue for political reasons.) In the case of the Bashkirs, of the 377,000 who had given up Bashkir, 350,000 had adopted Tatar. Among the 94,000 linguistically denationalized Uzbeks, twice as many declared Tajik their native tongue as Russian.

consequently see no reason to aspire to national self-preservation. *Mutatis mutandis,* the same may be said of the Jews, four-fifths of whom acknowledge Russian as their native tongue—at any rate to the census taker. More than one-quarter of all the Russified non-Russians belong to this category.

The nationalities with a medium "Russification index" may also be divided into two groups. One consists of the two largest minorities, the Ukrainians and Belorussians, both closely related to Great Russians in terms of origin and culture. If we compare the linguistic data for these two nationalities in the 1926 and 1959 census reports, we find that the proportion of those who consider Ukrainian and Belorussian their native tongues has actually *increased.* In 1926, 87.1 per cent of the Ukrainians spoke their native language; in 1959, 87.7 per cent. In the case of Belorussians, the increase has been even more significant: from 71.9 to 84.2 per cent. Figures by age groups indicate, moreover, that Ukrainians and Belorussians under 20 years of age (i.e., those educated between approximately the end of the war and the year of Stalin's death) are more loyal to their native languages than those of middle age (who had been educated in the 1920's and 1930's—an indication that there has been no progressive de-nationalization of youth.

The other group in this category consists of nationalities inhabiting the Volga-Ural region, including both Turkic Moslems (Tatars and Bashkirs) and Finnic Christians (Mordvins, Chuvash, etc.). These nationalities have for several centuries been under Russian rule. In fact, they were the first minorities to be conquered by Russians in the sixteenth and seventeenth centuries. They now find themselves in the midst of

Russian population centers, cut off from the main body of their Turkic and Finnic relatives, and consequently have a difficult time preserving their identity. Among them the proportion of those who are shifting to Russian is growing, though not dramatically (e.g., Tatar-speaking Tatars have declined from 98.9 to 92.0 per cent, Chuvash-speaking Chuvash from 97.7 to 90.0 per cent, with the Mordvins showing the greatest decline, from 94 to 78 per cent).

If we next turn to the minorities with distinct cultures, living in borderland areas, and with historic roots on their present territories, we find that Russification either has made little or no progress or has lost ground. The Turkic inhabitants, who constitute the single most numerous minority bloc after the Ukrainians, show an astounding loyalty to their native languages. Except for the Volga Tatars, whom we have discussed above, they show between 97 and 99 per cent adherence to their own languages. In some cases (e.g., the Azeri Turks and Turkmens) the percentage of native-speaking citizens is up a bit compared to 1926, in others (e.g., the Kazakhs and Kirghiz) it is a bit down, but in general no linguistic assimilation has taken place. Of the 20 million Moslems (Volga Tatars excepted) in the Soviet Union, only 200,000, or 1 per cent, have become linguistically Russified. The same situation prevails in the Caucasus. The percentage of Georgians who consider Georgian their native tongue has increased from 96.5 (1926) to 98.6 (1959). This also holds true of the Azeri Turks (from 93.8 per cent in 1926 to 97.6 per cent in 1959). The Armenians, on the other hand, seem to be slowly Russifying, though it is more than probable that the decrease in percentage of those who consider Armenian their native tongue (from 92.4 in 1926

to 89.9 in 1959) has occurred among Armenians residing outside the Armenian republic. Among the Baltic peoples, the proportion of those who adhere to their native languages varies between 95 and 97 per cent.

IMPLICATIONS FOR THE FUTURE

The principal conclusion which emerges from these statistics may be formulated as follows: both on territories predominantly occupied by Russians (RSFSR) and on those predominantly occupied by major minority groups, the lines separating the Russians from the nationalities in matters of language are becoming sharper and more distinct. The Russians as well as the national minorities are gaining linguistic hegemony in the areas where they enjoy numerical and administrative preponderance. What is occurring may be described as a process of the emergence of modern nations within the Soviet Union. The smaller nationalities are slowly giving ground by dissolving either among the Russians or among the ethnic groups whose language and culture are most closely related to their own. The major nationalities, on the other hand, among whom one must include the Ukrainians, Georgians, and Turkic peoples of Central Asia, are gaining in cohesion.

Language, of course, is only one of several criteria of national viability, and it would not be sound to base one's whole evaluation on the pattern of linguistic development. But it is a most important criterion. The transition from one language to another is, perhaps, the single most dramatic manifestation of a shift in national allegiance. The fact that it is not occurring among the major peripheral nationalities gives some ground for arguing that the burden of proof in discussing the fate of Soviet nationalities lies on those who foresee the imminent dissolution in a single Soviet nationality.

The practical conclusions which this evidence suggests have bearing not merely on the Soviet Union but on all those areas where a nascent sense of national identity emerges simultaneously with a drive for modernization. It is difficult to conceive how the contrary pulls implicit in modernization, to which reference has been made above, can be reconciled in any other way than through the establishment of independent national states. The national state alone provides within its confines outlets for both economic and other forms of rationalization on which material well-being and power depend, and for the national sentiments and loyalties which rationalization brings to the surface. Such has been the experience of Western Europe and of all the great multinational states and empires. In Russia, the breakdown of empire almost occurred in the course of the Revolution and Civil War. It was averted partly by force of arms and partly by the creation of a novel political system which combined outward decentralization with unprecedented inner centralization. But from the long-term historical point of view, there is no reason to assume that this solution was anything but a temporary one.

69

SOVIET RELIGIOUS POLICY

By Liudmila Anokhina and Margarita Shmeleva; Harry Willetts

After half a century of Soviet rule religion remains a viable force in the Soviet Union. Despite repeated waves of persecution and endless subtle pressure some Soviet citizens (we do not know how many because the Soviet census does not ask questions about religious belief and no statistics on religious affiliation are published) continue to profess and practice various forms of religion, both Christian and other. The regime is clearly both annoyed and embarrassed by all this, but has never found any clear-cut solution to the problem. For decades, however, it has spoken with great assurance about the ultimate disappearance of all religious belief among Soviet citizens. This conviction animates the small piece which we reprint as the first selection below; written by two Soviet lady anthropologists and sociologists, it is based, they write, on extensive field trips of 1956–60 during which a questionnaire was administered to over five hundred families totaling 2,162 persons. The reader will note, however, that the two investigators again fail to give any figures concerning the number of believers among those questioned. It should be added that the piece deals only with one part of European Russia, and only with the Russian Orthodox Church. The author of our second selection is a recognized British expert on the Soviet Union and is on the faculty of St. Antony's College at Oxford. It should be noted that his article (and a companion piece on Judaism in the USSR which we omit) is richly illustrated by samples of Soviet antireligious propaganda.

For a general study of church-state relations in the USSR see John Curtiss, *The Russian Church and the Soviet State, 1917–1950*; Walter Kolarz, *Religion in the Soviet Union*; Matthew Spinka, *The Church in Soviet Russia*; Nikita Struve, *Christians in Contemporary Russia*; Michael Bordeaux, *Religious Ferment in Russia: Protestant Opposition to Soviet Religious Policy*; William Stroyen, *Communist Russia and the Russian Orthodox Church, 1943–1962*; William Fletcher and Anthony Strover, *Religion and the Search for New Ideals in the USSR*. For superb photographs see Patricia Blake, "Russian Orthodoxy: A Captive Splendor," *Life*, September 14, 1959.

Important articles include the following: Vladimir Gsovski, "The Legal Status of the Church in Soviet Russia," in Sidney Harcave (ed.), *Readings in Russian History*, Vol. II (paperback); Paul Anderson, "The Orthodox Church in Soviet Russia," *Foreign Affairs*, January, 1961; Ethel and Stephen Dunn, "Religion as an Instrument of Cultural Change," *Slavic Review*, September, 1964; "The Results of the Persecution of the Orthodox Church," as well as "Further Proof of the Incontrovertible," *Bulletin of the Institute for the Study of the USSR*, May, 1965, and July, 1966; Michael Bourdeaux, "Reform and Schism," *Problems of Communism*, October–November, 1967; Joshua Rothenberg, "The Status of Cults," *ibid.*; and *St. Vladimir's Seminary Quarterly*, December, 1965, for the full text of letters by two Soviet priests on the actual state of the Russian Orthodox Church today.

For Soviet writing on the subject see U.S. Joint Publications Research Service, *The Atheist's Handbook* (a translation of a Soviet manual for atheists); *The Russian Orthodox Church: Organization, Situation, Activity* (published in Moscow in 1959); an article in *Atlas*, April, 1967; and "Atheist Agitation Weakness," *Current Digest of the Soviet Press*, February 28, 1968.

ANOKHINA AND SHMELEVA: RELIGIOUS SURVIVALS

The most harmful survivals of the past are those connected with the ideology of religion. These continue to poison the minds and affect the actions of a part of the rural population. At present the bulk of the population of the Soviet countryside hold atheist views, and another substantial group, made up of people now wavering in their faith, is, in fact, on the road to atheism. The rejection of religion is a broader movement now than it was in the twenties and thirties when it attained an increasingly popular character. And the meaning of religious faith is a far cry from what it was earlier. Today most believers have, typically, a vague idea of some kind of supreme power, to which they turn in the face of difficulties "just in case." This fundamentally utilitarian approach is a sure sign of the gradual withering of the religious attitude among even those collective farmers who think of themselves as believers.

Similarly indicative is the drop during the Soviet period of regular church attendance, daily prayers, the worship of icons, and the keeping of fasts— rules that spring from the heart of Orthodoxy. For the most part, believers today find such rules bothersome and

old-fashioned and generally do not observe them. The rupture between religious and political beliefs is further evidence of religious decline. Religious faith retains its reactionary character, but the faithful are patriots and, like the rest of the Soviet people, are devoted to the construction of communism. The danger of religious influence on some elements of the population is, nevertheless, real. The Kalinin countryside is no exception in this regard.

As a rule, believers are collective farmers of the older generation, among whom there are those who carry the system of religious ideas more or less intact, though their beliefs have been seriously shaken by socialism and the accomplishments of science. An old collective farmer of the village of Ignatovo, Kalinin District, expressed his ambivalence this way: "I believe and don't believe in God. For a long while I stuck to my religion, but now I don't know: Sputniks go off—but where is God?

The first selection is translated by Howard Goldfinger from L. Anokhina and M. Shmeleva, *Kul'tura i Byt Kolkhoznikov Kalininskoi Oblasti* (Moscow, 1964), pp. 313–18. The second selection is from H. Willets, "De-Opiating the Masses," *Problems of Communism*, November–December, 1964. Footnotes have been omitted. Published with the permission of the United States Information Agency.

Why would God let man do whatever he wants to?" These uncertainties and second thoughts are confined to the men of this generation. By and large, the women of the older group hold strictly to their religious views. They are unable to overcome prejudices instilled by the old family under the old social system. But even they failed to resist the general movement away from religious ceremonial.

In regard to religion, the collective farmers of forty-five to sixty years of age are even more heterogeneous. A variety of historical conditions shaped their attitudes (the Revolutionary years, the twenties and thirties) and this manifests itself, for example, in the ideas of the women. Unlike the women of the older generation, there are many convinced atheists among the women of thirty to forty, though there are believers as well. The latter, however, rarely have had any religious training and know next to nothing about prayers, holidays, and rites. They are unable to explain what they believe in and often fall back on the saving authority of their elders: "The old ones say so. . . ." The faithful of this generation are characterized by blind adherence to tradition.

Lack of general culture explains much of this clinging to religion among the middle-generation women. Without the knowledge necessary to handle questions of meaning and value on their own, they rely on the old religious explanations and customs. The young generation is being damaged by the attempts of some older members of the family to maintain religious traditions at home.

It must be said, however, that the majority of those who have broken with religious superstitions belong to the middle generation, which is the back- bone of rural society and the working collectives. The steady, vitalizing effect of Soviet reality acts on these people first of all. Even the believers among them perceive the incongruity of their outworn beliefs with their real interests and the demands of society.

K., a collective farmer of the Il'ich farm, Bezhetsky District, and one of its best flax workers, made a most relevant comment. By her own word, she still clings to religion, but she finds something definitely awkward about it: "In the collective farm I am always in the public eye. People look to me as an example. How could I go to church? I don't even especially want to."

The men of the middle generation do not believe in God, a believer being a rarity in this group. At the same time, not all the men are militant atheists, and many are indifferent about religious survivals.

Collective farmers of the younger generation (20–35 years of age) grew up during the period of a mass rejection of religion. They formed atheist views without the internal doubts and struggle that their elders experienced. But this "inborn" quality of their atheism contains its special weakness, and not all of the young fully understand the real harmfulness of religious survivals, and this allows the church to influence some of them through believers in their families. At the urging of parents, some of the youth (especially girls) go to church, participate in the services, sometimes as principal performers (e.g., marrying in church), and attach no significance to their actions. The outward, decorative aspect of religious ceremonies captivates some of these youths. Bound materially and spiritually to parents and family, they are hard-pressed to stay independent. When a young married woman sets out to accommodate herself to her husband's family (her mother-in-law chiefly), she can easily be swayed by the believers. She takes up religious duties as her relatives insist, though she had not earlier given religion a thought. To exemplify this, there is an incident that occurred on the "Awakening" Collective Farm, Bezhetsky District, in 1957. Several schoolchildren refused to become Pioneers. They had been forbidden to do so by their parents. As the teacher found out, the mothers (women of 30–35 years) were under the influence of the old believing women. The influence of believers on youth should, of course, not be exaggerated. The infected youth are an insignificant minority among a collective-farm youth population completely free of religious superstitions.

More solidly entrenched survivals are the religious beliefs and rituals which are woven into the very lives of the people and are seen as inseparable parts of it. Such religious acts as baptism, funeral and memorial services, the worship of icons, name days, and marriage (to a lesser extent) are part of numerous and varied traditions surrounding the chief events in the life of a peasant family. Thus, despite the undoubted victory of the atheist world view in our country, some religious survivals are apparent in segments of the collective-farm population. The backward influence at times overcomes unbelievers, who have to cope with the bearers of superstitions. Often, they are pushed into compromise by that philistine substitute for public opinion which continues to exist in the countryside, a network of family, relatives, and neighbors—indeed, every resident of this or that village—which is the pipeline of all kinds of conservative attitudes and customs and constitutes a genuine obstacle

to the development of socialist habits in the rural areas. The individual who neglects the unwritten village law runs the risk of the judgment of his relatives. Newly married youth, just setting up their own household, feel this factor keenly, as they try to attach themselves to the middle generation with whom they have common interests.

Real Soviet public opinion wages an irreconcilable struggle with philistine views, and in many localities, thanks to its penetration not only into productive collectives but also into family life, it has fully paralyzed the influence of individual believers.

A new phase in the religious struggle on the collective farms became sharply evident in 1960, when Party and public organizations began to develop more flexible forms of educational work and antireligious propaganda on the basis of the resolution of the Central Committee of the Communist Party of the Soviet Union on party propaganda in modern conditions. Without curtailing lecture programs, agitators and propagandists made the most of opportunities for informal, impromptu discussions with individual collective farmers or with small groups during meal breaks, or, after hours, in homes. Similarly a vanguard of atheists formed a club in Maksatikhinsky District, outfitted a planetarium, and organized lectures from among the local intelligentsia to visit the collective farms on a regular basis. At the discretion of the lecturers, specially selected films are shown. At the antireligious gatherings, the local teachers of biology, chemistry, and physics conduct experiments or give reports. Atheist clubs now exist in nearly every village with a church in its vicinity. Lecture topics vary: "The Harm of Religion," "Religion and Children," "Recent Achievements in the Conquest of Space," "The Origins of Religious Holidays," and so on. Atheist club productions have become very popular among the collective farm population.

The atheist theme is central to the programs of collective-farm clubs, agitation and propaganda centers, and Red Reading Rooms. It is also part of the curriculum of the people's universities of culture. The university in Bezhets is one among several that have created a department of scientific atheism. The newly created Soviet holidays and festivals for collective farmers, imbued with meaning and celebrated happily, play their important role in the liquidation of religion.

The development of the Communist world view among the toilers is impossible without a struggle against religion and other survivals of the past. This was reiterated by the plenum on ideology of the Central Committee in June, 1963. Peaceful coexistence of the world views of socialism and hostile capitalism is inconceivable.

The comprehensive work of building communism is creating all the conditions for the complete victory over old ideas and ways, including religion. The leading collective farms already are using their opportunities in this regard to the maximum. Gradually, comradely criticism of antisocial behavior is becoming the chief means of extirpating bourgeois ideas. The influence of Soviet public opinion grows ever more powerful.

WILLETS: DE-OPIATING THE MASSES

In the autumn of 1963, the Ideological Commission of the CPSU Central Committee reviewed the progress of the war on religion and decided to throw in reinforcements. A new Institute of Scientific Atheism, to be attached to the Cen-

tral Committee's Academy of Social Sciences, would coordinate all antireligious research and teaching; a regular quota of university students would be trained as professional atheists, and all students in universities and medical schools would be required to take courses in atheism; a number of learned and political journals would publish regular antireligious features; and the radio and television networks would put on more antireligious programs. Finally, at the local level, party organizations were to set up councils or sections "on atheistic work" whose task would be to draw all interested bodies and the public at large into the struggle.

There have been more savage attacks on religion in the Soviet Union in the past, but never has the regime mounted such a massive and heavily equipped campaign. How should we understand this apparently disproportionate effort to deal with what is nowadays supposed to be a minor and rapidly dwindling nuisance? If it is true that "the overwhelming majority of the Soviet people have broken with religion" and "become conscious atheists," that the religious are for the most part elderly people, peasants in remote rural areas, unskilled laborers, semiliterates, and housebound women, and if it is true. moreover, that most believers, in spite of their religion, are loyal to the regime and accept its social ideals, that education, the reclamation of rural slums, and the emancipation of still more women will in time dispel the lingering remnants of religious belief and practice, then why need the party do more than patiently exhibit the truths which, it insists, all mature human beings must acknowledge?

There are, of course, believers whose hopes of salvation depend on defiance of Soviet laws and norms of social behavior. The "True Orthodox Church," for instance, considers that Anti-Christ was enthroned in Russia in 1917, and it continues to deal with the Soviet authorities as if they were his representatives. A variety of sects—among them Jehovah's Witnesses and the numerous Adventists and Baptists who refuse obedience to the leaders in Moscow—do their best to scamp the demands made on them by Soviet society. There are sectarians who refuse to perform military service, sectarians who will pay no taxes, sectarians who withhold their children from the "Godless" Soviet schools, sectarians who think it wicked to keep body and soul together, sectarians who condemn all secular reading and entertainment, sectarians who reject medical aid in favor of prayer, and sectarians who try to avoid all intercourse whatsoever with the profane. Nor is it surprising that the Soviet authorities relentlessly pursue the orgiastic sects—the Molokane with their hysterogenic "jumping," the "shaking" and glossolalian Pentecostalists, the Innocentians and Murashkovites, who reputedly practice self-mutilation and sometimes fast unto death. But these intractable enthusiasts are few in number compared, for instance, with the Orthodox, who live orderly lives, render unto Caesar, and are regularly assured by their clergy that the Soviet system, far from contradicting Christ's message, is in some sense a fulfilment of it. Why, then, should the party want to bully these and other sedate churchgoers into renouncing their faith before it evaporates, as the party claims it will?

For one thing, the Soviet state is by nature irritable. Any foreign body sets up in it an intolerable itch which sooner or later must be relieved by a violent scratch. To Soviet officialdom generally, and more especially to the professional agitprop man, religion is often very irritating. It inevitably makes its adherents less amenable to the purposes of the regime. No matter how law-abiding and loyal to the state, the believer shudders when his child puts on the red kerchief of the Komsomol (though he may not go so far as the Baptists and call it "the Devil's mark"), and he certainly will try to keep the child out of an organization which would want him to disown his religious upbringing. But it is not just that religion, even in its least challenging forms, cannot help impinging on the authority of the regime; its prevalence also shows up the failure of the regime to fulfill for many of its subjects the promise on which its authority is supposed to rest—the promise to provide them with the good life. Millions of people still look to religion for the help and solace and reassurance that they cannot obtain, or think they cannot obtain, from the state or the "collective."

For many people everywhere, religion is a refuge from "the world," from a society which they, for whatever reason, dislike. It is, of course, infuriating to an exorbitant temporal power that some of its subjects find comfort in meditating on its transience, in squinting at its pretensions in the light of eternity. The theologians of present-day Orthodoxy "affirm that there are no contradictions between communism and Orthodoxy," but at the same time they "reduce communism to a matter of the 'external structure' of human existence," thus making it "an insignificant social factor in comparison with the absolute and eternal teaching of Christ." Perhaps the attitude of the tiny splinter group calling itself "True Orthodox," which teaches outright hatred of the Communists, is less annoying to the party than that of the powerful parent church, which teaches that the Communists are not too bad but should not be taken too seriously.

The religious denominations are the only large and fairly coherent opposition groups in the Soviet Union offering varying degrees of resistance to certain official policies and openly preaching rival philosophies and sets of values. I once heard a leading Soviet ideologist tell a foreign scholar that there existed in the Soviet Union a "flourishing school of idealist philosophers" whom he identified, on request, as "the Orthodox Church." He was joking, but the jest underlines the fact that only the religious now make any sustained public challenge to the official ideology. Perhaps this would matter less, from the official point of view, if religion were confined to the uneducated. But while it is frequently stressed that "the vast majority of believers are semi-literates," we learn on occasion that "there are also intellectuals among them."

These, then, are some of the reasons why L. F. Ilichev, head of the Ideological Commission, believes that "we cannot and do not have the right to wait for [religious] survivals to vanish without the action on them of our practical successes." And it is quite clear that the official strategists now believe some of their past efforts to have been misconceived. Often they have lopped off all of the plant that shows, but left the roots to grow again, sometimes freakishly. The province of Kostroma had 800 churches before the Revolution and now has only 80. At first sight, this seems a famous victory for militant atheism, but most of the dead churches were put out of action by force in the 1920's or by administrative harrassment in later years. There is, moreover, no correlation in the Soviet Union between the number of believers in a locality and the number of places of worship. The Orthodox Christian whose church has been padlocked against him or desecrated by being turned into a storehouse, stable, or workshop, may continue to worship surreptitiously in a private house together with his coreligionists, or quite often with the sectarians, who are well skilled in organizing such activities. Even if he no longer joins in congregational worship, he will very often continue to light the lamp before his icons and will impart to his children what he can remember of the church's teaching. And all the while he will feel insulted and deprived and will resent the brutality of the state.

Besides these secret worshippers, there are very many Soviet citizens for whom vestigial religious trappings and observances—ikons, mezuzahs, ritual foods, christening or circumcision, religious weddings and burials, excursions to local shrines—have a nostalgic and semireligious charm even when they have ceased to be imperatives of conscience. Frequently one reads of "intellectuals," officials, even party members who, though they may think the teachings of religion ridiculous, connive at or even attend religious ceremonies, and who tolerate the accessories of religion in their homes as though they were just traditional domestic ornaments. As long as there are such people—i.e., those who remain believers even though they have no place of worship, those who are in the "mixed and middle state" between belief and unbelief, and the Laodicean atheists who neither believe in nor fight against religion—the Communist educator's work is obviously far from done. Hence Ilichev's declaration that "the formation of a scientific outlook is our most urgent task. Its fulfillment demands, in particular, the furtherance of atheistic education by all possible means."

Many of the excesses of Soviet agit-prop campaigns are surely traceable to the feeling that whatever ideas people are abandoning, or half-abandoning, they are not firmly adopting a consistent Marxist-Leninist world view instead. To encounter in a work of anti-religious propaganda the chapter heading "Agnosticism in the Service of Modern Orthodoxy" is to be reminded that nothing less than total mental surrender can satisfy the Communist ideologue. Looking around him, he finds not only that religion is still vigorous, but that where it has been cut down a degenerate growth has sometimes sprung up in the same soil. The Soviet pundits are not the first to find that when traditional faiths are shown the door superstition flies in at the window.

At a more sophisticated level, imported religious fads or homegrown religio-scientific fantasies may move into minds emptied of their old faith. Thus Yoga, spiritualism, and white magic have been heard of lately in Leningrad. One well-known antireligious professional, reporting these phenomena, also views with alarm the recent currency of stories about "flying saucers," of the hypothesis that biblical accounts of miraculous ascents to and descents from heaven are in fact garbled records of visits from outer space, and even of "the legend of the Abominable Snowman." "In our circumstances," writes Shakhnovich, "such myths, although they may themselves contain no element of mysticism, nonetheless clear the way for it." The same writer goes on to report an extraordinary example of religio-scientific speculation:

In 1962 A. I. Grigoriev . . . sent to the Philosophical Faculty of Leningrad Uni-

versity a project for the foundation of a new religion. He argues that since "all things develop triadically," "we cannot stop at atheism, which is "only the antithesis of theism," and that therefore a "synthesis combining theism and atheism must be thought up." . . . in the light of dialectical materialism. God should be understood as a man living on some planet, but with milliards of years of evolutionary development behind him which have ensured him the attributes of omnipotence, omniscience, etc. Grigoriev accompanies his project for an "atheistic religion" with some absurd speculations on the mystical properties of numbers.

The cranky—or possibly humorous—Grigoriev is worth mentioning for two reasons. One is that Shakhnovich's deliberate choice of a particularly absurd example of religio-philosophic speculation leads one to wonder whether other such exercises, more intelligently conceived and rigorously conducted, are not quite common. If they are, they would obviously testify to a serious speculative interest in religion among the Soviet intelligentsia. But whether the answer to this question is yes or no, one other observation needs to be made, namely, that this sort of thing surely cannot be of the slightest real concern to the Soviet authorities. Shakhnovich is plainly making work for himself. Piety, ideological vacillations, and mere crankiness may, as I have suggested, genuinely irritate the professional zealot. But we can be sure, too, that for professional reasons he will exaggerate his irritation. The Ideological Commission, once established, had to justify its existence by doughty deeds on all the well-trampled ideological fronts, including that of scientific atheism. This, of coure, does not make the onslaught any easier for the religious to bear. But no one should infer from the violence of the campaign that religion is in fact a serious political or social problem from the point of view of Soviet officialdom—with the exception perhaps of some inquisitors.

This, however, is not to suggest that the war on religion has no serious political objective. It may be, as much as anything, a way of generating and channeling support for an officially decreed purpose and thus encouraging feelings of identification with the regime. Young people in particular have become rather bored with the regime's exhortations to workaday virtue, with its stereotyped self-congratulation and its nebulous promises, and it may be hoped that they will respond better if they are shown an enemy—a picturesque one at that—and a host of benighted fellow beings to be rescued. (For while religion is to be crushed, the religious are to be cherished—or, according to some sources, the religious rank-and-file are to be cherished, but not the incorrigible fanatics. We shall see below that there is cause for misgiving as to how this works in practice.)

Some Western readers of the egregious T. K. Kichko have wondered for whom exactly his book was intended, since, as one commentator observes, very few Jews read Ukrainian. But the Soviet press has often told us that believers do not go to antireligious lectures, and we may suppose that they are not major consumers of antireligious literature either. Some 70,000 "agitator-conversationalists" were recently mobilized in the Ukraine; and Kichko's book was published in 12,000 copies. There can be little doubt where most of them were intended to go.

The principle was laid down long ago —and re-emphasized in "Khrushchev's Decree" of 1954—that the fight against religion must be conducted by education and persuasion, without crude administrative pressures and without offense to the susceptibilities of believers. But in practice the rules have been loosely interpreted. The Soviet press has publicized a large number of cases in which a local antireligious drive was climaxed by the closing of a place of worship and the flight of its discomfited incumbents. The following shows the process at its most democratic and "spontaneous":

The synagogue ceased its activity, and its premises were turned into a recreation hall. This was preceded by extensive explanatory work among the believers. We began from the leadership, the ruling twenty elders. After the members of the ruling group had been persuaded that the further existence of the congregation was inexpedient, we used some of them to influence the rest of the believers. The whole congregation was then divided into groups, and each group was taken care of by agitators. As soon as the ruling twenty had signed an announcement of their resignation, it was comparatively easy to convince the rank-and-file of the congregation.

There is no need to spell out the many questions that this narrative raises. But it should perhaps be made clear that if the members of a congregation which had been disbanded in this fashion were to continue worshiping together in some other place, they might be charged with breaking the law since "ministers of religion do not have the right to open churches, mosques or houses of prayer on their own initiative, without the express permission of the organs of state power, nor . . . to hold prayer meetings in buildings not specifically designed for that purpose." Nor would it be safe for the priest, presbyter, rabbi, or mullah to canvass for support. If he were to visit members of his flock in their homes for this purpose, he would be infringing the law against conducting religious propaganda outside places of worship, for which the penalty might be severe.

Although in theory only moral pressures may be brought to bear on the religious, the press occasionally refers, disapprovingly, to strong-arm methods which have miscarried. For instance, the Krasnograd Ispolkom, after highhandedly ordering the demolition of a prayer house in the interests of urban development, was criticized for "trying to extinguish a fire with petrol." Its hasty action had only made the believers "more fanatical," it was stated, and the government had had to restore (for how long?) their place of worship. In another case of premature closure, the believers were said to have "greatly obstructed us, and though we succeeded in taking away the furniture more or less peacefully, the last truck got away only after certain difficulties. The activist believers, more than sixty of them, began to shower the raiispolkom with demands . . . and what scurrilities did they not utter!"

There is also evidence that administrative and social pressures are exerted on individuals as well as on communities. Thus, the Soviet periodical *Nauka i Religia* has on various occasions condemned the practice of dismissing workers for their religious beliefs, but its disapproval was apparently based on expediency rather than elementary justice or humanity since it pointed out in one issue that an employed person "can be worked on at a meeting and threatened with dismissal." We learn elsewhere that collectives contending for the title of "Brigade of Communist Labor" can earn marks by taking believers into their bosom and converting them.

Ruthless interference in the family lives of believers is not only permitted but officially encouraged for the purpose of "saving" children from pernicious religious influences. "Freedom of conscience," a high Komsomol official declared, "applies only to adult citizens who are responsible for their acts. But

no one can be allowed to cripple children spiritually, to exert pressure on their immature minds." The authorities, said the Komsomol's official organ, must "step in" to protect children who become the "victims of spiritual and moral violence at the hands of their parents."

It is, of course, a crime under existing Soviet legislation for a priest to give religious instruction to children, or to recruit them as choristers. Technically parents are still allowed to take their children to a place of worship, but the Ideological Commission's 1963 decisions called for "intensified measures of control to protect children and adolescents from the influence of churchmen and from coercion at the hands of their parents to perform religious rites." Various practical steps in this direction have been reported, including Komsomol patrolling of places of worship in order to dissuade children from attending services, or to report those attending to the school authorities for special indoctrination. In some cases (usually involving sectarians), children may even be taken away from their parents. One such case came to light when a young Leningrad worker named Malozemov was commended by Ilichev and others for acting to remove six of his younger brothers and sisters from the care of their parents, who were charged with nothing worse than being Baptists. (The Ideological Commission, however, *did* think that a Minsk court had been overhasty in awarding custody of three children to their drunken father rather than their Baptist mother.)

Among the gentler methods of persuasion, formal public lectures are now regarded as unprofitable, but atheistic films, amateur comedy acts ridiculing the clergy and their ways, and evenings of "unmiraculous miracles" (in which the performer utterly discredits the thaumaturges of all time with such marvelous tricks as the apparent conversion of water into boiling milk) are all highly recommended. But perhaps the method which the authorities would like to see most widely adopted is that of tactful house-to-house agitation, working from a (tactfully compiled) local register of believers. The agitator should proceed cautiously, showing sympathy for the believer, giving him material help and moral support if necessary, not thrusting atheistic tracts on him too soon, but trying first to interest him in unprovocative secular literature and then gradually sowing doubt in his mind.

The literature on which the atheist agitator relies breaks down broadly into three levels—"scientific," semipopular, and popular. The authorities are beginning to recognize that much of it is too general and too old-fashioned. In the pragmatic manner characteristic of the Khrushchevian era, they now call for "a clear view of the extent and nature of religious beliefs in each particular area," and also for attention to "contemporary religious literature" and (more important) to "the actual form in which belief in God manifests itself in the consciousness and behavior of the masses of believers."

It is unlikely, however, that these practical needs will be satisfactorily met unless there is first a great improvement in the techniques of the scientific study of religion and a considerable broadening of its scope. There has been, in the Soviet period, very little original anthropological research in the field of religion, and no inquiry at all, it seems, into the psychology of belief. Learned Soviet symposia on religion often resurrect works old enough to be museum pieces: it is surely rather remarkable that a fairly ambitious recent publication of the Academy of Sciences on Judaism should include Sir James Frazer's musings on Exodus 34 ("Thou shalt not

seethe a kid in his mother's milk"), and that its best offering should be a piece by Orchansky (died 1875) on Hassidism. Antireligious classics are copiously reprinted. No doubt the poetic power of Lucretius can still help to create a godless mood, however quaint his arguments seem; but could anyone except a professional historian of ideas endure, for instance, Holbach?

Similarly, Soviet critiques of the Jewish, Christian, and Moslem scriptures are largely parasitical on foreign—and sometimes, from the scientific rationalist's point of view, obsolete—sources. A better than average example of the genre, I. Kryvelev's *Kniga o Biblii* (Book about the Bible), is based almost entirely on Western (rationalist or modern Christian) biblical scholarship, ranging from Spinoza through Robertson, Wellhausen, and Delitsch to Holscher and C. H. Dodd. Such studies follow well-established lines, setting out to show the relatively late origin, purely human authorship, and all-too-human motivation of the scriptures, with a glance at the indebtedness of Jewish—and hence of Moslem and Christian—tradition to earlier Eastern systems of belief. Many Britons will find much of Kryvelev nostalgically familiar, having first heard it in boyhood from a teacher in holy orders as part of a course in religious knowledge.

At the semipopular and popular levels, poking fun at the Old Testament is a flourishing industry. The seminal work is E. Yaroslavski's *Biblia dlya Veruyushchikh i Neveruyushchikh* (Bible for believers and unbelievers), originally written in 1922 and reprinted again in an eleventh edition of 850,000 copies in 1962. There was undoubtedly a time when Yaroslavski's jokes about the discrepancies in the Old Testament, the comicality of its cosmogony, the eccentricities of its deity, and the uncouthness of its leading personages would have scandalized most pious Jews and Christians and reinforced any free-thinking velleity. But, for want of information on the "beliefs actually held" in the Soviet Union, we can have no idea who, except atheists, would be affected one way or another by, let us say, "the sacred history of the Jewish priest and his concubine who was cut into twelve pieces and was the occasion of the almost total destruction of the tribe of Benjamin."

As a rule, the most offensive antireligious literature of the "scientific" and semipopular varieties is that directed against Roman Catholicism. There are perhaps two reasons for this. First, the Soviet writings in this field draw heavily upon—though they do not outdo—western European anticlerical literature, medieval and modern. Second, we should be evading an unpleasant truth if we did not note the persistence of anti-Catholic animus which in Russia antedates communism. The typical anti-Catholic tract (Sheinman's brochure is a good example) dwells lovingly on the decadence of the papal court in the Middle Ages and its alleged corruption in our own times, on the Inquisition, the church's "persecution of science," witch hunts, the traffic in indulgences, the "fabrication of saints, miracles and holy relics," the "usurious commercial activities of the Holy See," the "alliance of the Vatican with fascism," and so on. It also plays upon Russian patriotic themes, such as the "subversive activity" of the Vatican in Russia in the late sixteenth and early seventeenth centuries and "the Papacy's alliance with the Turkish sultans."

The official Soviet view, no doubt, is that such works are offensive only to the clergy, but of course devout laymen must also be hurt by attacks on institutions and persons whom they feel bound to respect. In any case, it is not always easy for the propagandist to maintain the pretense of distinguishing between the "professional religious" and the rank-and-file. Some sectarians, the Baptists for instance, with their doctrine of universal priesthood, pose a problem. And the special· character of the Jewish religious community is one reason why anti-Judaic literature often attacks not just the rabbinate and the synagogue servants, but all practicing Jews.

Beyond question the most vicious anti-religious book of recent years is T. K. Kichko's *Iudaizm bez Prikras* (Judaism without embellishment), published in 1963. Even its outer cover administers a physical shock, illustrated as it is by the first of a profusion of "anti-Judaic" or, more accurately, anti-Semitic caricatures undistinguishable in many cases from those produced by the Nazi Jewbaiters of the 1930's. This seems to be an unusual feature in specialized anti-religious literature, although precedents can easily be found in the Soviet provincial press.

Kichko's points are drawn from the professional atheist's common stock: religion is, above all, a ruthless swindle, and its ministers are greedy charlatans; religion degrades women, sets up barriers of prejudice and hatred between peoples, and so on. Kichko does not add an original stroke to the conventional picture; he merely lays on his colors a little thicker. Thus, inspired no doubt by the press treatment of "economic crimes" involving Jews, he represents the synagogue as, above all, a thieves' kitchen. And writing on the doctrine of "The Chosen People," he is not content with referring to the usual *locus classicus* in Exodus, but distorts a Talmudic gloss to mean that the Jews have a divine right to exploit and rob other peoples.

To an outsider, some of the simpler popular literature looks shrewder and more telling than the heavy-handed "scientific" works. There are, for instance, a number of cleverly written pamphlets and articles which gently and humorously quiz the believer about his funny, old-fashioned and illogical religious practices. Those addressed to the Jews are particularly interesting and seem to owe a good deal to Yiddish literary tradition. Propaganda of this kind is no doubt intended mainly for the semi-believer who may be fairly easily teased into breaking with religion altogether.

A favorite genre with popular anti-religious writers is scandal-mongering about the clergy. Much of the material is provided—and a good deal of it written up—by former priests, pastors, rabbis, and mullahs. It is surprising how these high-minded citizens managed to endure, in some cases for many years and very profitably, their association with colleagues who "lead a shut-in life bounded by food, drink, church services, scandal and money-grubbing," who "instead of increasing their knowledge . . . strive to "outspit" one another [by boasting] about the sums they earn"; who try to outdo each other not in the number of books they read but in the "number of tots they drink." The clergy (of all denominations) are accused of profligate habits. "In every new parish he set himself up with mistresses." The Bishop of Astrakhan and Stalingrad has figured frequently in antireligious writings since 1959, when he was accused in the press of cohabiting with "adopted daughters" and "nieces" especially recruited by a local monk. Sodomy is said to be rife in Catholic and Orthodox monasteries.

The most lovingly elaborated tales, however, are of rapacity and cynicism. To quote a few examples: "I will not hide from my readers that I [an ex-priest] got from two to fourteen thousand rubles (old currency) a month." "Father Ioann uses the money he gets like a real businessman. . . . Not content with one house, he soon acquires another at a cost of 35,000 rubles. . . . God's servant Ioann laughs at such 'behests' of Christ as 'Lay up no treasure in this world'—his whole faith consists in his urge to get rich by fraud." [Father] Pavel Ivanov said to me, "I don't believe in God because he does not exist, but for money I am prepared to serve the devil." "He had a capacious pocket sewn inside his vestments . . . and during 'divine' service surreptitiously tucked away money from the collection plate." "Teper [chairman of a Jewish community] demanded from the grief-stricken husband 3,000 rubles for burying her [his deceased wife]." "The priests, 'nothing doubting,' take the offerings [in kind] of the faithful, which they themselves have sanctified with prayer and the smoke of incense, and feed them to their pigs." And so on without end.

For the benefit of Soviet Catholics (mostly Lithuanians and Poles), the Roman curia is subjected to the same sort of vilification. Lavretski's *Kardinaly Idut v Ad* (Cardinals go to hell) is the most striking recent example and should be noted particularly for its no-nonsense treatment of Pope John XXIII (at a time when the Communist press generally was showing a certain cautious friendliness toward him) and also for its illustrations, which are a more skillful application of the visual shock tactics used by Kichko.

We may be sure that persistent denigration of this sort has its effect, at least on those of feeble faith. Some of the "unmaskings" reported are probably quite genuine, since no religious denomination, any more than any other human institution, can keep itself entirely free of rogues and charlatans. But the wholesale denunciations which we find in Soviet antireligious literature would tax the credulity of most hardened secularists. Those attacked are, of course, given no chance to defend themselves. Perhaps the more thoughtful Soviet citizen, adept in judicious reading, often gives them the benefit of the doubt, but against this we may suppose that the very blatancy of the professional apostates helps to bring religion into disrepute. Whether the reader of Yakushevich, for example, thinks, "What scoundrels Orthodox priests are!" or merely, "So this wretch was an Orthodox priest," Ilichev has scored a small victory.

No popular antireligious work is complete without charges of treason, past and present. Some denominations—notably the Catholics and Jehovah's Witnesses—are represented in current Soviet propaganda as instruments of imperialist subversion. Most religious groups (including, in Kichko's farrago, even the Jews) are accused of collaboration with the Nazi invaders during the Second World War.

The religious cannot, of course, enter into detailed polemics with their assailants even if they wished to do so. The Baptists, it is true, are reported to have experimented with the presentation, in dramatized form, of an argument between a believer and an atheist critic of the Bible, but this seems to have been an isolated counterpropaganda enterprise. As a rule, the religious can reply only indirectly and in general terms. They, or at any rate the denominations which deign to argue, tirelessly insist that there is no incompatibility between religious belief on the one hand and modern science or Soviet social ideals on the other. Ilichev has called for special efforts to refute these contentions.

It will probably not be the most rigorous Soviet thinkers, however. who attempt to validate, by argument or demonstration, the conviction casually adopted by millions of laymen that science has somehow demolished religion. The scientific atheist in the Soviet Union is nowadays often guilty of crudities scarcely distinguishable from those which he could previously impute to some clergymen. A Moscow churchman, for instance, once opposed the construction of an underground railway for fear that it might debouch on the corridors of hell, but this is really no sillier than the triumphant conclusions drawn by militant atheists from the fact that Soviet cosmonauts have found no "firmament" and met no angels.

Much the same can be said of some Western well-wishers of the Soviet regime, whose views have perhaps caused even their Soviet friends a little—though probably purely literary—embarrassment. The former Dean of Canterbury, for instance, is quoted as holding that "if the Soviet regime rejects the name of Christianity, it is only because in Tsarist Russia this name had become the antithesis of the teaching and ideas of Christ." The ordinary Soviet believer, no doubt, will consult his experience and his conscience, rather than the Dean or his critics, as to whether religious belief is compatible with good citizenship.

The efforts of the religious to reach a *modus vivendi*, or rather a truce, with Soviet science and Soviet social ideals, and their modifications of certain practices (for instance, in the case of the Orthodox Church, the relaxation of rules concerning fasts and holidays of obligation, the acceptance of group confession, and the admission of women to the altar), are represented as signs of conscious weakness, desperate concessions to modernity, and renunciations of positions previously regarded as sacrosanct. But it is, perhaps, not in itself a very good argument against religion that, like everything else, it evolves.

The Soviet atheistic literature of recent years suggests a wistful preference for religion in its older and cruder forms, together with an awareness that the older and cruder forms of atheistic propaganda are no longer adequate. Indeed, militant atheists might ask themselves whether the old forms of antireligious work were not always counterproductive. For the Soviet Union, on the evidence of its antireligious literature, is still a long, long way from that deliverance, promised in *Das Kapital*, when religion will vanish because "the practical relationships of everyday life express themselves in clear and rational connections between people, and between people and nature."

70

ARE WE FLIRTING WITH CAPITALISM?

By Evsei Liberman

During the last decade the Soviets have begun to experiment with various economic reforms which are changing the more rigid aspects of economic life in the USSR. These reforms have been debated both in the Soviet Union and abroad, and there is no agreement on their ultimate significance. The Soviets claim that the reforms have nothing to do with any basic change in their economic system, but are designed to rationalize the socialist economy. The author of the piece below is professor of economics at Kharkov University, and is the man most often associated with the initiation of economic reforms. It should be noted that he is only one of many Soviet planners who, in the past years and even today, continue to debate the reforms.

For more by Liberman in English see the following: "Plan, Direct Contacts, and Profitability," *Reprints from the Soviet Press*, December 30, 1965; "The Truth Always Prevails," *ibid.*, December 2, 1965; "Liberman Offers Cure for Queues," *Current Digest of the Soviet Press*, April 10, 1968; "Liberman Proposes Modifications to the Reform," *ibid.*, April 17, 1968; "The Soviet Economic Reform," *Foreign Affairs*, October, 1967. For further Soviet views see "On Increasing Economic Incentives to Industrial Production," *Reprints from the Soviet Press*, October 21, 1965; L. Leontyev, "Plan and Economic Initiative," *ibid.*, June 9, 1966; "The Implications of Economic Reform in Construction," *Current Digest of the Soviet Press*, August 9, 1967; "Fedorenko Weighs Criteria of Reform's Effectiveness," *ibid.*, May 31, 1967; *The Soviet Economic Reforms: Main Features and Aims* (published in Moscow) ; and a special section on the reforms in Harry Shaffer, *The Soviet Economy: A Collection of Soviet and Western Views*.

For Western studies of Libermanism see Jan Prybyla, "From Libermanism to Liberalism?" *Bulletin of the Institute for the Study of the USSR*, July, 1966; Alec Nove, "The Liberman Proposals," *Survey*, April, 1963; Alfred Zauberman, "Liberman's Rules of the Game for Soviet Industry," *Slavic Review*, December, 1963; Ernst Halperin, "Beyond Libermanism," *Problems of Communism*, January–February, 1967; and Egon Neuberger, "Libermanism, Computopia, and the Visible Hand," *American Economic Review*, May, 1966.

For general studies on the reforms see Margaret Miller, *The Rise of the Russian Consumer*; George Feiwel, *The Soviet Quest for Economic Efficiency*; Jere Felker, *Soviet Economic Controversies*; Eugene Zaleski, *Planning Reforms in the Soviet*

Reprinted from Evsei Liberman, "Are We Flirting with Capitalism?" *Soviet Life*, July, 1965, pp. 37–39.

Union, 1962–1966; Alexander Balinky et al., *Planning and the Market in the USSR: The 1960's*; and Myron Sharpe, *Planning, Profit, and Incentives in the USSR*.

For articles see Morris Bornstein, "The Soviet Price Reform Discussion," *Quarterly Journal of Economics*, February, 1964; Theodor Frankel, "Economic Reform: A Tentative Appraisal," *Problems of Communism*, May–June, 1967; Alfred Zauberman, "Changes in Economic Thought," *Survey*, July, 1967; "Soviet Economic Performance and Reform," *Slavic Review*, June, 1966; Robert Campbell, "Marx, Kantorovich and Novozhilov," *ibid.*, October, 1961; Marshall Goldman, "Economic Controversy in the Soviet Union," *Foreign Affairs*, April, 1963; and Jan Tinbergen, "Do Communist and Free Economies Show a Convergent Pattern," *Soviet Studies*, April, 1961.

See also "The Politics of Libermanism," *Soviet Studies*, April, 1968.

In its February 12 issue this year *Time* magazine carried my picture on its cover, with the prominent caption, "The Communist Flirtation with Profits." The cover story, entitled "Borrowing from the Capitalists," made many references to my writings and statements, and drew conclusions vastly different from those I make. I therefore asked the editors of *Soviet Life* and *Ekonomicheskaya Gazeta* to permit me to comment on the *Time* article in their publications. To do a proper job, I shall have to go rather deeply into the essential character of profits.

Profits are the monetary form of the surplus product, that is, the product which working people produce over and above their personal needs. The surplus product is, therefore, an expression of the productivity of labor. Primitive man ate or used up what he produced. As civilization and technology progressed, labor began to create not only the equivalent of the working people's means of subsistence but something more. This something more was the surplus product, the very same surplus product that supports the entire nonproductive sphere, from the watchman to the banker and cabinet minister. But the surplus product is also the

source of means essential for the development of society. That applied to feudal and capitalist society, and it applies to socialism and communism.

Under socialism, products and services are also produced as commodities and also sold chiefly for money. Therefore, the surplus product inevitably assumes the monetary form of profits. But since profits in our country are used in the interests of society, they become less and less an expression of surplus (unpaid) labor and come more and more to express socially necessary labor.

What is the difference between capitalist and socialist profits?

BONUS "FOR RISKS"

The difference is not, of course, that private enterprise stands for profit while socialism "denounces" it, as economists in the West often claim. To make the difference clear, let us examine (1) how profit is formed, (2) what it signifies, and (3) for what purposes it is spent.

From the private entrepreneur's viewpoint, all profit belongs to the capitalist. To support this view, economists built the theory of the three factors that create value: capital, land, and labor. In *The Theory of Economic Development* Joseph A. Schumpeter says that profit is everything above cost. But his "cost" includes "wages" for the labor of the entrepreneur, land rent, interest on capital, as well as a bonus "for risks." On top of that, the entrepreneur reaps a profit if he succeeds, by a new combination of production elements, in reducing the cost to below the existing price level.

What kind of "combination of elements" this is can be seen from the fact that the main part of the profit under the private enterprise system now comes not so much from production as from the process of exchange. For instance, high profits come most readily from advantageous buying of raw materials, the raising of retail prices, the tendency of unemployment to lower wages, nonequivalent exchange with developing countries, the export of capital to countries where wages are low, the system of preferential tariffs and customs duties, raising the prices of stocks on the stock exchange, and so-called *Grunder* (speculator's) profits.

DOES MONEY SMELL IN THE SOVIET UNION?

All these sources of profit are ruled out in the Soviet Union owing to the very nature of socialism, under which there is neither private ownership of the means of production nor stock capital and, consequently, no stock market. The level of payment for labor depends on its productivity and is regulated by law. The prices of raw and other materials are planned; market conditions that could be taken advantage of in purchasing raw materials or hiring labor do not exist. Nor can the prices of finished articles be raised by taking advantage of market conditions. Exchange with other countries is conducted on the basis of equality and long-term agreements. Legend has it that the Roman Em-

peror Vespasian decided to impose a tax on public toilets when he saw that his treasury was running low. His son Titus, who later succeeded to the throne, waxed indignant at such an evil-smelling source of revenue. Vespasian then held up to his son's nose the first receipts from the toilet tax. "Non olet!" ("It doesn't smell!") Titus exclaimed in surprise. Ever since then the view that "money doesn't smell" has been gospel in the commodity world. Indeed, under private enterprise nobody really cares how money is made. The important thing is to make it, the important thing is how much of it you can make.

But in the Soviet Union "money does smell." That will be seen if we look into the nature of profit. In our country profit testifies, in principle, only to the level of production efficiency. Profit is the difference between the selling price of articles and their cost. But since our prices, in principle, express the norms of expenditure of socially necessary labor, the difference is an indicator of the comparative economy with which an item is produced. Behind Soviet profits there is nothing except hours of working time, tons of raw and other materials and fuel, and kilowatt-hours of electrical energy that have been saved. Our profits cannot "smell" of anything but that. We do not justify profits obtained through accidental circumstances—for example, excessive prices —and we do not consider such profit a credit to the factory or other enterprise which makes it. We look on such profits, rather, as the result of an insufficiently flexible practice of price fixing. All such profits go into the state budget, without any bonus to the enterprise concerned.

Capitalist profit is a different matter altogether. As the reader knows very well, profits in the West can indicate anything under the sun over and above purely technical and organized efficiency. Commercial dexterity, successful advertising, profitable orders for military production—that is what the history of present-day big capital testifies to sooner than to anything else. Surely it must be clear that in essence and origin profit under socialism bears only a superficial resemblance to profit under private enterprise, while by its nature and by the factors to which it testifies it is fundamentally different from capitalist profit.

Where do profits go in the Soviet Union? First of all, neither a single individual nor a single enterprise can appropriate profits. Profits are not arbitrarily invested by any persons or groups for the sake of private income.

Profits belong to those to whom the means of production belong, that is, to all the citizens, to society. Profits go, first and foremost, for the planned expansion and improvement of production and scientific research, and to provide free social services for the people: education, health, pensions, scholarships. Part is spent on the management apparatus and, unfortunately, a rather large part goes for defense needs. We would gladly give up this last expenditure if a program of general disarmament were adopted.

INDICATORS IN INDUSTRY

There is nothing new in that use or profits in the Soviet Union. Our enterprises have been making profits in money form for more than forty years, ever since 1921. It is with these profits that we have built up our giant industrial potential, thanks to which we have moved to a leading position in world science and technology. And we have accomplished this without major long-term credits from other countries.

Why has the question of profits been so widely discussed in the Soviet Union lately? Not because profits did not exist before and are only now being introduced. *The reason is that profit was not, and still is not, used as the major overall indicator of the efficient operation of our enterprises.* Besides profit, we have been using a fairly large number of obligatory indicators—among others, gross output, assortment, lower costs, number of employees, size of payroll, output per employee, and average wages. The multiplicity of indicators hamstrung the initiative of the enterprises. Their main concern often was to turn out as great a volume of goods as possible, since they would be rated chiefly on gross output. Furthermore, enterprises did not pay much attention to how they used their assets. Trying to meet their output quotas in the easiest way for themselves, they asked for, and received free from the state, a great deal of plant, which they did not always use efficiently or to full capacity.

How do we explain that?

VIRTUE BECOMES VICE

For a long time the Soviet Union was the only socialist country. We stood alone, surrounded by a world in which there were many who wanted to change our social system by force. We had to build up our own industries and secure our defenses at all costs and in the shortest possible time. Such considerations as the quality and appearance of goods, or even their cost, did not count. This policy completely justified itself. The Soviet Union not only held its own in the war of 1941–45 but played the decisive role in saving the world from fascism. That was worth any price. And that was our "profit" then.

But, as Lenin often said, our virtues, if exaggerated, can turn into vices. And that is what happened when we held to the same administrative methods of economic management after we entered the stage of peaceful economic competition with the industrial countries of the West.

We want to give every citizen, not only the well-to-do, a high standard of living, in the intellectual as well as in the material sense. In other words, we want everyone to have the fullest opportunity to develop his mental and physical capacities and his individual (I emphasize individual, and not group) inclinations and interests. We want every person in our country to be able to do the work he wants most to do. We want to reach the point where it will not be possible to draw a hard and fast line between a person's vocation and his avocation.

Before we can bring people's intellectual capacities to full flower, we must satisfy their material needs, place goods and services of high quality within everyone's reach. These needs must be satisfied, moreover, with the lowest possible production outlays and the fullest possible utilization of all assets.

WHAT IS THE WAY OUT?

All that cannot be done through the old methods of administrative direction and highly centralized management. We must change over to a system whereby the enterprises themselves have a material incentive to provide the best possible service to the consumer. It is clear that to do this we must free the enterprises from the excessive number of obligatory indicators. In my opinion, the criteria for rating the work of enterprises should be, first, how well they carry out their plans of deliveries (in actual products); and, if these plans are fulfilled, then, second, their level of profitability. I believe that out of their

profits, enterprises should have to pay into the state budget a certain percentage of the value of their assets as "payment for use of plant." The purpose would be to spur enterprises to make the most productive use of their assets. Part of the remaining share of the profits would go into incentive pay system funds, the amount depending on the level of profitability. The rest of the profits would accrue to the state budget to finance the expansion of production and to satisfy the welfare needs of the population.

PLAN, PROFIT AND BONUS

Why do I choose profit as the indicator?

Because profit generalizes all aspects of operation, including quality of output. The prices of better articles have to be correspondingly higher than those of articles that are outmoded and not properly suited to their purpose. It is important to note, however, that profit in this case is neither the sole nor the chief aim of production. We are interested above all in products with which to meet the needs of the people and of industry. Profit is used merely as the main generalizing and stimulating indicator of efficiency, as a device for rating the operation of enterprises.

Yet Western press comments on my writings blare away about the term "profit," very often ignoring the fact that the title of my *Pravda* article of September 9, 1962, was "The Plan, Profits and Bonuses." They make a lot of noise about profit but say nothing about planning.

Actually, my point is to encourage enterprises, by means of bonuses from profits, to draw up good plans, that is, plans which are advantageous both to themselves and to society. And not only to draw them up but to carry them out, with encouragement from profits. It is not a question of relaxing (or rejecting) planning but, on the contrary, of improving it by drawing the enterprises themselves, first and foremost, into the planning process, for the enterprises always know their real potentialities best and should study and know the demands of their customers.

The contractual relations with consumers or customers that we are now starting to introduce in several branches of light industry by no means signify that we are going over to regulation by the market. We have better ways of predicting consumer demand because we know the wage fund of the urban population and the incomes of the collective farmers. Therefore, we can draw up scientific patterns of the population's income and expenditure. In our country consumer demand, in terms of total volume, is a factor that lends itself to planning. However, the various elements of that volume—for instance, the colors of sweaters or the styles of suits factories should produce, or how best to organize their production—need not be the prerogatives of centralized planning but matters on which the stores and the factories concerned come to terms. Thus, the consideration of consumer demand and the planning of production are not only compatible in the Soviet Union but can strongly substantiate and supplement each other.

THE SUBSTANCE OF OUR DEBATES

The *Time* cover story is full of contradictions. It admits that the Soviet people now have more money and that there is a growing demand for better and more fashionable clothing and for private cars. One would think that pointed to an improving economy, yet the article claims that the switch to profits is a result of "unsettling prospects,"

of "waste, mismanagement, inefficiency and planning gone berserk," and so on and so forth.

There are, of course, no few instances of waste and mismanagement in the Soviet economy, just as there are in private enterprise; think of the thousands of firms that go bankrupt every year. But in the Soviet Union we focus public attention on instances of waste and mismanagement. We publicize and criticize them openly. Some Western commentators take advantage of that fact. What better way can there be of distorting an over-all picture than to pick haphazard details and offer them as representative of the whole? The over-all picture shows that the Soviet Union increased its output by 7.1 per cent in 1964. *Time* admits that this is a very good growth rate for a highly developed economy. It is not good enough for us, however. We are used to growth rates expressed in two digits, *Time* does not mention that the reason for this 7.1 per cent growth rate, a relatively modest one for us, was the 1963 crop failure.

We are turning to profits not because we need a "sheet anchor." We are not in any danger. The fact remains, however, that we have to improve our methods of economic management. This is the substance of our debates and our searches.

THE MAIN FUNCTION OF PROFITS

Under socialism, profits can be a yardstick of production efficiency to a far greater degree than in the West, for in the Soviet Union profits follow, in principle, only from technological and organizational improvement. This also means that profits here will play an important but subsidiary role, like money in general, not the main role. After providing a yardstick of production achievement and a means of encouraging such achievement, profits in the Soviet Union are used wholly for the needs of society. They are returned to the population in the form of social services and expanded production, which guarantees full employment and better and easier working conditions for everyone.

In the Soviet Union nobody accumulates profits in money form—neither the state nor enterprises. This is an important point to grasp. If, for instance, at the end of the year the state as a whole has a surplus of budget revenue over expenditure, the surplus does not stay in the form of accumulated currency but is immediately used for two purposes: (1) to increase State Bank credits for material stocks; in other words, the surplus takes the material form of expanding inventories in production or trade, while money only measures this increase; and (2) to withdraw paper money from circulation, that is, to increase the purchasing power of the ruble on the free collective farm markets, where prices are determined by supply and demand.

Consequently, profits cannot become either capital or hoarded treasure in the Soviet Union. They are not, therefore, a social goal or a motive force in production as a whole. The motive force in production under socialism is the satisfaction of the steadily growing material and cultural needs of the population. However, profit can be, and should be, an indicator (and the key indicator, moreover) of production efficiency. It should serve to encourage workers to raise their efficiency. But it should be understood that encouragement from profits is not distribution of the results of production on the basis of capital. Distribution is still on the basis of work; it is work that rules distribution under socialism.

THE GOAL AND THE MEANS

The significance of profit in the Soviet Union was underestimated owing to a certain disregard of the law of value. Some Soviet economists incorrectly interpreted that law as an unpleasant leftover from capitalism and said we had to get rid of it as quickly as possible. Shelving the law of value led to arbitrary fixing of planned prices and to prices that operated over too long a period. As a result, prices became divorced from the real value of goods, while profits fluctuated greatly from enterprise to enterprise, even on comparable articles. Under those conditions profits were poor reflections of the actual achievements in production. Because of this, many economists and economic managers began to consider profit as something completely independent of production and, hence, as a poor guide in matters of economic management. This is the delusion many Soviet economists, among them the present author, are now trying to expose. We do not intend to go back to private enterprise but, on the contrary, to permit the economic laws of socialism to operate. Centralized planning is wholly compatible with the initiative of enterprises. This is as far from private enterprise as private enterprise is from feudalism.

The law of value is not a law of capitalism but a law of all commodity production, including planned commodity production under socialism. The difference from capitalism is that the goal and the means have changed places. Under capitalism, profit is the goal, and the satisfaction of the needs of the population is the means. Under socialism it is just the other way around. Satisfaction of the needs of the population is the goal, and profit is the means. The difference is not one of terms but of substance.

TIME AND THE SOVIET ECONOMY

Soviet economists can only smile when they read how *Time* interprets the socialist planning system. It says: "A knitwear plant ordered to produce 80,000 caps and sweaters naturally produced only caps: they were smaller and thus cheaper and quicker to make." In other words, the factory had freedom of choice. But elsewhere the same article says that factories are tied hand and foot by the plan, and that the plans account for each nail and electric bulb. Where is the logic?

Another example: "Taxi drivers were put on a bonus system based on mileage, and soon the Moscow suburbs were full of empty taxis barreling down the boulevards to fatten their bonuses." But every Moscow schoolboy knows that the bonus of taxi drivers is based on the amount they collect in fares. Empty runs are a disadvantage. As a matter of fact, there is a restriction on the mileage of empty runs. Taxis in Moscow and many other cities are radio dispatched, the purpose being to reduce empty runs. Such lack of knowledge on the part of the *Time* staff can hardly make for an objective appraisal of the Soviet economy.

The magazine's statements on more serious matters are just as informed. Experimental garment factories, it says, "showed a resounding improvement in efficiency—and such 'deviationism'—that many Kremlinologists assumed they had contributed to Nikita's downfall."

In the first place, these factories did not show any "resounding" improvement in efficiency. On the contrary, their output dropped owing to a greater outlay of labor for more painstaking manufacture and finishing of the articles. The only thing they showed is that "deviationism" is it if the "deviation" was made in conformity with instructions issued by the Economic Council of the USSR in March, 1964—without any direct participation by Professor Liberman, whom the Western press cites, without having sufficient grounds when given the right to plan their output on the basis of orders from stores, they can make good suits of wool and man-made fiber mixtures at a lower price. Customers readily buy these suits.

In the second place, what kind of for doing so, on every occasion when steps are taken to improve the Soviet economy. My modest role, like that of many other of our economists, is to study methods of improving economic management on the basis of the principles and economic laws of socialism.

RIVERS DON'T FLOW BACKWARD

Soviet economists have no intention of testing the economic methods of private enterprise. We expect to get along with our own methods, sharpening the tried and tested instrument of material incentive on the grindstone of profit. This has been one of our instruments for a long time, but it has grown dull, chiefly because we didn't use it enough. Now we are sharpening it and it will, we hope, serve socialism well. But this does not mean that we are either giving up a planned economy or turning toward the system of private enterprise. Rivers do not flow backward. And if, at high water, rivers make turns, they are simply cutting better and shorter channels for themselves. They are not looking for a way to go back.

71

ON THE EVENTS IN CHINA

"Pravda," November 27, 1966

For some years now the Sino-Soviet split has been a major fact of international life. Beginning with the 1950's the two great Communist powers found it increasingly impossible to agree on anything. The split is now at its most bitter, and it is difficult to foresee what the future holds in store. As *Pravda* wrote on February 16, 1967: "On more than one occasion in the past half-century our Party and our people have had to endure the fierce attacks of hostile forces. But except for periods of direct armed aggression against the Soviet Union it can be said that never before has such a furious campaign been carried on against it as the one China's present leaders have launched." The Soviet statement on the situation reprinted below was chosen for its moderate tone, and because it summarizes the long-range trends of the relations between the two giants.

For another recent Soviet piece see "The Anti-Soviet Policy of Mao Tse-tung and His Group," *Reprints from the Soviet Press*, March 23, 1967. There are three Soviet journals in English which specialize in problems of foreign policy: the weekly *Moscow News*, and the monthly *New Times* and *International Affairs*. For a collection of Soviet documents on foreign policy which include China see Alvin Rubinstein, *The Foreign Policy of the Soviet Union* (paperback). For a chapter on "Stalin and China," see George Kennan, *Russia and the West under Lenin and Stalin* (paperback). The literature on the Sino-Soviet split is growing daily; only a sample can be included here. See Morton Halperin, *Sino-Soviet Relations and Arms Control*; the same author's *China and the Bomb*; Raymond Garthoff, *Sino-Soviet Military Relations*; Clement Zablocki, *Sino-Soviet Rivalry: Implications for U.S. Policy*; Donald Treadgold, *Soviet and Chinese Communism*; M. Klochko, *Soviet Scientist in Red China*; David Floyd, *Mao against Khrushchev* (paperback); Donald Zagoria, *The Sino-Soviet Conflict, 1956–1961*; Edward Crankshaw, *The New Cold War: Moscow vs. Peking*; W. A. Jackson, *The Russo-Chinese Borderlands*; D. Doolin, *Territorial Claims in the Sino-Soviet Conflict*; and Klaus Mehnert, *Peking and Moscow* (paperback).

The events in China are causing ever greater anxiety in the world communist movement, in the countries of the socialist community, and amidst the progressive public throughout the world. The press has published and is publishing information on what is going on in

From *Moscow News, Supplement*, December 3, 1966, pp. 2–14.

China, and also on the reaction of the world communist movement to the decisions taken by the 11th Plenary Meeting of the Central Committee of the Communist Party of China, which approved the so-called cultural revolution and the "hung wei ping" ("Red Guards") movement launched on directives from Mao Tse-tung. The Central Committee of the Communist Party of the Soviet Union has duly published a statement appraising those decisions. The events that have taken place in China since the 11th Plenary Meeting of the CPC make it necessary to consider the problem once again.

This article is not concerned with the interpolitical problems of China mentioned in the decisions of the Plenary Meeting of the CPC Central Committee. As for the foreign policy aspects of those decisions, there is good reason to say that the Plenary Meeting had given its official blessing to the great-power anti-Leninist course of Mao Tse-tung and his group, directed against the unity of the countries of socialism, against the entire world communist movement.

The Plenary Meeting of the Central Committee of the CPC declared that the main aim of the CPR foreign policy is to combat "three enemies"—"imperialism, world reaction, and modern revisionism." The further context shows that imperialism is mentioned merely as a matter of form. Under the guise of fighting the "revisionists" all the fire is leveled against the CPSU and the Soviet Union, the "rout" of which has been declared to be a precondition for the struggle against imperialism. Simultaneously, a course is followed openly at splitting the international communist and the entire liberation movement. The decisions of the Plenary Meeting abound in concoctions about our Party and its Central Committee which are insulting to all

Soviet people.

The international communist movement highly appraises in its documents the policy of our Party, and stresses that the Soviet Union is shouldering the main burden of the struggle against imperialism, that the Soviet people have achieved history-making victories for socialism and are successfully building a communist society, and giving tremendous support to all the revolutionary forces in the world. But in defiance of the truth the decisions of the Plenary Meeting of the CPC Central Committee slanderously allege that the CPSU line is "a line directed at preserving the domination of imperialism and colonialism in the capitalist world and at restoring capitalism in the socialist world."

The CPSU and the Soviet state serve as the main bulwark for nations in their resistance to the expansion of U.S. imperialism, and the imperialists are spearheading their struggle and their aggressive plans against the land of the Soviets, but the authors of the Chinese document go to the length of alleging that our Party "has joined forces with imperialism, led by the U.S.A. and world reaction, and is knocking together an anticommunist counter-revolutionary union directed against the people, an anti Chinese new holy alliance." The CPC leaders need all these ridiculous concoctions only to be able, under cover of the slogan of struggle against "modern revisionism," to declare the CPSU and the Soviet Union "enemy No. 1," against whom they intend "to struggle to the end."

Concentrating their fire on the CPSU and the Soviet Union, the leaders of the CPC at the same time make no secret of their hostility for the communist parties of other countries of socialism, which are following the general line of the world communist movement. They are labeling the overwhelming majority of the Communist parties of socialist countries and communist and workers' parties throughout the world as so-called modern revisionists.

The forces which took the upper hand at the 11th Plenary Meeting are openly proclaiming that the CPC rejects the general line of the world communist movement and will intensify the struggle against all communist parties consistently upholding this line in their activity. As distinct from the previous documents of the Communist Party of China, which, at least in words, declared that it supported the 1957 Declaration and the 1960 Statement, the decisions of the 11th Plenary Meeting do not even mention those documents. They state bluntly: "The 'Proposal on the General Line of the International Communist Movement' put forward by the CPC Central Committee on June 14, 1963, is a programme document." In this document, evolved under the guidance of Mao Tse-tung, in nine editorial articles of the newspaper *Jen Min Jih Pao* and the *Hungchi* magazine in connection with the Open Letter of the CPSU Central Committee, in the article "On the March Meeting in Moscow" and in other articles, the line of the world communist movement is being openly replaced by a special course laid down by Mao Tse-tung and his group.

The leaders of the CPC—contrary to the genuine interests of the struggle against U.S. imperialism in Vietnam— have rejected all the proposals made by the communist and workers' parties, aimed at strengthening international solidarity in defence of the Vietnamese people and the revolutionary cause the world over. The Plenary Meeting's decisions underscore that "there can be no talk about any kind of joint action" with the CPSU and other communist parties which urge unity of action.

The Communist Party of the Soviet Union considers the strengthening of the unity of the world communist movement and the promotion of its international influence to be a sacred cause. Marxist-Leninist parties all over the world have highly assessed the efforts of the CPSU directed at overcoming the difficulties which have lately arisen in the communist movement and at consolidating it on the principled basis of Marxism-Leninism. But the authors of the resolution adopted at the Plenary Meeting of the CPC Central Committee dare to slander the CPSU and declare openly that "there is no place in the united front" for the USSR.

The Plenary Meeting endorsed the campaign launched by the Chinese leadership against the CPSU and the other fraternal parties and declared that it would be continued in the future, too. Thus, the anti-Soviet line, the line to split the ranks of world communism and undermine the international solidarity of the working class, is being made official policy.

Today, the views of Mao Tse-tung are being put forward in China as an official ideology underlying the entire policy of the Party and the country. A special section of the decisions of the 11th Plenary Meeting reads: "The study on a broad scale by the entire Party and the entire country of the works of Comrade Mao Tse-tung is an event of outstanding historic significance."

The arrogant attempt of the Chinese leadership to proclaim the views of Mao Tse-tung as the acme of Marxism-Leninism and to impose them on the world communist movement cannot but evoke legitimate protest on the part of Communists everywhere in the world.

Lin Piao, Minister of Defense of the CPR and Mao Tse-tung's closest assistant, declared that "Chairman Mao stands much higher than Marx, Engels, Lenin," and that his ideas "are Marxism-Leninism of the highest standard." Lin Piao went on to allege that a study of the classics of Marxism-Leninism should by 99 per cent consist of learning the works of Mao Tse-tung. And in point of fact all this "mastering of theory" boils down to a study of the "works of Chairman Mao."

In the past, Mao Tse-tung disguised his personal participation in the struggle against the CPSU and the other Marxist-Leninist parties. Now it is being stressed that the anti-Leninist and anti-Soviet course has been evolved by Mao Tse-tung and leaders closest to him. The greetings to the Fifth Congress of the Albanian Party of Labor, signed by Mao Tse-tung, expressed in a concentrated way the substance of China's present anti-Soviet course.

Thus, the decisions taken by the 11th Plenary Meeting of the CPC Central Committee, which on the surface are devoted to the problems of the so-called cultural revolution, actually concern cardinal problems of the policies pursued by the CPC in the international arena, in the socialist community and the world communist movement.

The Chinese press makes no secret of the fact that according to the plans of the organizers of the "cultural revolution" it must transcend the borders of the country. "The cultural revolution" is "a great cause affecting the destinies of the Chinese people and, speaking on a broad plane, is a great cause affecting the destinies of all nations in the world," writes *Jen-Min Jih Pao.*

And, indeed, the events in China concern not only that country but the whole of world socialism, all Communists, but not in the sense as is thought in Peking. The fact that the entire policy of the CPC Central Committee is quite openly directed against the basic principles of Marxism-Leninism, against the Soviet Union, against the CPSU and other communist parties, against international unity in the ranks of the communist movement and the political line it has evolved cannot fail to evoke legitimate anxiety.

Lately, the communist and workers' parties have deemed it necessary to issue statements on the current policy of the CPC leadership. These statements thoroughly censured the policy directed against the Soviet Union and the other socialist countries, a policy which impedes unification of the forces for a collective rebuff to imperialist aggression in Vietnam. Fraternal parties the world over have arrived at the conclusion that the events taking place in China under the guise of a cultural revolution conflict with Marxism-Leninism, are detrimental to the cause of socialism, and can only compromise the ideas of scientific communism.

It should be stressed that the CPC leaders are insistently trying to aggravate relations with the Soviet Union, despite the tireless efforts of the CPSU and the Soviet government to normalize relations with the CPC and People's China. Our Party has displayed maximum patience and profound and sincere interest in overcoming existing difficulties and differences, in consolidating unity of action with the Communist Party of China, the unity of the entire communist movement on the basis of Marxism-Leninism and the principles of proletarian internationalism.

The principled course taken by our Party in respect to the Chinese People's Republic and the Communist Party of China is well known. It is a course of unity and solidarity of the CPSU and the CPC, of the USSR and China, a course of strengthening friendship and cooperation between the Soviet and the Chinese peoples. The CPSU considers the Chinese Revolution an important integral part of the world revolutionary process and does its utmost to promote its success. Ever since the emergence of the Chinese People's Republic, the Soviet Union has constantly rendered assistance in building up a new life in China, and in strengthening its positions in the international arena. The line followed by the CPSU Central Committee and the Soviet government in the sphere of Soviet-Chinese relations conforms to the interests not only of our two parties and countries, but also of the whole socialist community and the international communist movement.

The Communist Party of the Soviet Union has invariably made efforts to strengthen unity with the Communist Party of China and find ways of overcoming the difficulties that have cropped up. The efforts of our Party were especially persistent and consistent after the October Plenary Meeting of the CPSU Central Committee. For over two years, our Party has not engaged in polemics, notwithstanding that anti-Soviet propaganda in China did not cease for a single day, for a single hour.

Immediately after the October Plenary Meeting of the CPSU Central Committee, our Party put forward a broad program for normalizing Soviet-Chinese relations. This program, however, has been rejected by the leaders of the CPC. We took another step to improve relations between our two parties and countries during the meeting between the Soviet delegation and the Chinese leadership in February, 1965, in Peking. But that meeting, too, brought no success. The participants in the Consultative Meeting of nineteen parties in March, 1965, made an important proposal to act jointly, despite the existing differences,

in support of the struggle of the Vietnamese people against U.S. aggression. This idea was supported by the overwhelming majority of communist and workers' parties, but the leading group of the CPC Central Committee came up in arms against it.

On November 28, 1965, the CPSU Central Committee addressed a letter to the CPC Central Committee which also proposed improving Soviet-Chinese relations. The CPC Central Committee rejected that proposal too. The Chinese leaders refused to send a delegation to the 23d Congress of the CPSU. Despite that, our Party declared at the Congress that it was prepared at any moment to consider, together with the CPC leadership, the existing differences, so as to find ways to overcome them on the principles of Marxism-Leninism. The CPC Central Committee ignored the constructive proposals of our Party Congress and attacked its decisions.

A systematic anti-Soviet brainwashing of the Chinese population is today going on, on an unprecedented scale. Hostile demonstrations of "hung wei ping" outside the Soviet Embassy in Peking and provocative outbursts against Soviet people arriving in China have become a system.

The Chinese leaders are trying to spread their anti-Soviet activities onto the territory of our country. Dozens of radio stations are incessantly broadcasting hostile slanderous propaganda to the Soviet Union.

The continuous curtailment of economic, scientific, and engineering cooperation between the CPR and the USSR is another practical outcome of the anti-Soviet course followed by the CPC leadership. Today, the sole form of economic contact between our two countries is trade. The Soviet share in the CPR foreign trade has dropped from 50 per cent in 1959 to 15 per cent in 1965. Meanwhile the CPR trade turnover with the capitalist countries has been growing year by year. The volume of Soviet-Chinese cultural exchanges has been reduced to an extreme minimum because of the inimical stand taken by the CPC leadership.

Such are the facts. They provide irrefutable evidence that the Communist Party of the Soviet Union and its Central Committee have done everything possible to achieve stronger unity and cohesion between the CPSU and the CPC on the principled basis of Marxism-Leninism, with an eye to normalizing relations between the USSR and China. And if no success was achieved, the blame rests squarely with the leadership of the Chinese Communist Party.

The Soviet press has on more than one occasion informed our public about the specific trends and aims which today underlie China's foreign policy. This is especially evident in the matter of supporting the Vietnamese people. The intervention of the U.S.A. in South Vietnam and its aggression against the Democratic Republic of Vietnam tend to increase international tensions and jeopardize peace not only in Southeast Asia, but throughout the world.

The CPSU and the other fraternal parties hold that joint action by the socialist states is needed to support the Vietnamese people effectively in their struggle for freedom and independence. At its 23d Congress our Party again appealed to the Communists of all countries to close their ranks still more in the face of the expanding aggressive machinations of imperialism. The other fraternal parties have also implemented measures to strengthen the unity of the socialist countries in rebuffing American aggression. In November last year, the Central Committee of the Polish United

Workers' Party came forward with an important initiative aimed at achieving agreed action of the socialist countries in rendering assistance to the DRV, and proposed to the fraternal parties that a summit meeting on the problem be convened. But our proposals, just as the proposals of the PUWP and the other fraternal parties, were turned down by the CPC leadership.

Had there been united action on the part of the entire mighty socialist community, the assistance given the Vietnamese people would have been immeasurably more telling and effective. Instead of rallying in a united front with all socialist countries in the struggle against the U.S. aggressors, the leaders of the CPC are stubbornly continuing their splitting policies.

The Chinese leadership is making no little effort to smear the effective aid and support rendered to the Vietnamese people by the Soviet Union and the other socialist countries. By calling for "disassociation" from the CPSU and other fraternal parties, the Chinese leaders, essentially speaking, are demanding that the nations waging a just struggle for the national independence of their countries should reject assistance from the Soviet Union and other socialist countries and should be guided solely by the aims and objectives of Peking.

It may be asked—with whom then does the Chinese leadership which declares of the need of "the broadest united front of struggle against U.S. imperialism," wish to join forces, if it rejects all the proposals on joint action with the forces that are shouldering the brunt of the struggle against imperialism? All that is in fact helping escalation of U.S. aggression against the Vietnamese people.

The double-faced policy pursued by the Chinese leaders in the international arena is becoming ever more pronounced. On the one hand, they are trying to foist on the fraternal parties a course which would lead to a continuous aggravation of the international situation and, in the long run, to war, allegedly in the name of world revolution. The Peking leaders themselves are, however, following a course calculated to keep clear of the struggle against imperialism.

While declaring that all contacts the Soviet Union has with the U.S.A. are "collusion" with imperialism, the Chinese leaders miss no opportunity to develop relations with capitalist countries, including the U.S.A. Chen Yi, China's Foreign Minister, according to the Japanese agency Kyodo Tsushin, declared in a talk with the representatives of the Japanese Liberal-Democratic Party, that Peking was maintaining contacts with Washington in Warsaw, and "did not necessarily exclude the idea of talks with the U.S.A." This is not the first time Chen Yi has made such declarations. It is noteworthy that the Western press is repeatedly stressing that Peking's noisy campaign against the U.S.A. bears the imprint of a purely verbose "escalation." Meanwhile this selfsame press is persistently harping on the subject of tensions on the Soviet-Chinese border resulting from Chinese territorial claims. No wonder that today the bourgeois press is disseminating information on a tacit agreement between China and the U.S.A. and other capitalist countries, which are quite content with China's present-day policies.

Quite a few important events have taken place in the international arena ever since the CPC Central Committee came forward with its own platform. Life has more than once put to the test the correctness of the course evolved by the world communist movement at the Moscow meetings in 1957 and 1960. The present course of the Chinese leaders has also been tested in practice. There can be no two opinions on the results of this test.

International developments in recent years have affirmed anew the complete validity, realism, and effectiveness of the course taken by the Marxist-Leninist parties, which stand for peace, national freedom, democracy, and socialism. The socialist countries which in their development are guided by Marxism-Leninism and are following a course of all-round advancement of their economy, of strengthening their defense potential and of consistently applying Leninist principles of economic management, have achieved major successes. That is an irrefutable fact. At the same time the policy based on the concepts of Mao Tse-tung has led to grave failures in China's economy. Suffice it to say that this policy has resulted in a sharp decline in China's industrial and agricultural production which has only now attained the 1957–58 level.

The communist and workers' parties which are truly struggling against imperialism have still more consolidated their ranks, strengthened still more their alliance with all the peace-loving forces, and further enhanced the prestige of socialism. They are actively and effectively supporting the heroic Vietnamese people in their just struggle against the aggression of U.S. imperialism. They are putting up a united front in the struggle for European security and are rebuffing the machinations of American and West German imperialism. The socialist countries which abide by the line expressed in the 1957 Declaration and 1960 Statement, have consolidated even more their forces with the national-liberation movement and are furthering its successes.

At this same time the Chinese leaders have launched an unprecedented campaign aimed at splitting the international communist movement, hampering in fact the fight waged by the anti-imperialist front.

Guided by the principle "the end justifies the means," the CPC leaders are resorting to the most underhand means of political struggle. They are feverishly recruiting supporters. Peking writes that "the revolutionary peoples of the world are closely rallied around Chairman Mao." But the facts show that the utter majority of fraternal parties have resolutely rejected the present platform of the Chinese leaders.

The repeated appeals made by the CPC leadership to "disassociate organizationally" from the Marxist-Leninist parties aimed at setting up a bloc of parties and groups headed by the CPC. But the further events develop, the clearer one sees that they have no one to align with within the communist movement. The pro-Chinese splitter factions which preach borrowed ideas alien to the working class were not destined to become organizations with any sizable following and to win a position for themselves within the working-class movements of their countries. Lately strife started in the splitter organizations and many of them are falling apart.

Nor did the Chinese leaders meet with success in their attempts to establish control over international democratic organizations—the World Council of Peace, the World Federation of Trade Unions, the women's, youth, and other associations. The attempts to make those organizations operate on a narrow sectarian basis, and to foist on them slogans and forms of activity absolutely alien to them, were rejected.

The hopes the Chinese leadership pinned on the national-liberation movement also fell through. The major fiascos suffered by the Chinese policy in the na-

tional-liberation movement, and the failures of those leaders who had blindly supported it, seriously alerted the progressive forces in the young national states, in the revolutionary-democratic parties, and helped them to discern the danger of the Peking leaders' course. As a result, instead of achieving hegemony in the Asian, African, and Latin American countries, which the CPC leaders sought, there took place a sharp decline in the prestige of the CPR.

Aware of the obvious fact that the CPC leadership is becoming more and more isolated in the international communist and liberation movement, Mao Tse-tung, as if challenging the entire socialist world, declared in his greetings to the Congress of the Albanian Party of Labor: "We have no fear of isolation." But this course of isolating the CPR and the CPC shows most strikingly that the basic demands of proletarian internationalism are being ignored. It also conflicts with the interests of the Chinese people. Marxist-Leninists cannot be interested in the isolation of any socialist country, for that would mean taking the line of severing it from the socialist community, of disunity among the countries of socialism.

The struggle of the Chinese leaders against the Soviet Union and the other socialist countries, their splitting activities in the communist movement, and their failures in internal and foreign policies could not pass without consequence, and, as the Chinese press admits, caused mounting discontent among Party cadres, intellectuals, in the army, and among broad sections of the Chinese population.

In these circumstances, Mao Tse-tung and his group, instead of heeding the opinions of the Party masses and amending their erroneous course, took the road of taking this line still further, of carrying it to extremes. They considered the Party activists, the Party cadres to be the main obstacle along this path.

Mao Tse-tung and those who surround him could not but take into account the fact that the Party cadres, who had gone through the school of revolution, were beginning more and more to understand, despite the anti-Soviet campaign of recent years, the harm which the policy of splitting with the Soviet Union and the other socialist countries was bringing to China itself. It is hard to fool them with inventions about some sort of "collusion" of the Soviet Union with the U.S.A. or about the "restoration of capitalism" in our country. That is why Mao Tse-tung and his group have taken the line of defaming and attacking the Party cadres and the best representatives of the working class and intelligentsia, employing for this purpose some of the school-children and students as well as the military-administrative apparatus.

Meeting with resistance to their course, Mao Tse-tung and his adherents did not even stop short of jeopardizing the leading role of the Party in the state. They want to turn the Communist Party from an organization of people united by a common ideology, of conscious, principled fighters for the implementation of ideas of socialism, into an obedient, unthinking tool for fulfilling the will of Mao Tse-tung. Those who attempt to struggle for the principles of Marxism-Leninism and for Leninist norms of inter-Party life are hounded from the Party.

The things going on in China under the guise of a "cultural revolution" have nothing in common with it. The cultural revolution is one of the most important tasks facing any country building socialism. It is a dire necessity for China, too, for that country still has millions of illiterates and is in great need of skilled scientific and engineering personnel. The work of raising the cultural standards of all people, the training of personnel necessary for managing the economy, constitutes one of the most important aspects of a party's ideological work. Lenin wrote that it was necessary to "take the entire culture that capitalism left behind and build socialism with it. We must take all its science, technology, knowledge, and art. Without these we shall be unable to build a communist society" (*Collected Works*, Russian ed., Vol. 38, p. 55). He never tired of repeating that the Party alone, as the most advanced and conscious detachment of society, can lead and implement this. As for the campaign in China, it directly conflicts with Lenin's teaching, in both content and methods.

In the past few months many of the Party committees in the provinces, cities, industrial enterprises, and higher educational establishments, and the editorial offices of national and provincial newspapers and magazines were either "reorganized" or dispersed altogether in China. At present, Party organizations are quite often replaced by "working groups" and "cultural revolution committees." Numerous Party workers and government officials, workers in science, literature, and the arts have been dubbed "black bandits," "rightist elements," and "revisionists." These labels are designed to conceal the true meaning of the charges brought against them, but from the Chinese press it is becoming evident that it is mainly a question of many Communists and cultural workers disagreeing with the course of Mao Tse-tung which is being implemented, and the grave consequences of which they are well aware.

It is characteristic that people are subjected to repressions for the slightest expression of sympathy for the Soviet Union.

In order to make the purge appear to be a mass movement instigated from below, the so-called Red Guards—14–18-year-old youngsters brought up in a spirit of unbridled lauding of Mao Tse-tung's personality, arbitrariness, nationalism, and anti-Sovietism—have been employed. But actually behind them stands the leadership of the army and the state security bodies.

The events in China are very complicated and contradictory. But it is already clear that the nationalistic and great-power course of Mao Tse-tung and his group is inflicting great harm to the people of China and jeopardizing many of the gains of the revolution in the country, that it has seriously damaged the unity of the entire communist movement and the cause of the struggle against imperialism. This cannot but profoundly grieve and cause anxiety among those who had welcomed the great Chinese revolution, who had considered it their most urgent duty to help the Chinese people in the struggle against imperialism and in socialist construction, and who had always aspired toward unity and friendship with the Chinese Communists.

China is a great country, and it is clear that the weakening of the positions of socialism in that country could adversely affect the interests of the international revolutionary movement. Bourgeois propaganda is utilizing the negative processes in China to discredit the ideas of socialism throughout the world. Particularly dangerous are China's reckless actions in foreign policy. All this is damaging to the Chinese people themselves.

The interests of unity of all the revolutionary forces in their struggle against imperialism demand the overcoming of the nationalistic, anti-Soviet policies, the overcoming of the attempts to distort Marxism-Leninism and to replace it by the ideology and the practices of Maoism.

As for the CPSU it is fully resolved to do everything necessary to surmount the difficulties created by the policies pursued by the CPC leadership in the communist movement and the socialist community. The CPSU, like the other communist and workers' parties, is fully resolved to defend unflinchingly the ideas of Marxism-Leninism, of proletarian internationalism.

. . . The Soviet people entertain feelings of profound respect for the Chinese people, for the Chinese Communists. We are full of the feeling of solidarity with the heroic Chinese people, who have great experience in revolutionary struggle.

Being true internationalists, we hold dear the gains of the Chinese Revolution. We are firmly convinced that ultimately our parties and our peoples will be marching in the same ranks in the struggle for the common and great revolutionary cause.

The world communist movement has more than once met with grave trials. It is strong and viable enough to defend the great banner of Marxism-Leninism in the name of new victories of communism.

72

WHITHER THE SOVIET UNION?

By Zbygniew Brzezinski; Frederick Barghoorn

The Soviet regime is now fifty years old. It has survived many crises and has undergone substantial changes, and yet some of its features appear rather permanent. In the jubilee year of 1967 countless observers, both Soviet and foreign, have been casting a horoscope for the first socialist country in the world, and the oldest one. What is the future of the Soviet system? What is the nature of the changes which have taken place since the death of Stalin? Is Russia still a revolutionary society or is she deeply conservative in her own way? Is Soviet communism a model for the underdeveloped world, or are Soviet methods not applicable elsewhere? These are some of the questions which are being asked and answered. The two essays below are part of a series of articles printed in *Problems of Communism* in 1966 and 1967; many scholars took part in the debate. We reproduce only the leading article and one of the comments upon it. Professor Brzezinski teaches at Columbia University and is at present (1968) Special Assistant to President Johnson; Professor Barghoorn teaches political science at Yale University. Both are authors of numerous books and articles.

For alternate interpretations which appeared in 1967 see Isaac Deutscher, *The Unfinished Revolution, 1917–1967* (paperback); Y. Marin, "The USSR in the Jubilee Year," *Bulletin of the Institute for the Study of the USSR*, August, 1967; a series of articles in *Foreign Affairs*, September, 1967; "The Soviet Revolution, 1917–1967: A Balance Sheet," *Survey*, July, 1967; and Bertram Wolfe, "Reflections on the Future of the Soviet System," *Russian Review*, April, 1967. For Soviet views see all the 1967 issues of the Soviet monthly, *Soviet Life*; "The 50th Anniversary of the October Revolution," *International Affairs*, 1967, No. 8; "Fifty Heroic Years," *New Times*, July 5, 1967; and "Historic Significance of the Great October Socialist Revolution," *World Marxist Review*, August, 1967.

See also *The Impact of the Russian Revolution, 1917–1967* (paperback) by Arnold Toynbee and others.

From Z. Brzezinski, "The Soviet Political System: Transformation or Degeneration?" *Problems of Communism*, January–February, 1966, pp. 1–15; F. Barghoorn, "Changes in Russia: The Need for Perspective," *ibid.,* May–June, 1966, pp. 39–42. Published by permission of the United States Information Agency.

BRZEZINSKI: THE SOVIET POLITICAL SYSTEM

The Soviet Union will soon celebrate its 50th anniversary. In this turbulent and rapidly changing world, for any political system to survive half a century is an accomplishment in its own right and obvious testimony to its durability. There are not many major political structures in the world today that can boast of such longevity. The approaching anniversary, however, provides an appropriate moment for a critical review of the changes that have taken place in the Soviet system, particularly in regard to such critical matters as the character of its top leadership, the methods by which its leaders acquire power, and the relationship of the Communist Party to society. Furthermore, the time is also ripe to inquire into the implications of these changes, especially in regard to the stability and vitality of the system.

THE LEADERS

Today Soviet spokesmen would have us believe that the quality of the top Communist leadership in the USSR has been abysmal. Of the forty-five years since Lenin, according to official Soviet history, power was exercised for approximately five years by leaders subsequently unmasked as traitors (although later the charge of treason was retroactively reduced to that of deviation); for almost twenty years it was wielded by a paranoiac mass-murderer who irrationally slew his best comrades and ignorantly guided Soviet war strategy by pointing his finger at a globe; and, most recently, for almost ten years, by a "harebrained" schemer given to tantrums and with a propensity for wild organizational experimentation. On the basis of that record, the present leadership lays claim to representing a remarkable departure from a historical pattern of singular depravity.

While Soviet criticism of former party leaders is now abundant, little intellectual effort is expended on analyzing the implications of the changes in leadership. Yet that, clearly, is the important question insofar as the political system is concerned.

Lenin's biographers[1] agree that here was a man characterized by total political commitment, by self-righteous conviction, by tenacious determination and by an outstanding ability to formulate intellectually appealing principles of political action as well as popular slogans suitable for mass consumption. He was a typically revolutionary figure, a man whose genius can be consummated only at that critical juncture in history when the new breaks off—and not just evolves—from the old. Had he lived a generation earlier, he probably would have died in a Siberian *taiga*; a generation later, he probably would have been shot by Stalin.

Lenin was a rare type of political leader, fusing in his person several functions of key importance to the working of a political system: he acted as the chief ideologist of the system, the principal organizer of the party (indeed, the founder of the movement), and the top administrator of the state. It may be added that such personal fusion is typical of early revolutionary leaderships, and today it is exemplified by Mao Tse-tung. To his followers, Lenin was clearly a charismatic leader, and his power (like Hitler's or Mao

---

[1] Angelica Balabanoff, *Impressions of Lenin* (Ann Arbor: University of Michigan Press, 1964). Louis Fischer, *Life of Lenin* (New York: Harper, 1964). S. Possony, *Lenin, the Compulsive Revolutionary* (Chicago: Regnery, 1964). Bertram D. Wolfe, *Three Who Made a Revolution* (New York: Dial Press, 1948).

Tse-tung's) depended less on institutions than on the force of his personality and intellect. Even after the Revolution, it was his personal authority that gave him enormous power, while the progressive institutionalization of Lenin's rule (the Cheka, the appearance of the *apparat*, etc.) reflected more the transformation of a revolutionary party into a ruling one than any significant change in the character of his leadership.

Under Stalin, the fusion of leadership functions was continued, but this was due less to his personal qualities as such than to the fact that, with the passage of time and the growing toll of victims, his power became nearly total and was gradually translated also into personal authority. Only a mediocre ideologist—and certainly inferior in that respect to his chief rivals for power —Stalin became institutionally, the ideologue of the system. A dull speaker, he eventually acquired the "routinized charisma"[2] which, after Lenin's death, became invested in the Communist Party as a whole (much as the Pope at one time had acquired the infallibility that for a long time had rested in the collective church). But his power was increasingly institutionalized bureaucratically, with decision-making centralized at the apex within his own secretariat, and its exercise involved a subtle balancing of the principal institutions of the political system: the secret police, the party, the state, and the army (roughly in that order of importance). Even the ostensibly principal organ of power, the Politburo, was split into minor groups, "the sextets," the "quarters," etc., with Stalin personally deciding who should participate in which subgroup and personally providing (and monopolizing) the function of integration.

If historical parallels for Lenin are to be found among the revolutionary tribunes, for Stalin they are to be sought among the Oriental despots.[3] Thriving on intrigue, shielded in mystery, and isolated from society, his immense power reflected the immense tasks he succeeded in imposing on his followers and subjects. Capitalizing on the revolutionary momentum and the ideological impetus inherited from Leninism, and wedding it to a systematic institutionalization of bureaucratic rule, he could set in motion a social and political revolution which weakened all existing institutions save Stalin's own secretariat and his chief executive arm, the secret police. His power grew in proportion to the degree to which the major established institutions declined in vitality and homogeneity.[4]

The war, however, as well as the postwar reconstruction, produced a paradox. While Stalin's personal prestige and authority were further enhanced, his institutional supremacy relatively declined. The military establishment naturally grew in importance; the enormous effort to transfer, reinstall, and later reconstruct the industrial economy

---

[2] For a discussion of "routinized charisma," see Amitai Etzioni, *A Comparative Analysis of Complex Organizations* (Glencoe, Ill.: Free Press, 1961), pp. 26 ff.

[3] Compare the types discussed by J. L. Talmon in his *Political Messianism: The Romantic Phase* (New York, Praeger, 1960), with Barrington Moore, Jr., *Political Power and Social Theory* (Cambridge, Mass.: Harvard University Press, 1958), especially Chapter 2, "Totalitarian Elements in Pre-Industrial Societies," or Karl Wittfogel, *Oriental Despotism* (New Haven: Yale University Press, 1957).

[4] It seems that these considerations are as important to the understanding of the Stalinist system as the psycho-pathological traits of Stalin that Robert C. Tucker rightly emphasizes in his "The Dictator and Totalitarianism," *World Politics*, July, 1965.

invigorated the state machinery; the party apparat began to perform again the key functions of social mobilization and political integration. But the aging tyrant was neither unaware of this development nor apparently resigned to it. The Byzantine intrigues resulting in the liquidation of the Leningrad leadership and Voznesenski, the "doctors' plot" with its ominous implications for some top party, military and police chiefs, clearly augured an effort to weaken any institutional limits on Stalin's personal supremacy.

Khrushchev came to power ostensibly to save Stalinism, which he defined as safeguarding the traditional priority of heavy industry and restoring the primacy of the party. In fact, he presided over the dismantling of Stalinism. He rode to power by restoring the predominant position of the party apparat. But the complexities of governing (as contrasted to the priorities of the power struggle) caused him to dilute the party's position. While initially he succeeded in diminishing the political role of the secret police and in weakening the state machinery, the military establishment grew in importance with the continuing tensions of the cold war.[5] By the time Khrushchev was removed, the economic priorities had become blurred because of pressures in agriculture and the consumer sector, while his own reorganization of the party into two separate industrial and rural hierarchies in November, 1962, went far toward undermining the party's homogeneity of outlook, apart from splitting it institutionally. Consequently, the state bureaucracy recouped, almost by default, some of its integrative and administrative functions. Khrushchev

thus, perhaps inadvertently, restored much of the institutional balance that had existed under Stalin, but without ever acquiring the full powers of the balancer.

Khrushchev lacked the authority of Lenin to generate personal power, or the power of Stalin to create personal authority—and the Soviet leadership under him became increasingly differentiated. The top leader was no longer the top ideologist, in spite of occasional efforts to present Khrushchev's elaborations as "a creative contribution to Marxism-Leninism." The ruling body now contained at least one professional specialist in ideological matters, and it was no secret that the presence of the professional ideologue was required because someone had to give professional ideological advice to the party's top leader. Similarly, technical-administrative specialization differentiated some top leaders from others. Increasingly Khrushchev's function—and presumably the primary source of his still considerable power—was that of providing integration and impetus for new domestic or foreign initiatives in a political system otherwise too complex to be directed and administered by one man.

The differentiation of functions also made it more difficult for the top leader to inherit even the "routinized charisma" that Stalin had eventually transferred to himself from the party as a whole. Acquiring charisma was more difficult for a leader who (even apart from a personal style and vulgar appearance that did not lend themselves to "image building") had neither the great "theoretical" flare valued by a movement that still prided itself on being the embodiment of a messianic ideology nor the technical expertise highly regarded in a state which equated technological advance with human progress. Moreover, occupying the posts of First

[5] For a good treatment of Soviet military debates, see Thomas Wolfe, *Soviet Strategy at the Crossroads* (Cambridge, Mass.: Harvard University Press, 1964).

Secretary and Chairman of the Council of Ministers was not enough to develop a charismatic appeal, since neither post has been sufficiently institutionalized to endow its occupant with the special prestige and aura that, for example, the President of the United States automatically gains on assuming office.

Trying to cope with this lack of charismatic appeal, Khrushchev replaced Stalin's former colleagues. In the process, he gradually came to rely on a younger generation of bureaucratic leaders to whom orderliness of procedure was instinctively preferable to crash campaigns. Administratively, however, Khrushchev was a true product of the Stalinist school, with its marked proclivity for just such campaigns at the cost of all other considerations. In striving to develop his own style of leadership, Khrushchev tried to emulate Lenin in stimulating new fervor, and Stalin in mobilizing energies, but without the personal and institutional assets that each had commanded. By the time he was removed, Khrushchev had become an anachronism in the new political context he himself had helped to create.

Brezhnev and Kosygin mark the coming to power of a new generation of leaders, irrespective of whether they will for long retain their present positions.[6] Lenin's, Stalin's, and Khrushchev's formative experience was the unsettled period of conspiratorial activity, revolution, and—in Khrushchev's case —civil war and the early phase of communism. The new leaders, beneficiaries of the revolution but no longer revolutionaries themselves, have matured in an established political setting in which the truly large issues of policy and leadership have been decided. Aspiring

[6] See S. Bialer, "An Unstable Leadership," *Problems of Communism*, July–August, 1965.

young bureaucrats, initially promoted during the purges, they could observe— but not suffer from—the debilitating consequences of political extremism and unpredictable personal rule. To this new generation of clerks, bureaucratic stability—indeed, bureaucratic dictatorship— must seem to be the only solid foundation for effective government.

Differentiation of functions to these bureaucrats is a norm, while personal charisma is ground for suspicion. The new Soviet leadership, therefore, is both bureaucratic in style and essentially impersonal in form. The curious emphasis on *kollektivnost rukovodstva* (collectivity of leadership) instead of the traditional *kollektivnoe rukovodstvo* (collective leadership)—a change in formulation used immediately after Khrushchev's fall—suggests a deliberate effort at achieving not only a personal but also an institutional collective leadership, designed to prevent any one leader from using a particular institution as a vehicle for obtaining political supremacy.

The question arises, however, whether this kind of leadership can prove effective in guiding the destiny of a major state. The Soviet system is now led by a bureaucratic leadership from the very top to the bottom. In that respect, it is unique. Even political systems with highly developed and skillful professional political bureaucracies, such as the British, the French, or that of the Catholic Church, have reserved some top policy-making and hence power-wielding positions for nonbureaucratic professional politicians, presumably on the assumption that a freewheeling, generalizing, and competitive political experience is of decisive importance in shaping effective national leadership.

To be sure, some top Soviet leaders

do acquire such experience, even in the course of rising up the bureaucratic party ladder, especially when assigned to provincial or republican executive responsibilities. There they acquire the skills of initiative, direction, integration, as well as accommodation, compromise, and delegation of authority, which are the basic prerequisites for executive management of any complex organization.

Nonetheless, even when occupying territorial positions of responsibility, the *apparatchiki* are still part of an extremely centralized and rigidly hierarchical bureaucratic organization, increasingly set in its ways, politically corrupted by years of unchallenged power, and made even more confined in its outlook than is normally the case with a ruling body by its lingering and increasingly ritualized doctrinaire tradition. It is relevant to note here (from observations made in Soviet universities) that the young men who become active in the Komsomol organization and are presumably embarking on a professional political career are generally the dull conformists. Clearly, in a highly bureaucratized political setting, conformity, caution and currying favor with superiors count for more in advancing a political career than personal courage and individual initiative.[7]

Such a condition poses a long-range danger to the vitality of any political system. Social evolution, it has been noted, depends not only on the availability of creative individuals, but on the existence of clusters of creators who collectively promote social innovation. "The ability of any gifted individual to exert leverage within a society . . . is partly a function of the exact composition of the group of those on whom he depends for day-to-day interaction and for the execution of his plans."[8] The revolutionary milieu of the 1920's and even the fanatical Stalinist commitment of the 1930's fostered such clusters of intellectual and political talent. It is doubtful that the CPSU party schools and the Central Committee personnel department encourage, in Margaret Mead's terms, the growth of clusters of creativity, and that is why the transition from Lenin to Stalin to Khrushchev to Brezhnev probably cannot be charted by an ascending line.

This has serious implications for the Soviet system as a whole. It is doubtful that any organization can long remain vital if it is so structured that in its personnel policy it becomes, almost unknowingly, inimical to talent and hostile to political innovation. Decay is bound to set in, while the stability of the political system may be endangered, if other social institutions suceed in attracting the society's talent and begin to chafe under the restraints imposed by the ruling but increasingly mediocre *apparatchiki*.

THE STRUGGLE FOR POWER

The struggle for power in the Soviet political system has certainly become less violent. The question is, however: Has it become less debilitating for the political system? Has it become a more regularized process, capable of infusing the leadership with fresh blood? A

---

[7] Writing about modern bureaucracy, V. A. Thompson (*Modern Organization* [New York, 1961], p. 91) observed: "In the formally structured group, the idea man is doubly dangerous. He endangers the established distribution of power and status, and he is a competitive threat to his peers. Consequently, he has to be suppressed." For a breezy treatment of some analogous experience, see also E. G. Hegarty, *How to Succeed in Company Politics* (New York, 1963).

[8] Margaret Mead, *Continuities in Cultural Evolution* (New Haven: Yale University Press, 1964), p. 181. See also the introduction, especially p. xx.

closer look at the changes in the character of the competition for power may guide us to the answer.

Both Stalin and Khrushchev rode to power by skillfully manipulating issues as well as by taking full advantage of the organizational opportunities arising from their tenure of the post of party First Secretary. It must be stressed that the manipulation of issues was at least as important to their success as the organizational factor, which generally tends to receive priority in Western historical treatments. In Stalin's time, the issues facing the party were, indeed, on a grand scale: world revolution vs. socialism in one country; domestic evolution vs. social revolution; a factionalized vs. a monolithic party. Stalin succeeded because he instinctively perceived that the new *apparatchiki* were not prepared to sacrifice themselves in futile efforts to promote foreign revolutions but—being for the most part genuinely committed to revolutionary ideals —were becoming eager to get on with the job of creating a socialist society. (Moreover, had the NEP endured another ten years, would the Soviet Union be a Communist dictatorship today?) Stalin's choice of socialism in one country was a brilliant solution. It captivated, at least in part, the revolutionaries; and it satisfied, at least partially, the accommodators. It split the opposition, polarized it, and prepared the ground for the eventual liquidation of each segment with the other's support. The violence, the terror, and finally the Great Purges of 1936–38 followed logically. Imbued with the Leninist tradition of intolerance for dissent, engaged in a vast undertaking of social revolution that taxed both the resources and the nerves of party members, guided by an unscrupulous and paranoiac but also reassuringly calm leader, governing a

backward country surrounded by neighbors that were generally hostile to the Soviet experiment, and increasingly deriving its own membership strength from first-generation proletarians with all their susceptibility to simple explanations and dogmatic truths, the ruling party easily plunged down the path of increasing brutality. The leader both rode the crest of that violence and controlled it. The terror never degenerated into simple anarchy, and Stalin's power grew immeasurably because he effectively practiced the art of leadership according to his own definition:

> The art of leadership is a serious matter. One must not lag behind the movement, because to do so is to become isolated from the masses. But neither must one rush ahead, for to rush ahead is to lose contact with the masses. He who wants to lead a movement and at the same time keep in touch with the vast masses must wage a fight on two fronts—against those who lag behind and those who run ahead.[9]

Khrushchev, too, succeeded in becoming the top leader because he perceived the elite's predominant interests. Restoration of the primary position of the party, decapitation of the sceret police, reduction of the privileges of the state bureaucrats while maintaining the traditional emphasis on heavy industrial development (which pleased both the industrial elite and the military establishment)—these were the issues which Khrushchev successfully utilized in the mid-1950's to mobilize the support of officials and accomplish the gradual isolation and eventual defeat of Malenkov.

But the analogy ends right there. The social and even the political system in which Khrushchev came to rule was relatively settled. Indeed, in some re-

[9] J. V. Stalin, *Problems of Leninism* (Moscow, 1940), p. 338.

spects, it was stagnating, and Khrush-chev's key problem, once he reached the political apex (but before he had had time to consolidate his position there) was how to get the country mov-ing again. The effort to infuse new so-cial and political dynamism into Soviet society, even while consolidating his power, led him to a public repudiation of Stalinism which certainly shocked some officials; to sweeping economic re-forms which disgruntled many adminis-trators; to a dramatic reorganization of the party which appalled the *apparat-chiki;* and even to an attempt to circum-vent the policy-making authority of the party Presidium by means of direct appeals to interested groups, which must have both outraged and frightened his colleagues. The elimination of vio-lence as the decisive instrumentality of political competition—a move that was perhaps prompted by the greater insti-tutional maturity of Soviet society, and which was in any case made inevitable by the downgrading of the secret police and the public disavowals of Stalinism —meant that Khrushchev, unlike Stalin, could not achieve both social dynamism and the stability of his power. Stalin magnified his power as he strove to change society; to change society Khru-shchev had to risk his power.

The range of domestic disagreement involved in the post-Stalin struggles has also narrowed with the maturing of social commitments made earlier. For the moment, the era of grand alterna-tives is over in Soviet society. Even though any struggle tends to exaggerate differences, the issues that divided Khrushchev from his opponents, though of great import, appear pedestrian in comparison to those over which Stalin and his enemies crossed swords. In Khrushchev's case, they pertained pri-marily to policy alternatives; in the case of Stalin, they involved basic con-ceptions of historical development. Com-pare the post-Stalin debates about the allocation of resources among different branches of the economy, for example, with the debates of the 1920's about the character and pace of Soviet industriali-zation; or Khrushchev's homilies on the merits of corn—and even his undenia-bly bold and controversial virgin lands campaign—with the dilemma of wheth-er to collectivize a hundred million reti-cent peasants, at what pace, and with what intensity in terms of resort to violence.

It is only in the realm of foreign affairs that one can perhaps argue that grand dilemmas still impose them-selves on the Soviet political scene. The nuclear-war-or-peace debate of the 1950's and early 1960's is comparable in many respects to the earlier conflict over "permanent revolution" or "social-ism in one country." Molotov's removal and Kozlov's political demise were to a large extent related to disagreements concerning foreign affairs; nonetheless, in spite of such occasional rumblings, it would appear that on the peace-or-war issue there is today more of a consensus among the Soviet elite than there was on the issue of permanent revolution in the 1920's. Although a wide spectrum of opinion does indeed exist in the in-ternational Communist movement on the crucial questions of war and peace, this situation, as far as one can judge, obtains to a considerably lesser degree in the USSR itself. Bukharin vs. Trotsky can be compared to Togliatti vs. Mao Tse-tung, but hardly to Khrushchev vs. Kozlov.

The narrowing of the range of dis-agreement is reflected in the changed character of the cast. In the earlier part of this discussion, some comparative comments were made about Stalin,

Khrushchev, and Brezhnev. It is even more revealing, however, to examine their principal rivals. Take the men who opposed Stalin: Trotsky, Zinoviev, and Bukharin. What a range of political, historical, economic, and intellectual creativity, what talent, what a diversity of personal characteristics and backgrounds! Compare this diversity with the strikingly uniform personal training, narrowness of perspective, and poverty of intellect of Malenkov, Kozlov and Suslov.[10] A regime of the clerks cannot help but clash over clerical issues.

The narrowing of the range of disagreement and the cooling of ideological passions mean also the wane of political violence. The struggle tends to become less a matter of life or death, and more one in which the price of defeat is simply retirement and some personal disgrace. In turn, with the routinization of conflict, the political system develops even a body of precedents for handling fallen leaders. By now there must be a regular procedure, probably even some office, for handling pensions and apartments for former Presidium members, as well as a developing social etiquette for dealing with them publicly and privately.[11]

More important is the apparent development in the Soviet system of something which might be described as a regularly available "counter-elite." After Khrushchev's fall, his successors moved quickly to restore to important positions a number of individuals whom Khrushchev had purged,[12] while some of Khrushchev's supporters were demoted and transferred. Already for a number of years now, it has been fairly common practice to appoint party officials demoted from high office either to diplomatic posts abroad or to some obscure, out-of-the-way assignments at home. The total effect of this has been to create a growing body of official "outs" who are biding their time on the sidelines and presumably hoping someday to become the "ins" again. Moreover, they may not only hope; if sufficiently numerous, young, and vigorous, they may gradually begin to resemble something of a political alternative to those in power, and eventually to think and even act as such. This could be the starting point of informal factional activity, of intrigues and conspiracies when things go badly for those in power, and of organized efforts to seduce some part of the ruling elite in order to stage an internal change of guard.[13] In addition, the availability of

[10] One could hardly expect a historian to work up any enthusiasm for undertaking to write, say, Malenkov's biography: *The Apparatchik Promoted, The Apparatchik Triumphant, The Apparatchik Pensioned!*

[11] Can Mikoyan, for example, invite Khrushchev to lunch? This is not a trivial question, for social mores and political style are interwoven. After all, Voroshilov, who had been publicly branded as a military idiot and a political sycophant, was susbequently invited to a Kremlin reception. Zhukov, against whom the Bonapartist charge still stands, appeared in full regalia at the twentieth anniversary celebration of the Soviet victory in World War II.

[12] F. D. Kulakov, apparently blamed by Khrushchev in 1960 for agricultural failings in the RSFSR, was appointed in 1965 to direct the Soviet Union's new agricultural programs; V. V. Matskevich was restored as Minister of Agriculture and appointed Deputy Premier of the RSFSR in charge of agriculture; Marshal M. V. Zakharov was reappointed as Chief of Staff of the Armed Forces; even L. G. Melnikov reemerged from total obscurity as chairman of the industrial work safety committee of the RSFSR.

[13] Molotov's letter to the Central Committee on the eve of the 22d Party Congress of October, 1961, which bluntly and directly charged Khrushchev's program with revisionism, was presumably designed to stir up the *apparatchiki* against the First Secretary. It may be a portent of things to come.

an increasingly secure "counter-elite" is likely to make it more difficult for a leader to consolidate his power. This in turn might tend to promote more frequent changes in the top leadership, with policy failures affecting the power of incumbents instead of affecting—only retroactively—the reputation of former leaders, as has hitherto been the case.

The cumulative effect of these developments has been wide-ranging. First of all, the reduced importance of both ideological issues and personalities and the increasing weight of institutional interests in the periodic struggles for power—a phenomenon which reflects the more structured quality of present-day Soviet life as compared with the situation under Stalin—tends to depersonalize political conflict and to make it a protracted bureaucratic struggle. Second, the curbing of violence makes it more likely that conflicts will be resolved by patched-up compromises rather than by drastic institutional redistributions of power and the reappearance of personal tyranny. Finally, the increasingly bureaucratic character of the struggle for power tends to transform it into a contest among high-level clerks and is therefore not conducive to attracting creative and innovating talent into the top leadership.

Khrushchev's fall provides a good illustration of the points made above, as well as an important precedent for the future. For the first time in Soviet history, the First Secretary has been toppled from power by his associates. This was done not in order to replace him with an alternative personal leader or to pursue genuinely alternative goals, but in order to depersonalize the leadership and to pursue more effectively many of the previous policies. In a word, the objectives were impersonal

leadership and higher bureaucratic efficiency. Khrushchev's removal, however, also means that personal intrigues and cabals can work, that subordinate members of the leadership—or possibly, someday, a group of ex-leaders—can effectively conspire against a principal leader, with the result that any future First Secretary is bound to feel far less secure than Khrushchev must have felt at the beginning of October, 1964.

The absence of an institutionalized top executive officer in the Soviet political system, in conjunction with the increased difficulties in the way of achieving personal dictatorship and the decreased personal cost of defeat in a political conflict, create a ready-made situation for group pressures and institutional clashes. In fact, although the range of disagreement may have narrowed, the scope of elite participation in power conflicts has already widened. Much of Khrushchev's exercise of power was preoccupied with mediating the demands of key institutions such as the army, or with overcoming the opposition of others, such as the objections of the administrators to economic decentralization or of the heavy industrial managers to nonindustrial priorities. These interests were heavily involved in the Khrushchev-Malenkov conflict and in the "anti-party" episode of 1957.

At the present time, these pressures and clashes take place in an almost entirely amorphous context, without constitutional definition and established procedures. The somewhat greater role played by the Central Committee in recent years still does not suffice to give this process of bureaucratic conflict a stable institutional expression. As far as we know from existing evidence, the Central Committee still acted during the 1957 and 1964 crises primarily as a ratifying body, giving formal sanction to decisions already fought out in the Kremlin's corridors of power.[14] It did not act as either the arbiter or the supreme legislative body.

The competition for power, then, is changing from a death struggle among the few into a contest played by many more. But the decline of violence does not, as is often assumed, automatically benefit the Soviet political system; something more effective and stable has to take the place of violence. The "game" of politics that has replaced the former mafia-style struggles for power is no longer murderous, but it is still not a stable game played within an established arena, according to accepted rules, and involving more or less formal teams. It resembles more the anarchistic free-for-all of the playground and therefore could become, in some respects, even more debilitating to the system. Stalin encouraged institutional conflict below him so that he could wield his power with less restraint. Institutional conflict combined with mediocre and unstable personal leadership makes for ineffective and precarious power.

PARTY AND GROUP INTERESTS

In a stimulating study of political development and decay, Samuel Huntington has argued that stable political growth requires a balance between political "institutionalization" and political "participation": that merely increasing popular mobilization and participation in politics without achieving a corresponding degree of "institutionalization of political organization and procedures" results not in political development but in political decay.[15] Commenting in passing on the Soviet system,

he therefore noted that "a strong party is in the Soviet public interest" because it provides a stable institutional framework.[16]

The Soviet political system has certainly achieved a high index of institutionalization. For almost five decades the ruling party has maintained unquestioned supremacy over the society, imposing its ideology at will. Traditionally, the Communist system has combined its high institutionalization with high pseudo-participation of individuals.[17] But a difficulty could arise if division within the top leadership of the political system weakened political "institutionalization" while simultaneously stimulating genuine public participation by groups and institutions. Could this new condition be given an effective and stable institutional framework and, if so, with what implications for the "strong" party?

Today the Soviet political system is again oligarchic, but its socio-economic setting is now quite different. Soviet society is far more developed and stable, far less *malleable* and atomized. In the past, the key groups that had to be considered as potential political participants were relatively few. Today, in addition to the vastly more entrenched institutional interests, such as the police, the military, and the state bureau-

---

[14] Roger Pethybridge, *A Key to Soviet Politics* (New York: Praeger, 1962). See also Myron Rush, *The Rise of Khrushchev* (Washington, D.C.: Public Affairs Press, 1958).

[15] Samuel P. Huntington, "Political Development and Political Decay," *World Politics* (Princeton, N.J.), April, 1965.

[16] *Ibid.*, p. 414.

[17] The massive campaigns launching "public discussions" that involve millions of people, the periodic "elections" that decide nothing, were designed to develop participation without threat to the institutionalized political organization and procedures. The official theory held that, as Communist consciousness developed and new forms of social and public relations took root, political participation would become more meaningful and the public would come to govern itself.

cracy, the youth could become a source of ferment, the consumers could become more restless, the collective farmers more recalcitrant, the scientists more outspoken, the non-Russian nationalities more demanding. Prolonged competition among the oligarchs would certainly accelerate the assertiveness of such groups.

By now some of these groups have a degree of institutional cohesion, and occasionally they act in concert on some issues.[18] They certainly can lobby and, in turn, be courted by ambitious and opportunistic oligarchs. Some groups, because of institutional cohesion, advantageous location, easy access to the top leadership, and ability to articulate their goals and interests, can be quite influential.[19] Taken together, they represent a wide spectrum of opinion, and in the setting of oligarchical rule

there is bound to be some correspondence between their respective stances and those of the top leaders. This spectrum is represented in simplified fashion by the chart on this page, which takes cumulative account of the principal divisions, both on external and on domestic issues, that have perplexed Soviet political life during the last decade or so.[20] Obviously, the table is somewhat arbitrary and also highly speculative. Individuals and groups cannot be categorized so simply, and some, clearly, could be shifted left or right with equal cause, as indeed they often shift themselves. Nonetheless, the chart illustrates the range of opinion that exists in the Soviet system and suggests the kind of alliances, group competition, and political courtship that probably prevail, cutting vertically through the party organization.

---

[18] A schematic distribution of these groups is indicated by the following approximate figures: (A) amorphous social forces that in the main express passively broad social aspirations: workers and peasants, about 88 million; white collar and technical intelligentsia, about 21 million. (B) specific interest groups that promote their own particular interests: the literary and artistic community, about 75 thousand; higher-level scientists, about 150 thousand; physicians, about 380 thousand. (C) policy groups whose interests necessarily spill over into broad matters of national policy: industrial managers, about 200 thousand; state and collective farm chairmen, about 45 thousand; commanding military personnel, about 80 thousand; higher-level state bureaucrats, about 250 thousand. These groups are integrated by the professional *apparatchiki*, who number about 150–200 thousand. All of these groups in turn could be broken down into sub-units; e.g., the literary community, institutionally built around several journals, can be divided into hard-liners, the centrists, and the progressives, etc. Similarly, the military. On some issues, there may be cross-interlocking of sub-groups, as well as more or less temporary coalitions of groups. See Z. Brzezinski and S. Huntington, *Political Power: USA-USSR* (New York: Viking Press, 1964), Chap. 4, for further discussion.

[19] An obvious example is the military command, bureaucratically cohesive and with a specific esprit de corps, located in Moscow, necessarily in frequent contact with the top leaders, and possessing its own journals of opinion (where strategic and hence also—indirectly—budgetary, foreign, and other issues can be discussed).

[20] The categories "systemic left," etc., are adapted from R. R. Levine's book, *The Arms Debate* (Cambridge, Mass., Harvard University Press, 1963), which contains a suggestive chart of American opinion on international issues. By "systemic left" is meant here a radical reformist outlook, challenging the predominant values of the existing system; by "systemic right" is meant an almost reactionary return to past values; the other three categories designate differences of degree within a dominant "mainstream."

In the chart below (unlike Levine's), the center position serves as a dividing line, and hence no one is listed directly under it. Malenkov is listed as "systemic left" because his proposals represented at the time a drastic departure from established positions. Molotov is labeled "systemic right" because of his inclination to defend the essentials of the Stalinist system in a setting which had changed profoundly since Stalin's death.

TABLE 2

Policy Spectrum USSR

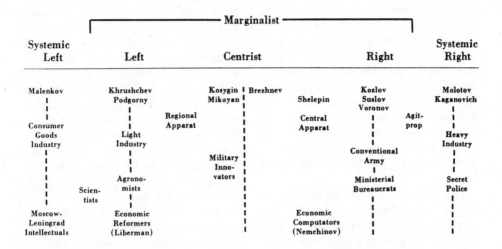

Systemic Left	Left		Centrist			Right		Systemic Right
Malenkov	Khrushchev Podgorny		Kosygin Mikoyan	Brezhnev	Shelepin	Kozlov Suslov Voronov		Molotov Kaganovich
Consumer Goods Industry	Light Industry	Regional Apparat			Central Apparat		Agit-prop	Heavy Industry
			Military Inno-vators			Conventional Army		
	Scien-tists	Agrono-mists				Ministerial Bureaucrats		Secret Police
Moscow-Leningrad Intellectuals	Economic Reformers (Liberman)				Economic Computators (Nemchinov)			

Not just Western but also Communist (although not as yet Soviet) political thinkers are coming to recognize more and more openly the existence of group conflict even in a Communist-dominated society. A Slovak jurist recently observed:

The social interest in our society can be democratically formed only by the integration of group interests; in the process of this integration, the interest groups protect their own economic and other social interests; this is in no way altered by the fact that everything appears on the surface as a unity of interests.[21]

The author went on to stress that the key political problem facing the Communist system is that of achieving integration of group interests.

[21] M. Lakatos, "On Some Problems of the Structure of Our Political System," *Pravny obzor* (Bratislava), No. 1, 1965, as quoted in Gordon Skilling's illuminating paper, "Interest Groups and Communist Politics," read to the Canadian Political Science Association in June, 1965.

Traditionally, this function of integration has been monopolized by the party, resorting—since the discard of terror—to the means of *bureaucratic arbitration*. In the words of the author just cited, "the party as the leading and directing political force fulfills its functions by resolving intra-class and inter-class interests." In doing so, the party generally has preferred to deal with each group bilaterally, thereby preventing the formation of coalitions and informal group consensus. In this way the unity of political direction as well as the political supremacy of the ruling party have been maintained. The party has always been very jealous of its "integrative" prerogative, and the intrusion on the political scene of any other group has been strongly resented. The party's institutional primacy has thus depended on limiting the real participation of other groups.

If, for one reason or another, the party were to weaken in the performance of this function, the only alternative to anarchy would be some *institutionalized process of mediation*, replacing the party's bureaucratic arbitration. Since, as noted, group participation has become more widespread, while the party's effectiveness in achieving integration has been lessened by the decline in the vigor of Soviet leadership and by the persistent divisions in the top echelon, the creation and eventual formal institutionalization of some such process of mediation is gaining in urgency. Otherwise participation could outrun institutionalization and result in a challenge to the party's integrative function.

Khrushchev's practice of holding enlarged Central Committee plenums, with representatives of other groups present, seems to have been a step toward formalizing a more regular consultative procedure. (It also had the political expedient effect of bypassing Khrushchev's opponents in the central leadership.) Such enlarged plenums provided a consultative forum, where policies could be debated, views articulated, and even some contradictory interests resolved. Although the device still remained essentially noninstitutionalized and only ad hoc, consultative and not legislative, still subject to domination by the party *apparat*, it was nonetheless a response to the new quest for real participation that Soviet society has manifested and which the Soviet system badly needs. It was also a compromise solution, attempting to wed the party's primacy to a procedure allowing group articulation.

However, the problem has become much more complex and fundamental because of the organizational and ideological crisis in the party over its relevance to the evolving Soviet system. For many years the party's monopoly of power and hence its active intervention in all spheres of Soviet life could

indeed be said to be "in the Soviet public interest." The party provided social mobilization, leadership, and a dominant outlook for a rapidly changing and developing society. But, in the main, that society has now taken shape. It is no longer malleable, subject to simple mobilization, or susceptible to doctrinaire ideological manipulation.

As a result, Soviet history in the last few years has been dominated by the spectacle of a party in search of a role. What is to be the function of an ideocratic party in a relatively complex and industrialized society, in which the structure of social relationships generally reflects the party's ideological preferences? To be sure, like any large sociopolitical system, the Soviet system needs an integrative organ. But the question is, What is the most socially desirable way of achieving such integration? Is a "strong" party one that dominates and interferes in everything, and is this interference conducive to continued Soviet economic, political, and intellectual growth?

In 1962 Khrushchev tried to provide a solution. The division of the party into two vertically parallel, functional organs was an attempt to make the party directly relevant to the economy and to wed the party's operations to production processes. It was a bold, dramatic and radical innovation, reflecting a recognition of the need to adapt the party's role to a new state of Soviet social development. But it was also a dangerous initiative; it carried within itself the potential of political disunity as well as the possibility that the party would become so absorbed in economic affairs that it would lose its political and ideological identity. That it was rapidly repudiated by Khrushchev's successors is testimony to the repugnance that the reorganization must have stimulated among the professional party bureaucrats.

His successors, having rejected Khrushchev's reorganization of the party, have been attempting a compromise solution—in effect, a policy of "muddling through." On the one hand, they recognize that the party can no longer direct the entire Soviet economy from the Kremlin and that major institutional reforms in the economic sphere, pointing toward more local autonomy and decision-making, are indispensable.[22] (Similar tendencies are apparent elsewhere—e.g., the stress on professional self-management in the military establishment.) This constitutes a partial and implicit acknowledgment that in some respects a party of total control is today incompatible with the Soviet public interest.

On the other hand, since obviously inherent in the trend toward decentralization is the danger that the party will be gradually transformed from a directing, ideologically oriented organization to a merely instrumental and pragmatic body specializing in adjustment and compromise of social group aspirations, the party functionaries, out of a sense of vested interest, have been attempting simultaneously to revive the ideological vitality of the CPSU. Hence the renewed stress on ideology and ideological training; hence the new importance attached to the work of the ideological commissions; and hence the categorical reminders that "Marxist education,

Marxist-Leninist training, and the ideological tempering of CPSU members and candidate members is the primary concern of every party organization and committee."[23]

However, it is far from certain that economic decentralization and ideological "retempering" can be pushed forward hand in hand. The present leadership appears oblivious to the fact that established ideology remains vital only when ideologically motivated power is applied to achieve ideological goals. A gradual reduction in the directing role of the party cannot be compensated for by an increased emphasis on ideological semantics. Economic decentralization inescapably reduces the scope of the political-ideological and increases the realm of the pragmatic-instrumental. It strengthens the trend, publicly bemoaned by Soviet ideologists, toward depoliticization of the Soviet elite.[24] A massive indoctrination campaign directed at the elite cannot operate in a "de-ideologized" socio-economic context, and major efforts to promote such a campaign could, indeed, prompt the social isolation of the party, making its dogmas even more irrelevant to the daily concerns of a Soviet scientist, fac-

---

[22] See the report delivered by A. Kosygin to the CC Plenum on September 27, 1965, proposing the reorganization of the Soviet economy. Also his speech at a meeting of the USSR State Planning Committee, *Planovoe khoziaistvo* (Moscow), April, 1965; and the frank discussion by A. E. Lunev, "Democratic Centralism in Soviet State Administration," *Sovetskoe Gosudarstvo i Pravo* (Moscow), No. 4, 1965.

[23] "Ideological Hardening of Communists" (editorial), *Pravda*, June 28, 1965. There has been a whole series of articles in this vein, stressing the inseparability of ideological and organizational work. For details of a proposed large-scale indoctrination campaign, see V. Stepakov, head of the Department of Propaganda and Agitation of the Central Committee of the CPSU, "Master the Great Teaching of Marxism-Leninism," *Pravda*, August 4, 1965.

[24] Stepakov, *ibid.*, explicitly states that in recent years "many comrades" who have assumed leading posts in the "directive aktivs" of the party have inadequate ideological knowledge, even though they have excellent technical backgrounds; and he urges steps against the "replacement" of party training "by professional-technical education."

tory director, or army general. That in turn would further reduce the ability of the party to provide effective integration in Soviet society, while underscoring the party *apparatchik's* functional irrelevance to the workings of Soviet administration and technology.

If the party rejects a return to ideological dogmas and renewed dogmatic indoctrination, it unavoidably faces the prospect of further internal change. It will gradually become a loose body, combining a vast variety of specialists, engineers, scientists, administrators, professional bureaucrats, agronomists, etc. Without a common dogma and without an active program, what will hold these people together? The party at this stage will face the same dilemma that the fascist and falange parties faced, and that currently confronts the Yugoslav and Polish Communists: in the absence of a large-scale domestic program of change, in the execution of which other groups and institutions become subordinated to the party, the party's domestic primacy declines and its ability to provide social-political integration is negated.

Moreover, the Soviet party leaders would be wrong to assume complacently that the narrowed range of disagreement over domestic policy alternatives could not again widen. Persistent difficulties in agriculture could some day prompt a political aspirant to question the value of collectivization; or the dissatisfaction of some nationalities could impose a major strain on the Soviet constitutional structure; or foreign affairs could again become the source of bitter internal conflicts. The ability of the system to withstand the combined impact of such divisive issues and of greater group intrusion into politics would much depend on the adaptations that it makes in its organization of lead-

ership and in its processes of decision-making. Unless alternative mechanisms of integration are created, a situation could arise in which some group other than the top *apparat*—a group that had continued to attract talent into its top ranks and had not been beset by bureaucratically debilitating conflict at the top —could step forth to seek power; invoking the Soviet public interest in the name of established Communist ideals, and offering itself (probably in coalition with some section of the party leadership) as the only alternative to chaos, it would attempt to provide a new balance between institutionalization and participation.

THE THREAT OF DEGENERATION

The Soviet leaders have recognized the need of institutional reforms in the economic sector in order to revitalize the national economy. The fact is that institutional reforms are just as badly needed—and even more overdue—in the political sector. Indeed, the effort to maintain a doctrinaire dictatorship over an increasingly modern and industrial society has already contributed to a reopening of the gap that existed in prerevolutionary Russia between the political system and the society, thereby posing the threat of the degeneration of the Soviet system.

A political system can be said to degenerate when there is a perceptible decline in the quality of the social talent that the political leadership attracts to itself in competition with other groups; when there is persistent division within the ruling elite, accompanied by a decline in its commitment to shared beliefs; when there is protracted instability in the top leadership; when there is a decline in the capacity of the ruling elite to define the purposes of the political system in relationship to society and to express them in effective institutional terms; when there is a fuzzing of institutional and hierarchical lines of command, resulting in the uncontrolled and unchanneled intrusion into politics of hitherto politically uninvolved groupings.[25] All of these indicators were discernible in the political systems of Tsarist Russia, the French Third Republic, Chiang Kai-shek's China and Rakosi's Hungary. Today, as already noted, at least several are apparent in the Soviet political system.

This is not to say, however, that the evolution of the Soviet system has inevitably turned into degeneration. Much still depends on how the ruling Soviet elite reacts. Policies of retrenchment, increasing dogmatism, and even violence, which—if now applied—would follow almost a decade of loosening up, could bring about a grave situation of tension, and the possibility of revolutionary outbreaks could not be discounted entirely. "Terror is indispensable to any dictatorship, but it cannot compensate for incompetent leaders and a defective organization of authority," observed a historian of the French revolution, writing of the Second Directory.[26] It is equally true of the Soviet political scene.

The threat of degeneration could be lessened through several adaptations designed to adjust the Soviet political system to the changes that have taken place in the now more mature society. First of all, the top policy-making organ of the Soviet system has been tradi-

[25] For a general discussion and a somewhat different formulation, see S. Huntington, "Political Development and Political Decay," pp. 415–17.

[26] G. Lefebvre, *The French Revolution* (New York: Columbia University Press, 1965), II, 205.

tionally the exclusive preserve of the professional politician, and in many respects this has assured the Soviet political system of able and experienced leadership. However, since a professional bureaucracy is not prone to produce broad "generalizing" talents, and since the inherent differentiation of functions within it increases the likelihood of leaders with relatively much narrower specialization than hitherto was the case, the need for somewhat broader representation of social talent within the top political leadership, and not merely on secondary levels as hitherto, is becoming urgent. If several outstanding scientists, professional economists, industrial managers, and others were to be co-opted by lateral entry into the ruling Presidium, the progressive transformation of the leadership into a regime of clerks could thereby be averted, and the alienation of other groups from the political system perhaps halted.

Second, the Soviet leaders would have to institutionalize a chief executive office and strive to endow it with legitimacy and stability. This would eventually require the creation of a formal and open process of leadership selection, as well—probably—as a time limit on the tenure of the chief executive position. The time limit, if honored, would depersonalize power, while an institutionalized process of selection geared to a specific date—and therefore also limited in time—would reduce the debilitating effects of unchecked and protracted conflict in the top echelons of power.

The CPSU continues to be an ideocratic party with a strong tradition of dogmatic intolerance and organizational discipline. Today less militant and more bureaucratic in outlook, it still requires a top catalyst, though no longer a personal tyrant, for effective operations. The example of the papacy, or perhaps of Mexico, where a ruling party has created a reasonably effective system of presidential succession, offers a demonstration of how one-man rule can be combined with a formal office of the chief executive, endowed with legitimacy, tenure and a formally established pattern of selection.

Any real institutionalization of power would have significant implications for the party. If its Central Committee were to become in effect an electoral college, selecting a ruler whom no one could threaten during his tenure, the process of selection would have to be endowed with considerable respectability. It would have to be much more than a mere ratification of an *a priori* decision reached by some bureaucratic cabal. The process would require tolerance for the expression of diverse opinions in a spirit free of dogmatism, a certain amount of open competition among rivals for power, and perhaps even the formation of informal coalitions—at least temporary ones. In a word, it would mean a break with the Leninist past, with consequences that would unavoidably spill over from the party into the entire system and society.

Third, increased social participation in politics unavoidably creates the need for an institutionalized arena for the mediation of group interests, if tensions and conflicts, and eventually perhaps even anarchy, are to be avoided. The enlarged plenums of the Central Committee were a right beginning, but if the Committee is to mediate effectively among the variety of institutional and group interests that now exist in Soviet society, its membership will have to be made much more representative and the predominance of party bureaucrats watered down. Alternatively, the Soviet leaders might consider following the

Yugoslav course of creating a new institution for the explicit purpose of providing group representation and reconciling different interests. In either case, an effective organ of mediation could not be merely a front for the party's continued bureaucratic arbitration of social interests, as that would simply perpetuate the present dilemmas.

Obviously, the implementation of such institutional reforms would eventually lead to a profound transformation of the Soviet system. But it is the absence of basic institutional development in the Soviet political system that has posed the danger of the system's degeneration. It is noteworthy that the Yugoslavs have been experimenting with political reforms, including new institutions, designed to meet precisely the problems and dangers discussed here. Indeed, in the long run, perhaps the ultimate contribution to Soviet political and social development that the CPSU can make is to adjust gracefully to the desirability, and perhaps even inevitability, of its own gradual withering away. In the meantime, the progressive transformation of the bureaucratic Communist dictatorship into a more pluralistic and institutionalized political system—even though still a system of one-party rule—seems essential if its degeneration is to be averted.

BARGHOORN: CHANGES IN RUSSIA

This symposium confronts the difficult but rewarding task of evaluating several thoughtful studies pertaining in one degree or another to the Soviet future.

Before commenting in detail on the fundamental issues posed by the studies in question, especially Professor Brzezinski's ingenious and original analysis, I should identify my point of view. Since political systems are the product of men's experience, they can change when there are changes in the environment by which they have been shaped. When political structures and the belief systems which legitimate them cease to be "functional," tensions develop between them and their internal and external environments. Institutions and practices which become obsolete must be either modified or replaced by new ones more appropriate to the tasks which confront them. Of course, political behavior is influenced not only by the experience of the living but also to some degree by living memories of the experiences of earlier generations. Hence, practices which have outlived much of their earlier relevance may, because of historical inertia, persist for a very long time indeed.[1] The concept of the political system as a set of interdependent processes and structures, adapting to but also influencing its domestic and foreign environments, is of course no magic key to political analysis. Its usefulness in the study of any system depends upon scrupulous regard to the unique history and characteristics of the particular system examined.

I shall comment briefly on the essays in the "Progress and Ideology" issue of *Problems of Communism.* These competent surveys of post-Stalin developments in several fields of social and natural sciences suggest, in my opinion, that the Soviet "creative intelligentsia" is an increasingly autonomous and po-

litically influential sub-community of the over-all political community. However, Soviet intellectuals are still constrained to seek limited objectives, pursued largely by such indirect means as behind-the-scenes pleading with party overseers, who are sometimes inclined for various reasons to support particular aspirations of the intelligentsia. The limited but real progress toward intellectual freedom made by the groups whose problems and prospects are examined in these essays tends to confirm Robert C. Tucker's view that the contemporary Soviet political system, having at least partly shaken off the heritage of the unique pressures of Stalin's personal rule, "should be pronounced, at least provisionally, post-totalitarian."[2] Still, the continued, if diminishing, frustration by the party and state of unfettered intellectual inquiry and artistic expression—especially Moscow's obstructiveness toward the practical application of innovative thinking—indicates how vigilantly the party still shepherds "its" intellectuals. The satisfaction of Soviet liberal intellectuals—and their well-wishers abroad —with post-Stalin gains must be tempered by realization that these gains are still not protected by firm legal guarantees or even by explicit revisions of obsolete and stifling ideological dogmas. Some of the partial reforms granted by the Soviet Establishment were, after all, reluctant, possibly temporary concessions, impelled by domestic economic difficulties and by such expediential foreign policy calculations as the desire to achieve respectability in the eyes of leftist French and Italian intellectuals.[3]

I share so fully Michel Tatu's skepticism, expressed in his review of M.

---

[1] A tentative application of these concepts to the USSR was made by this author in "Soviet Russia: Orthodoxy and Adaptiveness," (see Lucian W. Pye and Sidney Verba, eds., *Political Culture and Political Development* [Princeton, N.J.: Princeton University Press, 1965], pp. 450–511). A book by this writer on Soviet politics, applying the "political culture" and "political system" concepts to the Soviet Union, to be entitled *Politics in the USSR*, is scheduled for publication by Little, Brown & Co., in May, 1966.

[2] Robert C. Tucker, "The Dictator and Totalitarianism," *World Politics* (Princeton, N.J.), XVII, No. 4, 555–83, esp. p. 571.

Garder's *L'Agonie du régime en Russie soviétique*, about Garder's prediction of the collapse of Soviet communism by 1970 that I can deal very briefly with his article also. Garder's book is the latest of a long line of apocalyptic predictions of the collapse of communism. Such prophecies ignore the fact that great revolutions are most infrequent, and that successful political systems are tenacious and adaptive. Vigorous elites, such as the Soviet party and police cadres, also are ruthless in acting to suppress threats to their power. Perhaps the most sensible aspect of Garder's analysis is his insistence that the disappearance of the Soviet regime would still leave Russia a very great power. Even this assumption is perhaps somewhat debatable, for the collapse of Soviet authority might be accompanied by the breaking away from Russia of some of the non-Russian nationalities. Tatu's observations—especially his succinct discussion of a possible military takeover in Russia, and his opinions on the political implications of economic reform—are very perceptive, but since they closely resemble those of Professor Brzezinski, I shall confine myself to registering general approval without elaborating. Tatu is, however, less convinced than Brzezinski that the Kremlin stands at a crossroad of historical destiny.

Brzezinski's brilliant article may well signal a new stage in Western analysis of Soviet politics. It deserves most careful scrutiny. Brzezinski combines systematic analysis of the development and present state of the Soviet policy, with provocative forecasts of its various possible futures. Forecasting the political

[3] On the latter point, see Priscilla Johnson, *Khrushchev and the Arts* (Cambridge, Mass.: Harvard University Press, 1965), pp. 44-45, 62-64.

future is hazardous, and many scholars regard it as an idle exercise. However, the hypothetical futures forecast by Brzezinski have considerable value in helping to orient us toward various contingencies. Moreover, they may spur us to a sharp look at the warp of the past in search of intimations of the woof of the future. Brzezinski avoids overcommitment to a particular hypothesis by making his predictions contingent upon a variety of possible conditions. However, I think that his use of the "ideal type" mode of analysis, which for clarity and effectiveness selects aspects of a problem considered particularly significant, leads to some oversimplification. I share what I regard as his underlying assumption that a political system designed for the conduct and consolidation of a revolution is not necessarily suited to the needs of a relatively modernized society. The latter may be most simply characterized as a society whose members would like fewer jails and jailers, more comforts and conveniences, less propaganda, and more uncensored information.

Brzezinski frames his analysis largely in terms of the concepts of political "degeneration," or decay, and "institutionalization," a proper level and quality of which he regards as essential to the constructive guidance and control of the emerging demands of productive social groups for access to the making of national policy. I agree with Brzezinski that important adjustments, and perhaps fundamental reforms, are necessary if the Soviet Union is to preserve stability and achieve continued dynamic growth in popular welfare. I believe also that without such reforms the USSR will eventually lose ground in international competition.

However, it seems to me that Brzezinski exaggerates the clear and present danger of "degeneration" in the Soviet political system. Incidentally, or perhaps not so incidentally, it is very difficult to gather from Brzezinski's article any very precise indication of just when political decay began to set in and how far it has proceeded or will, within any specific period of time, develop. Possibly Brzezinski will wish in the future to further refine his predictive techniques.

Second, Brzezinski's somewhat schematic use of the concept of institutionalization leads him to exaggerate the imminence of decay, and to underestimate the difficulties of institutionalizing the fundamental reforms which he regards as anti-decay prophylactics. The reforms which he suggests are so fundamental as to amount, in effect, to the adoption by Soviet Communists of some sort of limited parliamentary or constitutional regime. Certainly this would be highly desirable, but how likely is it to occur in the foreseeable future?

The Russian political tradition is woefully defective in the prerequisites for gradualism. Russia's tragic history hindered the acquisition of a mature, balanced political character. Both the Tsarist and the Soviet political cultures have exalted the virtues of a stern social discipline and of unquestioned acceptance of the ruler's commands by his subjects. Most citizens, in my opinion, are still so awed by authority and so unsophisticated politically as to be easily manipulated or at best cowed by a display of determination from on high. In the Soviet era especially, citizens have been heavily indoctrinated in an antiliberal spirit not calculated to foster sympathy for a wide sharing of authority and responsibility among even highly placed elite groups, and still less receptive to notions of governmental responsiveness to the wishes of the "masses." The elite elements are probably united both

against internal subversion of their privileges, and against "imperialist" threats from abroad. If the present Soviet political system disintegrates within the next few years, it will probably be replaced at least for some time by a nationalistic oligarchy, representing a coalition of forces, dominated by moderate, production-oriented party leaders, scientists, industrialists and military figures. However, I think that the more desirable outcome envisaged by Brzezinski as one of his hypothetical variants, namely, gradual constitutional development, might eventuate after a long period of international tranquility and increasingly rewarding Soviet contact with the West.

In my opinion, fundamental change —or collapse—can only occur when at least the following conditions exist. First, the leadership must be badly split, or paralyzed by indecision. Second, there must be widespread loss of respect and support for the political authorities. Finally, it must become possible for some sort of organized political opposition with a clear conception of an alternative to the present system to organize, covertly or overtly, for effective political action. It seems reasonable to assume that some years will pass before these conditions are fulfilled.

Moreover, it will probably be possible to make partial reforms, short of those suggested by Professor Brzezinski, which will enable the present Soviet political system to continue to function fairly effectively for at least another ten or fifteen years. I am not persuaded that it would be impossible to retain the present centralized system of policy formation for some time, while granting increasing autonomy to the economic bureaucracy, to the scientific community, etc. Also, it seems to me that within the party itself, improved training and a more efficient method of recruitment of party executives, especially those assigned to coordinating the efforts of and maintaining liaison with the leaders of the various professional communities, could go far toward gaining increased support by the latter for the political authorities. To the extent that the party can recruit top executives capable of perceiving early enough the need for adjustments and taking initiatives to make them before pressures become explosive, it may be able to survive, and even to flourish. The burden of proof is upon anyone who takes the view that the Soviet political elite has lost or will soon lose the touch that has enabled it to perform its functions thus far with a relatively high degree of effectiveness. It is not irrelevant to note that the post-Khrushchev leadership, despite its perhaps excessive caution, has taken important steps toward improving the relationship between the political system and the Soviet national economy. If the reforms instituted at the September, 1965, plenum prove successful, the economy, and indirectly the political system, will be considerably strengthened —even though the uneasy compromise effected at the plenum between centralized organization and managerial autonomy is likely to fail.

In foreign affairs, at least, the Brezhnev-Kosygin leadership has displayed considerable skill in steering a course between the other two giants of the international arena, Communist China and the United States. Kosygin, in particular, seems a more skillful diplomat than any of us would have predicted before his mediation between India and Pakistan.

Despite my reservations, I agree with Brzezinski that existing Soviet political structures and the ideology which serves as a major source of their legitimacy are increasingly irrelevant to a more and more diversified society. Whether or not the specific institutional changes he regards as necessary for the effective processing of social demands by the polity are necessary or feasible remains largely unpredictable. There are so many unknowns and unknowables! For example, how sure can we be that a dynamic leader may not arise in the coming years—or months—to replace the colorless Brezhnev-Kosygin team and once again get Soviet society moving?

We must beware of confusing the desirable with the real. Fundamental social and political changes usually occur slowly, unevenly, and in a zig-zag fashion. Some parts of the system may change more rapidly, or more slowly, than others, although it is doubtless true that profound changes, for example, in the recruitment of leaders, eventually affect the functioning of all the structures of a system.

Institutional changes are usually preceded by broad changes in attitudes and ways of thinking. The erosion of ideological dogma among intellectuals is undoubtedly helping to undermine the psychological foundations of rule by a party which still makes a demigod of a man who died almost fifty years ago. There has recently been an encouraging revival of rational and empirical thinking in many fields. Its exponents, however, still constitute a small if growing minority, and they function in a considerable degree of isolation from one another. Still, empiricism, in science and social science, in economic administration and even in such fields as law is increasingly challenging traditional Communist orthodoxy.[4] Related to these positive developments is the tendency for liberal, nonconformist Soviet writers to ally themselves with, and in a sense to act as spokesmen for, Soviet natural scientists—a trend symbolized by the fact that physicists are among the best patrons of avant-garde writing and "abstract" art.

However, the dominant political culture in which the rational, liberal factions of the Soviet intellectual community must cautiously maneuver is still characterized by a great deal of arbitrary administrative behavior, cloaked in secrecy and justified with sacrosanct dogma and official lies. I was vividly reminded of the seamy side of the political culture when on October 31, 1963, I was abducted on a Moscow street and detained in total isolation for nearly three weeks on a fabricated charge of military espionage.

The growing demand of various segments of the Soviet intellectual community for greater autonomy has forced the Kremlin to recognize grudgingly the need to relax controls over the trained and talented professionals upon whose willing and efficient performance national power depends. Concessions have even been made to that most troublesome group, the creative writers, at least to those not openly in opposition to official doctrine and policy.[5] Party spokesmen still warn that "groupism" (*gruppovshchina*) is incompatible with the proper behavior of Communist intellectuals, thus acknowledging the existence of group consciousness among professionals. However, Soviet social scientists, and even *Pravda* editorial

writers, instruct researchers and youth leaders to take account in their work of the diversity of interests of Soviet society.[6]

There has been a great deal of behind-the-scenes bargaining between the Kremlin and the Soviet intelligentsia since the death of Stalin. One of its products has been the creation for the first time in the history of the USSR of the rudiments of a free, critical public opinion. Although still shackled, the Soviet intellectual community today is at least free to defend its views and interests against the cruder forms of arbitrary political interference, provided its members do not openly flout doctrines and symbols still regarded by the party leadership as above criticism. A poor sort of freedom? Yes, but almost un imaginable when measured by the Sta linist yardstick.

The possibility that the progress which has been achieved since the death of Stalin—toward personal security, the rule of law, limited intellectual freedom, and partial access to the exciting "bourgeois" world—might still be swept away by a relapse into Stalin-like terror seems remote even if it cannot be completely excluded. In terms of a rational Kremlin approach to the Soviet national interest, the price of such a relapse would be prohibitively high. Its consequences could be dire for the lives and fortunes of many party and government leaders. It would cripple an increasingly sophisticated economy, and it could undermine support for Kremlin policies among important segments of Soviet society and among Western intellectuals, including many Communists.

The foregoing considerations seem to

---

[4] In the field of law, see for example the remarkable article in *Izvestia* of November 24, 1965, by the jurist V. Kudriavtsev, chiding the advocates of a "get-tough" policy toward criminals and urging empirical analysis as the only useful tool in analyzing the causes of crime.

[5] The ground rules were provisionally set forth in A. Rumiantsev's article, "The Party and the Intelligentsia," *Pravda*, February 21, 1965.

[6] See, for example, the article on "concrete" research by the prominent economist, V. Shubkin, in *Kommunist*, No. 3, 1965, and a *Pravda* editorial of June 16, 1965.

me to support the view that the Soviet political system will continue to adapt more or less successfully and positively to pressures arising in the intrasocietal and extrasocietal environments. It seems likely that the CPSU will be with us for a while before it accepts Professor Brzezinski's blithe recommendation that it wither away.[7]

[7] Perhaps it is needless to point out that party spokesmen still deny the possibility that the party can disappear before the achievement of communism on a worldwide scale. See, for example, E. Bugaev, B. Leibzon. *Besedy ob ustave KPSS* (Moscow, 1964), p.

CHRONOLOGY VOLUME III

1917 (March)		**PROVISIONAL GOVERNMENT** (Prince Lvov)
		Petrograd Soviet of Workers' Deputies
		Order No. 1
		Kamenev and Stalin return from Siberia
	(April)	Lenin returns to Russia
		Lenin's April Theses
	(May)	Miliukov's note to Allies
		Coalition Provisional Government
	(June)	Election of Constituent Assembly set for September 30
	(July)	Russian offensive against Germans
		Uprising against Provisional Government
		Prince Lvov resigns
		Kerensky becomes premier
	(August)	Kerensky becomes dictator
		Constituent Assembly election postponed to November 25
	(September)	Kornilov *putsch*
		Bolsheviks dominate Petrograd Soviet
	(October)	Bolsheviks decide on armed uprising
	(November)	**BOLSHEVIK SEIZURE OF POWER**
		Decree suppressing hostile newspapers
		Patriarchate re-established
		Constituent Assembly elections begin
	(December)	Armistice negotiations at Brest-Litovsk
		Establishment of Cheka
		Left S.R.'s enter coalition with Bolsheviks
1918 (January)		Constituent Assembly meets for one day and is then dissolved
	(February)	Patriarch Tikhon anathematizes Bolsheviks
		Separation of church and state
	(March)	Treaty of Brest-Litovsk
		British land at Murmansk
	(April)	Japanese land at Vladivostok

1918	(June)	"Committee of the Village Poor" Decree on nationalization of industry
	(July)	Allied Supreme War Council decides on intervention Murder of Tsar and entire family
	(August)	American troops land in Vladivostok
	(September)	American troops land at Archangel
	(October)	Patriarch Tikhon under house arrest
	(November)	End of World War I Soviets repudiate Treaty of Brest-Litovsk French troops land at Odessa
	(December)	British troops land at Batum
1919	(March)	FOUNDING OF THE COMINTERN Kolchak launches drive against Bolsheviks
	(April)	French withdraw from Odessa
	(June)	Height of Denikin advance
	(October)	Allies withdraw from Murmansk and Archangel
1920	(January)	Kolchak shot by Bolsheviks Allies lift blockade
	(April)	Wrangel takes over from Denikin
	(October)	Treaty of Riga with Poland
	(November)	Wrangel evacuates Crimea End of civil war
1921	(March)	Kronstadt mutiny Party Congress orders purge New Economic Policy
1922		Cheka replaced by GPU Stalin becomes secretary general Treaty of Rapallo with Germany Arrest of Patriarch Tikhon Lenin's first stroke; his testament
1922		FORMATION OF U.S.S.R.
1923		Lenin's second stroke
1924		Lenin's death U.S.S.R. constitution U.S.S.R. recognized by Great Britain, France, Italy
1925		Trotsky removed as war commissar
1926		Trotsky, Zinoviev, Kamenev ousted from Politburo
1927		Trotsky and Zinoviev expelled from Party Communist revolt in China crushed
1928		Five-Year Plan adopted
1929		Trotsky deported Bukharin ousted from Politburo Forced collectivization begins
1930		Stalin's speech: "Dizzy with Success"
1931		Famine
1932		Famine

Dissolution of Russian Association of Proletarian Writers

Prokofiev returns from abroad

First mention of "socialist realism"

1933	U.S.A. RECOGNIZES U.S.S.R.
1934	Birobidzhan becomes autonomous Jewish state Second Five-Year Plan First Congress of Russian Writers Zhdanov speech Kirov assassinated
1935	Collective farm statute Campaign of Stakhanovism
1936	Gorky dies Stalin constitution promulgated Trial of Zinoviev, Kamenev, *et al.*
1937	Trial of Radek *et al.* Much of Soviet army command executed
1938	Eisenstein's *Alexander Nevsky* Trial of Bukharin *et al.* Beria becomes secret police chief
1939	Minimum labor days set for collective farms Nazi-Soviet Pact Soviet occupation of Estonia, Latvia, and Lithuania Soviet attack on Finland
1940	Sholokhov completes *Silent Don* End of war with Finland Baltic states annexed Bessarabia annexed Trotsky murdered in Mexico Tuition fees in higher education State labor reserves created
1941	GERMAN INVASION OF U.S.S.R.
1942	Churchill visits Moscow Lend-Lease in full operation
1943	German surrender at Stalingrad Dissolution of the Comintern Sergius becomes Patriarch Teheran Conference
1945	YALTA CONFERENCE Vienna and Berlin taken by Russian troops Potsdam Conference Eisenstein's *Ivan the Terrible*, Part I, wins Stalin Prize
1946	First elections to Supreme Soviet since 1937 Churchill's "Iron Curtain" speech Zhdanov attacks Zoshchenko and Soviet composers Eisenstein's *Ivan the Terrible*, Part II, withdrawn Fourth Five-Year Plan

1947   Rationing abolished
              Cominform established
1949   U.S.S.R. has atomic bomb
1952   Nineteenth Party Congress
              Presidium replaces Politburo

1953   DEATH OF STALIN

              Malenkov, premier; Khrushchev, first secretary
              Beria executed
1954   Ehrenburg's *The Thaw*
1955   Malenkov replaced by Bulganin
              Summit Conference in Geneva
1956   Twentieth Party Congress
              Khrushchev's "Secret Speech"
              Cominform dissolved
              Party condemns "cult of the individual"
              Molotov resigns
1957   Malenkov, Kaganovich, and Molotov ousted
              Decentralization of economic organization
              Sputnik
1958   Bulganin resigns

1958   KHRUSHCHEV PREMIER

              Doctor Zhivago awarded Nobel Prize
1959   Mikoyan, Kozlov, and Khrushchev visit U.S.A.
              Nixon visits U.S.S.R.
              Twenty-first Party Congress
              "Anti-Party Group" denounced
1960   Khrushchev at UN Assembly in New York
1961   Gagarin first man into space
              Twenty-second Party Congress
              New Party program and rules
              Stalin's remains removed from Lenin Mausoleum
1962   Solzhenitsyn's *One Day in the Life of Ivan Denisovich*
1963   Russo-Chinese split deepens
              Central Committee Conference on Ideology
              Ehrenburg, Evtushenko, and others attacked for non-
                 conformity
1964   KHRUSHCHEV DEPOSED. Replaced by Brezhnev and
                 Kosygin
              One third of clothing and shoe factories converted from
                 central planning to consumer orientation

1965   Soviet astronaut takes man's first "walk in space"

1966   Unmanned Soviet spacecraft lands on moon
              Twenty-third Party Congress endorses new Five-Year
                 Plan

1967   Svetlana Allilueva arrives in the U.S.A.

Premier Kosygin meets with President Johnson in Glass-
boro, N.J.

The trial of Soviet writers Siniavsky and Daniel

Launching of Soviet artificial earth satellites. Soviet astronaut Komarov killed

FIFTIETH ANNIVERSARY OF THE BOLSHEVIK
REVOLUTION

1968   Soviets announce industrial production rose 10 per cent
in previous year

Death of cosmonaut Yuri Gagarin

Trial of Soviet writers Alexander Ginzburg and Yuri
Galanskov

U.S.S.R. ratifies consular convention with U.S.A.

Soviet troops invade and occupy Czechoslovakia

CORRELATION *of* READINGS IN RUSSIAN CIVILIZATION

Vols. I, II, and III with Representative Texts

CLARKSON, JESSE D., *A History of Russia*, Random House, 1964

Chapter Nos.	Related Selections in READINGS IN RUSSIAN CIVILIZATION	Chapter Nos.	Related Selections in READINGS IN RUSSIAN CIVILIZATION
1	I: 16	19	II: 36, 37
2	I: 1	20	II: 35
3	I: 2	21	II: 39–41
4	I: 3–5	22	II: 38
5	I: 6, 10, 15	23	II: 42, 43
6		24	III: 44
7	I: 7–9	25	III: 45
8		26	III: 46
9	I: 11–13	27	
10	I: 14, 17	28	III: 47
11		29	III: 48
12	II: 18	30	III: 49–51
13	II: 19	31	III: 55, 56
14	II: 20–22	32	III: 52–54
15	II: 23–27	33	
16		34	III: 57, 58
17	II: 28, 30	35	III: 59–62
18	II: 29, 31–34	36	III: 63–69
		37	III: 70–72

DMYTRYSHYN, BASIL, *USSR: A Concise History*, Scribners, 1965

Chapter Nos.	Related Selections in READINGS IN RUSSIAN CIVILIZATION	Chapter Nos.	Related Selections in READINGS IN RUSSIAN CIVILIZATION
1		5	III: 47, 48
2	III: 44, 45	6	III: 49–56
3	III: 46	7	III: 57–62
4		8	
		9	III: 63–72

ELLISON, HERBERT J., *History of Russia*, Holt, Rinehart, and Winston, 1964

Chapter Nos.	Related Selections in READINGS IN RUSSIAN CIVILIZATION	Chapter Nos.	Related Selections in READINGS IN RUSSIAN CIVILIZATION
1	I: 16	13	III: 44–45
2	I: 1–5	14	III: 46
3	I: 6–10, 15	15	III: 47
4	I: 11–14, 17	16	III: 48
5	II: 18	17	
6	II: 19–22	18	III: 49–56
7	II: 23	19	
8	II: 24–27	20	III: 57, 58
9	II: 28–31	21	III: 59–62
10	II: 32–37	22	
11	II: 38–41	23	III: 63-70
12	II: 42–43	24	III: 71, 72

FLORINSKY, MICHAEL T., *Russia: A History and an Interpretation*, 2 vols., Macmillan, 1953

Chapter Nos.	Related Selections in READINGS IN RUSSIAN CIVILIZATION	Chapter Nos.	Related Selections in READINGS IN RUSSIAN CIVILIZATION
1	I: 1, 2	25	
2		26	
3	I: 15	27	II: 23
4	I: 6	28	II: 24
5	I: 3, 4	29	
6	I: 5, 10	30	
7		31	II: 25–27
8	I: 7–9	32	
9		33	
10	I: 13	34	
11	I: 11, 12, 14, 16, 17	35	
12		36	II: 33
13	II: 18	37	II: 28–32
14		38	II: 34, 36, 37
15		39	II: 35
16		40	II: 38–41
17		41	II: 43
18	II: 19	42	II: 42
19		43	
20		44	
21	II: 20, 21	45	III: 44
22		46	III: 45
23	II: 22	47	
24		48	III: 46

FLORINSKY, MICHAEL T., *Russia: A Short History*, Macmillan, 1964

Chapter Nos.	Related Selections in READINGS IN RUSSIAN CIVILIZATION	Chapter Nos.	Related Selections in READINGS IN RUSSIAN CIVILIZATION
1	I: 1, 2, 16	15	II: 28–33
2	I: 3–5	16	II: 34–42
3	I: 15	17	
4	I: 10	18	II: 43
5	I: 6	19	III: 44, 45
6	I: 7–9	20	III: 46–48
7		21	III: 52–56
8	I: 13	22	III: 49–51
9	I: 11, 12, 14, 17	23	
10	II: 18	24	III: 57, 58
11	II: 19	25	III: 59–62
12	II: 20–22	26	III: 63–72
13	II: 23, 24	27	
14	II: 25–27		

HARCAVE, SIDNEY, *Russia: A History*, 6th ed., Lippincott, 1968

Chapter Nos.	Related Selections in READINGS IN RUSSIAN CIVILIZATION	Chapter Nos.	Related Selections in READINGS IN RUSSIAN CIVILIZATION
1	I: 16	17	II: 36, 37
2	I: 1–5, 15	18	II: 33
3	I: 6–10	19	II: 31
4	I: 11–14, 17	20	II: 39–41
5	II: 18	21	II: 42
6	II: 19	22	II: 43
7	II: 20–21	23	III: 44, 45
8		24	III: 46
9	II: 22	25	III: 47

HARCAVE, SIDNEY, *Russia: A History*, 6th ed., Lippincott, 1968

Chapter Nos.	Related Selections in READINGS IN RUSSIAN CIVILIZATION	Chapter Nos.	Related Selections in READINGS IN RUSSIAN CIVILIZATION
10		26	III: 48
11	II: 23	27	III: 49–51
12	II: 24	28	III: 52–56
13	II: 25–27	29	III: 57, 58
14		30	III: 59–62
15	II: 28–30	31	III: 63–72
16	II: 34, 38		

MAZOUR, ANATOLE G., *Russia: Tsarist and Communist*, Van Nostrand, 1962

Chapter Nos.	Related Selections in READINGS IN RUSSIAN CIVILIZATION	Chapter Nos.	Related Selections in READINGS IN RUSSIAN CIVILIZATION
1	I: 16	19	II: 37
2	I: 1, 2	20	II: 35, 38
3	I: 15	21	II: 39–41
4	I: 3–5, 10	22	
5	I: 7–9	23	II: 25–28
6	I: 6	24	
7		25	
8	I: 11–14, 17	26	
9	II: 18	27	II: 42–43
10		28	III: 44, 45
11		29	III: 46
12	II: 19	30	III: 47, 48
13	II: 20–22	31	
14		32	III: 49–51
15	II: 23	33	III: 52–56
16	II: 24	34	
17	II: 29–31	35	III: 57
18	II: 32–34, 36	36	III: 58
		37	III: 59–62
		38	III: 63–72

PARES, BERNARD, *A History of Russia*, Vintage Books, 1965

Chapter Nos.	Related Selections in READINGS IN RUSSIAN CIVILIZATION	Chapter Nos.	Related Selections in READINGS IN RUSSIAN CIVILIZATION
1	I: 16	15	II: 22
2	I: 1, 2	16	II: 23
3	I: 15	17	II: 24
4	I: 3, 4	18	II: 25–27
5	I: 5, 10	19	II: 28
6	I: 7–9	20	II: 29–33
7	I: 6	21	II: 34–37
8		22	II: 38
9	I: 11–13	23	II: 39–41
10	I: 14, 17	24	II: 42, 43
11		25	III: 44–48
12	II: 18	26	III: 49–56
13	II: 19	27	III: 57–72
14	II: 20, 21		

PUSHKAREV, SERGEI, *The Emergence of Modern Russia, 1801–1917*, Holt, Rinehart, and Winston, 1963

Chapter Nos.	Related Selections in READINGS IN RUSSIAN CIVILIZATION	Chapter Nos.	Related Selections in READINGS IN RUSSIAN CIVILIZATION
1	II: 23	7	II: 36, 37
2		8	II: 35, 39–41
3	II: 24–27	9	
4		10	II: 38, 42
5	II: 28	11	II: 43
6	II: 29–34		

RAUCH, GEORG VON, *A History of Soviet Russia*, 5th rev. ed., Praeger, 1967

Chapter Nos.	Related Selections in READINGS IN RUSSIAN CIVILIZATION	Chapter Nos.	Related Selections in READINGS IN RUSSIAN CIVILIZATION
1	III: 44–46	6	III: 52–56
2		7	
3		8	III: 57, 58
4	III: 47–51	9	III: 59–62
5		10	III: 63–72

RIASANOVSKY, NICHOLAS V., *A History of Russia*, Oxford University Press, 1963

Chapter Nos.	Related Selections in READINGS IN RUSSIAN CIVILIZATION	Chapter Nos.	Related Selections in READINGS IN RUSSIAN CIVILIZATION
1	I: 16	22	II: 20, 21
2		23	
3	I: 1	24	II: 22
4		25	II: 23
5	I: 2	26	II: 24
6		27	
7		28	II: 25–27
8	I: 15	29	II: 29, 31
9	I: 3, 4	30	II: 34
10		31	II: 35, 39–42
11		32	II: 30, 36–38
12		33	II: 28, 32, 33, 43
13	I: 5, 10	34	III: 44, 45
14		35	
15	I: 7–9	36	III: 46–48
16		37	III: 49–56
17		38	III: 57–58
18	I: 6, 13, 14	39	III: 59–62
19	I: 11, 12, 17	40	III: 63–66
20	II: 18	41	III: 67–71
21	II: 19	42	III: 72

SETON-WATSON, HUGH, *The Russian Empire, 1801–1917*, Oxford, 1967

Chapter Nos.	Related Selections in READINGS IN RUSSIAN CIVILIZATION	Chapter Nos.	Related Selections in READINGS IN RUSSIAN CIVILIZATION
1	II: 18–22	11	II: 29–31
2		12	
3	II: 23	13	II: 32–34
4		14	II: 36, 37
5	II: 24	15	II: 35
6		16	
7		17	II: 39–41
8	II: 25–27	18	II: 38
9		19	II: 42
10	II: 28	20	II: 43

TREADGOLD, DONALD W., *Twentieth Century Russia*, 2d ed., Rand McNally, 1964

Chapter Nos.	Related Selections in READINGS IN RUSSIAN CIVILIZATION	Chapter Nos.	Related Selections in READINGS IN RUSSIAN CIVILIZATION
1		16	
2	II: 22–29, 31–33	17	III: 49–51
3		18	III: 52–56
4	II: 35	19	
5	II: 34, 39–41	20	
6		21	
7	II: 30, 36, 37	22	
8	II: 38, 42, 43	23	III: 57
9	III: 44, 45	24	III: 58
10	III: 46	25	
11		26	
12		27	III: 59–62
13	III: 47, 48	28	III: 63–66
14		29	III: 67–72
15			

VERNADSKY, GEORGE, *A History of Russia*, 5th ed., Yale University Press, 1961

Chapter Nos.	Related Selections in READINGS IN RUSSIAN CIVILIZATION	Chapter Nos.	Related Selections in READINGS IN RUSSIAN CIVILIZATION
1	I: 1, 16	10	II: 28–34
2	I: 2	11	II: 36–38
3	I: 3–5, 15	12	II: 35, 39–41
4	I: 7–9	13	II, III: 42–46
5	I: 6, 10–14, 17	14	III: 47–51
6	II: 18–21	15	III: 52–56
7	II: 22, 23	16	III: 59–62
8	II: 25–27	17	III: 57, 58
9	II: 24	18	III: 63–72

WREN, MELVIN C., *The Course of Russian History*, 3d ed., Macmillan, 1968

Chapter Nos.	Related Selections in READINGS IN RUSSIAN CIVILIZATION	Chapter Nos.	Related Selections in READINGS IN RUSSIAN CIVILIZATION
1	I: 16	12	II: 28–33
2	I: 1	13	II: 34–38
3	I: 2, 5	14	II: 39–43
4	I: 3, 4	15	III: 44–46
5	I: 6, 10	16	III: 47, 48, 52–56
6	I: 7–9	17	III: 49–51, 64, 66, 67, 70
7	I: 11–17	18	III: 59–62
8	II: 18	19	
9	II: 19–22	20	III: 57, 58, 65, 71
10	II: 23	21	III: 63, 68, 69, 72
11	II: 24–27		

WALSH, WARREN B., *Russia and the Soviet Union*, University of Michigan Press, 1958

Chapter Nos.	Related Selections in READINGS IN RUSSIAN CIVILIZATION	Chapter Nos.	Related Selections in READINGS IN RUSSIAN CIVILIZATION
1	I: 16	16	II: 32–34, 36–37
2	I: 1, 3, 4	17	II: 35
3	I: 2, 5	18	II: 39–41
4	I: 15	19	II: 38, 42, 43
5	I: 7, 8, 9	20	III: 44–45
6	I: 6, 10–14, 17	21	III: 46
7	II: 18	22	
8	II: 19	23	III: 47, 48
9	II: 20, 21, 22	24	III: 49–56
10	II: 23	25	
11	II: 24	26	III: 57, 58
12		27	III: 59–62
13	II: 25, 26, 27	28	
14	II: 28–31	29	III: 63–72
15			

INDEX VOLUME III

HOW TO STOP
THE BATTLE
WITH YOUR CHILD

HOW TO STOP
THE BATTLE
WITH YOUR CHILD

A Practical Guide to Solving
Everyday Problems with Children

DON FLEMING, Ph.D.
with Linda Balahoutis
Illustrations by Bill Melendez

PRENTICE
HALL
PRESS

New York   London   Toronto   Sydney   Tokyo   Singapore

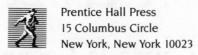

Prentice Hall Press
15 Columbus Circle
New York, New York 10023

Published in 1987 by Prentice Hall Press
A Division of Simon & Schuster, Inc.
Originally published by Don Fleming Seminars Publishing Co.

PRENTICE HALL PRESS and colophon are registered
trademarks of Simon & Schuster Inc.

Library of Congress Cataloging-in-Publication Data

Fleming, Don.
  How to stop the battle with your child.

  Bibliography: p.
  Includes index.
  I. Child rearing. I. Balahoutis, Linda. II. Title.
HQ769.F538 1987   649'.1   86-17020
ISBN 0-13-435009-X

Text design by C. Linda Dingler
Cover design and illustrations by Bill Melendez

Manufactured in the United States of America

10 9 8 7 6 5

I dedicate this book to the five most important women in my life: my mother, Genevieve—I'll always remember her caring and loving ways; my wife, Pamela; my sister, Millicent; my niece, Denel; and my newest love, my grandniece, Nicole, who was born April 24, 1986.

Acknowledgments

I want to thank Berea St. John, who encouraged me to become a psychotherapist and who, for many years, gave me the kind of inspiration that enabled me to achieve many of the goals in my life. Second, thanks to Estelle Sudnow, who was my first-year supervisor in graduate training at Florida State University and for whom I have the greatest respect. She gave me excellent supervision for which I will always be grateful. I am particularly indebted to Susan Schuster and Marilyn Lebow, who read the manuscript and contributed suggestions and criticism. Thanks to my sister, Millie Lupiani, who encouraged me and who has been one of my biggest boosters. My love to Denel Duprez, my niece, who is so important to me. My love to Brian Lupiani, my terrific nephew, for his interest in the success of the book. My deepest appreciation to Edward Lupiani, my brother-in-law, director of Elementary Education, Baldwin Park Unified School District, for his professional contribution in assisting with the development of this book.

I would also like to acknowledge Al Cartwright, director of Career Education and Special Projects, and Joe Spirito, director of Instructional Services, Baldwin Park Unified School District, for their concern and interest in the book. I wish to acknowledge Dr. Susan Brown for her inspiration over the years and for her friendship as a colleague. Also, thanks to Dr. Frank Williams for his long-time support as both colleague and friend. A special thanks to my wife, Pamela, for putting up with me during the writing of this book and for being very loving and understanding.

I'd also like to thank all those who through the years have assisted me in my career. And I cannot forget the many parents with whom I have worked, and who helped me develop the kind of experience and knowledge that has made this book possible.

Last, I would like to give a special thanks to my agent, Sherry Robb, who with humor, intelligence, and sincerity helped me get my book published. Thanks must also go to PJ Dempsey, my editor, who is great to work with and really made the process of publishing this book a very enjoyable and positive experience.

Contents

Introduction

What—another book on parenting? You might be thinking, "Aren't there enough of those? Haven't we read everything there is to read about it already?" Yes, there have been many books on parenting. Most give excellent suggestions. Some work at least part of the time.

However, if you are reading this book, I assume that nothing is working. By this time you have armed yourself with countless helpful hints from different sources. Then your child confronts you with a variation of the standard crisis, leaving you thinking, "Now what? This is different from situation No. 46!" After all your preparation, *your kid is still winning*! This may lead you to believe that he, too, is boning up on the subject of parenting. Maybe he is even attending seminars on "How to Make Life More Difficult for Your Parents."

This is a book for the average parent, whether single or with an intact family. It is for you if you have become locked into a chronic, unending battle with your child over specific attitudes or behavior patterns in daily routines such as going to the market, going to bed, or picking up toys. It presents step-by-step methods of unlocking the struggle. Children's deep psychological problems are not dealt with in this book. Instead, practical suggestions are offered about everyday dilemmas that parents have difficulty controlling. Also, this book will be of benefit to teachers and other professionals who work with parents.

Experiencing frustration more than once may have given you a strong desire to run away from home. But you are not crazy or a bad parent! Ambivalence, anger, and frustration are all understandable results of this continuous locked-in struggle with your child.

You may still ask how this book is different from other parenting books. Let's look at four basic categories with differing approaches to child-rearing and examine their values and drawbacks.

The Developmental Approach. Developmental psychology tells us what to expect from children at various stages of development. Books based on this approach are very informative about every aspect of normal child development, such as what age your child should start toileting and when he should stop sucking his thumb. They do not help you deal with the child who picks a fight with his brother every time you take him somewhere in the car. If you are locked into a struggle with your five-year-old, you do not want to know how bad (or good) he'll be when he is eight years old.

The Behaviorial Approach. This approach stresses changing behavior through the use of a punishment and reward system. This technique has value and may at first glance seem similar to the approach presented in this book. The drawback to the behaviorist approach is that the parent relies too heavily on punishment and reward, and fails to incorporate feelings. Also, the parent does not see how his own behavior impacts on the child. In the behaviorial approach, the system can become more important than the relationship.

The Firm Discipline Approach. Currently there are a number of popular books that suggest very firm discipline. In part this is a reaction to the very permissive approach. The point of this approach is that parents are really in charge, and the only way to make this clear to kids is with strong discipline. However, this method does not allow parents the flexibility to be firm and at the same time tender and sensitive. Secondly, and most important, this approach ignores the impact of the parent's behavior on the child. It fails to make parents take a hard look at their behavior patterns, which might prolong the problem even when there is strong discipline.

The Permissive Approach. In the permissive approach, the child's feelings are foremost in importance. Parents are taught to